The Huguenots in Later Stuart Britain

The Huguenots in Later Stuart Britain

VOLUME I
Crisis, Renewal, and the Ministers' Dilemma
HARDBACK 978-1-84519-618-9 (2015)

VOLUME II
Settlement, Churches, and the Role of London
HARDBACK 978-1-84519-619-6 (2018)

VOLUME III
The Huguenots and the Defeat of Louis XIV's France
HARDBACK 978-1-84519-620-2 (2023)

The Huguenots in Later Stuart Britain

Volume III – The Huguenots and the Defeat of
Louis XIV's France

Robin Gwynn

LIVERPOOL UNIVERSITY PRESS

First published 2023 by
Liverpool University Press
4 Cambridge Street
Liverpool
L69 7ZU

British Library Cataloguing-in-Publication data
A British Library CIP record is available

ISBN 978-1-84519-620-2 (cased)

Typeset by Carnegie Book Production, Lancaster
Printed and bound by CPI Group (UK) Ltd, Croydon CR0 4YY

Contents

List of Map, Tables and Figures

The Cover Illustration
To convey the experience of the Huguenot refugees, the cover highlights the cross, which came to symbolize what they stood for. The Huguenot cross presents their Calvinist Christianity. It is the *croix boutonné* of Languedoc; most representations of the cross show its spokes separated by *fleur-de-lis*, depicting France. The dove stands for the Holy Spirit descending from God to humanity, but can also serve as an allusion to the flight of the refugees. The dislocation that defined the refugees' situation and the uncertainty of their prospects is captured in Jan Luyken's contemporary depiction (1696) of Huguenots fleeing France around the time of the Revocation of the Edict of Nantes.

Preface

This, the final volume of *The Huguenots in Later Stuart Britain*, focuses on the political aspect: royal policy, the relationship between the Huguenots and the later Stuarts, and how the refugees helped defeat the monarch from whom they had fled and so shape the future of the Britain to which they came. Since the publication in 1960 of Warren C. Scoville's classic *The Persecution of Huguenots and French Economic Development 1680–1720*, his contention that the 'revocation of the Edict of Nantes did much less harm to the French economy … than most historians … have heretofore believed' has been widely accepted.[1] Against this, the present volume argues that the flight of the refugees damaged Louis XIV's government to a much greater degree than is now generally allowed, and that for a few brief years in the 1680s and 1690s they made a contribution that proved to be of critical, enduring importance for the future of England, Ireland and France.

'Memory' and 'networks' have been hot topics in recent years among scholars interested in the Huguenots, as can be seen in the collections edited by Bertrand Van Ruymbeke and Randy J. Sparks (*Memory and Identity: The Huguenots in France and the Atlantic diaspora*, 2003), David Trim (*The Huguenots: History and memory in transnational context*, 2011), and Vivienne Larminie (*Huguenot Networks, 1560–1780: The interactions and impact of a Protestant minority in Europe*, 2018).[2] These valuable works all include some outstanding essays, and they share a multinational approach and an interest in drawing comparisons between the settlements of the Huguenot Refuge in different countries. However, there is an inherent problem in such an approach that is particularly acute regarding Britain. Multinational comparisons depend on the assumption that there is a body of broadly reliable information shared by the international scholarly community, so that a firm basis exists from which

---

1 Scoville (1960), 446.
2 Published respectively by the University of South Carolina Press, Brill and Routledge.

comparisons can be made. Within Europe, there is indeed a broad scholarly consensus about Huguenot settlement in Germany, the Netherlands and Switzerland. However, the present trilogy has revealed a startling degree of misunderstanding when it comes to writings about the situation in Britain.

From the outset, one of the aims of *The Huguenots in Later Stuart Britain* has been 'to provide a proven evidential base from which the next generation of scholars can approach the subject with confidence they have a firm foundation with regard to sources'.[3] Each of its three volumes incorporates substantial new information that was never previously available. In the first book, this took the form of a biographical dictionary of French Protestant ministers in later Stuart England. The second volume included a brief history of each of the many French-speaking churches existing in England between 1640 and 1713 and listed for the first time the known lay officers helping to govern them. Volume III now provides a much more detailed look at the extraordinary group of laymen who served as elders and deacons of the largest French church in the country, at Threadneedle Street in the city of London. The result of half a century's research, this reveals the economic muscle and also the familial and European connections concentrated in the consistory room of that church towards the close of the seventeenth century. It highlights surprisingly close ties between the church and the Bank of England, which would later come to be located, like the church, in Threadneedle Street.

The present book also incorporates a list of Huguenot military officers known to have been fighting in the armies of William III and Anne. This would have been quite impossible but for the detailed unpublished research written up in longhand and deposited in the library of the Huguenot Society of Great Britain and Ireland by the late American history professor George Hilton Jones, whose publications included *Charles Middleton: The Life and Times of a Restoration Politician* (Chicago: University of Chicago Press, 1967) and *Convergent Forces: Immediate Causes of the Revolution of 1688 in England* (Ames: Iowa State University Press, 1990). The listing of officers is entirely reliant on his work.

The previous volumes of *The Huguenots in Later Stuart Britain* showed that recent estimates of the number of Huguenot refugees in Britain suggested by continental scholars are too low. Even such a basic statistic as the number of their churches has been seriously underestimated. Our study of ministers in Volume I showed that considerably more French pastors came to later Stuart England than was previously believed.[4] Volume II revealed that England surpassed the Netherlands in numerical terms as the

3 Gwynn (2015), 1.
4 Gwynn (2015), 148–52, 171–2.

primary host country of the Refuge during the 1690s, and showed how confusion and misrepresentation have plagued continental descriptions of Huguenot settlement in Britain over the past half century and more.[5] Some reasons underlying the misrepresentation have to do with the slight but significant differences in the timing of refugees coming to Britain, where the Catholic James II had become king in 1685 shortly before the Edict of Nantes was revoked in France. In many parts of Europe, refugee immigration peaked in 1686. England, though, was slow to offer any real welcome compared to other Protestant centres in Europe in 1685–6, although earlier it had been quick to do so under James's brother Charles II when the *dragonnades* started in 1681. In England migration peaked in 1687 and continued into the 1690s.

A welcome recent publication bears directly on numbers. In Volume II, while evaluating the scale of Huguenot settlement in Britain, we discussed 'imponderable' categories for which hard evidence was lacking. One of those imponderables concerned Huguenots in the Channel Islands, which I suggested would have added 'a thousand or more refugees to our figures'.[6] The lack of evidence has since been directly addressed in Robert Nash's *Directory of Huguenot Refugees on the Channel Islands 1548–1825*, a formidable work based on credible detailed research and databases of individuals in Jersey and Guernsey which was published in 2020. Nash shows that the number of Huguenots in the Islands is likely to have been depressed during the years of war with Louis XIV, with which I was particularly concerned, but that the number of refugees peaked in the period 1716–20 so that by 1720 there were 'at least 1000 refugees on Jersey … and at least 500 on Guernsey'.[7]

The earlier volumes of *The Huguenots in Later Stuart Britain* centred on the refugees themselves. The books discussed how the French-speaking communities in England survived the difficult years of the Civil War, Interregnum and post-Restoration period, and how the Protestant churches that defined them were organized. Then they investigated when the new Huguenot *réfugiés* from Louis XIV's France arrived, where they settled, how many of them there were, how they were received and how the multitude of many very poor refugees were assisted and enabled to survive. This final volume moves in a different direction and has a different focus. It is framed around the history of the new homeland to which they came, and tackles two related questions of wide English and European historical interest. From 1689 to 1713, with a pause between

---

5 Gwynn (2018), 1–3, 100–1, 159, 199–202. See also Gwynn (2019), 1–14.
6 Gwynn (2018), 196.
7 HSQS LXIII, pp. 14–22, especially pp. 21–2.

1697 and 1701, Britain and France were continuously at war. Against that background, what did the refugees contribute to the Britain to which they came, and what were the implications of their flight for the France they had abandoned?

The book argues that even in their own lifetimes, in the short but vitally significant period from the early 1680s to the mid-1690s, the refugees made a contribution so central that it proved to be at the heart both of a major reshaping of the course of English (and Irish) history, and of the eventual resultant defeat of Louis XIV, the French monarch from whose lands they had fled. After an introductory chapter, this volume is divided into three sections. The first looks at the Revolution of 1688–89 and suggests that but for the French background and the arrival of so many Huguenot refugees it is impossible to explain how James II, who in 1685 enjoyed the strongest financial and military position of any Stuart monarch, could have been forced to flee England so precipitately just three years later. The monarchs who replaced James, William and Mary, were immediately faced by military conflict in Ireland, and the second section investigates the direct contribution made by the refugees in the Irish wars of 1689–91. It shows that William's first general in Ireland, the Duke of Schomberg, far from being the dithering 'tired old man' portrayed by recent historians, was a consummate and energetic professional who played a significant part in ensuring the relief of the besieged city of Londonderry and later, confronted by appalling disease devastating his ill-supplied and inexperienced army, made rational and intelligent decisions that provided the platform on which success could be built the following year at the Battle of the Boyne. From there we turn to the little-known but bloodiest battle of the Irish wars at Aughrim in 1691, where Huguenot troops were largely responsible for transforming possible disastrous defeat into improbable and brutally decisive victory for the Williamites. Retracing our path across the Irish Sea, the final section of the book moves to the City of London and the foundation of the Bank of England in 1694, a development fundamental to Britain's ability to continue fighting until Louis XIV was forced to accept terms, first at the temporary Peace of Ryswick in 1697 and later at the lasting Treaty of Utrecht in 1713. These chapters show the importance in the genesis of the Bank of a closely knit group of earlier refugees who had long known and long intermarried and interacted with one another as members of the community centred on the Threadneedle Street church. The volume explores the motivation underlying the actions of the refugee military officers in Ireland and of the merchants of Walloon and French background who assisted in the creation of the Bank of England, and suggests why, in each of these very different cases, their motivation proved of great significance.

Volume I of our trilogy opened with a prologue describing the growing despair of the minister Gilbert Primerose in 1642 as he watched his life's work and his church in London undermined and engulfed by the forces that resulted in the English Civil War. The epilogue to this final volume reflects our story through the eyes of Gilbert's grandson David Primerose, appointed pastor of the same Threadneedle Street church in 1660, who by the time of his death in 1713 had witnessed the Restoration of the monarchy, the 'Glorious Revolution' and the arrival of a new century, and lived throughout the entire reigns of Charles II, James II and William and Mary, and almost all that of Queen Anne. Following the epilogue are appendices on the lay elders and deacons who served Primerose's church between 1640 and 1713, and on Huguenots in the service of the Crown in the armies of William and Anne. The work ends with a note of errata and corrigenda for the first two volumes, and a consolidated bibliography (volumes I–III).

As I wrote in the preface to Volume I, no work that results from half a century's research can possibly express all the thanks that are due for assistance in a great variety of different contexts. For this final volume, in addition to George Hilton Jones mentioned above, I have again incurred specific debts of gratitude. One, of depth and long standing although deriving from only brief acquaintance, is to P.G.M. Dickson, author of the seminal *The Financial Revolution in England: A study in the development of public credit, 1688–1756*, published by Macmillan in 1967. Many years ago, he was kind enough to provide me with copies of some of his notes relating to Huguenot contributions to the early English Funds. The notes were immensely helpful, not least in enabling me to see whom he had and had not included as 'Huguenot' in his work. Other debts are much more recent. In London, special thanks are due to Barbara Julien for drawing my attention to the document in the Huguenot relief papers at the London Metropolitan Archives that allows us a rare snapshot of some rank-and-file Huguenot soldiers in 1699,[8] and to Leslie Du Cane for sharing his deep family knowledge and providing enlightenment about the genealogical intricacies of the Du Quesne and Houblon families. Bénédicte Fougier kindly made special provision to allow research at the French Church of London library. Stacey Porter prepared the map of Ireland.

Military history is not an easy field for a scholar more used to studying ecclesiastical documents, and the Irish wars of 1689–91, studded as they are by conflicting accounts, frequently incompetent actions involving poorly trained soldiers and clouded by a great weight of nationalistic

---

8 Below, pp. 226–37.

myth, would be difficult enough for anyone. All the more thanks, then, to Vivien Costello and John Vignoles for many useful suggestions, discussions and copies of documents on the Williamite army in Ireland, and to Kenneth Ferguson, Marie Léoutre and Harman Murtagh for advice and hospitality in Dublin. Harman later kindly conveyed me to the battlefield of Aughrim and guided me around it. It was a great surprise to me when I found that my researches resulted in a favourable reassessment of both the Huguenot general Marshal Schomberg in 1689 and the French Catholic general (and Huguenot persecutor) Saint-Ruth at Aughrim in 1691, but none of those so kindly offering assistance are to blame for anything that may be amiss with my conclusions.

Abbreviations

Agnew	(1886) *Protestant Exiles from France, chiefly in the Reign of Louis XIV*, 3rd edn.
Arch.	Archive.
BEA	Bank of England Archive.
BGE	Bibliothèque de Genève.
BL	British Library.
BR	Bodleian Library, Oxford, Rawlinson MSS.
BSHPF	Bulletin de la Société de l'Histoire du Protestantisme Français.
BT	Bodleian Library, Oxford, Tanner MSS.
CCEd	Clergy of the Church of England website.
CCL	Canterbury Cathedral Library.
ChChL	Christ Church Library, Oxford.
CJ	*Journals of the House of Commons.*
CSPD	*Calendar of State Papers, Domestic.*
CTB	*Calendar of Treasury Books.*
DNB	*Dictionary of National Biography.*
Dubourdieu (1718)	*An Appeal to the English Nation.*
DWL	Dr Williams's Library, London.
Estat(s)	*Estats de la Distribution ... aux Pauvres Protestants François, printed 1707–10, covering the years from 1705 to March 1710.*
FCL	French Church of London Library, Soho Square.
Félice (1898)	*Les Protestants d'Autrefois ... Les Pasteurs.*
Foster (1891)	*Alumni Oxonienses: the members of the University of Oxford, 1500–1714.*
GH	Guildhall Library, London.

Haag (1846)	*La France Protestante (ou Vies des Protestants Français ...)*, 1st edn.
Haag (1877)	*La France Protestante (ou Vies des Protestants Français ...)*, 2nd edn.
Hessels	Hessels, Joannes H. (1897). *Ecclesiae Londino-Batavae Archivum. Tomi Tertii, Pars Secunda. Epistulae et Tractatus cum Reformationis tum Ecclesiae Londino-Batavae Historiam Illustrantes.* Cambridge.
HL	Huguenot Library, University College, London.
HMC	Historical Manuscripts Commission.
HSJ	Huguenot Society of Great Britain and Ireland, *Journal* (continuation of its *Proceedings*).
HSP	Huguenot Society of Great Britain and Ireland (formerly of London), *Proceedings*.
HSQS	Huguenot Society of Great Britain and Ireland (formerly of London), Quarto Series Publications.
huguenot.fr	http://www.refuge-huguenot.fr website, base de données du refuge Huguenot.
La Mothe (1693)	*Two Discourses .... Whereunto are added some Articles subscribed by all the French Divines in or about London, in Opposition to the Socinians.*
Livre Synodal	*Livre Synodal contenant les Articles résolus dans les Synodes des Eglises Walonnes des Provinces Unies du Pais-Bas* for the 1690s and eighteenth century. See Bibliography, section 2.
LJ	*Journals of the House of Lords.*
LMA	London Metropolitan Archives.
LP	Lambeth Palace Library.
Mours (1968)	'Les Pasteurs à la Révocation de l'Édit de Nantes', *BSHPF* 114 (1968), 67–105, 292–316, 521–4.
Newcourt (1708)	*Repertorium Ecclesiasticum Parochiale Londinense.*
NS	New style.
pers. com.	personal communication.
PRO	Public Record Office, see TNA.
R.O.	Record Office.
Schickler (1892)	*Les Églises du Refuge en Angleterre.*

SHPF   Library of the *Société de l'Histoire du*
                      Protestantisme Français, Paris.

TNA   The National Archives, Kew.

Venn (1922)   *Alumni Cantabrigienses ... Part I, from the earliest*
                      times to 1751.

Wallonnes   Commission de l'Histoire des Eglises Wallonnes,
                      Livre Synodal contenant les Articles résolus dans les
                      Synodes des Eglises Wallonnes des Pays-Bas, vol. I
                      (1896) or vol. II (1904). See Bibliography, section 3.

Wood (1813)   *Athenae Oxonienses*, new edition.

For fuller details of the printed works above, and for abbreviations of other works specific to individual footnotes, such as 'Hart (1952)', see the Bibliography.

Chronological Table and Note on Dates

Background

1550	Foundation of French and Dutch churches of London.
1559	Acts of Supremacy and Uniformity provide the legal foundations of the Elizabethan Church.
1598	Edict of Nantes.
1609	12-year truce in Netherlands.

The foreign communities in Britain in a world turned upside down: 1640–60

1640	Long Parliament meets (–1653).
	Archbishop Laud impeached.
1642	Outbreak of English Civil War (–1646).
1645	Laud beheaded.
1649	Trial and execution of Charles I; England declared to be a Commonwealth.
1653	Oliver Comwell established as Protector.
1658	Death of Cromwell.
1660	Charles II's Declaration of Breda promises amnesty and religious toleration.
	Restoration of the monarchy and of bishops.

New threats, new challenges, new starts: shifting foundations, 1661–79

From 1660s	Increased legal pressures against Huguenots in France.
1661	Louis XIV begins personal rule in France.
	Cavalier Parliament meets, predominantly royalist (–1678).
	Foundation of the conformist church of the Savoy.

1662	Act of Uniformity accepts revised English Prayer Book. Ejection of Nonconformist ministers.
1665	Great Plague.
1666	Fire of London.
1670	Secret Treaty of Dover between England and France.
1672	Declaration of Indulgence for Roman Catholics and Nonconformists (–1673).
	William of Orange becomes Stadtholder of Zeeland and Holland.
1673	Test Act excludes Roman Catholics from office in England.
1678	Popish Plot.
1679	Attack on Huguenots in France intensifies.
	'Exclusion crisis' in England (–1681); terms 'Tory' and 'Whig' come into use.

Period of the crisis of French Protestantism, 1680–85

1681	Onset of *dragonnades* in France.
	Large-scale influx of refugees into England begins.
	First brief for financial collection for refugees.
1683	Rye House Plot to assassinate Charles II and James is discovered.
	Charter of City of London declared forfeit.
1685	Death of Charles II, succeeded by openly Catholic James II.
	Monmouth's rebellion put down.
	Edict of Fontainebleau revokes the Edict of Nantes.

The crisis of French Protestantism within Britain, 1686–88

1686	Second brief for financial collection for refugees.
1687 (Apr.)	Declaration of Indulgence for Liberty of Conscience. Maximum intensity of Huguenot immigration into England.
1688 (Nov.)	William III invades England.
(Dec.)	James II escapes to France.

The Huguenot Refuge in an age of freedom: The reigns of William III and Anne, 1689–1714

1689	Bill of Rights.
	Toleration Act.
	England at war with France (–1697).
1690	Louis XIV sends troops to fight for James in Ireland.
	Battle of the Boyne; James flees to France.
1691	Battle of Aughrim.
1694	Foundation of the Bank of England.
1695	Government censorship of the press ended in England.
1697	Peace of Ryswick.
1702	England at war with France in the War of the Spanish Succession (–1713).
	Death of William III, succeeded by Queen Anne.
1709	Protestant refugees from the Palatinate reach England.
1713	Treaty of Utrecht.
1714	Death of Queen Anne.
1175	Death of Louis XIV.

Note on Dates

In 1582, much of continental Europe adopted the 'New Style' Gregorian calendar, which advanced the calendar by ten days to compensate for a growing difference between the calendar and the solar year. Britain however kept the old Julian calendar, which began the calendar year on 25 March, throughout the period with which we are concerned. Since the present work is based on the British experience, dates have been kept 'Old Style' but with the assumption that the calendar year began on 1 January. For documents such as continental correspondence, the date used are those of the writers themselves.

Glossary of Terms

Abjuration	Use of this word in the French church records most commonly refers to the conversion to Protestantism of long-standing Roman Catholics.
Brief	Royal letters patent authorizing a collection through the churches of the country for a specified charitable object such as refugee relief.
Censures	Quarterly meetings of church officers for the maintenance of church discipline.
Coetus	The public organ of the old-established foreign churches in London, especially in the defence of their rights and privileges.
Colloquy	A meeting of representatives of all the old-established French-speaking (or, of all the Dutch-speaking) churches in the English mainland.
Confederated churches	Name assumed by the old-established French congregations in England after the Restoration to distinguish themselves from newer foundations.
conformists	French Protestants worshipping in accordance with the Anglican Prayer Book translated into French.
Consistory	The governing body of a church, usually consisting of all ministers and elders.
deacon (or *diacre*)	In non-conformist churches, deacons were unpaid, lay officers charged with the administration of poor relief. In conformist churches, deacons were junior Anglican clergy.

denization	The process by which aliens might become Englishmen through executive action, by letters patent.
Dragonnades	From 1681, the deliberate policy in areas of France of billeting dragoons (light cavalry) on Protestant households to intimidate them, ruin them financially and force their conversion.
elder (or *ancien*)	Unpaid, lay officers of a church, central to its organization.
English Committee	Oversaw poor relief for the refugees, laying down criteria for relief and checking records of accounts.
French Committee	In control of the detailed process of administering poor relief to the refugees.
General Assembly	The General Assembly of French churches in London came into being in the late 1690s to provide a forum in which all those churches, whether conformist or non-conformist, could discuss common problems. It had no power to override the independence of its constituent churches.
Lecteur	A paid officer who read from the Scriptures and led Psalms in services; in non-conformist churches the *lecteur* was a layman, but in conformist churches he was often an Anglican deacon.
Maisons de Charité	Houses of Charity, established in Spitalfields ('La Soupe') and Soho to provide soup, bread and meat to poor refugees.
Mereau(x) or *Marque(s)*	Communion token(s).
naturalization	The process by which aliens might become Englishmen through legislative action, by Act of Parliament.
Nonconformists	English Dissenters.
non-conformists	French Protestants, legally authorized in Britain, using the form of service to which they were accustomed in France.
Proposant	A student of theology or minister in training, not yet called by a church.

proselyte	A convert, in the present work normally from Roman Catholicism.
Quo Warranto	Legal process requiring a body to show by what right it existed, frequently used in the 1680s to ensure greater royal control.
Reconnaissance	Acknowledgement of a fault committed. During our period, many refugees making *reconnaissance* were acknowledging they had been forced to abjure their faith in some way in France.
Socinianism	Similar to Unitarianism. Socinians denied the orthodox doctrine of the Trinity, believing Christ to be no more than a remarkable man, and emphasized the role of human reason in interpreting the Scriptures.
Synod	Joint meeting of the French and Dutch colloquies in the English mainland.
Témoignage	Certificate of sound doctrine and good behaviour.

For Margaret

The Huguenots in Later Stuart Britain is dedicated in deepest appreciation of constant assistance, love, patience and support over what is now more than half a century.

Enfin

This final volume is also dedicated with gratitude to Anthony Grahame, founder and until recently Editorial Director of Sussex Academic Press, who has supported this project since its inception and was responsible for setting the two earlier works in the trilogy, *Crisis, Renewal, and the Ministers' Dilemma* (2015) and *Settlement, Churches, and the Role of London* (2018).

I

Introductory Chapter

The preface noted that one major aim of *The Huguenots in Later Stuart Britain* has been to provide a proven evidential groundwork for the refugees and their communities settled across the Channel. As this groundwork has been developed, it has become clear that more refugees came to England than has been previously accepted, and that more Huguenot communities were established in England than modern continental historians have recognized. The biographical dictionary of French Protestant ministers in later Stuart England in our first volume more than doubled their relevant number compared with the only previous attempt at a listing, although the author of that effort had believed his attempt was 'as comprehensive as ... possible'. The dictionary also showed how historians had misclassified the destinations of several ministers fleeing France, failing to realize that they settled in Britain.[1] The second volume included a brief history of each of the French-speaking congregations existing in England under the later Stuarts. It concluded that the total number of refugees settling in Britain (excluding Ireland) was about 50,000, rather more than writers (including myself) had previously suggested. It will always be possible to argue about the precise number of refugees, since the surviving evidence does not allow certainty. What cannot be disputed, however, is the number of French congregations, which grew from seven in 1680 to over fifty in the early years of Anne's reign. Meanwhile, England surpassed the Netherlands in numerical terms as the primary host country of the Refuge during the 1690s.[2] Failure to comprehend this has plagued continental descriptions of Huguenot settlement in Britain over the past half-century and more.

The present book incorporates a list of over fourteen hundred Huguenot military officers identified as fighting for the British Crown in the armies of William III and Anne, the work of the late George Hilton Jones. Before Jones's research, most historians would have been

---

1 Gwynn (2015), 148–52, 171–2.
2 Gwynn (2018), 1–3, 100–1, 159, 199–202. See also Gwynn (2019), 1–14.

startled to learn that so many individuals can be identified. This book will also demonstrate that although the initial depositors with the Bank of England in 1694 have been closely examined by historians, the number of Huguenot foundation depositors has been underestimated by over 15 per cent.[3] At no stage of our enquiries, in any aspect, has it appeared that Huguenot numbers in England have been exaggerated by serious historians in recent years. Rather, what stands out is that previous recent accepted estimates of the number of Huguenot refugees settling in later Stuart England are demonstrably on the low side. This raises the question, if there were more Huguenot refugees and communities in the country than previously thought, and if refugees are found turning up in greater numbers than expected at critical junctures at the end of the seventeenth century, could it be that their significance in broader English history has been underestimated?

This volume argues that this has indeed been the case, and particularly that the refugees helped make a significant contribution to the defeat of the monarch from whom they had fled and so shape the future of the Britain to which they came. This is no new argument. It would have been accepted without hesitation by most writers before the mid-twentieth century. However, since the publication in 1960 of Warren Candler Scoville's classic *The Persecution of Huguenots and French Economic Development 1680–1720*, his contention that the 'revocation of the Edict of Nantes did much less harm to the French economy ... than most historians ... have heretofore believed' has been widely accepted.[4] Against this, the present volume argues that the flight of the refugees damaged Louis XIV's government to a much greater degree than is now generally allowed.

SCOVILLE AND THE MINIMIZATION OF DAMAGE CAUSED TO FRANCE BY THE HUGUENOT EXODUS

Scoville came to his subject from the background of deep study into the spread of capitalistic production in eighteenth-century French glassmaking, and at a time when, he wrote, 'I have discovered that many people have quoted quite unrealistic figures for the number of Huguenots who fled France. The figures are often larger than the total number of Protestants ever living in France at any one time.'[5] He set out to re-examine the hypothesis that the Revocation of the Edict of Nantes seriously retarded

---

3 Below, p. 158.
4 Scoville (1960), 446.
5 Scoville (1960), viii.

French economic development, and then to reach 'certain tentative conclusions' about its significance by comparison with other factors that operated simultaneously to create 'a long period of economic stagnation and depression, lasting approximately from 1684 to 1717'.[6]

By the end of the work, Scoville was wondering whether any 'segment of the French economy felt the impact of the Revocation so keenly as to warrant listing the persecution of Protestants as the most significant factor, or even a prime factor, in the prolonged stagnation that affected the French economy after 1683'. He suggested that the decline was due, rather, to prolonged and costly involvement in warfare and the market disruption it caused; to bad harvests and famines; to excessive and unimaginative government leadership, red tape and bureaucracy; to changes in consumer taste and decreased demand for luxury goods; and to growing prosperity in England and the Dutch Republic. 'Almost any one of these factors could have caused or deepened the depression as much as the revocation of the Edict of Nantes', he wrote; 'taken together, they certainly exerted more influence'. He concluded that the Revocation 'did much less harm to the French economy, both in the short run and in the long run, than most historians of the nineteenth and twentieth centuries have heretofore believed'.[7]

Scoville's work has many virtues, in particular its admirable foundation developed through dedicated, well-footnoted research on French archives. He was certainly right to question the exaggerated numbers that are too often tossed lightly into discussion. That same problem is also evident in claims made by early writers about Huguenots coming to England, where the Spitalfields minister Jacob Bourdillon roundly asserted in 1785 in writing to the Bishop of London that some 150,000 refugees came after the Revocation, and the nineteenth-century suggestions of 120,000 (by Samuel Smiles) and 100,000 (by Baron Fernand de Schickler) lacked foundation and remained too high.[8] Scoville was also well aware of formidable problems in his path: of how incomplete is the evidence, how lacking the quantitative data for the period, how difficult it is to separate out the many independent variables in historical causation with cause and effect closely interrelated, and how hard to assign the correct weight to each variable. As he says, 'there are not enough reliable data either to "prove" or "disprove" any pertinent hypothesis. One can only "test" or examine different hypotheses in the light of existing data.'[9]

---

6 Scoville (1960), 12, 26–7.
7 Scoville (1960), Summary; quotations from pp. 435, 444, 446.
8 LP, Fulham Palace papers, Lowth 2, f.245r; Smiles (1867), 287; F. de Schickler, 'Les Églises du Refuge', extract from *L'Encyclopédie des Sciences Religieuses* (1882), p. 34.
9 Scoville (1960), 23–5, 437.

Often he shows himself similarly cautious in his conclusions. For example, while our present work has not attempted to tackle the question, I am in complete agreement with his assessment that 'it is extremely difficult, if not altogether impossible, to evaluate the overall effect of the Huguenots on the English economy'.[10]

Regarding his main thesis, however, Scoville's conclusions are not cautious, but clear cut. He does not attribute particular significance to the Revocation in causing France's financial depression, and views other issues, especially war, as 'much more important'.[11] Given his book's many merits and formidable annotation, it is of lasting value, so it is not surprising that his work has held sway for the last two generations. Its widespread acceptance continues to dominate the thought of today's professionals interested in the Huguenots, and a recent historian summed up the prevailing orthodoxy when he applauded Scoville in 2015: 'in reality the economic losses incurred by the Revocation were limited.'[12] The general acceptance of that view during the last half century has helped spark a marked shift away from any focus on what contribution, if any, the refugees might have made to their host countries.

Instead, modern approaches tend to highlight a 'myth' or 'legend' consciously developed by the refugees themselves and a hagiographical 'awareness of a glorious Huguenot past' created in the nineteenth century and fostered by societies of descendants 'born of an intense need to celebrate the past and of a sense of sharing the same heritage'. This supposed 'legend' and 'need', it is suggested, has resulted in a 'biased and introspective Huguenot memory' that exaggerates the contribution of the refugees to their host societies. In an extreme form, these approaches imply that any attempt to argue that the refugees might have offered substantial commercial or other advantages is so old-fashioned that it should necessarily be dismissed as mere 'glorification'.[13] Any readers inclined towards such a view might care at this point to run their eyes, just quickly, over the entries for trade, wealth and social status in the analysis of the lay officers of one particular church, that at Threadneedle Street in London, presented as Appendix 3 in this book (pp. 238–356). The appendix is factual and has no space for 'glorification', but even a

---

10 Scoville (1960), 331. My earlier work *Huguenot Heritage* drew attention to the range of crafts, trades and professions in England influenced by the refugees, but any serious attempt at an accurate evaluation of their economic impact would require a cooperative effort involving specialists in many different fields.
11 Scoville (1960), 441.
12 Van der Linden (2015), 40.
13 See for instance Van Ruymbeke and Sparks (2003), Introduction (quotations from pp. 14–15); Van der Linden (2015), 3–6; Yardeni (1993), 79–96.

quick glance provides enough chapter and verse to suggest that, at the very least, there is room and need for further discussion about the Huguenots' possible economic contribution to their new homelands. This is a discussion that needs to be undertaken with an open mind, not approached from any blinkered obsession with 'myth'.

Scoville's approach conceals fundamental problems. The facts he provides do not always support the conclusions he reached. He tended to ignore 1681, the year in which the *dragonnades* began, and with them, refugee emigration on a major scale. His study of the effects of immigration in the countries to which the refugees went lacked the requisite depth, especially insofar as England was concerned. The only way to demonstrate these problems is to take a case study, and we will begin by taking for such a study the extent of the loss suffered by France in terms of seamen and sailors. This was a major political issue of international concern, a subject of great interest to the royal players Louis XIV in France and James II and William III in England, and to Louis's principal emissary sent to England to examine the Huguenot situation there, François d'Usson de Bonrepaus, who was intendant-general of the marine.

In each of his studies of different areas of economic activity, Scoville can be relied upon to provide a framework and give an idea of contemporary thinking, and this is no exception. He notes how Louis's concerns predated the onset of the *dragonnades*, and how in December 1680 the French king forbad French pilots, caulkers, gunners, sailors and fishermen to serve under foreign flags, under penalty of service in the galleys for life. He highlights the anxieties of Seignelay, Colbert's son and minister of the marine, who was particularly worried about the situation around La Rochelle and Rochefort, where a third of all seafaring men and over half the 1200 marine officers were Huguenots, and at Bordeaux, where nearly all the vessels travelling to and from the American islands were owned and operated by Huguenots. Seignelay did what he could to ameliorate royal policy where it risked encouraging seamen to leave the country, and Louvois, the other principal royal minister, was also concerned about their loss.[14]

Another major figure of the day, the distinguished military engineer Marshal Vauban, was one of the few highly placed members of the French establishment prepared to tackle his king directly on the Huguenot question, and he provides the only contemporary overall estimate of the loss of sailors, which Scoville is able to quote. In 1689 Vauban drew up a memorandum urging a change in policy direction, 'Pour le Rappel des Huguenots', and sent it to Louvois in the hope that it would gain Louis

---

14 Scoville (1960), 52–7, 98, 135, 282–3.

XIV's attention. Vauban reviewed it several times thereafter but saw no reason to change what he had written, which included the assertion that in military terms, the persecution had benefited France's enemies to the tune of between eight and nine thousand sailors ('des meilleurs du royaume'), and between five and six hundred army officers and ten to twelve thousand soldiers.[15] Scoville is also aware that the Venetian ambassador reported home in 1688 that most sailors on the west coast had left. He may well be right in dismissing the ambassador's comment as a probable exaggeration, but it is surprising that he should not take more seriously the evident concern of Seignelay, Louvois and Vauban. Of the latter's estimate of eight to nine thousand seamen, while acknowledging that other well-informed historians had accepted it, Scoville simply says brusquely that it 'seems much too large'. Instead he proposes a figure of two to three thousand.[16] Yet Vauban was likely to make himself unpopular with the king by raising the subject at all, and surely he would not have put forward his figures unless he believed they were reliable or at least defensible.

Since Scoville gives little reasoning in support of his own suggested figure, it is impossible to know on what (if anything) it may have been based. That is a fundamental oversight, because he goes on to use his estimate as if it was a proven base from which to draw rather precise comparisons with other problems affecting the French marine until he concludes that 'in the absence of convincing evidence to the contrary ... religious persecution was not the paramount depressant of French shipping'. He agrees that in reality, 'evidence is scanty'. The one hard relevant figure he cites is an early (1686) report by Bonrepaus that the number of seamen serving England and Holland probably did not exceed 800, but Bonrepaus – as Scoville rightly remarks elsewhere – had good reason to underestimate the effects of the Revocation, since by so doing he emphasized his own successes and minimized the general failure of his mission.[17]

Writers have normally suggested that most refugee seamen went to the Netherlands, which is reasonable enough. Scoville's book is focused on France, just as this present work is focused on Britain. Setting the relevant evidence for France and England together is no simple matter, but is there any helpful evidence in British sources which might contribute towards an understanding of the overall picture? Volume II of *The Huguenots in Later Stuart Britain* showed that

---

15 *BSHPF* XXXVIII (1889), 194–5.
16 Scoville (1960), 284–7.
17 Scoville (1960), 284, 286, and see 123, n.92.

1. Captain Greenhill, one of the Commissioners of the Navy, and the merchant Nathaniel Dowrish certified in Plymouth that the refugees 'have brought up many of their families to the sea, and at this time many of them are actually in the service of their Majesties' ships of war' and 'imprested into their Majesties' sea service' (p. 55);
2. sailing folk predominated in the early history of the Bideford settlement (pp. 43, 323–5);
3. nine specific ships owned by Huguenots complete with their crews can be identified as sailing to Stonehouse and relocating there (p. 41);
4. Dartmouth and most other western settlements are also likely to have had significant maritime elements (p. 48);
5. 31 per cent of the Bristol refugees whose trade is known were sailors (p. 45);
6. following the onset of the *dragonnades*, seven boats of fishermen had been settled at Rye before the end of 1681, and fishing remained the prime occupation of the Huguenot settlement there (pp. 69–70);
7. the principal occupation of the Wapping congregation (formed from Channel Islanders who were likely to have included refugees) was also as seamen, of whom most, according to a petition of 1705, 'serve on board your Majesty's Fleete' (p. 152);
8. a survey of published church registers that included erratic entries about trades showed 60 seamen and naval employees in East London out of a total sample of 841, or 7.13 per cent (p. 214);
9. the same survey showed eleven such employees in west London out of a total sample of 1081, or just over 1 per cent (p. 214).

If we apply the percentages indicated in the last two of those bullet points to the numbers of Huguenots in London we established in the third and fourth chapters of our second volume, it would be reasonable to suggest that in the closing years of the seventeenth century there were perhaps rather more than a hundred refugee seamen and naval personnel in the western suburbs and about eleven hundred in the eastern suburbs of the capital. Lest it be thought the East London figure is too high, the published church registers used in the original survey, volumes XI and XXXII of the Huguenot Society Quarto Series, were revisited to ensure there really were 60 individual identified seamen named in the registers of the two churches of La Patente, Spitalfields (53) and Crispin Street (7). In fact, the 60 proved to be rather an understatement than an exaggeration. Eight, not seven men are named in the Crispin Street records as *marinier* or *matelot*;[18] the five of them whose place of origin is given all came from the Saintonge region. The tally for La Patente is five short. It seems the given figure of 53 had

18 Baty, Bau, Biaud, Ducq, Janson, Le Lieure, Meniel, Vignaud.

not included two men described as *hommes de mer* and one who was said to have been absent from his son's baptism simply because he was 'sur la flotte', while a *marinier* and a *matelot* attending as witnesses were also ignored. Each congregation also included a ship's carpenter. The La Patente registers, better than most at recording places of origin, give them for 41 of the relevant individuals. Twenty-nine of those, or 70 per cent, came from Saintonge, including ten from La Tremblade and six from Royan. Six sailors came from Normandy, of whom four were from Dieppe.

Since the sample proves sound, the suggestion of over a thousand French sailors in the London region is likely to have merit. It would also seem reasonable to allow roughly a further thousand to cover those in Bristol, Plymouth and Stonehouse, other Devon ports, Rye and other places in England outside the capital, not all of which have been previously considered. For example, Gregory Stevens Cox's study of St Peter Port, Guernsey, notes that 'at least three Huguenot refugees commanded island privateers in the wars against the French; but it is not easy to determine how many refugees served as ordinary sailors because there were those who employed *noms-de-guerre*'.[19]

If we accept a little over a thousand mariners in the London area and a further thousand for the rest of the country, that would make a total of over two thousand seamen in England alone. One other piece of evidence makes that appear a fair estimate. Roger Morrice reported in his *Entring Book* on 5 March 1687 that 'this last weeke it is very credibly reported there is full 2000 French Protestants fled out of France into Plymouth, Falmouth, Sussex and London whereof about 600 are Seamen'.[20] There is independent supporting evidence that the figure of two thousand-plus as the overall number crossing the Channel at this particular time is justifiable; that very day, 68 refugees made *reconnaissance* at Threadneedle Street, the largest group since the Revocation, and they proved to be the harbingers of successive waves so that 2237 new arrivals made their peace in this one church during 1687.[21] If the total figure is correct, it is reasonable to assume that Morrice's informant was exceptionally well informed and therefore likely also to have been right in his estimate that some six hundred seamen arrived immediately following the Declaration of Indulgence in early 1687.

As far as we can tell, then, rather over two thousand French seamen in all took refuge in England. That was very likely considerably fewer

---

19 Cox (1999), 88. The practice of using such *noms-de-guerre* was encouraged by the fact that any refugee sailors caught by the French on English ships suffered severe penalties.
20 DWL, Roger Morrice's *Entring Book*, Q, p. 79.
21 HSQS LVIII, pp. 2, 184–5.

than the number of Huguenot mariners who had gone to live in the Netherlands, and there were other refugees in the navies of the Elector of Brandenburg and the King of Denmark, and in coastal towns in Ireland and elsewhere. Scoville's unsupported estimate of two to three thousand refugee seamen in total leaving France is quite inadequate. It is noticeable that none of the Devon ports, Bristol or Rye appears in the index to his work, and he does not consider London in relation to maritime or naval employment. His book has accurately captured the concerns of high French officials well placed to understand the problems they faced, but the available evidence simply does not substantiate his conclusion. Indeed on this issue, as on other occasions in Scoville's book, his conclusions and summary defy rather than reflect the evidence he has brought together.

The fact that the refugee settlement at Rye was set up and functioning before the end of 1681 highlights a further problem with Scoville's approach, one that is particularly acute insofar as Britain is concerned. In the case of the French marine he asks 'whether the situation anywhere [in France] was appreciably different after the Revocation from what it had been before'. He then compares figures for Bordeaux for 1682 and 1686–8. Rarely does his book incorporate 1681 in its figures. However, many French Protestants had already fled their homeland before and during 1681. A high percentage of these crossed the Channel, as is demonstrated by Figure I.1, which shows an annual breakdown of the number of new members joining the French Church of London, Threadneedle Street, between 1680 and 1705. In other European countries, the year 1686 normally witnessed the peak of Huguenot immigration in the 1680s. England was a special case with twin peaks, an early one in 1681 (when the *dragonnades* started in France) and a later and much larger one in 1687 (following the Declaration of Indulgence for Liberty of Conscience in England). Thus when Bonrepaus reported back to France in March 1686 that only some 4500 refugees had arrived in England since 1682,[22] the exclusion of 1681 from his calculations would have robbed his figures of real meaning even had they been accurate in other respects.

Regarding seamen, it should be noted that Henry Savile, English envoy at Paris, wrote to secretary of state Sir Leoline Jenkins in July 1681 advocating a royal declaration encouraging Protestant refugees to come to England. He emphasized particularly the number of French Protestant seamen, and also 'the considerable number of wealthy people ready with great sumes to come over to you'.[23] Savile was well placed to know what he was talking about and, given the speed of Charles II's action in

---

22 TNA, Baschet transcripts, 31/3/165, Bonrepaus to Seignelay, 11 March 1685 NS.
23 Cooper (1858), 210.

welcoming refugees, his views were certainly shared at the English Court. So from the point of view of Scoville's subject as a whole – the effect of the persecution on the French economy – the absence of data for 1681 and his chosen starting point a year or two later seriously weakens his argument. The significance of 1681 is enhanced by the fact that it was easier then to send wealth out of France than would later be the case after persecution intensified, and by the end of the year King Charles II was recommending to the East India Company that new French Protestant refugees who had arrived with money should be allowed to buy stock as though they had been naturalized, notwithstanding any clause in its charters to the contrary.[24] French historians have followed Scoville in downplaying early emigration. Elisabeth Labrousse, for example, viewed it before 1685 as small scale and not significant – 'le nombre des fugitifs ne représenta une sérieuse hémorragie qu'après l'Édit de Fontainebleau', she wrote.[25] Set against the English context, such views need reassessment.

Figure I.1

New members of the French Church of London, Threadneedle Street, 1680–1705[26]

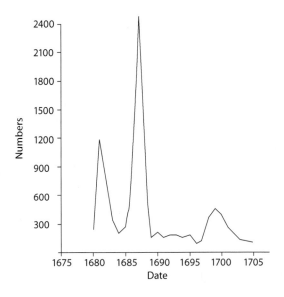

---

24 *CSPD*, 1682, p. 9 (4 January).

25 Labrousse (1985), 207.

26 The figure is taken from Gwynn (1968A), 372; an annual breakdown of new members follows on p. 373, showing that 1182 new members came to this one church in 1681, and 2497 in 1687. The only other years in which it witnessed over five hundred arrivals were 1682 (691), 1686 (607) and 1688 (715).

Our case study has revealed significant and fundamental flaws in Scoville's approach. He ignored the immediate consequences of overt persecution in 1681. He needed to review the consequences of emigration in the lands where refugees settled in greater depth. Moreover, in the case of the French marine, Scoville offered – and eventually used as if they provided an established basis – figures that simply have no justification. The problem with his figures is not confined just to France's loss of seamen. What he suggests about the overall numbers of Huguenots coming to England confirms the need for caution in accepting Scoville's own estimates except in those cases where he provided clear supporting evidence. He asserts that 'from 20,000 to 50,000 would be a cautious estimate of the number who settled throughout England, and an actual count would most likely have placed the figure somewhere between 40,000 and 50,000'. The 40,000 to 50,000 was indeed a reasonable and very defensible estimate given the evidence available to him. In the paragraph in which this quotation appears, he refers to three contemporary estimates, one of 33,000 with more refugees arriving daily, a second of 40,000–50,000 and a third of 90,000, including children born by 1713. The same paragraph cites two historians who each estimated 50,000. But how could his lower figure of 20,000 ever have been justified, on any grounds? 'Cautious' it certainly is, but it is also purely imaginary and fictitious, based on no evidence whatsoever. It does not reflect but flies in the face of such evidence as does survive. It is as seriously misleading as the more obviously exaggerated figures, which he (rightly) summarily dismissed. The analysis provided in Volume II of *The Huguenots in Later Stuart Britain*, based on evidence not all of which was available to Scoville, shows that this lower figure is simply untenable. His upper estimate of between 40,000 and 50,000 remains possible, but something slightly over 50,000 is more likely and higher numbers are not impossible.[27]

Revocation and Revolution: The Revocation as an International, Not Only a French Event

Scoville's argument, then, is not so 'solidly documented' as some otherwise well-informed writers have suggested.[28] More importantly, there is a fundamental problem with Scoville's approach of far greater concern than occasional low estimates or numbers that may have lacked evidential

---

27 Scoville (1960), 122–3, 324; compare Gwynn (2018), chap. IV, 'The Scale of Settlement'.

28 For example, Yardeni (1993), 79.

support but been advanced simply to bolster his argument. His evidence is based on France, and the statistical information he provides is convincing in demonstrating how French industries that had been temporarily damaged by the disruption caused by war, famines, Huguenot emigration and other factors frequently recovered – often quite speedily – once peace returned in the eighteenth century. Our present book, which ends in 1713, is concerned only with the short term and with Britain, and in those regards Scoville's argument is much less convincing. Britain also suffered severe economic distress, hugely increased taxation and harvest failure resulting in sharp increases in the price of bread in the 1690s. The real problem, though, is that Scoville treats the annulment of the Edict of Nantes purely as an internal French matter. It was not.

E.S. de Beer, the editor of John Evelyn's *Diary* and later of John Locke's correspondence, had argued ten years before the publication of Scoville's book that the Revocation was critical in the formation of the English public opinion that would be expressed in the Glorious Revolution in 1688 through widespread failure to rally to James II's cause. De Beer concluded that 'more than anything else ... [it was] the conduct of Louis that made up Englishmen's minds for them; the Revolution was in many respects their answer to the Revocation'.[29] Another historian writing a major work on England in the reigns of James II and William III, David Ogg, similarly commented a few years before Scoville wrote on how the religious policies of Louis XIV were 'so clearly evidenced by the many proofs of atrocities brought by the refugees, that Englishmen were able to form their own conclusions about the likely results of a Bourbon–Stuart absolutism, conclusions which had some influence on the Revolution of 1688'.[30]

Scoville knew of De Beer's article, which is listed in his bibliography, but he never made any attempt to come to terms with it. Yet it is devastating for his whole line of argument. When Scoville did consider international relations, he acknowledged there was a case to be made that French religious policies may have helped unite Louis's enemies (before he then set out to try to minimize that factor).[31] However, he simply ignored the possibility that without the Revocation in France, there might never have been the Revolution in England; and the Revolution in 1688 in Britain can be seen as the turning point of Louis's reign. Before it, the French king was always on the front foot, making persistent acquisitions both in Europe and overseas through the 1660s, 1670s and 1680s. For a few years after the Revolution William was desperately trying to consolidate, but once he

29 De Beer (1950), 310.
30 Ogg (1955), 42.
31 Scoville (1960), 311 ff.

had done so, Louis could no longer dictate terms. The French king began to put out feelers for peace at the end of 1693, and William's recapture of Namur in 1695 signalled a power shift that was confirmed during the War of the Spanish Succession in the first decade of the following century.

Taken together, the Revocation of the Edict of Nantes in France and the Revolution in England helped create and cement an international realignment strong enough to neutralize the advantages and economic strength of France, Europe's greatest power. The Huguenot Refuge played a major part in that process. This book will follow De Beer in arguing that without the Revocation of the Edict of Nantes in France, coming as it did just months after the accession of a Roman Catholic king across the Channel, it is highly unlikely that William could ever have dispossessed James II and seized the British thrones. Even after the Revolution, William remained in great peril, and we will see how significant the refugees were, first in defeating the immediate military counter-thrust he faced in Ireland, and then later in promoting and supporting the economic developments, especially the creation of the Bank of England, which eventually empowered the major role played by England as the forces opposing France ground out Louis's defeat. For a very short but decisive period, not much more than one single decade, the Huguenots were of real importance in British and European political history. Just as the Revolution in England and the consequences that followed undermined Louis's position in Europe, so Scoville's failure to look at the broader political picture and analyse the role of the refugees in the process fatally undermines his eventual overall conclusions.

In other words, much that Scoville says is sound, especially regarding developments within France, but his conclusion that the Revocation was not a major factor in France's long economic depression cannot stand. On the contrary, it was central to it. We have seen that Scoville attributed the country's economic woes to prolonged and costly involvement in warfare and the market disruption it caused; to bad harvests and famines; to excessive and unimaginative government leadership, red tape and bureaucracy; to changes in consumer taste and decreased demand for luxury goods; and to growing prosperity in England and the Dutch Republic. Of these, religious persecution had little directly to do with the bad harvests and famines and with failings in government leadership and bureaucracy. It had, however, a great deal to do with the other factors that Scoville lists, and especially with the costs and perpetuation of war.

By contributing towards the peaceful acceptance of William III in England at the time of the Revolution, the Huguenot Refuge helped cement a very dangerous opponent as a central force in William's alliance against Louis. As part of the 'Protestant International' that ringed France, it assisted with communications and intelligence. Huguenot merchants helped disrupt French markets. They had a part to play in changes in consumer taste; eventually they would help Britain prosper. In the shorter term they encouraged and helped promote the Bank of England in its early years when it was vulnerable. The availability of Huguenot army officers willing to serve in the early 1690s was of particular importance in England by comparison to other centres of the Refuge because well over half of the English officers who had served James II, having taken oaths of loyalty to him, would not serve against him.[32] To the damage that persecution caused within France must be added the benefits it handed to other lands, and especially England, which by 1700 was numerically the most important place of refuge.[33] It is therefore time to rebalance the ledger and to rein in the exuberance with which historians since Scoville have sought to belittle the economic significance of the Revocation and the persecutions that accompanied it in France.

GROWING NEGLECT OF THE REFUGEES IN TWENTIETH-CENTURY ENGLISH HISTORICAL WRITING

At this point we run into the second theme of this introductory chapter, a strange silence that cries out for explanation. If the refugees in England had a significant role to play in the late 1680s and early 1690s, why is it that they feature so rarely in modern mainline histories of Britain? Consider the books likely to have been studied by school students and undergraduates with an interest in the later seventeenth century across the past two generations. The Huguenots were responsible for the English word 'refugee' and provide one of the outstanding examples of successful integration of a large immigrant group in an increasingly cosmopolitan world, but the two-volume *Oxford Children's History* (Oxford University Press, 1983) could find no place to mention them in its 700 pages. Why should it have, when highly competent professional specialist writers of the 1960s and 1970s were quite ambivalent in their treatment of the Huguenot influx? Professor J.P. Kenyon, for example, did not consider them worth mention in his wider works on the Stuarts,[34] although his biography of the Earl of Sunderland shows he was well aware that 'it was probably

---

32 Childs (1980), 85, reports that a biographical study of 500 officers who served continuously with the English army from 1685 to 1688 shows that only 127 of them took commissions under William, while 147 fought in Jacobite armies in Ireland and Scotland and the remainder resigned their appointments and retired from military life.
33 Gwynn (2018), 200–202.
34 J.P. Kenyon, *The Stuarts* (1958 and 1966) and *Stuart England* (Harmondsworth, 1978).

the conduct of Louis XIV which finally wrecked James's relations with his subjects ... [by driving] across the English Channel a host of living witnesses to the reality of religious persecution under a Catholic king'.[35] Similarly, J.R. Jones agreed that 'at a time when the Huguenots were suffering so severely, all connections with French Catholicism were highly damaging', yet his *Country and Court* locates the refugees primarily in the context of xenophobia.[36] Even the chronologically confined detailed work by J.R. Western, *Monarchy and Revolution: The English State in the 1680s*, while it suggests Huguenot troops were useful to William after the Revolution, did not consider the effects on the host population of the arrival of so many new refugees.[37]

The publication of Barry Coward's *The Stuart Age* might have inaugurated a change in approach, since he made the point that 'without the Revocation ... the successful intervention of William of Orange in England in 1688 (and therefore the "Glorious Revolution") would have been impossible', and highlighted the importance of the refugees in bringing 'concrete proof, in Louis XIV's *dragonnades*, of the truth of Protestant allegations of the cruelty and intolerance of rampant Catholicism'.[38] There has also been renewed interest in the Huguenots since the tercentenary commemoration of 1985, while in 1997 Tim Harris wrote that in order to understand how English public opinion came to be shaped in the later Stuart period, 'we need to go outside England, to investigate the European context more generally'.[39] Yet, to date, the refugees and their background can hardly be said to have been reintegrated into mainstream English history. Even Harris's own works, so brilliant at weaving together our understanding of Scottish and Irish developments with those occurring in England, have not progressed far in this regard. Tony Claydon's *William III and the Godly Revolution* argued that theological language remained critical in the 1690s and that Protestant beliefs need to be kept centre stage by historians rather than ignored on the grounds that the decade was a time of marked secularization, and it notes that the promotion of William as a righteous instrument of God was a vital factor in sustaining the national struggle on the international scene;[40] but it has little to say about the Huguenots and barely mentions the Revocation.

Historians from the eighteenth and nineteenth centuries would have found such neglect most puzzling. Lord Macaulay highlighted the deeply

---

35 Kenyon (1958), 123–4.
36 J.R. Jones (1972), 91, and (1978), 93, 306–7.
37 Macmillan, 1985 (first published by Blandford Press, 1972), 337, 390.
38 Barry Coward, *The Stuart Age* (Longman, 1980), 274, or 2nd edn (1994), 317.
39 Tim Harris (1997), 191.
40 Claydon (1996), 5, 233.

embarrassing effect of the Revocation and continuing persecution of French Protestants for the policies James II wished to pursue in England. He also discussed James's attitude to the refugees, understood the significance of the public generosity shown in collections for them, noted Huguenot willingness to lend resources to William and appreciated the importance of Schomberg and of the Huguenot regiments in Ireland.[41] Macaulay was rebuked by some contemporaries for his handling of their contribution, but the rebuke came for what he had omitted, not out of concern he might have exaggerated their significance. It came from the great French historian Jules Michelet, who criticized Macaulay's account of William's invasion of England in 1688:

> Surely great England, with all her glories, her lineage of ancient liberties, will acknowledge handsomely the part played by us French in her deliverance. In his Homeric account of William's companions the historian includes everyone: English, Germans, Dutch, Swedes, Swiss, with picturesque details about weapons and uniforms, down to 300 negroes in turbans with white plumes in the trains of rich Englishmen and Dutchmen. He doesn't see our men. Evidently our expatriates paid little honour to William by their costume. A number, no doubt, wore the clothing in which they had taken refuge, dusty, shabby, tattered.[42]

Michelet went further, discerning the fundamental importance of the Revocation for Britain in the preface to his first volume, which focused on the personal reign of Louis XIV. In examining the significance for France of the Revocation of the Edict of Nantes in comparison to the 1789 Revolution, he noted how the Revocation caused the diaspora of Huguenots 'and the Revolution in England which was its consequence'.[43] Camille Rousset's *Histoire de Louvois* picked up on the 'fatal coincidence' of James's accession in Britain and the Revocation in France.[44] Another nineteenth-century French historian who reached the same conclusion had spent many years studying both English history and the story of French Protestants who took refuge across the Channel. Baron Fernand de Schickler concluded his three-volume work *Les Eglises du Refuge en*

---

41 Lord Macaulay (1913–15), 675ff, 732–4, 868, 1074ff, 1100–2, 1686–95, 1875, 1880–1.
42 Michelet (1860), 418–19.
43 'et la Révolution d'Angleterre qui en fut le contrecoup'; Philippe Joutard recently drew attention to Michelet's comment in *La Révocation de l'Édit de Nantes...* (2018), 418.
44 C. Rousset (1865), II, p. 2.

Angleterre with the sentence 'The Revocation of the Edict of Nantes would result in the revolution of 1688 and the fall of the Stuarts'.[45]

It is hard to know why this insight into the interrelationship between the Revocation in France and the Revolution in England should have become forgotten or obscured, but that is what had happened by the later twentieth century. In both England and France, the massive displacements caused by two world wars provided more immediate subjects of urgent interest. Scoville's work consciously minimizing the economic significance of the loss of the refugees is part of the picture, and in France it fitted well with scholarly concern that estimates of Protestant numbers in the country had been unduly exaggerated. England had engaged with the refugees in the later nineteenth century, when economic historians like William Cunningham were interested in their contribution, the Huguenot Society was founded in part to encourage study of them and the books of Samuel Smiles (of 'Self-help' fame) were best-sellers going through repeated editions. But, and in retrospect quite suddenly, the situation changed. It is hard to think of any significant book on the Huguenot refugees in England published between the start of the century and the 1980s. Scholarly work continued apace, and the same period saw the publication of editions of virtually all the extant French church registers, as well as of other important materials such as records of denizations and naturalizations. Yet in the public eye, the Huguenots in England largely vanished. Sometimes they did not even appear in local studies where one might have supposed they should, so that for example the fine book by John Evans, *Seventeenth-century Norwich ... 1620–1690* (1979), ignored the aliens and their descendants in the city even though there were substantial foreign churches both French and Dutch there and the aliens had comprised about a third of the city's population in later Elizabethan England.

What our current work does is to resume the long-standing historical narrative that Scoville and too many subsequent historians on both sides of the Channel chose to ignore, a narrative that sets the Revocation in France and the Revolution in Britain beside one another in a wider European context. The Huguenots crossing the Channel from France came to a land in turmoil. Their new country witnessed in a few short years Titus Oates's 'Popish Plot' and the Exclusion Crisis, the brief but turbulent reign of James II, the 'Glorious Revolution' that replaced him with William and Mary, subsequent hard-fought victory in Ireland, and a foreign war on the continent that in intensity, duration and cost was far beyond anything Stuart England had previously experienced, occurring

---

45 'La Révocation de l'Édit de Nantes aura pour conséquences la révolution de 1688 et la chute des Stuarts' (in Schickler (1892), II, 359).

(in the 1690s) during a time of scarcity and high prices. And all that in the long shadow of a Civil War in England, which was still part of living memory. James was England's only overtly Roman Catholic monarch after 1558, and he came to the throne in the same year in which the Edict of Nantes, which had long given legal protection to Protestants in France, was revoked. William and Mary by contrast were perceived as champions of Protestantism, and their foreign war was waged against the French king responsible for the Revocation. Under the circumstances, it is reasonable to expect that the refugees should have had some significant part to play in these dramas. This volume shows that indeed they did.

In particular, the book underlines a critical contribution made by the refugees to the Williamite cause in Britain across a very limited period, from 1685 to 1697, a few years that, though short, proved nevertheless fundamental for the fortunes of England, Ireland, France and indeed the whole of Europe. Sometimes the refugees' impact was unintentional and unwitting, simply the consequence of their presence. On other occasions their conscious assistance in political, military and economic matters had an effect. Overall their input is shown to have had such force that without it, Louis might never have faced the defeat which in the second half of his reign tarnished and outweighed his earlier successes. The next chapter investigates James II's policies and relationship with his Huguenot subjects. Then we will see how the refugees helped render his position untenable and so prepare the ground for the Revolution of 1688–9. After that we will consider the Huguenots' very real contribution during the Irish wars that followed the success of William's invasion, and their financial impact through their support of the foundation of the Bank of England, which became so important in the war effort against Louis XIV in the longer term.

PART ONE

REVOLUTION

II

The Royal Need, 1687

King Charles II, as we saw in Volume I, gave the first refugees reaching England in 1681 a warm, positive and remarkably prompt welcome, regardless of the fact that his actions might cause affront to Louis XIV.[1] The only downside, from the Huguenots' point of view, was that Charles persisted with his long-standing policy, decided shortly after the Restoration, not to license any new French churches unless they conformed to the Church of England in the manner of the Savoy church in Westminster.[2] We went on to examine the contrast at the time of the Revocation in 1685, eight months after Charles's death. While the refugees' necessity was more obvious than it had been four years earlier, the new King James II acted with none of the speed and urgency that Charles had shown. On the contrary, he made sure any brief in the refugees' support was delayed as long as possible and, when he could procrastinate no longer, hedged it in with restrictions and interpretations consciously designed to discourage both Huguenot immigration and English charitable donations. At the same time James and his mouthpiece, Lord Chancellor Jeffreys, sought to promote a very precise type of conformity, which had little support among the refugees and threatened to undermine the Savoy church.[3]

James II has been represented in sharply differing ways by his many biographers, and his treatment of the Huguenots has been used to justify opposing arguments. In this chapter we will look at the key features of the reign as seen through the eyes of the refugees, commenting on those events that enable us to shed light on the king himself and on the interpretations of his actions offered by historians. Then we will look closely at James's particular hopes and needs in 1687 as he struggled to make a new policy, startlingly different from the one he had originally pursued when he came to the throne two years earlier, work to his advantage. From there we will

---

1 Gwynn (2015), 126–8.
2 Gwynn (2015), 93–4.
3 Gwynn (2015), 129–37.

pursue his failure to carry his subjects with him in the months leading towards the Revolution that ousted him in 1688.

James's biographers are agreed that compared to his brother, he was very serious and much more religious, and lacked Charles's wit and sense of humour. James was hard-working but only of average intelligence, and, in the words of W.A. Speck, 'English to the core'.[4] He held a high view of monarchical power and was keen to enhance his own authority; having survived the Exclusion Crisis and the rebellions he faced on coming to the throne, he maintained a much-increased army in peacetime to awe his subjects. He was a poor judge of character, and the bad choices he made for diplomatic appointments came back to haunt him in 1688, when Louis XIV was far better informed than he was about William's preparations to invade England.

One thing of which we can be quite sure is that James did not like the Huguenots, although he also did not like the way they were treated in France. His words to Sir William Trumbull on the latter's appointment as envoy in Paris in 1685–6 ring true:

> His Majesty added, that though he did not like the Huguenots (for he thought they were of anti-monarchicall principles), yet he thought the persecution of them was unchristian, and not to be equalled in any Historie since Christianity: That they might be no good men, yet might be used worse than they deserved, and it was a proceeding he could not approove of.[5]

This agrees with the Earl of Ailesbury's report that he personally heard James exclaim against Louis XIV's severity towards the Huguenots in France.[6] What is much less certain is that one can go on from there to say that James genuinely believed in religious toleration, although a case can be made. J.P. Kenyon thought that 'James's policy of toleration was so disastrous, politically so counter-productive, that we just have to assume a quite strong element of moral sincerity behind it'.[7] This fits well with William Penn's report that James 'ever declared to me it was his opinion that conscience should be free'.[8] Up to a point, it also fits with the King's statement in the 1687 Declaration of Indulgence that 'conscience ought not

---

4 Speck (2002), 132.
5 BL, Add. MS 52,279, 30 Oct. 1685 (Old Style).
6 Ailesbury (1890) I, 103.
7 Introduction to Cruickshanks (1989), 2.
8 Speck (1988), 174; Buranelli (1962), 127. The actions of some members of John Locke's circle also suggest they believed that James's commitment to toleration was sincere, see Goldie (1992).

to be constrained, nor people forced in matters of mere religion'. Those last five words, though, raise a problem. Who defined what was 'mere' religion? James might have answered that it was up to the king to decide, but since he was a man who thought in very black and white and often simplistic terms and tended to view Nonconformists as seditious, ultimately I accept John Miller's judgement that 'the suddenness of James's conversion from persecution to toleration is ... a sufficient argument against claims that he consistently favoured toleration'.[9]

The formal exchanges between the new Roman Catholic king and his French Protestant subjects in existing churches in his realm went off smoothly. Speaking on behalf of the long-standing non-conformist Dutch and French congregations within days of Charles's death in February 1685, the minister David Primerose assured James of their loyalty and obedience, promising prayers for a long and happy reign. James for his part promised the same protection as his brother and ancestors had provided, saying he would show he regarded their members as good subjects.[10] From the point of view of most refugees, the first reliable indication of whether James truly meant his kind words came in October, when the Edict of Fontainebleau revoked the Edict of Nantes in France. The indication was not positive. It came, not in instant action to match that of Charles II in 1681, but in the form of censorship and the strange 'silence' noted by John Evelyn in his diary, which ensured that not 'one syllable of this wonderful proceeding in France' was publicly reported.[11] So comprehensive was the silence that even the consistory minutes of the French church of Threadneedle Street make no mention of the Revocation, although it must have been the subject of much heart-searching and debate within the congregation.

Both at the time and since, some defenders have argued on James's behalf that he was a plain-speaking man whose word could be trusted, that he was well disposed and generous towards the Huguenots, and that key policies against their interests were not really his own but should be ascribed to intolerant Anglicans.[12] This chapter will demonstrate that these arguments are not supported by his decisions and actions in the aftermath of the Revocation, when the royal attempts in 1685–6 to confine relief to conformist refugees alone dishonoured the promises James had

---

9 Miller, 'James II and Toleration', in Cruickshanks (1989), 19.
10 HSQS LVIII, p. 143.
11 The full extract from Evelyn's diary is given in Gwynn (2018), 245.
12 In an extreme modern case, Ashley (1977, p. 187) persuaded himself that James showed genuine generosity towards the Huguenots and suggested that 'nothing has been more completely misrepresented in James's life than his attitude' towards them. James's failure to follow the precedents set by his brother in 1681 and the hard evidence from his own reign presented in this chapter tell a different story.

made in response to the address of the nonconforming churches following his accession. If he did harbour any favourable disposition towards the refugees, his brother had provided a clear template for what could be done on their behalf, and James had no wish to follow it. We have previously evidenced that the long delay between the Privy Council's approval of a brief on their behalf (6 November 1685) and its actual issue months later in the first week of March 1686 was the result of intentional inaction for which the king and his mouthpiece Lord Chancellor Jeffreys were responsible. The careful and deliberate rewording of the drafts prepared by Archbishop Sancroft, invariably in ways that were damaging to the refugees and aimed to discourage support for them, further shows the extent of royal interest and control over what happened. The archbishop had highlighted the severities to which the Huguenots had been exposed, the difficulties in the way of their flight and their urgent need for assistance, and he would have allowed sermons on their persecution 'upon the Account of their Religion'. So the policy that was being pursued cannot be blamed on intolerant Anglicanism. Rather it was the king who did not want these matters to come before the public eye.[13]

The Huguenots themselves obviously understood the finer points of the policy that James II and Jeffreys were driving, but most contemporary Englishmen would not have appreciated them. One who did comprehend their import very clearly was the Presbyterian Roger Morrice, who noted that the 1686 brief issued by James that authorized financial collections throughout the country for refugees applied only to those Huguenots accepting some degree of conformity to the Church of England.[14] Morrice was an exceptionally well-informed man with no known French family connections, although he did have contacts among the refugees.[15] For James's reign, the *Entring Book* he maintained is the single most important source available to historians for our day-to-day knowledge of what was happening in the kingdom, so he will feature prominently in this chapter and the next. Morrice's bias is plain, and Mark Knights has described his narrative as 'suffused with an underlying conspiracy theory, in which the High Churchmen (or 'Hierarchists', as he often called them) sought to triumph over those who truly followed the national interest and the interest of Protestantism'.[16] Clearly, this must be considered where relevant. Nevertheless, insofar as the refugees are concerned, Morrice's information has been shown to be exceptionally accurate.[17] He

---

13 The Court's amendments to the archbishop's drafts are analysed in Gwynn (2015), 130–1.
14 *Entring Book*, P, p. 492. The brief is in the British Library, 190.g.13 (394).
15 *Entring Book*, P, p. 242.
16 Knights (2006), 216.
17 Detailed examples are analysed in Gwynn (2006B).

never set out with any intention to reflect on them, though, and for most of the time his massive 'Historical Register of Occurrences',[18] which runs from 1677 to 1691 and contains some 925,000 words, has little to say about the Huguenots. So their frequent appearance specifically in James's reign provides eloquent testimony to just how significantly they loomed in the English psyche during the king's short period of rule.

Following hard on the heels of the long-delayed 1686 collection for the refugees came an event that was bound to cause great concern throughout Protestant Europe: the public burning in London, on 5 May 1686, of a book attributed to the Huguenot minister Jean Claude, *Les Plaintes des Protestans, cruellement opprimez dans le Royaume de France* (Cologne, 1686), promptly translated into English as *An Account of the Persecutions and Oppressions of the Protestants in France*. Jean Claude was unacceptable to Louis XIV, and (as Morrice reported)[19] the French king unsuccessfully demanded his return from the States General of the Netherlands, where he was in exile, to answer treason charges. Both French and English editions of the book were seized and burnt in London.

The French ambassador, Barrillon, personally claimed responsibility for inciting the English authorities to burn Claude's book and stated that the Lord Chancellor spoke against burning the French edition on the grounds that it had not been printed in England. James silenced discussion by remarking that there was an English proverb that dogs defend one another when they are attacked, and he thought kings should do the same.[20] Barrillon reported James's strong personal intervention to his master, and the French Court duly expressed its gratitude to Sir William Trumbull, the English ambassador in Paris.[21] *The London Gazette* also confirmed Barrillon's role,[22] and John Evelyn, pondering that 'so mighty a power & ascendent here, had the French Ambassador', observed that no evidence had been produced to show the *Account of the Persecutions* was false.[23]

---

18 So subtitled, perhaps not by Morrice himself. The manuscript extends over three large folio volumes, MSS P, Q and R. The printed edition [Mark Goldie and others, 2007] consists of seven volumes including the index, all with different editors. The two printed volumes covering James II's reign are volumes III (1685–7, covering manuscript pages P 458 to Q 83), edited by Tim Harris, and IV (1687–9, covering manuscript pages Q 84–469), edited by Stephen Taylor. References that follow are to the original manuscript but can be readily followed in the printed edition, see the Reader's Guide in each volume.

19 *Entring Book*, P, pp. 542–3.

20 TNA, 31/3/166 (f. 311); Sér. Angl., vol. 158, f. 290.

21 BL, Add. MS 52,279, 21 May 1686 NS.

22 No. 2136, 6–10 May 1686.

23 De Beer (1955), IV, 510.

Morrice provides far more information than any other source on this event. Only from him do we know that the *Account* was burnt by the Common Hangman in 'severall other places' besides the Exchange, 'presses haveing been broken before, and many of the pamphlets seized upon'. Only from him do we learn of the translator, 'Mr. Rayner a Minister, lately made a petty canon of St Paules worth about 60l. per annum'. 'Strict enquiry and proces' having gone out against him, Rayner went into hiding, but quickly became 'wearie of his Sculking', returned home and was apprehended.[24] Later he was bailed, and on 5 June he defended himself at the King's Bench along the lines

> that he confessed he did translate and publish that booke, but did it not seditiously nor maliciously against the Government, but being full of compassion towards his suffering fellow Christians and Protestants, having not estate wherewith to relieve them himselfe, he did translate and publish that book, in purpose to raise the affections and enlarge the bowells of Compassion in Protestants here towards their relief, and did not publish it till after his Majesties Letters Patants for a Collection for them came out, and that this and no other was his reason and end, and he did not thinke that it would have been a crime in a Protestant Kingdome to have done it for that purpose &c.[25]

Eventually, Morrice recorded, Rayner was fined

> only one Marke, for applycation was made to Monsieur Barillion, That he was a poore man of no understanding in Polliticks etc That he did not know or Consider that it would be any offence &c, begged pardon, and Barrillion acquiessed therein, having had publick Satisfaction given to his Master, by the publick information.[26]

Given that one of Morrice's key Court sources was Sir John Baber, whom Morrice was later to describe in a shorthand passage as 'so thoroughly in with the French imbassador',[27] there is every reason to suppose this is an accurate account. Barrillon's evidence confirms that the responsibility for choosing to proceed to the burning of the book in French as well as English lay personally and solely with James, who had overridden Jeffreys' objections.

The extra layers of Morrice's information about this incident underline the value of the *Entring Book*: and all the more, so far as the Huguenots

---

24 *Entring Book*, P, pp. 533, 535, 537.
25 *Entring Book*, P, pp. 542–3.
26 *Entring Book*, P, p. 557.
27 *Entring Book*, Q, p. 492.

in England are concerned, because the story of Rayner's arrest is almost immediately followed by a statement under the date of Saturday 22 May 1686, 'There is a Quo Warranto gone out against the French Church, to be served upon foure or five of their most conspicuous Elders'.[28] The French church in question was the oldest in the land, the French Church of London at Threadneedle Street, which had been founded in Edward VI's reign in 1550 and so predated the Church of England as by law established. This is one time when Roger Morrice's information may not be entirely accurate. Normally when Morrice had doubts he prefaced his record with some such statement as 'It is said that ...', but not on this occasion. His assertion is unequivocal. Yet there is no hard evidence that a *Quo Warranto* was issued, although two other references show what a desperately close-run thing it must have been and it may have been issued but then immediately recalled.

On the same day as Morrice's entry, Edward Harley reported to his father, Sir Edward Harley, that David Primerose, a minister at Threadneedle Street since 1660, 'tells me that the difficulties of the escape has kept most of the tradesmen in France. Those that are come over that want employment are soldiers, dyers, and linen weavers. I hear a *quo warranto* is intended against the French Church in the City.'[29] The other source that refers to the *Quo Warranto* is an unsigned newsletter from Whitehall in the State Papers, dated just over a week later, on 1 June 1686.[30] The newsletter reports that one means suggested to 'rid this kingdome of the French Hugonetts here, who are by the Cabalistical Councill represented as dangerous to the Government' was to send out writs of *Quo Warranto* against the 'French Hogonett Church in London and other partes of England which did not confirme in ceremony to the Church of England'. It seems, the newsletter continued, that these measures were actually taken, whereupon the merchants who gave financial support to the Threadneedle Street church told its ministers and elders that if they conformed, they would withdraw their maintenance:

> Upon which its thought, they will be forced to breake up and retire else where, which will not only force away abundance of those Hugonetts, many of which are substantial merchants ... but many other of our merchants dissenters, who resorted to the said church, and discourage all the rest, who will take this for a forerunner of a greater storme, and will thereupon discontinue their trade and withdraw their money

---

28 *Entring Book*, P, p. 538.
29 HMC 29: Portland III: p. 396.
30 TNA, SP 8/1, pt.2, ff. 72–3.

which is thought to be att least 6 partes of tenn of the moveing cash
that drives the trade of the whole nation which cannot but much deaden
our traffick, and extreamly diminish the Kings customes, but as it is
thought this nor no other emergent obstacle whatever will be capable
to deterr the King from his fixed resolution of pursueing to the utmost
the point of relegion.

The report concluded that the French merchants supporting the church
had tried to get the ablest lawyers available to plead their case against the
Quo Warranto, but for fear of offending the Court the lawyers did 'excuse
themselves from so ticklish an employ'.

That such a *Quo Warranto* should have been considered by the Court
makes perfect sense. Its objective would have been to place management
of the people governing the congregation in the king's hands. After
1683, when judgement had been entered against the City of London, a
systematic policy was developed that used *Quo Warranto* proceedings to
control not only boroughs but organizations such as livery companies,
overseas trading companies and colleges of Oxford and Cambridge. By
calling in and remodelling the charters on which institutions depended,
their governing bodies and internal affairs could be controlled through
the ability that then fell into Court hands of removing office holders at
will. Royal policy in the capital in the 1680s has rightly been described
as 'overwhelmingly and ... unprecedentedly intrusive'.[31]

From the point of view of James II, or of the Tory Anglican establishment
that was in power at this point of the reign, there was every reason for
the French Church of London to be a prime target. We saw in Volume I
how it had been a thorn in the side of royalists at the time of the Civil
War and Interregnum, when one of its ministers was calling publicly for
the king's execution at the remarkably early date of 1645, and another
had been a Cromwellian agent in Europe.[32] The Restoration Court had
been informed frequently by the royalist minister Louis Hérault that the
consistory was ill-disposed to monarchy. The Whig leanings of leading
members could not be hidden at the time of the Exclusion Crisis; their
number included Thomas Papillon and John Dubois, at the centre of the
disputed shrievalty elections of 1682. In 1683 a discussion in the church
about whether rebellion could ever be justifiable came to the ears of the
Court.[33] Two years later, at the time of Monmouth's rebellion, four past

---

31 Levin (1969), 16. For the Livery Companies see Knights (1997) (quotation from
p. 1143). Fifty-six writs of *Quo Warranto* were issued against borough corporations
between 1682 and 1685 (Speck (2002), 31).
32 Gwynn (2015), 39, 84.
33 HSQS LVIII, 7–8, 104–12.

or present church officers were arrested and another had his premises searched,[34] while Papillon continued in exile in the Netherlands.

The threat of *Quo Warranto* proceedings in late May 1686 came just days after the burning of Claude's book on 5 May. It may be that the Court considered the French Church of London to have been implicated in some way in the book's production, and this brought the matter to a head. Unfortunately for those at Court who wished to proceed by way of *Quo Warranto*, there were formidable pitfalls in the way of calling in the foundation document of the Threadneedle Street church. Doing so would equally have affected the inoffensive Dutch Church of London, since the two congregations shared a common charter that had originally been made out for 'Germanorum et aliorum peregrinorum' ('Germans and other foreigners'). Controlling a body of elders and deacons, some of whom changed every six months was a dauntingly time-consuming prospect that would have required a degree of personal knowledge of the available suitably qualified people, which it was unlikely that the Court possessed. Besides, where were suitable replacements – supporters of the Court line – to be found in the Threadneedle Street congregation? In so far as its members participated in English politics, the church must have been one of the most staunchly Whig-dominated institutions in all England, its officers including numerous certain and undeniable Whigs but not one in the last quarter of the seventeenth century for whom there is any evidence to suggest Tory leanings.[35]

Beyond these practical matters, there were deeper considerations. A frontal attack on the independence of the French and Dutch churches, which had always been of European significance in the Reformed community, would have sent reverberations throughout Protestant Europe. It would have given weight and substance to the arguments of pamphleteers who had claimed in relation to the attack on London's charter that the purpose of the whole *Quo Warranto* campaign was to subvert the Protestant religion. It would have sharpened the fears of those who already saw James as on the same road that had led Louis through legal manipulation to the *dragonnades* and the Revocation. Above all, as the Whitehall newsletter argued, such an action could have had incalculable effects on trade. The Revocation had led to severe disruption of the trade of France – there had been 'great alteration in the French Exchange, by reason of the

---

34 Guillaume Carbonnel, Jacques Deneu, Pierre Houblon, Humfroy Willett, Isaac (II) de Lillers [LMA, CLA/050/02/002, pp. 37, 42, 61]. In 1686 an order was issued for the search and arrest of a deacon, Pierre Fauconnier, and the seizure of any arms found at his house [TNA, SP/44/337, p. 125].
35 See Appendix 3.

severe proceedings against the Protestants'[36] – and, as Appendix 3 shows, any large-scale withdrawal of refugee and existing French merchants in England would certainly have been very damaging.

Clearly, a *Quo Warranto* was planned against the Threadneedle Street church at James II's Court in 1686. Papers are likely to have been prepared, ready to be served. Probably a message was passed to the consistory through David Primerose or other church officers, to gauge whether the church would yield without a struggle. Then at the last minute, perhaps it was decided that the practical difficulties and potential consequences outweighed the possible gain, and the papers were either never served or immediately withdrawn. If that is an accurate assessment of the situation, the question arises, why is there no mention of the proposed *Quo Warranto* in the church's consistory minutes? They are extant, and very full, and what was known to David Primerose and Roger Morrice was undoubtedly known also by the elders in the Threadneedle Street Consistory. To judge from the newsletter report quoted, there must have been much turbulence in the church. Yet its records are silent, in mute but eloquent testimony to its fear of the authorities.

The evidence we have examined for the years 1685 and 1686, when James was not under pressure, shows that the king thoroughly disliked the Huguenots. This was demonstrated publicly when he abandoned his brother's policy of encouraging refugee immigration, but his actions suggest a more personal aversion. On their own, the delays in allowing a brief for refugees following the Revocation might simply be set down to a lack of charity. However, the qualifications carefully thought through to ensure that any relief that the public did offer was minimized and restricted, the attempt to use the precise conformity of the 'Lambeth model' to undermine the main conformist church at the Savoy, the proposed use of a *Quo Warranto* to undermine the main non-conformist church at Threadneedle Street, the burning of Claude's account of the persecutions in France – these add up to a conscious attack on a broad front, and a potential crisis for French Protestantism in England. Actions speak louder than words, and from the Huguenot viewpoint these actions were deliberate and malign. A year later the poet John Dryden, poet laureate and recently converted to Catholicism, would defend James:

> Behold! how he protects your Friends opprest,
> Receives the Banish'd, succours the Distress'd:
> Behold, for you may read an honest open Breast.[37]

---

36 Thomas Papillon to Sir James Oxenden, 16/26 September 1685, cited in Emily Papillon (1923), p. 756.
37 *The Hind and the Panther* (1687), iii, lines 876–8.

A twentieth-century defence of the king, written on the eve of the Second World War, attempted the same line of argument, but was woefully deficient in its understanding of the import of the monarch's actions.[38] Such defences of James do not hold water when set against the hard evidence of 1685–6.

Where we can determine the source of these actions, they all lead back to the king himself. To them can be added one more damning piece of evidence – his part in undermining the linen manufactory at Ipswich, investigated in Volume II.[39] For that we have the word of Louis XIV's agent Bonrepaus, who reported home that James consciously turned a blind eye to his activities and allowed him freedom to act because he viewed the refugees as his enemies, even though king and parliament both regarded the matter 'comme capital pour ce Royaume'.[40] James's early supporters often defended his actions on the grounds of his special concern for the national economy. Ailesbury, for example, claimed that 'trade he had much at heart, and his topic was, liberty of conscience and many hands at work in trade'. William Dicconson echoed that 'trade which is so beneficial to the Nation, was so peculiarly his care, that never Prince understood it better, or advanced it more'.[41] Yet regarding the Ipswich settlement, in a matter of significant economic concern to both France and England, James fostered an action undoubtedly detrimental to English interests. There is no possible reason to doubt Bonrepaus, whose self-interest lay in underlining the difficulties in his path rather than explaining that the king had opened the way for him. If the argument of most biographers that James was no mere puppet of either the French king or his English councillors is accepted,[42] then there is only one conclusion to be drawn. The king's personal antipathy towards the Huguenots overrode any concern he might have had for trade or the national interest.

When he came to the throne in 1685, the new king declared that he would support the Church of England, knowing that its principles were favourable to monarchy. He repeatedly assured his subjects that he would 'Preserve this Government both in Church and State, as it is now by Law Establish'd'.[43] This was an excellent platform for immediate Tory support,

---

38 Malcolm V. Hay (1938), chap. VII.

39 Gwynn (2018), 76–9.

40 TNA, 31/3/166, Sér. Angl., Reg. no. 157, f. 128; 31/3/164, Sér. Angl., Reg. no. 157, f. 53; and 31/3/171, Sér. Angl., Reg. no. 163, f. 93.

41 Ailesbury (1890) I, 103; [William Dicconson] (1816), II, 609.

42 See for instance Miller (1978), 140, 161, 194; Turner (1948), 344–5; Speck (1988), 126.

43 *An Account of what His Majesty said at His First Coming to Council* (Broadside, London, 1684 i.e. 1685 NS). See also Grey, *Debates* (1769), VIII, 344.

and very soon an overwhelmingly Tory House of Commons voted him revenues so generous that he faced no significant financial difficulties for the rest of his rule, especially as trade and consequently customs revenues expanded. At the start of the reign he was both powerful and popular. Rather pathetic rebellions by the Duke of Monmouth and the Earl of Argyle were despatched with ease. James's English army consisted of fewer than nine thousand men at the time of his accession, but more than doubled in size during 1685, and the king was so well provided that he could afford to maintain it without reduction thereafter. Indeed, no other Stuart monarch ever held a position of such strength as did James in the autumn of 1685, which makes his abject flight just over three years later all the more extraordinary. Had he fulfilled the assurances he gave on coming to the throne, it is inconceivable he could ever have lost it in the way he did.

The problem for James was that what motivated him, what drove him on, was guaranteed to rouse massive opposition and to alienate Tories and Whigs alike. A zealous convert to Catholicism himself, his convictions had been strengthened during his second exile (1679–82) at the time of the Exclusion Crisis.[44] He was determined above all to do away with the Test Acts which excluded his fellow Roman Catholics from parliament and from all kinds of public office, together with the penal laws that prohibited Catholic worship. That meant having a parliament willing to pass the necessary legislation. At the start of his reign he hoped this could be achieved through the same Tory Parliament that had proved so obliging with its financial grants. He assumed that its members' attachment to the doctrine of non-resistance must imply unconditional obedience, and expected that, since they professed principles of loyalty to the Crown, they would simply do as he wished and repeal the laws that he found objectionable. However, he completely failed to comprehend the enduring power of the Reformation and the depth and long history of anti-popery in the country, and to understand that Anglican Tories might be as staunch in defence of the law as in defence of the king. He was blind to the fact that the Tories were at least as loyal to the Church of England as to the monarchy, and as fiercely anti-Catholic as they were anti-nonconformist.

By the end of 1685, James had realized he could not win over the parliament, which he prorogued in November; it was not to meet again during his reign. He had already begun to commission Catholic officers in the army by dispensing them from the provisions of the 1673 Test Act using the royal prerogative, and he was blunt with parliament that he would retain them. It was around this royal demand for an army in which

---

44 HMC, Dartmouth I, 36; Speck (2002), 27.

Roman Catholics would have commissions that an opposition developed in the 1685 House of Commons. The military historian John Childs estimates that by the end of 1685, 141 Catholics held commissions in the English army.[45] James steadily widened the use of his dispensing powers, using similar powers to dispense some English Nonconformists (especially Quakers) as well as Roman Catholics from the penal laws. By purging the judicial bench, he managed in June 1686 to obtain a favourable verdict in the test case of *Godden v. Hales*, when Lord Chief Justice Herbert decided that it was 'an inseparable prerogative in the Kings of England to dispense with penal laws in particular cases, and upon particular necessary reasons' and that 'of those reasons and those necessities the king himself is sole judge'.[46] These were steps along the path that led to an open and complete reversal of James's earlier policies.

That startling transformation was revealed to the world on 4 April 1687, when James promulgated his first Declaration of Indulgence, *his gracious declaration to all his loving subjects for liberty of conscience.* In it he declared that 'it is and hath of long time been our constant sense and opinion ... that conscience ought not to be constrained, nor people forced in matters of mere religion'. He promised to protect and maintain his Anglican subjects 'in the free exercise of their religion as by law established, and in the quiet and full enjoyment of all their possessions', but he ordered the immediate suspension of the execution of the penal laws. Any subjects could worship publicly in their own manner provided that local JPs were informed which buildings were to be used and there was no preaching or teaching that might 'alienate the hearts of our people from us or our government'. The oaths of supremacy and allegiance and other tests and declarations ordered by law were not to be 'required to be taken, declared or subscribed by any person ... employed in any office or place of trust either civil or military under us, or in our government'. All English nonconformist subjects and recusants were granted pardon and indemnity for anything in the past that might have infringed the penal laws concerning religion.[47]

In one stroke, the Declaration suspended all the penal laws, the Test Acts and the Corporation Act. Yet it was impossible that this could be the end of the matter: there was too much past history, vested interest and constitutional law involved. Instead James found himself embroiled in more and more contentious issues as he continued and extended plans to intrude Catholics into the universities, purge commissions of the peace

---

45 Ogg (1955), 160; Childs (1980), 22.
46 Kenyon (1966), 439.
47 Kenyon (1966), 410–13.

and lieutenancies in the counties of those who would not favour his policy, and try to obtain a parliament that would actually repeal the Test and Corporation Acts.

The Declaration of Indulgence impacted directly on the Huguenots, both those who had stayed in France and those who had already taken refuge in England. The Declaration claimed that religious intolerance undermined government 'by spoiling trade, depopulating countries and discouraging strangers'. One of its stated objectives was that it should be 'for the increase of trade and encouragement of strangers'. It served, therefore, as the invitation to Huguenots to come to England which had been so notably lacking in 1685–6. As for existing refugees, there was now no block to the foundation of new non-conformist French churches, at least as far as central government was concerned, and no reason why conformists should receive any special favoured treatment should they enthusiastically adopt Anglican ways.

The king's ultimate aim had not changed. He still wanted the penal laws removed, and the disadvantages suffered by his Catholic co-religionists gone. His immediate requirement in the new world that his Declaration had created was to show there was a real possibility of an alliance with the Dissenters, smarting under years of Anglican persecution, which might support that aim. He therefore positively encouraged addresses of thanks which were delivered by some eighty English nonconformist churches and groups glad to have been relieved from unwelcome attack and prepared to acknowledge at least that much. The Huguenots did not need to present addresses to the Crown, since their churches enjoyed their own legal authorization and were not subject to the penal laws. However, they were not slow to show appreciation of James's new direction through their actions. The Threadneedle Street congregation sought and obtained permission to erect a daughter church, l'Eglise de l'Hôpital, in Spitalfields. Ministers who had not been re-ordained into Anglican orders opened new non-conformist churches in the eastern and western suburbs of London in 1687–88, in St John's Street, Spitalfields and Glasshouse Street, Piccadilly respectively.[48] More importantly, new refugees now poured in from France in immediate response to the Declaration, in what was the peak concentration of Huguenot emigration to England (see Figure I.1, p. 10).

Unfortunately for James, addresses of thanks and refugees voting with their feet were not nearly enough for his purposes. What he desperately needed were clear indications of positive support, tangible political support that could be expressed in remodelled local government and

---

48 Gwynn (2018), 105–6, 120–3.

in parliamentary votes that would change the law. New refugees were irrelevant to such purposes, and many English Dissenters, even if prepared to thank the king that they were no longer under active persecution, had no interest in the rest of his agenda and no wish to support his catholicizing policies. Notable exceptions included the Presbyterian journalist Henry Care, who had written anti-Catholic literature at the time of the Exclusion Crisis but now promoted religious toleration,[49] and the Quaker William Penn. There were also some Whigs who now embraced the king's side, such as William Williams, who as a former Speaker of the House of Commons had opposed any extension of the royal prerogative but in 1687 was knighted and promoted to be James's Solicitor General; he was made a baronet the following year. Dissenters and Whigs were divided in their response to the dilemma that confronted them, but a significant number proved willing to accept positions in local government, or to lodge formal complaints against the way they had been treated by their Tory social betters.[50] Many, though, avoided acknowledging the suspending and dispensing powers, showing that they were following their own agenda, not the king's.[51] James found the amount of positive support he received from such sources less than he wished, even after official pressure was used to encourage specific support for his prerogative, not merely general expressions of thanks.[52] Too many of those whom James was now wooing simply did not trust him and opposed the arbitrary suspension of parliamentary legislation. Too many believed, with reason, that the only real purpose underlying his actions was to benefit Roman Catholics. Too many looked to the example of France to interpret where his policies were leading. Too many sympathized with the view of the Earl of Halifax, whose influential *Letter to a Dissenter* (1687), distributed simultaneously in towns throughout the country, suggested the Dissenters were 'to be hugged now' only so they could 'be the better squeezed at another time'.[53]

Still worse for James, the events of 1687 confirmed that the Tories and the Anglican leadership were not prepared passively to fall in line with what he had done. On the contrary, Archbishop Sancroft wrote against the Declaration, urging his clergy not to subscribe any addresses to the king thanking him for including in it his promises to protect the Anglican Church. Bishop Compton of London had already been suspended in 1686 for refusing to act on a royal order that he proceed against

49 See Lois G. Schwoerer (2001), chap. 8.
50 Goldie (1993).
51 Gary S. De Krey, 'Reformation and "Arbitrary Government": London Dissenters and James II's Polity of Toleration, 1687–1688', in McElligott (2006), 17.
52 *Entring Book*, Q, pp. 120, 132, 149.
53 Kenyon (1969), 106.

John Sharp, rector of St Giles in the Fields, for anti-Catholic preaching. Other London clergy showed their views by mounting a campaign of anti-Catholic propaganda. The Lord High Treasurer, the Earl of Rochester, had supported Compton's suspension but was dismissed in 1687 when he refused to turn Catholic.

Major issues of principle emerged as the king moved towards and then implemented his change of direction. The Declaration promised Anglicans 'the free exercise of their religion as by law established', but how did that square with James's campaign to force Magdalen College, Oxford, and Sidney Sussex College, Cambridge, to appoint Roman Catholic presidents and so breach the Anglican monopoly of the universities? Was it acceptable that the king should 'closet' individuals specifically to try to secure a parliament that would repeal the Test and Corporation Acts when a packed parliament would simply have been a rubber stamp rather than a representative institution? What is not in doubt is that James was personally at the forefront of the decisions that were made, big and small alike. Roger Morrice reported the process whereby the Commission for the Peace was purged and altered in November 1686:

> There was but two bookes of all the Justices in England at the Board, and his Majesty had one of them in his hand, and read the names himselfe, and with his own pen did marke, or alter them as he thought fit, and trusted not the Clark of the Counsell to read the names.[54]

Matters came to a head after James issued his second Declaration of Indulgence in late April 1688, following it up the following month by an Order in Council requiring that it be publicly read in churches on two successive Sundays. The Archbishop of Canterbury and the Bishops of Bath and Wells, Bristol, Chichester, Ely, Peterborough and St Asaph responded with a widely distributed petition requesting they be excused. They stressed that their unwillingness to publish the Declaration was due not to 'any want of duty and obedience', nor to 'any want of due tenderness to Dissenters', but especially because it was 'founded upon such a dispensing power as hath been often declared illegal in Parliament'.[55] They were promptly sent to the Tower on the grounds that their petition was a seditious libel, that is, a publication likely to bring the ruler or government into hatred or contempt. However, their stance was public knowledge and few clergy read the Declaration. Their arrest united the country as few other things could have done. The bishops were supported on their way to imprisonment by

---

54 *Entring Book*, P, p. 658.
55 Kenyon (1966), 441–2.

a 'very great' crowd, with 'the Watermen generally crying God bless the Bishops', while a delegation of ten nonconformist ministers visited them in the Tower to bear witness to their constancy in the Protestant faith.[56] Their eventual acquittal was met by cheering in the court that lasted over half an hour, a great shout of joy from the soldiers encamped at Hounslow Heath, the ringing of church bells, bonfires in the streets of London that night (contrary to specific royal order) and subsequent echoes of rejoicing around the country. Bishop Lloyd of St Asaph made a triumphant progress through his diocese after his acquittal.[57]

England was in disarray, with 'the nation in high discontent' according to the Tory John Evelyn on 12 July, and 'publick affaires ... in a very tottering posture', with 'no party engaged to the Crown' according to the Presbyterian Roger Morrice the following month.[58] For James, the die was cast. At the same time as the bishops were acquitted, seven prominent men sent an invitation to William of Orange in the Netherlands, pledging support if he invaded and assuring him that the invasion would succeed. They covered a diverse range of opinions and backgrounds: Henry Compton, the suspended Bishop of London; the Tory Earl of Danby, a former Lord Treasurer; Lord Lumley, who had become a Protestant in 1687; Edward Russell, who had joined William's service earlier in the 1680s; Henry Sidney, brother of Algernon Sidney and general of British regiments in Dutch service 1681–5; the Earl of Shrewsbury, who was to take £12,000 to Holland for William's cause; and the Earl of Devonshire, who had been active in the Popish Plot proceedings of the late 1670s.

Well before he received the invitation, William had already made the decision to invade. He could not afford to ignore the pregnancy of James's wife, Mary Beatrice of Modena, but probably at first did not take it too seriously in view of her previous miscarriages. However, the birth in June 1688 of James's namesake son and heir changed the situation fundamentally. It demoted William's wife Mary from the position of heir apparent to the British thrones; and it raised the possibility of a long succession of Catholic kings.

In any event there was a still more basic political consideration. The two rulers James II and William III matched each other in one respect. Each had one overriding aim governing their policy, for which they would risk anything. For James, it was to remove all obstacles in the way of his fellow Roman Catholics. For William, it was to check French power under Louis XIV and so secure the continuing independence of the

56 *Entring Book*, Q, p. 277; Harris (1993), 129.
57 Miller (1978), 187; Turner (1948), 403–4.
58 De Beer (1955), IV, 590; *Entring Book*, Q, p. 286.

Netherlands. In terms of restraining Louis, the position of Britain was critical. Louis had won victory after victory over many years, and so long as James or a Catholic successor ruled in England, Dutch prospects for long-term success against their powerful neighbour were very poor. Access to British resources through a firm alliance had the potential to make a major difference. William, therefore, had long kept a close eye on what was happening across the Channel, and in 1687 he sent special envoys, first Dijkveld and later Count Zuylestein, to sound out both Anglicans and Dissenters in the aftermath of the Declaration of Indulgence. Their reports suggested the Dutch leader could hope for support in England, although they would also have shown him that it might be lukewarm and fickle.

The invasion of England in 1688 was an extraordinary, massive gamble. It came exactly a century after the comprehensive failure of the Spanish Armada. It was little over three years since James had put down Monmouth's rebellion with ease. But for William, it was a gamble that had to be taken, and luckily for him the cards fell his way. The Channel crossing late in the year in November eventually proved possible. James panicked, lost his nerve and fled. In January 1689, the English parliament voted that the throne was vacant, and offered it to William and Mary, who were crowned the following month. That was not the end of the matter, for international consequences immediately followed as the Dutch declared war on France and Louis gave assistance to James. In March 1689 James landed at Kinsale in south-west Ireland, and the scene was set for the Irish conflict that we will consider in Part Two of this book. In 1688, though, William's success had been remarkable for its speed and (in England) for how little bloodshed had accompanied it. The next chapter shows the critical role Huguenot refugees had played, largely unintentionally, in what unfolded at the time of the Revolution.

III

The Crisis of the Age: A Climate of Fear, Developments in the 1680s and the Refugee Presence

The sheer speed of the Glorious Revolution of 1688 demands attention. The suddenness with which James's position collapsed, the surrender of the substantial army that he had developed with so few shots being fired in England, the failure of any substantial group of Englishmen to come to his defence: these all require explanation, and many biographies of James and books about the Revolution have been written in consequence. What this chapter adds to the jigsaw of factors that must be considered is the recently increased number of refugees that were in England by 1688, the significance of the timing of their arrival, and the way Louis XIV's actions constantly undermined what James hoped to achieve. English historians have not always considered these matters seriously, but they are too significant to be neglected.

THE CRISIS OF THE AGE AND A CLIMATE OF FEAR

'It is really to be feard', preached Thomas Sharp in Leeds on Christmas Day 1679,

> that there is a Great day coming upon us of these Lands, that in al probability may exceed in terror that of the Jews ... because it hath been the Lot of all the Protestant churches in all nations about us, the Netherlands, Valtoline, Savoy, the whole Empire, Germany, Bohemia, Ireland, Scotland, & why should impenitent England be left unpunished?

The preacher was reflecting on the Popish Plot 'as an apocalyptic struggle between the true Gospel and popery, by placing it within the Reformation narrative and giving it an historical and international framework'.[1] Many others thought along such lines, such as Henry Care, whose *History of the Damnable Popish Plot, in its various Branches and Progress* argued that there was a general Roman Catholic design under French leadership to overwhelm and pluck down Protestantism.[2] Echoes of such thinking can be heard with increasing frequency over the next decade.

'The year 1685 was such an epoch', wrote Jacques Pineton de Chambrun, a Protestant minister in the principality of Orange, 'that future ages shall look upon to be the most dreadful that hath happened'.[3] He was not referring merely to the afflictions and misfortunes of his own family, although the introduction to our second volume showed that those were severe enough in all conscience.[4] Rather his reference was to the whole state of Europe, and especially to the Revocation of the Edict of Nantes and its accompanying atrocities. The feeling Pineton voiced was common to most of Protestant Europe, and there was a growing awareness through the 1670s and 1680s that this was a time of decisive importance, a crisis for the whole international Protestant community in the face of the threat of a universal Catholic despotic monarchy.

In England, in 1675, the House of Commons was assured by Mr Mallet, one of its members, that 'the French sword is guided by Antichrist'. In 1680 the House reminded Charles II how the murderous tendencies of popery placed all European Protestants 'in the same common Danger'. The following year another member, Sir Henry Capel, spelled out the 'universal design against the Protestant Party': 'We see France has fallen upon the Protestant Party there', he said. 'The Emperor has mastered them in Hungary, and what has been done in Bohemia, they say, broke the Prince-Elector's heart'.[5]

Writing in exile in the Netherlands, Thomas Papillon confided similar thoughts to his diary in September 1685:

> Oh what mourning should there bee at this day, and what crying to the Lord in regard of the taking away the means of grace from them in France, the sad feares concerning England and other parts, God's Church and people beeing everywhere oposed and designed for Ruine.[6]

---

1 David L. Wykes, 'Dissenters and the Writing of History: Ralph Thoresby's "Lives and Characters"', in McElligott (2006), 180–1.
2 Second edn, 1681, 73–6.
3 Pineton (1689), 12.
4 Gwynn (2018), 5.
5 Grey, *Debates* (1769), III, 336, and VIII, 328; *CJ* IX, 642.
6 HL, Emily C. Papillon (1923), p. 768.

From the refugees' perspective, they and their people lived near the heart of this crisis.

On both sides of the Channel, it was widely recognized by people living through the 1680s that theirs was no ordinary decade, but an exceptional, momentous one. The language of the day was extravagant beyond any normal frame of reference. In France, it was expressed in the whole cult of the Sun King, in architecture at Versailles and in words when Louis XIV was compared with the gods and heroes of classical mythology like Apollo and Hercules, or praised (as he was by Bossuet following the Revocation of the Edict of Nantes) as 'this new Theodosius, this new Marcion, this new Charlemagne'.[7] We have already noted the extreme polarization of opinion caused by such language and the extraordinary hostility displayed towards Louis by English people of every shade of religious and political opinion.[8] Just as Catholics in France drew on ancient and classical examples to praise their king, so on the Protestant side an undated French attack on him maintained that the cruelties, inhumanities and torments he inflicted and maintained on his Protestant subjects surpassed even those of pagan tyrants, a sentiment reflected also by John Evelyn in his *Diary* when he commented on the 'unheard of cruelties to the persecuted protestants of France, such as hardly any age has don the like even amongst the pagans'.[9]

Gilbert Burnet, writing his *History of His Own Time*, likewise thought that 1685 was a point of the greatest moment, a year that 'must ever be remembered, as the most fatal to the protestant religion'. Taking a European perspective, he pointed to a Catholic monarch acceding to the English throne, the electoral dignity in the Palatinate going to 'a most bigoted popish family', the Revocation of the Edict of Nantes in France and the Duke of Savoy (under French pressure) recalling the edict his father had granted to the Vaudois.[10] Burnet believed the Protestant religion had suffered five great crises, the first in the time of the Emperor Charles V, the second in the late 1550s, the third in the late 1580s and the fourth in the 1620s. The fifth and (he hoped) final crisis he saw as beginning in 1672 with Charles II's Declaration of Indulgence and the emergence of a ministry in England whose members were bribed by Louis XIV, coinciding with Louis's armies sweeping through the Low Countries and bringing the Protestant northern states of the Netherlands 'very near the extremities of despair'.[11]

Europeans could be in no doubt that Roman Catholicism was in the ascendant. France had emerged from the Thirty Years War as Europe's

---

7 Burke (1992), 6, 104–5.
8 Gwynn (2018), 235–6.
9 BL, King's MS 140, f. 203b; De Beer (1955), IV, 498.
10 Burnet (1833), III, pp. 74–5.
11 Burnet (1833), I, p. 563–4, 569–88, 594.

most powerful state, and its power was marked by growing absolutism. Everywhere Protestantism seemed on the defensive, and its deterioration never seemed more striking than in the late 1680s. In May 1686 John Evelyn envisaged a 'universal designe' with France at its centre:

> The Duke of Savoy, instigated by the Fr[ench] King to exterpate the Protestants of Piemont, slew many thousands of those innocent people, so as there seemed to be a universal designe to destroy all that would not Masse it, thro[ugh]out Europ, as they had power.

Four days later Evelyn returned to the subject with an addition that would hardly have pleased King James II: 'The Duke of Savoy, instigated by the French [king], put to the sword many of his protestant subjects: No faith in Princes.'[12]

In January 1688 Roger Morrice was in tune with the same sentiment when he reviewed the state of the 'Protestant Interest' across the continent, especially in the light of very recent events since 1684, and concluded it should be 'often and seriously' taken to heart,

> for in most Kingdomes and States it is utterly suppressed, and in others dangerously threatned, in Bohemia, Walacia, Moldovia, all Hungary and severall other Countries it is quite utterly destroyed. So it is in France ... so are also the Albigences, and Waldences in the Duke of Savoys Territories ... And Geneva is now in great hazard ... And as thus the Protestants are universally weakened, so they are in most places utterly suppressed in some others utterly destroyed, and in some others cruelly tormented or Persecuted as in France Savoy Hungary etc, where the Emperour has already during the War prohibited the Protestants.[13]

Plainly, there were powerful reasons to fear for the future of European Protestantism. As for England, when we examined in Volume II why the welcome encountered by the Huguenot refugees in Britain was far more affirming and positive than past precedent suggested was likely, our explanation involved analysing the phenomenon of anti-popery. We found that phenomenon had little to do with contemporary English Roman Catholics, who were generally harmless and unthreatening, but it had a great deal to do with historical memory and how past English experience was interpreted. The long roots of anti-popery stretched back to the persecutions of Queen Mary's reign in the mid-sixteenth century

---

12 De Beer (1955), IV, 511.
13 *Entring Book*, Q, pp. 232–3.

as presented to English men and women through John Foxe's 'Book of Martyrs', and then through the Massacre of St Bartholomew, the threat of Catholic Spain with its Armadas, and into the seventeenth century with the Gunpowder Plot of 1605 and the massacres of Protestants in Ireland in 1641 and in the Piedmont in the 1650s. The popular identification of Catholicism with absolutism, tyranny, persecution and bloodshed undoubtedly helped inspire the welcome widely offered to the new refugees of the 1680s and the notably generous public collections made on their behalf.[14] It also helps account for why 'paranoia about popery' meant that 'religion was at the heart of the Revolution' in 1688.[15]

In the 1670s new developments added to English fears, causing anti-popery to be expressed in an increasingly hysterical and violent manner. Louis XIV's growing power made him a much greater threat to European Protestantism than Philip II of Spain had ever been in Queen Elizabeth's reign. In 1673 Charles II's brother James, then heir apparent, confirmed his Catholicism openly when he declined to take the Anglican sacraments, resigned office under the terms of the Test Act, and married the Catholic princess Mary Beatrice of Modena, who was a French protégée. These developments transformed the potential political future of Britain and increased the French threat, at a time when there were already pressures on Protestants in France, Germany and Hungary.

John Miller's study *Popery and Politics in England 1660–1688* shows how it was against such a background that, in the winter of 1677–8, Andrew Marvell's *Account of the Growth of Popery, and Arbitrary Government in England* was published. The *Account* reminded its readers of the horrors of popery, which Marvell defined as 'such a thing as cannot, but for want of a word to express it, be called a Religion: nor is it to be mentioned with that civility which is otherwise decent to be used, in speaking of the differences of humane opinion about Divine Matters'. Marvell added together signs of Catholicism at Court, arbitrary tendencies in government and a persecuting Anglicanism. The sum, he suggested, added up to a plot to bring in popery and absolutism, and he claimed that affairs were moving towards a crisis. Miller points out that fears of 'Popery and Arbitrary Government' had a serious rationale, since Charles II's long-term alignment with France developed just as Louis was emerging as the 'epitome of absolutism and the greatest enemy of European Protestantism'.[16]

Marvell's opening sentence talked of a long-standing design 'to change

---

14 Gwynn (2018), 236ff.
15 Speck (1988), 233–5.
16 Marvell (1677), 5; Miller (1973), 93, 149–51.

the Lawfull Government of England into an absolute Tyranny, and to convert the established Protestant Religion into down-right Popery'.[17] His *Account* struck home, providing fertile soil for the imaginings of Titus Oates's supposed 'Popish Plot', and for many pamphlets and speeches in the House of Commons which repeated the stereotypes of the day and underlined the danger popery posed to the state. One such speech by a Cornish MP, probably Hugh Boscawen, was recorded by Roger Morrice in May 1679:

> This is the time, so I must repeat it, that it is indeed the time, that is to say the Moment of time, for if wee Suffer it to slip from us, it may never be in our power to regaine it, and then our children may be bound to curse us, for I must tell you it is utterly impossible ever to secure the Protestant religion under a Popish Successour for unlesse you do totally disable him from inheriting the Protestant Countrey, The tyranny of the Sea of Rome will infallibly steale upon You.[18]

The events of the 1670s and the 'Popish Plot' had shown the strength of Protestantism deep within the psyche of later Stuart Englishmen. Passing over the Exclusion Crisis and jumping to James's reign, little imagination is required to appreciate how quickly it could again be aroused. The Huguenots provided extra fuel for the fire, which had not previously been present. There were now some thousands of refugees in the country, and they had been arriving sporadically since 1681, when their advent had been accompanied by intensive news coverage.[19] Every individual refugee was by his or her very presence a silent advertisement for the real pain a Catholic king could inflict. Some Englishmen would have remembered how they had been warned, in sermons at the time of the 1681 collection for the first refugees, that 'you know not how soon your own condition may be the same with theirs'.[20]

There was real reason to fear popery at the Royal Court in view of its connections with the persecuting policies of the French king. Moreover, in English eyes, Louis had demonstrated very clearly that no reliance could be put on any promises by a Catholic monarch. Had he not just repealed a 'perpetual and irrevocable' edict? So when James promised to maintain the Church of England but proceeded against the Fellows of Magdalen College, the future Bishop Burnet commented:

---

17 Marvell (1677), 3.
18 *Entring Book*, P, p. 193.
19 Gwynn (2018), 243–4.
20 Bolde (1682), 33.

we must crave leave to remember, that the King of France, even after he had resolved to break the Edict of Nantes, yet repeated in above an hundred Edicts, that were real and visible violations of that Edict, a clause confirmatory of the Edict of Nantes, declaring that he would never violate it.[21]

When the scholarly printed edition of the *Entring Book* was imminent, a conference at Cambridge, 'The World of Roger Morrice', resulted in an accompanying volume. Edited by Jason McElligott, it was published by Ashgate in 2006 and entitled *Fear, Exclusion and Revolution: Roger Morrice and Britain in the 1680s.* The title is appropriate, for in addition to telling us much about anti-popery and the increasing attention paid in Jacobean England to events in France, Roger Morrice's *Entring Book* offers a wider perspective on the fears that beset the country's people. Indeed his whole work might be said to be framed by fear, opening as it does with the genesis of Oates's 'Popish Plot', which greatly increased public alarm, and winding down in early 1691 after some pressing fears had been temporarily relieved following William's victory the previous year at the Battle of the Boyne and James's consequent withdrawal from Ireland to France. The Popish Plot was characterized, Jonathan Scott rightly remarked, by 'pitiless determination and a cold-blooded cruelty'.[22] Thereafter, as McElligott says, there was 'a palpable sense of ... fear and foreboding in the 1680s', which helps to explain why the Revolution took the form it did, a fear all the stronger because 'men and women of the 1680s from a variety of different backgrounds habitually read their present in terms of past events, and, as a result, were frightened for their future'.[23] There were even prophecies of future trials confounding Protestants to keep the cauldron of fear bubbling.[24]

Fear is a very strong emotional and motivating force, and there is no doubt that it powerfully affected Morrice and his contemporaries. Brilliantly if unintentionally, the *Entring Book* exposes the climate of fear in which English Nonconformists – and their French refugee counterparts – lived in the 1680s. It is never easy to penetrate through to the real emotions of people in the past. Morrice is an amazingly impersonal author who refuses to let the reader into the secrets of what he is doing or where exactly he is living. After 925,000 words, a careful reader would still not know whether he was married. At first glance, he does not seem a likely source to reveal human emotions. But one thing that comes through loud

---

21 Burnet (1688), 8.
22 Scott (1990), 109.
23 McElligott (2006), 3–4.
24 *The Prophecy of Bishop Usher* (London, 1687), 1–3.

and clear, page after page, is the strain under which he and his friends lived in the 1680s. It is even more telling when his reticence briefly slipped in February 1689 and he rejoiced that he was

> never at Westminster Hall, nor at the Parliament house since Anno 1679 ... till Monday Feb[ruary] 4 instant, nor have scarce ever walked one turn in that Hall without feare since Anno 1662, till the day aforesaid, when I walked with true liberty and freedome ...[25]

Early in 1688, thinking back to the aftermath of Monmouth's rebellion, Morrice recalled how in 1685 'every man' was then 'not only affraid of his neighbour but almost of himselfe'.[26] Even without the added stress of rebellion, fears were well founded. They derived from the contemporary constitutional, legal and religious environment. Whether in great causes like the *Quo Warranto* against the City of London, or in small matters that impinged only on the individual, the law was being applied in a manner that was truly frightening. The decade of the 1680s was marked by packed juries and unfair trials. Defences might not be thoroughly heard; as Henry Cornish said when refused a postponement to bring from the north a witness he claimed could prove his evidence, 'it was the same thing to deny a man a tryall, and to put him under an utter impossibillity of defending himselfe'.[27] All too often judges browbeat witnesses and accused persons, imposed huge fines, like the £10,000 levied on Thomas Papillon or the £40,000 on John Hampden, and handed down vicious sentences like the murderous flogging to which Titus Oates was subjected. In one case the judges changed an opinion they had already given following the demotion of the Lord Chief Justice, and a seventeen-year-old soldier was executed in consequence.[28] In treason cases, where the interpretation of intent was all important, mere suspicion could be assumed to be grounded fact.

The legal situation was not as frightening in England as it was in Scotland, where the state could inflict torture and did so without conscience or restraint.[29] Yet even in England, no one was safe. The full severity of the law could be felt right across the spectrum, by great Whig leaders like Sidney (executed on the strength of his as yet unpublished *Discourses Concerning Government*) or the Earl of Shaftesbury (who died in exile on the continent), by the Roman Catholics Viscount Stafford and Oliver Plunket (executed on perjured or inadequate evidence), by merchants like

---

25 *Entring Book*, Q, p. 458.
26 *Entring Book*, Q, p. 239(2).
27 *Entring Book*, P, p. 485.
28 *Entring Book*, Q, pp. 99, 104, 108.
29 See for example *Entring Book*, P, pp. 441–2.

Patience Ward and Thomas Papillon, forced into exile overseas, by hapless lesser folk like those caught up in Monmouth's rebellion. The head and quarters of Alderman Cornish, a victim of weak and disputed evidence who proclaimed from the scaffold that the information against him was 'falsely and maliciously sworn', were exhibited for over two years from 1685 to 1687 on the gates of London and on the Guildhall.[30] His rotting remains warned evil-doers of the power of the Crown. They must also have served as a daily reminder of how the law could be abused and manipulated to give full play to royal vengeance.

Algernon Sidney said that 'we live in an age that maketh Truth pass for Treason', in which flourish 'such Constructions as neither agreed with Law, Reason or Common Sense'.[31] The 35-year-old George Jeffreys was promoted directly from the bar to be Lord Chief Justice of the King's Bench specifically to ensure that Sidney was convicted of treason. In his 'Apologie ... on the Day of his Death', Sidney commented that Jeffreys

> had overruled eight or ten very important points of lawe, and decided them without a hearing; whereby the lawe itself was made a snare, which noe man could avoide, nor have any security for his life or fortune, if one vile wretch could be found to sweare against him such circumstances as he required.[32]

Richard Greaves's close analysis of the Rye House Plot trials from the judicial perspective confirms that they did not serve the cause of justice: 'even in the laxer context of seventeenth-century jurisprudence, standards of justice were violated in three key areas'.[33]

Certainly the deliberate use and abuse of law as a political and religious instrument, supported by a powerful censorship of the printing press, was extremely alarming to Morrice, to English Nonconformists and Whigs – and the same tactics were only too well known to Protestant refugees from France. But during James's reign the sense of fear was not confined to such quarters, or to the English capital, or to any one point of time. Far to the north, on the Lincolnshire/Yorkshire border, another diary was being kept by a person of very different stamp to Morrice, the sixteen-year-old Abraham Prym or de la Pryme, a firm Anglican already in rebellion against his father's Presbyterianism. 'All the land quakes for fear!', Prym recorded in July 1687; 'never a day passes but one or other is asking concerning the French, they being thought to be those that K[ing] Jam[es] design's to ruin

---

30 Greaves (1992), 248–50, 407.
31 *Entring Book*, P, pp. 404, 406.
32 Cited in Carswell (1989), 229.
33 Greaves (1992), 250.

us all with, for the Jesuits and Papists here bear all down before them'. Later in the year, on the arrival in England of Irish soldiers, he wrote again that 'all the nation is in fear of being murder'd'.[34] Much earlier, it was from a Scottish ship's captain at Dover that John Erskine, a participant in Argyll's rebellion on his way to join the Anglo-Dutch Brigade in the Netherlands, heard that 'the French king was pulling down all Protestant churches, and designed to take a great army to Britain that he might reduce the people there to the Popish religion'.[35] Fake news abounded, and the rumour mill was widespread, persistent and enduring.

The physical presence of the Huguenot refugees brought home where James's policies might lead Englishmen, not just to the legal and verbal persecution that the Nonconformists had already been experiencing (and which the French Huguenots had experienced before them), but to physical violence through state action enforced by the army: to exile, and penury. The parallels between English Nonconformists and French Huguenots were for Morrice – and other Englishmen – all too real.[36] The time frame for these parallels drawn by Morrice is significant. They do not begin in 1685 with James's accession as a Catholic king. They start much later, after the Revocation of the Edict of Nantes and especially after mid-1686, as what Morrice termed the 'French party' gained influence at the English Court. Such parallels, therefore, must be seen as a vital part of the Dissenters' ambivalence and unwillingness to accept James's protestations regarding the Declaration of Indulgence. James has been the subject of many biographies, but comparatively few underline the importance of Louis XIV's activities in helping explain what happened in England in 1688. Roger Morrice would have found that oversight unaccountable.

Wherever the Huguenots landed – all along the south coast – inevitably the news of their sufferings spread, then followed them as they moved across country in search of work or relief. They were not silent about what had happened to them; on the contrary, Barrillon reported to Louis XIV that they disseminated what he called their exaggerations, rumours and falsities.[37] By 1688 French could regularly be heard spoken in the streets in the east and west London suburbs of Spitalfields and Westminster. However much the censors ensured that nothing was printed in the *London Gazette*, the refugees could not be hidden. A fortunate few were wealthy men, well-connected in the city and England's trade circles. Some brought skills appreciated by English high society, like the craftsmen employed by the

---

34 Cambridge University Library, MS Add. 7519.1, ff. 6v, 7r, and for Prym's religious orientation, f. 9v.
35 Glozier (2002), 94.
36 See for instance *Entring Book*, P, pp. 595, 628, 655; Q, pp. 39, 89, 104, 214.
37 TNA, Baschet transcripts, SP 31/3/162, 19 Nov. 1685 NS.

Earl of Montagu to work on Montagu House in Bloomsbury after it was partially destroyed by fire in early 1686.[38] The generality of the refugees were the subject of sermons reflecting on their faith and misfortune. The veracity of their claims was attested by their own destitution and distress, by responsible members of existing French-speaking congregations, many of whom were well integrated into broader English society, and by royal briefs ordering collections on their behalf. Those collections – three of them during the 1680s, two in James's reign itself – reached every single household in the country, for all three were conducted house-to-house by the local clergy and churchwardens. The amount of money they raised shows they struck home on the English consciousness in a special way, as the sufferings of the Huguenots 'fitted seamlessly into the narrative of Catholic persecution which informed the self-image of many Englishmen and Englishwomen'.[39]

Only occasionally can we actually catch sight of refugees in the action of passing on information to the host community or assisting the spread of Williamite propaganda. Our second volume included the reproduction of two contemporary personal experiences of the *dragonnades*, which ended up in the papers of Bishop Henry Compton of London.[40] One of these was a letter sent in 1685 from Thomas Bureau of Niort to his brother François, a London bookseller, and François must have been either directly or indirectly responsible for the letter reaching the bishop. Earlier, the same François had received from Amsterdam a parcel of about a hundred copies of Pierre Jurieu's *L'Esprit de Monsieur Arnaud*, a work considered very offensive by James and his ministers because it highlighted and exploited tensions and divisions within French Catholicism and laid all the problems of the Huguenots in France at the feet of Louis XIV himself: 'le Roi veut perdre les Huguenots'.[41]

By any standards, the tumultuous decade of the 1680s was unsettling and frightening for the English, as the country lurched from the hysteria of the Popish Plot to the Exclusion Crisis, from the Rye House Plot to the rebellions of 1685, from the accession of a Roman Catholic monarch to invasion and the Revolution. The actions of Louis XIV, the Revocation of the Edict of Nantes in France and the persecution and flight of many Huguenots in the 1680s could only make things worse. Precisely how much worse is not measurable, but if we turn to the actions of James's reign that aroused his subjects' concern, we can see how English fears were constantly sharpened by reflection on what was happening across

---

38 See Murdoch (1992).
39 Gwynn (2018), 264; quotation from McElligott (2006), 6.
40 Gwynn (2018), 330–5.
41 BL, Add. MS 41,809, ff. 178, 193; Jurieu (1684), II, 275.

the Channel. Nor would that cease immediately with the Revolution, for English fears of Louis were promptly given further substance by the angry French king's action in letting loose his troops to ravage the Palatinate (for the second time) in 1688–89.

James's Policies and the Unrest they Provoked

A major source of unease was James's army. The king's requirement to raise more troops to deal with the rebellions that he faced in 1685 was obvious and unquestioned, and his employment of individual Roman Catholic officers was also understandable under the emergency circumstances. It was what happened thereafter that gave cause for concern. The 1661 Militia Act had given Charles II the legal right to command, but it made no mention of a standing army in peacetime. So, officially unrecognized, the army was a department of the royal household, very much the king's force if he could raise enough money to pay for it. Charles had no interest in a standing army and was always short of funds, so any surplus soldiers were simply disbanded. The English army that James inherited in 1685 was a small force of 8865 men, but by the end of the year he had 19,778 men in arms in England, a figure that changed little until 1688.[42]

James had more than doubled the size of his army. He then kept it in being at a time when there was no threat, either internal or external, to justify such an action. That was unprecedented. James, who had no time for the local trained bands, could point to the need to have a more competent, better trained force that could also overawe his subjects to prevent any smouldering thought of rebellion reigniting. Louis XIV's activities in France, though, suggested a different scenario. The *dragonnades* would not have been possible without the French army. Now England had a Roman Catholic king and a substantial police force to do his will, could that force be used to impose Catholicism? It is highly unlikely that James ever thought along such lines. He knew perfectly well that too great a majority of English people were Protestant for force to be a practicable option, and anyway he believed that the situation would change of its own accord once he had established a more level playing field for his Catholic subjects. However, the fear was there. As Patrick Dillon remarks, 'the Whigs of the Exclusion Crisis had been successful in one thing at least: they had told England what to look for in a Catholic king. A powder trail had been laid in the public mind', and the annual army camps that James convoked on Hounslow Heath 'could not but recall the *dragonnades* by

---

42 Childs (1980), xvi–xviii, 1–3.

which French soldiers had forced Protestants to abandon their faith'.[43] The camps were large affairs – the one in 1686 had over 10,000 soldiers in a line of tents about a mile and a half long – and it can hardly be a coincidence that the same entry in John Evelyn's diary on 9 June 1686, which commented on 'many jealosies and discourse what the meaning of this incampment of an army should be', should also report on intensified persecution in France and the burning of Claude's book in England.[44]

English people aware of what was going on in Ireland in 1685–8 would have had extra reason to be scared about what James might be intending, because across the Irish Sea a major transformation of the army was taking place on a religious basis. James had never been to Ireland in his life, knew nothing about the country and depended heavily both for advice and its execution on Richard Talbot, Earl of Tyrconnell. Tyrconnell was an Irish Roman Catholic from an old English background, a man with a fiery temper who knew James well and had long been his servant. The Irish army in 1685 was an entirely Protestant army numbering 7500 men. During James's reign, Tyrconnell oversaw a determined and effective purge of over 7000 Protestant soldiers, who were dismissed and replaced by Catholics. The poor quality of the army did not improve, indeed worsened because the new officers had less experience than those they replaced, but the transformation did mean that the king's Irish troops now shared the king's religion and political aims. It also meant that the English perceived a further threat to their liberties and religion.[45]

The *dragonnades* in France involved very selective billeting accompanied by deliberate violence and pressure applied to extract conversions to Catholicism. In England, the 1679 Disbanding Act had insisted that no private householders could be 'compelled against their wills to receive soldiers into their houses ... without [their] consent', so the legal position was plain. Any subject could refuse to quarter or billet soldiers. However, it was objected during the November 1685 session of parliament that quartering in private houses was widespread and that people were left unpaid for what was taken. 'The Country is weary of the oppression of the soldiers, weary of free quarters, plunder and some felons, for which they have no complaint, no redress', said one MP in the House of Commons, while another coupled such objections with officers evading the Test Act:

The King declared, 'That no soldiers should quarter in private houses;' but that they did: 'That they should pay for all things they took;' but they

---

43 Dillon (2006), 61–2.
44 Childs (1980), 97; De Beer (1955), IV, 514–15.
45 Childs (1980), 2, 68, and chap. 3 *passim*.

paid nothing for almost all they took. And for Officers to be employed not taking the Tests, it is dispensing with all the Laws at once.[46]

In similar vein, Evelyn reported 'greate complaints' about the insolence of 'the forces disposed into severall quarters through the Kingdome' in his diary on 3 December 1685, and later in the same entry he commented on the persecutions raging in France. Early the following year James ignored the long-standing rights of the City of London by requisitioning some Dissenters' meeting houses for barracks and billeting troops within City limits in Fleet Street.[47] It was because the issue of billeting was so touchy a subject that, when he invaded, the Prince of Orange tried hard to ensure that no soldiers took free quarters or were quartered in private houses, especially in the London area. Very early in 1689 William issued a Declaration that, instead, soldiers should 'be disposed of by the Civill Magistrate'.[48]

An overlapping issue involved the use of troops to support King James's political objectives. For example, the unusually lengthy billeting of troops on Bristol in the winter of 1685–86 was apparently a rebuke for supposed support for the Duke of Monmouth, while soldiers supported the Ecclesiastical Commission in its proceedings against Bishop Compton in 1686 and regarding Magdalen College, Oxford in 1687.[49] James, then, made it plain that he wished to extend royal control, and that in so doing he was prepared to make use of the military even if that potentially trampled on legal rights. That, too, was a reminder on a small scale of how Louis XIV used his military power within his own country at the time of the Revocation. It was only a few years earlier that Marvell had identified Catholicism at Court, arbitrary tendencies in government and a persecuting Anglicanism as leading towards popery and absolutism in England and had claimed that affairs were moving towards a crisis. Those fears had not melted away, and the Revocation (and the refugees in its train) highlighted just how toxic Popery and arbitrary government could be, especially if supported by French power.

---

46 Grey, *Debates*, VIII, pp. 358, 365.
47 Childs (1980), 85–6, 88–9; De Beer (1955), IV, 490.
48 *Entring Book*, Q, pp. 364, 426.
49 Childs (1980), 88, 100.

THE IMPACT OF THE REFUGEES

It is important to recognize exactly when during James's reign the greatest number of refugees arrived. Morrice recorded in December 1685 that notwithstanding the renewal in France of 'such unheard of Crueltyes, as have hardly ever sounded in our eares', 'few' Protestants had crossed the Channel that year, 'for its treason for any Vessell to transport them'.[50] Only one other Englishman, Robert Harley, seems to have noted and recorded this,[51] while Bishop Burnet – who was overseas at the time – quite wrongly claimed later that there were large numbers of refugees arriving daily in England in 1685.[52] Burnet has often been followed by subsequent historians,[53] but it is Morrice and Harley who had the truth of the matter. Only 283 new arrivals joined the Threadneedle Street church in the year of the Revocation, for example.[54] The refugees came in greatest strength in 1687, continuing into 1688. That means the real flooding of the country with immigrants escaping Catholic tyranny, and the greatest English concern with news from France, occurred at the precise time when James was pushing most determinedly for his co-religionists to be allowed to hold greater power in the land, just months before William's invasion. Such timing must have been a significant factor in deterring Protestants from supporting James and in helping secure their neutrality during the Revolution. Bishop Burnet may have got the chronological details of the arrival of Huguenot refugees in England wrong, but his basic argument holds good: they were 'such a real argument of the cruel and persecuting spirit of popery, wheresover it prevailed, that few could resist this conviction'.[55] And we know that, excluding refugees who had arrived before the Revocation, fifteen thousand had received assistance between 1685 and the end of 1687, and there were still some twenty thousand French Protestants in England in distress in March 1688, with others continuing to arrive daily.[56]

Within England, we have seen how James did his best to suppress all information about the Revocation and persecutions in France. That was why the *London Gazette* never reported it, causing Evelyn to remark on the unconscionable 'silence' at such a time. It was why there is nothing on the Huguenots in the popular ballads of the moment, since even the word

---

50 *Entring Book*, P, p. 506.
51 HMC 29: Portland III, p. 390.
52 Burnet (1833), III, p. 87.
53 For example Ashley (1977), 187; Coward (1994), 338.
54 Gwynn (1968A), 373.
55 Burnet (1833), III, p. 88.
56 Gwynn (2018), 164–5, 336–8.

'Protestant' was censored from their pages. It was why even the consistory minutes of the French church at Threadneedle Street dared make no mention of the Revocation, at a time when the Lord Chief Justice argued that anything included in a private letter to a friend had been 'published'. Most obviously, it was why Jean Claude's book was marked out for public burning.[57]

For all the government's efforts, the censorship was an utter failure. Indeed, its effects were precisely the opposite of what its architects intended. The awareness of ordinary English men and women about what was happening to Protestants in France increased sharply, and what they came to believe can be charted through the entries made by Roger Morrice in his *Entring Book*. In earlier years, Morrice had had little to say or report about the situation of French Protestants in their home country, even though there were plenty of printed English publications that did so.[58] He offers no comment on the onset of the *dragonnades*; his account has gaps in July–August and early October 1681, probably because he was ill.[59] During the next three years and nine months, through 1682, 1683, 1684 and the first three-quarters of 1685, he refers to the troubles of Protestants in France just twice. The first of these entries (1 May 1682) did not talk about persecution; the second (16 October 1684) dealt specifically with the afflictions of ministers.[60] In other words, as Charles II's reign drew to its close, ordinary lay Huguenots and the persecution they faced in France were not of much interest to Morrice. They were not significant in English consciousness.

From October 1685 to the end of 1688, the situation changed dramatically. Across this slightly shorter period of three-and-a-quarter-years, the *Entring Book* discusses the French situation on no fewer than 35 occasions, with heavy emphasis on persecution and on the sufferings of ordinary lay people. Morrice reflects on the hardships the French Protestants faced, 'not of late yeares nor scarsely formerly … parallelled in all Circumstances'.[61] He describes their 'inexpressible' persecution, the 'unheard of cruelties' practised on them, how they were liable to be kept without food or sleep until 'distracted', or hung up by their toes and hands and fingers 'and other tender parts', or have their noses and lips split.[62]

---

57 Gwynn (2018), 245, 258, and above, pp. 23–7; McElligott (2006), 85.
58 Gwynn (2018), 242–4.
59 *Entring Book*, P, p. 372.
60 *Entring Book*, P, pp. 332–3, 442.
61 *Entring Book*, P, p. 480.
62 *Entring Book*, P, pp. 484, 498, 502.

He reports on the particular inhumanity of the persecution in Savoy,[63] and on increasingly severe edicts against the Protestants in France. Two illustrations will suffice. Morrice writes:

> (24 July 1686)   New French Edicts are issued out more seveare and bloudy then the former to this purpose. First, That no minister of the Protestant religion remaine in that Kingdome upon pain of death. Secondly That if any person of what quality soever does succour or harbour any such person they are condemned to the Gallies forever, and if Women, to the Cloysters and their Goods to be Confiscated. Thirdly Any that makes discovery of such &c shall have 500 Livers for such discovery ...[64]

> (6 August 1687)   Wee hear certainly by severall English Gentlemen lately come out of France that the cruelties are as great or greater if it can possible be there then formerly, That they actually kill none but put them to torments inexpressibly more dreadfull then death it selfe, keepeing them still without meat and sleepe, pricking and pierceing them with sharp instraments of Steele made on purpose, And that they lately brought two Barons in chaines into the Streets, and baited them as we use to do Bulls and Bears, and so they have used of late severall other Noble men, and Gentlemen of Condition.[65]

What Morrice's reports reveal is how what was happening across the Channel became an integral part of the thought pattern of the Jacobean English. Historians cannot ignore it, if they want to understand how James came to lose his throne with so little bloodshed. The 35 references discussed above are simply to the persecutions within France and her immediate borders. Even more important were the thousands of refugees in England itself, living witnesses to popish tyranny, natural subjects of news and sympathy, each with their own story of brutality, suffering and loss.

The timing of Morrice's aroused interest is highly significant. The earliest report was written in October 1685, when Morrice described how

> I have not heard that any considerable number of Protestans of France have been actually killed, but at Montaulban ... Souldiers are quartered upon them, and kept numbers together without sleepe or meate, and

---

63 *Entring Book*, P, pp. 537, 546.
64 *Entring Book*, P, p. 575.
65 *Entring Book*, Q, p. 164.

then in that disorder and distraction hurrey them to Mass, and if upon
reflection they recant it is fellony. Its said that many have fallen down
upon their knees and begged of the Souldiers immediatly to Shoot them,
or run them through with their Swords. Severall thence got away to
Sea, and ventured in open boates, some of which are come lately into
England ...[66]

The new awareness that French events mattered, therefore, did not start
immediately after a Roman Catholic came to the English throne with
James's accession. Its cause was specifically the persecution of ordinary
Huguenot men and women and the withdrawal of the legal protection that
the Edict of Nantes had previously offered them in France.

For James, Louis's actions were nothing short of disastrous. James
had started his reign successfully. He had been well supported by his new
subjects and well supplied by his Tory Parliament. Monmouth's rebellion
drew negligible gentry support and was soon doomed and destroyed. Now
the actions of a foreign king in a foreign land focused attention precisely
on those matters that James did not want discussed in England – on the
damage a Roman Catholic king could do to the Protestant religion, on
the dangerous potential power of an absolute monarch, on whether kings
(especially Catholic kings) could be trusted. Moreover, the timing could
hardly have been worse. James had emerged from the rebellions against him
with the strengthened conviction that God had chosen him for the task of
relieving the position of his Catholic subjects, and keen to act.[67] Thus the
Revocation of the Edict of Nantes in October 1685 became the immediate
background to the second and final session of James's parliament, which
lasted only two weeks and was marked by the absolute refusal of both
Houses to accept the continuing presence of Roman Catholic officers in the
English army. The Parliamentarians, and English people generally, could
not ignore what was happening on the continent. Surely a Catholic king,
with an army supported by Catholic officers and with possible financial and
military support from France, would be invited and tempted to follow the
example that Louis was setting? As such a thought pressed on their minds,
it did not help that news was arriving about persecutions of Protestants
in France and in Orange, about a day of fasting and prayer called in the
Netherlands and about action taken in Switzerland to support refugees.[68]

The overall unsettled atmosphere that came to envelop James's reign
thereafter was a combination of a fear of Roman Catholic government, of

66 *Entring Book*, P, p. 480.
67 Miller (1978), 142–3.
68 Morrice, *Entring Book*, P, p. 488; *CSPD*, 1685, pp. 345, 353, 358, 372, 375–6.

arbitrary rule and of bloody persecution. Behind each of these alarms lay historical experience and how the English understanding of their world and its perils had matured. Behind each of them loomed the shadow of Louis XIV, which hung over not only England but the whole of Protestant Europe. It was nurtured by his huge army and his actions, such as the occupation of Strasbourg (in peacetime, in 1681) and of Orange, the territory that gave William the title of an independent prince. That was supplemented by the Revocation and the diaspora, which spread refugees extensively throughout Protestant Europe and to the New World and elsewhere. A widely reported speech by the Bishop of Valence praising Louis in July 1685 for his work for Catholicism was read as foreshadowing an anti-Protestant crusade in England. The accumulating anxiety built up over years helps explain the abject and wholly groundless terror that seized London and then England more widely in the second week of December 1688, when people 'sate up most of the nights' fearing 'their throats should be cut' by English and Irish Papists.[69]

Protestants argued that since oaths could be annulled by the Pope, the words and promises of a Roman Catholic king could never be trusted. No better illustration of that argument was needed than the Revocation of the long-standing Edict of Nantes that the French kings and Louis XIV himself, as well as his predecessors, had promised again and again to respect.[70] James's own undertakings on coming to the throne were well remembered,[71] and had been shown to be false by his actions after Monmouth's rebellion. If subjects could not trust their king's word, if arbitrary use was to be made of the prerogative, and if ultimately there was no protection to be had through the law, how then could they be safe? Back in 1681, *The Currant Intelligence* had reported Louis XIV's response to the Marquis de Ruvigny and other Huguenot petitioners in France: 'Gentlemen, I have nothing more to say to you, but that I will have all my subjects to be of one religion'. Compare that with the scene in 1687, when a furious James II addressed the Fellows of Magdalen College:

> Get you gone, know I am your king. I will be obeyed and command you to be gone. Go and admit the Bishop of Oxford head, principal, what do you call it of the college, I mean president of the college. Let them that refuse look to it; they shall feel the weight of their sovereign's displeasure.[72]

---

69 De Beer (1955), IV, 486; *Entring Book*, Q, p. 359; Levillain (2006).
70 Gwynn (2015), 165–6.
71 For example, they were cited by Sir Thomas Clarges in Parliament on 12 November 1685; Grey, *Debates*, VIII, p. 356.
72 *The Currant Intelligence*, no. 24 (1681); Miller (1978), 170.

Louis was measured, James apoplectic, but the message was the same. Nothing was to stand in the way of the royal will.

Three issues that alarmed the English political nation during James's reign involved the king bypassing or undermining established understandings and legal protections. First, he repeatedly purged the bench of judges to secure his way. Taken to an extreme, such action must lead inevitably to the appointment of timeservers willing to do the royal bidding, so the conclusion could only be that no legal protection could suffice against determined absolutist action. Second, despite his early promises to preserve the government in church and state as by law established, James's policies soon led him to undermine the Anglican monopoly of higher education by appointing Catholics to key roles at Christ Church, Oxford, Sidney Sussex College, Cambridge, and most notably Magdalen College, Oxford, where his appointment of the President met such resistance that eventually most of the original fellows were deprived of their fellowships for refusing to act illegally, while Anglican services ceased and mass was publicly celebrated.[73] Third, from the end of 1686 James began personally to call individual members of both houses of parliament into his closet and interrogate them about their views and their willingness to support his policies. A later variant of this technique was widely extended to include JPs and deputy lieutenants, officers in corporations and others, in order to produce a compliant parliament. The clear intent of these approaches was to exert such pressure that parliament would be reduced to a rubber stamp in support of the royal will.

Each of these three issues evoked echoes of French events. The path to the Revocation of the Edict of Nantes had been prepared by a long, deliberate process of legalistic interpretations of the law, regulations and applied pressure, and this was clearly understood in England. After the issue of the Declaration of Indulgence in April 1687, Morrice reported the Marquis de Ruvigny's comment that by including in it promises to the Church of England,

> The method they have taken ... is perfectly like that of France, for that King issued out an Edict at first to Confirm the Edict of Nants that gave the Protestants such ample Privilledges and immunities, but in a while after began to Quarrell with some Churches, as built before that first Edict was made, and with some others because they were without

---

73 G.V. Bennett, 'Loyalist Oxford and the Revolution' in L.S. Sutherland and L.G. Mitchell (eds.), *The History of the University of Oxford, v: The Eighteenth Century* (Oxford, 1986), 18.

the Jurisdiction and extent of that Edict, which allegations were both notoriously false, and with others upon the like colour.[74]

The Edict of Nantes that was now cancelled had been proclaimed for nearly a century as 'perpetual and irrevocable'. Plainly, no legal protection could suffice to stand against Louis's simple intent that he would have all his subjects to be of his religion. As for James's intrusion of Catholics into the leadership of the university colleges, it would have served as a reminder that the Revocation was accompanied by the destruction of the Protestant Academies in France.

The years from 1681 to 1686 were characterized by a bitter and intense Anglican persecution of Dissenters. Then in 1686–88 there are three occasions when evidence shows the whole English political nation coming together, notwithstanding that background of deep hostility. The first of these concerned the new refugees directly, and took the form of the strong public response to the 1686 brief for a collection for their support, which raised the remarkable sum of nearly £43,000.[75] This was three times what had been raised by the 1681 brief, even though in 1681 the *dragonnades* had been a new phenomenon and the arrival of many new *réfugiés* was then being extensively publicized in print, whereas in 1685–6 news was being censored and the number of new arrivals was smaller. Given that James II and Jeffreys went to considerable trouble to delay and actively discourage contributions in 1686, the amount given was far more than a generous acknowledgement of the plight of the Huguenots. It was a conscious and heartfelt rejection of royal policy. The French ambassador Barrillon reported to his master that English people showed much zeal in the matter and that James understood that people who were ill-disposed towards him were likely to be those giving most generously.[76]

The second moment at which one can detect very different English groups coming together occurred a little later in 1686, when James oversaw Bishop Compton of London's suspension from office. Here again the refugees had a part, this time but a small one, to play in the story. There was no love lost between the bishop and the king. Compton had overseen the religious instruction of James's daughters, which had left

74 *Entring Book*, Q, p. 89.
75 Gwynn (2018), 264.
76 TNA, Baschet transcripts, SP 31/3/165, 29 April 1685 NS (Barrillon): 'On s'y porte avec beaucoup de chaleur et le Roy d'Angleterre connoist bien que les gens malinten-tionnez pour luy sont les plus prompts et les plus disposez à donner considèrablement.' See also the letter from Bonrepaus to Seignelay, same day and reference.

both Princess Mary and Princess Anne as convinced Anglicans, and the bishop had confirmed them in 1676 contrary to their father's wishes. James's opposition was one reason that Compton had not been appointed to the see of Canterbury after Archbishop Gilbert Sheldon's death in 1677. Amongst the bishops, Compton's biographer Edward Carpenter explains that he 'stood pre-eminent as the determined enemy of Rome'. So it was hardly surprising when in 1685 he was removed from his place as Dean of the Chapels Royal, and from the Privy Council, especially after he spoke strongly and at length in the House of Lords against James illegally appointing Roman Catholic army officers.[77]

Compton was well known to be a good friend of the French refugees, which would hardly have endeared him to James, and in May 1686 he further offended the king when he refused to force changes in the constitution and practices of the French church of the Savoy in compliance with the detailed plans that James and Jeffreys had developed to impose on it a new, stricter form of Anglican conformity.[78] At the same time, the bishop's conferences with his clergy were discussing issues the king did not want raised, such as responses to Roman Catholic propaganda and James's 'notion of having a dispensing Power in himself'. Shortly thereafter, perhaps as a result of deliberate entrapment, John Sharp, rector of St Giles in the Fields, preached severely against the claims of Rome. James ordered Compton to suspend him, which the bishop could hardly legally do without holding a hearing. Compton was then suspended during royal pleasure for disobedience.[79] The instrument used for the suspension was the Ecclesiastical Commission, itself of dubious legality in the eyes of many contemporaries. Political, religious and constitutional issues all coalesced. Roger Morrice commented that Compton's case 'has the whole body of the Kingdome for its defence and support', and on how the bishop was supported by Dissenters as well as his old Anglican friends, 'for indeed it was never known of late yeares that so universall an Interest of Churchmen, Trimmer and Dissenters did follow any one Cause as now follows his'.[80]

The same combination of political, religious and constitutional issues resurfaced still more strongly with the trial of the seven bishops, the last of these three examples evidencing a growing consensus between former rivals. As Halifax wrote to William of Orange in July 1688,

the several parties, though differing never so much in other things, seem to agree in their resolution of preserving by all legal means the

---

77 Carpenter (1956), 82, 84.
78 Gwynn (2015), 132ff.
79 Carpenter (1956), 87ff.
80 *Entring Book*, P, pp. 602, 613.

securities of their religion and their laws. The late business concerning the bishops hath such an effect that it is hardly to be imagined; the consequences are not seen to their full extent by the men in power, though they are not a little mortified by the ill success of it. I look upon it as that which hath brought all the Protestants together, and bound them up into a knot that cannot easily be untied. It is one of those kinds of faults that can never be repaired; all that can be done to mend it will probably make it worse, as is seen already by every step that hath since been made to recover the reputation they have lost by it. It is given out that there will be yet some further proceedings against the bishops; but in that I am an unbeliever.[81]

At the end of the day, historians of James's reign must answer two fundamental questions. Why was it that the Tories decided their loyalty to the Church of England outweighed their loyalty to the monarch? And why were so many Dissenters not willing to trust James and joyously grasp the olive branch – and freedom from persecution – they were offered in 1687? Louis's treatment of the Huguenots in France is a key component of the answers to both questions. It may not have been reasonable for the English to have measured the conduct of their own Roman Catholic king by Louis's persecution of his Protestant subjects, but that is what they did. James's personality, his determination to push the bounds of royal power at every opportunity, his failure to understand the sincerity of those whose views did not tally with his own, his employment of Catholic officers in his armies, his actions both in great matters and in lesser ones like his vindictiveness towards the Monmouth rebels or the combination of petulance and ignorance he displayed before the Magdalen Fellows, inflamed and aggravated the situation.

Ultimately, the combined fear of Roman Catholic rule, arbitrary rule and bloody persecution was so strong that rather than closing ranks behind James as it would have done had William invaded England in 1685 at the start of his reign, the political nation chose in 1688 to stay on the sidelines and simply wait to see what would happen when their king's professional army clashed with William's invasion force. A high percentage even of Anglican clergy then accepted the Revolution settlement. Very recently, Tim Harris argued that 'if we are searching for a turning point in Anglican royalist thinking, we need to look not to 1642 but to 1688', because 'whereas in the 1640s the Anglican royalist position remained so entrenched as to make a negotiated settlement impossible, by 1688 there was enough movement in the Anglican royalist position so as to avoid

---

81 Kenyon (1969), 341–2.

thrusting England into civil war once more'.[82] The evidence presented in this chapter suggests that the turning point for which Harris is searching is rooted less in 1688 than in 1685. Jules Michelet in the nineteenth century and Edmond de Beer in the twentieth were right to observe that the 'Glorious Revolution' was in many respects the English answer to the Revocation of the Edict of Nantes.[83]

82 Harris (2019), 37.
83 Above, pp. 12, 16.

PART TWO

THE IRISH WARS, 1689–92

IV

1689: Schomberg in Ireland

The 'royal need' in 1687, which we examined in chapter II, had been entirely the result of James II's personal wishes and priorities. There was no pressure on James in the spring of that year when he chose to abandon the policy of cooperation with the Anglican establishment that he had inherited two years earlier. No external necessity or compulsion forced him to adopt the very same policy of indulgence towards Roman Catholics and Nonconformists, which had previously been shown to be unworkable in 1672. That was entirely his own choice. By comparison, in 1689 the position of the new king and queen of England, Scotland and Ireland, William III and Mary II, was very different. Their invasion had been a success beyond all realistic expectation, as the English political nation decided that its fears of what a firmly established Catholic dynasty might do with French support outweighed its dislike of the thought of a Dutch ruler. The new king and queen were crowned at Westminster on 11 April 1689. That same day, they learned that James had landed in Ireland with an army of French and Irish troops. Now their need was both obvious and urgent. They had to hold on to their conquests and consolidate.

Two months earlier, John Locke had seen how 'the great concernes of my Country and all Christendom' justified William's invasion, 'for the redeeming [of] England and with it all Europe'. He sought urgent foreign policy action, for even 'if we be, France will not be Idle', so the English had to adopt 'a posture of defence and support of the common interest of Europe'.[1] Not many English Whigs emphasized the Revolution's significance for Europe's future in such a way, but the Huguenot international network thought along similar lines. Jean Le Clerc urged the same argument in his *Bibliothèque Universelle et Historique*, arguing in 1689 that France's enemies should take advantage of what had happened 'to deliver Europe from the slavery into which it was falling'. Philip van

---

1 S.J. Savonius-Wroth, 'Corruption and Regeneration in the Political Imagination of John Locke', in Champion and others (2019), 145.

Limborch, another of Locke's intellectual companions, likewise hoped that once the resources of the three kingdoms could be added to the fight against France, 'at last the excessive power of the Frenchman ... may be restrained by the united forces'.[2] The *République des Lettres* had no frontiers, and the publications produced in the Netherlands educated like-minded readers across Protestant Europe, helping foster agreement for action against Louis XIV.

By the time Louis XIV was defeated and the Treaty of Utrecht signed in 1713, Europe had become accustomed to large-scale engagements and had witnessed the great battles of the Duke of Marlborough at Blenheim, Ramillies, Oudenarde and Malplaquet in the first decade of the eighteenth century. By comparison, the battles fought in Ireland in the early 1690s by the two kings William III and James II were small-scale, and in numerical terms fairly insignificant. At Landen in the Netherlands in 1693, 66,000 French troops faced about 50,000 Williamite soldiers,[3] while at Blenheim in 1704, over 100,000 men were involved and defeat cost the French 40,000 men killed, wounded or captured. By contrast the major battle of the Irish wars, at the tiny village of Aughrim in 1691, was fought out between perhaps 40,000 combatants in all on both sides combined and may have left seven or eight thousand bodies strewn around Kilcommodon Hill.[4]

Small though those statistics may be by continental standards, they make Aughrim the bloodiest land battle ever to have been fought in Ireland, and arguably in the British Isles.[5] It was a far costlier affair than the much better-known Battle of the Boyne. Taking a more strategic view, in the wider scheme of things there can be no doubting the importance of William's victory in Ireland. In 1689, when his campaign there started, William's position in England remained insecure and civil war in Scotland was highly likely, while in Dublin James's viceroy Richard Talbot, Earl of Tyrconnell, was well in control. Defeat in Ireland would have been disastrous for William, leaving the way open both for Louis to pen him in the British Isles and harass him there, and for James to take his army to Scotland with the intention of invading England from the north. William's success, by contrast, took James out of the equation, denied Louis a substantial advantage, confirmed William's own position and reputation

---

2 Savonius-Wroth (2019), 146.
3 Childs (1991), 233.
4 Childs (2007), 332, 337; Wauchope (1992), 223, 233; McNally (2008), 108, 112, 172–3 (McNally argues for a lower death toll of some 5000, but the contemporary accounts support the higher figure).
5 Goldie (2016), 27.

in Britain and allowed him to concentrate on his major lifelong task of holding the French king in check on the Netherlands border.

On both sides, the troops who fought in Ireland were an extraordinary mixture. Their international spread was reflected in their leaders. The Williamite forces were led originally by Frederick Herman, first Duke of Schomberg, a German-born Calvinist and lifelong career soldier who had served Louis XIV as a marshal of France before the Revocation of the Edict of Nantes forced him into exile from that country. He died at the Battle of the Boyne in July 1690, shortly after William had arrived to take command of his Irish army in person. When William returned to England in early September, it was a Dutchman, Godert de Ginkel, later Earl of Athlone, who became the commander-in-chief; he would be replaced by a Huguenot, Henri de Massue, second Marquis de Ruvigny, as the wars came to an end. On the other side, while Tyrconnell was James's viceroy, in 1691 effective control of the army came to lie with the French lieutenant general Charles Chalmont, Marquis de Saint-Ruth.

The troops themselves involved an even wider spread of nationalities. The Williamites included the English, the Dutch, Huguenots, Protestant Scots and Irish, and later Danes (whose regiments incorporated many Germans). The Huguenot component of this force, apart from individual officers who might spring up elsewhere, was concentrated in one cavalry and three infantry regiments. The infantry were under the command of François du Cambon, formerly a chief engineering officer; Pierre Massue de La Caillemotte, younger brother of the Marquis de Ruvigny; and Isaac de la Melonière, who had served as colonel of a French regiment before the Revocation. Schomberg led the cavalry. As for the 6000 men of Louis XIV's French brigade who arrived in 1690 in support of the Irish Jacobite army, their brigade consisted of three battalions of French, one of Walloons, and two of (chiefly Protestant) Germans who had until recently been prisoners of war in French camps.[6]

There was little that could be called glorious about the campaigns in Ireland. The historian is faced, rather, by scenes of confusion, ignorance and incompetence, and by clashes all too often bedevilled by floods and bogged down in mud. The confusion was not caused only by the multiplicity of nationalities and languages on the battle fields, although they certainly did not help. There were other basic problems. For example, in an age when there were no national uniforms, each regiment dressed in its own colours, making it hard to know what was happening in the heat of battle, 'the cloaths of friends & foes are soe much a like', as Sir

6 Wauchope (1992), 94.

Robert Southwell commented.[7] Isaac Dumont de Bostaquet, a Huguenot gentleman from Normandy, who recounted his service in Ireland in his memoirs written between 1688 and 1693, describes how at the Boyne, he nearly stabbed an ally; it was only after the latter had called out in alarm that he saw and recognized 'the green which he wore on his hat which was our rallying signal as well as our sign of recognition'.[8] The two sides endured many problems in common. Both suffered from a lack of ammunition and supplies. Both had inadequate medical support. Both lacked good, reliable intelligence, and might be planning on false assumptions, as was William when, shortly after his victory at the Boyne, he was given misleading information about the result of the naval battle of Beachy Head. Especially in the early stages of the war, neither side knew the size or true capacity of their enemies' forces, although over most of Ireland the Jacobites had an edge in local intelligence.

Modern historians inevitably suffer from the same confusion and ignorance as the combatants in the war since that confusion tainted the sources available for them to study. Contemporary accounts of local actions were mostly written from a markedly biased standpoint and generally made little attempt to provide a balanced picture. The best original report is widely acknowledged on all sides to be that by the Reverend George Story, chaplain to a Williamite foot regiment and later Dean of Limerick, who was prepared to explore the situation around him for himself and reported what he had seen and heard first-hand in his *Impartial History of the Wars of Ireland, With a Continuation thereof. In Two Parts. From the Time that Duke Schonberg landed with an Army in that Kingdom, to the 23d of March, 1691/2, when their Majesties Proclamation was published, declaring the War to be ended*.[9] Story was prepared to be very critical of aspects of the English performance in Ireland, and if in doubt I have tended to prefer his account to others. However, on all too many matters the modern historian lacks key evidence. For example, we know next to nothing about the composition of the rank and file of the army: one single document, which allows us a brief glimpse of some men from Huguenot regiments dissolved ('broken') in Ireland who were assisted in London in the spring of 1699, is so unusual that it has been summarized as Appendix 2 of this volume. It is virtually impossible to obtain certainty about numbers. Michael McNally, the military historian who is the author of the only published book-length work specifically focused on the clash at Aughrim, laments that 'regrettably no single, definitive list exists for either

---

7 BL, Add MS 38.146, f. 97v.
8 Ressinger (2005), 230. Dumont's memoirs were written with no thought of publication and were not published in French until 1864 and in English until 2005.
9 Published in London, 1693.

of the combatant armies which fought at Aughrim. Instead we are faced with a number of contemporary documents which were drafted after the battle, most of which have as many differences as they have similarities.'[10]

Both sides, from time to time, displayed noteworthy incompetence that highlighted their desperate need for better trained officers. The officer corps leading William's English troops who formed the bulk of his original forces in Ireland had been left severely weakened by the refusal of many officers to serve against James, to whom they had taken oaths of loyalty while he was king.[11] Besides, William's priority had been to send troops to the Netherlands for war against Louis XIV, and that effort had creamed off most of the best and most experienced men available before the force for Ireland was assembled. By early February 1689, there were signs of people 'dayly deserting and quitting their commands' in the army.[12] March witnessed a mutiny at Ipswich, where the Scots Guards refused either to embark for Holland or to serve under the Duke of Schomberg, which led to the passing of the first Mutiny Act. All the same, some 10,000 troops commanded by the Earl of Marlborough were sent off to the continent between March and May 1689.[13] As for the Jacobite army in Ireland, 'the long exclusion of Roman Catholics from military life' before James's reign 'left the army chronically short of experienced officers and non-commissioned officers'.[14]

As one small example of the problems on the Williamite side, consider the position of the Huguenot infantry from La Melonière's regiment of grenadiers, commanded by Captain Saint-Sauveur, who were sent to reinforce Sligo in October 1689. The place might have been defensible in the short term, but the garrison commander Colonel Thomas Lloyd had not bothered to supply it with ammunition, powder or provisions and left as soon as he could, so the reinforcements reached the stone fort in the town only to discover the lack of everything necessary, won one small skirmish and then had no option but hastily to accept generous terms, which would surely have never been offered had their opponents understood their dire straits. The boot was on the other foot at Aughrim, where the Jacobite general Saint-Ruth had established an excellent defensive position, but some Irish defenders in one critical spot apparently found that they were provided with fresh ammunition which was useless because it was for English muskets and would not fit into their French flintlocks.[15]

---

10 McNally (2008), 198.
11 Childs (1980), 85, 206.
12 Browning (1991 edn), 547.
13 Childs (1991), 101.
14 Murtagh (1995), 71.
15 These examples are highlighted in Wauchope (1992), 83–4, 229.

An inescapable problem faced by both sides was the Irish topography and climate. Wherever they went, it seemed, the armies found themselves confronted by rivers and bogs. The river Shannon and midland bogs were almost impassable in the winter. The weather was especially bad in the autumn of 1689, full of 'extreamly violent' and 'very tumultuous' winds and rain; De Bostaquet recounted how on the march to Dundalk, at Newry, 'most of the tents in our camp' were blown over.[16] The soldiers' lack of food was often severe, compounded by scorched earth policies that desolated the land. Lacking adequate food, clothing, boots, sanitation and shelter, and following heavy rains, dysentery ('the bloody flux') devastated both armies, especially during the first winter, when 'the most active men on both sides were the chaplains who conducted the services for the dead'.[17] King William wanted a speedy victory, but Irish conditions thwarted any such ambition and confined active campaigning months to less than half a year, from May or June to September or October.[18]

Few encounters can ever have had so many generals on both sides keen *not* to serve as the Irish campaigns of 1689–91. Except for Tyrconnell, none of the leading participants was predominantly interested in Ireland. James had never previously set foot in the country, and quickly showed that his principal concern was to use it as a stepping-stone back to Westminster via Scotland – a stance disastrous for his relationships with would-be Irish subjects, since they wanted him to be Francophile and Catholic but his potential English subjects wanted neither. As for William, Ireland was simply a distraction from what really mattered to him, the situation in the Low Countries. Henry Hyde, second Earl of Clarendon, who had served as James's Lord Lieutenant in Ireland in 1685–86, remarked in 1689 on how William 'has very little curiosity, or sets a very small value on Ireland', while the king himself told the Elector of Bavaria that it was a 'terrible mortification' for him to have to go to Ireland where he would be 'as it were out of knowledge of the world'. Likewise, Louis XIV's only interest was to distract William and force him to waste time and resources away from the continent, and many of his servants in Ireland, like his envoy the comte d'Avaux and the courtier general the comte de Lauzun, were pleased to be recalled as soon as possible.[19]

---

16 Story (1693), *i*, 13, 15, 18, 22, 29–30; Ressinger (2005), 216, 220.
17 Wauchope (1992), 75.
18 Lenihan (2001), 121–3; Childs (2007), 15–16.
19 Simms (1969), 52, 135, 139, 173.

THE START OF HOSTILITIES IN IRELAND

Some of the problems on both sides related to the disorganization with which events unfolded. No one could have envisaged the Irish wars before the surprising speed of the Glorious Revolution in England, so there was no advance planning. There were, however, plenty of tensions and anxieties in Ireland awaiting violent release, following massacres there around the time of the English Civil War and Interregnum, and recent massive purges of Protestants from the Irish army, judiciary and local and central government during James's reign. During the last two months of 1688, Protestants in Derry became aware that local Irish blacksmiths were producing half-pikes and Gaelic daggers and that priests were encouraging their flocks to arm themselves, while across Ireland Protestants gathered what weapons they could, and some fled to England with tales of impending doom.[20]

The war that followed was precipitated not by any determined leader on either side pursuing an intentional plan of action, but by a few 'apprentice boys' in Londonderry. This city in the far north lay in the one part of Ireland where Protestants and Catholics were reasonably evenly matched numerically – by contrast, Tyrconnell estimated that in Munster and Leinster, excluding Dublin, Catholics were in the majority by forty to one, and in Connaught by two hundred to one.[21] With feelings running high, great uncertainty and deep-rooted fears of a repetition of the massacres of 1641 in Ulster, Protestant resistance in Londonderry was to be expected after the existing garrison, which was led by a Protestant, was ordered south to Dublin by Tyrconnell, and a new force of Catholic Irish and Scots under the Earl of Antrim directed to replace it. However, the Protestant leaders in the town were divided about what they should do. They were faced by greatly superior numbers, uncertain about William's situation in England and acutely aware that to refuse admission to the city by the king's army was treason. The decision was taken out of their hands by nine 'apprentice boys', immediately joined by four others, who saw that the Earl's troops had crossed the river and were landing some three hundred yards from the Ferryquay gate. Drawing swords, they dashed to the main guard and seized the keys, then rushed to the gate, hauled up the drawbridge and locked the gate. The leading elements of Antrim's forces were left stupefied just 60 metres outside the gate, having shown no awareness that there might be some cause for haste. A loud shout from within the walls for someone to bring up a 'great gun' was enough

20 Childs (2007), 3–5.
21 Macrory (1980), 119.

to decide them hastily to retrace their river crossing, while the rest of the town was secured.

The apprentices' precipitate action might have backfired, for an inventory taken that night, the night of 7 December 1688, revealed that there were only 300 (mostly untrained) men capable of bearing arms in the city, while the magazine contained just nine barrels of gunpowder and 150 weapons fit for use (as well as a thousand 'very much out of order').[22] However Captain Thomas Ash, who kept a diary throughout the siege, noted that the closing of the gates 'acted like magic and roused an unanimous spirit of defence; and now with one voice we determined to maintain the city at all hazards, and each age and sex conjoined in the important cause',[23] while reinforcements began to come in from the surrounding countryside. Londonderry had proclaimed its Protestantism and adherence to William in what became the prelude to the siege of the town the following year.

The siege lasted over a hundred days, from 18 April until 28 July 1689. It was the longest and most significant siege in the history of the British Isles. The death rate in Londonderry was frightful. The town suffered from continuous mortar fire day and night, one account suggesting that 'five hundred and eighty seven Bombs were thrown into the city' between 24 April and 22 July.[24] The inhabitants, however, suffered far more from starvation and from a particularly virulent fever. By July 1689, the price of quarter of a dog (fattened by eating dead Irishmen) was five shillings and six pence; of a dog's head, two shillings and sixpence; of a cat, four shillings and six pence; and of a rat or mouse, respectively one shilling or six pence. In contrast, as soon as Londonderry was relieved, a pound of good beef would sell for three halfpence. And relief came only in the nick of time, Ash recording in his diary on 27 July that through lack of food, 'of necessity we must surrender the city ... next Wednesday is our last if relief does not arrive before it'.[25] Jacobite intelligence confirms that James's men also expected the defenders of Londonderry to run out of food before the end of July.[26]

The siege of Londonderry was the essential preliminary to the War of the Two Kings. The city had comparatively modern fortifications dating from the early seventeenth century, and there was at the time no bridge across the river Foyle, which was tidal and not fordable. Its defence was

---

22 Childs (2007), 6.
23 Macrory (1980), 130–1.
24 *History of the Wars in Ireland* (1690), 22. The 'bombs' varied greatly in size, with the largest claimed to be '273 pound weight apiece' (Walker (1689), 28).
25 Macrory (1980), 291, 312, 356; Doherty (2008), 195.
26 Royal Irish Academy, MSS H.I.3, 28 July 1689, and see also 24.G.1, 20 July 1689.

vital to the Williamite cause. No other location offered such protection or communications with England, which might lead to relief by sea should the need arise, while the failure of the siege meant that the Jacobites lost their best hope of crossing to Scotland and infiltrating England from the north. Nevertheless, the details of the siege need not detain us. Our purpose is not to rewrite the whole history of the wars in Ireland but to focus on the role of the Huguenots, paying particular attention to 1689, when a large body of troops was first sent from England, and 1691, when the battle at Aughrim was decisive. However, the extraordinary confusion and incompetence that had marked the beginning of hostilities, the lack of advance planning, poor intelligence, the absence of adequate supplies and the real suffering of participants both military and non-combatant, were enduring features of the entire war. They provide the background against which the Huguenot contribution must be judged.

SCHOMBERG AND THE 1689 CAMPAIGN

The first part of the Huguenot contribution was led by the man whom William put in charge of fighting against James in Ireland in 1689, Frederick Herman von Schomberg. Some might raise their eyebrows at the suggestion that this international mercenary soldier from a family with a long and distinguished German ancestry should be considered 'Huguenot'. Born at Heidelberg in the Palatinate in 1615, he was the son of a German father with powerful international connections and of a high-born English mother. He had spent his life in the honourable service of those who needed his military talents, fighting at different times for the armies of Sweden, the Dutch Republic, France, Portugal, Brandenburg and Britain. His high military reputation had been earned fighting to achieve Portuguese independence in the 1660s. Between his birth in Germany and his death in Ireland, his extraordinary career made him a count of the Holy Roman Empire, a count of Mertola and a grandee of Portugal, a French duke and marshal, and an English duke and, in 1689, commander-in-chief of the British forces in Ireland.

Nevertheless, by the time he landed at Torbay in 1688 as William's second in command, there is good reason to classify Schomberg as a Huguenot refugee. He had always been a Calvinist, educated at the Protestant Academy of Sedan and at the University of Leiden. He was naturalized in France in 1664 with his sons Meinhard and Charles. In 1669, he married a Huguenot as his second wife, Susanne, daughter of Daniel d'Aumale, seigneur d'Haucourt. Five years later he purchased the lordship of Coubert, near Paris. The early 1670s saw him created duke and peer of France, appointed commander of the French army in Roussillon, and made Marshal of France. In 1676, he was in sole command of the French forces arrayed against William of Orange. He petitioned the French Crown against the persecution, and *The Humble Petition of the Protestants of France, lately presented to His Most Christian Majesty, by the Mareschal Schomberg, and the Marquis de Ruvigny*, was translated and printed in England in 1685. It was the growing persecution of Protestants and the Revocation of the Edict of Nantes that forced him to move. Many at the French court, including members of his wife's family, were successfully pressured to convert. Schomberg refused to follow suit, saying his religion was fundamental and he would not exchange it for high office. As a mark of special royal favour he was formally granted dismissal from the French army in 1686 and enabled to retire with his family to Portugal. His estates in France, which at first he was allowed to retain, were confiscated by Louis in 1688.[27]

Schomberg did not remain long in Portugal, where the authorities were encouraged by Louis XIV's ambassador to make further unsuccessful attempts to convert him. At the beginning of 1687 he visited William of Orange in the Netherlands, and thereafter travelled to Berlin where the Elector Frederick William made him commander-in-chief of the armies of Brandenburg. Schomberg's background, his long-held Europe-wide reputation, his military experience and the knowledge of his staunch resistance to Louis's overtures combined to make him an ideal choice as both William's second in command for the descent on England at the end of 1688, and commander-in-chief of the army sent to Ireland the following year.

General Percy Kirke, perhaps as a reward for his part in the conspiracy that arranged for substantial elements of James II's English army to desert to William following his landing on English soil, had been appointed to secure the relief of Londonderry. It was his first independent command, and he was wholly indecisive in his actions after sailing from Hoylake at the end of May. The warrant for Schomberg's commission to conduct the campaign in Ireland was not formally issued until 16 July 1689,[28] but he intervened earlier in ways that were of great significance in leading towards the relief of Londonderry. He was already acting towards that end at the beginning of May.[29] Then, on 3 July, he sent Kirke a pointed reproof and clear instructions in the king's name that he was to consult

---

27 For this paragraph and Schomberg's life as a whole, see the biography by Matthew Glozier (2005).

28 *CSPD, 1689–90*, 188.

29 Royal Irish Academy, MS H.I.3, 'A Journal. From London to the Relief of London-Derry. 1689', 2 May 1689; Doherty (2008), 108.

the sea officers 'whether it may not be possible to break the boom and chain and to passe with the ships, and that you attempt the doing of it for the reliefe of the Town'. Had Schomberg personal insight into the desperate conditions in the town, where one of his sons was serving within as a captain?[30] In any event his words compelled Kirke, who 'maintained friends in the Jacobite officer corps' and whose loyalty was perhaps dubious,[31] to take the obvious steps he had so notably failed to undertake. Schomberg doubled down on the absolute need for urgency, requiring that Kirke advise him 'what may be fitt to be further done for the Reliefe of the Town, which is a matter of so great a consequence'. Schomberg's insistence and sense of urgency were clearly important in the story of Londonderry's relief, although most historians have not paid them much attention.

There is an extraordinary contrast between Schomberg's first and second months in command of the military expedition to Ireland; in August and early September he acted decisively, then he became bogged down at Dundalk. In making an estimate of his contribution to the Williamite War in the country we need to consider his performance in both periods and try to explain the apparent contrast between them. His conduct of affairs during the first month was almost impeccable; by any standards, he acted intelligently and speedily. He and his force embarked at Hoylake on 8 August, but contrary winds made it impossible to sail for four days. Making up for lost time, he then bypassed a prearranged rendezvous with miscellaneous transport and artillery ships, horse boats and merchantmen, sending them a message that the fleet was making straight for Ireland. Anchoring next day (13 August) opposite Carrickfergus, a walled town with a castle which was garrisoned by the Jacobites with 1200 men,[32] he immediately disembarked, and spent the 14th landing stores and organizing men for the reduction of the town. On the 15th he occupied Belfast, which his enemy had abandoned, and over the next four days detailed patrols to deal with Irish robbing and plundering. On the 20th, returning to Carrickfergus, Schomberg summoned the garrison to surrender, and, on their refusal, began the siege. The surrender, which cleared Ulster of all regular Jacobite forces, came one week later.

August 28 and 29 found Schomberg's army marching back to Belfast, where recently disembarked reinforcements were incorporated and the army was mustered on the last day of the month. Through

---

30 Bodleian Library, Oxford, Carte MS clxxxi, f. 238; Macrory (1980), 307–8; Doherty (2008), 145.

31 Doherty (2008), 161. Schomberg considered Kirke 'un homme capricieux' (*CSPD*, 1689–90, 199).

32 Kazner (1789), II, 331.

Map IV.1: Ireland, showing key places mentioned in chapters IV–V.

the first week of September, the general set what the raw English levies would have found a cracking pace, leaving Belfast for Lisburn and thereafter camping at Dromore (3 September), Loughbrickland (4th), and at Newry, which he found abandoned and burnt by the Jacobites (5th–6th). On the 7th, he reached Dundalk, after a series of long, hard marches in bad weather, the last along causeways that had been deliberately broken up to delay his passage by forces under the Duke of Berwick, the illegitimate son of King James II and Arabella Churchill.[33] The Jacobite *Relation of what most remarkably happened*

---

33 Story (1693), *i*, 6–15; Kazner (1789), II, 298–301.

during the Last Campaign in Ireland described the highway as having been left 'almost impassable'.[34] The challenge was too much for some of the Williamite troops who collapsed along the way.

The basic details of the army movements and their timing described in the previous paragraph are set out in chapter 10 of *The Williamite Wars in Ireland 1688–1691* by the English military historian John Childs, published in 2007. The relevant chapter is entitled, 'A tired old man', hardly an appropriate description for what we have just related: Schomberg had established himself effectively and was proceeding southwards at a fast rate, with every intention of capturing Dublin before winter. However, at Dundalk he stopped, and some days later created an entrenched camp. Why did he do so, and were his actions indeed those of a tired old man, or a professional response to the realities of changing conditions?

There were certainly reasons for Schomberg to take stock of his new position. Further north, he could reasonably expect the military intelligence reaching him from the surrounding countryside to be at least equivalent to that of his adversaries. The farther he moved into strongly Catholic country, the less true that became. Had this not already been plain to him, it would have become clear when he found to his surprise that the strategic points of the Moyry Pass and the crossing of the River Clanrye at Newry Bridge, which (with good reason) he had expected to be defended by the Jacobites, had been simply abandoned and left wide open to him. However, he faced more fundamental problems than uncertain intelligence. We need to assess his supply situation; the physical state of his army; the troops at Schomberg's disposal and what he knew of the enemy opposing him; disloyalty both within his force and in England; and the overall European strategic situation in late 1689. In each case we should examine the extent to which difficulties and deficiencies can be laid at his door.

As Schomberg moved south, he had increasing difficulties with supplies. When he set off southwards, his provisions, transport horses and wagons had still not reached him, so he gave the necessary orders and relied on supplies being sent promptly by sea to meet him at Carlingford. Provisions, however, were already found 'very scarce' at Newry, because 'there wanted horses to bring them after us'.[35] By the time the army reached Dundalk, it had little food, being saved from acute embarrassment by the fortunate arrival of 2000 sheep driven into camp from a nearby fortified house that had been occupied. The countryside had been ravaged by the scorched-earth tactics pursued by Berwick and the Jacobites, so living off the land was not an option. The only solution was a direct supply from England,

34 *A Relation of what most Remarkably happened* (1689), p. 6.
35 Story (1693), *i*, 13.

which had always been intended – it was how Oliver Cromwell's forces in Ireland had been victualled a generation earlier – but 'Schomberg's army was accompanied by neither horses nor wagons whilst the provision ships docked at increasingly distant Carrickfergus rather than Carlingford Lough'.[36] Well aware of the potential problem, the general had ordered before leaving Belfast that his artillery horses 'and all necessaries for the army' coming from England be shipped to Carlingford Lough,[37] but horses had to be sent back towards Belfast to fetch bread because the supply ships failed to arrive at Carlingford Lough as they had been directed.

In other words, far from acting as a tired old man, Schomberg had moved so energetically that he had outstripped his supplies, and he had issued the appropriate orders but they had not been followed. The difficulty with the lack of horses and wagons was out of the general's control; it went back to decisions taken in England and to deep-rooted, persistent problems with an incompetent commissariat.[38] The most significant positions were held by John Shales, Commissary General of the Provisions, and the Paymaster, William Harboard. Shales was particularly unsatisfactory. He had London experience – he had been the contractor for James II's military camp at Hounslow Heath – but had no Irish experience and proved both corrupt and incompetent, so that when Schomberg reached Chester there were no provision ships awaiting him and when provisions did arrive, they were inadequate and many weapons were defective.[39] Shales was replaced in December, Harboard the following year. The contemporary historian of the war, George Story, confirms that he personally was at Chester a week after Schomberg had landed in Ireland with his army, 'and all or most of the Waggon-Horses, and some of the Train-Horses were there then: Nor did they come over till we had been some time at Dundalk'.[40] The immediate reason for the original decision not to advance from Dundalk was the absence of bread which, Schomberg informed William's trusted advisor William Bentinck, Lord Portland on 13 September 1689, had halted his march for four days.[41] De Bostaquet's memoirs confirm the explanation: 'the army had no supplies and we had to wait at Dundalk for ships to come from Belfast with provisions. Contrary winds delayed the arrival of supplies and the Duke decided to stay at Dundalk – when our

---

36 Childs (2007), 155.
37 Story (1693), *i*, 11.
38 See for example BL, Egerton MS 3340, f. 86v; *CJ* X, 262–3; *CSPD*, 1689–90, 294; James Scott Wheeler, 'The Logistics of Conquest', in Lenihan (2001), 202–4.
39 Childs (2007), 18.
40 Story (1693), *i*, 42.
41 Childs (2007), 18, citing *Correspondentie van Willem en van Hans Willem Bentinck*, ed N. Japikse (The Hague, 1927–8), ii, pp 27–8.

provisions were gone it was difficult for everyone. The peasants brought us nothing and the army had no food.'[42]

The four lost days were a serious matter, because the army was daily becoming more immobilized by sickness. Illness in the ranks had become apparent a week earlier, when soldiers began collapsing from a combination of hunger, fatigue and the 'bloody flux', worsened by long marches and bad weather. On reaching Dundalk, Schomberg immediately ordered a party to backtrack and pick up the sick who had collapsed while coming from Newry.[43] Now disease took hold, and already by 24 September Story reported how 'several regiments were grown pretty thin' as a result.[44] Thereafter the situation only worsened as disease spread; it ravaged Schomberg's army and – for both sides[45] – became the dominant feature of the winter months. Childs lists typhus, typhoid, malaria, plague, smallpox, pneumonia, influenza, dysentery and food-poisoning as all being prevalent and asserts that 'disease killed at least 20 times more people than military action' during the Irish war. He comments,

> no contemporary military medical organization could have coped with the scale of disease suffered at the Dundalk camp. The sick were left to die in their tents, bodies lay unburied and the small, tented hospital was soon full to overflowing. Towards the end of September, the sick were shifted to Carlingford with a view to shipping them to Belfast and Carrickfergus. Quite how many died at Dundalk is unclear but the epidemic continued throughout the winter and not until the spring of 1690 was the army reasonably clear of infection.[46]

One can argue about the precise nature of the illnesses. Another military historian, Pádraig Lenihan, in a detailed, interesting and grisly examination of their nature, denies that plague could have been involved on the grounds that the disease had already receded from Ireland as well as Britain, while Kenneth Ferguson questions whether typhus was much to blame since contemporaries did not point to its characteristic swellings.[47] In any event, there is no doubt that the cocktail of diseases, very probably first nurtured

42 Ressinger (2005), 216.
43 Childs (2007), 157–8; Story (1693), *i*, 15. See also Lenihan and Sheridan in *Irish Studies Review* 13 (2005), 484.
44 Story (1693), *i*, 24.
45 James's army had already lost many men to sickness before it went to winter quarters; National Library of Ireland, MS 4166, p.8.
46 Childs (2007), 23–4.
47 Lenihan (2009), 45, 52; Ferguson (1990), 67.

in Londonderry during the siege,[48] and spread far beyond Dundalk. The fever accompanying them proved particularly brutal. Most casualties died in Belfast, rather than at Dundalk itself. De Bostaquet, who was not struck down until Christmas Eve, when he was in Armagh, described how his fever 'lasted 28 days with terrible transports of delirium and nausea' and left him weak 'with so many complications and ulcerations that I languished all winter'.[49] In retrospect, as things turned out, Schomberg might have usefully spent July 1689 studying possible dire medical problems. But he could not foresee the future, and instead, his attention was focused on the production of the new *Rules and Articles For the better Government of Their Majesties Forces within the Kingdom of Ireland, during the present rebellion*, the printed code of 69 articles that would later become the basis for all future standing orders.[50]

Were there steps that Schomberg could have taken to combat the disease? He could have selected a drier, less boggy site, but Newry had been burnt by the Jacobites and Dundalk offered good military defensive possibilities once he decided he could not advance; as Richard Kane noted, there was a good haven for small ships to bring in supplies, while the Newry mountains protected the army's rear.[51] Schomberg could, and did, take actions to try to protect the men, such as ordering the building of huts, repeatedly ordering the officers to take care of the rank and file, allowing huts to be moved to higher ground, and ordering fit men to collect ferns to make beds for the sick. Story claimed he took 'all imaginable care … that the sick should be well look'd after'.[52] Lenihan disputes this, arguing that the one move to a new camp site during the Dundalk period was insufficient. The same historian also questions whether the recommendations made in Luca Porzio's *De Militis in Castris Sanitate Tuenda* ['How to keep soldiers healthy in camps'], the most authoritative contemporary treatise on the subject, were carried out, pointing out that this work came to be reprinted six times in the eighteenth century. The reprints are irrelevant, since Schomberg was long dead before they first appeared. More to the point would be to ask whether this work, first published at Vienna in 1685, had even reached Ireland by 1689. In any case it is unlikely that Schomberg, who was pushed out of France in 1685 and then Portugal in 1686, and thereafter moved to major new challenges in Brandenburg, the Netherlands and England before coming to Ireland in 1689, would have had any time to study and assess it.

---

48 Story (1693), *i*, 24; Lenihan (2009), 49.
49 Ressinger (2005), 223.
50 TNA, SP 63/352, f. 24.
51 Kane (1747), 2.
52 Story (1693), *i*, 27; Bellingham (1908), 90.

Other considerations ensured that Schomberg's advance got no further than Dundalk. The first was a matter of numbers. As was necessary in a hostile country, he had left units in garrisons at Londonderry, Enniskillen, Sligo, Belfast, Carrickfergus and Newry, with other detachments defending his lines of communication. At Dundalk he had 2000 horse and dragoons, and 12,000 infantry.[53] He believed from the intelligence reports reaching him that the Jacobite army in his path outnumbered him by at least two to one, and might have as many as 35,000 men although 5000 of those were armed only with skeans (Gaelic daggers) and half-pikes. He knew the Jacobites had been confident enough to advance speedily from Drogheda to Ardee to meet him. He could see for himself that they showed good discipline when, on 21 September, James's army deployed efficiently to the south-west of Dundalk in an orthodox professional manner with cavalry on both wings and two lines of infantry in chequer-board formation and 'in excellent order'.[54]

An appendix to John Stevens's manuscript *Journal of my Travels since the Revolution* provides a breakdown showing that Stevens believed that James's army before Dundalk consisted of some 28,250 men.[55] Of modern estimates, one Irish military historian, Harman Murtagh, estimates 36,000 men for the Jacobite army in 1689, while Lenihan argues for far fewer. The discrepancies can be taken as a commentary on just how hard it is to be certain about actual numbers, but James appears to have had a numerical edge, although he rejected the advice of Rosen, one of his French generals, that he should attack Schomberg where he was at Dundalk.[56] What is agreed is that the Jacobites had a marked advantage in cavalry, for whom the open and largely level terrain between Dundalk and Dublin was well suited. The mettle of the Irish cavalry had already been demonstrated in a rout of Londonderry defenders at Claudy-ford (modern Clady) in April, and would be shown again at the Boyne the following year – unlike the other branches of the Jacobite army, its horsemen were well up to the best European standards.[57] The number of his opponents alone might not have worried Schomberg unduly, but the numbers taken in combination with

---

53 Story (1693), *i*, 41, is accepted by Childs (2007), 160. Story had first-hand knowledge, and Lenihan's suggestion (2009, p. 39) that Story's estimate was too low is unconvincing.
54 Childs (2007), 159–60, 162–3; *A Relation of what most Remarkably happened* (1689), p. 8.
55 BL, Add. MS 36,296, ff. 128–30.
56 Murtagh (1995), 70; Lenihan (2009), 41; 'A Light to the Blind', National Library of Ireland, MS 476, p. 572.
57 D'Avaux (1934), 461; Doherty (2008), 63–7; Diarmuid and Harman Murtagh (1990), p. 41.

the underfed, under-supplied and diseased state of his own infantry, and the superiority of the Irish cavalry, surely did.

The final straw ensuring that the general did not seriously reconsider his decision to advance beyond Dundalk was located within his own ranks, and worse, within the Huguenot ranks on which he placed particular trust. On 22 September, he was presented with demonstrable proof of a serious, long-planned Roman Catholic conspiracy within the Huguenot regiment commanded by du Cambon. To understand how this came about, we need to return to the speed with which events had unfolded earlier in 1689. The instability of England in the aftermath of the Revolution and the new regime's lack of immediate resources, coupled with the greater instability of the Scottish situation and the fact that King William's clear priority was to send troops to the continent, made organizing the Irish expedition a difficult matter. Parliament voted money in March, and most commissions for troops were dated that month; but while some expected Schomberg to leave for Ireland in April,[58] the expedition only began to assemble at Chester in mid-July, when Schomberg received his warrant and took his leave of the House of Commons.[59] William did not trust the English regular army sufficiently to use it in Ireland, instead sending the Earl of Marlborough with English troops to the Netherlands to replace Dutch forces in England.[60] The English infantry who formed the bulk of Schomberg's army were therefore wholly new, and also lacked experienced officers, since most of those available had left with Marlborough. In contrast, the Dutch troops were settled, professional and experienced. The Huguenot regiments who were part of the English force included many highly experienced soldiers, but the regiments themselves were entirely new.[61]

The raising of the new regiments needed to be done quickly, and English recruiting officers clearly did not stop to investigate the background of new recruits, since those they enlisted in their regiments included former Irish troops, presumably remnants of those who had gone to England in 1688, who promptly deserted on reaching their homeland. The Huguenot regiments in William's service included deserters from regiments in the Dutch army.[62] At Dundalk some of these were proved to be part of a serious, intentional, coordinated attempt to destabilize the Williamite army. Their conspiracy was planned in secret so our knowledge of it

---

58 Morrice, *Entring Book*, Q, p. 545.
59 *CJ* X, 223–4.
60 HMC, Twelfth Report, Appendix, Part VI: *The Manuscripts of the House of Lords, 1689–90* (London, 1889), p. 174; Story (1693), *i*, 5–6; Simms (1969), 120–1.
61 Glozier (2002), 121.
62 Childs (2007), 165.

is incomplete, but it is plain that it started on the continent; that the conspirators intentionally and specifically came to England in order to infiltrate the new regiments as they were levied; and that at Dundalk the leader was named Du Plessis. The *London Gazette* reported that 'most of these had deserted the French service this summer, and passing to Holland, and thence to England, upon the report that three French regiments were levying there, had listed themselves in the same'.[63]

The *Gazette* suggested it was simple haste that prevented their discovery when they enlisted in England. That was also the spin put on events by Jacobite sources,[64] but it underrates the boldness and intentionally deceptive actions of the conspirators themselves. Roger Morrice investigated further in October 1689 and found that Du Plessis had personally approached Schomberg in London asking the honour to be his 'vauntguard' and with others had 'qualified themselves by receiving the Sacrament, which was Administered to them by Dr Tennison' [later Archbishop of Canterbury]. Morrice underlined that the conspirators hanged at Dundalk had 'received the Sacraments in the way of the Church of England'.[65] Since they had taken the trouble to equip themselves with authentic papers proving their status and supposed support for the Williamite cause, there was no way any Huguenot recruiting officers could have identified the danger they posed.

The plot unwound rapidly after it was discovered at Dundalk. On 21 September, two French grenadiers were caught deserting to the enemy. The next day, one of the men in a Huguenot infantry battalion informed his captain that four soldiers and a drummer, all Roman Catholics, planned to desert to the Irish garrison at Charlemont. They were arrested, and the captain then found letters addressed to the comte d'Avaux, one of Louis XIV's leading diplomats, among the possessions of one of them. During interrogation the man revealed he also had letters from Du Plessis, who was serving as a private soldier in Du Cambon's regiment. Du Plessis was seized. He confessed under examination he had written to both King James and to D'Avaux promising to bring many Catholics in the Huguenot regiments over to the Irish army if he was pardoned by Louis and given a commission. Another report says Du Plessis had a map of the camp in his pocket with data about unit strength. Twenty-one Huguenot soldiers were arrested, several with letters from Du Plessis to either James or D'Avaux, and they confessed how James's letters had reached Dundalk. On 26 September, Du Plessis was hanged with five others following trial

---

63 *London Gazette*, no. 2496, 10/14 October 1689; Kane (1747), 3.
64 *A Relation of what most Remarkably happened* (1689), p. 10.
65 *Entring Book*, Q, p. 610.

by a Council of War. When Schomberg was first informed, he immediately ordered a proclamation read to every regiment that all Roman Catholics must declare themselves, on pain of instant execution if they did not and were later found to be of that religion; he also ordered that no Huguenots were to leave Dundalk camp without a pass. Between 150 and 200 men surrendered themselves and were sent under escort to England and thence to the Dutch Republic where they were used for garrison duty. The colonels of the three Huguenot infantry battalions then investigated, but no more Roman Catholics were found.[66]

Lenihan is strangely silent about the conspiracy in his article on 'Schomberg at Dundalk', but a plot involving careful preparation and communication with the enemy at the highest level could not be ignored by any responsible commander, especially one in such close geographical proximity to an army he believed was substantially larger than his own. This was no case of individuals deserting to save their skins by getting themselves out of the firing line, but a substantial plot with a clear military aim, one that carried a real possibility of achieving serious damage. The plot was black and white; there could be no doubt about it. Story describes how the six principal members of the French conspiracy who were hanged all died as Papists

> and confessed their design to take over as many to King James as they could, and that this was their intentions when they first Listed themselves; and that if we had engaged the Enemy the Saturday before [21ˢᵗ], they were to have put our Army into Confusion by firing in the Rear, and so deserting.[67]

In England the previous year during the Revolution, John Childs explains elsewhere, the effect of quite a small number of desertions on the morale of King James and his army had proved 'out of all proportion', and it broke the ice for more timid and cautious conspirators. The army was rendered useless with 'each man suspecting his neighbour'.[68] James himself, perhaps recalling how the desertions had shaken him to the core and left him psychologically broken and with acute nose bleeds, held high expectations of the impact of the conspiracy now unveiled at Dundalk, of which he had advance knowledge. Story continues his account by saying that Colonel Wolseley 'some time before this, had sent a Spy to Dublin, who had brought him a particular Account … [that] the Irish had great hopes of

---

66 Story (1693), *i*, 24; Childs (2007), 165–6; *History of the Wars in Ireland* (1690), 49–51; Luttrell (1857), II, 508.
67 Story (1693), *i*, 25.
68 Childs (1980), 187–8.

the French revolting to them'. The colonel reported this to Schomberg. The general would not believe it without evidence, but the advance warning may help explain why he would not stir when challenged by the Jacobite army on Saturday 21 September. If so, he probably made a good call. He did not turn and flee in the face of conspiracy, as James had fled England in 1688. Instead he acted immediately to suppress it, dug in, accepted the cost to his army and reputation, forced James to move to winter quarters, and made sure that the Williamite army kept control of the north of Ireland and – despite all its losses to disease – remained formidable and ready for what he doubtless hoped would be a final thrust the following year.

A related, constant major headache for Schomberg in Ireland, especially in the months following his appointment, was to know whom he could trust, something that could only come over time through experience. Even within England, King William 'could not even command the best service of his supporters, nor could he always be sure who were his worst enemies', and found his subjects were split by intense personal rivalries. A year later, at the Boyne, despite William's personal presence, Williamites were seriously concerned and afraid about the possibility of treachery. As late as 1692, Queen Mary and her cabinet 'scarcely knew whom to trust' as they tried to plan a descent on France.[69] The situation was much worse for Schomberg across the Irish Sea in 1689. He was not invested with any aura of royal majesty and had no obvious English power base other than royal support. He could not simply assume the loyalty of the officers around him. How many were crypto-Jacobites, deliberately disrupting his communications and transportation or even 'totally alienated from King William and ... entirely in King James's Interest'?[70] How many harboured ill-will at their regiments being placed under the command of a foreign general? How many were competent?

Historians have understood many of Schomberg's problems in Ireland, but no author seems previously to have drawn attention to other difficulties the general faced back in England. Without anyone able to give him much support in Ireland, Schomberg desperately needed to maintain good communications with William. However, there were hostile elements in London looking out for opportunities to intercept his mail and damage him if they could. Roger Morrice reported on 14 September 1689 how

About 14 dayes since Duke Schomberg sent a Paquet of Letters forth of Ireland to King William by a Gentleman, who rode Post with the Postboy, and betweene Barnet and Highgate three Gentlemen met the

---

69 Ogg (1955), 228, 230, 363; McElligott (2004–5), 41, 43.
70 See *Entring Book*, Q, pp. 597–8, 611, 659.

Gentleman with Schombergs Paquet, knock'd him off his horse, opened his Paquet and all the Letters, and tooke away those from Schomberg to the King.

Morrice continued with an explanatory note of his own:

Schomberg clearly apprehends that there are those that practise upon him and Clogg all his affaires, and keepe his foot and his Horse from him etc and he has a natural plainnesse, and states matter of fact clearly as it is ... and writes with that freedome to his Majesty as scarce any other Subject does, and therefore it's believed that those that robbed the Paquet were set on worke by some of the Regents, who are greatly concerned that no such frank Letters should come to his Majesty.

By 'the Regents', Morrice meant those who claimed 'that there is a Cess[ation] of all Regall Authority', which included the Jacobites. It is a sharp reminder of the suspension and disarray of normal processes during the period when William was not fully accepted as king and political discourse and power in England remained volatile and uncertain. A little later (26 October), Morrice reported once more that 'the last Letters that came to our Court from Ireland beare date 4th instant. Duke Schomberg could never of five Weekes after he went into Ireland, get any Letter Writ with his own hand delivered to the King, though the Ordinary Post kept its times'. Eventually the general sent first Colonel Scravenmore and then a Mr Nichols as individual couriers.[71] Not only had Schomberg's life and faith led him with his army to an Irish bog, they had also brought him into a mire of conflicting factional and personal interests in an England where political instability continued in the aftermath of the Revolution, and all too many of the politicians and soldiers who publicly served William and Mary were also in covert communication with James.

The last of the major issues that Schomberg had to keep in mind was not of his making but was arguably the most significant. This concerned the overall European strategic situation by the autumn of 1689. William and Mary had been proclaimed king and queen in England, but the capture of the general's own despatches so close to London and the conspiracy at Dundalk highlight how active and widespread Jacobitism remained. Little progress had been made during a year of stalemate on the continent, where the British corps under Marlborough suffered massive desertion and entered the field with less than half its official establishment, another

---

71 *Entring Book*, Q, pp. 598–9, 612, 620.

consequence of the Revolution.[72] Ireland, where the siege of Londonderry had been relieved and the north was now firmly held by the Williamites, was the brightest spot, but the appearance of James with French support meant that a significant threat remained. Taken overall, William's cause had made some progress during the year. That was something that Schomberg would not put at risk. As he wrote to William, if he advanced with his raw, diseased and ill-equipped troops against a significantly larger army equipped with much superior cavalry, the risk of losing all Ireland (and encouraging the rebels in Scotland) outweighed the possible gain.[73]

How, then, are we to sum up Schomberg's contribution? Irish conditions did not treat him kindly in September 1689. Nor have subsequent historians done so. They have tended to ignore his part in achieving the relief of Londonderry, and to downplay the speed with which he acted to reach Dundalk when he did. Fundamentally predisposed to be sympathetic to William's rosy expectations of a quick victory, they have shared the king's disappointment and exasperation that his general failed to progress further towards Dublin without adequate consideration of the problems confronting him in England as well as Ireland. The last generation of historians has been particularly unkind to Schomberg. His one biographer during the last two centuries, Matthew Glozier, concludes that 'his judgement was clearly failing him'.[74] John Childs suggests 'his nerve faltered when opposed by a supposedly superior force' and calls him 'tired, over-cautious and pedestrian' and 'elderly, timorous, indecisive and supine', a view cited with approval by Lenihan.[75] The general modern consensus has it that all Schomberg achieved was 'a reputation for "masterly inactivity" in refusing battle'.[76]

In my view it is much too easy to be wise after the event, and the more closely I have examined those opinions, the less I agree with them, although I endorse the earlier assessment of J.G. Simms that Schomberg's 'temperament was cautious, professional and fussy'.[77] In particular, any suggestion he was too old and tired can be ruled out immediately. It simply does not fit with Schomberg's actions before he reached Dundalk. Nor does it fit the contemporary descriptions of either George Story, who stressed Schomberg's conscientiousness, or Lieutenant General Ferdinand-Wilhelm,

72 Childs (1991), 101.
73 Kazner (1789), II, 333, 335.
74 Glozier (2005), 143.
75 Childs (2007), 173; Lenihan (2009), 41–3.
76 D.W. Hayton, 'The Williamite Revolution in Ireland, 1688–91', in Israel (1991), 201.
77 Simms (1971), 14.

Duke of Württemberg-Neustadt, commander of the Williamite Danish forces, who landed in Ireland on 13 March 1690 and reported to the Danish king that Schomberg was 'very vigorous in spite of his great age, so that no business is a burden to him'.[78] In 1689, Schomberg rode out virtually every day, took a forward position to spy out the land and was active in reconnoitring the enemy. Lenihan comments that he sited his headquarters unusually far forward at Dundalk. The general paid great attention to detail, and regularly stayed up late to deal with business, meeting with brigade majors at night. His initial embarrassment at Dundalk was caused because he had moved too fast for his supplies to keep up. Once encamped there, he took prompt action to deal with the conspiracy when it was revealed, while Story claimed it was 'scarce in the power of any man' to care more for his soldiers. Unlike the Jacobites, Schomberg did not waste the winter, but reformed his regiments in January, toured the frontier posts, and in April moved on the Jacobite enclave at Charlemont, catching Tyrconnell and the Jacobites by surprise because they did not expect action so early in the year. It capitulated in May 1690.[79]

When he arrived at Dundalk in September 1689, Schomberg expected to continue his march. He could not do so because his army lacked food and supplies, and he had no other option but to await them since the surrounding countryside had been desolated by the Jacobites. It was not as though he had a well-trained force experienced in looking after itself. On the contrary, his officers were clearly unreliable, and when he ordered firing practice, it was found that many of the new recruits who had been equipped with matchlocks 'had so little skill in placing of their Matches true, that scarce one of them in four could fire their Pieces off; and those that did, thought they had done a feat if the Gun fired, never minding what they shot at'.[80] They also needed boots; on 6 October Schomberg contemplated a march for the Shannon, but his generals advised against it 'because half the men lacked shoes and the footwear of the remainder would disintegrate within two days'.[81] One modern historian considers this a 'trivial' matter, a judgement that Schomberg would surely have strongly disputed. Since gangrene was so bad that Story reported several sufferers as having 'had their Limbs so mortified in the Camp, and afterwards, that some had their Toes, and some their whole Feet that fell off as the

---

78 Danaher and Simms (1962), 31.
79 Story (1693), *i*, 21, 44, 46, 64; Kazner (1789), II, 302–3; Lenihan (2009), 42; Childs (2007), 188, 190, 200–2.
80 Story (1693), *i*, 24.
81 Childs (2007), 167, 174.

Surgeons were dressing them', the contemporary evidence suggests the generals' concern was well founded.[82]

The steady spread of virulent disease was decisive. To take the initiative with an army in such disarray against forces he believed to be twice the size of his own would indeed have invited decisive defeat that could leave James as the master of all Ireland and do serious damage to William's cause, as the general tried to tell his unsympathetic royal master. Whether Schomberg chose to stay at Dundalk, advance or retreat, the disease was already spreading in his camp and would have decimated his army in any event, as it also did the Jacobite army in its winter quarters.[83] He expected James to mount an attack, and chose to receive it at the entrenchments he had created at Dundalk, because whichever side 'gave the Attacque ... it was odds against them'.[84] He had always been a methodical and personally brave rather than a dashing soldier, and that did not change in Ireland. I conclude he made the best decision that as a military professional he could make in the adverse circumstances and held to it, even though by so doing he lost the confidence of the king.

Some of the criticisms that historians have levelled against the general seem less than reasonable. J.G. Simms, one of the most judicious writers on the subject, reached the entirely understandable conclusion that the general's mistake 'had been to allow himself to be so ill served in transport, equipment, provisions and men'.[85] What remains very questionable, of course, is whether Schomberg had the time, power and relevant backing at Whitehall to have done anything about those issues; he reported and complained about them often enough to the right quarters, but without effect. John Childs accuses Schomberg of lacking 'grip' and failing to make sure that his instructions were obeyed. Yet Childs acknowledges that the general 'lacked a professional, efficient staff and had neither authoritative nor trustworthy advisers'.[86] To that should be added that his English officers were frequently inexperienced, often unenthusiastic and reluctant, sometimes downright and perhaps deliberately obstructive. At the siege of Carrickfergus, for example, Schomberg wanted an English sapper to accompany the battery being advanced towards the castle but no one would volunteer, so next day Huguenot sappers (two of whom were

---

82 Lenihan (2009), 42; Story (1693), *i*, 39.
83 Bellingham's Diary reports the Irish as 'in a lamentable condition' with 'great numbers of their men' dying in mid–late October (Bellingham (1908), 89, 92, 94). See also National Library of Ireland, MS 4166, pp. 7–8.
84 Story (1693), *i*, 45.
85 Simms (1971), 25.
86 Childs (2007), 183–4.

wounded in the assault) were given the duty instead.[87] After the fall of the castle, Schomberg ordered both the artillery and the provision ships to rendezvous with the army at Carlingford; but although the wind stood fair, the ships took ten days to clear Belfast Lough and it was only after the army had been at Dundalk for a week that the first ships came into Carlingford Lough, and even then, only four of them appeared.[88] The general showed himself quite willing to take action to underline his orders. After Carrickfergus fell, Schomberg personally rode into the crowd, pistol in hand, to ensure that the agreement for safe conduct he had made was observed. On the march to Dromore two men were hanged in front of the army for deserting, while a Lieutenant-Colonel was broken for insolence towards Lieutenant-General Solms and for misdoings in his regiment.[89] Given the multitude of responsibilities that fell on him, it is hard to see what more Schomberg was supposed to do. With time, no doubt the problems could have been resolved, but time was a luxury he did not have.

More serious might be considered the complaint developed by Glozier, Childs and Lenihan, that Schomberg's judgement and nerve failed him at Dundalk, and that he was over-cautious and indecisive. Against this view one should set another work by John Childs, *The British Army of William III*. That book cites key accepted maxims of seventeenth-century warfare: a general should 'never fight without manifest advantage', and 'always encamp so as not to be forced to it'; 'Warfare in the late seventeenth century did not seek the destruction of the opponent's army as its first aim' because usually 'it was unattainable by contemporary methods'. Lenihan has cited the very same references with approval.[90] In other words, these historians are taking Schomberg to task for doing at Dundalk exactly what his professional training told him was the correct course of action. The general had not been appointed to lead the Irish expedition because he was a dashing young officer ambitious to make a name for himself. He was given the job because he was a thorough-going, exceptionally experienced professional who shared the king's ambitions and whom William could trust to hold his untried army together and use his best judgement in local conditions, which proved to be unlike anything either of them had previously met.

Schomberg fulfilled his obligations to the best of his professional ability. He had not lost his nerve, and his actions the next year at the Boyne, where he died, do not support any suggestion he had suddenly become timorous. He shared William's wishes but, at Dundalk, found that the speed of his

---

87 Kazner (1789), II, 297–8.
88 Story (1693), *i*, 18.
89 Story (1693), *i*, 10; Kazner (1789), II, 299, 303.
90 Childs (1987), 243, 255; Lenihan (2005), 45–6.

advance had outrun his supplies. Forced to pause, confronted by an army that he believed was substantially larger than his own and that had clearly superior cavalry, his analysis showed he did not have a manifest advantage – far from it – so he played things by the book and stayed encamped. He then found himself confronted by desperately serious disease developing at alarming speed, and by clear evidence of his infantry's shortcomings in handling their arms and their shortage of boots. The revelation of the conspiracy affecting some of his best units was the last straw. So he stayed where he was, and the army suffered with him. His decisions can be challenged, but it is wholly unreasonable to base any such challenges on spurious personal attacks that lack serious evidence and belie the professionalism that was the hallmark of his conduct throughout his long career. It is noteworthy that however disappointed William was that Dublin was not taken in 1689, the king realized full well how Schomberg remained essential to his cause as the only man who could hope to hold his force in Ireland together without his own presence, and told him that unless he remained there over the winter, all would be lost.[91]

Schomberg fell victim to unreasonable English expectations, which had been sufficiently widespread to infiltrate William's early planning. Perhaps he was also a victim of his own high reputation. The king's advisors tended simply to assume that such an experienced general would have no problem in subduing Ireland, regardless of local conditions, how late in the year he was sent and the poor quality of the troops of which most of his army consisted. The supply problem then ensured that Schomberg received at Dundalk what in rugby parlance might be called a 'hospital pass', that is, a pass made by a team-mate to a player certain to be instantly and heavily tackled by the opposition. Unable to break through the opponent's lines, such a player then becomes wide open to criticism by spectators or reporters for failure to progress.

Even with the benefit of hindsight, I also believe that the general's decision to stay at Dundalk – although it would eventually mean that close to half his army was lost to disease (mostly not at Dundalk itself but further north)[92] – was nevertheless probably the best available option. Had he gone back to the burnt remnants of Newry across the broken causeway with the same troops who had already struggled over it to reach Dundalk, there were neither supplies nor shelter there, and retreat could very easily have turned into rout. Had he gone forward towards Dublin, his army was likely to be caught by superior cavalry in terrain much more favourable to them than to his own infantry. After witnessing the impact

---

91 Kazner (1789), II, 321, 323–4.
92 Story (1693), *i*, 38–9.

of Jacobite charges against well-trained infantry at the Boyne, even the
chaplain George Story could appreciate the likely disastrous consequence
of such an encounter.[93]

Story's reaction is most revealing. He was close to the action, both to
the troops and the decision-makers. He visited the sick, described the piles
of dead as 'the most Lamentable Sight in the World', and was very much
aware of the butcher's bill. He well understood the arguments mounted
against Schomberg's decision by the afflicted men and their friends and
families and others who disagreed with it:

> That if he had gone on at first, he might certainly have got to Dublin,
> and what he did was only to protract the War, and that he cared not
> how many died, so he was well himself, ... [and] that he was so old that
> he was not fit for Action.

Nevertheless, Story rejected all those 'most false and ignorant suggestions'
and concluded that 'the General acted ... according to the Rules of Art
and Prudence' in not advancing on James's army at Dundalk:

> Whatever the World may think, yet I can attribute those Distempers
> amongst us to nothing else but the Badness of the Weather, the moistness
> of the Place, the unacquaintedness of the English to hardships, and
> indeed their lazy Carelessness ... Upon the whole Matter, I doubt not
> but it will appear to any Man that pleases to consider it, that the Duke
> did better in not hazarding that in a moment, which may be was not
> to be redeemed again in many Ages, since not only the Safety of these
> Kingdoms did in a great measure depend upon it, but a great part of the
> Protestant Interest in Europe had a Concern in it.[94]

Story was chaplain to an English regiment, and the English suffered
particularly badly from disease at Dundalk. There was no reason why he
should have been biased in favour of Schomberg. In any case, though, the
last word can be left to King William, whose commentary was not spoken
but enacted the following year.

William left England for Ireland in June 1690, two months earlier in
the year than Schomberg, who had been despatched in the August of 1689.
Before William came, he focused serious attention on Ireland, in contrast to
the neglect for which, John Evelyn noted, the king was being 'much blamed'

93 Story (1693), *i*, 45.
94 Story (1693), *i*, 23, 32–3, 35, 38, 41–2, 46.

in the spring of the previous year.[95] Schomberg's corps was sent to Ireland without an effective commissariat and with dated or poorly made weapons, without an adequate medical service for a known problem area, and with a badly supplied fleet so that when his troops began to embark they lacked bread, food and water; several hundred men immediately became ill and a number died.[96] These matters were all addressed. In November 1689 Schomberg recommended using civilian victualling contractors, and Isaac Pereira signed the initial contract to provide bread on 9 April 1690.[97] From the beginning of March 1690, a 'Marching Hospital to attend Our Army in Ireland' was instituted.[98] In 1689, £14,937 had been spent on transport. William had £100,000 of transport support in 1690, nearly seven times as much, so there were plenty of wagons and horses: 450 wagons for bread and 100 for artillery, and 2500 carriage horses.[99] Schomberg embarked on his quest for positive action with some 10,000 men; William embarked with similar intent with 15,000 men to join Schomberg's forces already in being, and the king's eventual army of 36,000–37,000 men was clearly dominant, half as large again as James's and better equipped, especially in artillery. William had also ensured he had more well-trained troops who were not involved in English politics, renting 6000 infantry and 1000 cavalry from the King of Denmark after negotiations in which Huguenot connections were involved.[100]

Each of these changes, each of the steps that the king took to set to rights the problems that had bedevilled Schomberg, was in effect an acknowledgement that he had presented his general with a well-nigh impossible situation once it was compounded by the outbreak of exceptionally severe disease. While William started much earlier in the year, he too found that campaigning in Ireland was no simple matter. He never ran into anything like the conditions of disease and weather that Schomberg encountered at Dundalk, but despite his far larger army and his victory at the Boyne, William too was unable to wind up the Irish offensive, his army becoming bogged down at Limerick. Victory had to await a much bloodier battle, at Aughrim, and a second and successful siege of Limerick, in 1691.

Meanwhile, notwithstanding the miseries of Dundalk, Schomberg retained the full respect of his men. Jean François de Morsier, a Swiss

---

95 De Beer (1955), IV, 630.

96 The problems are clear from Schomberg's reports to William printed in Dalrymple (1773), part 2, appendix book 4, 23 ff, and from BL, Egerton MS 3340, f. 86, and Add. MS 5540.

97 Childs (2007), 18–19, 23; Kazner (1789), II, 286–7.

98 TNA, W.O. 24/884, p. 131.

99 Lenihan (2005), 58; Ferguson (1990), p. 69.

100 Childs (2007), 148, 193–4; Wauchope (1992), 98; Simms (1969), 136, 147.

Calvinist whose journal presents a rare view from the rank and file, knew all about the lack of supplies – he seems to have thought and probably dreamed about little else than food – and like most of his fellows also suffered from disease, falling sick with a burning fever although he 'managed fairly well on the two bowls of gruel we were brought every day'. De Morsier, though, had only praise for Schomberg, whose 'formidable name', he believed, was all that prevented King James from launching an attack at Dundalk. Both de Morsier and Schomberg were in action again at the Boyne the following year, when after the general's death de Morsier commented he died 'mourned by the whole army who looked on him as a general in whom they could have complete trust'.[101] As for the officers, Schomberg remained to the Huguenots, in the words of Dumont de Bostaquet, a 'great man' – 'our hero'.[102]

---

101 Lenihan and Sheridan (2005), 484, 487.
102 Ressinger (2005), 229.

V

The Irish Campaign, 1690–92[1]

Schomberg always thought highly of the Huguenot regiments in the English army: too highly, indeed, for the liking of other commanders and their troops.[2] He reported to William in October 1689 that the three regiments of French infantry and their regiment of cavalry 'do their duty better than the others', and later again that the king got 'more service' from them 'than from twice the number of any others'.[3] At the first encounter at Carrickfergus, when he needed sappers, he had quickly discovered that they would tackle front-line work at which others might baulk, while the loss of one of his aides-de-camp, the marquis de Venours, and other Huguenot officers before its walls also showed they were willing to die for their cause.[4] He therefore tended to use them when situations required initiative or particular bravery, a precedent followed by other Williamite commanders in the Irish wars. Another illustration of what they had to offer came when, in March 1690, Colonel La Caillemotte took a party to burn the wooden bridge at Charlemont, where the castle was in Jacobite hands, in order to prevent Irish excursions. The bridge was within musket shot of the castle, and two redoubts captured by La Caillemotte's party were even closer, but the mission was successfully accomplished, although casualties included Major De La Borde de La Villeneuve (killed) and Lieutenant-Colonel Pierre de Belcastel and Captain Paul de Rapin de Thoyras (wounded). John Childs says that the effrontery of this attack made it a *cause célèbre* among the army. This success was followed up the following month when Jacobite attempts to break the

---

1 This chapter is best read in conjunction with Harman Murtagh, 'Huguenot Involvement in the Irish Jacobite War, 1689–91', in Caldicott and others (1987), 223–38, which provides a better overall view of that subject as a whole. I have focused in detail on Schomberg in 1689 (in the previous chapter), and the Battles of the Boyne and Aughrim and the First Siege of Limerick (in this).
2 *CSPD*, 1689–90, 201.
3 *CSPD*, 1689–90, 288, 401.
4 Above, pp. 89–90; Kazner (1789), II, 296.

blockade of Charlemont left it over-garrisoned and under-provisioned. Ambushes mounted by Huguenot infantry then defeated successive sallies by the defenders and trapped them until the castle surrendered in May, in the last significant development before the Battle of the Boyne.[5]

WILLIAM IN IRELAND AND THE BATTLE OF THE BOYNE, 1690

The Boyne was not a great battle, rather an extraordinary muddle studded with poor judgement on both sides. Eyewitness accounts of what happened are both confused and wildly contradictory. The improvements made to William's forces following Schomberg's failure to reach Dublin were such that it was hardly possible for them to lose, and the closest they came to doing so occurred before battle was joined, when William decided to sit down on the grass to refresh himself for an hour while viewing the enemy's positions. That gave time for the Jacobites to bring up two field cannons, one of which fired a shot that struck a ricochet blow to the king's shoulder, drawing a small amount of blood but leaving him just 'a little soar'.[6] James had decided to fight at the Boyne, where the river provided the last useful natural line of defence before Dublin and he had the advantage of choosing the ground. However, he and his generals failed to prepare any defensive positions in advance. Nor did they agree to designate a rallying point in case of need. Indeed, Pádraig Lenihan describes William as having blundered at the Boyne, but James's incompetence as 'almost delusional'.[7]

It is widely agreed that there were some 60,000 men involved in the battle, making it a far larger affair than any other encounter ever experienced in the British Isles. Thirty-six thousand of these troops were Williamites, 14,000 mounted and 22,000 infantry, and they were accompanied by a well-equipped artillery train. An early estimate from the Williamite side, from its recently appointed Principal Secretary of State for Ireland, was that 'the slaughter on the place was not 1000 men of the enemy, nor half as many of ours'. Most modern estimates have been in the range of 1600–2000 losses between the two sides. Even if one takes a high modern estimate of 2800 losses in total, the question remains why the Boyne was such an indecisive battle, and how the Irish were able to

---

5 Story (1693), *I*, 56; Childs (2007), 193, 201–2.
6 Story (1693), *i*, 74–5; BL, Add. MS 38,146, f. 94.
7 Simms (1969), 145; Lenihan (2005), 110, 177.

withdraw with a low body count and their artillery intact, allowing them to rally on the river Shannon soon afterwards.[8]

Once William arrived in Ireland in June, he moved to force battle as fast as he could. His rival King James was advised by Tyrconnell that he should delay and avoid battle, prolonging matters as long as possible, yet James was torn by a wish to do something heroic. As William came on faster than the Jacobites expected, the two sides ended pitched into a battle for which neither had thoroughly prepared. Some of the Jacobite field guns were actually on their way back to Dublin as the battle took place. A last-minute Williamite council of war on 30 June decided not to attack that night but to cross the river the following day, when a sizeable detachment under the Marshal's son Count Meinhard Schomberg marched westwards early in the morning to cross the river at Rosnaree or Slane. William always intended his main attack to be at the fords at Oldbridge, but James completely mistook Meinhard Schomberg's column for William's main body. The resulting redeployment of James's forces left roughly two-thirds of them facing little more than one-third of the Williamite troops in an area where marshy ground and bottomless ditches prevented active engagement. It also meant that only one-third of the Jacobite troops were left to face William's main army and artillery in the real battle at Oldbridge.[9]

First to move forwards at Oldbridge were William's Dutch Blue Guards, shortly followed by the Huguenot infantry regiments of La Melonière, La Caillemotte and du Cambon a little lower down the river, then the Northern Irish Enniskillen and other English, Dutch and Danish regiments. The Dutch Guards and Huguenot and Enniskillen troops met heavy fire from the Irish soldiers once they were halfway across the river; it would have been heavier still had not Williamite artillery been pounding the further bank for a considerable time.[10] As they struggled ashore the regiments were then confronted by an Irish counter-attack in the form of successive charges by Tyrconnell's cavalry, resulting in fierce and confused fighting. The Huguenot infantry had neither *chevaux de frise* to act as a barrier nor pikes to check cavalry charges, and the Irish cavalry burst through

---

8 BL, Add. MS 38,146, f. 98; Lenihan (2005), 8, 179, 202–3; Childs (2007), 206, 223.

9 The many modern accounts of the battle include Simms, *Jacobite Ireland* (1969); Hayes-McCoy, *Irish Battles* (1969); Shepherd, *Ireland's Fate* (1990); Lenihan, *1690 Battle of the Boyne* (2005); and Childs, *Williamite Wars* (2007). Harman Murtagh, *Battle of the Boyne 1690* (2006), includes excellent maps.

10 Lenihan (2005), 118. An eye-witness account by Sir Henry Hobart, an equerry in William's household and deputy lieutenant of Norfolk, commented on how 'the enemy had lined all the hedges, and filled the houses' on the other side of the river with foot and dragoons (Roger Morrice, *Entring Book*, R, p. 167).

La Caillemotte's regiment with dash and courage, mortally wounding the colonel, who was carried from the field still urging his men on 'à la gloire'. La Caillemotte's death wound had two significant consequences, one immediate, one longer term. On the battlefield, the Duke of Schomberg saw the danger and rode across the river to rally the Huguenots with an unusual battle cry: 'There are your persecutors: forward, lads! Forward!'. Caught in the mêlée and a clear target since he was wearing the Order of the Garter, the Duke himself was killed, taking two sabre cuts and a shot to the head. As Raymond Pierre Hylton and Marie Léoutre have argued, in the longer term La Caillemotte's death together with other Huguenot losses may well have been what determined his elder brother Henri de Massue, second Marquis de Ruvigny and later Earl of Galway, to replace Schomberg as colonel of his horse regiment. The significance of this will become apparent as we consider what happened at Aughrim.[11]

Their infantry having established a bridgehead, William and his cavalry crossed the river and gave them much-needed relief. Tyrconnell reached the conclusion that the battle was lost and ordered his men at Oldbridge to retreat southwards to Duleek on the way towards Dublin, leaving some of his horsemen to delay pursuit. After news of the defeat at Oldbridge reached the main part of the Jacobite army, it followed suit, keeping sufficiently good order to hinder attack. There was considerable chaos as both parts of the army had to cross the single stone bridge at Duleek, and disarray continued as the Jacobites streamed back to Dublin. The limited casualties suggest they managed to maintain some cohesion. That was certainly assisted by the early efforts of the Irish horse, and by the marshy ground, which had not previously been reconnoitred and prevented active pursuit by the Williamites who had crossed at Rosnaree.

This has been a very abbreviated account of the most celebrated encounter of the Irish War. Almost every individual detail of what happened at the Boyne can be contested, depending on one's perspective and what primary source one is inclined to trust. The original sources available are not only biased, but often blinkered simply because those writing them saw only a small part of the overall picture. The two kings themselves did not know what was going on. The deep layer of black smoke from the firing near Oldbridge; the mud, which was in some places so thick that William got stuck and had to dismount and get assistance to release his horse; the ignorance of the participants and the self-interest of commentators combine to present an impenetrable fog separating the modern reader from what actually happened on the field of battle. However, what stands out at the end of the day is that few other battles

---

11 Hylton (2005), 51; Léoutre (2018), 40.

can ever have been fought with so much incompetence or involved so few casualties in comparison to the number of troops employed, and yet have had such significant consequences. The long-term shadow it cast on Irish history is beyond our scope, but we cannot ignore what the Boyne meant for the Williamite cause.

The battle attracted Europe-wide attention because it pitted two crowned monarchs head to head against one another, each supported by an international army. The presence of the two kings highlighted the significance of this conflict in a region of Europe that rarely received much notice, as part of the War of the Grand Alliance. There could not be the slightest doubt that William was the victor. He may have been lucky in how he achieved decisive superiority at the key point, but in any event, it was obvious that his tactics had fooled his adversary. His personal courage had never been questioned and had now again been proved in battle. (Some might suggest this image was carefully crafted, but my reading of the sources is that his followers were genuinely struck by 'how desperately he ventured all the day', even if a few also wondered whether he was wise to take so much on himself.[12]) His success won him Dublin. It justified his presence in Ireland rather than the Netherlands. One English newsletter crowed prematurely, 'we believe the war to be at an end'.[13] The value of the victory in preserving the Grand Alliance and confirming William's leadership was enormous, especially since it came hard on the heels of the French naval victory over the English and Dutch fleets at Beachy Head.

Divine judgement had been passed on the field of battle, and the Boyne was as disastrous for James as it was successful for William. Against the advice of his allies, James had fought and lost. He had fled from England; now he fled again from Ireland, even though the Jacobite army remained in being. Even worse was his manner of leaving. The battle at the Boyne had not in itself been decisive, and the Irish army was intact or regrouping on the day after the encounter. It did not fail its leadership, rather it was deserted *by* its leadership. On reaching Dublin, James spoke to his Privy Council, and the next morning similarly to the Lord Mayor and some others, saying

> that in England he had an Army which durft have fought, but they proved false and deserted him; and that here he had an Army which was Loyal enough, but would not stand by him; he was now necessitated to provide for his Safety, and that they should make the best Terms for

12 BL, Add. MS 38,146, f. 97r; Ressinger (2005), 230; Story (1693), *i*, 82–3.
13 HMC, 12th Report, Appendix, Part VII (1890), Le Fleming, p. 281, Newsletter from London dated 19 July 1690.

themselves that they could, and not to burn or injure the Town'; and immediately after took Horse, and ... so, to Waterford; where he took Shipping for France.[14]

Thus James not only fled, but wrongly blamed the army that had fought for him, and actively urged surrender. The king was a broken man. All that can be put forward in James's favour is the one gift he gave Ireland, his insistence that Dublin be left untouched – how to preserve Dublin from being razed by fire, as was advocated by James's French allies, had been a particular worry of the newly appointed Williamite Principal Secretary of State for Ireland.[15]

The First Siege of Limerick, 1690

Initially distracted by reports that greatly magnified the defeat at Beachy Head and raised the spectre of a possible French invasion of England, William took five weeks to reach Limerick. That gave the Irish army time to rally. Improbably, it did so, assisted by a political error by William in offering terms that Jacobite officers were bound to reject since they failed to guarantee property in return for surrender. The army gathered in Limerick, where the Jacobite commander was a French major-general, the marquis de Boisseleau. He organized improvements to the defences before William arrived and declined to surrender, so William had to organize a regular siege. For that he needed the eight heavy guns (six 24-pounders and two 18-pounders) that were winding their slow way from Dublin, and their passage was obstructed in the most celebrated Jacobite action of the war, 'Sarsfield's Ride'.

Patrick Sarsfield was a cavalry commander in County Clare, an officer with flair and some continental experience who had joined with Boisseleau and the Duke of Berwick in arguing that Limerick should be defended. He crossed the Shannon with a picked force of Irish cavalry and dragoons and brought them through the Tipperary mountains to Ballyneety, fourteen miles south-east of Limerick. There he intercepted the Williamite artillery convoy at two o'clock in the morning of 12 August 1690, taking it completely by surprise, with the guns strung out in the open with few sentries. The two accompanying cavalry troops put up little resistance, many being killed in their tents. John Childs reports the damage done in the raid as 120 wagons destroyed, 500 horses driven off or killed, five

---

14 Story (1693), *i*, 88. A different version of the speech is given in Simms (1969), 153.
15 BL, Add. MS 38,146, f. 93.

and a half tonnes of gunpowder burnt together with match, grenades and bombs, 3000 cannon balls scattered or lost, three days' supply of bread and flour destroyed, two cannon ruined and others temporarily damaged. Sarsfield used an unexpected route to return safely to his lines.

The raid much improved the morale of the defenders at Limerick, who now fought with great courage, women joining in to throw stones and bottles. It also left the Williamites short of gunpowder and delayed the siege by long enough to ensure that after rain came in the last week of August, it had to be raised. Impatient as ever, William mounted a general attack on the counterscarp before an inadequate breach on 27 August. The attack was met by furious and concentrated fire from the defenders, whose losses (some 500 killed) were significantly less than those of the attackers (over 500 killed and 1000 injured). Heavy rain then fell, and the siege had to be abandoned. William left Ireland, to which he would never return, and the war was prolonged into a third year.[16]

The siege at Limerick was much the worst Williamite defeat of the war, with casualties far exceeding those at the Boyne. The regular fighting units were sometimes rearranged during the siege – grenadiers from across the army were grouped together to lead the attack on the counterscarp, for example – but, although they are hardly mentioned by Childs, the Huguenot regiments were plainly in the thick of things. Dumont de Bostaquet was present throughout, and his *Memoirs* highlight both the lack of competence of the king's high command and the savagery of the fighting. On the evidence of his account, Sarsfield's Ride should never have been successful:

An Irish Protestant brought news to the King that Sarsfield had been detached to cross the river and take our cannon ... The King gave orders that someone from our regiment be sent for news, and a sergeant was sent who confirmed the report after he had seen the enemy. The King ordered a detachment to be ready by 9 o'clock that night; it was Major-General Lanier's turn to march. La Bastide and Moliens were called from our regiment and were ready at the appointed hour but the rest arrived late and as a result they did not leave until 2 o'clock in the morning. This gave Sarsfield time to surprise the men who were guarding the cannon.[17]

Dumont de Bostaquet had no command responsibilities, was not writing with publication in mind and is recording events that directly affected his

16 Childs (2007), 249 ff.
17 Ressinger (2005), 237.

regiment and individuals he knew well. There is every reason to suppose
he can be trusted. His evidence shows that William not only knew that an
attack was imminent but had sought and obtained confirmation and had
issued the necessary, time-specific orders. Lanier, who had been a favourite
of James II, was strongly suspected of treachery at the time. Dumont's
account supports that accusation, since there was no reason for the delay,
nor for several unnecessary halts after Lanier had started off.[18]

The *Memoirs* also highlight the role played by the Huguenots at
Limerick and the ferocity of the encounters in which they were involved.
A detachment under Paul Didier de Boncour was joined by twenty officers
of Dumont's regiment, who found themselves

> exposed to fire from the ramparts for too long and many officers and
> troopers and their horses were killed or wounded. Boncour was slightly
> wounded. La Roche, Hautcharmois, and La Roquière, incorporated
> captains from our regiment, were killed immediately – at least the first
> two – but La Roquière was brought back to camp where he died the next
> day. Couterne, Cuissy's cornet, was wounded and his horse killed under
> him. He could not get free without help and was abandoned on the field.
> He remained in this sad condition for three days and three nights before
> he was pulled from beneath his horse during a cease-fire for the purpose
> of burying the dead. He was brought back to camp where he died the
> same night. He had been a handsome trooper. Of this whole troop there
> was only Bernard who was not wounded and nor was his horse – all the
> others as well as their horses were either wounded or killed.[19]

When it came to the assault on the counterscarp, a decision with which
'many officers disagreed', Dumont explains that 'a detachment of grenadiers
was selected from the whole army and divided into several platoons, each
commanded by an officer from one of the three French regiments. La
Barbe, a brave man and a good officer, commanded all.' When the assault
failed,

> the enemy charged our troops as they retreated, killing or wounding
> more than fifteen hundred men ... Many were killed in this offensive; the
> Dutch guards regiment lost many officers, but La Caillemotte's (which
> had become Belcastel's) and Cambon's French regiments lost more than
> any. Belcastel was wounded.[20]

18 Kane (1747), 6.
19 Ressinger (2005), 238–9.
20 Ressinger (2005), 240–1.

According to a Jacobite account, du Cambon's regiment was left after the first siege of Limerick with only six officers out of 77 able to serve, the other 71 being killed or wounded.[21]

Aughrim and the Williamite Victory, 1691

William had failed at Limerick, but he regained the initiative thanks to a splendidly executed combined land and sea operation organized by the Earl of Marlborough that seized Cork and Kinsale, the ports that provided the best communications between France and Ireland, in September–October 1690. The winter that followed witnessed many bitter but small-scale local raids and operations both by and against the rapparees, Catholic irregulars whom Story defined as 'such of the Irish as are not of the Army, but the Countrey People armed in a kind of an hostile manner with Half-pikes and Skeins, and some with Sythes, or Musquets'.[22] Such operations, however, had little impact on the overall strategic situation. Godard van Reede, baron de Ginkel, the senior lieutenant general in the Dutch army, now had command of the Williamite forces. Two new senior officers in his force who would play important roles in what was to follow were Lieutenant General Hugh Mackay, who had been William's commander-in-chief in Scotland, and Henri de Massue, second Marquis de Ruvigny, who was now appointed colonel of what had previously been Schomberg's cavalry regiment.

The new campaign also saw the arrival, in May 1691, of a new Jacobite general, who was needed because the Irish leaders Tyrconnell and Sarsfield were at odds with one another. This was Charles Chalmont, Marquis de St Ruhe, pronounced Saint Ru. He is more commonly known as Saint-Ruth. Saint-Ruth had made a name for himself in France in the years 1683–86 as a committed persecutor of the Huguenots, especially in Dauphiné and Languedoc. Don't worry about quoting old preachers if you want to hold the Huguenots to their duty, a contemporary French epigram on the *dragonnades* concluded: 'Just cite Saint Ruth: his is the right way'.[23] De Tessé, his second in command at Aughrim, had also assisted him in the persecutions in Dauphiné.[24] There can be no doubt that their reputation would have been well known to the Huguenots serving in Ireland, and

21 Gilbert (1892), 265.
22 Story (1693), *i*, 16.
23 'Ne citez que Saint Ruth: c'est la bonne méthode'; *BSHPF* I (1852–3), 476. See also *BSHPF* IV (1855–6), 611; X (1861), 450; XXVI (1877) 69; XXVIII (1879), 408; and XXXIV (1885), 607.
24 [Pierre Jurieu], (1684), 347, 354, 358.

it must have strengthened their motivation and determination. Later in the 1680s Saint-Ruth had been sent to Savoy, where he displayed similar rough and brutal tendencies while also showing himself to be an active, brave and effective general. In Savoy, he had commanded Irish regiments, got on with them and found they served well, so he would not have been unhappy with his new posting.[25]

The two armies were roughly of the same order of magnitude, rather over 20,000 men, and both had received supplies by sea during the winter: arms, ammunition, food, clothing. The Williamites, however, were better prepared to fight, and were now backed by an exceptionally powerful siege train, described by Story as 'such an one as never had been seen before in that Kingdom'.[26] Ginkel's first objective was to capture Athlone, a key crossing point of the Shannon, and his attack there began on 20 June. Athlone was a strong position and defended by Saint-Ruth's whole army. It consisted of an English town and an Irish town, connected by a stone bridge. The English town, on the Leinster side of the river, was taken relatively quickly. A lieutenant of du Cambon's Huguenot regiment led the advance party of 30 grenadiers attacking the first breach, losing his life in the process.[27] Moving on from there to the Irish town was a difficult matter, the river so deep and fast-flowing that the French general believed it could not be forded in the face of enemy fire. The bridge was only partial, the Jacobites having broken down two of its nine arches, and energetic defence defeated successive Williamite attempts to cross it and caused significant losses. Eventually a way was found to ford the river, and the town was then captured on 30 June.

Although Ginkel's 32 siege guns had expended 12,000 cannonballs and 600 bombs in the attack, Saint-Ruth should never have allowed Athlone to be taken, as he knew very well. He had the geographical advantage. The Jacobite defence of the bridge had been determined and effective; the courage of his men was not at fault. He had not been present in the city when it had been captured, and he had failed to ensure that, in the event of successful infiltration by the enemy, there was a clear passage for his army beyond the town to enter it quickly to charge the Williamites and force their immediate withdrawal. Some historians have also argued that Saint-Ruth's arrangement for a succession of regiments to relieve one another in turn, rather than having a regular garrison, meant that raw and inexperienced troops were at the critical point at an unfortunate time,

---

25 *Journal du Marquis de Dangeau* (vol. III, 1689–91) (Paris, Firmin Didot Frères, 1854), 225.
26 Story (1693), *ii*, 80.
27 Story (1693), *ii*, 96–8.

but Michael McNally gives strong reasons for suggesting this was not in fact the case.[28]

Following the fall of Athlone, Saint-Ruth had a practical need to hold his army together and limit the desertions that often followed a defeat. He also had a strategic need to save Galway and Limerick, and a personal need to restore his reputation at Louis XIV's court and his credibility in Ireland. His solution was to fight at Aughrim. The battle was his choice, no one else had responsibility. Ginkel had no idea what his opponent intended, and the Williamites did not even know where Saint-Ruth was until their scouts found his army arrayed before them. As for the other Jacobite leaders, they did not agree with Saint-Ruth. Sarsfield, the highest profile Irish soldier, always at his best as a 'hit and run' cavalryman, wanted mobility and to ensure that the war continued until 1692. He argued that Ginkel's army was more numerous and better disciplined, with veteran European troops and 'also a considerable party of Protestants out of France, bred up in arms and inured to war'.[29] Tyrconnell, likewise, did not want to risk the campaign on a single battle.

The battle at Aughrim was bloody and at the end of the day utterly one-sided, devastating in its results for the Irish. Simms quotes a contemporary Irish poet:

In Aughrim of the slaughter they rest;
Their skeletons lying there, uncoffined,
Have caused the women of Ireland to beat their hands.
The children to be neglected, and the fugitives to wail.[30]

Yet Aughrim was also the one event in the wars when the Williamite army came close to suffering a major defeat: a defeat on a scale that would have kept a Jacobite army in being, undoubtedly with continuing French support, into a fourth year, 1692: a defeat that might then arguably have toppled William, who was already feeling sharp financial pressures in 1691, when Sir Charles Porter, one of the ruling Lords Justices in Ireland, considered it 'absolutely necessary, upon any terms, to end the war in [Ireland] this summer'.[31] So we will pay the battle close attention. This is the more important because although Aughrim was the decisive encounter of the war – certainly for the Jacobites – there has been far less written

---

28 Contrast Simms (1969), 207–10, and Childs (2007), 325, with McNally (2008), 89–91.
29 Wauchope (1992), 214–15.
30 Simms (1969), 229.
31 *CSPD*, 1690–91, 393.

on it than on the Boyne.[32] It was not in anyone's interest to dwell on it. From Louis XIV's perspective, he had suffered a blood-stained defeat, and there was nothing glorious about it. For the Irish, the loss and pain were too great to be borne, and there were no positive outcomes. Even for the Williamites, the battle was far more costly than they would have liked and highlighted the arrogance of English expectations ever since the successes of the Cromwellian regime. However, a study of what happened at Aughrim is essential to an understanding of the wider contribution of the Huguenots to William's cause, because three facts point towards this hard-fought encounter being, in particular, *their* victory. First, the refugee troops, both infantry and cavalry, appear prominently in the most hotly contested areas of the battlefield. Second, the Williamite commander the baron de Ginkel publicly embraced Ruvigny after the battle, expressing his pride in his bravery and conduct and congratulating his troops.[33] The third compelling piece of evidence, as we will see, lies in the casualty list of Williamite officers compiled immediately after the battle and printed by the English chaplain George Story in his *Continuation of the Impartial History of the Wars of Ireland* (1693).

It may come as a surprise that the present book on the Huguenots would rehabilitate Louis XIV's general, their persecutor Saint-Ruth, but the charge of which he has been accused that he was simply a 'foolhardy French gambler' is less than reasonable.[34] Not only did Saint-Ruth choose to fight, he also selected the battlefield. Near the small village of Aughrim he found exactly what he was looking for. It was a site that the Williamite army could not bypass on the road from Athlone to Galway. Above the village was Kilcommodon Hill, over a mile long and protected at its foot by a stream running through a wide bog impassable to mounted troops or artillery. Hayes-McCoy describes it as a 'natural defensive position [which] must in 1691 have stood up like a bulwark above a waterlogged countryside'.[35] The road to Galway ran along a narrow causeway that was only wide enough for two horsemen to ride abreast and went past the ruins of Aughrim castle just 40 yards away, well within effective musket shot. The two armies were comparable in size, but the Williamites had

---

32 The only book-length study is Michael McNally, *The Battle of Aughrim 1691* (2008); it is well written and well informed but not footnoted in detail. Other accounts include Simms (1969), chap. XIII; Childs (2007), chap. 20; Wauchope (1992), chap. XVII; Hayes-McCoy (1969), pp. 238ff. Historians' detailed knowledge of the battle can only be termed unsatisfactory; Hayes-McCoy remarks (p. 261) that 'we know very little about the disposal, unit by unit, of the Irish troops in any part of the field'.
33 Ressinger (2005), 252; *Oxford Dictionary of National Biography* (Oxford University Press, 2004), vol. 37, entry *sub* Massue de Ruvigny by Harman Murtagh.
34 Wauchope (1992), 236.
35 Hayes-McCoy (1969), 249. There is a readable map of the battle on p. 241.

more cavalry and artillery, and such a site was ideal for negating those strengths, since neither the cavalry nor the artillery could cross the bog. Moreover, Saint-Ruth had enough time before Ginkel arrived to improve the site still further. The hill was lined with successive rows of hedges, and the French general caused communication gaps to be cut in them so that the Irish infantry could repeatedly fall back from one defensive position to another. Story describes how the hillside above the bog was

> cut into a great many small Enclosures, which the Enemy had ordered so as to make a Communication from one of them to another, and had lined all those very thick with Small Shot [i.e. muskets]; this shewed a great deal of Dexterity in Monsieur St Ruth, in making choice of such a piece of Ground as Nature it self could not furnish him with a better.[36]

The official Williamite account, the *Particular and Full Account of the Routing of the whole Irish Army at Aghrim*, published 'by authority' in Dublin after the battle, confirms that the Jacobites 'encamped upon the side of a Hill very well ditched, and the Ditches as well lined with Shot to the very edge of the Bogg'.[37]

The Jacobites did not have the detailed training to carry out complicated battlefield manoeuvres, but they had shown at Limerick and again at Athlone that they could maintain a defensive position with courage and determination. On Kilcommodon Hill, Saint-Ruth believed that would be enough for victory, and he did not order his encampment to be struck before the battle.[38] As for the causeway, its narrow width made it a potential death trap for the Williamites, since their horses could only tackle it two abreast, there was no room to turn or manoeuvre, and the Jacobite cavalry could be positioned unchallenged at the far end.

The battle at Aughrim took place on the evening of 12 July 1691. Ginkel's army, infantry in the centre and horse (or perhaps a mixture of horse and infantry) on the wings, was in place facing its opponents by mid-afternoon, and the first attack was made by his most consistent and reliable infantry shortly before 5 pm when the three Huguenot battalions (Belcastel, du Cambon, Melonière) and the Danes did their best to advance through the bog and up the hill. Under constant fire and with the sun in their eyes, that proved very difficult, and little progress was made, although testimony to the ferocity of their attempt is evident in the name still attached to the place where the fighting was fiercest, 'Bloody Hollow'.

---

36 Story (1693), *ii*, 122.
37 *A Particular and full Account of the Routing the whole Irish Army at Aghrim* (1691), 1.
38 McNally (2008), 112.

After an hour and a half of indecisive fighting, four English regiments were also sent into the bog nearby. Although most of their men were 'up to their Middles in Mudd and Water', they gained a foothold in the lower hedges, only to be thrown back into the bog and beyond by the Irish, with heavy losses. Story conceded that at this stage an observer would have given victory to the Irish, since they had now 'driven our Foot in the Centre so far back, that they were got almost in a Line, with some of our Great Guns', putting the latter out of action 'because of the mixture of our Men and theirs'. Up to this point, events had fallen out just as Saint-Ruth had envisaged. His infantry had fulfilled or exceeded his expectations, and he was more certain than ever of victory, telling those around him that he would now beat the Williamite army 'back to the Gates of Dublin'.[39]

Battles, however, can be desperately unpredictable, and three things now happened within a short time frame which, between them, spelled utter ruin for the Jacobite cause. First, a stray cannon ball removed Saint-Ruth's head as he rode down Kilcommodon Hill to lead what he expected to be the decisive cavalry charge of the war that would send the Williamites packing. Those around him were more concerned to cover his corpse and remove it out of sight than to pursue the battle. The loss of leadership was disastrous. Some of his subordinates lacked a clear understanding of his intentions, others were slow to discover what had happened or were not clear about their responsibilities, and his second in command, René de Froulay, comte de Tessé, was wounded shortly afterwards. Second, the Marquis de Ruvigny broke through the causeway and immediately seized the initiative from the now paralysed Irish army, turning against the exposed Jacobite infantry. Third, many of the Irish horse made only token resistance or did not fight but simply left the field, instead of vigorously attacking the Williamite horse who had successfully crossed the causeway while they were still in disarray near Aughrim castle. The combined result of these three developments was a slaughter of the unfortunate Irish infantry that continued until nightfall and decided the whole Irish campaign.

It is the lists of officers killed and wounded in action at Aughrim that best highlight the determination with which the Huguenots fought. There were 22 units of Williamite foot, and between them they returned a total of 136 killed and wounded officers. The two units suffering most were both Huguenot regiments, those of Pierre de Belcastel and François du Cambon.[40] Between them, these two regiments had 39 officers killed and wounded, between a quarter and 30 per cent of the total for

---

39 Story (1693), *ii*, 128–33.
40 Belcastel – 1 killed, 22 wounded; du Cambon – 4 killed, 12 wounded.

all 22 Williamite infantry units combined. Even more striking are the statistics for Ruvigny's cavalry, which suffered twenty officers killed and four wounded. There were in all nineteen Williamite horse units, and between all of them, 33 officers lost their lives and nine were wounded. So Ruvigny's unit suffered 60 per cent of all the Williamite Horse officer fatalities in the Aughrim battle. As a percentage of officers involved, the figure must have been even higher, since a squadron of Ruvigny's force had been detached and sent to reinforce other units early in the battle.[41]

Table V.1

Williamite cavalry officers killed or wounded at Aughrim[42]

Unit	Officers killed or wounded
Earl of Oxford	4
Edward Villiers	6
Francis Langston	0
Marquis de Ruvigny	24
Sir John Lanier	0
Robert Byerley	1
William Wolseley	0
La Forest-Suzannet	1
Moritz Melchior von Donop	2
Jens Maltesen Sehested	0
Paul Didier de Boncour	0
Earl of Portland	2
Marquis de Montpouillon	0
Baron van Ginkel	0
Bogislaf Sigismund Schack	1
Erik Gustaaf van Steinbeck	0
Baron Ittersum tot Nyenhuis	1
Willem Frederick van Nassau-Zuylenstein	0
Abraham van Eppinger	0

41 McNally (2008), 128; Story (1693), *ii*, 131.
42 Story (1693), *ii*, 140.

It would be entirely reasonable to expect that the Huguenot officer casualties would be high because their regiments included many *incorporées*, supernumeraries who were not full-time soldiers but paid only for time in active service. Even so, one could hardly ask for a clearer statistical statement of their determination and vital contribution at Aughrim.

If there was one man whose decisions and actions were of critical importance, it was Ruvigny, in joint command of seven regiments of horse and three of dragoons on the right wing of the Williamite army, and in charge on this part of the field after Mackay was thrown from his horse. He ordered Villiers's brigade to engage in the hazardous advance along the causeway, then joined it himself. The difficulties they faced are captured in Story's account:

> The Right wing of our Horse ... [made] what Haste they could to succour our Foot; for seeing their Danger, and indeed that all was in hazard by reason of the Difficulty of the Pass, they did more than Men, in pressing and tumbling over a very dangerous place, and that amongst Showrs of Bullets, from a Regiment of Dragoons, and two Regiments of Foot, posted conveniently under Cover, by the Enemy, to obstruct our Passage ... It's reported, that Monsieur St. Ruth, seeing our Horse draw that way, and then begin to scramble over at a place where only two a Breast could pass, and that too with great difficulty; after all which, they had no other way to march, but to go within thirty yards of the Castle. The French General seeing our men attempt to do this, askt 'What they meant by it?' And being answered, That they would certainly endeavour to pass there, and Attack him on the Left; he is said to reply with an Oath, 'They are brave fellows, its a Pity they be so exposed' or Words to that purpose.[43]

The *Particular and Full Account of the Routing of the whole Irish Army at Aghrim* confirms that the path of the causeway 'was passable no way for Horse, but just at the Castle, by reason of a River, which running through a moist ground, made the whole a Morass or Bogg'. It was therefore right beside the castle that the pass had to be forced,

> though defended by a regiment of Dragoons, and so narrow, that our Horse were forced to march it by a defile of two a breast ... till at last recovering the firm part of the Bogg, our men formed a line, and some of them advanced under the walls of the Castle, and lodged themselves in a dry Ditch, though the Enemy poured volleys of their Small Shot upon

---

43 Story (1693), *ii*, 131–2.

them, the rest of that Brigade with great Bravery attackt their Ditches, and pressed so far upon the Enemy, beyond what they ought to have done, unless they had been supported with Horse, that they were forced back to the Bogg, but when they were reinforced by our Horse ... they drove the Enemy to the top of the Hill, where their Horse and Foot mixed with ours, but after a short dispute we totally routed them, and beat their Horse out of the Field.

The Jacobite account of the battle in 'Light to the Blind' likewise emphasizes the 'extraordinary valour' with which the whole overall engagement at Aughrim was fought on both sides. As for the broken causeway, it agrees it would only allow one or two horses at a time, that it was very close to the castle, which was defended by Colonel Bourke with two hundred men, and that close behind were the Jacobite forces of Luttrell's dragoons and Major-General Shelden's horse guards, stationed specifically to defend the Causeway Path.[44] The picture that seems to emerge from the rival accounts is not of one mad dash up the causeway, but rather of repeated surges, one getting through the causeway, another advancing against the castle, a third occupying the 'dry ditch' under heavy fire, and finally the Williamite breakthrough on to the top of the hill. What is plain is that once across the causeway, Ruvigny did not allow his initiative to slacken, but charged Luttrell's dragoons, who could not stand against his offensive. His determination could not have been better timed, with the Irish leaderless and uncertain. Even Gilbert Burnet, not renowned for any partiality for the French, acknowledged that Ruvigny played a major part in the victory.[45] While part of his force masked the Jacobite horse, the remainder now broke onto the hill and charged the unprotected Irish infantry. Some Jacobites stood firm and fought to the end, and Story relates finding bodies clustered in groups in ditches and behind hedges, up to 150 in some enclosures. Gradually, though, the Jacobite army disintegrated and as night fell defeat turned into rout, many of the infantry throwing away their weapons as they ran.[46]

Plainly, Ruvigny and his Huguenot officers were leading by example and shared a united resolve that this was the battle which had to be won at all costs. That raises an interesting question about motivation. Modern historians are quick to reject any idea that the Williamite wars were wars of religion. They rightly note how William and the Dutch Republic were at great pains to reject any suggestion that they might be

---

44 National Library of Ireland, MS 476, pp. 681–5.
45 Burnet (1833), IV, 146.
46 McNally (2008), 113, 158; Wauchope (1992), 228, 232; Story (1993), *ii*, 133, 135, 137; *Particular and Full Account*, p. 2.

leading an anti-Catholic crusade. After all, the Grand Alliance to check the ambitions of Louis XIV included major Roman Catholic powers and was sometimes assisted by papal diplomacy, while imperial and Spanish recognition of William as king in England was not forthcoming until William provided reassurances that English Roman Catholics would be tolerated.[47] Nevertheless, Aughrim does appear as an outlier from the earlier age of the Reformation. The battle was fought on a Sunday, and for the Jacobites began with mass. Saint-Ruth's secretary, who lost his life that day, was said to have had amongst his papers a speech by the French general urging his men to fight for the Catholic Church, for James, for their families and country and for honour. Burnet claims that Saint-Ruth sent priests through his troops who made them 'swear on the sacrament, that they would never forsake their colours'.[48] On the opposite side, in another speech that was a mirror image of Saint-Ruth's, the Scot Hugh Mackay urged his men on as the last hope of the Protestant Church, for their honour and to protect their church, and to protect both their families from France and the liberty of England.[49] The Catholic bishop of Cork confirmed that 80 priests were killed at Aughrim, crucifix in hand, while urging on their troops to fight for their faith. J.G. Simms concluded that 'the crusading spirit must have made its contribution to the courage and resolution with which the Irish fought',[50] but he ignored that the same might be equally true of their Huguenot counterparts on the other side and indeed barely mentions Ruvigny in his account of the battle. Looking at the Irish losses and Ruvigny's casualties, one wonders if there may not have been at Aughrim a foretaste of an encounter that would take place in Spain sixteen years later, when during the battle of Almanza in 1707 a Huguenot refugee regiment recently raised by Jean Cavalier found itself confronting French troops whom its members had known only too well in their homeland. The Duke of Berwick was the experienced and victorious Catholic commander that day. He never forgot the bloody clash he witnessed as the two sides did not even bother to fire but simply rushed at one another with bayonets, Cavalier losing over half his men.[51]

Religion was a powerful motivating force, but it was not the only one in play on Kilcommodon Hill. Another was shared historical experience. Ruvigny had succeeded his father as Deputy General of the Huguenots at the French court and was the true representative of the French Protestant nobility whom Louis had scorned. To that he added the mantle of

---

47 See for instance Israel (1991), 20, 123, 137–8, 141.
48 Burnet (1833), IV, 141.
49 Story (1693), *ii*, 123–5; McNally (2008), 154; Mackay (1833), 164.
50 Simms (1969), 220.
51 *DNB sub* Cavalier.

Schomberg, whose cavalry regiment he had inherited together with his determination, military leadership and preparedness if necessary to die for the Williamite cause. Their ghosts fought alongside him when the conditions of Aughrim presented half a chance to transform possible defeat into improbable victory. Ruvigny's utter conviction that the opportunity must at all costs be seized was embraced by his men. They were no ordinary group of professional soldiers, although their professionalism and cohesion had been enhanced and forged anew during their time in Ireland. These were independent volunteers who shared a common background of rejection in France, men who had been forced from their homeland, men whose goods had been seized and whose families had been shattered. Since coming to Ireland they had developed and strengthened personal friendships and ties and a shared understanding of what needed to be done, which meant that they trusted and fought for one another, and for former friends now lying dead on Irish soil, as well as for their leaders and beliefs. In the evening hours of 12 July 1691, fighting under their rightful leader against known persecutors of their fellow Huguenots in their homeland, they were not to be denied.

The determination with which both the Irish Jacobite foot and the Williamite Huguenots fought at Aughrim is plain. That highlights the question, what happened to the Jacobite horse guards, who should have made Ruvigny's success at the causeway impossible? The author of 'Light to the Blind' spelled out how they had waited all day to fulfil the one objective for which they had been placed in position, 'to secure that very pass' and so ensure that James II's army was not endangered. They had witnessed the remarkable bravery of their compatriots elsewhere on the field of battle. They knew their orders and their duty. Rather than fulfil it they deserted their charge and handed victory to the Williamites.[52] Other Jacobite accounts spoke even more darkly of treachery.[53] Modern historians have preferred to blame low morale or self-interest rather than deliberate treachery, although it is hard to see why morale should have been low after the day's efforts by the Jacobites or how self-interest could possibly be allowed to override the inevitable bloody fate of the Irish foot once their horse deserted them.[54] In any case, it is hardly possible to argue with Simms's conclusion that 'negligible resistance was offered at the causeway and that this was fatal for the whole Jacobite army'.[55]

---

52 National Library of Ireland, MS 476, pp. 693–7, and MS 477, 'To the Catholicks of Ireland', p. 87.
53 Gilbert (1892), 146–7; Lenihan and Sidwell (2018), Book 6, lines 1214–16, 1255 ff, 1695–6.
54 Childs (2007), 336–7; Lenihan and Sidwell (2018), Book 6, nn.114–15.
55 Simms (1969), 225.

The sacrifices of the Huguenots at Aughrim were of real consequence. The crushing nature of the Jacobite defeat at the battle destroyed Irish morale,[56] and the aftermath can be quickly summarized. A week after the battle, Ginkel reached Galway, and the town was captured with little resistance a few days later. That left Limerick as the principal Williamite target. Its defences had been repaired and strengthened by French army engineers with new entrenchments, bastions and demi-lunes following the successful defence of the city by the Jacobites in 1690, so it had the potential to be a real problem for the Williamites in 1691. However, as was noted at the time and as the historian Pádraig Lenihan has echoed this century, while the defences might have been strengthened, the Irish had lost heart and showed none of the spirit they had displayed on the earlier occasion: 'Aughrim had made the difference in a way that the Boyne had not.'[57] Truce terms were under discussion by late September, and Limerick was formally occupied by the Williamites on 4 October.[58] Aughrim, then, brought the Williamite wars in Ireland to a close. But what if Saint-Ruth had lived, and led the successful cavalry charge he anticipated? That question cannot be answered. Saint-Ruth would have had reason for optimism, for the Irish horse had performed nobly at the Boyne and would have been much fresher than their opponents. It was once speculated that a Jacobite victory at Aughrim might have changed the course of Irish, even European, history, drawing the response that the greater resources of the Williamites must eventually have prevailed.[59] All that is certain is that Jacobite victory at Aughrim would have prolonged the war in Ireland into a fourth year. The historian has no way of telling whether William could have sustained the financial and diplomatic pressure which that would have entailed.

CONCLUSION: THE HUGUENOT CONTRIBUTION IN IRELAND, 1689–92

There can be no doubt that the Huguenot troops in Ireland were well trained and professional in their approach. They stood alongside the Dutch and Danish troops as the most reliable in the Williamite forces. They did not believe, unlike the otherwise dependable Enniskilleners,

56 John Jordan, 'The Jacobite Wars: Some Danish sources', in *Studies: An Irish Quarterly Review* (winter 1954), pp. 436–7.
57 Lenihan (2005), 195.
58 For the details of the second siege of Limerick, see the concluding chapters of Childs (2007).
59 Simms (1969), 228.

that 'they should never thrive so long as they were under orders', nor did they suppose, like the novice English troops, that it did not matter if they chose to ignore orders that they build huts.[60] Rather, the Huguenots were sufficiently well organized and prepared to dig, erect huts or tackle an apparently impossible challenge if ordered to do so. Dumont de Bostaquet prided himself that 'it was a point of honour and even pleasure for me to do my duty with great precision', and his memoirs suggest that he and his colleagues sought to prevent looting and be punctual and in a state of readiness when required for action.[61] Schomberg and William trusted them in a way they did not always trust their other soldiers in Ireland, and retained that trust even after the carefully planned hostile conspiracy implanted into some of the Huguenot ranks had spluttered briefly into life at Dundalk in 1689. In April of that year the refugees had claimed in a submission to the House of Commons to have shown their loyalty through the recent formation of three regiments 'ready to lay down their Lives in Defence of the Protestant Religion, and the Liberties of England',[62] and the history of the regiments in Ireland showed that this was no idle boast. They expected to be used, and from first to last, from Carrickfergus in 1689 to Aughrim in 1691 by way of Charlemont, the Boyne and the first siege of Limerick in 1690, they showed themselves willing to put their lives on the line.

Just how many officers and men were involved, and how many casualties resulted, is impossible to assess accurately. We know most about the officers, and thanks to the research of George Hilton Jones, Appendix 1 of this book reveals that over 1400 Huguenot officers can be individually identified as fighting in the armies of William III and Anne across the period 1689–1713 in all the various theatres of war. The true figure will be higher, with those most likely to have escaped the records being men killed very early in their military careers. Well over five hundred of the 1400 officers recorded in the appendix took part in 'the reduction of Ireland'. Not all the Huguenot Williamite officers who were fighting in Ireland were doing so for the British Crown. For example, the Williamite left wing at Aughrim was commanded by Frédéric-Henri, marquis de La Forest-Suzannet, a Huguenot officer in Dutch service, whose troops included Huguenot horse. Many of the 'Danish' officers were German, with a scattering of French Protestants. Nor were all the Huguenots who were in British service concentrated in the specifically 'Huguenot' regiments; Lenihan estimates that up to 15 per cent of the English officer corps were

---

60 Simms (1970), 16; Story (1693), *i*, 12, 26.
61 Ressinger (2005), 219, 232, 237.
62 *CJ* x, p.103, 24 April 1689.

French Protestants.[63] It might indeed be suggested that the wide distribution of Huguenots amongst the officers of different Williamite forces helped to create bridges in a divided international situation. Dumont de Bostaquet comments at one point on how difficult it was to keep his troops to their duties 'because they included men from almost all the nations of Europe: the lieutenant spoke French, the cornet Dutch and German'.[64] One thing that can be said specifically about the Irish situation is that by the end of 1691 pensions had been established for former serving officers in the one horse and three Huguenot infantry regiments in Ireland who still lived but had 'by wounds or otherwise become uncapable of further service' during the previous two and a half years. The list consisted of 147 men – 1 colonel, 2 lieutenant colonels, 47 captains, 61 lieutenants, 10 cornets and 26 ensigns.[65]

If there are serious gaps in our knowledge of the officers, the same is much truer of rank-and-file soldiers. Indeed, under normal circumstances there are no surviving sources that allow the historian to view individual refugees serving in such a capacity, and Appendix 2 of this book is provided precisely because of its unusual nature. It derives from a charity relief document, created because of the temporary need of a group of largely southern French soldiers whose regiments had been broken in Ireland and who came to London in 1699 in consequence. Because there is no other source with which to compare it, we cannot say how typical or unusual is the picture it provides. As to total numbers of casualties, again we have no hard evidence. Our second volume drew attention to the estimate by the generally well-informed Hilaire Reneu that 'in the reduction of Ireland ... upwards of 7000 [refugees] perish'd either by sword or sickness'.[66] That seems high, but Reneu was not normally given to exaggeration. The only other indication of possible relevance I have seen comes from the anonymous *The Cevenois Relieved, Or else, Europe Enslav'd*, published in London in 1703. The author claimed that there were over 300 French Protestant officers on half pay in England and Ireland, who would undertake to raise at least 8000 men for service in the Piedmont. The author also noted how quickly the captains of the Duke of Schomberg's regiment had completed their companies the previous year, even though 'that abundance of Refugees in Soho and Spittlefields' had not then enlisted because they expected that they would be needed

63 McNally (2008), 113; Lenihan (2005), 67. For some examples, see pp. 177–8.
64 Ressinger (2005), 235.
65 The individuals are itemized in *HSP* IX no. 3 (1912).
66 Gwynn (2018), 195–6.

to go to the Camisards' aid.[67] A prominent recent military historian has suggested that 'the Huguenot regiments were no different from many other corps in contemporary armies, most of which took whatever soldiers they could from whatever source', but the references presented in this paragraph do not support such a suggestion, which appears to be a misrepresentation based on over-emphasis on the deliberately planned, treasonable infiltration of the 1689 Huguenot regiments (below, pp. 82–3), as if that were a standard occurrence.[68] Another misconception that seems to have misled some writers is that 'Huguenot émigrés were disproportionately drawn from the better off so the lower ranks were necessarily filled out with non-Huguenots'.[69] The fact of the matter is that the overwhelming majority of Huguenot refugees were not 'drawn from the better off' at all, but the very poor, and overall the evidence suggests the Huguenot regiments were indeed very largely composed of Huguenot refugees.

From King William's point of view, perhaps the single greatest gift that the Huguenots offered was that they came at exactly the right time. When he invaded England in 1688, he did not know whom in Britain he could trust, and in any event after the Revolution the English troops suffered a desperate shortage of trained officers after many of those who had been in James's army had decided they could not serve against their former king, to whom they had tendered oaths of loyalty. But the Huguenots were to hand in 1689, more than adequately trained and officered, highly motivated and happy to serve under the Duke of Schomberg and later under Ruvigny.

There were not enough of them for the king's purposes, and William found a further solution when he employed the Danes. They too were excellent troops, well trained, well led and moreover well equipped with modern flintlock weapons and socket bayonets. They also had the advantage that they were wholly unconnected with English politics. However, they suffered from one major disadvantage: they came at a high price. William was not in a good position to worry about financial details when his envoy Robert Molesworth negotiated the lease of 1000 Danish cavalry and 6000 infantry with the Danish king Christian V in August 1689. The terms of the agreement signed the following month were much in the Danes' favour. The payment for the lease was fixed at 240,000 rixdollars, to be raised to 325,000 rixdollars if the corps was transferred to Ireland. After the war compensation was to be paid of 60 crowns

---

67 *The Cevenois Relieved, Or else, Europe Enslav'd* ... (John Nutt, London, 1703), 44.
68 Childs (2007), 166–7. It is likely, as Childs implies, that the composition of Huguenot regiments in the Netherlands became less coherent after they were redeployed in Flanders in the Spanish Netherlands in 1693.
69 Lenihan (2005), 68.

for any missing horse and cavalryman and 18 crowns for each missing infantry soldier. 'In comparison with similar leasing arrangements at the time the rent for the corps was exorbitantly high.'[70] The Huguenots came with the same professional dedication as the Danes, but they were far cheaper. The pay of the incorporated captains, lieutenants and ensigns in the Huguenot infantry regiments was set in 1689 respectively at five shillings, two shillings and sixpence and two shillings a day, 'to be paid unto them during their service as Incorporated Officers ... and no longer'. Their brother cavalry officers did little better at six shillings and three pence, three shillings and nine pence, and three shillings and two pence respectively.[71] Nor were they always paid in timely fashion.[72]

Inexpensive, instantly available at just the right moment of time, profoundly loyal to his cause, the Huguenots were a godsend to William. The king knew what was owed to them, and in March 1692 Lieutenant General Ruvigny returned to Ireland as Lord Galway and commander-in-chief of the remaining forces in the country. If we agree with Matthew Glozier's conclusion that 'the campaign in Ireland was the determining factor in King James II's ultimate failure to regain his throne',[73] then the Huguenots must be given a prominent place. Their determination, professionalism and courage were at a premium in the boggy plains and uplands of Ireland. Clifford Walton, writing his *History of the British Standing Army* (1894), put his finger on the one characteristic marking them out from all others that gave them a special edge, when he remarked on how the Huguenots added to whatever military skill they brought with them 'the bitter ferocity and desperate invincibility of excommunicated exiles'.[74] That phraseology is justified by their performance in Ireland, and never more so than in the decisive victory at Aughrim, where their infantry slugged out a stalemate against better positioned opponents in the mud of Bloody Hollow and their cavalry won victory through Ruvigny's determined surges along the dangerous causeway.

---

70 Knud J.V. Jespersen, 'Surviving in a World of Great Powers: Denmark, England and Europe in the late Seventeenth Century', in Bernadette Whelan (ed.) (1995), 57–8.
71 TNA, W.O. 25/3146, pp. 17, 21, 33, and W.O. 24/884, pp. 117, 120.
72 See for example Ressinger (2005), 222, 238, 245.
73 Glozier (2002), 115.
74 Walton (1894), 108.

PART THREE

FINANCE

VI

The Huguenot Presence at the Birth of the Bank of England (I): The Threadneedle Street Church

However many lives were laid down in Ireland, England could fight for only so long as it had resources to do so. In this section we turn from the boggy battlefields of Ireland to the city of London, where the Bank of England was founded in 1694, less than a decade after Louis XIV destroyed open Protestant worship in France. New Huguenot arrivals and the descendants of earlier Protestant refugees joined in contributing significantly to the Bank's immediate success, and the Bank was critical to England's survival because without it, the country could not have borne the huge cost of almost continuous land war with France from 1689 to 1713. This chapter is a story about a Bank that was not quite what readers might expect in a modern bank, a nearby church that was not simply what they might expect in a modern church, and the surprisingly numerous links that the two institutions had in common. It provides new insights into the strength and extent of the connections between the two in the Bank's foundation years.

The Bank of England has been characterized as the 'Old Lady of Threadneedle Street' since a famous cartoon by James Gillray was published in 1797. However, when the Bank was founded a century earlier in the 1690s, it was not located at Threadneedle Street, but first at Mercer's Hall (for the second half of 1694), then in Grocer's Hall for some forty years thereafter. Meanwhile, in Threadneedle Street there already existed an 'old lady', the French Church of London, which worshipped a hundred yards down the road from where the Bank would eventually make its home. We have seen how the ancestry of that church predated the Church of England as by law established, and how its leadership and direction was driven largely by its Consistory. The majority of the Consistory's members were lay elders who devoted a remarkable amount of their time and energy to running the church.[1] It was not until 1734, when the young Bank of England moved its house of business to Threadneedle Street, that the Bank and church became close neighbours, but as we will find, this later proximity was more than just an accident of geography.

Church historians and economic historians do not normally start from the same point or study the same records. In my own case, I reconstructed the membership of the Consistory of the Threadneedle Street church back in the 1960s when writing my doctorate on the ecclesiastical organization of French Protestants in late seventeenth-century England. In recent years I have tried to learn more about the lives, concerns, work and professions of the laymen serving as elders and deacons, and it is in the course of those studies that the connections between the church and the Bank – institutions that at first glance have nothing in common – have stood out with increasing clarity.

At any one time in the 1690s the French Church of London had up to five ministers, usually elected for life; eighteen lay elders whose work was to govern and run the church and its two congregations, a daughter congregation in Spitalfields as well as the one in Threadneedle Street; and eighteen lay deacons whose role concerned poor relief. The lay elders and deacons both usually served for a term of three or three and a half years at a time before being replaced, although individuals might be elected once or twice as a deacon and later repeatedly as an elder during their lives. This is not a church structure that will necessarily be familiar to readers accustomed to more hierarchical systems such as those of the Roman Catholic and Anglican churches.

An important role played by the Threadneedle Street church was that it seamlessly brought together French-speaking Protestants from different backgrounds, regions and countries. Understanding this is an important antidote to attempts by some French writers to demand a sharp differentiation between 'Walloons' and 'Huguenots'. Defining national identity in the seventeenth century is perilous, especially in the refugee community. To the English diarist John Evelyn, the future Bank director Sir James Houblon was a 'French' merchant.[2] That was not because the diarist was 'ignorant of or indifferent to continental history'.[3] It was not because Evelyn failed to comprehend the Houblons' Walloon family origins. Nor was it because he supposed him to be trading primarily with France – the Houblons' trading interests were widely known to be Iberian. Rather, Evelyn considered Sir James 'French' because he was by his background a

---

1 Gwynn (2015), chap. 2.
2 De Beer, (1955), IV, 162, 306.
3 Compare Crouzet (1996), 228.

French-speaking Protestant, a member of the French Church of London. The church itself made no distinction between its members unless specific legal situations required it. By ignoring the Threadneedle Street church, a key institution through which French-speaking Protestants of the sixteenth and seventeenth centuries (wherever they were born) were gradually transmuted into Englishmen, historians risk losing a vital part of the story that led to the foundation of the Bank, and in this chapter and the next we will see that both the descendants of earlier immigrants and the new influx of Huguenot refugees played an important part in the Bank's foundation.

Those accustomed to high street banks in the modern western world will find themselves surprised by some of the activities of the Bank of England in its infancy following its foundation. For example, they would not expect a modern bank to concern itself with reducing the interest on pawns against which loans had been advanced, as did the Bank of England in its early years. Far more startling, however, is the entire purpose for which the Bank of England came to see the light of day. What is now known as the 1694 Bank of England Act did not come into existence because the then rulers King William and Queen Mary, their ministers or parliament had determined that it would be a great thing for commerce, or for the economy, to have an English bank. True, some far-sighted individuals advanced that idea. However, why the Bank came to exist is very clear from the original title of the Act, as embedded in the Charter of the Corporation of the Governor and Company of the Bank of England:

An Act for granting to their Majesties several Rates and Duties upon Tunnage of Ships and Vessels, and upon Beer, Ale and other Liquors: for securing certain Recompenses and Advantages, in the said Act mentioned, to such persons as shall voluntarily advance the Sum of £1,500,000 towards carrying on the War against France.[4]

In other words the Bank came into being because of the government's imperative need to pursue the war with France into which it had been plunged by the Glorious Revolution, and which (with a short break around the turn of the eighteenth century) would continue through to 1713. In enabling that purpose, it was spectacularly successful and wonderfully dedicated. Every single halfpenny of its initial £1,200,000 was promptly used for the intended purpose: £536,746 9s. 3½d for marine services, £663,253 10s. 8½d for land services.[5] Writing his history of the Bank, John

4 Giuseppi (1966), 11.
5 BL, Lansdowne MS 1215, ff. 61–2, 'Apporcionment of the Fonds for the Warr in

Giuseppi commented that 'the sudden availability of such substantial sums, in what was practically hard cash, had results on both services which were immediate and far-reaching', and created 'revolutionary improvement' in the fighting abilities of the navy.[6]

Long before the 1690s, goldsmiths had developed practices offering safe deposit, exchange and loan facilities, and honouring their customers' 'drawn notes'. But there had always been problems. Shortly before the Civil War, King Charles I seized the treasure owned by individuals that had been deposited in the Tower of London for safe keeping. In 1672 his successor's government once more undermined public trust through the 'Stop' of the Exchequer, and the harm and disruption caused to government credit were substantial. By the 1690s, there was therefore a long-standing debate about the need for a London bank, balanced by equally long-standing fears that any such bank might allow a king to obtain money without parliamentary sanction. It could be guaranteed that goldsmiths and others who stood to lose would oppose the foundation of any such bank. As the broadside *Account of the Bank of England* put it c.1695, it was only natural that 'a Thing of so great a Nature' should produce both much discussion and also attack from those who previously obtained 'exorbitant profit by advancing money on the publick revenues'.[7] However, Charles Montagu, from 1694 Chancellor of the Exchequer, considered that the proposal for a 'Bank of England' had merit. Its promoters, after all, were prepared to back the venture with their own money. They were Protestants, solid in their support for the Revolution. They were also prominent merchants with close associations with the city government. Above all, the government was desperately in need of money to conduct the war and could see no other way of getting it.

With that in mind, as we return to the French church in Threadneedle Street, we can begin to appreciate the natural 'fit' between it and the Bank. Of the church officers holding positions in 1694, the year the bank was founded, no fewer than nine – six elders, one deacon and two ministers – were subscribers to the initial call for money by the Bank. The six elders present a clear demonstration that the people we are dealing with were substantial individuals of significance in the society of their day. Further details about them, and about all the lay officers of the church between 1640 and 1713, will be found in Appendix 3, where full references are provided; here we simply present some highlights. Alphabetically, we find:

1. The merchant Joseph Ducasse de la Couture, who had served previously as a deacon at the Threadneedle Street church. He was

---

the Year 1694'.
6 Giuseppi (1966), 21.
7 BL, CUP.21.g.39/63.

the eldest son of Jérémie Ducasse of Nérac, *avocat au Parlement.* He had left France in the livery of the future Republican martyr, Algernon Sidney, joining his household in London in 1680–81 where he became Sidney's valet and trusted secretary – and sole servant at the scaffold when Sidney was beheaded for high treason on Tower Hill in 1683.

2. Also a merchant was Daniel Hays from Calais. According to family tradition, he came to England in the same ship as William of Orange. He became wealthy enough to leave £20,000 to his son, and £10,000 apiece to his five daughters, after having earlier put £20,000 at his wife's disposition.

3. Jean Le Platrier was an elderly man in his eightieth year, serving an unusually long term in office after being elected elder in 1688. A goldsmith and bourgeois of Rouen, he had been specifically targeted by the French authorities and suffered substantial losses in the persecution, abandoning two houses when making his escape.

4. In a similar situation to the last was François Mariette from Orléans, a wine merchant of Place Maubert in Paris, also elderly and also serving an unusually long term in office after being elected elder in 1688. He too had been specifically targeted by the French authorities and suffered major losses in the persecution, leaving behind several properties and vineyards in France worth over 90,000 livres.

5. Besides being a wealthy merchant and, later, stock dealer, Pierre Reneu (I) was exceptionally active in organizing charity relief for the refugees. He used his mercantile activities as cover for gathering intelligence in France for the Williamite cause, which he then passed on to the English Secretary of State and to Pierre Jurieu in the Netherlands.

6. The last of the six elders in office when they responded to the initial call for subscriptions to the Bank, Etienne Seignoret, formerly a silk merchant at Lyons, was probably the wealthiest refugee who came to England, where he was naturalized in 1686 and established himself at Lombard Street. His wife Elizabeth Got was very rich, and he was a substantial import/export merchant with business activities in Germany and the Low Countries and in the Mediterranean – Spain, Portugal and Italy. In the later 1690s he was estimated to be worth between £50,000 and £100,000.

This is a notably wealthy and geographically diverse group of people. Their mercantile connections are obvious, but it is also striking that all except perhaps Seignoret had evident personal reasons or clear intent to oppose Louis XIV. Nor should we overlook the two ministers of the church who subscribed, David Primerose and Aaron Testas, although their financial resources were far smaller. Of the first, the historian Alice Clare Carter wrote 'he built for himself a respectable Bank Stock holding of over £1,000 in the space of three years', and 'his services were often at the disposal of lady members of his congregation who needed an attorney to assist in their investment business'.[8] In other words Primerose – the church's longest-standing, best connected and most influential minister – was not only subscribing himself, but actively spreading the word to those he could reach that the Bank should be supported.

Of the 1268 initial subscribers to the Bank of England, just 27 are listed in the Bank's verified index as 'clerk' or 'minister' or 'doctor of divinity'. Nine of those 27 men were Huguenot pastors – Asselin, Baignoux, Jean Dubourdieu, Gilbert, Graverol, Claude Groteste de la Mothe, Primerose and Testas, and one man from Rotterdam.[9] (A tenth was Samuel Biscop, a minister of the Dutch Church of London, which was closely allied to the Threadneedle Street church.) One third of all ministers who were initial subscribers to the Bank, therefore, were Huguenots – a far stronger statement of immediate support than was forthcoming from Church of England clergy. In this matter, there was no split between Huguenots who worshipped in their original French manner and those who worshipped using the Anglican liturgy in translation. Asselin, Jean Dubourdieu, Graverol and La Mothe were conformist ministers; Baignoux, Primerose, Testas and (at this stage) Gilbert led non-conformist worship. The Bank drew positive support from both camps.

If we widen our scope beyond those in office in 1694 and consider all who previously or subsequently served as church officers of the Threadneedle Street church, then nineteen were initial subscribers to the new Bank in 1694. One also acted as his brother's agent. To them we might add ten others, not themselves church officers, who were sons of past elders and whose families maintained significant connections with the French Church extending into the late seventeenth century, one of whom was agent for multiple subscriptions from the Lethieulliers. In total, this group put up over £66,000 towards the Bank's initial capital. See Table VI.1.

---

8 *HSP* XIX (iii), 36.
9 For these men, see the Biographical Dictionary of Ministers in Gwynn (2015).

Table VI.1

Initial depositors in the Bank of England with connections to the Consistory of the French Church of London

Name	Born	Connection	£ subscribed
Jacques Auguste Blondel	Paris	5	400
Isaac Bonourier	Saintes	5	500
David Boucheret	London?	6	100
Jean Delmé	Canterbury	4	500
Jacques (James) Deneu	London	4, 7	2000
John Dubois	London	6	2000
Joseph Ducasse de la Couture	Nérac	1	500
Jacques Dufay	Boulogne	4, 5	2800
Jean Du Maistre	Bordeaux	4	500
Peter Du Quesne (1646–1714)	London	6	4000
Same as agent for James Du Cane			2000
Same as agent for Lethieulliers			5500
Louis Gervaize (I)	Chauny, Picardy	4	150?
Louis Gervaize (II)	Paris	4, 5	650?
Daniel Hays	Calais	1	1000
Abraham Houblon	London	6, 7	10,000
Jacques (Sir James) Houblon	London	6, 7	4000
Jean (Sir John) Houblon	London	6, 7	10,000
Jean Le Plastrier	Rouen	1	500
Robert Le Plastrier	Rouen	2	200
Benjamin Le Quesne (Le Cane)	London	6	1000
Samuel Lethieullier	Amsterdam	6, 7	2000
Benjamin Lordell	London	6	3000
Jean Lordell	London	6, 7	4000
François Mariette	Orléans	1	500
Pierre Nepueu	Dover	4	300
David Primerose	Rouen	3	200
Pierre Reneu (I)	Bordeaux	1	2000
Same as agent for brother Hilaire			2000
Etienne Seignoret	Lyons	1	2950
Aaron Testas	?	3	400
Humfroy Willett	Rouen	4	1200
Total			66,850

Connections: (1) in office as elder in 1694; (2) in office as deacon in 1694; (3) in office as minister in 1694; (4) in office earlier than 1694; (5) in office later than 1694; (6) never a lay church officer but son of a former elder; (7) original Bank director.

This was a significant contribution to a new and potentially controversial exercise. The church officers' interest in the Bank remained unabated after its initial foundation, and new investment continued. Pierre Lombard put up £500 in late 1694, Jean Drigué £1400 in 1695, Bennet Metcalfe £1200 in 1695–6 and Daniel Brulon £500 in 1696. By 1697 John Girardot de Tillieux held £1850 of bank stock, Benjamin de Jennes £845, and Robert Caillé £2450. All these men served as either deacon or elder or both between the 1680s and 1700. Then, in 1697, the Bank sought new contributions as it enlarged its capital stock. Once again, the Threadneedle Street church featured prominently, with six former investors increasing their deposits and thirteen new depositors coming forward from amongst those who served the church as elders or deacons between 1680 and 1700. Between them, these provided over £30,000; see Table VI.2.

Table VI.2

Contributors to 1697 enlargement of Bank capital stock who served as lay officers of the French Church of London at some point between 1680 and 1700.

Name	Born	Increased holding (I) or New depositor (N)	£ subscribed
Louis Augier	Bordeaux	N	313
	+ for a family member overseas		500
Claude Baudouin	Tours	N	225
Jacques Auguste Blondel	Paris	I	125
David Careiron	Uzès	N	929
François Touvois dit Dechamp	Tours	N	960
Jean Delmé	Canterbury	I	4020
Jacques (James) Deneu	London	I	2810
Jean Deneu	London	N	260
Philippe Ferment	Dieppe	N	255
Jacob de Lillers	London	N	142
Pierre Lombard	Nîmes	I	2682
Pierre Marescoe	Lille	N	1125
Samuel Monck	London	N	510

Name	Born	Increased holding (I) or New depositor (N)	£ subscribed
Abraham Monfort	Chinon	N	125
Etienne Noguier	Nîmes	N	375
Herman Olmius	Lochem, Gelderland	N	1511
Pierre Reneu (I)	Bordeaux	I	3920
Etienne Seignoret	Lyons	I	5365
	+ for his partnership with R. Baudouin		4438
John Strang (?)	Pittenweem, Fife	N	662 10s
Total			£31,252 10s

Between the £66,850 from Table VI.1, £8745 from seven individuals between 1694 and 1697, and the £31,250 from Table VI.2, the total put into the Bank through the church officers and their connections amounts to £106,845 in the crucial four-year period that saw the Bank firmly establish itself. It is a striking amount to come out of one congregation.

Beyond the sums that found their way from the elders and deacons of the Threadneedle Street church to the Bank, there are other revealing aspects of the connections between the two institutions. It is interesting, for instance, that the French church may be the first customer that made use of the Bank for safe deposit purposes, and that this development arose out of the urgent need for immediate funds for refugee poor relief. In October 1696, tallies were deposited with the church consistory by the Archbishop of Canterbury, Lord Keeper and Bishop of London (members of the English Committee supervising the relief process) for safe keeping as the security for raising a loan of £2200. The Consistory resolved to keep them at the Bank of England, with Mr Deneu keeping the necessary accounts. (Jacques Deneu, an original director of the bank, had twice served as an elder of the church, and was involved in refugee relief.) The Bank's receipt for the tallies reached the Consistory the following month. It is plain from the church records that several office holders who had already subscribed to the Bank – Ducasse, Daniel Hays and Pierre Reneu (I), as well as Deneu – took part in working through this process.[10]

Other church officers also showed particular interest in the new Bank's activities or worked with it already. One of the Bank's earliest

10 FCL, MS 8, ff. 42–3. The earliest Bank records referring to items held for safekeeping begin in September 1702.

paid servants was Michel Fallet, who was employed in its accountancy office from February 1694. Born in Caen, he had served as a deacon of the Threadneedle Street church through 1686–9. His high salary (£160 per annum from August 1697) attests that he was one of the small group of key Bank employees. He ran into trouble on his initial appointment in 1694; the Bank records show that he successfully defended himself against unspecified accusations made against him, revealing in the process that he was involved in a successful privateering operation during the war against France.[11] Jean Delmé, a merchant factor with an important role in marketing the goods produced by Canterbury weavers, attended the Bank's second General Court.[12] And there were two men named Louis Gervaize, father and son. They lodged together, and both had served as officers of the Threadneedle Street church before 1694. Early Bank records show a Lewis Gervais of London, Esquire, as depositing £150 on its first morning of business, 21 June 1694, and a Lewis Gervaize of London, merchant, as depositing £50 on 23 June.[13] I take the first to be Louis the father, and the second to be Louis the son. If so, they were both initial subscribers to the Bank, but later entries are hard to distinguish. (In Table VI.1, all their early deposits except the £150 from the first morning have been assigned to Louis Gervaize II.) Four months later, one of the two personally attended a meeting of the bank's directors and engaged in unusually detailed discussion with them about its specific workings, as its minutes show:

> 24 Oct 1694 Mr Lewys Gervaize attending was called in, and presents a Book to each of the Directors present, with a Paper this day directed to the Governor Deputy and Directors, which was read in his presence … after a Debate it was Resolved That it be left to the Discretion of the weekly Comittee to allow to such as keep their Cash with the Bank, running-cash-notes, or Bank Bills, for Inland Bills or Goldsmiths notes which are due. And to Discount Inland Bills or Goldsmiths Notes of such as keep their Cash with the Bank which are not due, at 6 per cent per annum, for the time they have to runn, at the Discretion of the said Comittee.[14]

As the Bank became more firmly established, another connection between it and the French church developed. We have already seen Louis Augier, Pierre Reneu (I) and David Primerose acting as attorneys or agents purchasing stock on behalf of others. In the 1694 initial bank stock

---

11 BEA, G4/1, pp. 156–9, 166–9.
12 BEA, G7/1 1694–1701, 10 Aug. 1694.
13 BEA, M1/3.
14 BEA, G4/1, p. 85. Abbreviations have been silently extended.

subscription, Pierre Deschamps (a deacon from 1697 to 1700) acted as agent for three other Huguenots but did not subscribe himself. Before the 1690s were out these would be joined by other officers acting in similar capacities. Most, like Jacques Auguste Blondel, Jacob Coutris or Adrien Lernoult (II) acted on a small scale, but Robert Caillé and Jean Girardot de Tillieux became active traders in bank stock.

Significantly, and taking us a generation back before the foundation of the Bank itself, there are also several vital connections between the church at Threadneedle Street and the initial and early directorship of the Bank. The most critical of these concerned the family of Houblon or Houbelon. According to the family chronicler Alice Archer Houblon who wrote in 1907, the family's origins lay in France, in Picardy, but its Protestant members who took refuge in England in the sixteenth century came from the Lille area of Flanders. The first in the direct line that would lead to four initial directors of the Bank was Jean Houblon, who had been born before 1523 and fled from the persecution imposed by the Duke of Alva on behalf of Philip II of Spain in 1567. Like his father before him, Jean had been a *bourgeois* of Lille, and in exile he was sufficiently wealthy to contribute £100 to the City's loan to Queen Elizabeth in 1588. His son Pierre, born in Lille in 1559, followed him to London, and became a member of the Dyer's Company and, in 1590, a denizen. Both father and son died of the plague in 1593. Pierre's wife, Marie, also died that same year, but they left a young family of orphans who included the redoubtable Jacques (James) Houblon (1592–1682). He would become the father of three and grandfather of a fourth of the initial directors of the Bank of England in 1694. (See Figure VI.3.)[15]

In an informal arrangement hurriedly made just before his death in 1593, Pierre Houblon left his younger brother Nicolas to be 'overseer' of James and his other children. Like Pierre, Nicolas had followed their father to London, where he too was a merchant, living in Lime Street near Leadenhall Street South and Cornhill.[16] The actual care of the children is likely to have fallen to their grandmother, Marie de La Fontaine. Fortunately, there was no lack of resources. Pierre had left his children well provided with an ample fortune, and Nicolas too was well off; in 1601 he provided £200 towards the repayment of money due to the Queen by direction of an order under the privy seal.[17]

---

15 Houblon (1907), chaps I–V and pp. 355 ff.; HSQS VIII, 126. For the identification of the foundation director John Lordell as grandson rather than son-in-law of James Houblon (1592–1682), see below, pp. 136–7.
16 Strype (1720), I, ii, 73.
17 HSQS vol. X part III, 109.

Figure VI.3

Simplified Houblon genealogy showing some connections with the Bank of England and the French Church of London, Threadneedle Street

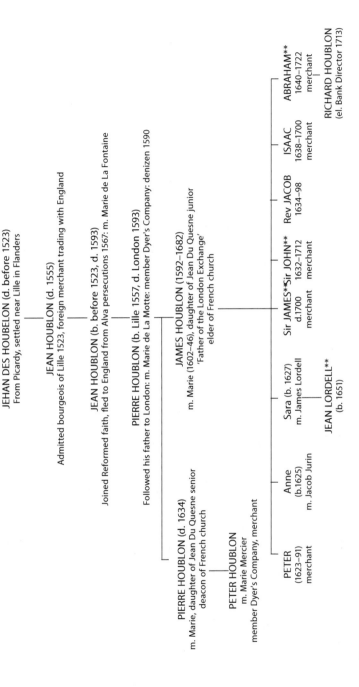

JEHAN DES HOUBELON (d. before 1523)
From Picardy, settled near Lille in Flanders

JEAN HOUBLON (d. 1555)
Admitted bourgeois of Lille 1523, foreign merchant trading with England

JEAN HOUBLON (b. before 1523, d. 1593)
Joined Reformed faith, fled to England from Alva persecutions 1567: m. Marie de La Fontaine

PIERRE HOUBLON (b. Lille 1557, d. London 1593)
Followed his father to London: m. Marie de La Motte: member Dyer's Company: denizen 1590

JAMES HOUBLON (1592–1682)
m. Marie (1602–46), daughter of Jean Du Quesne junior
'Father of the London Exchange'
elder of French church

PIERRE HOUBLON (d. 1634)
m. Marie, daughter of Jean Du Quesne senior
deacon of French church

PETER HOUBLON
m. Marie Mercier
member Dyer's Company, merchant

PETER
(1623–91)
merchant

Anne
(b.1625)
m. Jacob Jurin

Sara (b. 1627)
m. James Lordell

JEAN LORDELL**
(b. 1651)

Sir JAMES** Sir JOHN**
d.1700   1632–1712
merchant   merchant

Rev JACOB
1634–98

ISAAC
1638–1700
merchant

ABRAHAM**
1640–1722
merchant

RICHARD HOUBLON
(el. Bank Director 1713)

Note
** = Foundation Director

Not only was Jacques (James) Houblon brought up in near proximity to the French church in Threadneedle Street, he remained closely attached to it throughout his long life. The church was where Nicolas's own children were baptized, as James had been. James's elder brother Pierre served as a deacon of the church in the 1630s. James himself will have held that office at some stage before twice serving as an elder. James remained a lifelong church member, contributing £50 towards its rebuilding after the Great Fire and leaving it a legacy of £100. Preaching James's funeral sermon in 1682, Gilbert Burnet commented that he was a regular monthly communicant and weekday as well as Sunday attender, and that when in the city he worshipped with the French church, while in the country he joined the Anglicans.[18] It was at Threadneedle Street that in 1620 James married Marie Du Quesne, like himself a London-born descendant of refugees. The marriage of her parents twenty years earlier is the first in the church's surviving registers.[19] He urged his children to 'be especially charitable to the French Church: I know not any charity better bestowed or more faithfully managed ... There your ancient father was baptized, there, in a happy day, was he married, and in that congregation were ye all christened.'[20]

Children can forget their parents and brothers can argue ferociously, but James's family always remained exceptionally close, renowned in the London of their day alike for their commercial success and their mutual affection. Both aspects are captured in repeated entries in Samuel Pepys's *Diary*. Pepys first met the future Sir James Houblon in discussions about chartering a ship to take goods to Tangier early in 1665, when James junior struck him as 'a pretty serious man'. Within a year the diarist noted he was 'a man I love mightily, and will not lose his acquaintance', and they became fast friends in later years after the close of the diary. From the start, it is clear how closely the brothers worked together, as is also the joint impression they made on Pepys. On 5 February 1666 he went to *The Sun* behind the Exchange 'where I find all the five brothers Houblons, and mighty fine gentlemen they are all, ... their discourses (having been all abroad) very fine'. Four days later 'the five brothers Houblons came ... and a fine sight it is to see these five brothers thus loving one to another, and all industrious merchants'. Again and again, the *Diary* entries show two, three or all five of the Houblon merchant brothers working together. They were just as close when away from work, as at the time of the Great Fire in 1666 when Pepys saw 'Mr Isaccke Houblon, that handsome man

---

18 See the appendix entry (p. 302).
19 HSQS IX, 1, 19.
20 *Pious Memoirs of Mr. James Houblon, Senior... who died ... 1682 ...* (1886), p. 12.

– prettily dressed and dirty at his door ... receiving some of his brothers things whose houses were on fire', or in July 1667 when the diarist went 'to church, where ... none I knew but all the Houblon brothers'. When Pepys saw the elder Jacques Houblon for the first time in 1668, it is no surprise to find he was surrounded by 'all his sons about him'.[21] Burnet's funeral sermon shows this was again the case at the time of the old man's death.[22]

Apart from his faith and his family, the life of the patriarch who died in 1682 was dominated by his mercantile pursuits, which laid a platform of success and trust on which his sons could build. John Strype described him as 'a very eminent merchant of London, and as eminent for his plainness and piety ... his family descended from confessors on both sides'. Burnet's funeral sermon commented that James had 'as visible and long a share of the good things of this Life as, all things being put together, any Man in this Age hath had'. Pepys, requested by James junior to write the epitaph for his father, called him *Londinensis Bursae Pater*, the 'Father of the London Exchange', highlighting how the elder Jacques Houblon had identified himself with the Royal Exchange all his life.[23]

The formative years of the three Houblon brothers who were to become initial directors of the Bank – James, John (the first governor) and Abraham – fell in the period of the Civil War and Interregnum. In the year in which King Charles I was beheaded, James was aged eighteen, John sixteen, and Abraham was nine. The English political environment could not escape their attention, nor were they ignorant that the French church of Threadneedle Street had its own troubles in which their father was heavily involved. Jacques senior had served as an elder in 1637–40 and did so again in the particularly difficult years of 1643–6. In 1643, polarized views were being propounded from the pulpit of the French Church of London by the extreme Parliamentarian Jean de La Marche and the ultra-royalist Louis Hérault. Later, after Civil War conditions meant that Hérault fled while La Marche became entrenched in his position, the latter's lack of moderation caused strong opposition to him to develop.[24]

There is not the slightest doubt about where the elder James Houblon stood in these travails of his adopted nation and his church. He was a committed Parliamentarian. A member of the Honourable Artillery Company, he had been seriously injured in the mid-1630s by an explosion in the Artillery Garden during training near Moorfields, which forced his

21 Latham and Matthews (1970), VI, 27, 336–7; VII, 36, 39, 44–5, 52, 64, 98, 270, 368, 371; VIII, 1–2, 337; IX, 68, 405.
22 Burnet (1682), 36.
23 Strype (1720), I, ii, 162; Burnet (1682), 33; Houblon (1907), I, 166.
24 See Gwynn (2015), chap. I.

retirement from service.[25] Unable to take the field himself, he immediately paid for and equipped a cavalry soldier to serve in his place when a regiment of horse was enlisted in 1642, and later loaned a horse and man for Cromwell's New Model army. He used his organizational skills for the Parliamentarian cause, becoming a member of the City Committee for the Affairs of Ireland. In June 1644 he had custody of 'arms, ammunition, and other provisions made for the armies in Ireland now lying in the stores in Bucklersbury and Smart's Quay in London'.[26]

Within the Threadneedle Street church, his stance was equally clear-cut. He was at the heart of the group of elders lending full support to the outspoken Parliamentarian minister Jean de La Marche. It was in 1645 that La Marche first called for the execution of the king in his sermons and the pastor was attacked by his opponents in the anonymous *Complainte de l'Eglise Francoise de Londres sur l'Assechement des Eaux de Siloè*. In that year the seven elders who gave him the narrowest of majorities in the Consistory governing the church were Jean Beauvarlet, Barthélemi Caulier I, Jacques Dambrin, Jacques Houblon, Isaac and Jean de Lillers, and Jean Du Quesne II. La Marche died in 1651, but the faction who had supported him regrouped around another minister, Elie Delmé. When eventually a Colloquy managed to effect a general reconciliation in 1658, five men who had served as elders in the 1640s initially refused to accept it. They were Jacques Houblon, Jean de Lillers, Pierre Du Quesne (1609–72), Jacques Dambrin and Daniel Desmarets. They came from interrelated families well assimilated into English society, and the overlap of personnel with the more extreme Parliamentarian supporters of 1645 is plain: the Houblon–Du Quesne–De Lillers interest was critical.

The Houblons came from Lille, whence Jacques's grandfather had fled Alva's persecutions. The Du Quesnes came from Hainaut, escaping the same threat in the late 1560s. The two families were deeply interwoven through much more than family background and the experience of persecution. They were united also by marriage alliances, church attendance and in common beliefs, interests and mercantile activities and other actions and pursuits. As the simplified Houblon genealogy shows, not only was Jacques Houblon married to Marie Du Quesne, daughter of Jean Du Quesne junior, but Jacques's elder brother Pierre was married to another Marie Du Quesne, daughter of Jean Du Quesne senior. Both families worshipped at Threadneedle Street, produced lay office holders of the French church in the early to mid-seventeenth century, and supported La Marche and later Elie Delmé. Both were openly and proudly Parliamentarian. Pierre

---

25 Burnet (1682), 33–4.
26 Houblon (1907), I, 106–7, 112–14. See *CSPD*, 1625–49, Addenda, pp. xxxvii, 658.

Houblon, son of Jacques's brother Pierre, fought with his regiment as Captain of the Blue Trained Band and was painted in armour.[27] Modern descendants of the Du Quesne family have a near contemporary portrait of Pierre Du Quesne, perhaps by the same artist, depicting him in dark, sober Puritan dress. It can hardly be coincidence that, as Civil War drew imminent, Benjamin Du Quesne, Peter Houblon senior and Peter Houblon junior were all admitted members of the Honourable Artillery Company on the same day, 29 March 1642; it has been suggested that all three may have been sponsored by Jacques Houblon.[28]

The close relationship of James Houblon's youthful family to the lay leadership of the Threadneedle Street church is also indicated by the marriages he made for Anne and Sara, his two surviving daughters. Anne, who had been born in March 1625, married Jacob Jorion, son of Jean, in March 1644.[29] Jean was an elder in 1640–4 (and on three later occasions), and Jacob served as a deacon in 1644–6. The marriage produced a daughter but did not last long due to Jacob's early death, and Anne remarried in 1653. Sara was born in August 1627, and married Jacques Lordell, son of Jean, in January 1645.[30] Jacques Lordell was serving as a deacon at the time and would later also serve as an elder.

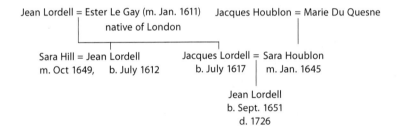

Figure VI.4

Descent of the Bank foundation director Jean Lordell

A Jean Lordell was a foundation director of the Bank in 1694, and it has long been asserted that this was the brother of Sara's husband. The writings of Houblon (1907), Acres (1934) and Crouzet (1996) all make or imply this claim,[31] but they create an impossible situation by doing

---

27 The portrait is reproduced in Houblon (1907), I, opposite p. 101.
28 Reese (2015), 364.
29 HSQS IX, 140, and XIII, 26s.
30 HSQS IX, 150, and XIII, 27k.
31 Houblon (1907), I, 174–5; Acres (1934), 240; Crouzet (1996), 228.

so. Jean junior and Jacques Lordell were brothers, sons of Jean Lordell senior and his wife Ester Le Gay, and they were baptized at the French church in Threadneedle Street respectively in 1612 and 1617.[32] That makes Jacques aged 27 at the time of his marriage to Sara Houblon. There is no problem with that age, which also corresponds with the normal kind of time for a man to be admitted to office as a deacon of the church. The difficulty is that the Jean Lordell who was a director of the Bank did not die until 1726, by which time Jacques's brother Jean, born in 1612, would have been aged 114. That is so unlikely as to be unacceptable. However, Jacques Lordell and Sara Houblon had a son Jean, who was baptized at Threadneedle Street on 7 September 1651.[33] This Jean would therefore have been 42 when the Bank of England was founded, and about 75 when he died in 1726. I conclude that he, and not his father's brother, is the true Bank director Jean Lordell.

It follows that Jacques (James) Houblon (1592–1682) was the grandfather of one initial director of the Bank of England as well as the father of three others: an extraordinary legacy to his family's adopted country. Moreover one of the three sons, Sir John, was the first governor of the Bank. It is on the site of Sir John's home in Threadneedle Street (perhaps originally chosen by him in part because of its convenient location near the French church?) that the Bank now stands, and the Bank livery derives from that of his household. The whole family had long been accustomed to banking, eight Houblons appearing regularly in the ledgers of the goldsmith Alderman Edward Backwell in the 1660s.[34] There remains real substance to François Crouzet's reflection that 'one might say that the Bank of England started as a Houblon family business!'.[35]

This generation of Bank directors played less of a role in the governance of the French Church of London than their predecessors. That did not, however, mean they lost their connections, far from it. Even apart from religious considerations, the dispersion of the Huguenots from Louis XIV's persecution in the 1680s and 1690s meant that the church, crowded with new arrivals, would have been a wonderful source of accurate, up-to-date European information that was of value in the course of business. In the early 1680s John, James and Peter Houblon became 'adventurers' in the Ipswich refugee linen-weaving settlement following an approach to the first two from the Consistory of the London church.[36] Sir John donated money to the poor of the church from time to time in the early 1690s.

---

32 HSQS IX, 86, 107.
33 HSQS XIII, 125a.
34 Houblon (1907), I, 171–2.
35 *HSP* XXV, 168.
36 HSQS LVIII, 61; Papillon (1887), 119.

Sir James left it £50 on his death in 1704, and Isaac £100 to its poor and £200 for Huguenot refugees more generally in 1702. His brother Abraham, as Isaac's executor, entrusted the distribution of both sums to the church elders, and it is significant that he knew the poor well enough to make specific recommendations about individuals when handing over the money.[37] When Sir John Houblon was chosen as Lord Mayor in 1695, the delighted Consistory made a special separation in the ministers' pew to seat him. Over a decade later, he remained an important channel of communication with the English authorities on contentious matters to do with charity distribution and the French 'prophets'.[38]

Besides the Houblons, other Bank directors also had firm connections with the Threadneedle Street church stretching both backwards and forwards in time. The Houblons were closely linked to the Du Quesnes, and the Du Quesnes in turn were especially close to the Lethieulliers. All three refugee families shared the same origins in Alva's persecution in the Low Countries in the 1560s. The Jean Letheuillier who was an officer of the Threadneedle Street church and the man who settled his family in England was the grandson of the man of the same name who was martyred in that persecution. The tie with the Du Quesnes came about through the marriage of his son (later Sir) Christopher Lethieullier (1639–90) to Jane (1644–1718), the daughter of Peter Du Quesne (1609–72) and Jeanne Maurois. Christopher and Jane married just after the Restoration, in 1661, and spent the early years of their marriage living with Peter Du Quesne (1661–63) and then with Christopher's father John (1663–65).[39] The Lethieulliers maintained their connection with the Threadneedle Street church, celebrating three family baptisms there in the late 1680s.[40] Of the £8200 that the family contributed towards the initial funds of the Bank, £5500 went through the hands of Peter Du Quesne (1646–1714) as agent, the remaining £2700 coming direct from three merchants in the family including £2000 from Samuel, Christopher's closest brother, who was elected as a foundation director.

We have already named Jacques Deneu as another foundation director. He had served as deacon, then elder, of the church between the 1650s and 1680s. Like the families of the Houblons, Du Quesnes and De Lillers, he had supported Elie Delmé at the church in the 1650s; he married into the De Lillers family. Like the Houblons he had been an 'adventurer' in the Ipswich refugee linen weaving settlement in the early 1680s and, again like them, he was an Iberian merchant – their connections were close on all

37 HSQS LVIII, 347; FCL, MS 8, ff. 32v, 180–2, 200v.
38 FCL, MS 8, ff. 31–2, 245, 251r, 263v.
39 Agnew (1886), I, 180.
40 HSQS XVI, 45a, 62w, 63o.

counts. He was also tied to Guillaume Carbonnel of Caen, a significant merchant and outspoken church officer between the Restoration and the early 1680s; the baptisms of Guillaume's children show strong links with the Deneu family. Jacques Deneu was the uncle of Delillers Carbonnel, a Bank director from 1722, deputy governor in 1738–40 and governor in 1740–41.

Other connections between the Threadneedle Street church and the Bank directorate can be tabulated more briefly:

Samuel Bulteel, elected a director in 1697, was the son of Pierre Bulteel, who had served as an elder in the 1630s, 1640s and 1650s. François Crouzet describes Samuel as a 'shadowy figure', but his father appears as a 'merchant stranger' and as one of the 'first and best sort of men' in the Broad Street Ward in a 1640 list of the principal inhabitants of London.[41]

Sir Peter Delmé (1667–1728) was elected a director of the Bank in 1698 and rose to become Deputy Governor (1715–17) and Governor (1715–17). He was the son of the wealthy Whig merchant Pierre Delmé, who had served as a deacon of the church in the 1660s and an elder in the 1670s and 1680s. Sir Peter became Lord Mayor of London (1723) and was worth over £300,000 on his death in 1728.

Sir Richard Houblon (1672–1724), the son of Abraham, became a Director in 1713.

Jacques (James) Gaultier, a church deacon and elder in the opening decade of the eighteenth century, was a Director 1728–48.

Benjamin Longuet was the son of Jean Longuet from Bayeux. Jean was an elder of the church 1687–90. Benjamin became a Bank director 1734–61, Deputy Governor 1745–7 and Governor 1747–9.

Such connections show that relationships between the church and the bank continued well into the eighteenth century, but they were never again as close or as significant as they had been at the Bank's foundation. That is why the initial directors matter so much. The 1690s were years of crisis, and to have men at the top who shared not only commercial ability but a very clear sense of what they were doing (and why it was necessary) gave their leadership special importance.

To fully appreciate why so many of these leading men whose background lay in the French Church of London came also to give a lead that was

---

41 Crouzet (1996), 229; W.J. Harvey (ed.), *List of the Principal Inhabitants of the City of London 1640* (Pinhorns, Isle of Wight, 1969), 4.

accepted in the wider context of London society at the time of the Bank's foundation, we need to understand something of English political and London civic events over the previous generation. At the time of the English Civil War, some of the English descendants of Walloon refugees rediscovered the truth by which their forefathers had lived and died, that there were times in their lives when they had to stand up for what they believed. By going back to the surroundings in which the three Houblon brother directors grew up, we have been able to witness the confirmation of family alliances and the formation of a common shared trust and vision at the difficult time of the Civil War and Interregnum, which would again be of relevance as the Bank was founded in the aftermath of the Revolution. The Civil War was very much a British concern, but by the 1640s the people we have been considering were English born, strongly associated with the City and generally thought like Londoners although perhaps it might be suggested that Archbishop Laud's deliberate and conscious attacks on the foreign Protestant churches in England and their lay eldership may have encouraged them to take sides earlier than most English people.[42] In any event, the War highlighted and reinforced close ties of thinking and interest binding together the native English and the descendants of the sixteenth-century refugees who were now ruling the French Church of London.

During the half-century between the 1640s and 1690s, new crisis points again brought the same families together and reminded them of what they shared not only with one another but also with other Londoners who looked to the Whig interest and feared the direction of government policies. At the same time, Catholic advances and the power of Louis XIV in Europe loomed as increasingly threatening, and the arrival of large numbers of new refugees provided a sharp reminder that the whole Protestant Cause was in peril. The early 1680s made these trends increasingly apparent, as the *dragonnades* began in France, while in England the government targeted the Whig leadership and the city of London was confronted by challenges to its charter.

From the perspective of the Threadneedle Street church, the aftermath of the Exclusion Crisis highlighted that it was in a particularly difficult situation. On the one hand, the arrival of many new refugees meant that it needed good relations with the Crown. On the other, in the 1680s court proceedings and government moves were increasingly following paths that were anathema to the church's senior members on whom its government and leadership relied, men who did not feel they could fail to fulfil their responsibilities in helping lead London life. In 1681,

42 For Laud's attack, see Gwynn (2015), 26–30.

the government proceeded against the Whig leaders, especially Anthony Ashley Cooper, first Earl of Shaftesbury. During preliminary moves leading up to Shaftesbury's arraignment for high treason, an elder of the Threadneedle Street church, Guillaume Carbonnel, offended the Court as a member of a Grand Jury considering a bill presented against John Rouse, another Whig similarly accused, in October 1681.[43] Shortly afterwards the members of the Grand Jury of Middlesex that considered the charges against Shaftesbury and refused to find a true bill against him were nominated by two Whig sheriffs, which was the only reason the Earl escaped execution. (He fled to the continent, where he died shortly afterwards.) The 'forty substantial men' offered to the court by the sheriffs for a jury were largely influential Whigs, including John Houblon, Thomas Papillon, John Dubois and Michael Godfrey, and the 21 members of the Grand Jury included Papillon, Dubois, Godfrey and also John Cox, who was Pierre Reneu's father-in-law.[44] Papillon played an important part in the *ignoramus* verdict.[45]

Both cases highlighted the crucial role played by the sheriffs, which set the scene for the disputed election of 1682, when Dubois and Papillon twice gained a clear majority as sheriffs over candidates supporting the royal interest but were met by fierce counter-attacks, resulting in Papillon being faced by a £10,000 fine and fleeing to Holland until the Revolution, and Dubois's death in 1684.[46] When Papillon and Dubois were summoned before the Lord Mayor in 1683, they were supported by Peter Houblon and Jacques Deneu, and King Charles II sent a barely veiled warning to the church by way of Bishop Compton of London that it seemed to encourage rebellious principles. The Consistory was forced to grovel.[47] However as we have noted, that did not prevent Joseph Ducasse de la Couture from being Algernon Sidney's sole servant attending him on the scaffold when he met his death that same year.

The personnel and forces that would unite to make the Bank a reality gathered together in a range of organizations and circumstances that criss-crossed with one another. One such organization, largely ignored by the historians who have written on the Bank, was the Dyers' Company of London. While its company records are scanty before 1667, its membership in the 1650s and 1660s included multiple freemen drawn from each of the Deneu ('Denew'), Du Quesne ('Ducane') and Houblon families. Amongst

---

43 HSQS LVIII, 65. In Carbonnel's defence, the Consistory noted his extensive work on behalf of the new refugees, and the complaint was allowed to drop.
44 Godfrey would become the first deputy governor of the Bank of England.
45 Haley (1968), 677, 679; *A Complete Collection of State-Trials* (1730), III, p. 414.
46 See Gwynn (2018), 254–5.
47 HSQS LVIII, 101.

the prime wardens of this company for the generation before the Bank's foundation were Jean Jurion or Jurin, Pierre Du Quesne, Pierre Houblon, 'J. Houblon Esq', Jacques Denew and Captain Peter Houblon.[48] These men came not only from mercantile families connected with the French church at Threadneedle Street, but also from families with a particularly strong Parliamentarian and Whig background. The index to the company register of admissions of freemen (1650–1728) includes six Lethieulliers, five Carbonnells, four Deneus, three Houblons, two members each from the De Lillers, Jurin and Le Keux families and a Delmé.[49] Subscribers of the Dyers Company to the 1696 Association to defend the succession of William and Mary included J.A. Houblon and Peter Houblon (Assistants) and John Jurin, John Denew, J.N. Carbonnel, and Abraham and William Lethieullier (members of the livery).[50] The political and social role of the livery companies has not been greatly explored for the seventeenth century,[51] but surely, here we have a concentration of wealth, interest and political activity too great to be ignored.

Mercantile groups naturally also had an important part to play, and the economic historian François Crouzet has emphasized the 'Scheme of Trade' presented to the House of Lords in 1674, signed by fourteen merchants including James Houblon, John Houblon, Thomas Papillon, John Dubois, Benjamin Delaune and Michael and Benjamin Godfrey, whose spokesperson was Sir Patience Ward.[52] One should also consider the petition of 'the Merchants Trading to the Kingdom of Portugall' of the same year, where sixteen of the 35 petitioners were from families with French church connections – William and Edward Des Bouverie; John, Abraham and two Peter Houblons; John Lordell; Isaac Jurin; Samuel, William and Abraham Lethieullier; James Denew; James Ducane; Jacob and James De Lillers; and Samuel Boulteel.[53] Not all these signatories of foreign descent were initial subscribers to the Bank twenty years later, but sixteen of the original petitioners were, between them putting up £45,800. Another historian, D.W. Jones, has emphasized the Iberian connection as critical, noting that while all merchants were adversely affected by the Williamite wars in different ways, amongst the most affected were wine merchants, who

---

48 See the company website. I am indebted to Leslie Du Cane for drawing my attention to this concentration of men with French Church and/or Bank connections in the Dyers' company.

49 LMA, CLC/L/DC/C/003/MS 08168/001.

50 Daynes (1965), 83–4.

51 Perry Gauci, *The Politics of Trade: The Overseas Merchant in State and Society, 1660–1720* (Oxford University Press, 2001), 142.

52 Crouzet (1996), 236–7.

53 TNA, SP/31/5, f. 11r.

suffered a serious slump in business. He points out that the largest single contribution from active London merchants to the Bank of England and also the East India loan in the mid-1690s came from this sector.[54]

Following the Revolution, the pace of events brought together those who would be concerned with the Bank's foundation with greater frequency and left them well placed to circulate and discuss their ideas. Peter, James and John Houblon, Michael Godfrey, Sir John and Christopher Lethieullier and James Denew were all among the 94 men nominated in March 1689 to be on the Lieutenancy for the City of London. John Houblon and Christopher Lethieullier were the first sheriffs of London elected after the Revolution, in June 1689,[55] both being knighted by William III shortly thereafter. At the same time, the Crown was seeking loans to meet its pressing commitments, based on various parliamentary grants – the 'Present Aid', 'First Poll', '12d. Aid', '2s. Aid' and 'Additional 12d. Aid'. Such loans provided a demonstration that the mercantile community, both native English and naturalized French, was willing to support the new regime. Sixteen of the French church officers featuring in Appendix 3 lent money to the Crown in 1689–90:

Jean Delmé
Jacques Dufay
Abraham Dugard
Louis Gervaize
Claude Hays
Pierre Houblon
Daniel Jamineau
Benjamin de Jennes
Adrien Lernoult
Pierre Lernoult
Pierre Lombard
François Mariette
Herman Olmius
Thomas Papillon
Pierre Reneu
Etienne Seignoret.[56]

Other familiar names in the lists of those who loaned to the Crown at this time include all five of the Houblon brothers, Peter Du Quesne, and

54 D.W. Jones (1988), 274–5, 302, 306.
55 *Entring Book*, Q, p. 579.
56 *CTB*, 1689–92, Appendix 2, pp. 1972–2008.

Christopher and Sir John Lethieullier. These loans had the advantage of finding the government immediate cash while providing a good return of interest to those making them. It was, though, a clumsy way of raising money, one that had to be repeated endlessly. The Bank would provide a standing organization continuing in business, would be open to many more individuals subscribing, would provide greater security and so hopefully lower interest rates, and would raise money faster. In 1694 it took only twelve days for the Bank to reach its initial target of £1,200,000.[57] Most importantly, in the long run it would create a National Debt. Through their personal vested interest, the debt would eventually bind the English commercial and ruling classes who loaned money to the Bank to support it in maintaining national security.

Previous historians have debated whether the Huguenots assisted the 'Financial Revolution' in England, and have sought to measure the extent of their economic contribution. None, however, have juxtaposed the French Church of London and the Bank of England in a long-term seventeenth-century context in the way this chapter has done. Yet the juxtaposition is essential and shows us why the Houblons and those around them had confidence they could succeed. The descendants of the old refugees knew from the experience and history of their own families that the influx of new skills, trading networks and resources could be turned to the financial advantage of their adopted country, and were well placed to appreciate the value of the networks of communication that coexisted and interacted in the communities centred on their churches. It was no accident that the Bank provisions specifically allowed and encouraged overseas residents to invest in England, although only English-born or naturalized English subjects could be directors. The descendants of previous generations of refugees understood the potential of new immigrant skills and the importance of systems in place to help new Huguenot arrivals find their feet and help guarantee to their hosts that the newcomers were genuine in their Protestantism and upright in their behaviour.

Above all, looking at their past family histories explains what motivated the leading members of the Threadneedle Street church, why they were so willing, even eager, to offer support to the Bank right from its inception, even though its stock price could fluctuate wildly (it dropped from 148 in early 1696 to 51 the following year),[58] and there was real risk that the Bank could fail and their investment be lost should Louis XIV be victorious. Refugees and their descendants, old and new alike, shared

---

57 Giuseppi (1966), 12. The sum had been amended from the £1,500,000 in the Bank charter.
58 Ogg (1955), 435.

an absolute certainty based on personal and family experience that their world faced a Roman Catholic threat that was real and dangerous and needed to be averted at all costs for their long-term security and prosperity. Their commitment was genuine: they could not afford failure; they had nowhere else to turn. Sometimes one can see that commitment expressed in ways other than helping with government finance or direct personal military service. We have noted how bank clerk Michel Fallet was involved in financing a privateering venture against French shipping. The initial Bank director, Jacques Deneu, likewise was part-owner of two ships engaged in privateering in the 1690s. Sometimes there must have been a very personal motivation for the choices that were made. The refugee David Garric, grandfather of the future actor David Garrick, was a native of Montpellier and former *bourgeois* of Bordeaux who was an elder at Threadneedle Street when the Bank of England was founded in 1694. He did not invest in bank stock but was part-owner of a privateer christened with the unusual name *The Protestant Cause*. Similarly Jean de Grave (II), a deacon of the Threadneedle Street church shortly before the Bank's foundation, an English-born but French-naturalized merchant who was specifically and nastily targeted by the *dragonnades* at Rouen, did not invest at all in the funds but was a member of a highly successful syndicate outfitting privateers on a grand scale that had 60 captures to its credit.[59]

It is easy to understand why the Houblons and their friends should have been appreciated in the circles of past and present immigrants, but the high regard in which they were held obviously also extended to English and other international merchants. Their family background had much to do with that, especially James Houblon's integrity, his long life promoting the London Exchange and the fact that his whole family had worked together harmoniously for so long. It was now over a century since their ancestors had crossed the Channel, so they could hardly be viewed as other than English; and they had been fully involved in London life and were widely known. In all that time they had not wavered in their principles, earning the moral authority implied by John Strype when he noted how they were 'descended from confessors on both sides': there was a sense of certainty that the family commitment to its sworn word was absolute.

We return to the real original purpose for which the Bank came into existence, to allow the war against France to be pursued with vigour. It was essentially a political purpose, a purpose that derived from fears of Catholic absolutism and the perception of a real Catholic threat, a purpose that was associated particularly with the Whigs. It would have been impossible to find a single institution in the country so clear in its

---

59 See the entries for Garric and Jean de Grave (II) in Appendix 3.

support for that purpose and perception as the French Church of London in Threadneedle Street, its pews packed with refugees who had personally suffered from Catholic absolutism, its leadership in the late seventeenth-century Whig almost to a man so far as our evidence can tell. Historians agree that the Bank of England was a Whig stronghold, 'a bulwark of the revolutionary settlement and of the Protestant succession'.[60] They have ignored, however, that the same description applied equally to the French church, and that many connections tied these two very different institutions closely together. The entire consistory and church knew how close to the wind it had sailed during the 1680s. They were aware how leading members had been attacked during the Exclusion Crisis (Guillaume Carbonnel, Jean Dubois, Thomas Papillon), or arrested as a government precaution at the time of Monmouth's rebellion (Carbonnel, Jacques Deneu, Pierre Houblon, Isaac de Lillers (II), Humfroy Willett):[61] how close the church had come to suffering *Quo Warranto* proceedings in James's reign. Its relief after the Revolution was palpable, and its support for the Bank, significantly engineered by a family it had long known intimately, was remarkable. As P.G.M. Dickson noted, the first subscription to the Bank 'must have been regarded as a test of the new regime's ability to survive'.[62] The church and its members were determined that it should not only survive, but thrive.

---

60 Giuseppi (1966), 13–14; Crouzet (1996), 238.
61 James and John Houblon were also briefly detained in June 1685 (*Entring Book*, P, 469).
62 Dickson (1967), 256.

VII

The Huguenot Presence at the Birth of the Bank of England (II): The Wider Picture

Notwithstanding the particular significance of the Threadneedle Street church with its long historical background, by the time the Bank of England was founded the church was just one – although much the largest – of many French-speaking congregations in London and beyond. In 1694, there were 23 in England outside London, and 19 in the London-Westminster metropolis. Besides Threadneedle Street, three others of the total of 42 were sixteenth-century foundations: Canterbury, Norwich and Southampton. Two more had their origins in the mid-seventeenth century, Thorney and the Savoy church in Westminster. All the others owed their existence to Louis XIV's persecutions. Plainly, then, we have not yet presented the full picture insofar as the relationship between the Bank and the new Huguenot refugees is concerned. This chapter will examine that wider picture and show that 11 per cent of the initial subscribers to the Bank were recently arrived Huguenots.

One new Huguenot arrival became an initial Bank director: Theodore Janssen from Angoulême. He was not mentioned in the previous chapter because he seems to have had little special connection with the Threadneedle Street church other than that he presented his *témoignage* there in 1683 and made *reconnaissance* there in August 1694 for having abjured. Even the fact of that *reconnaissance* is most surprising, since it was a full eleven years since he had presented his *témoignage* and nine years since he had been naturalized.[1] The timing suggests that his election as a Bank director focused attention on disreputable past behaviour and raised mutterings that needed to be silenced through a public statement

---

1 FCL, MS 8, f. 20v; HSQS XVIII, 170, and XXI, 145. I can find no record of any other church attachment for Janssen.

of commitment to the Protestant cause. A few years earlier, during James's reign, when he appears to have been working in league with the French ambassador Barrillon, Janssen had been successfully prosecuted by the English Company of White Papermakers for causing three of their workmen to abscond to France.[2] At that time, he had claimed he could not afford the £500 fine. In 1694, however, he contributed £10,000 to the Bank subscription, and there is no doubt about his value to the Bank in its early years. The records show he was a very active director. His *Discourse concerning Banks* (1697) highlighted the particular advantages of the Bank of England, while his strong Dutch connections made him a valuable member of its 'Committee for the Remisses', set up to oversee payment of £200,000 to Flanders for military purposes.[3] Dickson describes Janssen and Sir Henry Furnese as the two key agents in remitting government money to pay the troops overseas.[4]

The highest amount permitted for initial subscriptions was £10,000, and only twelve such sums were received in 1694. One of those came jointly from King William and Queen Mary; one from the king's friend and advisor William Bentinck, Earl of Portland; two from Houblons, Sir John Houblon and Abraham Houblon; six from Englishmen (one of whom was an initial director, Sir William Scawen); and two from recently arrived Huguenots. The background of the second wealthy new Huguenot, Jacques de la Bretonnière, has long proved particularly elusive. François Crouzet could establish no more than that by 1695, when he died, he had increased his Bank holding to £21,800.[5] However, new research makes it possible to flesh out the picture. La Bretonnière had reached England as early as July 1689, when he made the first of several £1000 loans to the government.[6] He assisted poor refugees, donating £100 through a member of the French Committee in 1693 and leaving them a legacy of £300, which was distributed at the end of 1695. On the latter occasion he was described as James Baudet de la Bretonnière.[7] He lived at Suffolk Street, Westminster, in the parish of St Martin in the Fields,[8] and the combination of wealth, social position and location makes it likely that he was a member of the substantial Savoy congregation, for which all too few records of the later seventeenth century have survived.

---

2 *CTB, 1685–9*, pp. 1465, 1607, 1677; Coleman (1956), 222–3.
3 Giuseppi (1966), 21. The other members of the Committee were Michael Godfrey, James Denew and Abraham Houblon.
4 Dickson (1967), 264–5.
5 Crouzet (1990), 175.
6 *CTB, 1689–92*, pp. 1979, 1982, 1986–7, 1992, 1995, 2002.
7 HL, Bounty MS 6, *sub* 20 Dec. 1693, and MS 11.
8 *CTB, 1693–6*, p. 1148.

La Bretonnière's death set off a series of events that are revealing about his personal entourage. On 27 June 1695, La Bretonnière's will was proved by his executors, Nicholas Gambier, a Westminster apothecary and member of his own parish, and Gambier's wife Ester or Hesther Le Heup. He had been living with them.[9] The government entered a caveat on 4 July against legacies amounting to £9000 of bank stock, which would have gone to alien enemies in France. The next month, the executors transferred La Bretonnière's £21,800 of stock to Paul Fenoulhet of London, gentleman, at which time David Devarenne Esq., 'brother and heir at law' to La Bretonnière, declared his free consent and approval. The very next day, the same sum was transferred back from Fenoulhet to Gambier.[10] From early February 1696, a new style was in use for Devarenne in the Bank records, 'David Devarenne de la Bretonnière', and he was naturalized the following month as 'David Devarenne la Bretonniere *alias* Baudet, born at St Lo in Normandie, son of Peter Baudet and Susanna, his wife'.[11] The personal connections provided by the new evidence indicate that Jacques de La Bretonnière probably came from Normandy, and that he was closely linked with a wealthy group of refugees living in the Westminster area. Devarenne, Fenoulhet, Gambier and Thomas Le Heup were all themselves immediate subscribers to the Bank of England, although not on the scale of La Bretonnière. As for his family, the Wagner wills summaries in the Huguenot Library refer to Devarenne, to whom he left £3000, as La Bretonnière's brother 'David de Bande al[ia]s de Varennes'. La Bretonnière also left all his silver plate to 'Thomas Le Heup my brother', and £8000 to his 'kinswoman' Esther Le Tellier, wife of Michael Dieu.[12]

The events following La Bretonnière's death also say a great deal about the care taken by William's government to protect the Bank's position and the national interest. The speed with which it took legal action suggests that it had been monitoring the position closely, possibly as a result of another very recent case in which Francis La Pierre *alias* Stone, a merchant also variously described in the Treasury records as 'Lepair Stone', 'La Parystone' and 'Le Pairston', had died around the end of May 1695 and left some £5000 to French Roman Catholic relatives. Unlike La Bretonnière, Stone was not a Huguenot and his estate did not involve bank stock, but the government believed the executors had concealed his will and 'not

---

9 HL, Wagner wills, A.318. I am most grateful to Micol Barengo for tracking this valuable entry down for me under the difficult recent conditions. It refers to La Bretonnière as Jacob rather than James.
10 *CTB*, 1693–6, pp. 1148, 1154, 1171; BEA, AC28/1513, 26 Aug. 1695, and AC 28/32233, 27 Aug. 1695 (p. 435) and 11 Feb. 1696.
11 BEA, AC 28/32233, 11 Feb. 1696; HSQS XVIII, 241.
12 HL, Wagner wills, A.318.

brought [it] to the Prerogative Court as it ought to be', and entered a caveat against granting administration of the estate until the Crown had been heard. The authorities dealt with both cases together in late 1696, conveying the Crown's title to the forfeited estates to two nominees 'to assign and dispose of same, or such part thereof from time to time as shall be recovered, according to such directions as they shall receive under the privy seal or royal sign manual and to no other use, intent or purpose whatsoever'. Evidently William was determined to keep as tight a personal grip on proceedings as possible.[13]

Theodore Janssen and Jacques de La Bretonnière were exceptional in their wealth and status, but they were not alone in being newly arrived refugees committed to supporting the Bank in 1694. Just as King William sought to understand what resources might have reached his new kingdom, so historians have tried to grapple with how much wealth the Huguenots took out of France, and – within that – with the more limited question of how much they contributed to the Bank of England's establishment. The broader question of how much wealth the Huguenots took from France is fraught with difficulty, as Graham Gibbs commented:

> To what extent Huguenots managed to move their capital outside France, and how, remains one of the most obscure problems connected with the Huguenot exodus. It seems agreed that there was a great displacement of capital from France, and that it may have taken the form of apparently normal banking and commercial transactions.[14]

Scoville noted that the number of depositors in the Bank of Amsterdam increased by about a third between 1671 and 1701 and that the interest the bank paid fell somewhat after 1685. He concluded that 'although it would be unwise to attribute all this to the revocation ... certainly the Huguenots arriving in Holland appreciably increased the supply of liquid capital and helped lower interest rates'.[15] Historians are rarely in total agreement, and a different approach emphasizes the importance of technical changes in the facilities offered by the Amsterdam Bank in helping explain those developments. On two relevant matters, however, historians share almost unanimous consensus. First, that the great majority of exiles during the Huguenot Refuge were very poor, indeed struggling to survive from the depths of poverty, so that a giant gap separates them from the fortunate few with spare resources to invest in bank stock.[16] Second, that those

---

13 *CTB, 1693–6*, pp. 1170–1, 1384, and *1696–7*, pp. 53, 91, 196, 266, 289, 311.
14 Gibbs (1975), 259, n.12.
15 Scoville (1960), 348.
16 See for instance Archdeacon (1976), 49, for New York; Van der Linden (2015),

seventeenth-century contemporaries like Michel Levassor who claimed that the Huguenots took with them 'immense summs, which have drawn dry the fountain of commerce' were guilty of gross exaggeration.[17] While the present work makes no attempt to estimate the overall loss to France of the Huguenot exodus, it cannot shy away from the English side of things. What did the new refugees from Louis's persecution contribute to the Bank and other early English funds? The first serious attempt to tackle that question was made by Charles Weiss in the early 1850s. He was aware of the poverty attending most refugees, but also appreciated that a small number of rich families did bring real resources. He cited as evidence that 50,000 pistoles reached the London mint ('La Monnaie de Londres') in the first four months after the Revocation, and a 23 October 1687 despatch from Louis's well-informed agent, the comte d'Avaux, that 960,000 louis d'or had already been melted down in England ('fondus en Angleterre').[18] These same references were used by Scoville, and by Herbert Lüthy in his study of French banking.[19]

Other historians have concentrated more closely on the situation regarding the Huguenot contribution to the Bank of England, notably A.C. Carter (1954, 1975), F.M. Crouzet (1990, 1996) and P.G.M. Dickson (1967). Dickson's seminal work *The Financial Revolution in England* concluded that in 1694, 'allowing for some uncertainty of classification, there were … 123 [Huguenots] lending £104,000 in the subscription to the Bank'. He spelled out his criteria: Huguenot names were identified from the careful lists in W.A. Shaw's *Letters of Denization and Acts of Naturalization*,[20] while 'recent domicile' for the Huguenots was taken as after 1650.[21] Crouzet, while critical of aspects of Carter's arguments, cites Dickson's findings approvingly. They have been widely accepted as showing that the Huguenots were less significant in the Bank's foundation than contemporaries believed.

At this point I must acknowledge my own personal debt to Professor Dickson, whom I met only once, in 1976, when I was completing my doctorate. On that occasion, with great generosity, he gave me a copy of his working notes which showed who were the 123 relevant subscribers to the Bank in 1694 he had identified as Huguenot. Without that gift,

---

pp. 41, 226, for the Netherlands; Gwynn (2018), pp. 155, 165, 221, for England.

17 [Levassor], *The Sighs of France in Slavery, breathing after Liberty* (1689), Memorial I.

18 Weiss (1853), I, 283–4.

19 Scoville (1960), 292, 299, 331–2; Lüthy (1959), I, 29.

20 HSQS XVIII, XXVII, XXXV; the first of these volumes covers the seventeenth century.

21 Dickson (1967), 259 and n.2.

Tables VII.1, VII.2 and VII.3 in this chapter could not have been compiled. Professor Dickson's expertise on banking and the early English funds is far greater than mine, and it covers a wider time span – his *Financial Revolution* extends to the 1750s. On the other hand, he did not spend so much of his life as I have in studying the Huguenots in Britain in the later seventeenth century, so perhaps it was to be expected that I would identify some newcomers who subscribed and had been overlooked.

The group of Huguenot gentry around La Bretonnière had negligible association with the French Church of London in Threadneedle Street in the City. That would also have been true of many other Huguenot residents to the west of London, including a phalanx connected with the medical profession. From the area of the City, the medical doctor Jacques Auguste Blondel was an initial subscriber to the Bank with £400, while Philippe Guide, a 'Doctor in Physick' living off Fleet Street,[22] provided £200 as did Andrew Le Roy.[23] The western suburbs were the home of a more formidable group of medics who supported the Bank in 1694, as Table VII.1 shows.

Women form another group who stand out from the statistics for the western suburbs of the metropolis. The great majority of the 1268 initial Bank subscribers in 1694 were of course Englishmen, but amongst them were 149 women (and two young daughters). In most cases the Bank's verified index provides their name, place of residence and quality – their title, if they had one, ranging from a marchioness and two countesses to 61 widows and 37 spinsters. In a few cases they are described as someone's wife, daughter or sister. Only one woman, the Huguenot Jeanne de La Perelle, is described by her trade: she was a grocer. As one would expect, by far the largest number of female subscribers lived in or near the metropolis. Huguenot women are not especially prominent in the ranks of those listed as living in 'London', but there is a significant grouping among those who lived in Westminster and the western suburbs; see Table VII.2. To the names originally supplied by Professor Dickson, we can add two more recently arrived Huguenots. Suzanna Duplex, a widow of St Ann's Westminster, who subscribed £250, had been endenized with her then husband, Abraham, and four children (including another Suzanna) in December 1687; one of the two Suzannas married Jean Maret in 1700 at the French church of the Savoy.[24] Another widow, Elizabeth Marchant of Covent Garden, whose subscription of £200 was delivered through her

22 See Leslie G. Matthews, 'Philip Guide, Huguenot Refugee Doctor of Medicine', *HSP* XXII, 345–52.
23 Perhaps the 'Andrew Roy' endenized in 1688, who was described as French [HSQS XVIII, 214].
24 HSQS XVIII, p. 196, and XXVI, p. 139.

Table VII.1

West London medical professionals identified by Professor P.G.M. Dickson as Huguenots and initial subscribers to the Bank in 1694

Isaac Aimé	Surgeon	£500
James De Batts[a]	Surgeon	£500
David Boucheret	Apothecary	£100
Paul Buissiere	Surgeon	£600
Charles Coliner[b]	Apothecary	£100
Dr Theodore Colladon[c]		£2000
Nicholas Gambier	Apothecary	£600
Isaac Garnier[d]	Apothecary	£700
Christianus Harel[e]	Doctor in Physick	£2000
Total		£7100

a) Jacobus De Bat was endenized in 1691 [HSQS XVIII, 225]. He frequently helped treat French refugees and was probably the Debat who was an elder of the Savoy church in 1698 [Gwynn (2018), 273, 299].
b) Described as a French Protestant when endenized in 1684 [HSQS XVIII, 164].
c) Theodore's father Jean had been an elder of the Savoy, signing the 1660 petition for its use; both father and son were endenized in 1662. Theodore attended William III [Gwynn (2018), 110; HSQS, XVIII, 89; *HSP* XIX, 121].
d) See Rosemary Baird Andreae, 'From Huguenot Apothecary to English Squire: The Garniers ...', *HSJ* 31 (2018), 17–20.
e) 'Christianus Hazel' when naturalized in 1685 [HSQS XVIII, 172, but see *HSP* XIX, 258]. Harel had been born at The Hague but took the qualifying sacrament through the French Church.

son Peter, is identifiable with the Elizabeth Marchant who was endenized with her sons Peter and Paul in 1698.[25]

It is most unfortunate that there are so few records for the Savoy and other west London conformist churches to allow a proper comparison with the French Church of London in Threadneedle Street. Nevertheless, as Table VII.3 shows, Bank records reveal plenty of supportive activity from others of a superior social quality who were not part of La Bretonnière's inner circle or the medics and women discussed above.

How do our findings modify Professor Dickson's conclusion that 123 recently arrived Huguenots provided £104,000 in the initial subscription to

25 BEA, M1/1, p. 36; HSQS XVIII, 288.

Table VII.2

West London women identified as Huguenots and initial subscribers to the Bank in 1694

Mme Louise Vareilles Beauchamp, widow[1]	St James's Westminster	£600
Madelaine Olimpe Beauchamp, spinster[2]	St James's	£100
Madam Mary Blancard[3]	St James's Westminster	£100
Barbara Anna de Calvart, spinster	Somerset House	£200
Judith de Courcy, spinster	St Ann's Westminster	£100
Judith Dergnouth, spinster[4]	Pall Mall	£100
Suzanna Duplex, widow	St Ann's Westminster	£250
Renée Duvall, wife of John D.	Golden Square	£100
Anne Gendrault, widow	St James's Westminster	£200
Lady Hesther Hervart, Marchioness de Gouvernet[5]	St James's	£500
Mary Lefort, widow	St James's Westminster	£100
Katherine Lorren	St Martin's in the Fields	£200
Elizabeth Marchant, widow	Covent Garden	£200
Mary de Monceau, spinster	St Martin's in the Fields	£300
Elizabeth Guilbert de Montargier, widow	St James's Westminster	£100
Jeanne de la Perelle, grocer	St Ann's Westminster	£200
Total		£3350

1 'Lewisa Beauchamp Vareilles' when endenized in 1696 [HSQS XVIII, 242].
2 'Magdalen Olympea Beauchamp' when endenized in 1696 [HSQS XVIII, 242].
3 She was the daughter of Jean Blancard, also an initial subscriber to the Bank; they were both endenized in 1691 [HSQS XVIII, 226].
4 'Judith Dergnoult de Pressinville' when endenized in 1691 [HSQS XVIII, 226].
5 'Relict of the Sieur Charles de la Tour, late Marquis de Gouvernet' when endenized in 1690 [HSQS XVIII, 224]. By the end of 1697 she held £7000 in the Bank [Crouzet (1996), 242].

Table VII.3

Other West Londoners identified as Huguenots and initial 1694 subscribers to the Bank

Marc-Antoine de la Bastide, gentleman	Piccadilly	£1000
Daniel Bernard Esq[1]	Whitehall	£500
James Beschefer[2]	St James's Westminster	£200
John Blancard, gent.	St James's Westminster	£200
Paul Boyer, gent.	St James's Westminster	£700
John Braguier	Covent Garden	£200
Simon de Brienne Esq	Kensington	£3000
James Cardonnel Esq	Westminster	£500
Abraham Casenave, linen draper[3]	St Martin's in the Fields	£500
Sir John Chardin	Westminster	£2000
Francis le Cog Esq.	St James's Westminster	£500
Theodore le Cog de St Leger	St James's Westminster	£3000
Alexandre Duroure Desbonnaux, gent.	Soho	£200
René Desclousseaux, gent.	Soho	£500
George Nicolaus Dobbertin, gent.	St Clement Danes	£500
John Dubourdieu, clerk	The Savoy	£200
Francis Duprat, gent.	Westminster	£400
John Faure, hosier[4]	St Clement Danes	£100
James Frontin Esq	Whitehall	£2000
Jacob Gedeon de Sicqueville, gent.	St Ann's Westminster	£100
Capt. John Germain	Westminster	£5000

1 Perhaps the Daniel Bernard from Montauban, aged 46, who made his *reconnaissance* at the Savoy church in 1687 [HSQS XXII, 10], but there are several different French Protestants of this name who were endenized or naturalized between 1681 and 1700 [HSQS XVIII, 131, 158, 219, 299, 306–7].
2 Beschefer, endenized in 1697 [HSQS XVIII, 247], was an elder of the Glasshouse Street/Leicester Fields church (1693–1704) [Gwynn (2018), 304].
3 Cazenave, aged 41, from Béarn, made *reconnaissance* at the Savoy church in 1687 [HSQS XXII, 12], and was an elder of the French church of St James Square, 1690–4 [Gwynn (2018), 301].
4 A John Alexander Faure was endenized in 1693 [HSQS XVIII, 230]. John Faure was a lay elder of the French church of the Savoy in 1701 [Gwynn (2018), 299]. (Another John Faure, an army lieutenant, is listed in Appendix 1.)

Abraham Gilbert, clerk[5]	St James's Westminster	£500
John Graverol, clerk	St James's Westminster	£500
Peter de Gualy, gent.	Soho Square	£500
Thomas Guenault, gent.	St James's Westminster	£500
Salomon de Guerin Esq	St James's	£500
Abraham Hallée, gent.	St Anne's Westminster	£100
Louis, Marquis de Heucourt	Soho	£1000
John Lafargue, gent.	St Giles's in the Fields	£250
Richard Le Bas[6]	Whitehall	£600
Alexandre Mariette	Usher to the King, St James's House	£500
Abraham Meure, gent.	Frith Street	£600
James Misson Esq	St Anne's Westminster	£550
Nicolas de Monceau de l'Etang	Whitehall	£4000
John de Remy de Montigny Esq	Whitehall	£400
James Partheriche, gent.	St Giles's in the Fields	£500
Charles Rampaine, gent.	Westminster	£200
Samuell de Ravenell Esq	St James's Westminster	£600
Peter la Roche, gent.	St Martin's in the Fields	£1000
Alexander Sasserie, gent.	St James's Westminster	£700
John Thuret, jeweller[7]	Covent Garden	£200
Paul Vaillant, grocer	Covent Garden	£100
Bernard de Vignau, gent.	St Martin's in the Fields	£100
Charles de Vignoles Esq	St Ann's Westminster	£200
Total		£35,400

---

5 Gilbert, son of a former pastor at Charenton, was a foundation minister of the French Chapel Royal at St James's Palace, 1689–1711; he was endenized in 1694 [Gwynn (2015), 300].
6 Endenized 1685 (HSQS XVIII, 173); he has not been located in the surviving records of West London French churches, but see HSQS LX, 232–3, for his will and that of his brother Charles which reveal Huguenot connections.
7 Thuret, born at Senlis, was endenized in 1683 and made his will in July 1717 [HSQS XVIII, 160; TNA, PROB 11/562, ff. 148–9]. His family in England were Huguenots, silversmiths in the eighteenth century [*HSP* XV, 520; TNA, C 11/2100/38; Tessa Murdoch, pers. com.].

the Bank? Both these figures are shown to have been low. We cannot add to his list of West London medical professionals, but the two Threadneedle Street ministers David Primerose and Aaron Testas mentioned in the previous chapter were not included in his lists. We have also been able to add two women (Suzanna Duplex, Elizabeth Marchant) and seven men (Richard le Bas, Daniel Bernard, James Beschefer, Abraham Casenave, John Faure, Abraham Gilbert and John Thuret) in the western suburbs. Nine others that should be accepted as Huguenot under the relevant criteria, but were not included in Professor Dickson's original calculations, are:

Isaac Beranger, major[26]		£500
John Fargeon, merchant[27]		£500
Isaac Girardin La Font, major[28]		£1000
John Lambert, merchant[29]	London	£500
Major-General de la Melonière[30]		£1000
Susanna Pain, widow[31]	Spitalfields	£100
Nicholas Tourton, merchant[32]	London	£2000
Peter Valette, gentleman[33]	London	£100
Humfroy Willett, merchant[34]	London	£1200
Total		£6900

---

26 Beranger was serving as a major with Danish troops in Flanders in 1694, but was endenized in 1696 [HSQS XVIII, 245]. His sister Elizabeth had a power of attorney dated February 1696 from 'Major Isaac Beranger Lieutenant Colonel of the Regiment of Nassau in the service of his Majestie of Great Brittain' [BEA, AC28/1513, 9 Jan. 1699].
27 Endenized 1687 [HSQS XVIII, 197].
28 Naturalized as a refugee officer from Angoumois; commissioned major Feb. 1694 [HSQS XVIII, 267 and note]. His agent in lodging his subscription was Theodore Janssen.
29 From St Martin, Ile de Ré, Lambert was naturalized in 1696 [HSQS XVIII, 240]. See Crouzet (1996), 260–1, n.5.
30 Previously colonel in command of one of the Huguenot infantry regiments in Ireland.
31 The Huguenot family of Pain was based in Spitalfields; she was perhaps the Suzanne who was sponsor at the baptism of Suzanne Grimaudet in 1698 [HSQS XVI, 172b].
32 From Lyons, endenized 1687, in a list of French Protestants taking oaths towards a naturalization bill that did not proceed 1690, naturalized 1691 [HSQS XVIII, 192, 218, 224].
33 From Bergerac, endenized 1694, naturalized 1698 [HSQS XVIII, 235, 253].
34 Willett had been elected deacon of the Threadneedle Street church in 1672 and elder in 1687. He was born in Rouen, and in 1702 claimed to have been a London merchant for the past 38 years. He seems therefore to have come to England in the 1660s, but he does not appear in the records of denizations and naturalizations. See below, p. 355.

At least twenty people, then, can be added to Professor Dickson's estimate. Rather than 123 Huguenots lending £104,000 in the initial Bank subscription, 143 Huguenots – a little over 11 per cent of the total number of subscribers – lent £114,500. That is not a sufficient increase to change the overall tenor of Dickson's argument, but it does confirm a clear pattern that has been apparent at every stage of our present study: the numbers of Huguenots in England accepted by recent historians are once again on the low side and need upwards revision. Out of the initial total of £1,200,000, £114,500 amounts to 9.54 per cent. The tally may still not be complete. Dickson's reliance on denization and naturalization records will have captured most merchants but means that others might escape identification, and some uncertainty of classification will always remain unavoidable. We might reasonably also consider the special efforts of individual newly arrived Huguenots to support the initial Bank float by bringing in money from family and other connections overseas. Two substantial cases stand out. Theodore Janssen brought in subscriptions totalling £6000 from his brothers in Hamburg and Amsterdam – they are the earliest powers of attorney in the Bank's archives.[35] In addition to the £3000 that Theodore le Cog de St Leger subscribed personally, he passed on another £2000 from Guillaume Heroward de Moystelles and £1000 from Alexander Gigon de Vezancays, both living at The Hague. On a much smaller scale, the king's usher Alexandre Mariette seems to have written to his continental contacts urging them to support the Bank, since as well as subscribing £500 himself he provided the small foundation deposits from Elizabeth Gebert, spinster of Rotterdam, Susanna de Laage, wife of Moses Cherboneau at Delft, and Jeanne Juliot, wife of the sieur de St Germain, also at Delft, a total of £400.[36] All in all, newly arrived Huguenots in England can be said to be responsible for about 10 per cent of the initial subscriptions to the Bank of England as well as making up 11 per cent of the initial subscribers.

If we now set these newly arrived Huguenots from France alongside the role played by the descendants of refugees – both Walloon and French – from previous generations, we are confronted by fewer individuals but more formidable concentrated wealth. By far the largest contributors to the initial subscription were the Houblons; five family members put up £25,700. Eight Lethieulliers produced £8200, Lady Jane setting up three younger family members with £500 each besides investing £3000 herself. Eight thousand pounds came from three Lordells, and £6000 from two Du Canes. So these four families alone were responsible for just

---

35 BEA, M6/87.
36 BEA, M1/1, p. 27.

under £48,000. If we accept Crouzet's calculation that the whole contribution of these earlier refugee descendants was £64,400,[37] then the total subscription provided by new refugee families and their contacts together with the old refugee families was £188,350, nearly 15.7 per cent of the Bank's first funds. This figure is made up of

123 newly arrived Huguenots identified by Dickson	£104,000
Descendants of earlier immigrants, estimated by Crouzet	£64,400
20 further newly arrived Huguenots now identified	£10,550
Money brought in from overseas (as previous paragraph)	£9400
Total	£188,350

Crouzet goes on to show how the longer established families consolidated and increased their holdings over subsequent years, but this is arguably of less importance in that the years of real danger for the Bank, the years when it could quite possibly have failed, came right at its beginning. Once the problems of recoinage had been overcome in 1696–7 and the Bank's second subscription had been successfully raised in 1697, it is hard to envisage it collapsing. The refugee contribution no longer retained the significance it had in 1694, even though the history and fortunes of many refugee families would continue to intertwine with those of the Bank (and other newly established Funds) long into the eighteenth century.

What was the real significance of the presence of the refugees (both the new, and the descendants of the old) at the birth of the Bank of England? It did not lie in the amount of cash they produced: £188,350 was certainly a useful sum, but on its own it would not have been enough to make the Bank the successful venture that it became, and the almost farcical failure of its potential rival the Land Bank showed how quickly grand schemes could collapse.[38] What mattered much, much more was something that cannot be so easily measured. It lay deep in their motivation and was expressed in their unshakeable confidence and commitment when the Bank was first founded and during its early months while it was vulnerable. That commitment and confidence were common to the descendants of the earlier refugees and recent arrivals from Louis's France alike; they were shared by the French church of London and the newer French congregations. Undoubtedly the leadership of the Houblons and their circle was important, and it is evident that the Houblon family was united in agreement that John, the third son, was the right man to

---

37 Crouzet (1996), 239.
38 Ogg (1955), 432; Giuseppi (1966), 26–8.

lead the venture as the first governor. However, immediate support for the new bank was not confined to the Houblons and their circle, or indeed to others accustomed to dealing with money on a professional basis. We have seen that it came too from more unexpected groups like medics, ministers and women, while an estimated 28 Huguenots who were initial contributors deposited just £100 each.[39]

Such commitment mattered just because it was by no means certain that the Bank would be a success. True, there had long been suggestions advanced by thoughtful people that a bank would be desirable. Sir William Petty had argued in 1681 that should England lack adequate money, 'we must erect a Bank, which well computed, doth almost double the Effect of our coined Money: and we have in England Materials for a Bank which shall furnish Stock enough to drive the Trade of the whole Commercial World'.[40] Yet the City of London Bank proposed in 1682 had not come to fruition, and different rival plans failed to gain traction. True also, there was plenty of money in London in the 1690s looking for an advantageous home. As John Houghton put it in 1694, 'trade being obstructed at sea, few that had money were willing it should be idle, and a great many that wanted employments studied how to dispose of their money, that they might be able to command it whensoever they had occasion'.[41] Nevertheless, experience under the Stuart kings Charles I and Charles II had made potential investors wary about the risks of political manipulation. Moreover, since the foundation purpose of the bank had been to enable the war against Louis XIV to be pursued, what would happen to subscriptions to the Bank if the French monarch then defeated William in battle?

Only with hindsight can we be tempted to view the Bank as a secure investment. Potential subscribers in the 1690s who had lived through the shock of the Revolution and knew that one major battle could threaten every penny of their investment did not have the comfort of seeing things that way. Sir John Clapham's history vividly describes the Bank's desperate situation in the mid-1690s when it was still new and inexperienced, the government was at its wits' end for cash to pay its troops, inflation had taken hold, no dividend was paid and its stock fell steeply. Shortly afterwards tallies were selling at all sorts of discounts averaging some 40 per cent in 1696–7, and the Bank's own notes were discounted by 16 or 17 per cent. Meanwhile the whole coinage of England cried out for reform, yet the silver recoinage left the Bank unable to make prompt

39 Asselin, Baignoux, Beauchamp, Blancard, Boucheret, Brisac, Coliner, De Courcy, Dergnouth, Du Thoit, Duvall, de Farcy, Faure, de Sicqueville, Guilbert, Hallée, Juliot, Laage, Lefort, Louvigni, Pain, Petitot, Prevost, Saffre, Simon, Vaillant, Valette, Vignau.
40 Clapham (1944), 4–5, citing Petty's *Quantulumcunque concerning Money*.
41 Cited in D.W. Jones (1971), p. 262.

repayment in cash. From the royal viewpoint, too, success hung on the slimmest margin of financial balance. In May 1696, William warned his key administrative officer, the Duke of Shrewsbury, that the troops in Flanders 'are so much in want of money, that they can scarcely move'. The following month William instructed him, 'in the name of God, determine quickly to find some credit for the troops here, or we are ruined ... there is no alternative, but to perish, or find credit', and in July he advised 'that if you cannot devise expedients to send contributions [to prevent the army mutinying], or procure credit, all is lost, and I must go to the Indies'.[42] The 1690s were indeed a decade during which English minds 'were agitated with fearful recollections of the past, anxiety for the present, and alarm for the future'.[43] As Clapham concluded, 'the Bank of the early years was a speculation with an uncertain future',[44] while David Ogg wrote,

> Many contemporaries were amazed that, with its tenuous resources, the Bank remained solvent ... it was dependent on its reputation and the forbearance of its creditors ... of all the gambles in this reign of gamblers, the Bank of England was the most risky.[45]

Whether new economic ventures succeed or fail very often depends as much on public confidence as on rational analysis, and the unhesitating support from new refugees and the descendants of earlier ones undoubtedly assisted in the Bank's speedy establishment, especially at a time when the Revolution had left many English people confused, uncertain and rudderless. The acknowledged historical financial success of the first wave of refugees could not be denied and was encouraging, as was also the reputation of the Houblons. The French church at Threadneedle Street had a well-earned reputation for good financial management – its members did not beg – and for strict personal ethics and responsibility,[46] and its strong endorsement would have counted for something. The instant support from some of the new refugees – La Bretonnière, Le Heup, Gambier, Janssen, Girardin, Gervaize, Sasserie, Seignoret and Meure were all among those who deposited money on the first possible day, 21 June

---

42 Coxe (ed.) (1821), 115, 119, 129.
43 Coxe (ed.) (1821), p. i.
44 Clapham (1944), I, 44–7, 228.
45 Ogg (1955), 421. The complexity, novelty, internal divisions, and evasions and sharp practices that accompanied Parliament's dealings regarding the Bank in the 1690s are clarified in William A. Shaw's 1934 introduction to volumes XI–XVII of the *Calendar of Treasury Books*.
46 An illustration from Pepys's Diary is given below, p. 270 *sub* De Santhuns.

1694[47] – highlighted the potentially important fact that assets of the new refugees who still had money might be available in comparatively ready cash rather than entailed in property and fixed commitments. Doubtless, too, it would have helped that some of them were also known to be writing to continental contacts urging their participation (and indeed by 1697 the Dutch-domiciled Marc Huguetan, with just over £10,000, would be the second largest Huguenot holder of bank stock).[48] Time would demonstrate that the early support would not waver or be deterred by fluctuations in the price of bank stock, as more new Huguenot money reached the Bank and the Houblons built up their own holdings, until in 1702 fifteen members of the family held stock totalling £54,760.[49]

Sir John Houblon was the first Governor of the Bank of England, a Lord Mayor of London and a Lord of the Admiralty, but he has never been the subject of a major biography. It is clear he possessed understanding and discretion, wisdom and energy. He was helpful when consulted, trustworthy and prepared to accept responsibility, but not someone to push himself forward, flaunt his abilities or set his own interests above the common good. Perhaps these were precisely the qualities his family and other contacts discerned which made them agree that he was the right man to be at the helm of the new bank. He must certainly have had a remarkable ability to remain calm and measured under extreme pressure, for as Ogg put it, while the Bank was performing a national service virtually from its inception in helping finance the war,

> it was a hand-to-mouth business, with constant objections by king and Treasury regarding the high exchange rates, and protests by the Bank at the remoteness of the funds offered as security. Only the public spirit of the directors prevented a breakdown.[50]

It is hard to disagree with the conclusion reached by the family chronicler Alice Archer Houblon over a century ago, that probably no one but his brother James really understood 'the true motives of John Houblon's devotion to the spirit of the Revolution and his systematic support of the war'. Events largely outside their control had tied their own interests firmly

---

47 BEA, M1/3.
48 Carter (1954), 40; Crouzet (1996), 261–2 n.13.
49 Crouzet (1996), 228.
50 Ogg (1955), 422. BL, Harleian MS 7421 (the Earl of Ranelagh's 1696 report on the demands made by the Bank for its losses by remittances to the army in Flanders), and the published correspondence between the Duke of Shrewsbury and the king, show how immensely difficult it was for the two sides to reach a mutually satisfactory agreement.

into those of the Protestant succession and the success of William and the Revolution. The love of liberty they had inherited from their forbears inspired a total devotion to the business of financing the war as something vital and essential, and

> in the sacrifices they made and the risks they ran, they recognised that they had no choice but to carry through boldly what they had begun. This they accomplished in the face of the manifest disapproval and jealousy of their subscribers, whilst the distrust of the public is shown in the fluctuations of Bank stock, and in the virulent abuse of tracts and pamphlets.[51]

In their own way, the Houblon brothers showed the same determination as the Huguenot soldiers at Aughrim to do all they could to ensure that William's gamble succeeded.

---

51 Houblon (1907), I, 253–4.

Conclusion
The Huguenots and the Defeat
of Louis XIV

The preface to this volume posed the questions: 'what did the refugees contribute to the Britain to which they came, and what were the implications of their flight for the France they had abandoned?'.

We have answered them by studying three key areas where the Revolution of 1688–89 could have stalled, William's planning could have gone seriously awry and Louis XIV's ambitions could then have been achieved unchecked by any effective coalition. First, we saw how Louis XIV's treatment of the Huguenots, combined with the large numbers of refugees who had fled France and crossed the Channel during the 1680s and especially in 1686–88, was a major factor in discouraging the English from rallying to James II's support when William invaded. This was not so much a matter of action deliberately taken by the Huguenots in their new home, rather the simple fact that they had been forced to flee, viewed in the context of how the English interpreted their own history after the Protestant Reformation. Without the refugee presence and sufferings, we have argued, James could never have so quickly lost the popular support he had enjoyed when he came to the throne little more than three years previously.

James might have fled in 1688, but that did not mean that William was either popular or secure, and he and Mary were instantly faced by a war in Ireland that it was imperative that they won, and won quickly. We have argued that their first general in Ireland, the Duke of Schomberg, himself an exile from France after the Revocation, was not the 'tired old man' portrayed by recent historians but an experienced and energetic professional. He helped ensure the relief of the besieged city of Londonderry and later, confronted by appalling disease devastating his ill-supplied and inexperienced army in 1689, made sensible, intelligent decisions that provided the platform on which success could be built the following year at the Battle of the Boyne at which he himself died. We then focused on the key battle of Aughrim in 1691, where Huguenot troops suffered heavy casualties but were largely responsible for transforming possible disastrous defeat into what at one stage seemed an improbable and conclusive Williamite victory.

The final section of the book took us back to London in 1694. If the immediate challenge had been military, once Ireland had been secured William's biggest worry was financial, how to keep up the fight against such a rich and powerful adversary as France. The answer proved to lie in the foundation of the Bank of England. It was this that would enable the huge cost of war, far greater than anything in Britain's experience, to be borne and sustained to a victorious conclusion over the next twenty years. By examining the bonds between the Bank and the French Church of London in Threadneedle Street and the confirmation of wider Huguenot contributions to the endeavour, our findings shed new light on the role played by both descendants of earlier Protestant refugees and new arrivals in the Bank's foundation and early years. Between them, they subscribed over 15½ per cent of the Bank's initial funds, while recently arrived Huguenots made up 11 per cent of the initial individual contributors. Yet our argument has been that the actual money they contributed was of less significance than their confidence and their immediate and unwavering support for the venture, and the leadership provided by the Houblons and their associates.

Our evidence has led us to reject Warren Scoville's assessment in 1960, which minimized the significance of the Revocation in damaging Louis XIV's France, despite his book's popularity with many historians in recent years. We showed in the introductory chapter how Scoville frequently excluded the year 1681 (when the *dragonnades* began) from his calculations, how his estimated numbers sometimes lacked the backing of any serious evidence, how limited was his understanding of the English situation, and how he chose to ignore important, relevant work published during the decade before he wrote. Once it strayed beyond the French archives on which it was principally based, Scoville's work did not have the 'solid documentation' with which it has been credited. The overall argument of his thesis demands reappraisal and major revision.

Undertaking such a reconsideration has led *The Huguenots in Later Stuart Britain* trilogy in two directions. Our work throughout has offered new detailed research to provide a firm groundwork of evidence in areas where scholarship has been weak. Our final volume now brings together evidence on Huguenot seafarers coming to England, lists over 1400 military officers in the service of the British Crown under William and

Mary and Queen Anne, investigates funding that supported the Williamite regime especially in relationship to the foundation of the Bank of England and supplies a detailed analysis of the lay officers of the Threadneedle Street church – the oldest, largest, wealthiest and most important in the country – across the later Stuart period. While providing this new evidence, the present volume also looks backwards in time to interpretations that prevailed before Scoville's work, finding real merit in earlier understanding on both sides of the Channel that the Revocation in 1685 was not simply a French event but one that needs to be understood in the wider context that it found its counterpoint in England in the Revolution of 1688.

Within that framework of event and counterpoint, we have focused in the current book on two specific and very different issues of the 1690s, the wars in Ireland and the creation of the Bank of England, chosen because both were fundamental to Williamite success and both involved a significant refugee contribution. Other historians might have chosen a wider time frame or different aspects. They might, for instance, have decided to emphasize the role of the refugees in William's army of invasion in 1688, which we have largely ignored.[1] Then, since the Huguenot military contribution did not end in Ireland, they could have followed it through in Flanders, in Marlborough's campaigns from Blenheim to Malplaquet, and in the wars in the Spanish peninsular in Queen Anne's reign. In the process they might have developed the refugees' importance in providing intelligence to support the war effort.[2] I preferred to focus on Ireland because the Huguenots' efforts in the campaigns there have been underrated and were of critical significance. Economic historians might have put a magnifying glass on the refugees' craft skills and on commercial and mercantile gains, but I have previously written briefly on this subject[3] and a longer time frame is needed to develop it. In contrast, the major danger period for the Bank of England had passed by the end of the 1690s, and the subject fitted naturally with the analysis of the lay officers of the Threadneedle Street church always planned for this volume.

---

1 For this, see Glozier (2002) and Israel (1991).

2 Daniel Finch, Earl of Nottingham, Secretary of State, made much use of refugees for naval information (see *Historical Manuscripts Commission 71: Report on the Finch Manuscripts vol. V*). A striking example has been examined in detail by Sonia P. Anderson, 'The Adventures of Peter Fontaines, Naval Surgeon and Intelligence Agent', *HSP* XXVIII:3 (2005), 336–49. Fontaines provided a detailed military appreciation of the strengths of towns between Brest and Rennes, a route he had travelled four times while on trial in France with his hands manacled and his feet tied under his horse's belly. Later, at his own suggestion, he was locked up among French prisoners of war in English prisons and continued a dangerous game of counter-intelligence through the mid-1690s.

3 Gwynn (2001), 74–5, 81ff.

Both the Irish wars and the early history of the Bank highlight the historian's problems in working on the Huguenots. Refugees are, by definition, stateless people with no home. Until they re-emerge as newly fledged members of another nation, they live in the shadows, and can be hard to see for that reason. Historians' attempts to peer back across more than three centuries are not helped by different spellings of names – we recall the specific ruling of the company of deacons at the Threadneedle Steet church for the guidance of its members writing entries in its records that it did not matter how they spelled a name provided the pronunciation was unchanged.[4] Some Huguenot surnames might be translated into English soon after their arrival or were identical in French and English and so effectively disappear immediately from view in English records.[5] A problem with far wider ramifications is that the great majority of surviving contemporary records, and later commentaries, were written by writers who had no reason to see things from the refugee viewpoint. This is particularly apparent in relation to the Irish wars, where contemporary descriptions on both sides were usually presented from either an English (Protestant) side or an Irish (Catholic) one. The refugees could hardly be called 'French' since they had abandoned France, and anyway there were Catholic French troops fighting in Ireland at the same time. Both Williamite and Jacobite writers on Ireland found their answer to this dilemma by not considering the refugees too carefully and largely setting them aside when they could. Thus in discussing the battle of Aughrim, the Jacobite 'Light to the Blind' referred to 'the forraigners' with the English army who were 'the better moyety of the army', and to the Irish use of 'club musketts whereby the Forraigners suffered much', while the official Williamite account described the 'left wing of our Army' as 'being most Forraigners'.[6] Only when the accounts of the two sides agree in naming Ruvigny as the leader of the assault up the narrow causeway at Aughrim does it become clear where the drive to victory originated.[7]

During our three-volume journey, *The Huguenots and Later Stuart Britain* has redrawn important aspects of what we know about the Refuge. It has shown that within a decade of the Revocation of the Edict of Nantes, England rather than the Netherlands had emerged as the most populous Huguenot centre outside France – and that many scholars have failed to understand the extent of refugee settlement across the Channel or even

---

4 FCL, MS 52, p. 252.
5 Examples are given in Gwynn (2001), 222–3.
6 National Library of Ireland, MS 476, pp. 685, 688; *A Particular and Full Account of the Routing the whole Irish Army at Aghrim*, p. [2].
7 National Library of Ireland, MS 476, p. 690; Story (1693), 133.

comprehend basic facts about the number of new refugee congregations formed in England between the 1680s and the reign of Queen Anne.

At the same time, a series of detailed investigations has greatly extended our knowledge of key aspects of the Refuge in Britain. In Volume I, a biographical dictionary of professionals involved in the ministry of French Protestant worship in Britain 1640–1713 had 737 entries.[8] Volume II followed with a review of all Huguenot worshipping communities in later Stuart Britain, examining their history and providing a listing of known lay church officers. This present book features a detailed study of the lay elders and deacons who governed the Threadneedle Street church, revealing not only their work for the congregation but much about their family interconnections, wealth and social status. The difference to our understanding made by these investigations is major. The 737 men in the biographical dictionary in the first volume represent more than double the number that would have been expected from the only previous attempt to provide a list of ministers. The second volume sought to provide as accurate an assessment as possible of the total number of new refugees arriving in Britain. It showed that about 50,000 came to Britain (excluding Ireland), that 43 of the 50 French churches in Britain by the end of William's reign were founded by new refugees, and that in the 1690s England surpassed the Netherlands as the home of the largest displaced Huguenot community. The number of congregations can hardly be open to dispute, but it stands in startling contrast to different, much smaller figures put forward by French writers at the time of the 1985 Huguenot tercentenary commemoration and repeated even very recently.[9]

The closing decades of the seventeenth century seem a period like no other, during which the network of descendants of the sixteenth century Walloon and Huguenot immigrants, bolstered by some recent arrivals, came to have a particular significance in the activities and thinking of the City of London. The study of the Threadneedle Street church lay officers in the present volume is suggestive in explaining why this should have become the case, especially in relation to the establishment of the Bank of England. Meanwhile in Ireland, the Huguenot regiments were of central importance to the Williamite campaign. Within a few short years the English army would emerge victorious from the Duke of Marlborough's great campaigns of Queen Anne's reign, but in the early 1690s it was short of officers and had to develop a new professionalism on the battlefields of Europe. Meanwhile the Huguenot troops helped to buy the time it needed through their efforts in Ireland.

---

8 Gwynn (2015), chaps V–VI and pp. 203–423.
9 Gwynn (2018), 199–202.

Unlike many other aspects of the Refuge in England, the contribution to the Bank of both earlier Protestant immigrants and new Huguenot refugees has been examined closely by highly qualified professional historians and economists since the Second World War. It might therefore have been expected that there would be little new to say on the subject in this book. However, we have shed an entirely new light on the Bank's foundation by setting the very different institutions of the Bank of England and the French Church of London alongside one another. In the process we have also established that, while P.G.M. Dickson concluded that 123 recently arrived Huguenots were foundation subscribers to the Bank, there were at least twenty more who had remained unidentified. That so many of these foundation subscribers could be overlooked in such a detailed and intensive study again confirms how the refugees were people of the shadows, easy for the historian to miss.

In fact the one thing that stands out from *The Huguenots and the Later Stuarts* is that whenever we have paused to make a special study, we have invariably found more Huguenots than expected, not fewer: more French-speaking ministers in later Stuart Britain than previous work suggested, far more French congregations in England than continental scholars have allowed, more refugee officers in the armies of William and Anne than might have been expected. These findings should ring warning bells for professional historians. We are taught, for good reason, to beware exaggeration. In the shadowy refugee world, minimization can be just as damaging a threat to true understanding. Low numbers are not in themselves intrinsically any better or worse, or even 'safer', than high ones. What we need are simply the most accurate figures we can offer, based on good evidence, judiciously interpreted and properly footnoted, and subject to revision should new information appear.

In an earlier work, *Huguenot Heritage*, I wrote about the refugees in Britain across the centuries, concluding that they

> were likely to share an exceptional degree of determination and to have particular reason to work long and hard to create for themselves a new life in a strange land. Consequently they proved to be a productive people, highly motivated, who provided a major economic impetus to Britain, as to other countries wise enough to adopt them.[10]

The Huguenots in Later Stuart Britain has been confined to two generations between the English Civil War and the Treaty of Utrecht, and this final

---

10 Gwynn (2001), 5.

volume to just one decade from the mid-1680s to the mid-1690s. The time constraint has had the advantage of placing the refugees firmly amidst the immediate challenges of their own day. Its disadvantage, of course, is that it makes it very difficult to follow through long-term consequences. However, considerable attention has again been paid in this volume to the importance of motivation. During the few brief years in the 1680s and 1690s on which we have concentrated, the sacrifices of the Huguenot troops in Ireland and the speed of the response of Huguenots in London to the creation of the Bank both demonstrated a strong inner drive, determination and commitment that proved of critical, enduring importance to the future of England, Ireland and their former homeland, France.

For the Huguenots, the backcloth to their motivation lay in their religion, and bound up with that, their immediate family histories. In studying the foundation of the Bank of England and its close ties with key members of the Threadneedle Street church, we unwound that thread as far back as the English Civil War, noting how family alliances then formed – alliances that would help lead towards the Bank's foundation – were later renewed and strengthened by political developments under Charles II and James II. Perhaps we should have gone back even further in time. The prime purpose underlying the Bank's foundation was to pursue the war against the Catholic threat posed by Louis XIV's France. It would certainly not have escaped the attention of the three Houblon brothers who became initial Bank directors that over a century earlier, back in 1588, their great grandfather Jean, forced into exile following Alva's persecution, had contributed towards the City of London's loan to Queen Elizabeth's government at the time of the Catholic threat posed by Philip II's Spain and its Armada. Looking not backwards but onwards in time, the refugees' commitment proved not only real, but enduring. The Jacobites of 1715 would still point to the Huguenots as their most implacable enemies, Lord Bolingbroke describing 'the whole body of the French refugees' in a memorial to the Pretender James III as 'more desperate and better disciplined than any other class of men in England' and those most ready at once to oppose Jacobite invasion. Huguenot men were again quick to volunteer when threat loomed anew in 1745.[11]

A great social gulf separated the Marquis de Ruvigny, who played a vital role at the battle of Aughrim, from the Houblon family members so significant in the foundation of the Bank of England. Yet there is more in common between them than one might expect. All lived by their parents' values, values that had been shaped by persecution and its effects on their families and friends and those dependent on them. All had been brought

---

11 HMC 56: *Stuart I*: p. 527; Gwynn (2018), 210–11.

up to believe they must put God before self. Shortly after the English Revolution, all experienced the same growing certainty that they must act, and that their time was now or never. Once they had reached that conclusion, all fought for it with immense determination. While many English people did not understand or like their new Dutch king, both Ruvigny and the Houblons recognized and admired William's absolute determination to oppose to the end Louis XIV and the Catholic threat he represented, and were prepared to give him all the support they could. As we considered the battle of Aughrim, we envisaged Ruvigny fighting with the ghosts of his father and General Schomberg at his side. The Houblons were not military men, but they too lived with the ghosts of ancestors who had endured persecution at their side.

The contribution of the very presence of so many refugees in making what happened in 1688 thinkable, the efforts of the Huguenot soldiers in Ireland and the impact of the support of both descendants of earlier Protestant refugees and the enthusiastic engagement of newly arrived Huguenots with the nascent Bank of England were all critical in the success of the Revolution. Each of these three contributions was so significant that it might reasonably be argued that without the refugee presence, the Revolution would have failed or stalled. Taken together, they amount to a powerful argument that the French king's revocation of the Edict of Nantes and his willingness to encourage the *dragonnades* damaged him so severely that his actions against his peaceful Protestant subjects were the single major reason why Louis could not win the wars that dogged him and undermined the French economy for the rest of his reign.

Epilogue

In the prologue to the opening volume of *The Huguenots in Later Stuart Britain*, we witnessed the anxieties on his deathbed of Gilbert Primerose DD (c.1568–1642), minister of the Threadneedle Street church, as he contemplated the recent deaths of his two colleagues, which had undermined his personal security, and the approaching Civil War, which promised violence and national disunity on a scale that had the potential to destroy his church and refugee community, and with them, his life's work.

We have enough historical evidence to be sure that such concerns clouded the end of Gilbert's life. There is no equivalent evidence for the frame of mind of his grandson David Primerose (1639–1713), also a minister of the Threadneedle Street church, as he came to the close of his life 71 years later. All we can say with certainty is that David's will was made on 17 December 1712, that he was buried on 17 August 1713 in the body of St Stephen's church, Coleman Street, and that his will was proved three days later.[1]

There were remarkable parallels between the lives of the grandfather and grandson, parallels underlining the change and challenge that formed the constant framework of both their personal and their professional lives. Both died in London, but neither had been born in England; Gilbert's origins had lain in Scotland, David's in France. Both lived long lives well into their seventies. Both had buried two wives and remarried a third time. Both had spent a substantial part of their adult lives in serving the French Church of London and defending it against potentially terminal threats.[2]

As David Primerose reflected on his life during the year of his death, he would surely have agreed that God had sent him to live through times that were truly remarkable, rarely lacking in fear and hope, in interest and variety and danger. Indeed it may have seemed to him like several

---

1 *Miscellanea Genealogica et Heraldica*, 3rd series, II, 1898, 78; HSQS LX, 313.
2 For their lives, see Gwynn (2015), 380–2.

lifetimes since, as a bright-eyed promising young minister, he had arrived in London in 1660 at the dawn of the Restoration of the Stuart monarchy. Since then the rulers Charles II, James II, and William and Mary had come and gone, the Revolution of 1688 had overturned the state of England and Anne's reign was near its end.

Barely had David Primerose served his apprenticeship as minister to his large refugee congregation in a major cosmopolitan centre uncertain of its future in the aftermath of civil war when the first major challenges appeared. The earliest were physical, one the most personally frightening of his entire life – the Plague, which killed off about one in every five members of the congregation in 1665. He married as his first wife the widow of another promising young fellow minister who had not survived the year. There was little time to mourn, because the following year saw his church and the whole central city burnt to the ground in the Great Fire of London.

If recovering from those shocks and planning and fundraising the money needed to rebuild the church was not enough, David Primerose then entered the time of his life most challenging in terms of the personal and political subtleties and skills needed for survival. The same waves of change that had brought him to the English capital in 1660 had also reinstated Louis Hérault, an extreme royalist forced out of his ministerial position at Threadneedle Street by the Civil War, who had strong connections at Court. Hérault was an embittered man determined on revenge and prepared to undermine the whole ecclesiastical *Discipline* of the French churches in England to achieve it. David Primerose inevitably became the Consistory's spokesman and defender before the state and episcopal authorities and found himself accused of being a traitor to the king.

By the time Hérault finally retired from Threadneedle Street in 1676, the perilous condition of the Huguenots in France was becoming apparent, and from 1681 the congregation was confronted by new refugees in unprecedented numbers, Primerose becoming deeply involved in their relief. As this volume has shown, the 1680s were also a time of political danger in England, and Primerose again had to defend the church and some of its leading members in very difficult interviews with the state authorities.

The political upheavals of the late 1680s relieved that situation but brought their own challenges: the building and care of the large new church annexe, l'Eglise de l'Hôpital, in Spitalfields; how to cope with all the refugees who continued to pour in; the new arrangements needed to work in harmony with the multitude of new refugee congregations. Yet by the time of Primerose's death there were clear signs all around him of a new world dawning. Spitalfields was now a suburb so crowded with refugees and their descendants that it was served by not one but numerous non-conformist Huguenot churches. The rebuilding of London after the Fire was nearly achieved, with the city's new St Paul's Cathedral completed just three years before his death. Louis XIV had been humbled, the threat he had posed to European Protestantism lifted – not least by Huguenot sacrifices in Ireland and their commitment to the new Bank of England.

Looking at the number of refugees in today's world and after living through the inhumanity and needless violence of Ukraine's recent troubles, an author of a work on the Huguenots in later Stuart Britain – the people who brought with them to England the very word 'refugee' – can only reflect on how little our race has progressed between 1685 and 2023. Yet David Primerose may have come to the end of his long life in a far more positive frame of mind. No doubt he and his grandfather would be pleased to know that the church they served still survives, now located in Soho Square across the London they knew. Perhaps they would agree that while God had presented them with challenges and dangers far beyond anything they had ever envisaged or wanted to face, He had also given them and many of their fellow Huguenots the health and vigour, the support, and the faith and strength of conviction to enable them to meet those challenges to the best of their ability.

APPENDIX 1

Huguenot Army Officers in the Service of the Crown in the Later Stuart Period

The following list is based on filing cards lodged in the Huguenot Library at University College, London, in the 1990s by the late Professor George Hilton Jones III (1924–2008). The Library's reference for the cards is Huguenot Army Officers T/28. Dr Jones was an American college professor who specialized in Later Stuart history and was the author of works including *Charles Middleton: The Life and Times of a Restoration Politician* (Chicago: University of Chicago Press, 1967) and *Convergent Forces: Immediate causes of the Revolution of 1688 in England* (Ames: Iowa State University Press, 1990). There is no introduction to the cards, no indication of what he hoped to do with them, no complete list of the sources he used in compiling them. Written in longhand, their value lies in the huge amount of detailed information, invariably with sources given, which they provide. Manuscripts studied by Dr Jones include MSS at the Bodleian Library, British Library and National Archives, and these manuscripts form the basis for the cards. He has also incorporated relevant information from printed sources such as army lists, the Huguenot Society Quarto Series, Charles Dalton's *English Army Lists and Commission Registers, 1661–1714*, the *Calendar of Treasury Books*, the Index to Irish Wills, and the London *Gazette* during the Irish wars.

As an example, consider the case of John Comarque or Comargues. The four cards for him show:

> *Comarques, [John], was listed for a pension of 2s 6d p[er] d[ay] (£45/12/6 p.a.) on the Irish Civil Establishment commencing May 1, 1699. He is listed among officers of Galway's regiment of horse. P[ublic] R[ecord] O[ffice], T.14/8, fol. 8v.*

Comargues was listed for 2s 6d. p. d. (£45/12/6 p.a.) on an Irish Civil Establishment of August 1, 1701.

Comarques had a commission as a reformed lieut[enant] on the Irish Civil Establishment and a pension of 2s 6d. p. d. He had served six years, including time in Ireland and Flanders. He had £160 and a rent of £8: 10 st[erling]. He was supporting his wife and three children. He was able to serve. Disbanded in March, 1698/9. Abstract... French pensioners [1702] P.R.O., T.37/7, p. 2.

Lieut. Commarques [in 1706] was an officer of horse on the Irish Establishment in a condition to serve. Brit[ish] Lib[rary], Add 38,848, fol. 170r.

Commarques was to be recalled from Ireland [to England, perhaps for employment] with the same advance on his pension as foot officers had had. April 27, 1706. P.R.O., SP. 67/3, fol. 125 r & v.

Comargue, John, was ordered a commission to be a captain in Lieut.-Col. Balthazar de Foissac's regiment of Portuguese dragoons, March 7, 1708/9. P.R.O., W.O. 25/122, p. 86.

John Comarque, of Foissac's dragoons, had a captain's commission dated February 23, 1708/9, given by the Queen. He had produced the act of naturalization and was apparently on half pay [before Christmas, 1714]. P.R.O., W.O. 25/2984, fol. 17r.

Captain John Comarques of Foissac's regiment was on the British half-pay establishment for 1721. P.R.O., W.O. 25/2986, fol. 430v.

Captain John Comarque, a half-pay officer of Foissac's regiment, was examined 25 May, [1726?]. He was then 60, with 35 years service, including time in Flanders, Spain, and Portugal. Ibid, fol. 11v.

John de Comarque, born at Montauban, was naturalized by 4 and 5 Anne, No.94. Shaw, ed., D[enizations] and N[aturalizations], 1701–1800, p. 49.

His son was James Comarque, q.v.

The present Appendix simply records the names of those active in the later Stuart period for whom Jones produced cards, providing an idea of the individuals identified and the range of ranks or roles they indicate. (It should be noted that ranks given are far from clear-cut, since men could be breveted to a higher rank than they really held; they could also be paid at a rank below that which they held.) The date references are to the information provided, <u>not</u> to years of active service. My particular interest has been to get an approximation of the total number of identified Huguenot army officers over the period from 1689 to 1713. Hopefully, further research will be facilitated as other scholars become aware of the groundwork Dr Jones has laid, and the cards offer a most useful starting point.

All the entries in this appendix have cards indicating military activity within the period up to 1713. Individuals for whom the cards lack satisfactory evidence that the men in question served actively within this period are bracketed. Any known to have died on active service are indicated by an asterisk (*).

It must again be stressed that the dates are those referred to on the cards or extrapolated from information on them; they are not necessarily dates of active service, and could be very misleading if taken as such. This can be illustrated by the entry for the example above, which is listed simply as

COMARQUE[S], John   1690s – 1726   Lt – Capt.

To give another example, the dates given in the entry for Charles Boileau Castelnau are 1694–1733, but although he died in the latter year, he left the army in 1711.

There are particular difficulties with names of army officers. Doubtless this is largely because each list was compiled by one clerk, who [whether English or from some particular district of France] may not have had occasion to discover how they were normally spelled. The problem is compounded by the number of men claiming titles, "sieur de" this or that, who entered army service as officers. Dr Jones simply started each card with the entry in front of him, which is not necessarily the spelling he ended up with as normative for the officer. The order of the cards [which often indicates what he <u>did</u> end up with] can therefore be significant.

Other problems confronting the researcher include the fact that family traditions may mean successive elder sons carried the same Christian name as their father and followed him into the army. In a refugee situation, it would not be impossible for grandfather, father and son to enter William's service simultaneously: or, again, two brothers might enter the same regiment at the same time.

It is important to recognize that Huguenots were not only to be found in French regiments. They may for instance appear (like Stephen Taillourdean de St Paul) in the Grenadier Guards; or (as was Jacques Gabriel de Montresor when he was wounded at the battle of Malplaquet in 1709) in the Royal Scots Fusiliers; or (like Colonel John Montargie in 1706) in the Welsh Fusiliers. Those dependent on the English crown might not obviously even be in English service. Soldiers might switch between English and Dutch service, like Henry Lislemarais, or Henri de Monteze who took the oaths prescribed for naturalization in Ireland in 1699 but later, as Major-General, commanded the troops of the Dutch Republic in Catalonia. They might be sent to fight in Savoy and the Piedmont with the troops of the Duke of Savoy in 1690, like Salomon de Loches, or again at the express command of Queen Anne, like Claude Lavabre. They may turn up in other, stranger places; for example, the engineer John Massé was directed to Rio de Janeiro in 1712. Those like Gaspard Paudin, Charles de Quinsac or Paul Randon who embarked at Nice in 1704, having originally intended to assist the Cevennois, were specifically promised that should they fight for Victor Amadeus of Savoy, and survive the war, they would be treated on the same terms as other officers in the Queen's service. David Montolieu, Baron de St Hipolitte, who was to die a full General in the British army in 1761, made his name as a young Lieutenant-Colonel appointed Lieutenant-Governor of the Citadel of Turin by the Duke of Savoy at the time of the siege of the city in 1706.

Much of our surviving evidence derives from the need to pay pensions. Many men killed in action, or not requiring pensions, or who moved elsewhere, are therefore hardly known. A survey made in about 1726, showing length of service of surviving officers on half pay, is most revealing in the way it pushes back the time of service that the other surviving records would indicate. This is shown in John Comarque's case. For another example, the first reference in these cards to Daniel Mauco, cornet of dragoons, is dated 1711: yet in the 1720s it was established he was aged 66 with 37 years' service including time in Ireland, Flanders and Portugal, so he had fought right through the campaigns of William's and Anne's reigns from 1689 onwards.

The listing that follows cannot, then, be considered definitive. It will certainly be incomplete. The high percentage of officers within it who attained the rank of captain and above is notable. (Such rank in many cases – 675 out of 1426 - was of course attained under the Hanoverians). This may partly be ascribed to the sudden arrival of many comparatively experienced French soldiers, but it is also harder to overlook senior officers. Many cornets, ensigns and lieutenants – especially if killed in the front line early in their service – must simply have disappeared without trace. Even so, the listing shows over 1,400 Huguenot officers in the armies of William and Anne.

ABBADIE [Dabbadie], Daniel	1690s–1717	Cornet
[ABBADIE, James (d')	1689–90	Chaplain]
[ABBADIE, John James (d')	1706	Secretary]
ABESNIE, d'	1695	Lt
ABZAC, Henri d'	1690s–1739	Capt – Lt. Col

ADDEE, Daniel	1690s–1727	Capt – Lt. Col
AFFAU, Henry d'	1707–1714	Lt
DAGNEAUX, Louis	1695–1712	Ensign – Capt
DAGNEAUX, Jacob	1692–1695*	Ensign – Lt
D'AIGUILLON [d'Eguilhon], Estienne	1690s–1720	Lt
D'AGNIAUCOURT	1706	Ensign
D'ALBENAS, Charles	1709–1734	Lt. Col
D'ALBENAS, Charles jr	1697–1702	Lt – Cornet
D'ALBENAS, François	1690–1699	Adjutant – Capt
D'ALBENAS, Henry (Senior)	1697–1702	Capt
D'ALBON, Balthazar		Lt. Col
ALISIEUX, François d'	1709–1714	Quarter-Master
ALISIEUX, Peter	1694–1740	Capt – Major
D'ALLON, Dan.	1691–1692	Lt – Capt
ALOTTE or ALLOTTE, Charles	1698–1735	Quarter-Master
AMATIS, Abel	1690s–1720	Quarter-Master – Cornet
[AMYOT, Peter	1706]	
ANDOINS, James d'	1690s–1713	Lt – Capt
ANDRÉ, Theophilus d'	1699–1717	Lt
[ANGIBAUT or ANGEBAUD, Chas	1682–1705	Apothecary-General]
D'ANGILBAUT, Louis	1689–1726	Ensign – Adjutant – Lt
D'ANOU	1689–1690	Ensign
D'ANROCHES, Charles	1689–1716	Capt
D'ANROCHE LE CADET, Charles	1706–1721	Ensign – Lt – Cornet
D'ANTRAIGUES, Baron	1689–1702	Capt
DE APPELLES	1689	Capt
ARABIN (DE BARCELLE), Barth:	1678–1712	Cornet – Capt
D'ARBONNE	1699*	Lt
D'ARBONNE	1699–1701	
[on reverse of first d'Arbonne card:]		
D'ARTIQUENAVE, Charles	1688–1690	Capt
ARDESOIF, Abraham	1706–1707 ("lately dead")	Ensign
ARDESOIF, Abraham	1707–1742	Lt
ARDESOIF, Abraham de Courteille	1689–1717	Capt

ARDESOIF, Peter?	1694–1712	Lt (Marine officer)
DARENNES, Francois. Despierre	1689–1735	Capt
ARMAND, Lewis	1699–1742	Ensign – Lt – Capt
ARMAND, Pierre	1699	
ARMENAND	1692	Ensign
DARRAU (Darros)	1693–1699	Capt
DARSONVILLE	1689	Capt
DANCOUR, Paul Arundal	1700–1705	Ensign – Lt
DASSAS	1691–1712	Lt – Capt
AUBIN, Abraham	1706–1726	Lt
AUBIN, Elie	1689–1703	Capt
AUBRESPY or OBRESPIE, David	1706–1733	Cornet
D'AUBUSSARGUES, James	1689–1720	Lt.Col – Col – Maj.-Gen.
AUGEARD	1689	Lt
AUGIER, Seignuron	1690s–1717	Ensign
AUMONT, Augustin	1706	Ensign
AURELLE, Pierre	1689–1704	Adjutant
D'AUTEUIL, Florand	1706–1713	Capt – Major – Lt.Col
AVÈNE, Henry D'Espaigne d'	1689–1690*	Capt
D'AVESAN or DAVEJAN	1690	Lt.Col
BAÇALAN, David	1689–1709*	Lt – Capt – Col/A.D.C.
BAÇALAN, Tho. St Leger de	1690–1711	Lt – Capt – Lt. Col
BAÇALAN, Pierre	1698–1704	Major
BADEZ or BADESI	1690–1701	Ensign
BAGARS, Jean [Mazel] de	1711–1726	Cornet
BAIGNOULX, Paul	1684–1724	Lt
BAILHACHE, Anthoine de	1706–1726	Lt
BALANDRIE, Peter	1690s–1720	Capt
BALMIER, Solomon	1687–1702	Lt
BALQUERYES, Eleazar	1689–1699	Ensign – Lt
BALTHAZAR	1689–1698	Capt – Col – Brig.General
BANCART	1699	
BANCELIN	1689*	Cornet
BANCONS or BANCOURS, Isaac	1689–1720	Lt
BANCONS, Jean	1693–1726	Ensign
BANCONS, Jeremie	1689–1722	Lt – Capt – Lt.Col

BARBAT, Jean	1706–1726	Surgeon
BARBOT, Jacques	1690–1709	Capt
BARBUT, Francis	1709–1724	Lt
BARBUT, Pierre	1706–1726	Ensign – Lt – Capt
BARCUS (Bargust), Pierre	1699–1714	Ensign – Cornet
BARDON	1689	Ensign
BARMON	1689	Lt
BARNIER	1708–1714	Ensign
BARRARD	1691–1692	Lt
BARRATON, John	1693–1707*	Quarter-Master – Lt – Capt
BERENGER or BARRENGER, Ph:	1709–1730	Lt – Quarter-Master
BARRY or BARY, Jacques	1690s–1738	Ensign – Lt
BASIGNAC, Jean	1689–1706	Ensign – Lt
BASTIDE, John de	1706*	Capt
BAUDOUIN	1689–1706	Ensign – Col
BAULON	1689–1690	Capt
BAYSE or BAYLE, Jean	1689–1717	Lt – Capt
BÉARN, Baron de	1696	Major
BEAUBISSON, Peter Guenon de	1690s–1711	Keeper of Armoury
BEAUCHAMP, Jean or Jacques	1690s–1718	Trooper
BEAUCOUR, Estienne	1689–1717	Ensign – Lt
BEAUFORT, Solomon	1689–1731	Ensign – Lt – Capt
BEAUJEU or BAJU	1689–1702	Cornet
BEAULIEU, James de	1689–1742	Capt – Lt. Col
BEAUREGARD, Alpheus	1694–1706	Ensign
BEAUREGARD, John Peter de	1696	Lt
BAUVOISIN	1689–1690	Lt
BEAUSOBRE or BRAUSOBRE	1690–1699	Ensign
BEDORAT, Peter	1689–1706	Lt
BELARD, John	1690s?	
BELCASTEL, Peter, Marquis of	1689–1710*	Lt.Col – Col – Maj.Genl
BELCASTEL, de	1689–1690*	Capt – Major
BELLEAU, Louis Costard de ("Belleval")	1689–1717	Cornet – Major – Lt. Col
BELLCOTE	1689	Ensign
BELLAFOND, Sampson	1690s	

BELLEGARDE	1689–1694	Capt
BELLOC, Isaac	1703–1720	Capt
BELLOT, Etienne de	1694–1696	Lt
BELORIAN or DELORIAN, John	1691–1717	Lt
BERNASTRE, Daniel de	1690–1747	Capt – Lt.Col
BERNARD or BARNARD, James	1697	Lt
BERNAY, James	1691–1698	Lt
BERNIERE, John Anthony	1694–1726	Ensign – Capt
BESSIERE, Anthony	1711–1740	Adjutant – Capt
BESSIERE, Mark Antony	1711–1728	Ensign
BETEMCOUR, Charles de	1697–1700	Capt
BETTE, Grandry de	1697	Ensign
BETTE, Pierre	1709*	Lt
BLACHON	1689*	Capt
BLANCHAR or BLANCARD, Pier	1696–1699	Quarter-Master
BLANSAC or BLAUZAC	1689–1699	Capt
BLEVILLE, Jno Baptist	1710–1740	Cornet
BLOSSET, Paul	1706–1718	Col
De BODT, Jean	1688–1699 (and later elsewhere)	Engineer, Capt
BOIGNOLLE, Jean	1690–1694	Chaplain
BOILEAU de Castelnau, Charles	1691–1733	Ensign – Lt – Capt
[BOIRIBEAU, Jean	1699–1713]	
BOIROUX, Henry Auguste Helie	1693–1695*	Capt
BOISDAUNE, Philip	1702–1733	Ensign – Capt
BOISMORELL, André Costard de	1688–1739	Ensign – Capt – Brig.Gen
BOISRAGON, Daniel Chevaleau de	1695–1709	Lt
BOISRAGON, Louis Chevaleau de	1695–1730	Capt – Major – Lt. Col
BOISROND ST LEGIER, Henry	1706	Lt
BOISROND, Samuel de	1689–1737	Major – Lt. Col
BOITOUT, Lucas	1694–1706*	Engineer
De BOLEDE or BOYLE, David	1690–1702	Ensign – Lt
BOLROY	1689	
BONABELL, John	1706–1714	Lt – Capt.-Lt
BONAFOUS, Peter	1694–1715	Ensign – Capt
BONARD, Vincent	1695–1714	Lt – Capt
BONIFACE, Lewis	1698–1706	Ensign – Lt

BONVILLARS	1689	Ensign
BORD, John	1690	Lt
BORDA or BORDUC?, de	1689–1691	Capt – Lt.Col
BORDENAVE, Peter	1699–1706	(galley slave) – Capt
La BOUCHETIERE, Charles Janvre de	1694–1720	Col
BOURDIGUES or BORDIGUES	1689–1701	Lt – Capt
BRAGARD or BRAGARS, Cyrus	1688–1725	Capt – Major – Lt.Col
BRAINVILLE	1706	Capt
BRAQUELETS or BRAGLET	1689–1690	Lt
BRASSELAY, James	1701–1708	Ensign
BRASSELAY, Jean	1689–1708	Capt – Col
BRESSAC, John	1692	Cornet
BRISAC, Henry	1689–1701	Ensign
BRISAC, John Peter	1701–1708	Chaplain
BRISAC, Paul de	1695–1702	Capt
BRISAC or BRIZAC, Peter	1695–1739	Ensign – Lt – Capt
BROZET, John	1710–1769	Ensign
BROZETT, Peter	1709–1757	Lt
BRUGIERE, Elias	1699–1709*	Major
BRUGNIER, Jacques	1690s–1736	Cornet
BRUNEL or BRUNETT	1693–1738	Cornet – Lt – Capt
BRUNEQUIL, Abraham	1689–1726	Cornet – Lt
BRUNEVAL, Pierre, Sieur de DU PUY	1687–1722	Capt – Lt. Col
BRUNEVALL, Mons de	1693–1706	Lt – Capt.Lt
BRUNEVALL, Daniel	1711–1726	Cornet
BRUNVILLE, Michael	1689–1720	Ensign – Lt – Capt
BRUSE, Pierre (de)	1699–1726	Capt
[BUISSIERE, Paul	1689	Surgeon-General]
BUOR, Charles	1711–1714	Lt
BUREAU, Pierre	1696–1717	Ensign
BURJAUD or BURJANDS, Jno	1702–1740	Capt
BUSEVILLETTE, Louis de	1693–1698	Ensign
CABANOIS, Paul	1709–1735	Ensign
CABROL, Daniel	1696–1723	Surgeon
CABROL, Francis	1689–1750	Capt

CADOUL or CADOLLES	1690–1702	Capt
CADOUL, Francis	1690–1706	Engineer
CADROY, Noah	1692–1712	Cornet – Lt – Capt
CADROY, Stephen	1696–1709	Ensign – Lt – Capt.Lt
CAGNY	1706	Lt
CAILHOT or CAILHOTT, Jean	1689–1717	Quarter-Master
CAILLAUD, Reuben	1698–1732	Lt – Capt
CALAIS or CALLAISE, René	1704–1707	Quarter-Master – Cornet
CALADON, Paul	1690s–1717	Lt
CALVAIRAC, David	1689–1729	Ensign – Lt
CAMBEROSE/COMBRECROZE, Pierre de	1693–1732	Lt – Capt
CAMBES, Henry	1699	Lt
CAMBOLIVE, Stephen	1688–1690	Lt
CAMBREE, Piercy	1689–1726	Cornet – Lt – Capt
CAMONT	1689	Ensign
CAMPAGNE, Daniel	1695–1700	Ensign – Lt
CAMPAGNE, Samuel	1693	Lt
CANDALE, Francis	1706–1726	Ensign – Cornet
CANITROT [no.1]	1689–1690	Ensign
CANITROT [no.2]	1689–1690	Ensign
CANET or CANNET, Daniel	1702–1726	Lt
CARCASSONET, Jean Fran: de	1694–1701	Lt
CARIES, Moses	1689–1717	Lt – Capt
CARLE, Peter	1689–1730	Lt – Capt – Col – Brig. Genl
CARNAC or CARNAT, Peter	1699–1756	Surgeon – Captain
CARMOULD, Charles	1707–1757	Surgeon
CARYETTS	1689	Lt
CASAUBON, Etienne de	1689–1692	Lt.Col
CASAUBON(E), Isaac	1702–1726	Capt
CASSIN, Ami	1690–1691*	Capt
CASSAN or CASSEEN, Stephen	1689–1696*	Capt
CASSELL, Nicholas	1689–1730	Lt – Capt
CASTAGNIER, Aldebert	1690–1726	Quarter-Master
CASTELAIN, David	1694–Q.Anne	Lt
CASTELFRANC, Abel de	1695–1726	Cornet – Lt – Capt

CASTELFRANC, Gedeon	1698–1742	Cornet – Lt ?
CASTLEFRANC, Josias de	1691–1695	Ensign
CASTELNAU, Charles Boileau	1694–1733	Ensign – Lt
CASTILLON	1689	Capt
CASTRON	1689	Ensign
CAVALIER, Jean	1702–1716	Col
CAVALIER, Peter	1710–1727	Lt – Capt
[CAVALIER, Solomon	Former officer in Iberia]	
CAYRAN, Francis	1702–1726	Quarter-Master
CAZALET(TE), Estienne	1706–1721	Ensign – Cornet
CAZALET, Mark	1688–1700	Lt – Capt (cashiered)
[CAZALET, Pierre	1693	No evidence of military service]
CAZALET, Mr	d 1745	Engineer
CAZETTES, Alexander	1696–1725	Lt – Capt
CELERIES, Jean de	1689–1726	Ensign – Lt – Capt.
CELERIES, Louis de	1689–1701	Capt
CHABERT, Simon	1690s–1738	Ensign – Lt – Capt
CHABRIER, Anthony	1690s–1714	Quarter-Master
CHABRIERES, Isaac	1689–1742	Lt – Capt
CHABROL(LES), François?	1694–1706	Capt
CHALAMEL, Pierre	1690–1709	Lt – Capt
CHAMARD, Jean François	1689–1706	Ensign
CHAMLOR, Ceira	1691–1692	Capt
CHANLORGE l'ainé	1689	Lt
CHANLORGE le cadet	1689	Lt
CHAMPA[G]NÉ, Josias	1689–1737	Ensign? – Capt – Major
CHAMPFLEURY, John	1689–1715	Capt
CHAMPLORIER, Marc, le cadet	1691–1717	Ensign
CHAMPLORIER, Pierre Thibeaut, Sieur de	1699 –1701	Capt
CHANGUION	1690–1701	Capt
CHANTIGNE	1689	Ensign
CHAPELLE, Daniel	1689–1709	Quarter-Master – Lt – Cap
CHAPUY, Bernard	1689–1729	Ensign
CHAPUZETTE, Peter	1697–1708*	Surgeon
CHARDELOUP, Jean	1692–1717	Engineer – Capt – Lt.Col

CHARRIER, Isaac	1689–1717	Capt
CHASSELOUP, Peter	1687–1717	Lt – Capt
CHATEAU (de) VERDUN	1689–1691	Capt
CHATEAUVIEUX, Gaspard	1709–1726	Capt
CHATILLON	1689–1690	Lt
CHATINE, sr	1690s	Cadet
CHATINE, James [= jr?]	1690s –1714	Cadet – Lt
CHAUVYN, Peter	1694–1699	Lt
CHELAR, Peter	1688–1720	Quarter-Master
CHENEVIX, Philip	1689–1705*	Lt – Capt – Major
CLAPIES, [Jno] Philip de	1708–1726	Capt
CLAPIEZ, Savinee	1694–1726	Lt
CLAUSADE, Jean	1694–1754	Ensign – Lt
CLARIS, John	1695–1697	Engineer
[CLAVERIE, John Augustus	1710–1742	Capt]
CLAVIER or CLAVYE, Jean	1689–1720	Lt
CLAVIER, Pierre	1690s–1718	Cadet
CLAVIS, John or Samuel?	1709–1726	Cornet
CLERE, Pierre de	1699	
CLERVAUX or CLERVASE	1689–1703	Lt – Capt
COLOM or COLLOM, Thomas	1689–1699	Lt
COLUMBIERE	1690s–1706	Ensign – Lt
COLOMBIERE, Anthony	1689–1716	Lt – Capt – Major – Col – Lt.Col
COLUMBIERE, Daniel	1689–1717	Lt
COLUMBINE, Anthony	1708	Col
COLUMBINE, Ben	1697–1721	Lt – Capt – Major – Lt.Col
COLUMBINE, Edward	1702–1729	Quarter-Master – Ensign – Lt – Capt
COLUMBINE, Francis	1695–1746	Ensign – Capt – Major – Lt.Col – Lt.Gen
COLUMBINE, Henry	1692–1693	Ensign – Lt
COLUMBINE, Ventris [I]	1688–1704	Major – Lt.Col – Col – Brig.Gen
COLUMBINE, Ventris [II]	1697–1706*	Ensign – Capt
COLUMBINE, Ventris [III]	1712–1731	Lt
COMARQUE, James	1712–1714	Cornet

COMARQUE[S], John	1690s–1726	Lt – Capt
COMBREBRUNE, Peter	1689–1726	Lt – Capt – Major
COMPAING, Paul	1688–1714	Ensign – Lt
COMBRECROSE, Peter	1689–1732	Lt – (Capt)
CONSTANTIN(E), John	1689–1717	Lt
CONSTANTIN(E), Philip	1689–1717	Lt
COQUTSANTE, Samuel	1711–1739	Lt
CORBETTES, John	1695–1733	Cornet
CORBETT, Louis	1699–1719	Lt – Capt
CORNAUD, James	1690–1706	Lt – Capt
COSNE/CONE	1691–1692	Capt (Horse)
COSNE CHEVERNAY	1689	Capt.Lt (Foot)
COSNE, Peter de	1689–1717	Ensign – Lt
COSSAU, Peter	1709–1721	Cornet? – Lt
COSTEBADIE, John	1706–1726	Lt
COSTARD de Lignière, Louis	1688–1702	Capt
COSTARD de Belleau, Louis	1692–1694	Capt – Major
COTEREAU	1690	Lt
COTTIN, Daniel	1690–1703	Capt – Major
COTTIN, John	1711–1721	Lt
COULOM, Daniel	1690s–1717	Cornet
COULON, Jean Jacques	1689–1720	Lt
COULOMBIER, Isaac de	1691–1701	Ensign – Lt
COURAUD or COURRAND, Francis	1701–1717	Lt
COURSEL or COURCELLES, Philippe	1687–1707*	Ensign – Lt – Capt
COUSSEAU, James	1706	Ensign – Lt
COUSSEAU, Peter	1706–1726	Cornet
COUTEAU or COUTAUD, Charles	1690–1702	Major
COUTERNE, Charles de	1689–1691*	Cornet
COURTIERS, Auguste de	1697–1707*	Ensign – Lt
CRAMAHÉ, Hector F. Chataigner de	1688–1725	Capt
CREPIGNY (CRESPIGNY), Charles	1706–1733	Ensign – Lt
CREPIGNY, Gabriel (de)	1691–1722	Lt – Capt
CREPIGNY, Tho.	1689–1710	Cornet – Capt.Lt – Capt

CRESPIGNY, William	1707–1713	Ensign – Capt?
CRESPIN, Daniel	1700–1730	Cornet – Lt – Capt.Lt
CRESSERON, Charles Le Fanu de	1689–1738	Capt – Major
CROSAT, Jacques (James) de	1693–1717	Ensign
CROYE or CROY, Peter	1693–1704*	Ensign – Lt – Capt
CRUSEAU, Jean	1696–1708	Cornet
CUSSY or CUISSY, de	1689–1693	Capt
DAGAR, Abraham	1706–1726	Lt
DAGAR, Theodore	1688–1702	Brigadier & Lt – Capt
	(wife to 1717)	
DAILLON, Charles	1692–1701	Ensign
D'ALBINQUE, François	1689–1706	Ensign – Lt
DALBON, Baltazar	1689–1711*	Capt – Major – Lt. Col
DALBOS, John	1701–1737	Lt
DALLEZ SOUSTELLE, Baron	1695–1702	Cornet – Lt – Capt
d'ALMAN, Jacob	1694–1702	Ensign
DALMAS, John	1685–1737	Lt – Capt.Lt – Capt
DALON or DALLONS, Alexandre	1689–1715	Lt – Capt
DAMBON, James	1691–1715	Lt – Capt.Lt – Capt
DALTERAC, James	1690s–1718	Sergeant – Ensign
DAMBOIS, Francis	1689–1730	Lt
DAMPIÈRE, Stephen Monginot	1689–1717	Capt
DANCOURT, Paul	1692–1705	Ensign – Lt
DANDURAN, Louis	1689	Lt
DANROCHES, Estienne	1689–1711	Ensign – Lt
D'ANTILLY, John Adrian du Bosc	1689–1702	Lt – Capt
DAPILLY or DAPPELLY, Anthony	1690–1726	Ensign – Lt
DARASSUS, John	1689–1730	Ensign – Lt
[DARBONNE see d'ARBONNE]		
DARENNE, Francis Despierre	1692–1735	Capt
DARQUES, Lewis	1690s–1717	Cornet
DARQUIER, John	1695–1732	Surgeon
DARQUIER, Peter	1705–1739	Cornet
DARRAGAU, Sebastien	1689	Lt
DARRIPE, David	1690s–1731	Capt
DAUBARES	1689–1690	Lt

DAUGE or DANGÉ, James	1689–1717	Ensign – Lt – Capt
[1 or 2 men?]		
DAUBON	1690–1694	Lt
DAULHAT, Peter	1700–1725	Ensign – Surgeon
DAUNISE or D'AUNIX, Pierre	1691–1711	Capt
DAUSSY, Jean	1697–1703	Cornet
DAUSSY, Peter	1690–1714	Capt
D'AUTEUIL, Florand	1689–1731	Capt – Major – Lt. Col
DAVESSEIN DE MONCAL, Joseph	1689–1714	Cornet – Lt – Capt
DAVESSEIN DE MONCAL, Mark Anthony	1685–1742	Lt–Capt–Major–Col-Brig

["There was at least one other Marc Antoine Moncal". See below *sub* Moncal.]

DAVISE, David	1703–1713	Capt
DEBATZ	1689–1690	Ensign
DEBIE, Gisbert or Jasper	1689–1699	Ensign – Lt
DEBIZE, David	1694–1720s	Surgeon
DEBIZE, Roger Augustus	1711–1740	Ensign – Lt – Capt
DEDIER, John	1704–1716	Surgeon
DEGOINE, René	1692–1707*	Ensign – Lt – Capt
DEJEAN, Lewis	1706–1764	Ensign – Lt – Capt – Major – Lt.Gen
DEJOY or DEJOUS, James	1696–1702	Ensign – Lt
DE[S]LANDES, Albert	1690–1742	Capt
DELATE, John	1695–1736	Capt-Lt – Capt – Lt.Col
DELFIEU, Stephen	1710–1724	Ensign – Cornet
DELON, Louis	1694	Capt
DELPECH, Bernard	1700–1708	Surgeon
DELPY or d'ELPY, Jean	1689–1706	Ensign – Lt
DELRIEU	1691–1699	Ensign – Lt
[DEMARAIS see DESMARAIS]		
DENIE, Charles	1699 -1703	
DEPERAY, John Baptist	1692–1731	Ensign – Lt – Capt – Major
DE ROYERE, Samuel	1694–1733	Ensign – Lt
DESAULNAIS or DISNEY, Henry	1699–1731	Capt – Col
DESAZILES, Lewis	1709–1714	Capt

DESBORDES, James	1694–1705	Lt
DESBORDES, John Pierre	1688–1740	Ensign – Lt – Capt – Col – Maj.Gen – Brig.Gen
DESBRISAY or DEBRISAY, Théophile	1689–1720	Capt
DESBRISAY or DEBRISAY, [Samuel] Théophile jr	1713–1772	Capt
DESCAIRAC, Alexandre see d'ESCAIRAC		
DESBROSSES, Claude	1694–1701	Capt
DESCAZALS, John	1709–1726	Quarter-Master
DES CHAMPS, Jean Procureur, sieur	1696–1699	Lt
DESCLAUX, Noah	1689–1720	Lt
DES CLOUSEAU, Lewis René Royraud	1688–1720	Ensign – Lt – Capt
DESCORBIAC	1689–1690	Lt
DESCURY, Daniel Collot	1688–1715	Capt – Major
DESCURY, Simon	1702–1740	Lt.Col – Col
DESEMBLARS, André	1689–1737	Ensign – Lt
DESERS or DESERT	1699–1701	
DESFOURNEAUX, Alexandre de Raquet	1689–1742	Cornet
DES ETANGS, St Pol (Count)	1691–1709	Brigadier – Major General
DES GROIS, Mark Anthony de Gorron	1689–1691	Lt – Capt
DESHERBIERS [later BOROUGHS], Richard	1691–1742	Ensign – Lt – Capt
DESHIERES or DEZIERES, James	1710–1730	Lt – Capt
DES ISLES, Lewis	1693–1737	Cornet – Capt
DESLOIRE, Joshua	1689–1720	Capt
DE(S)MARAIS, Charles	1713–1718	Quarter-Master
DE(S)MARAIS, Henry	1689–1715	Cornet – Lt
DESMARCHAIS or MARCHAIS, Benjamin	1689–1714	Capt
DESMAREST or DEMAREST, Esaye	1689–1702	Capt
DESMARETTE or DE MARRETTE, James	1689–1726	Cornet – Lt – Capt

DESMINIERS, John	1694–1701	Ensign
DES MOULINS, Charles	1689–1696	Capt
DESODES, Estienne	1695–1723	Ensign – Lt – Capt
DESPARES, Lewis	1708–1714	Lt
DESPARON	1689–1690	Lt
DESPARON	1689–1690	Ensign
D'ESPERENDIEU, Henry	1689–1703	Lt – Capt
DESPIERE(S), William	1690s–1716	Capt
DEPRES or DESPREZ, Daniel	1689–1703	Ensign
DEPRES or DESPREZ, Lewis	1689–1720	Lt – Capt
DESROMANES, James	1691–1740	Lt – Capt – Major – Lt.Col
DES ROMAINES, John	1705	Ensign
DESTREMAS or DE ESTREMAS	1689–1690	Capt
DE VEILLE, Thomas	1703–1726	Capt
DE VOYE	1713	Capt
DEYAS, John	1708–1717	Ensign – Lt
DIGUES *alias* LA TOUCHE, David	1692–1745	Ensign – Lt – Capt
DOLON, Louis *le fils*	1689–1732	Cornet – Lt – Capt
DOLON, Louis *père?*	1689–1703	Capt
DOMERGUE, Henry	1690–1723	Ensign – Lt – Capt – Maj
D'ORGUEIL, Gaspart	1706	Ensign
DORNANT, Daniel	1697–1699	Lt
DORNANT, Samuel	1692–1716	Ensign – Lt – Capt.Lt
DORTOUX, Jean	1689–1718	Capt
DOUDART, James	1691–1693	Adjutant
DOUGLAS or DUGLAS, Dominique	1689–1706	Ensign – Lt
DROLENVAUX, Daniel	1699–1704	Lt
DROUART, Isaac	1695–1704	Ensign – Lt – Capt.Lt
DRULHON, Henry	1693–1717	Cornet – Lt
DUBARRY, Alexander	1690–1726	Lt – Capt – Major
DU BAY or DU BUY	1689–1701	Cornet – Lt
DU BOIS, Louis Gratien	1689–1690*	Capt
DUBOIS or DE BOY, Louis	1693–1699	Ensign
DUBOIS, Peter	early 1690s*	Capt

[noted at end of the previous card]

DU BORDA(S) or DUBORDAC, James	1689–1698	Capt – Lt. Col
DU BORDIEU, Gabriel	1695	Engineer
DU BORDIEU, Peter	1706–1718	Chaplain

[A reference to this man also as 'surgeon' is presumably an error. See Gwynn (2015), 271.]

DUBOS[C], Jacob	1706–1726	Quarter-Master
DU BOSC d'ANTILLY, John Adrian	1694–1700	Capt – acting Major
DUBOUCHET or DUBOCHET, Pierre	1696–1703	Engineer
DUBOURGAY, Charles	1691–1732	Ensign – Capt – Col – Brig.General
DUBUC or DUBUE, Nicholas	1689–1733	Lt – Capt
DU BUISSON, Paul	1692–1693	Capt
DU CAMBON, François	1688–1693*	Col – Engineer-general – Brig.Genl
DU CASSE, Daniel	1706–1717*	Cornet
DU CASSE, James	1694–1718	Lt
DU CASSE, Stephen	1708–1745	Lt
DU CAUSSE, Hannibal	1688–1717	Lt
DU CHESNE, Michel or jr	1689–1717	Cornet
DU CHESNE, Peter or sr	1689–1717	Cornet – Lt
DU CHESNE VAUVERT, Theophilus	1696–1723	Lt
DU CHESNOY, Salomon?	1691–1699	Capt
DUCLA, Peter	1690–1758	Ensign – Lt
DUCLOUSY, [Paul] Martin	1711–1726	Ensign
DUCROS, John	1690s–1718	Ensign – Lt
DUCROS, John	1692–1706	Surgeon
DUCROS, Peter	1703–1712	Surgeon
DU FALGA(S), Anthony	1689–1701	Ensign
DUFAU, Henry	1701–1726	Lt
DUFAU, John	1703–1731	Lt
DUFAUR or DUFAUX, Joseph or jr	1689–1726	Ensign – Lt – Capt
DUFAUR, Daniel	1689–1732	Lt – Capt.Lt
DUFAUR, Samuel	1689–1742	Ensign
DU FAUSSAT, Pierre	1689–1711	Ensign – Lt – Capt

DUFAY	1689–1694	Capt
DUFAY, Simon	1692–1742	Cornet – Lt
DUFAY d'EXOUDUN, Josué Benjamin	1694–1730	Cornet – Lt – Capt

[written variously as 'd'Issodum', 'd'Issondun', 'd'Ixoudun', 'd'Exoudun', 'Dessoudun'. Issoudun (Indre department, Centre-Val de Loire) and Exoudun (Deux-Sèvres department, Nouvelle-Aquitaine) are both French locations. The officer was born at Niort, which suggests 'd'Exoudun' is correct.]

DUFOUR, Louis	1698–1733	Lt
DU FRAT	1689	Lt
DU GARDIN	1689	Capt
DUHAUMEL	1689	Ensign
DU HOMMET(TE), James	1690–1717	Lt
DUMARESQUE, George	1702–1719	Capt
DUMARESQUE, John	1705–1727	Ensign – Lt – Capt.Lt
DUMAS, Charles	1709–1742	Lt
DUMAS Peter	1708–1740	Ensign – Lt – Capt.Lt – Capt

[another? Peter DUMAS appears on the Irish Establishment 1700–1701 – could this be the subject of the next entry?]

DUMAS de Roche, ---	1689–1706 (active service 1689–91)	Ensign – Lt
DUMAS de Roche, Jacques	1694–1716	Cornet – Lt – Capt
DUMAY De l'Epinasse, Marc	1689–1707	Cornet – Lt
DUMENY, John	1689–1729	Lt – Adjutant – Capt
DUMENY, Peter	1689–1705	Lt – Capt – Major
DUMONT, David	1708–1726	Capt
DUMONT DE BOSTAQUET, Isaac	1689–1709	Capt
DU PARC or DU PARE, Francis	1689–1717	Lt – Capt
DU PERAY, John Baptiste	1690–1731	Capt – Major
DU PILL DE VILLERS, Jean	1689	Capt
DUPIN, Francis	1703–1717	(Sub-) Brigadier
DU PLESSIS, Charles	1689–1701	Cornet
DUPLESSY, Lewis sr	1689–1726	Quarter-Master
DUPLESSY, Lewis jr	1711–1714	Ensign
DUPLEX, Isaac	1696–1705*	Ensign – Lt
DU PONCET DE LA VIVARIE, Guillaume	1689–1713	Lt – Capt – Major

DUPRAT(T), Isaac	1708–1722	Lt
DUPRAT, Peter	1706–1726	Ensign – Lt
DUPRÉ	[of Belcastel's regiment]	
DUPUY	1689–1702	Cornet [of horse]
DUPUY	1693–1702	Ensign – Lt [foot]
DUPUY, Matthew	1706–1740	Ensign – Lt
DUPUY, Peter	1689–1721	Capt – Lt.Col
DUPUY, Samuel	1704–1707	Lt – Capt
[perhaps the second Dupuy listed above?]		
DU or DE QUAVRE, John	1693–1694	Surgeon
DU QUERRY, Auguste	1694–1724	Ensign – Lt – Capt – Major
DU QUESNE, Gabriel, Marquis	1709–1740	Major – Lt-Col
DURAND or DURANT, Abraham	tempore Q. Anne	
DURAND, Charles	1708–1726	Lt
DURAND, John	1707–1726	Ensign – Cornet – Lt
DURAND or DURANT, Lewis	*tempore* Q. Anne–1737	Lt-Col
DURAND or DURANT, Peter	1696–1715	Engineer – Lt.Col
DU RASOY, Louis	1689–1693	Capt
DURBAN, Joseph	1689–1706	Lt
DUROURE DESBONNEAUX, Alexander	1689 or 1714–1740	Lt – Capt – Major
DUROURE, Francis	1689–1718	Lt – Capt
DUROURE, Scipio	1710–1745	Capt – Major – Col
DU ROY, Benjamin	1688–1701	
DUSSAU/DUSCAUD/DUSSAUX	1699–1701	Capt
DUSSAU/DUSCAUD/DUSSAUX	1696–1698	Ensign
[not Joseph, *may* be Henry or John]		
DUSSAU, Henry	1707	Lt
DUSSAUD, Isaac	1708–1717	Surgeon's Mate
DUSSAU, John	1706–1712	Ensign – Lt
DUSSAUX, Joseph	1696–1715	Ensign – Lt – Capt
DUSSAUX, Joseph jr	1711–1739	Ensign – Lt – Capt
DU SERRE/DUSCIRE	1692–1706	Ensign – Lt
DU SOLVAN	1689	Lt

DU SOUL, Samuel	1688–1734	Lt – Capt
DUTENS, Alexander	1694–1713	Ensign – Capt
DUTERME/DUTERNE, Charles	1707–1748	Ensign – Major
DUTERME/DU TERNE de la Court, Louis	1692–1714	Lt – Capt – Lt.Col
DUTERME, Steven Sarlande	1697–1730	Capt
DU TORAL or DU TERRAIL, Alexander de Bardel	1689–1715	Lt – Capt
DUVAL, Auguste	1689–1719	Cornet – Lt
DUVAL, Jacques	1706–1707	Cadet
DUVAL, Joseph	1706	Ensign
DUVERNET or De VERNET, Henry	1711–1726	Capt
[DUVERNET] ROMEGOUX, James Dezier or Dessire	*tempore* Q. Anne	
DUVERNET, John Francis	1711–1730	Ensign – Lt – Capt
DU VIVAS [or just VIVAS], Peter Archer	1699–1703	Ensign
DU VIGNEN	1689	Lt
DUVINOIS, Jedeon	*tempore* Q. Anne	
DU VIVIER(S)	1689–1692	Lt
DU VIVIER, John	1706	Ensign
d'EPPE or DEPPE, David de Proisy	1689–1712	Capt
d'ESCAIRAC, Alexandre [See also Gwynn (2015), 264–5, *sub* Descairac.]	1690–1694	Chaplain
ESCORONE	1691–1692	Lt
ESQUALET or SCALÉ, Peter	1691–1726	Capt
[ESPERENDIEU, Jacques	1680	No military-related evidence]
ESTAUNIÉ or STONIER, Isaac	1689–1742	Ensign – Lt
EYME, Isaac	1691–1712	Capt – Major – Lt.Col
EYMER or EYMAR, James	1706–1726	Cornet – Capt
FABRE, Louis	1694?–1733	Ensign – Lt
FALAISE, Ephraim	1689–1738	Lt – Capt
FALAISEAU	1689–1701	Ensign

FALGUEROLLES, Peter de	1708–1714	Capt
FALQUIER, Isaac	1699–1709*	Ensign
FARANGE or FARANGUE, Gabriel	c.1690–1730	Quarter-Master
FARCEY, John	1701–1731	Capt – Lt. Col
FARINEL, Baltazar	early 1690s–1718	Trooper
FARJON, David	1692–1726	Lt
FAUBARE, Mark Anthony (de)	1710–1714	Adjutant
FAURE, Daniel	1709–1714 [1742–3]	Cornet
FAURE, Jean	1689–1718	Lt
FAURE, Paul or Francis	1690s–*temp.* George I	Surgeon's Mate–Surgeon
FAVIERE, Maximilien Dubois	1695–1730	Engineer – Capt
FEIRAC or FAYRAC, Isaac	1706–1726	Capt
FENOUILLET, Jacques (James)	1696–1717	Cornet – Lt
FERMENT, Moise	1689–1697	Lt
FERRAND, Nicolas	1689–1720	Capt
FERRON, (de)	1689–1690	Capt
FIGUEL, Hosea	1696–1717	Surgeon
FLEURY, René	1694–1704	Ensign
FOISSAC or FOISAC, Balthazar	1689–1726?	Lt – Capt – Lt.Col – Col
FOISSAC, James	1689–1726?	Ensign – Capt
FOLLEVILLE, Henry	1688–1702	Ensign – Capt
FONBRUNE, Pierre	1689–1700	Ensign – Lt
FONJULIANE, Gedeon	1691–1717	Capt – Major
FONJULIANE (jr), Louis	1689–1715	Capt – Major – Col
FONRANCES, Louis Levesque	1689–*temp.* George I	Lt – Ensign – Capt
FONSUBRAN[E], James	1692–1732	Ensign – Lt – Capt
FONTAINE OR FOUNTAIN, Eloy de (Elias)	1706–1712	Capt
FONTAINE OR FOUNTAIN, James	1708–1738	Capt – Major – Lt.Col
FONTAINE OR FOUNTAIN, John (de)	1689–1720	Ensign -Lt – Capt
FONTALBA, Lewis	1689–1731	Lt – Capt
FONTANIER, John	1689–1720	Lt – Capt

FORTENIER or FORTAGNÉ, Daniel	1689–1726	Lt
FOUBERT, Henry (de)	1685–1743	Cornet – Lt – Capt – Major – Crown Equerry
FOUBERT, Peter	1707–1726?	Adjutant
FOUCAULT or FOUCAUTE, Peter	1706–1726?	Ensign – Lt
FOUQUET, Charles	1689–1704	Cornet – Lt
FOURESTIER, Daniel	1702–1714	Lt
(FOURNIER, John	1689–1699)	
FRAISINET or FRESSINET, Pierre Granier de	1689–1720	Lt – Adjutant – Capt
FRANCFORT, Pierre de	1694–1755	Lt – Capt
FRERE or FREYER, Jeremy	1695–1704*	Ensign – Lt
FRIARD, Charles	1688–1696	Lt
FULGHEM, Adrian	1689–1702	sub-brigadier – Cornet
GACON or GACONE, Isaac	1702–1728	Ensign
GACON or GACONE, Peter	1713–1718	Surgeon
GALLARY, Francis	1706–1726	Quarter-Master
GALLISIAN, Charles	1701–1718	Quarter-Master
GALLY or QUALY, Estienne Pinet de	1691–1694	Capt
GALLY DE LA GRUELLE, Paul de	1689–1737	Capt – Major – Col – Maj. Gen
GALLY DE GAUJAC, Peter [See also Gwynn (2015), 296–7]	1693–1715	Chaplain
GALLY, Peter/St Pierre de	1689–1765	Lt – Engineer – Capt
GALLY le père	1689–1701	Capt
GALLY, Joseph	1697 -1699	
GALLIPUY or GARRIPUY, Francis	1689–1742	Ensign – Lt
GASSAUD, Jacques	1689–1699	Cornet
GAST, Daniel	1709–1714	Ensign – Cornet
GASTINE, Matthew	1689–1708	Capt – Major
GAUBERT	1689–1706	Cornet – Lt
GAUME, Benjamin	1689–1717	Cornet
GAUSSERAND, Peter	1710–1718	Quarter-Master
GAUTERON, Gedeon	1689–1711	Capt

GAZEAU, John	1707–1726	Lt
GEFFRES LA GROIS or LA GROYE	1689?–1715	Ensign – Lt
GEFFRES DE LA TOUCHE, Alexandre	1691–1731	Lt – Capt
GENESTE, Louis	1689–1742	Ensign – Lt
GENEST, Peter	by 1710–1726	Surgeon
GERBETT, John	1698–1727	Lt – Capt
GERVAISET, Blaise	1695–1704	Lt
GERVERAU or JEFFRO, Isaac	1694–1743	Ensign – Lt – Capt
GIBERNES, Jean	1689–1717	Capt
GIDOUIN or GEDOIN or "JIDOIGNE", Jean	1706–1722	Ensign – Lt
GIGNOUX, Isaac	1695–1752	Ensign – Capt
GIGNOUX, John	1693–1731	Ensign – Lt – Capt
GIGNOUX, Peter	1689–1699	Capt
GINESTET, James	1689–1694	Capt
GIRANDEAU or GIRARDEAUX, Moses	1688–1699	Surgeon
GIRART, Philippe	1689–1730	Lt
GLATIGNY, Adam	1689–1742	Ensign – Lt
GORSE(S), Peter	1708–1726	Quarter-Master
GOUBET(T), John	1691–1695*	Capt – Engineer
GOUDET, Joachim	1694–1735	Ensign – Lt – Capt
GOULAINE or GOULENE, Charles de	1689–1720s	Lt – Capt – Major
[his son, another Charles, was an ensign by 1714]		
GOULIN, Pierre	1689–1715	Cornet – Lt
GOULON, Charles le	1689–1696	Lt-General (artillery)
GOUPILL, Daniel	1710 or earlier–1726	Surgeon
GRANCÉ or GRANÉE, Jean	1693–1717	Ensign
GRANDMAISON, Paul	1711 or earlier–1740	Quarter-Master – Ensign
GRANDPREY, Martin	1694–1711	Adj – Quarter-Master – Cornet – Lt – Capt
GRANDRY, Jean	1689–1743	Ensign
GRANGER, René	1693–1702	Ensign – Lt

GRANGUES, John Henry	1695–1754	Cornet – Capt – Major – Col – Gen
GRAVERON, Jacob de	1689–1696	Ensign – Lt – Capt.Lt
GRENIER, James	1695–1718	Cadet –Ensign
GRIMAUDET, Benjamin	1692–1710	Ensign – Lt – Capt
GROGNET or GROGUET, Isaac	1705–1709	Ensign
GROGNET, Vigor	1692	Capt
GUERIN, Mainhard de	1706–1749	Ensign – Regimental agent
GUERIN, Salomon de	1690–1702	Capt
GUIBAL, Peter	1708–1726	Ensign
GUIBERT de Sissac, Alexander	*temp.* Q.Anne–1742	Capt
GUIBERT, Isaac	1709–1740	Adjutant
GUYCHENON, Pierre	1699	
GUILHEM, Bernard de	1696–1699	Ensign
GUILHEM or GUILLIN, David de	1689–1726?	Ensign – Lt
GUILLERMIN or GUILHERMAIN, Pierre	1689–1733	Ensign – Lt
GULHON or DESGULHON, Estienne (de)	1695–1728	Capt.Lt
GUY, Scipio	1696–1706	Cornet – Lt
GUYON or GUION, John	1709–1730	Quarter-Master
GUYON, William	1690s–1740	Ensign – Capt
GUYRAUDET or GIRAUDET, Claude	1690s–1717	Quarter-Master
d'HANUS or de HANNUS, Louis	1689–1717	Capt
d'HARCOURT, Oliver	1692–1712	Engineer – Capt – Major – Lt. Col
HAUTECLAIRE, John	1689?–1714	Lt – Capt
HERBAUT, Peter	by 1709–1740	Lt
HOULEZ or OULES, John	1691–1699	Surgeon
d'HIER, Scipion	1710–1716	Ensign
De HOURS or d'HOURSE, Henry	1689–1733	Ensign – Cornet – Lt
d'HUISSEAU, Adam	1704–1730	Ensign – Lt
HURRY, Francis	1695–1706	Adjutant – Cornet
HUSSON, Paul Steven	1710–1721	Cornet

ISARNE, Jean	1689–1702	Lt – Capt
JAGMAR, John	by 1709–1721	Cornet – Quarter-Master
JALAQUIER, John	1690s–1717	Cornet
JAMES, Jeremiah	by 1711–1736	Quarter-Master
JARLAN, Mark	1706–1730	Ensign – Lt
JEMBELIN, Jacques	1706–1712	Ensign – Surgeon
de JOYE, John	1689?–1717	Ensign
JOYSELL or JOIZELL, (Du)	1690–1694	Capt
LA BALME, Gaspard	1689–1726	Capt – Major
LABAN, Gabriel de	1710–1730	Capt.Lt
LA BARRE, Louis Le Chivre, Marquis de	1689–1692	Cornet – Capt
LA BARTHE, Jean Thomas (de)	1690–1715	Capt – Lt. Col
LA BARTHE, John de L'ESTANG, his brother	by 1692	see card for Louis de
LA BASOCHE, Philip	1689–1718	Cornet
LA BASTIDE, Antoine Martin [de]	1689–1729	Capt
LA BASTIDE, Armand de	1689–1727	Lt – Capt – Lt. Col
LA BASTIDE St Sebastian, Pierre de	1689–1693	Capt – Major – Lt. Col
LA BASTIDE (de) BARBUT, Francis	1689–1718	Cornet
LA BASTIDE DELON, Paul	1694–1704	Capt
LA BASTIDE DE LOND DUPUY, Peter	1689–1726	Capt – Major – Lt. Col
LABAT or LABATTE, André	1689–1718	Lt – Capt
LABAT, Francis	1693–1709	Lt
LA BATTYE, Pierre?	1689–1702	Capt
LA BALME or LA BAUME LA SALLE	1689–1702	Capt
LA BALME or LA BAUME VIGNOLLE	1689–1702	Capt
LA BAUME, Jean	1691–1706	Lt
LA BEAUNE or LA BEAUVE, Philippes de	1701	Capt
LABAISSADE de MASSAS , Etienne de	1689–1694	Lt

LABEISSADE, John	1690–1716	Lt [Foot]
LABEISSADE or LA BESSÈDE. John (de)	1689–1699	Capt [Horse]
LA BENNE or DE LA BENE, John Lewis	1689–1722	Lt – Capt – Major – Col
LA BENNE or DE LA BENE, Michael	1709–1730	Ensign – Lt – Capt
LABILLIERE, Paul	1689–1726	Ensign – Lt – Capt
LABILLIERE, Peter	1705–1742	Capt
LA BLACHE BELET, St. Claude	1705–1735	
LA BOISSIERE, John (de)	1694–1721	Ensign – Lt – Capt
LA BOISSONADE, Samuel de Pechels	1689–1718	Lt
LA BORDE, Josias (de)	1705–1740	Ensign – Lt – Capt
LA BORDE VILLENEUVE, John	1689–1690*	Major
LA BOUCHETIERE, Charles Janvre de	1689–1720	Lt – Capt – Lt. Col – Col
LA BOUCHETIERE, Charles Janvre de	1708–1730	Cornet – Lt
LA BOUCHETIERE, Lewis	1710–1714	
LA BOULAY, l'ainé	1689–1699	Lt
LA BOULAY, le cadet or jr	1689–1702	Lt
[LA BOULAY, Charles	1713–1715	Likely to be one of the two above]
LA BOULAY, James Anthony de	1688–1722	Ensign – Lt – Capt
LA BOULAY DUCHAMP, Jean	1708	Lt
LA BOULAY, Roland de	1692–1694	Lt
LA BOUTINIERE, John	Queen Anne's reign–1726	Lt
LA BRISSONIERE, Peter de	1689–1719	Lt – Capt
LA BROSSE FORTIN	1689–1701	Lt
LA BROUSSE, Jean Paissen de	1689–1734	Capt
LA CAILLEMOTTE, Pierre de Massue, sieur de	1689–1690*	Col
LA CAILTIERE, Charles (senior)	1689–1725	Lt – Capt
LA CAILTIERE, Theodore (junior)	1689–1720	Cornet – Lt
LACAPELLE, Isaac	1706–1717	Lt
LACASSE or LACAZE, Jean	1694?–1726?	Cornet
LACATERIE, Elie de	1691?–1698	Lt

LA CAUX, John	Queen Anne's reign–1726?	Lt
LA CHANCELLERIE, Jean	1689–1715	Lt
LA CHAPELLE	1692?–1702	Cornet
LA CHAPELLE, Peter	1704?–1718	Quarter-Master – Ensign
LA CHERROIS, Daniel (de) or jr	1689–1717	Lt
LA CHERROIS, Nicholas (de)	1689–1703	Capt – Major
LA CLARIERE/CLARETIERE, Louis de	1692–1701	Ensign
LA CLAVELIERE	1698	Major
LA CLIDE D'ESTRILLE, Isaac de	1689–1717	Capt
LA CLIDE, John	1689–1717	Capt
LA CLOCHE DU MAREST, Charles	1689–1717	Lt
LA COLOMBINE, Achilles (de)	1690–1740	Ensign – Lt – Capt – Major
LA COMBE, John	1710–1726	Lt
LA COMBE, William	1706–1729	Lt
LA COSTE	1689–1701	Capt
LA COSTE	1689–1702	Ensign – Lt [La Melonière's regmt]
LA COSTE, Hercule de Gartoule	1709–1717	Lt – Capt
LA COSTE, Jean	1689–1742	Ensign – Lt [La Caillemotte/ Belcastel's regmts]
LA COSTE, Pierre [perhaps the La Coste of La Melonière's regiment above?]	1706–1735	Lt – Capt
LA COSTE, Stephen de	1695–1710	Lt
LA COUDE, John	1697–1712	Capt
LA COUDE, Theophilus Vauchin de	1695–1699	Ensign
LA COUDRIERE, Jean Rabault de [two men of this name, father and son, both served in the French regiments]	1689–1717	Adjutant – Capt – Lt. Col
LA COUDRIERE, Guillaume Rabault de	1695–1715	Capt
LA COUR, David de	1703?–1740	Ensign – Lt
LA COUR, John Malleville de	1694–1701	Capt

LA COUR, Theophile (de)	1692–1714	Capt
[possibly two officers of this name]		
LA COURT, Guy de	1689?–1715	Captain-Lieutenant
LA CREUZE, Stephen de	1713–1726	Cornet – Lt
LA CROIX, Charles	1712–1714	Surgeon
LA CROIX, John	1694–1704	Ensign – Lt
LA CROIX	1689–1691	Capt
LADEVEZE, Abel Rotolph de	1706–1740	Capt
LADEVEZE, Anthony Rotolph de	1706–1740	Ensign – Lt – Capt – Major
LA FABREQUE, Francis	1689–1709	Capt – Lt. Col
LA FARELLE, John Lewis	1688–1725	Ensign – Capt – Col
LA FARELLE, Paul de	1708–1726	Lt
LA FARGEZE, Peter	1704–1743	Capt
LA FAUSILLE, Henry	1710–1719	Capt
LA FAUSILLE, Jean de	1708–1763	Ensign – Col – Maj. General
LA FAUSILLE, René de	1689–1722	Capt
LA FERÈ, Salomon	1693–1696	Lt
LA FERRIERE, Hector de	1690–1699	Ensign – Engineer
LA FITTE, Jean	1689?–1717	Ensign
LA FITTE, Matthew	1693–1729	Lt – Capt
LA FITTE, Peter	1707–1740	Quarter-Master
LA FITTE, Timothy	1696?–1737	Capt
LA FOND, Samuel	c.1692?	Cornet
LA FONT, Armand	1691–1732	Ensign
LA FONT, Isaac Gabriel de	1694–1698	Ensign
LA FONT, Isaac de	1694–1701	Major
LA FONTAINE, Peter de la	1706–1730	Capt – Major
LA FONTAN[D], Daniel de [la]	1689–1719	Capt
LAFOUS or LA FORCE, Francis de	1689–1691	Capt.Lt – Capt
LAFOREY or LA FERRY, John or James	1705–1727	Lt – Capt – Major – Lt.Col
LA FORTELLE, Caesar	1689–1723	Lt – Capt
LA GARDE, Isaac	1703	Brig
LA GARDE, Jacques	1694–1707	Cadet – Ensign
LA GARDE, Pierre Ferré	1688–1710	Capt

LAIGER, Jean	1689–1761	Adjutant – Capt
LA GODINIERES or LA GAUDIERE	1689–1693	Capt
LA GRANCE, Lewis	1710	Ensign
LA GRANGE, William	1704–1715	Lt
LA GRAVIERE, Daniel	1710	Cornet
LA GROIS, Gabriel	1690–1694	Ensign
LA HAUTEVILLE, Jacques Quevermont de	1689–1707	Ensign – Lt
LA HOUSSAIE, James	1709	Ensign
LAIGLE, Isaac de	1689–1736	Capt – Major
LAISNÉ, Bertrand	1689–1717	Lt
LA JAUNIERE, Peter	1709–1726	Lt
LA JONQUIERE, David (de)	1689–1730	Cornet – Ensign
LA JONQUIERE	A second man of this name was serving in 1689.	
LA LANDE, François Daulnis, Sieur de	1689–1717	Lt – Capt
LA LANDE, Henry de	[1689–1737	Lt – Capt.Lt – Capt]
LA LANDE, Henry de (no.2)	[one died a Lt 1728, the other as a Capt 1737]	
LA LARGERE, Francis	1703–1726	Ensign – Lt – Capt
LA LAUZE, François Robert de	1689–1710	Lt
LA LO, Samson de	1691–1709*	Engineer – Capt – Lt. Col – Col – Brig.Gen
LA MAINDRIE, Peter (de)	1707–1742	Lt
LA MALQUIERE, Louis Guittard (de)	1689–1733	Lt – Capt
LA MARIA, Antoine (l'ainé)	1689–1733	Capt – Major
LA MARIA, Gédéon (le cadet)	1689–1707	Capt – Major
LA MARTINIÈRE, Alexander (de)	1692–1704	Engineer
LA MAUGERE	1689–1690*	Capt
LA MAUGERE, Michel	1689–1739	Ensign – Lt
LAMBERT, George	1694–1701	Lt
LAMBERT, Peter	1702?–1730	Quarter-Master – Lt
LAMECOURT, Charles David	1695–1717	Ensign – Lt

[Charles Lamecourt and David Lamecourt are the same man]

LA MELONIERE, jr, probably Anthony	1694–1740	Cornet – Ensign – Lt – Capt – Major – Lt. Col
LA MELONIERE, Isaac de Monceaux	1689–1712	Col – Brig. Gen – Maj. Gen
LA MENERIE, Daniel de	1692–1699	Capt
LAMENES, Peter	1690s?–1740	Quarter-Master
LA MERIE	1689–1706	Capt
LA MILLIERE, Alexander	1707–1714	Ensign – Lt
LA MILLIERE, Charles Guinebald de	1689–1703	Lt
LA MILLIERE, Cirus de	1695–1709	Cornet
LA MILLIERE, Florent Guinebald de	1687–1728	Capt
LA MILLIERE, Henry	1703–1739	Lt – Capt
LA MESSILLE, Jacques	1689–1699	Ensign
LA MONGOTIERE, Pierre Abraham	1703–1753	Capt
LA MORINIERE, Pierre Buor de	1694–1706	Ensign – Lt
LA MOTTE/MOTHE/MOTE, André (de)	1690–1703	Capt
LA MOTTE BELLEAU, Centurion (de)	1689–1717	Capt
LA MOTTE, François Philiponneau de	1690–1694*	Engineer – Col
LA MOTTE BROCAS, Gabriel	1689–1720	Ensign – Lt – Capt
LA MOTTE CHAMPY, Jean	1689–1717	Lt
LA MOTTE, Josias	1693–1705*	Gent: of Ordnance – Capt
LA MOTTE GRAINDOR, Samuel	1689–1736	Lt – Capt
LA MOULINE, Paul Robert	1688–1708*	Artillery Captain – Capt
LA MUSSE, Samuel, Comte de	1690 –1717	Capt
LAMY, Peter	1689–1717	Cornet
LA NALVE, Gaspar	1690s–1754	Lt – Capt.Lt
LANDAIS, Elias	1690–1706	Lt
LA NEGRERIE	1691–1701	Ensign
LANGÉ or LANGEAIS, Joseph	1689–1715	Lt
LANGON(S), François	1688–1713	Ensign
LA NOE, Charles	1704–1738	Lt – Capt – Major – Col
LA NOE, Nicholas de	1691–1709	Capt

LA PENOTIÈRE, Frederic de	1693–1716	Ensign – Capt – Major –Lt.Col
LA PLANCHE, Lewis (de)	1689?–1738	Lt – Capt.Lt
LA POINTELLE, Charles	1689–1706	Lt
LA POIRE, Peter de	1708–1726	Cornet
LAPORTE, Moses (no.1)	1689–1704	Lt
LAPORTE, Moses (no.2)	1709–1721	Ensign – Lt

[Assumed two Moses Laportes, to account for the discrepancies of rank and date]

LA PRADELL[E], John de Quarter-Master General	1689–1733	Ensign – Capt – Col –
LA PRIMAUDAYE, Maurice	1695–1705	Capt
LA RAMIER, Claude	1689–1693	Capt
LA RIMBLIERE, Jacques Defrottey	1689–1724	Capt
LA RISE, Paul	1689–1706	Capt
LA RISOLE FALENTIN, Germain	1689–1702	Lt
LA RIVALIERE, Theophilus	1694–1747	Lt – Capt
LA ROCHE BREVILLIETT or BREUVILLET	1693–1700	Capt
LA ROCHE LOURIE or LOUHERIE	1689–1690*	Capt
LA ROCHEQUA	1692–1693	Capt
LA ROQUE, Anthony (de)	1689–1720	Cornet – Ensign
LA ROQUE, Jean Porte de	1689–1720	Quarter-Master – Adj – Lt
LA ROQUE, Pierre (de)	1694–1704	Cornet – Capt
LA ROQUIERE	1689–1690*	Capt
LA ROUSSELIERE, Peter	1689–1720	Lt
LA ROUVIERE	1689–1706	Cornet – Lt
LA ROUVIERE, Jean Jacques Taissoniere de	1689?–d. 1716	Lt – Capt
LA ROUVIERE, Jean (de)	1692–1742	Capt
LA ROUVIERE, Jean Liron de	1699–d. 1713	officer on pension

[Could this be the same man as the first La Rouviere above?]

LA ROUVIERE, Jean	1709–d. 1736	Ensign
LARQUIER BORDA, James	1698–1702	Lt. Col
LA RUE, Peter de	1694–1698	Quarter-Master
LA SALLE, Daniel de	1710–(1726)	Quarter-Master

LA SALLE, Deine	1689–1699	Lt
LA SALLE, Henry	1706–1717	Cornet – Lt
LA SALLE, Isaac	1689–1702	Ensign
LA SALLE, Jean	1690s–1717	Ensign
LA SAUTIER, Anthony	1690–1742	Capt
LA SAUVAGIE, Pierre	1689–1706	Capt
LA SELLES, Marc	1692–1714	Cornet – Lt
LA SERRE, John	1689–1717	Cornet
LAS NAUZES or LA MAUZET, Jean Antoine	1690?–1712	Capt
LATANÉ, Daniel	1711–1726	Ensign
LA TEISSONIERE, David	1696–1699	Ensign – Engineer
LA TEISSONIERE	1689–1692	Lt
LA TERRASSE, Isaac de	1698–1701	Ensign
LA TOUCHE, David [Digges] de	1692–1706	Ensign – Lt
LA TOUR, James	1692–1715	Ensign – Lt
LA TOUR, John	1689–1707	Ensign – Capt
LA TOUR, Mathew	1691	Ensign
LA TOUR, Paul	1689–(1727)	Ensign – Lt
LA TUILLIERE or LATEUILIERES, Abraham	1706?–1726	Cornet
De LAUNAY, Joseph	1690s–1729	Lt – Capt – Maj – Col
De LAUNE, Henry	1706–1727	Capt
LAURANS, Samuel	1703(?)–1727	Brigadier
LAUSSAC, Antoine D'Astor de [See also Gwynn (2015), 336–7]	1698–1726	Chaplain
LAUSSAC, Peter	1713–1714	Chaplain
LAUSSAN, David	1690s–1709/12	Capt
LAUTAL, Theodorus	1690s–1717	Lt – Capt
LAUSTALE or L'HOSTAL, John	1706–1726	Ensign – Lt
LOSTAL, John Peter	1711–1726	Ensign – Lt
[both the two above men were examined in 1726]		
LAVABRE, Claude	Q. Anne's reign–1730	Capt
LAVAL or LAVALL[E], David	1689–1717	Ensign
LAVALL[E], Francis	1708–1726	Quarter-Master
LA VAL, Peter (de)	1690s–1717	Capt
De LAVALL, Thomas	1689–1699	Capt

LA VALLETTE, Charles Cabriere de	1691–1701	Lt
LA VALLETTE, Daniel de	1692–1701	Lt. Col
LAVERGNE, Isaac	1706–1712	Cornet
LA VERNEDE, Cezar	1694–1701	Ensign
LA VIVARIE, Poncet de	1689–1706	Capt – Major
LAYARD, Peter	1696–1740	Major
LAYMERIE, Vincent	1689–1715	Cornet
LEARMONT, Robert	1690s–1717	Ensign
LE BAS, Francis	1693–1702	Lt
LE BAS, Paul Pierre	1692–1702	Ensign
LE BLANC, Albert	c. 1706	Chaplain

[See also Gwynn (2015), 225, *sub* Blanc]

LE BLANC, Louis	1695–1706	Lt
LE BLANC, James	1689(?)–1726	Capt [foot]
LE BLANC	1689–1706	Lt [horse]
LE BRETON, Paul	1711–1721	Quarter-Master
LE BRUN, Jacques	1691–1701	Lt
LE CERCLE, Peter	1689–(1700)	Capt
LE CLERCK, Peter	1710–1739	Cornet
LE COMTE, Estienne	1690–1702	Ensign
LE COQ DES MOULINS, Henry	1692–1702	Ensign
LEFANU, James	1712–1726	Ensign
LE FERON, Paul	1689–1713	Cornet – Lt
LE GRAND, Henry	1710–1714	Cornet
LE GRAND, Peter	1709–1724	Quarter-Master
LE HEUP, Isaac	1706–1707*	Ensign – Lt
LE MAIGNAN, Pierre	1694–1705	Quarter-Master?
LEMPRIERE, Clement	1706?–1726	Ensign
L'ENFANT, Alexander David	1689?–1734	Ensign
LENTILLAC or LENTILHAC, Henry	1689–1712	Lt
LE PETIT, Lewis	1689–1717	Lt
LERMONT, Lewis	1689–1712	Ensign – Lt – Capt
LES FOURNIER, Charles	1697?–1726	Quarter-Master
LESPINAY, John August	Queen.Anne's reign–1728	Lt
LESPOIS, Auguste de	1694–1709	Lt – Capt

LESPOIS, Legous de	1689–1693	Lt -Capt
L'ESTANG, Louis de	1692–1721	Lt – Capt
L'ESTANG, Nicholas de	1690–1697	Lt – Col – Brigadier –
Major-General		
LESTANGUETTE, Jean Jacques	1697–1718	Capt – Maj
LESTABLERE, René la Douespe	1689–1726	Ensign – Lt
De LESTRILLES, Isaac	1688–1709	Capt
L'ESTRY or LYSTRY, Jean	1706–1721	Lt
LE SUEUR, John	1711–1714	Quarter-Master
LE SUEUR, Peter	1706–1740	Chaplain
LETETRE, Gedeon	1708–1721	Ensign
LETHIEULLIER, John	1708–1718	Capt
LE TORT, James	1708–1717	Capt
De LEUZE, James	1690–1735	Lt – Capt
LEVESQUE, Jacob	1690–1702	Lt
LEVESQUE, Noah	1685–1692	Surgeon
L'HIRONDELLE or	1706–1717	Chaplain
L'HERONDEL, Francis Alexander		
[see also Gwynn (2015), 344–5]		
LIART, Samuel	By 1709–1740	Ensign
LICHERE, Nicholas	1697–1712	Capt
LIFFORD, Frederic William de	1688–1742	Maj – Col
Roye de Rochefoucauld, Count de		– Major-General
Marton and Earl of		
LIGER, Salomon	1689–1722	Capt
LIGONIER, Francis	1711–1746	Ensign – Lt. Col
LIGONIER, John Lewis	1689–1701	
LIMAREST, Jacques de	1695–1720	Cornet
LION or LYONS, Alexandre	1710–1712	Capt
LISLE, Charles François de	1689–1693	Capt
LISLE, Pierre de	1694–1702	Capt
LISLE, De	1689–1702	Cornet – Lt [horse]
LISLE DU ROY	1689–1702	Lt [foot]
LISLE MARAIS, Henri Boybellaud de	1689–1722	Capt – Lt.Col – Col – Maj.Genl
LIVERNE, Edward [de Leuze de]	1689–1709	Lt – Capt
LIVRON, Abraham de	1688–1702	Ensign – Lt – Capt
LOCHES, Anthony de	1689–1717	Ensign – Lt

LOCHES, David de	1691–1707*	Lt – Capt – Lt. Col
LOCHES or LOCKE, Salomon de Blosset de	1689–1717	Col – Brig. General
LOM, Peter de	1695–1722	Lt – Capt
LOMBARD, Elias	1709–1721	Lt
LOMBARD, Peter	1710–1716	Capt
LONGCHAMP, Paul	1689–1742	Lt – Capt
LORME, François de	1691?–1712	Ensign – Lt – Capt
LORTHE or LORTE, Isaac de	1689–1722	Capt
LOSTAL/L'HOSTAL, John Peter	1706–1740	Lt
LOUPILLE d'Auteuil	1689–1695	Capt
LOUPREZ or LONPRE, Charles Reboul de	c.1690–1731	Cornet
LOUVIGNY, Henry	1689–1710	Lt. Col
LOUVIGNY, Nicolas de (le cadet)	1689–1703	Capt
LUBIERES, (Francis de Langes de?)	1689–1702	Cornet
MACHINVILLE, Abel Armenaux de	1689–1715	Lt – Capt
MADAILLAN	1690*	Lt
MADRONET, Elizée de	1689–1691*	Capt – Engineer
MAGNY, Constantin de	1689–1722	Capt – Major – Col
MAILHÉ or MALLIÉ, Peter de	1695–1720	Quarter-Master
MAINAUDUC or MENANDUC, Alcide	1689–1726	Lt
MAINBRAY, Peter de	1689–1717	Ensign – Lt
MAIRARGUES, Francis	1708?–1726?	Lt
MAJOU, John [see also Gwynn (2015), 352]	1702–1724	Chaplain
MALBOIS, Gabriel de	1689–1700	Capt
MALERARGUES, Baron de	1689–1697	Cornet – Lt – Capt
MALFAQUERAT, Benjamin	1694–1699	Surgeon
MALHERBE, Olivier	1689–1726	Quarter-Mstr – Lt – Capt?
MALIDE, Benjamin	1702–1718	Capt
MALIDE, Paul (de)	1712–1730	Lt – Capt
MALLERAY, Francis	1695–1709	Lt
MALLERAY (de MAILLE), Isaac	1689–1717	Cornet – Lt

MALLET	1691–1698	Col
MALLIET, Anthoine	1708?–1727	Quarter-Master
MANICHER, Nathaniel	1697–1699	Quarter-Master
MARCEL, Anthony	1708–1742	Capt
MARCEL, Louis	1710 –1730	Ensign
[MARCHAIS see DESMARCHAIS]		
MARCHEGAY, Ozee	1708–1709	Lt
MARCONNAY, Samuel Philemon	1691–1742	Capt – Lt. Col
MARCONY	1697*	Major – Lt. Col
MARESCHAL, Jean	1689–1737	Capt
MARET, Guillaume	1690s?–1750s	Capt
MARET DE LA RIVE, Jean	1690s–1728	Capt
MARGARET, Peter [I]	1702–1713	Surgeon
MARGARET, Peter [II, and possibly III]	1712–1740	Ensign – Lt – Capt.Lt
MARGARET, Paul	1688–1721	Surgeon
MARGOT, Phillip	1690s–1731	Surgeon
MARTELL, Anthoine	1708–1709	Ensign
MARTELL, David	1710–1721	Capt
MARTELL, John	c. 1691–1734	Ensign – Lt – Capt
MARTIN, Paul	1689–1710	Ensign
MARTIN, Peter	1690s?	
MARVAUD or MARVAULT, Jean	1706–1726	Ensign – Cornet
MASCARINE, Paul	1706–1760	Ensign – Lt – Capt – Maj – Lt. Col – Maj.Gen
MASCLARY, Henry	1693–1730	Brigadier – Lt – Capt – Maj
MASSÉ, François?	1689–1715	Lt
MASSÉ or MASSIE, John	1695–1712	Engineer – Col – Lt. Col
MASSE, Samuel	1706–1718	Quarter-Master
MASSILOS, John	1689–1738	Lt – Capt
MASSY, Joseph	c.1706–1738	Cornet
MASSUGNIES, Carlot	1706–1715	Lt – Quarter-Master
MATHURIN, Pierre	1697–1728	Chaplain
[see also Gwynn (2015), 356 sub MATURIN]		
MAUCLERE, John	1693–1706*	Engineer – Capt – Lt. Col
MAUCO, Daniel	1689?–1726	Cornet

MAUPAS, Abel de	1689–1701	Capt
MAURICE, William	1699–1700	Capt
MAURIES, Jean	1706	Ensign
MAZERES, Abraham	1689–1714	Lt – Capt – Major – Col – Brig.Gen
MAZUEL, David	1699–1726?	Ensign – Lt
MAZUEL, Jacques	1696–1712	Surgeon
MEHEUX, Francis	1689–1716	Ensign – Lt – Capt
MEHEUX, John	1689–1705	Ensign
MELANCHE, François	1689–1694	Ensign – Capt.Lt
MELON, Daniel	1691–1714	Lt – Capt
MELON, James	by 1705–1717	Lt
MELYER/MESLIER, Caesar	1689–1734	Lt – Capt
MEMVIELE, John	1698–1699	Quarter-Master
MENIVAL, François du Val de	1695–1720	Capt
MERCIER, Claudius	dead by 1710	Lt
MERCIER, François	1699–1714	Lt – Capt
MERCIER (l'ainé – Jacques?)	1689–1706	Lt [foot]
MERCIER (le cadet – Pierre?)	1689–1717	Lt [foot]
MERCIER [Possibly Claudius??]	1689–1702	Lt [horse]
MESTRE, John (Le or De)	1689–1717	Lt
MEURE, Charles Francis de	1688–1694	Lt – Capt
MEYRAN, John	1709–1716	Lt
MEZERAC, Marc Antoine	c. 1695–1740	Cornet
MICHEL, Jacques	by 1693–1717	Quarter-Master
MIGET, Henry (I) and (II): between them [one died 1723, the other 1755]:	c.1686–1755	Trooper? – Quarter-Master – Adj – Capt
MILLERY, Guy Alexander	1689–1717	Lt – Capt
MILLON, John de	1693–1706	Captain-Lt – Capt
MIMET, Cosme de	1689–1722	Capt
MIREMONT, Armand de Bourbon, marquis de	1688- 1732	Col – Major-General – Lieutenant-General
MOLIE, Estienne ("senior") [No information about Molie jr]	1689–1706	Ensign – Lt
MOLIENS, Jacques de	1689 -1701	Capt – Lieutenant-Col

MONBRISSON, Charles de Vulson, sieur de	1700–1706	Capt
MONCAL, André d'Avessein de	1689–1730	Lt – Capt
MONCAL d'Avessein, Mark Anthony [see also DAVESSEIN]	1692–1729	Cap – Maj – Lt. Col – Brig. Gen
MONCAUT, de [l'ainé]	1689–1700	Capt
MONCAUT, de [le cadet] [One of the two De Moncauts was named Jean]	1689–1700	Capt
MONCORNET, David	1689–1732	Lt
MONGINOT	1701–1707	Dr
MONGUION, Henry de Cordon de	1689	Capt
MONTGAUD or MONGAULD, James	1689?–1717	Ensign
MONTANDRE, François de la Rochefoucauld, marquis de	1693–1739	Capt – Col – Major-General – Lieutenant-General – Field Marshal
MONTARGIE, Gabriel de Philiponneau de	1689–1694	Capt
MONTARGIE, John de Philiponneau de	1691–1710	Lt. Col – Col
MONTAUBAN, Alexandre de Saint-Féréal de Chevrieres, marquis de	1693–1699	Col
MONTAUT, Jacques de	1689–1723	Capt – Lt. Col
MONTAUT, Jean de	1690–1702	Capt
MONTBRUN, Jean du Puy, marquis	1693*	Col
MONTEZE or MONTAISE, Henri de la Tremouille de	1689–1713	Capt.– Lt. Col – [Dutch] Major General
MONTFORT or MONFORT, Pierre	1690s–1742	Lt
MONTLEDIER, Jean	1690s–1731	Lt – Capt
MONTRESOR, Jacques Gabriel de	1689–1724	Ensign – Lt – Cap – Major
MONTROY, Abraham du Verge de	1689–1704	Capt
(MOREL) LA BAUVE, Philip	1689?–1742	Capt
MORELLE, Elie	by 1706–1726	Lt

MORELON, Etienne	1706–1726	Surgeon
MORIN, Guy	1692–1707	Adjutant – Lt – Capt
MORIN, Peter	1690–1715	Ensign – Lt – Capt
	[see also card *sub* BORD]	
MOZET(TE) or MUZETT, John	1698–1702	Quarter-Master
NAJAC, [Mark] Anthony de Gineste, sieur de	1694–1741	Cornet – Lt – Capt
NAVEZ, Peter	1699–1702	Ensign
NEAU, Martin	by 1691–1701	Lt
[NEVILL	1710–1713	Col., but why supposed French?]
NICHOLAS, John	1691–1739	Cornet – Lt – Capt
NISSOLE, Stephen	1694–1717	Ensign
NOIRAY or NORRY, Francis	1710–1726?	Lt
NOLLET, Constantin (de)	1706–1707*	Lt
NOUVELL, Peter	1708–1733	Quarter-Master
ODAT or AUDAT, Jean	1701–1714	
d'OFFRANVILLE, Peter	1693–1720	Ensign – Lt – Capt – Maj
OLIVIER, Jean	1692–1717	Adjutant – Cornet – Lt
OSMONT, Augustin	1706–1726	Lt
OURRY, Lewis	1709–1726	Ensign – Lt
PAGEZ, Peter Gilbert de	1689–1721	Engineer – Lt – Capt – Lt.Col
PAILLET, James	1710–1718	Quarter-Master
PAIN, Daniel or David	1706–1730	Quarter-Master – Lt – Capt
PAJON or PAJOU, Gaspard	by 1699–1726?	Ensign – Cornet
PAJON or PAJOU, Louis	1706–1721	Ensign – Cornet
PANDIN or PAUDIN, Gaspard	1703–1717	Lt
PANSIER, Andrew	1703–1730	Cornet – Lt – Capt
PAPIN or PEPIN, Jean	1689–1717	Lt – Adj – Capt
PAPIN, Louis	1689–1715	Lt
PAPOT, John	1693–1717	Quarter-Master
PARIS, [l'ainé]	1689–1704	Ensign

PARIS, [le cadet]	1689–1704	Ensign
PARIS, Ferdinando	1685–1712	Ensign – Lt – Capt
PASCAL, Benjamin	1689–1715	Lt – Capt?
PASCAL, Henry	1709–1726	Ensign
PASSY, Josiah (de)	1689–1694	Capt
PASSY, Louis (de)	1690–1742	Lt
PASTOURELLE, Peter	1689–1701	Capt
PASTRE, Peter	1709–1714	Lt
PAULIN, Charles de la Tour, Comte de	1689–1713	Cornet – Capt – Maj – Lt.Col
PAVILLARD, Jonas	1706–1729	Lt
[PAYZANT, James	1711]	
PECHELS, Jacob	1701–1740	Ensign – Capt – Lt. Col

[son of Samuel de Pechels La Boissonade, see La Boissonade]

PECQUEUR, Daniel	1708–1730	Lt – Capt
PEGAT or BEGAT, Charles de	1689–1714	Lt
PELLAT, Alexander	1689–1717	Lt
PELLISIER, Abel	1689–1727	Quarter-Master – Lt
PELLISIER, Abel jr	1708–1714	Adjutant (– Lt?)
PELLISIER, James	1704–1714	Lt – Capt
PELLISIER, Louis (de)	1689–1704	Capt
PELTIER or PELETIER, James	1690–1721	Cornet – Lt – Capt.Lt
PERRIN[ET], Estienne	1690s–1731	Ensign – Cornet
PERROT[E], Daniel	1690–c.1706	Ensign
PETIT, Isaac Francis	1693–1706*	Engineer – Capt – Lt. Col
PETIT, James	1696–1730	Engineer – Lt – Capt – Maj
PETIT, John	1695–1700	Engineer – Capt

[The cards also provide information about another? Capt John Petit in the 1720s]

PETIT des Etans, Lewis	1689–1720	Engineer – Ensign – Lt – Capt – Lt.Col – Brig
PETIT, Peter (I)	1689–1698	Col
PETIT, Peter (II)	1713–1758	Lt – Capt
PETIT	1688–1694	Capt [horse]
PETIT BOSC, Daniel le Grand de	1689–1737	Lt. Col
PETITOT, Stephen (I)	1690s–1731	Cornet – Capt
PETITOT, Stephen (II)	1711–1730	Ensign – Lt
PEYRAUBE, Francis	1710–1732	Lt – Capt

PHILIBERT, Paul	1690	see card *sub* BORD
PIAGET, Amy de	1690s–1739	Capt
PIAGET, Peter	1712–1740	Ensign
PINCHINAT, Abraham	1709–1727	Ensign – Lt
PINCHINAT, Isaac	c.1690?–1706	Quarter-Master – Lt
PINEAU	1689–1702	Quarter-Master
PINEAU, Paul	1689–1717	Lt
PINIOT, Augustus	1703–1749	Ensign – Capt.Lt – Capt
PINSON, Edward	1688–1726	Ensign – Lt – Quarter-Master
PINSUN, Peter	1689–1720	Lt
PIQUENIT, Cezar	1711–1726	Lt
PLAFOY, Claude	1690s–1747	Cornet
PLANTAT, Henry	1689	Chaplain
PLANTEAU, Estienne	1689–1693	Lt
POILBLANC, Henry	1695–1717	Ensign – Lt – Capt
[DU] PONCET, Guillaume	1689–1720	Capt
PONTBISSON, Jacques	1690s–1704	Quarter-Master
PONTEREAU, François (de)	1689–1720	Capt
PONTHIEU, Abraham (de)	1708–1732	Ensign
PONTHIEU, Charles (de)	1689–1726	Lt – Capt
PORTAL, John	1690s–1716	Lt – Capt
PORTAL, Peter	1689–1720	Lt
PORTEBISE	1689–1691	Ensign – Lt
POUCHAUD, Nicholas or Michael	1704–1719	Ensign
PRAT, Pierre [l'ainé]	1689–1710	Lt
[nothing here on any Prat le cadet]		
PRESSAC	1689–1702	Capt
[PREVEREAU, Gaspard	1711]	
PROU, Arnold	1689–1717	Capt
PRUEZ or PRUER	1689–1691	Lt
PUICHENIN, Japhet (de)	1689–1729	Lt – Capt
PUISARS or PUIZAR, Louis Jacques Vasseur Congné, marquis de	1695–1701	Col
PUJOLAS, Anthony	1693–1740	Engineer – Ensign – Lt – Capt – Maj – Lt. Col
PUJOLAS, [St] Denis	1694–1712	Ensign – Lt – Capt

PUJOR or PRYOR, Louis	1699–1701	
QUESTEBRUNE, John Pestallieur	1691–1699	Capt
QUINCHANT, John Janvre	1706–1727	Ensign – Capt.Lt – Capt
QUINSAC, Charles (de)	1690s–1745	Capt
QUINSON	1691–1702	Ensign
RABAR, Auguste de	1689–1694	Capt – Lt. Col
RABAR, Peter	1692–1694	Capt
RABAUD, Reney	1693–1697	Ensign
RABOTEAU, George	1694–1701	Lt
RABINIERE(S), James	1694–1698	Ensign – Lt
RABINIERE(S), Theophilus de	1691–1705	Major – Lt. Col
RADA, Henri de Caumont, Marquis de	1688–1695	Capt – Lt.Col – Col
RANDON, Paul	1703–1720	Lt (- Capt)
RAPIN, Jean de	1689–1695*	Capt – Major
RAPIN [-THOYRAS], Paul de	1689–1693 (d.1725)	Ensign – Lt – Capt
RAPIN, Salomon	1686–1719	Ensign – Capt – Maj – Lt. Col
RASINGUES, Jean	1706–1707	Ensign
RAVENAL, Daniel de	1694–1711	Cornet – Lt – Capt?
RAZE, Peter	1708–1713	
RAZOUX, Henry	1690s–1708	Quarter-Master – Lt
RAZOUX, James	1709–1731	Lt
REFFIER, Lewis	1709	Col
REGNAUT/REGNAUD, Noah	1706–1727	Cornet
REGNAUT/REGNAUD, Peter	1694–1718	Ensign – Lt – Capt
REGNIER, Lewis	1693–1710	Lt
RENOUARD, David	1697–1715	Cornet – Capt
RENOUARD, Peter	1701–1762	Cornet – Lt – Capt – Maj – Lt. Col
RIBIER, Gedeon	1693–1708	Ensign – Lt
RIBOT, Charles	1709–1726	Adjutant – Cornet
RIBOT, James	1709–1726	Cornet
RIBOT, Peter	1690s–1739	Quarter-Master – Lt – Capt.Lt

RICARD, John	1709–1726?	Ensign
RICHARD, Charles	1696–1704	Ensign – Lt
RICHIER, Andrew	1690–1740	Cornet – Lt – Capt
RICHIER, Nicholas	1710–1715	Quarter-Master
RICHON, Bernard	1706–1733	Chaplain
[see also Gwynn (2015), 387–8]		
RIEUTORT, Guillaume	1689–1726	Capt – Maj – Col
[There is a possibility of a second Rieutort, a Lt in 1689 –1690]		
RIFFIER, Lewis	1691–1717	Capt – Col
RIGAUDIE, Alexander	1690?–1706	Cornet – Lt
RIGAUDIE, Marc	1699–1717	Cornet
RIQUET, John	1711–1714	Quarter-Master
RIVAL(L) or RIVALS, Lewis [no.1]	1689–1717	Ensign – Lt
RIVAL(L) or RIVALS, Lewis [no.2]	1689–1711	Ensign – Lt – Capt
RIVAL(L), Peter	1688–1736	Chaplain
[see also Gwynn (2015), 388–90]		
RIVAS(S)ON, John	1693–1718	Ensign – [Capt.]Lt
RIVRY or RIVERY, Francis?	1689–1702	Cornet
ROBINAU, Denis	1706	Ensign
ROCHEBLAVE, Louis de	1690s–1721	Ensign – Lt
ROCHEMONT, James (l'aîné)	1689–1717	Cornet
[no information here about any Rochemont le cadet]		
ROISSY or ROIFFEY, John	1700–1726	Surgeon – Major
ROMAGNAC, John (de)	1689–1710	Lt. Col
RONDELET, Francis	1690s?–1726?	Lt
ROSOY	1689–1694	Capt – Major
ROSSET, Louis (de)	1690–1720	Capt
ROSSIERES or ROUSSIERS, Jean (de)	1689–1717	Capt
ROUSSET DE SOULEGRE, Andrew de	1695–1697	Capt
ROU or ROUX, Solomon	1689–1732	Ensign – Lt
ROUX, Abraham	1706–1717	Ensign – Lt
ROUX or ROUSSE, James	1689–1732	Ensign – Lt
ROUSSEAU, Anthony	1689–1696	Surgeon
ROUSSILLON or ROSSILLON, Henry	1689–1740	Ensign – Lt – Capt.Lt
RO(U)VIERE, Peter	1708–1710	Surgeon

RUFANE, Francis Duchesne *alias*	1688–1740	Capt.Lt – Capt – Major
RUYNAT, Daniel	1689–1726	Capt
RUVIGNY, Henri de Massue, Marquis de, later Viscount and Earl of Galway	1690–1720	Col – Maj. Gen – Lt. Gen
RYVES, Jean [I]	1697	Capt
RYVES, Jean [II]	1698–1708	Cornet
SACCONAY BURSINEL, Jean de	1694–1706	Lt. Col – Col – Brigadier
SAGEAUX, Charles de	1691–1699	Cornet
SAILLY, Charles de	1695–1726	pensioned "Officier" but did he serve?
SAILLY, Isaac	1706–1740	Lt – Capt
SAILLY, Michel de Bures	1689–1713	Lt
ST AGNAN, Alexander	1689?–1726	Lt
ST AMOUR, Claude	1707?–1726?	Cornet
ST AMOUR, James	1704?–1734	Quarter-Master
ST AUBIN, Guy de	1689–1700	Ensign or Lt
ST AUBIN, Jacques de	1689–1699	Capt – Lt.Col
ST BREST, Jean	1706–1709	Ensign
ST CHRISTOL de Liverne, James	1689?–1739	Cornet – Lt – Capt
ST CYRE	1692–1702	Capt
ST ELOY, Isaac Gouicquet de	1689–1728	Capt
ST ELOY, Moses Gouicquet de	1695–1702	Ensign
ST ESTIENNE, François?	1689–1701	Ensign
ST FAUSTE	1689–1702	Lt
ST FERIOL DE LA TOUCHE, Charles	1699–1742	Cadet – Capt
ST GABRIEL (LE LOU), Gabriel de	1689–1714	Capt
ST GEME(S) or ST JEME	1689–1702	Lt – Capt
ST GERMAIN, Gaston Pompée de Goron	1689–1717	Capt
[the cards also mention two brothers killed in Ireland]		
ST HERMINE, Henri Louis, marquis de	1689–1715	Major
ST HIPOLITTE, David Montolieu, Baron de	1689–1761	Ensign – Lt.Col – Col – Brig.Gen – Maj.Gen – Lt.Gen – General

ST JEAN, Philippe de	1692–1702	Lt
ST JUST, Peter de	1689–1704	Ensign – Lt
ST LEGER, Joseph de	1689–1706	Lt
ST LEGER DE BACALAN, Thomas de	1706–1711*	Capt – Lt. Col
ST MAISON, Philippe de Parantau	1689–1710	Capt
ST MAISON, Martial de Parenteau	1699–1700	Cornet
ST MARTIN, Claudius	c.1685–1702	Quarter-Master
ST MARTIN, Isaac	1695–1723	Lt – Capt
ST MARTIN, James	1689–1699	Ensign – Lt – Capt
ST MAURICE, Charles	1695–1740	Capt
ST MAURICE, Marc de Vulson	1693–1720	Capt
ST MEARD, Pierre La Gramere	1690s–1726?	Ensign – Lt
ST MESMIN, Etienne	1689–1736	Capt
ST PAU or PEAU, Girard	1689–1739	Lt
ST PAUL, Hannibal de	1689?–1695	Ensign
ST PAUL, Stephen Taillourdean (de)	1694–1705	Lt – Capt
ST PHELIX or FELIX, Pierre de	1690–1710	Lt – Capt
ST PHILBERT, Jacques Mauclere de	1689–1723	Capt
ST PIERRE, James, *alias* Peter Jaquin	1685–1713	Cornet – Capt – Maj – Lt.Col
ST PUY, Joseph	1689 –1717	Lt – Capt
ST SAUVEUR	1689–1710	Lt
ST SAUVEUR, Camille	1689–1690*	Capt
ST SIMON, John Lewis (de)	c.1707–1726?	Lt
ST YOUR or SAINTOUR or ST JORE, La Coste (de)	1689–1703	Lt

[one side of one card sub DESCLAUX also relates to this officer]

SALBERT DE MARSILLY, Peter	1710–1726?	Cornet
SALLES	1689–1702	Lt
SAMAZON, Andrew	1692–1706	Lt – Capt
SANDOS, Abraham	1694–1715	Ensign
SARLANDE, Joseph	1689?–1722	Lt. Col
SAUBERGUE, Jacques	1689–1723	Ensign – Lt – Capt

[There may have been another Saubergue, a Captain-Lieutenant in 1717]

SAURENCY, Euvert de Meausse de	1692–1702	Ensign – Lt – Capt

SAURIN, Estienne de Marraul(d)	1689–1741	Quarter-Master – Lt – Capt
SAUSSURE, John Francis de	1692–1707	Ensign – Lt
SAUTEL(LE), Francis	1690s–1726?	Ensign – Lt
SAUVAGE, John	1710–1728	Ensign
SAUVAGIE	1689–1712	Capt
SAVARY, John Tausia, sieur de	1699–1720	Lt. Col
SAVONETT, Jaque Daniel	1691–1702	Cornet
SCALÉ	see ESQUALET	
SEDIERE, Gabriel	1713–1740	Ensign – Lt
SEDIERE, Louis de	1694–1726?	Capt – Major – Lt.Col
SECQUEVILLE, Jean de	1689–1710	Capt
SENEBIER(E), Lewis	By 1709–1726?	Quarter-Master
SENEGAS or SENEQUA, Lewis de	1692–1699	Ensign
SENEGAS, Pierre de	1699–1703	
SERBIER or SORBIERE, Theophile	1702–1706	Lt
SERMENT or SARMAN, Claude	1689–1700	Capt
SEVE, Etienne	1690?–1707	Lt
SIGONIERE	1690s–1706	Lt
SILVESTRE, Peter	1690s–1704	Physician
SIMOND or SIMON, David	1689–1732	Lt – Capt
SINAULT, Daniel	1693–1703	Ensign – Lt – Capt
SISOL(L) or SYOLL, Pierre Vigne	1689–1714	Lt
SIVA(A), Jacques	1690s?–1735	Quarter-Master
SOLEIROL, Michel	Queen Anne's reign–1722	Cornet
SOLIGNÉE, François de	1701–1715	
SOUBERGNE or SOUBERGUE, Ja: de	1689–1697	Ensign – Lt
SOUBIRAN, John [Longuergine]	1698?–1740	Lt – Capt.Lt
SOUBIRAS, Peter	1689–1700	Lt
SOUCHES, Isaac de	1689–1708	Lt
SOULEGRE, de	1695–1697	Capt
STAMPLE, James	c..1706–1739	Lt
STONIER	see ESTAUNIÉ	
SUBERBIELLE or SUBERVILLE, Matthew	1711–1718	Lt

SURVILLE, John	1691–1722	Ensign
TASCHER René de	1693–1709*	Ensign [- Capt in Dutch service]
TAURANAC or TOURANAC, Jean [Louis de]	1690s–1720	Ensign – Lt
TAURIAC or TORIAC, Anthony de	1689–1699	Lt – Capt
TEISSIER, John	c.1703–1726?	Ensign – Lt
TEISSONIERE, David de	1697–1707*	Ensign – Lt – Capt
TEMPIÉ, Stephen	c.1696–1730	Lt – Capt
TERNAC, Francis Joly de	1693–1742	Ensign
TERNAC de St Eugene, Joseph	1689–1700	Lt
TERRONDET, Henry de	1707–1714	Ensign – Lt?
TERROT, Jean Charles	1689–1735	Lt – Capt
TERSON, Mark Anthony	1694–1702	Ensign
TERSON, Thomas	1689–1718	Lt – Capt
TERSON, Thomas jr	1689–1749	Ensign – Lt
TESTEFOLLE, Claudius	1694–1730	Cornet – Lt – Capt.Lt – Capt – Major
THAROT, Gabriel de	1689–1725	Capt
THENIE, Lewis de Garron de	1689–1706	Capt
THERMIN	c.1692–c.1705	Lt
THEROND, Durand sr	1690–1717	Cornet – Lt
THEROND, Durand jr	1710–1731	Ensign
THIAU DE BLEVILLE, John Baptist	1708–1740	Cornet
THOMAS, John	1695–1717	Engineer – Capt
THOMAS, Cesar	1699–1709	Ensign – Lt
TOUSSAINT, Peter	1699–1723	Surgeon
TRELLEBOIS (TRAILBOYS), Jacques Vigier sieur de	1689–1706	Ensign – Capt
TREMOLET, Jacques du	1690–1714	Capt
TREPSAC, John [see also Gwynn (2015), 416–7]	1706–1727	Chaplain
TRONCHAY, Paul	1692–1703	Ensign – Lt – Capt – Maj
TURPIN, Lewis	1702?–1727	Ensign – Lt
BRUNEVAL VALADA, de	1689–1702	Lt – Capt.Lt

VALADA, Joseph de	1689–1715	Lt – Capt
VAL(L)ADE, Timothy	c.1707–1727	Ensign – Lt
VALENTINE, Laurens	1712–1717	Quarter-Master
VALOGNE, Marc Antoine	1691–1740	Capt
VALSERY	1689–1702	Capt
VANDIERE, Charles Drouart	1698–1720	Cornet
VAREILLES, John (James)	1695–1709	Ensign
VARANGLE, John de	1689–1728	Capt – Lt. Col
VAUCLEN, Theophilus de	1695–1705	Ensign – Lt
VAURY, John	1690–1717	Capt
VAUX, Peter de(s) or D'AVAUX	1693–1716	Adjutant – sub-Lt
VEBRON, sieur de	1690–1694	Capt
VEDEAU, Andrew	1710–1728	Lt
VEILLE, Tho: de	1708–1709	Lt – Capt
VENDARGUES, Camille Ric: de	1694–1698	Ensign
VERCHAUD, Peter	1706–1714	Lt
VERDELLE(S) Joigny, de	1689–1702	Capt
VERDIER, John	1689–1695	Capt
VERNOUX, Moses	1690–1718	Lt
VESTIEU or VESTIEN, John	1689–1720	Ensign – Lt
VIALAS or VIALLARD, Jean	1700–1724	Quarter-Master
VIALAS, Jérémie	1689–1702	Lt
VICOZE, François, Baron de	1690–1713	Capt – Lt. Col [- Col – Maj.General in Dutch service]
VIGNALS, Abel Ligonier de	1706–1709	Lt
VIGNE, François	1690s–1717	Ensign
VIGNEAU, Pierre	1689–1749	Ensign – Lt – Capt.Lt
VIGNEAU, Theophilus	1710–1745	Major
VIGNEUL, Louis	1689–1720	Ensign
VIGNOLES, Charles (des)	1689–1725	Capt
VIGNOLES, Francis	1691–1709*	Capt – Major
VIGNOLES	1711	Cornet
[son of Francis, see that card: did he actually serve?]		
VILAS, François de	1690s–1705*	
VILLARNOUL, Philippe de Jeancourt, marquis de	1689–1706	Ensign – Capt.Lt – Capt – Maj
VILLE, Paul	1697–1717	Ensign – Lt?

VILLEBON de Fremont, John	1689–1704	Ensign – Capt
VILMISSON or VILLEMISSON, James	1689–1717	Quarter-Master – Lt
VILMISSON or VILLEMISSON, John	1702–1737	Lt
VILLENEUVE, Anthony	1689–1700	Capt
VILLENEUVE, Gideon	1689–1701	Capt
VILLENEUVE, John (I)	1713–1716	Quarter-Master
VILLENEUVE, John (II)	1706?–1726?	Quarter-Master
VILLENEUVE, Josias	1692–1717	Lt
VILLETTES or VILLATTES, Alexandre Auguste, Baron de	1696–1723	Brig – Capt – [– Maj – Maj/Lt.Gen in Dutch service]
VIMARÉ du Petit Bosc, Josias de	1689–1724	Maj – Lt. Col – Col – Brig. Gen.
VIMIELLE, Andrew	1702–1727	Surgeon
VINCENT, Peter	1690	Capt
VINOIES, Gedeon de la	1706?–1726?	Quarter-Master
[VIRAZEL, Jacques de Belrieu, Baron de	1693–1719	Military pension but no rank?]
VIRAZEL, Daniel de Belrieu, Baron de	1689–1742	Ensign – Capt
VISSOUSE, Francis	1709–1740	Ensign – Lt – Capt
VISSOUSE, Guy	1711–1721	Ensign – Cornet
VITRACK, James	[served in Spanish peninsula in Anne's reign]	
VIVENT/VIVENS/VIVAINS, Michael (le cadet)	1689–1699	Lt
VIVENT/ VIVENS/VIVAINS, Peter (l'ainé)	1689–1699	Capt
VIZER or VISIER, Bernard	1696–1701	Ensign
WARQUIN, Daniel	1698–1711*	Gunner – Adjutant – Lt
WIBAULT, Jacques	1695–1715	Engineer – Lt – Major

APPENDIX 2

Some Rank-and-file Huguenot Soldiers, 1699

Under normal circumstances, there are no surviving sources that allow the historian to view individual refugees serving as common rank-and-file soldiers. However, the London Metropolitan Archives house one fifteen-page unpaginated document (COL/CHD/PR/05/02/053 [bundle 5 no.42]) that provides a brief glimpse of one group of several hundred such men in April–May 1699 and notes their places of origin. It is so exceptional that the information it provides has been given in this appendix.

The document that has survived is not military in its nature and says nothing about rank apart from identifying one sergeant. Rather it is part of the extensive records kept by the French Committee administering public charity, whose activities were discussed in chapter 7, Volume II of *The Huguenots in Later Stuart Britain*. Normally the Committee had nothing to do with payments to soldiers, but the circumstances were extraordinary after various regiments had been broken in Ireland. One result was the appearance of this group of men in London, where they received some assistance. Some of them are specified in the record as going on to the Netherlands; these are indicated below by an asterisk (*) in the Comments column. Occasionally we learn that the soldier was accompanied by his wife (W) and children (W & C), or that he was given funding for apprenticeship (A) or 'pour estre placé' (P), or that he was ill (I).

The description in the master account presented by the French Committee to the English Committee for auditing (LMA, COL/CHD/PR/05/01/011) reads, 'To several poor disbanded soldiers both in England and Ireland, was distributed from the 12th April 1699 to 18th August ensuing as appears per account no.42, the sum of one hundred pound'. In fact, as the 789 entries in the accounts show, the money had all been spent by the end of May. Many of the soldiers had received several small payments, so the total of one hundred pounds allowed assistance to 309 individual men. A possibility of error exists if any entry in the following table masks two individuals or, conversely, if two separate entries refer to the same person, but any such errors should be statistically insignificant.

For all but fourteen individuals, the place or region from which they have come is given. The list includes one Vaudois from the 'vales de Lucerne', a Scotsman, a pair of brothers described as 'Walloon', eleven from Switzerland including six from Geneva and two from Metz. Otherwise, they came from all parts of France. Those from the north included seventeen from Picardy and 28 from Normandy. There were eight from Châtillon-sur-Loire and five from Paris. Most, however, came from the southern provinces, with about 120 from Languedoc and Dauphiné, including four from the Pragelas valleys on the Dauphiné–Italy border, and fifteen from Vivarès, the Occitan name for the Vivarais region, now the Ardèche.

SURNAME	FIRST NAME	FROM	COMMENTS
Algret	Phelix	Cévennes	
Aliaume, Aleausme	Jean	Normandy	(A)
Alison	Jean	Vivarès	
Amalere	Jean	Switzerland	
Ambroise	David	Metz	
André	Anthoine	Languedoc	(*)
André	Pierre	Poitou, Dauphiné	
Arnat, Arnal, Arnaul	André	Cévennes	
Arnault	Pierre	Dauphiné	
Arpenteur or L'Arpenteur	Batiste	Picardy	
Audry	Jean	Dauphiné	
Baissa, Beÿsa	Pierre	Languedoc	
Barbay	Christian	Lausanne	
Bardon	David	Languedoc	
Bart or Bard	Jean	Dauphiné	(*)
Basset	Jean	Saint-Antonin	
Beaufort	Anthoine	Dauphiné	(*)
Beaupois	Pierre	Poitou	
Belier	Jean		
Benoist	Anthoine	Millau, Rouergue	
Berard	Jean	Sainte Foy	(*)

Bernard	Abel	Dauphiné	
Bertain	Jacob	Normandy	
Bertain, Berthain	Paul	'vales de Lucerne', Vaudois	(W)
Berteau, Bertheau	Alexandre	Paris	
Bertheau	Salomon	Sedan	
Berthelot	Jean	Pragelas	(*)
Berthon, Berton	Jacques	Mer	
Beÿ	Abraham	Picardy	
Bezanson, Besançon	Jean	Provence	
Bidau	Jean	Beausse	
Bideault, Bideau	Jacques	Villeneuve	
Biron	Charles	Guise	
Bisset	Jacques	Saintonge	
Bisset	Jean	Saintonge, Languedoc	
Bissu, Bissus	Daniel	Picardy	
Blanc	Anthoine	St Martin, Dauphiné or Pragelas	(*)
Blanc or Le Blanc	Daniel	Pragelas, Dauphiné	(*)
Blanc	Pierre	Provence	
Blay	Anthoine	Poitou, Dauphiné	
Boissonnet, Boissonier, Bissonet	André	Dauphiné	(W) (*)
Bonsens	Louis	Lusignan, Poitou	(W)
Boucairan, Bouquairan, Bouqueran	Pierre	Nîmes	
Bouche	Daniel	Dauphiné	
Boulenier	Moïse	Clairac	
Boumier	Mathieu	Dauphiné	
Bourdon, Boiradon, Bouredon	Pierre	Tonin	
Bourel	Abraham	Dauphiné	
Branssillon	Pierre	Cévennes	
Breton	Jacques	Mer	

Brian	Denis	Roissy, Picardy	(*)
Brian	Thomas	Picardy	
Brieres or Bruguiere	Jacob	Cévennes	(W & C)
Brieres	Pierre	Rouen	(*)
Briger or Brugier	Etienne	Uzès, Languedoc	
Brives, Brive	Elie	Mazères, Guyenne	
Brossard	Jean	Picardy	
Broüet	Jacques	Languedoc	
Brun	Pierre	Dauphiné	(*)
Brunet	Etienne	Pragelas, Dauphiné	(*)
Calvet	Claude	Montauban	(*)
Camaret	David	Languedoc	
Camplan, Complan	David	Alès, Languedoc	(*)
Casting	Lancelot	Pithiviers or Gatinois	
Cause	Pierre	Languedoc	
Caussé	Pierre	Montpellier	
Cauvet	Jean		
Caÿran, Cairan	Daniel	Guyenne	
Celier	Jean	Orléans	
Chambon	Paul	Vivarès	
Chamerson	Jean Pierre	Vivarès	
Charpentier	Joseph	Sedan or Metz	
Charraux	Jean	Languedoc	
Chaslon	Jean Jacques	Geneva	
Chassé, Chasse	Mathurin	Languedoc	
Chastenay	Jacques	Bresse	
Chuchel, Chuché	Jean	Vivarès	
Colet	Jacques	Languedoc	Brother of Jean
Colet	Jean	Languedoc	Brother of Jacques
Combete	Gamaliel	Dauphiné	
Conjon, Conion	Moïse		
Cosson	Isaac	Blois	
Costé	Jean	Normandy	(W)

Cotterel	Claude	Normandy	
Darret, Darrette	Daniel	Picardy	
Daspre, D'aspres	Moïse	Dauphiné	(*)
Dauché, Daucher	Alexandre	Vivarès	
Dauchier	André		
David	Jacques	Paris	
Deban, Debanc	Jean Pierre	Iverdun	(*)
Debault	Pierre	Switzerland	
Deferné, de Ferné	André	Dauphiné	
Deferné, Desfernée	Abraham	Geneva	
Delaloix	Pierre		(A)
Deleray	Jean	Mazères	
Deleu, de Leu	Joseph	Nérac, Guyenne	
Delions	Louis	Vivarès	
Doit, Douët	Paul	Châtillon-sur-Loire	
Dombre	Abraham	Nîmes	
Droüet	Jacques	Languedoc	
Dubois	Elie	Neuchâtel	
Dubois	Pierre	Nérac	
Du Cros	Jacques	Vivarès	
Dugual	Jean	Languedoc	
Duisseau	Pierre		
Du Mas	Anthoine	Montauban	(*)
Du Mas, Dumas	Guillaume	Montpellier	
Du Moulin	Jacques	Languedoc or Dauphiné	(*)
Du Moutier	Jean	Normandy	
Du Pont, Dupont	Jacob	Dauphiné	
Du Saule or Doueson	Pierre	Châtillon-sur-Loire	
Echevel, Echavel	Jean Pierre	Dauphiné	(*)
Elier, Ellier	Jacques	Normandy	
Espert	Elie	Bordeaux	(I)
Evain	Phillipes	Picardy	(*)

Faurnes	Pierre		
Fauvain	Jean	Dauphiné	
Fabereau	Mathieu	Nîmes, Languedoc	
Ferrand	Louis		
Fillet, Fillot or Flotte	Jean	Périgord	
Flandrin	Jean	Dauphiné	
Flandrin	Michel	Bordeaux, Guyenne	
Fleurier, Flurrier	Jean	Normandy	
Foix	Jean	Picardy	
Forcade	Pierre (twice Jean)	Béarn	(*)
Fortin	Louis	Cherbourg, Normandy	
Foubert	Etienne	Châtillon-sur-Loire	
Fougeroles, Frigerole	Jean	Cévennes	
Fougeron	Paul	Orléans	(W)
François	Jean	Picardy	
Fransillon	Pierre	Dauphiné	
Frasier, Frazier	Pierre	La Ferté	(*)
Frechenet	Jacques	Nîmes	
Frichet	Guillaume	Dauphiné	
Frigerolle, Frigerole	Jean	Languedoc	
Galand	Samuel	Dauphiné	
Galeau	Pierre	Picardy	
Gamenet	Pierre	Dauphiné	
Gautier	Pierre	Montauban	
Gelly	David	Provence	
Gely	Pierre	Dauphiné	
Genest	Pierre	Guyenne	(*)
Geofroy	Louis	Rouen	(*)
Gilles	Pierre	Dauphiné	
Girault or Girou	Jacques	Poitou	
Girault or Gireau	Jean	Paris or Meslé	

Gireau	Pierre	Pays de Gês	
Giroust	Abraham	Meaux	
Gourdon	André	Scotland	
Gourgonneau	Louis	Dauphiné	
Gourmay	Jacques	Picardy	
Goutard	François	Dauphiné	
Goutinay	Jacques	Picardy	
Granget	Michel	La Perouse	
Guasche, Gâche	Pierre	Languedoc	
Hareaux	Jacques	Languedoc	
Heliard	Jacques	Normandy	
Hemard	Daniel	Dauphiné	
Ignard	Daniel	Dauphiné	
Jacodard	François	Bresse	
Jaulin	Samuel	Dauphiné	
Jolivet	François	Normandy	(*)
Juge	Pierre	Guyenne	
Juin	Jean		
L'Abraham	Jean	Languedoc	
Laborie	Anthoine	Montauban	(*)
Labry, L'abry	André	Languedoc	
La Chaumette	Louis	Poitou	
La Combe	Jean	Clairac	(I) Brother of Pierre
La Combe	Pierre	Clairac	(I) Brother of Jean
La Combe	Pierre	Agen	
La Coste	Jean	Normandy	
La Croix	Charles (de)	Issoudun	(*) Brother of Jacques
La Croix	Jacques (de)	Issoudun	(*) Brother of Charles
Ladague	Jacques	Sedan	(*) But also (P)

Lafitte	Mathieu	Guyenne	
Lafleur	Jean	Dieppe	
La Marque, Lamarque	Jean	Béarn	
L'Amour, Lamour	Jean	Montauban	(*)
Laprayrie, Laprairie	Jacques	Normandy	
Laprayrie	Jean	Normandy	
La Salle, Lasalle	Daniel (de)	Béarn	
Laurens, Laurend	Jean	Languedoc	
Lausanne	Jean	Paris	
Lautier	Abel	Montauban	(*)
La Val	Pierre	Alès	
Laverteaux	Louis	Champagne or Sauses	
Lebeau, Labeau, Lebault	Daniel	Picardy	(I)
Lebreton	Jacques		(I)
Lebreton	Jean	Gien	
Le Clerc	François	Picardy	
Lefevre	Anthoine	Champagne	(*)
Le Louay or La Loy	Pierre	Saint-Lô, Normandy	(P)
Le Moine	Hilaire	Meaux	
Le Moine	Jacques	Meaux	(*)
Le Mousle	Pierre	Normandy	
Le Noir	Moïse	Switzerland	(*)
(Le) Rossignol	Jacob	Guise	
(Le) Rossignol	Jacques	Picardy	
L'Espine	Pierre	Dauphiné or Vivarès	
Leuse	Alexandre or Abraham	Languedoc	
Leuse	Etienne de	Viguan	
Levesque	Isaac	Normandy	(*)
Liege	Jacques	Poitou	
Lioutre	Pierre		
Lombart	Claude	Nîmes	

Lorme	Charles or Claude de	Languedoc	
Magnan	Jean Pierre	Normandy	(*)
Magny, Magné	(Jean) Pierre or Paul	Geneva	(*)
Mambourg	Jacob	Picardy	
Marchand	Daniel (Le)	Caen, Normandy	
Marin	Jacques	Dauphiné	
Maro or Marc	François	Poitou	
Martin, Martine	Jacques	Nîmes, Languedoc	
Martin	Jean	Montélimar	
Martin	Pierre	Vivarès	
Martroy	Jean	Châtillon-sur-Loire	
Michau	Abraham	Champagne	
Mignairon, Migneron	Joseph	Rouergue	
Miramont	François	Languedoc	Aged 27
Montaigu	Pierre	Languedoc	
Montenon	Gedeon		
Morin	Mathieu	Dauphiné	(*)
Morisset	Jean	Orléans	
Mouchan, Mouchen, Mouchamp	Charles	Dauphiné	
Moucouffé, Moucaufé	Jean	Brittany	(*)
Moulenier, Molenier	Moïse	Clairac	
Mousle	Pierre	Normandy	
Neel	Nicolas	Normandy	
Nogelet or Nougalade	Arnault	Bergerac, Périgord	
Nouriguat or Novinquat	Guillaume	Languedoc or Dauphiné	
Olimpe	Gabriel	Uzès, Languedoc	
Olivier or Olive	Joseph	Clairac	
Pasques	Jacques	Pontas[?]	

Peigné	Jacques or Pierre	Normandy	(I)
Pelé	Jacques	Paris	
Pelet	Jacques	Dauphiné	
Pelet	Mathieu	Languedoc	
Pepin	Abel	Dauphiné	
Perret	Etienne	St Martin, Dauphiné	(*)
Perret	Imbert	Dauphiné	(*)
Perret	Jacob	Switzerland	
Perrin or Perren	Etienne	Languedoc	(*)
Peton	Peau	Sedan	
Picq	Jacques	Alès, Languedoc	
Pilet or Pile, Pille	Jean	Tonin, Guyenne	
Plaut	Salomon	Châtillon-sur-Loire	
Pocque(s), Poque	Jacob	Béarn	(I)
Poisdebon, Poidebon	Pierre (de)	Poitou	'Sergent'
Ponsset	Joel	La Rochelle	
Porte	Jacques	Languedoc	(*)
Portier	Jean	Montpellier	
Pouetier	Jacques		
Poulingue	Phillipes	Normandy	
Poulard	Jacques	Normandy	(*)
Prevost	Jacques	Champagne	
Raillier	Jean	St Jean d'Angély	
Rambour(g)	Jean	Sainte Foy	(*)
Ranc, dit Chabanel	Jean Pierre	Vivarès	
Raul, Rahoul	Paul	Montauban	
Rauy	Elie	Dauphiné	
Rayard	Jean	Languedoc	
Raynault	Jacques	La Rochelle	
Renault or Reneau	Pierre	Languedoc	(W)
Resnier	Moïse	Languedoc	
Richard	Jacques	Languedoc	

Roger	Samuel	Gien or Châtillon-sur-Loire	
Rosel	Amand	Saint-Antonin	
Roulard	Jean de	Sedan	
Rouslin	Jean	Champagne	
Rousset	Mathieu	Valentin	
Rouvieres, Rouviere	Jacques	Languedoc	(*)
Rou or Roux	David	Anduze, Languedoc	
Roux	Hercule	Languedoc	
Ruÿnat	Anthoine	Grenoble	
Ruÿnat	Daniel	Grenoble	
Saint Bonnet, Sabonnet	Claude (de)	Lyon, Dauphiné	
Saint Romain	François de	Coignac or Saintonge	
Salafranque	Daniel	Languedoc or Guyenne	
Samuel	Thomas	Dauphiné	
Saulnier	Simon	Vivarès	
Sauset, Sauzet	Pierre	Guyenne or Nérac	
Sautier	Louis	Geneva	
Savin, Cevain, Sevain	Jean	Cévennes or Languedoc	(*)
Segain, Seguain	Moïse	Nérac	
Servel or Servet	Samuel	Geneva (once, Lions)	
Sevestre	Daniel	La-Ferté-sous-Jouarre	
Sigoulet	Michel	Nîmes	
Sigoulet	Pierre	Agen	
Sonnet	Pierre	Geneva	
Soulier	Jacques (Jacob)	Vivarès	
Sourbier	Jacques	Languedoc	
Soyer	Michel	Dieppe, Normandy	
Suchel	Jean	Vivarès	(I)

Tauvois	Henry	Walloon	Brother of Pierre
Tauvois	Pierre	Walloon	Brother of Henry
Tibault	Osée	La Rochelle	
Tiffault	Jean		
Tinlan or Tinlault	François	Vivarès	
Tissier	Jean	Languedoc	(*)
Ustache or Eustache	Pierre	Dauphiné	
Valette	Etienne	Languedoc	(I)
Vansson, Vanson	Salomon	Châtillon-sur-Loire	(*)
Vastier	Pierre	Languedoc	(*)
Vianés, Vienes, Viennes	Jean	Cévennes or Languedoc or Viguan	
Vidal	Isaac	Dauphiné	
Vidars	Isaac	Nîmes	
Vidault	Jacques	Orléans	
Vilot or Villot(te)	Marc	Vivarès	
Vivier	Moïse	Normandy	

* = Going on to the Netherlands
A = Funded for an apprenticeship.
I = Ill.
P = 'pour estre placé'.
W = Accompanied by wife.
W & C= Accompanied by wife and children.

APPENDIX 3

Elders and Deacons of the French Church of London, Threadneedle Street, 1640–1713

Identification of the lay officers of the French Church of London 1650–1700 was originally set out in the author's unpublished London University PhD thesis, 'The Ecclesiastical Organization of French Protestants in England ...' (1976). The thesis entries remain of value to researchers interested in the *quartiers* to which individual officers were allotted, and its accompanying chart enables the reconstruction of the entire elected leadership of the church in any year between 1650 and 1700 at a glance. In other respects the entries are superseded by the present analysis, which has been greatly extended and covers a longer period.

Abbreviations used in these references that do not appear in the list of abbreviations at the start of the volume are as follows:

A	*Ancien* or elder
Bianquis	Jean Bianquis [and Emile Lesens], *La Révocation de l'Édit de Nantes à Rouen* (Rouen, 1885) [two works in one volume, separately paginated]
D	*Diacre* or deacon
De Krey (1978)	Gary Stuart De Krey, 'Trade, Religion, and Politics in London in the Reign of William III' (PhD Dissertation, Princeton University, 3 vols, 1978)
Douen	O. Douen, *La Révocation de l'Édit de Nantes a Paris d'après des Documents Inédits* (Paris, 3 vols, 1894)
Eg. 2734	British Library, Egerton MS 2734, the 1641 Discipline of the Church signed by ministers and elders from 1666 to the 1740s

End	Endenized
Glass	D.V. Glass, *London Inhabitants within the Walls 1695* (London Record Society, 1966)
Lesens	[Jean Bianquis and] Emile Lesens, *La Révocation de l'Édit de Nantes à Rouen* (Rouen, 1885) [two works in one volume, separately paginated]
Moens (1884)	William John Charles Moens (ed.), *The Marriage, Baptismal, and Burial Registers ... of the Dutch Reformed Church, Austin Friars, London* (Lymington, 1884)
Nat	Naturalized
Papillon	A.F.W. Papillon, *Memoirs of Thomas Papillon, of London, Merchant (1623–1702)* (Reading, 1887)
Roseveare	Henry Roseveare (ed), *Markets and Merchants of the Late Seventeenth Century: The Marescoe – David letters, 1668–1680* (Oxford University Press for the British Academy, 1987)
Wagner Pedigrees	Genealogical material regarding Huguenot families collected by Anthony Wagner and held at the Huguenot Library, University College, London

When available, information is tabulated under the following headings:
NAME
BORN
ENDENIZED/NATURALIZED
IN OFFICE
TRADE, WEALTH, SOCIAL STATUS
FAMILY OR TRADE CONNECTIONS WITH OTHER CHURCH
OFFICERS

SURNAMES given are those as signed by the officers on taking office [Eg. 2734] or as most frequently found in the church records of this period. There are many variations: the company of deacons specifically recorded that the spelling of names did not matter provided the pronunciation was not changed [FCL, MS 52, p. 252]. Only a few of these variations are indicated in brackets; 'de Lillers', for example, is spelled in at least fifteen ways in the records, two – Delier and Delliers – being potentially misleading. Where there are multiple entries with the same surname, variants are given only under the first. Christian names have normally been modernized.

PLACE OF BIRTH is normally taken from the consistory minutes recording election to office, and given in a modernized and Anglicized form. Where only the province of birth is certain, this is provided in brackets.

ENDENIZATION ('End') AND NATURALIZATION ('Nat'). Where the officer was almost certainly endenized or naturalized, but there is uncertainty as to the year because different people of the same name appear in the lists, a simple 'Yes' has been entered, rather than a date. In some cases two dates are given, since many who were endenized or naturalized during the Interregnum chose to repeat the process after the Restoration. The evidence is normally drawn from the Huguenot Society Quarto Series volumes XVIII and XXVII. They are well indexed, and specific page references have not been given here.

Election to CHURCH OFFICE took place some days after the December/ January and June/July *Censures* at which it was agreed which officers should be discharged, and the minutes recording that and the new elections of *anciens* (A) and *diacres* (D) are to be found in MSS 5, 7 and 8 of the French Church Library in Soho Square. After the end of MS 8 there is a gap in the splendid series of consistory records, and information about the elders' dates of election is then drawn from the copy of the Church Discipline signed by ministers and elders between 1666 and the 1740s, which has become separated from the church records and is now Egerton MS 2734 in the British Library ('Eg. 2734'). Again, specific page references have not routinely been given here. With the gap in the records it becomes difficult to find out about the election of deacons and about when elders were discharged; thus, for example, we know from MS 8 and Eg. 2734 that Daniel Alavoine, the subject of the first entry below, served as deacon 1701–4 and was elected elder in 1706 and again in 1716, but we do not know how long he served as elder on either occasion.

In April 1688, the company of elders and the company of deacons were each enlarged from thirteen to eighteen members. The new officers then appointed [listed in HSQS LVIII, pp. 259–60] are the only ones for whom researchers should normally need to look beyond the regular entries of appointments in January and July, although the disharmonies of the time resulted in a lessened standard of record-keeping during the period of the Interregnum.

TRADE, WEALTH, SOCIAL STATUS, ENGLISH POLITICAL AFFILIATION. Particular attention has been paid to available information from the 1690s about (1) loans to the Exchequer in the early part of William's reign before the foundation of the Bank of England in 1694, (2) bank deposits and (3) trading activities – figures are supplied comparatively often for the year 1695–96 simply because this is the one year for which a largely complete picture can be formed [D.W. Jones (1971), 174n].

FAMILY RELATIONSHIPS. Where the source of information on family relationships has not been specified, it has been obtained by working out family trees based on the HSQS publications of the registers of the Threadneedle Street church. Many more family interrelationships could undoubtedly be found, but enough are shown to indicate the intense degree of personal and family knowledge and connections running through the consistory.

A

NAME: **Daniel ALAVOINE**
BORN: St Quentin
ENDENIZED/NATURALIZED: Oath roll naturalization 1710
IN OFFICE: D 1701–4; A 1706–? and later again 1716–? [Eg. 2734]
TRADE, WEALTH, SOCIAL STATUS: Silk weaver, with business quarters in the Old Artillery Ground and a 'great house' at Tottenham. His will, dated 1726 and proved 1728, included a pension to his wife of £200, £1000 to his daughter, and £100 to the church [HSQS LX, 4–5].

NAME: **Pierre ALBERT**
BORN: Bordeaux
ENDENIZED/NATURALIZED: End 1686, Nat 1698
IN OFFICE: D 1690–3; A 1698–1701
Messrs Laloze and Reneu stood as witnesses for Pierre and Susanne Albert on their admission to the church in 1686 [HSQS XXI, 2]. Pierre's work as elder in 1699 included investigating the numbers and needs of French soldiers cashiered from Irish regiments, and wider discussions of the refugees' situation [FCL, MS 8, ff. 88r, 99–100]. In 1703 he loaned £10 to the establishment of the French church of St Martin Orgars [LMA, MS 00994/I, p. 46].
TRADE, WEALTH, SOCIAL STATUS: Albert was a substantial wine merchant, of Swithin's Lane, Walbrook Ward [HSQS XVI, 201], and contributed £7000 to the New East India Loan of 1698 [D.W. Jones (1971), pp. 358 n.172, 478]. He maintained connections with Bordeaux, where his family held *bourgeois* status [Meller (1902), 23 and (for the privileges and responsibilities of this status) p. 25; *BSHPF* XL (1891), 46, 49, 78, 81].

NAME: **François AMONNET** (Ammonet, Ammonier, Amonett)
BORN: Loudun, c.1637 [J.T. Du Pasquier, pers. com.]
ENDENIZED/NATURALIZED: End 1682 with his wife, five children and six servants [HSQS XVIII, 132].
IN OFFICE: A 1682–3; died in office, December 1683. His work in 1683 included deputations to the Mayor and Bishop of London and Secretary Jenkins [FCL, MS 7, pp. 134–5, 145–6, 180].
WEALTH, SOCIAL STATUS, ENGLISH POLITICAL AFFILIATION: Well-connected former Paris merchant ('marchand de points de dentelles'), brother of Mathieu Amonnet who was an elder at Charenton. After François left France, his country house at Charenton was used for informal meetings of the consistory after ordinary meetings were banned. He arrived in England with personal goods reputed to be worth 400,000 livres, according to a French police report [Douen, II, 24]; they certainly included some 700 ounces of plate [*CTB, 1681–5, 255*]. One of the 'principaux de l'Eglise' consulted about the refugees, 1681 [FCL, MS 7, p. 80], he gave the church £50 in 1682 [FCL, MS 218, p. 62]. He established manufactures to assist refugees in England. He had previously helped persuade the Dutch authorities to grant privileges to Huguenot refugees. He was a Gentleman of the Privy Chamber to King Charles II, as he had formerly been to Louis XIV [*CSPD, 1682, 531*; Douen, II, 23].
FAMILY OR TRADE CONNECTIONS WITH OTHER CHURCH OFFICERS: His widow Jeanne née Crommelin was remarried to Jacques Dufay, December 1684. His daughter Jeanne married Robert Caillé, while another daughter, Susanne, married François Grueber [HSQS XXVI, 122, and LX, 8; Wagner Pedigrees *sub* Grubert]. Together with Claude Hays (I) and Daniel Duthais, Amonnet patented an invention of the manufacture of 'draped milled stockings', 29 July 1682 [*Subject-Matter Index (made from Titles only) of Patents of Inventions ... 1617... to 1852* (2 vols, 1854), patent no. 221].

NAME: **François ANDRIEU** (Andrews)
BORN: Honfleur
ENDENIZED/NATURALIZED: End 1687, Nat 1698
IN OFFICE: D 1696–9; A 1705–7. Andrieu was elected deacon just two months after his admission to the church, when its minister Charles Bertheau had witnessed on his behalf [HSQS XXI, 4]. As deacon he was in charge of withdrawing the children kept at Ware at the church's expense, kept a register of the names of poor orphans, and was involved with charity distribution to refugees and soldiers [FCL, MS 52, pp. 216, 219, 260].

ANET, see HANET

NAME: **Jean ARNAUD** (Arnaut)
BORN: La Tremblade [FCL, MS 8, f. 176r]
ENDENIZED/NATURALIZED: Men endenized 1697 [HSQS XVIII, 249] and taking oath roll naturalization 1710 [HSQS XXVII, 104] are possibilities, but the name is not uncommon. Another John Arnaud was naturalized in 1698 as part of Parliament's thanks to Hilaire Reneu, whose birthplace was given as Rochelle, for uncovering silk smuggling with France [HSQS XVIII, 255].
IN OFFICE: D 1702–5
TRADE, WEALTH, SOCIAL STATUS: One Jean Arnaud, married to Marie, was a Spitalfields weaver in 1702; another, married to Ester, was 'teneur de livre de la Compagnie des Tafetas Lustres' in 1699 [HSQS XVI, 223i, 349q]. The latter may be the man naturalized in 1698, who was then described as an officer in Hilaire Reneu's family employed in the making of Alamodes and Lustrings. No clear evidence links the church deacon to either.

NAME: **Louis AUGIER**
BORN: Bordeaux [FCL, MS 8, f. 230r]
ENDENIZED/NATURALIZED: 'Lewis Augier, born at Bordeaux…, son of Paul Augier and Anna' was naturalized in 1698 [HSQS XVIII, 253], but see below.
IN OFFICE: D 1705–6
TRADE, WEALTH, SOCIAL STATUS: Louis Augier was active in trading Bank stock from its beginnings, when he subscribed for £200 of original stock on behalf of a widow, Martha Dufour [BEA, M1/1, p. 36]. He was described as a merchant of Bow Lane when he became an original subscriber to the enlargement of the Bank's capital stock in 1697 (£313 for himself and £500 for James Augier of Rotterdam, merchant) [BEA, M1/6, Book B, nos. 192–3], and when transferring £500 Bank stock [BEA, AC 28/1513, 8 Nov. 1698]. He held £800 Bank stock in 1709 [P.G.M. Dickson, pers. com.].

All the above references except the last come from the 1690s, and timing suggests the deacon of the Threadneedle Street church may be a cadet member of the family rather than the original Louis. Mrs Carter examines the Augiers' activities, describing them as 'a rich family with plenty of investment experience' [*HSP* XIX (iii), 37–8].

B

NAME: **Pierre BAR** or **BARR** (I) (Baz, Bare, Bair)
BORN: Rouen
ENDENIZED/NATURALIZED: Nat 1657, 1660 [see under Pierre Barr (II) below]
IN OFFICE: D 1651–4; A 1655–8, 1662–5, 1669–72, 1675–8. As a deacon, Barr was involved in an attempt to come to terms with Jean d'Espagne's congregation in 1651 [FCL, MS 5, pp. 355–6]. His many services as elder included being church representative at the 1656 Colloquy [FCL, MS 5, p. 375], deputations to the Weavers' Company and successive Secretaries of State [FCL, MS 5, p. 437, 472, 556, 572, 690], heavy involvement in completing the church's rebuilding [FCL, MS 5, pp. 551, 562, 568] and work on behalf of the Piedmont churches [FCL, MS 5, p. 660]. He became an 'Adventurer' in the stock raised to establish French refugee linen manufacture at Ipswich, 1681–2 [Papillon, 118].
TRADE, WEALTH, SOCIAL STATUS, ENGLISH POLITICAL AFFILIATION: Barr was a very substantial merchant and merchant banker, with a wide range of activities including carrying wine and spirits from La Rochelle to Barbados, and pitch and tar from the Baltic to Rouen, in the early 1650s [*CSPD, 1651–2, 575*, and *1652–3, 47, 54, 480*]. He supplied naval provisions at Portsmouth in the mid-1660s and was agent and attorney for the French West India Company in the 1670s [*CTB, 1669–72, 755*, and *1672–5, 115, 457*]. Notes were frequently drawn on him, as also on Guillaume Carbonnel, to convey Louis XIV's subsidy to the English government – over £50,000 was passed on in notes drawn on Barr in 1676–7 [*CTB, 1676–9, 1317–21*]. In 1687 he was referred to as a banker ('banquiere') [*CTB, 1685–9, 1210*].

Barr was a moderate in the English Civil War; his objections to the seditious preaching and millenarian opinions of Jean de La Marche caused him to be suspended from communion in 1645 [Hessels, 1971; FCL, MS 5, p. 303]. See also:

NAME: **Pierre BARR** (II)
BORN: Rouen
ENDENIZED/NATURALIZED: 'Peter Barré' was naturalized in 1657 and 1660, described on the latter occasion as the son of Peter Barr and Susan; this seems likely to be Pierre Barr (I). 'Peter Bar, of London, the younger, born in Rouen ... son of William Bar and Mary', also naturalized in 1660, is probably Pierre Barr (II) [HSQS XVIII, 71, 77–8].

IN OFFICE: D 1662–3
TRADE, WEALTH, SOCIAL STATUS: One Pierre Barr was married into
the wealthy Le Gendre family [HSQS XIII, 163; Agnew (1886), I, 260].

NAME: **Jean BASIN** (Bassin, Bazin)
BORN: London
IN OFFICE: D 1663–6; A 1673–6. In 1657 he was a supporter of Elie
Delmé [*Consistoire* [1657]].
FAMILY OR TRADE CONNECTIONS WITH OTHER CHURCH
OFFICERS: His son Jean married Lea, daughter of Pierre Baudry.

NAME: Claude BAUDOUIN (Baudowin, Beadouen)
BORN: Tours, c.1654 [Wagner Pedigrees]
ENDENIZED/NATURALIZED: Nat 1698
IN OFFICE: D 1689–91, having presented his *témoignage* from Tours in
1673 [HSQS XXI, 14]; elected A 1714 [Eg. 2734]
TRADE, WEALTH, SOCIAL STATUS: Foreign master weaver [HSQS
XXXIII, 60], gentleman. Original subscriber to 1697 issue to enlarge the
Bank's capital stock, with £225 [BEA, MS M1/6, A, no.123].
FAMILY OR TRADE CONNECTIONS WITH OTHER CHURCH
OFFICERS: Brother of René Baudouin.

NAME: **René BAUDOUIN**
BORN: Tours, 1650
ENDENIZED/NATURALIZED: Nat 1677–8
IN OFFICE: D 1682–5. He carried out the work of elder as well as deacon
for three months in 1682 following Samuel Despaign's death. He was in
France at the time of the October 1684 *Censures* [FCL, MS 7, pp. 180,
204 and MS 90].
TRADE, WEALTH, SOCIAL STATUS: René Baudouin was born in 1650
[*HSP* VII, 208] and presented his *témoignage* at the London church in
1673 [HSQS XXI, 14]. He became a substantial merchant of Lombard
Street, with a turnover of £2848 in 1695/6 as exporter and importer-
exporter, notably in cloth to the Baltic, Iberia and the Mediterranean
[D.W. Jones (1971), 390]. He was estimated to be worth some £15,000,
and fined £3000 when convicted by Parliament in 1698 for trading in silks
with France during wartime [*HSP* XV, 412, 420]. He subscribed £3000
to increasing the capital of the Million Bank in 1700 [TNA, C/114/16],
and held £7417 of East India stock in 1709 [Dickson (1967), 264]. He
contributed £50 to the loan at the establishment of the French church of
St Martin Orgars [LMA, MS 00994/I, p. 46], and was involved in the
foundation of the French Protestant Hospital, of which his brother Jacques

was the first deputy governor. His will, dated 22 June 1727 and proved the following February, included bequests of £300 and an Exchequer annuity of £14 p.a. to the Threadneedle Street church, £100 to 'La Soupe' and an Exchequer annuity of £28 p.a. to the Hospital [HSQS LX, 27].
FAMILY OR TRADE CONNECTIONS WITH OTHER CHURCH OFFICERS: In partnership with Etienne Seignoret in the 1690s. Brother of Claude Baudouin.

NAME: **Jacques BAUDRY** (I) (Bauldry, Bodree, Boudré, Boudrie, Bouldry)
BORN: Middelburg
IN OFFICE: D?–1639; A 1647–9, 1663–6
FAMILY OR TRADE CONNECTIONS WITH OTHER CHURCH OFFICERS: Father of Jacques (II) and of Pierre Baudry. His son Jacques married Suzanne, daughter of Deric Petit. His daughter Ester married Nicolas (de la Fontaine, dit) Wicart. His daughter Marie married Samuel Despaign.

NAME: **Jacques BAUDRY** (II)
BORN: London, 1630
IN OFFICE: D 1661–4, 1667–70; A 1676–9
TRADE, WEALTH, SOCIAL STATUS: Weaver [HSQS XXXIII, 21–2]
FAMILY OR TRADE CONNECTIONS WITH OTHER CHURCH OFFICERS: Son of Jacques Baudry (I). Half-brother of Pierre Baudry. Son-in-law of Deric Petit. Brother-in-law of Nicolas Wicart and of Samuel Despaign.

NAME: **Pierre BAUDRY**
BORN: London, 1644
IN OFFICE: D 1673–6; A 1686–9, when he held £100 on behalf of the consistory [FCL, MS 7, p. 472].
TRADE, WEALTH, SOCIAL STATUS: Weaver [HSQS XXXIII, 15, 24]
FAMILY OR TRADE CONNECTIONS WITH OTHER CHURCH OFFICERS: Son of Jacques (I). Half-brother of Jacques (II) Baudry. Brother-in-law of Nicolas Wicart and of Samuel Despaign. His eldest daughter married Jean, son of Jean Basin.

NAME: **Pierre BAUME** (Baulme, Beaume)
BORN: Paris
ENDENIZED/NATURALIZED: End 1682, Nat 1685
IN OFFICE: D 1679–81; A 1688–91, 1704–7. Baume had presented his *témoignage* from Paris in 1674 [HSQS XXI, 14]. He helped distribute public charity to refugees during his first term as elder [FCL, MS 7, p. 392].

TRADE, WEALTH, SOCIAL STATUS: He may have come to England via Amsterdam, where a Pierre Baume, goldsmith from Paris, had become established by 1670 [Douen, III, 314]. It is presumably another man of this name, possibly his namesake son, who was associated with the conformist church 'des Grecs' in 1695 [*HSP* XIV, 176].

NAME: **Etienne (de) BEAUMONT** (Beaumond)
BORN: Châlons-sur-Marne
ENDENIZED/NATURALIZED: End 1655
IN OFFICE: D 1644–7; A 1650–3, 1660–4, 1670–3. In 1656 he objected to Cisner's preaching on various doctrinal matters, church festivals, and the status of the minister within the church [LMA, CLC/180/MSO7412/001, pp. 67–9, and CLC/180/MSO7413, no. 9].
TRADE, WEALTH, SOCIAL STATUS, ENGLISH POLITICAL AFFILIATION: Merchant of St Botolph, Aldgate. In his will (dated 1677, proved 1681) he left specific legacies of £3650 [TNA, PCC PROB 11/365], including £1400 of which the consistory took charge until Etienne Allemand came of age [FCL, MS 7, pp. 61–3, and Misc. Papers 18]. Considered well affected towards Cromwell's government, 1655 [HSQS XVIII, 68–9].
FAMILY OR TRADE CONNECTIONS WITH OTHER CHURCH OFFICERS: When his will was made, he was owed bonds totalling £600 by Charles Trinquand, £400 by Marc Maubert and £200 by Nicolas Maubert. Trinquand was Etienne Allemand's guardian.

NAME: **Jean BEAUVARLET** (Beauvallet)
BORN: Cambrai
ENDENIZED/NATURALIZED: End 1632
IN OFFICE: D 1640–3; A 1645–7
TRADE, WEALTH, SOCIAL STATUS, ENGLISH POLITICAL AFFILIATION: Merchant [CCL, U47-H2–83]. Parliamentarian, strong supporter of de La Marche against Hérault and in 1646 [FCL, MS 5, f. 142a; Hessels, 1970].
FAMILY OR TRADE CONNECTIONS WITH OTHER CHURCH OFFICERS: son-in-law of Barthélemi Caulier (I) [HSQS V, 80, and IX, 21]; brother-in-law of Pierre Caulier, Barthélemi (II) Caulier and Pierre Hochart.

NAME: **Pierre BELLON** (Belon, Bellone, Belloune, Beslon)
BORN: Metz
ENDENIZED/NATURALIZED: End 1655
IN OFFICE: D 1632–4 [SHPF, MS 335/4, f. 68; HSQS IX, 194]; A 1661–4.

A strong opponent of Jean de La Marche [HSQS II, 106–7], he tried to reconcile the divisions in the London church following the minister's death in 1651 [FCL, MS 5, p. 356; SHPF, MS 785/3, transcribed letter of 16 Jan. 1652]. As elder, he was deputed to help pacify divisions at Canterbury [FCL, MS 5, p. 409].

TRADE, WEALTH, SOCIAL STATUS, ENGLISH POLITICAL AFFILIATION: Jeweller [HSQS XVIII, 68], with a 'labouratoire in Whitfriers' [Hessels, 2148] and a small country house [SHPF, MS 335/1, f. 152]. He became employed in the Jewel House [Mitchell (2017), 57]. A moderate during the Interregnum; he testified against seditious preaching by de La Marche, 1646 [Hessels, 1971], but was considered well affected towards Cromwell's government in 1655 [HSQS XVIII, 69].

NAME: **Louis BERCHERE** (Berchaire, Berchere, Berchier, Berchire)
BORN: Paris
ENDENIZED/NATURALIZED: End 1682, Nat 1685
IN OFFICE: D 1682–5, having presented his *témoignage* from Charenton in 1681 [HSQS XXI, 18]; A 1697–1700. In 1700 he questioned the doctrinal views of the minister Jacques Colas de La Treille on grace and predestination [FCL, MS 8, f. 132v].
TRADE, WEALTH, SOCIAL STATUS: Goldsmith, and 'an important Parisian jeweller and diamond merchant' [Mitchell (2017), 63]. Berchere had European connections – in 1692 he was unable to accept election as elder because he had to visit Holland and Germany [FCL, MS 7, p. 537]. He was admitted to the freedom of London by redemption in the Goldsmiths' Company, 1682 [LMA, Court of Aldermen, Rep. 87, f. 186]. He subscribed £100 to the Tontine, 1693 [P.G.M. Dickson, pers. com.].
FAMILY OR TRADE CONNECTIONS WITH OTHER CHURCH OFFICERS: Nicolas Maubert stood surety for him, 1682 [Mitchell (2017), 63]. Father of:

NAME: **Jacques** (James) **Louis BERCHERE**
BORN: Paris
ENDENIZED/NATURALIZED: Nat 1685
IN OFFICE: D 1701–5; A 1709–?, later elected again 1718 [Eg. 2734]
TRADE, WEALTH, SOCIAL STATUS: James Louis Berchere (1670–1753), merchant jeweller or banker in Broad Street, was said to be worth £120,000 ['Pedigree of the Huguenot Refugee Families of Berchere and Baril', *The Genealogist*, N.S., XXIII (April 1907). He was a foundation Director of the French Hospital [*HSP* VI, 71]. For further information about his family see Agnew (1886), II, 501, and for his will, HSQS LX, 31.

NAME: **Pierre BERNARD**
BORN: Paris
ENDENIZED/NATURALIZED: Yes [likely references in HSQS XVIII, 160, 218]
IN OFFICE: D 1688–90. At the *Censures* of 1690 his place was declared vacant since he was no longer a member [FCL, MS 7, p. 505].
TRADE, WEALTH, SOCIAL STATUS: Peter Bernard of Westminster, gentleman, appears in Bank of England records in mid-1695 [BEA, AC28/1513], and in December 1699 [ibid.] and June 1697 [BEA, M1/6, Book C] as attorney for Ann or Anna Formont [for whose Parisian banking family see Douen, III, 339–42]. Was this the same man?

NAME: **Henri BERTRAND** (Bertran, Bertram)
BORN: Angoulême
ENDENIZED/NATURALIZED: Nat 1699
IN OFFICE: D 1704–7, having been admitted to the church in 1701 on the testimony of Joseph Ducasse [HSQS XXI, 21]; A 1710–?

NAME: **Zacharie BERTRAND**
BORN: Guernsey
IN OFFICE: D 1649–51; A 1661–4
TRADE, WEALTH, SOCIAL STATUS: Apothecary [FCL, MS 101, Jan. 1665 and Feb. 1668].

NAME: **Frédéric BLANCART** (Blanchard, Blankart)
BORN: Calais
ENDENIZED/NATURALIZED: End 1687
IN OFFICE: D 1670–3

NAME: **Laurens BLANCART**
BORN: Calais
ENDENIZED/NATURALIZED: Nat 1657, 1660; given as the son of Lawrence Blancart, late of Sandwich, Kent [HSQS XVIII, 78].
IN OFFICE: D 1656–9
TRADE, WEALTH, SOCIAL STATUS: Perhaps the Sieur Blanchart who agreed to instruct those wishing to be admitted to communion, 1651 [FCL, MS 5, p. 354].

NAME: **Phinées BLIND** or **BLAND**
BORN: London
IN OFFICE: D 1646–8. In 1657 he was a supporter of Elie Delmé [*Consistoire* [1657]].

NAME: **Jacques Auguste BLONDEL** (Blondeau, Blondell, Blundale)
BORN: Paris
ENDENIZED/NATURALIZED: End 1687
IN OFFICE: D 1700–3. Prior to becoming a deacon, he had served as a director of the Spitalfields *Maison de Charité* in 1695 [HL, *Maison de Charité, Deliberations* 1695–1718, f. 1b]. He presented his wife Mariane as a member of the church two months after being elected deacon [HSQS XXI, 24].
TRADE, WEALTH, SOCIAL STATUS: Medical doctor; M.D. Leyden (1692), admitted a Licentiate of the College of Physicians (1711), author of treatises on pregnancy [Agnew (1886), II, 368; *DNB*]. An original subscriber to the Bank of England in 1694, with £400 [BEA, M1/1, p. 31], and to the 1697 issue to enlarge the Bank's capital stock, with £125 [BEA, M1/6, Book D]; he also acted as attorney for others [BEA, AC28/1513, 30 April 1696]. He died in 1734.

NAME: **Jean BLONDEL** (I)
BORN: Canterbury
IN OFFICE: D 1650–3, 1657–9; A 1661–4, 1667–9, 1674–6
TRADE, WEALTH, SOCIAL STATUS: Weaver, gentleman. His will (1698) left grounds in Coleman Street, freeholds in Bishopsgate Street, a copyhold estate in Stepney (the 'Angell and Trumpet') and six tenements in Gravel Lane, Houndsditch, as well as £1790 in specific legacies including £40 each to the French churches of London and Canterbury [Agnew (1886), II, 259]. One of the two Jean Blondels was an 'Adventurer' in the stock raised to establish French refugee linen manufacture at Ipswich, 1681–2 [Papillon, 119].
FAMILY OR TRADE CONNECTIONS WITH OTHER CHURCH OFFICERS: Father of Jean Blondel (II). His will shows he had numerous Baudry and Delfoss cousins and a Petit brother-in-law, and included a substantial legacy to his friend Pierre Le Keux (II) [Agnew (1886), II, 259].

NAME: **Jean BLONDEL** (II)
BORN: London, 1647 [HSQS XIII, 109. An earlier Jean, born 1644 [ibid., 96], had presumably died in infancy].
IN OFFICE: D 1679–81
TRADE, WEALTH, SOCIAL STATUS: Weaver [HSQS XXXIII, 25 *sub* Blundale]. See Jean Blondel (I).
FAMILY OR TRADE CONNECTIONS WITH OTHER CHURCH OFFICERS: Son of Jean Blondel (I).

NAME: **Nicolas BOCQUET**
BORN: Cerisy Montpinchon, Normandy
ENDENIZED/NATURALIZED: End 1687 or 1697
IN OFFICE: D 1706–?

NAME: **Jacques BOCQUOIS** (Boquoy, Bouquoi, Bourgeois, Buquois)
BORN: Valenciennes
ENDENIZED/NATURALIZED: Oath roll naturalization, 1709 [HSQS XXXV, 14]
IN OFFICE: D 1699–1702; A 1706–?
TRADE, WEALTH, SOCIAL STATUS: Weaver, living 1709 in the parish of St Dunstan, Stepney [*HSP* XX, plate V]. He had been married in London in 1681 [HSQS XIII, 59k].

NAME: **Jacques BOISSONNET** (Boissonet)
BORN: Nogent
ENDENIZED/NATURALIZED: End 1682, Nat 1685
IN OFFICE: D 1683–6, having arrived at the church in 1681 with a *témoignage* from Paris [HSQS XXI, 26].
TRADE, WEALTH, SOCIAL STATUS: Denis Papin, curator of experiments to the Royal Society, explained in 1687 that improvements to his invention of the pressure cooker or 'digester of bones' could be seen demonstrated at Mr Boissonet's, in Water Lane, Blackfriars [*HSP* XX, 190].

NAME: **Isaac BONOURIER** (Bonouvrier, Bonouvriet)
BORN: Saintes
ENDENIZED/NATURALIZED: Yes [see HSQS XVIII, 135, 217, 235, 240]
IN OFFICE: A 1697–1700. His specific tasks included maintaining an alphabetical register of church members [FCL, MS 8, f. 72v].
TRADE, WEALTH, SOCIAL STATUS: 'Eminent Wine-Merchant', whose son married into a fortune of over £30,000 [*The Historical Register*, XXIII (1738), Chronological Diary, p. 15]. An original subscriber to the Bank of England in 1694, with £500 [BEA, M1/1, p. 43]. Earlier in the decade he had been based in Dublin [*CTB, 1689–92*, 1451].

NAME: **David BOSANQUET** (Bouzanquet)
BORN: Lunel, 1661
ENDENIZED/NATURALIZED: Nat 1698
IN OFFICE: D 1694–7; while in office he donated eight silver communion cups to the church [FCL, MS 8, f. 56r], and during the next decade he was

a prominent contributor to collections for the relief of the galley slaves in France [FCL, MS 91, ff. 194–5].

TRADE, WEALTH, SOCIAL STATUS: Merchant, a Mercer and member of the Levant Company. He was proposed as surety for Goudet and Barrau, amongst the leading silk smugglers of the 1690s [*CJ* XII, 257]. He had been in the silk industry at Lyons before fleeing France, and was himself a substantial silk importer, with a turnover of £13,457 in 1695–6 [D.W. Jones (1971), 453]. He supplied nearly £2300 of Genoa velvets and damask for the coronation of George I. His assets amounted to some £100,000 on his death in 1732. For further information see Lee (1966), especially chap. 3.

FAMILY OR TRADE CONNECTIONS WITH OTHER CHURCH OFFICERS: Son-in-law of Claude Hays (I) and brother-in-law of Claude Hays (II) [Wagner Pedigrees *sub* Hays], as was Jean Deneu.

NAME: **Jacob BOSSU** (Bosseu, Bousseu)
BORN: Canterbury
IN OFFICE: D 1684–6; A 1690–2, died early in 1692 [FCL, MS 7, p. 546].

NAME: **Mathieu BOUCHERET**
BORN: Amiens
ENDENIZED/NATURALIZED: End 1655, Nat 1656 and 1662, when stated to be the son of Gedeon Boucheret of Lewes, Sussex [HSQS XVIII, 81].
IN OFFICE: A 1661–4; served on a deputation to Court regarding Roman Catholic monks in London [FCL, MS 5, pp. 466–7].
TRADE, WEALTH, SOCIAL STATUS: 'His Maiesties apothecary' [HSQS XVIII, 81].
FAMILY OR TRADE CONNECTIONS WITH OTHER CHURCH OFFICERS: Son-in-law of Florentin Tainturier, from whom he and his wife inherited extensive property, including the manors of North Willingham and Ludford in Lincolnshire. While Boucheret's £20 legacy reached the church only in 1686, he had died in 1671 [Jean Imray, 'The Boucherett Family Archives', *The Lincolnshire Historian*, 2:3 (1955–6), 12–13; FCL, MS 218, p. 76].

NAME: **Paul BOUILLY** (Bouillé)
BORN: Tours
ENDENIZED/NATURALIZED: Nat 1708 ('Paul Bovilly') [HSQS XXVII, 64]
IN OFFICE: D 1704–7; A 1710–?
TRADE, WEALTH, SOCIAL STATUS: weaver [HSQS XVI, 9g, 180t]

NAME: **David BOUQUET** (Bouchet, Boucquest, Bouget, Bouguer, Bowkett)
BORN: Dieppe
ENDENIZED/NATURALIZED: End 1627
IN OFFICE: A 1637–40, 1644–7, 1653–6, 1659–62, 1665, died in office. He represented the church in 1644 before the Walloon Synod of the Low Countries [FCL, MS 298, 14 March 1644], at the 1654 Colloquy [FCL, MS 5, p. 371], and at Dieppe in 1660 [FCL, MS 5, pp. 395–6].
TRADE, WEALTH, SOCIAL STATUS, ENGLISH POLITICAL AFFILIATION: A watch- and clockmaker of Blackfriars, Bouquet was first recorded in England in 1622, when he had two apprentices [David Thompson, *The British Museum Watches* (British Museum Press, 2008), 40]. He became a founder member of the Clockmakers' Company. A silver case lantern clock by him is in the Victoria and Albert Museum, and three of his watches can be seen at the Ashmolean Museum in Oxford and a spectacular example at the British Museum, all dating from the mid-seventeenth century period. A moderate in the English Civil War, he opposed Jean de La Marche's 'medling with state matters' in 1646 [Hessels, 1970].
FAMILY OR TRADE CONNECTIONS WITH OTHER CHURCH OFFICERS: Father-in-law of Isaac Maubert, and also of Nicolas Maubert [HSQS XIII, 35, 42]; they married his daughters Marie and Suzanne respectively. Another daughter, Marthe, married Isaac Romieu's namesake son [HSQS XIII, 44]. The year after David Bouquet's death, Marie was remarried to Esaie Pantin.

NAME: **Pierre BOURDEAU** (Bordeaux)
BORN: Tournai
IN OFFICE: D 1643–6
TRADE, WEALTH, SOCIAL STATUS: Weaver? [HSQS XXXIII, 12 ('Burdeux'), 20]

NAME: **Pierre BOURLA** (Bouilar, Bourlar, Bourlare)
BORN: Tournai
ENDENIZED/NATURALIZED: End 1632
IN OFFICE: D?-1639; A 1641–4, 1652–4, 1659–62. He was suspended from communion in 1645 for advising Philippe Delmé of Canterbury not to encourage his son Elie to become minister of the Threadneedle Street church [FCL, MS 5, p. 305, minutes crossed through dated 22 Aug.].
TRADE, WEALTH, SOCIAL STATUS: 'Weaver and husbandman' when endenized in 1632.
FAMILY OR TRADE CONNECTIONS WITH OTHER CHURCH

OFFICERS: Father-in-law of Nicolas (de la Fontaine, dit) Wicart [HSQS XIII, 26].

NAME: **Pierre BOUSINIE** (Boisinie, Bousigny, Busigni)
BORN: Valenciennes
ENDENIZED/NATURALIZED: Nat 1663 or 1677
IN OFFICE: D 1665–7; A 1677–80

NAME: **Samuel BRULÉ** (Bruslé)
BORN: Guise
ENDENIZED/NATURALIZED: Oath roll naturalization, 1709
IN OFFICE: D 1707–?; A 1713–? Either he or another Samuel Brusle had presented his *témoignage* at the church, from Amsterdam, in 1686 [HSQS XXI, 38].

NAME: **Daniel BRULON** (Broulon, Brullon, Bruslon)
BORN: Ile de Ré
ENDENIZED/NATURALIZED: End 1682, Nat 1685
IN OFFICE: D 1680–2; A 1691–4, 1698–1701. Active as deacon in assisting new refugees in 1681–2 [FCL, MS 7, pp. 58–9, 77, 81–2, 85, 89]. As elder he was deputed to Bishop of London three times in 1699–1700, once alone and unofficially on a sensitive matter [FCL, MS 8, ff. 84v, 97r, 119].
TRADE, WEALTH, SOCIAL STATUS: Merchant; 'His Majesty's Fishmonger' [G.D. Heath, 'Hampton Court Palace: the Huguenot Connections' (unpublished typescript in HL), p. 25, and see also p. 29 where Brulon requests permission to take over a captured French frigate and man it for the fishermen's protection]. He undertook to convey the whole catch of the Huguenot fishermen at Rye to London and Westminster, for which he was granted the Freedom of the City of London, 1682 [TNA, SP/44/66, p. 100].
Later he seems to have changed focus. 'Daniel Brulon of London, Haberdasher' held £500 of Bank stock [BEA, AC28/1513, 12 Nov. 1696 and 2 March 1698] and appears in the Threadneedle Street registers of 1700–04 variously described as tobacconist, haberdasher and distiller.

NAME: **Etienne BUIZARD** (Buisard, Buysart)
BORN: La Rochelle
IN OFFICE: D 1671–3
TRADE, WEALTH, SOCIAL STATUS: The available evidence suggests there were two different Etienne (or Stephen) Buizards in London

simultaneously. One, Stephen Buizard of La Rochelle, son of Stephen, was naturalized in 1667 [HSQS XVIII, 98]; perhaps it was his estate that was involved in the court case *Buizard v Dumaresque* in 1679, when he was described as formerly of Newington Butts, Surrey, gentleman [TNA, Prob. 18, 11/51–52]. Such an early naturalization date makes it unlikely he was the Estienne Buzard who, with Marie Toppin, his wife, presented *témoignages* from Amsterdam at the Threadneedle Street church in 1669 [HSQS XXI, 39]. This second Etienne was a watchmaker in Westminster, and his wife was endenized in 1672–3 [HSQS XVIII, 108; *CSPD, 1672–3*, 168]. Chronology would suggest the watchmaker as the French church deacon.

FAMILY OR TRADE CONNECTIONS WITH OTHER CHURCH OFFICERS: The Buizard family had connections with the Wanleys and with David Collivaulx [HSQS IX, 197, and XIII, 30, 124]. Marie Buizard, widow of Valentin Wanley, as his executrix, passed on £80 to the Threadneedle Street church in November 1669 [FCL, MS 222, f. 1].

NAME: **Pierre BULTEEL** (Bulteel, Bultel, Bulltell)
BORN: London, 1579
IN OFFICE: D 1611–14; A in 1632 [HSQS IX, 82, 89, 94, 174], 1640–3, 1652–4. Threadneedle Street church representative at the 1641 Colloquy and Synod [HSQS II, 72, 76].
TRADE, WEALTH, SOCIAL STATUS: A notably wealthy wool merchant, as had been his father Gilles [Vivien Allen, *The Bulteels* (Phillimore, 2004), 18, 30]. One of the 'first and best sort of men' in a list of the principal inhabitants of London, 1640 [*Miscellanea Genealogica et Heraldica*, 2nd series, II (1888), 52]. One of the largest contributors to the 1650 collection for the repair of the church [FCL, MS 62, f. 3r]. His grandson Samuel became a director of the Bank of England in 1697 [Allen, *The Bulteels*, 22].
FAMILY OR TRADE CONNECTIONS WITH OTHER CHURCH OFFICERS: Uncle of Anne Bulteel, widow of Jacques Maurois, who married Jacques Guyott in 1646.

NAME: **David BUTEL** (Buttel)
BORN: Dieppe
ENDENIZED/NATURALIZED: End 1687
IN OFFICE: D 1692–5; A 1699–1702. A signatory of the 1700 agreement between the French Committee and the French churches of London on behalf of Threadneedle Street [*Relation dans laquelle...* [1706], 8], he later objected that the Committee was denying the poor the assistance ordered

for them by the English Committee [*Malversations du Committé Francois* (1708), 26]. In 1706 he was the first to complain about the activities of the French 'Prophets' [FCL, MS 8, f. 251r].

NAME: **Isaac BUTEUX**
BORN: near Clermont
ENDENIZED/NATURALIZED: Most deacons were around the age of 30 when first elected, so the Isaac Buteux endenized with his wife and daughter in 1682 is likely to belong to an earlier generation than this church officer.
IN OFFICE: D 1701–4. He died in office during 1704 [FCL, MS 8, f. 211v].

C

NAME: **Robert CAILLE** or **CAILLÉ**
BORN: Geneva
ENDENIZED/NATURALIZED: End 1697, Nat 1698
IN OFFICE: D 1700–2 (discharged because going on a long voyage); A 1707–?. He was also a director of the Spitalfields *Maison de Charité*, 1705–8 [HL, Maison de Charité, Deliberations 1695–1718, ff. 76a, 87b], and a member of the French Committee administering public charity, 1707–9 [FCL, MS 8, f. 266v; *Estats* for 1707 and 1708].
TRADE, WEALTH, SOCIAL STATUS: Merchant and stock dealer. He had a personal holding of £2450 of Bank stock in mid-1697 and bought over £4000 and sold over £3000 in the latter part of the year, largely on behalf of Huguenot and Sephardic clients. He was also a considerable dealer in East India stock, 1706–8, and contributed £2500 to the Bank subscription of 1709 [*HSP* XIX (iii), 33, 39].
FAMILY OR TRADE CONNECTIONS WITH OTHER CHURCH OFFICERS: Trustee for Amonnet family. Married Jeanne, daughter of François Amonnet, whose mother had remarried to Jacques Dufay. Brother-in-law of François Grueber.

NAME: **Daniel CANION** (Cannion)
BORN: Valenciennes
ENDENIZED/NATURALIZED: End 1631
IN OFFICE: D 1642–?

NAME: **Delillers CARBONNEL** (Carboneale)
BORN: London, 1669

IN OFFICE: D 1698–1700

TRADE, WEALTH, SOCIAL STATUS, ENGLISH POLITICAL AFFILIATION: Banker – director of the Bank of England from 1722, becoming deputy governor 1738–40 and Governor 1740–1. Whig [*A List of the Poll for John Ward … for Members of Parliament For the City of London* (1713), p. 12].

FAMILY OR TRADE CONNECTIONS WITH OTHER CHURCH OFFICERS: Son of Guillaume Carbonnel and Elizabeth de Lillers. Nephew of Jacques Deneu. 'Cousin' of Pierre Delmé, as was noted at his baptism [HSQS XIII, 193].

NAME: **Guillaume CARBONNEL**

BORN: Caen

ENDENIZED/NATURALIZED: Nat 1657, 1660

IN OFFICE: D 1659–62; A 1666–70, 1674–7, 1681–3. His efforts as deacon and elder are discussed in vol. I of the present work, pp. 66–7.

TRADE, WEALTH, SOCIAL STATUS, ENGLISH POLITICAL AFFILIATION: Merchant in a range of goods including paper and brandy [*CTB, 1679–80*, 852]. He had wide connections in France, and his activities included organizing ships being laden in the Netherlands for direct consignment to French ports [FCL, MS 45, 28 Nov. 1667; *CTB, 1676–9*, 758]. Notes were frequently drawn on Guillaume Carbonnel, as also on Pierre Barr (I), to convey Louis XIV's subsidy to Charles II; over £47,000 was passed on through notes drawn on Carbonnel in 1676–77 [*CTB, 1676–9*, 1317–21]. Two of his ships in Barbados were taken into service in 1691 as fourth-rate men of war [*Calendar of Privy Council Acts – Colonial*, II (1680–1720), p. 275]. Administered over £7000 in poor relief for new refugees, 1681–3 [FCL, MS 63, and HSQS, LVIII, 125]. Member of the English Committee supervising public charity adminis-tration in the late 1690s [LP, MS 941, no. 87]. Described as 'of an antient gentleman's family' at Caen in the Visitation of London, 1687. His brother Jean was a titular secretary of Louis XIV for over 25 years before retiring to Holland. Of Guillaume's sons, five became London merchants, a sixth (David) was a groom of the Privy Chamber to King William III in 1694 [Agnew (1886), I, 198–9, and Wagner Pedigrees].

Outspoken Whig, considered by the Anglican Pierre du Moulin to be a 'perverse fanatick' in ecclesiastical matters. Carbonnel's behaviour on a Grand Jury in 1681 resulted in a call by the Court for him to be removed from his eldership [Gwynn (2015), 67]. Together with his son Jean and Claude Hays (I), he was a witness in 1681 to the will of Robert de Lunars, of whom the Hertford Quarter Sessions were informed the following year that he 'entertains Castair [the Scottish Presbyterian William Carstairs,

imprisoned and tortured in Scotland 1683 on suspicion of involvement in the Rye House plot] in his house' [Anthony Kirby, pers. com.]. Carbonnel was a 'disaffected and suspicious person' arrested and detained at the time of Monmouth's rebellion, 1685 [LMA, CLA/050/02/002, pp. 37, 42, 61]. By contrast he was also described as 'a person of very good reputation, great loyalty and affection to [William and Mary's] government' when granted a crest to his arms in 1694 [Wagner Pedigrees].
FAMILY OR TRADE CONNECTIONS WITH OTHER CHURCH OFFICERS: Son-in-law of Jean de Lillers. Father of Delillers Carbonnel [Agnew (1886), I, 42, 190–1]. Brother-in-law of Jacques Deneu – the baptisms of Guillaume Carbonnel's children reveal a strong connection with the Deneu's, to whom he was related along with the de Lillers family.

NAME: **David CAREIRON** (Careron, Carreiron, Carreyron)
BORN: Uzès
ENDENIZED/NATURALIZED: Nat 1696
IN OFFICE: D 1698–1700, having arrived at the church in 1695 with a *témoignage* from Amsterdam [HSQS XXI, 45].
TRADE, WEALTH, SOCIAL STATUS: Merchant of Throgmorton Street; subscribed £929 to the 1697 issue enlarging the Bank's capital stock, and £1700 to the expansion of the Million Bank's stock in 1700 [BEA, M1/6, Book A nos 62, 288, and Book B no.151; TNA, C/114/16].

NAME: **Pierre CAREIRON**
BORN: Montpellier
ENDENIZED/NATURALIZED: End and Nat 1685
IN OFFICE: D 1685–8; A 1692–5. As elder he served throughout his term as a member of the French Committee administering public charity [FCL, MS 8, f. 28r; HL, Bounty MS 6, 1 June 1692–4 April 1694].

NAME: **Nicolas CARLIER** (Carlié) [given as Antoine when elected, but signed as Nicolas and so named when discharged: FCL, MS 5, pp. 331, 353, and MS 135A].
BORN: Valenciennes
IN OFFICE: D 1647–50

NAME: **Jacques CARON** (Carron)
BORN: Rouen
ENDENIZED/NATURALIZED: End. 1675? [HSQS XVIII, 113].
IN OFFICE: D 1689–90; discharged early because of illness [FCL, MS 7, p. 505].
TRADE, WEALTH, SOCIAL STATUS: Gentleman; the records refer to

'Mr' Carron donating to the church in 1686 [FCL, MS 218, p. 87] and on his death in 1698, when he left the church property and a legacy of £40 [FCL, MS 52, p. 240; MS 140, f. 321a; and MS 218, p. 120].

Caron seems likely to be the French hatmaker James Caron, against whom the Feltmakers Company petitioned the London Court of Common Council in late 1682 when he had 'set up the trade of feltmaking at Lambeth' and then sought admission to the Freedom of the City [LMA, COL/CP/02/095, and (for the date) Court of Aldermen, Rep. 88, f. 10r]. This feltmaker was also a gentleman and a Threadneedle Street church member [FCL, MS 7, p. 214].

However, identification is made complicated by a second comparatively wealthy James Caron, weaver of Stepney parish, whose inventory following his death and that of his wife in 1700 included £210 ready cash, 30 Exchequer notes and 40 Million Lottery tickets, and totalled four figures [Parker (2014), 124–6].
FAMILY OR TRADE CONNECTIONS WITH OTHER CHURCH OFFICERS: Brother-in-law of François Touvoye dit de Champs, and of Nicolas Dufay? [HSQS XIII, 56–57, and XVI, 14].

NAME: **Pierre de (des) CARPENTRY** (Carpanterie, Carpentris)
BORN: London
IN OFFICE: D 1669–72, 1675–8; A 1682–5, 1688–91, 1695–7. On the last occasion he was discharged when leaving to live in Canterbury [FCL, MS 8, f. 48v].

NAME: **Abraham CARRIS** (Caries, Cairis, Caris)
BORN: Pittenweem, Fife, Scotland
IN OFFICE: D 1674–7; A 1680–3, 1687–90
TRADE, WEALTH, SOCIAL STATUS: Substantial London inhabitant, liable to surtax in 1695 Assessment as having a personal estate valued over £600 [Glass, 54]. Merchant, with Iberian connections; his imports in 1695/96 totalled £1803, with £789 of port and Spanish wine, £904 of currants and £110 of iron [D.W. Jones (1971), p. 440].
FAMILY OR TRADE CONNECTIONS WITH OTHER CHURCH OFFICERS: Uncle of David and Jean Strang [HMC 75: *Downshire I pt. I*: p. 71].

CASSE, see DUCASSE

NAME: **Michel CASTEL**
BORN: Canterbury
IN OFFICE: A 1639–43

TRADE, WEALTH, SOCIAL STATUS: A substantial contributor, with
£20, to the 1650 collection for the repair of the church [FCL, MS 62,
f. 3r]. He had died by 1661 [FCL, MS 218, p. 13], and his widow left £50
to the church a few years later [FCL, MS 101, Nov. 1668].

NAME: **Barthélemi CAULIER** (I) (Cawlier, Colier, Collier, Coulier)
BORN: Canterbury
IN OFFICE: A 1643–51. He was used on deputations sent to Norwich
and Canterbury in 1646–7 to try to resolve problems, in both cases with
another supporter of de La Marche, Jacques Danbrine [HSQS LIV, letters
41, 43, 51–3, 57; CCL, U47-H-1, no. 71]. The consistory sent the same two
officers to defend De la Marche against allegations made at the 1647 Synod
[FCL, MS 5, p. 333].
TRADE, WEALTH, SOCIAL STATUS, ENGLISH POLITICAL
AFFILIATION: Parliamentarian, strong supporter of De la Marche, 1646
[Hessels, 1970].
FAMILY OR TRADE CONNECTIONS WITH OTHER CHURCH
OFFICERS: Father of Pierre and Barthélemi (II) Caulier; father-in-law
of Jean Beauvarlet and of Pierre Hochart [HSQS IX, 21, 105, 114, and
XIII, 7g, 26p].

NAME: **Barthélemi CAULIER** (II)
BORN: London, 1619 [HSQS IX, 114].
IN OFFICE: D 1647–50, 1654–6. He abandoned his charge in June
1656 because he objected to the deacons being excluded from consistorial
debates concerning Elie Delmé [FCL, MS 135A; Hessels, 2401–2].
FAMILY OR TRADE CONNECTIONS WITH OTHER CHURCH
OFFICERS: Son of Barthélemi (I) and brother of Pierre Caulier. Brother-
in-law of Jean Beauvarlet and Pierre Hochart.

NAME: **Pierre CAULIER**
BORN: London, 1616 [HSQS IX, 105].
IN OFFICE: D 1644–7; A 1655–7
TRADE, WEALTH, SOCIAL STATUS: Merchant, seeking to export
silk to France with Jacob Gosselin, 1661 [*CTB, 1660–67*, 195]. Held an
extensive property in Bush Lane, which he was renting for £30 p.a. before
the Great Fire and which was in the possession of his son-in-law David
Griel; he rebuilt it in the late 1660s and was granted a longer lease at a
reduced rent [P.E. Jones (1966), II, 167–8]. He became 'a leading merchant
and shipowner in Great Yarmouth, Norfolk, becoming a freeman in 1667
and serving as joint Bailiff for the burgh in 1669 and 1678' [Roseveare,
238n].

FAMILY OR TRADE CONNECTIONS WITH OTHER CHURCH OFFICERS: Son of Barthélemi (I) and brother of Barthélemi (II) Caulier. Brother-in-law of Jean Beauvarlet and Pierre Hochart. Father-in-law of David Griel. Trade connections with Charles Marescoe and Jacob David, with whom he could 'evidently claim kinship ... through the Lethieulliers' [Roseveare, 238n, 269, 389].

NAME: **Jean CAZALET** (Casalet, Cazalett)
BORN: Sommières
ENDENIZED/NATURALIZED: End 1694, Nat 1702 [HSQS XXVII, 12].
IN OFFICE: D 1700–2; A 1710–?, later elected again, 1719–24 [Eg. 2734]. Also a director of the Spitalfields *Maison de Charité*, 1705 [HL, Maison de Charité, Deliberations 1695–1718, f. 76].
TRADE, WEALTH, SOCIAL STATUS: Merchant [Wagner Pedigrees, Cazalet folder 1].
FAMILY OR TRADE CONNECTIONS WITH OTHER CHURCH OFFICERS: Brother of Pierre Cazalet.

NAME: **Pierre CAZALET**
BORN: Sommières
ENDENIZED/NATURALIZED: End 1694, Nat 1696 [HSQS XVIII, 240].
IN OFFICE: D 1703–6; A 1714–? [Eg. 2734].
TRADE, WEALTH, SOCIAL STATUS: Admitted to the Freedom of the City 'as one due to the Lady Majoress this present yeare' by Redemption in the Company of Shipwrights, 1696 [LMA, Court of Aldermen, Rep. 100, f. 198b]. He subscribed £600 towards enlarging the capital of the Million Bank, 1700 [TNA, C/114/16].
FAMILY OR TRADE CONNECTIONS WITH OTHER CHURCH OFFICERS: Brother of Jean Cazalet.

NAME: **Jean CHARRON**
BORN: St Martin, Ile de Ré
ENDENIZED/NATURALIZED: End 1696
IN OFFICE: D 1698
TRADE, WEALTH, SOCIAL STATUS: Merchant? – left almost immediately, established at Rotterdam by June 1698 [FCL, MS 8, f. 67r].

NAME: **David COLLIVAULX** (Collivaux, Coliveau, Colliveaux)
BORN: Vitry-le-François
ENDENIZED/NATURALIZED: David Collivaulx (Callivaux) 'of London,

tailor' was endenized in 1655 (when he was described as well affected to the government), and naturalized in 1656 [HSQS XVIII, 69, 73]. After the Restoration, he was again endenized in 1662 and sought naturalization in 1667 [ibid., 88 ('Colmaulx') and 99n].

IN OFFICE: D 1657–60; he declined the charge of elder in 1673.

FAMILY OR TRADE CONNECTIONS WITH OTHER CHURCH OFFICERS: Marriage connection with the Wanley and Buizard families [HSQS XIII, 31, 134. David's wife was probably either sister or niece of Valentin Wanley].

NAME: **David CONGNARD** (I) (Cocgnart, Cognard, Coignard, Conyard)
BORN: Rouen
ENDENIZED/NATURALIZED: Nat 1660 [HSQS XVIII, 78]
IN OFFICE: D 1653–6, 1661–4; A 1670–3, declined a further term in 1677.
TRADE, WEALTH, SOCIAL STATUS: Merchant. Trading commodities included brandy [*CTB, 1679–80*, 853].
FAMILY OR TRADE CONNECTIONS WITH OTHER CHURCH OFFICERS: Father of David Congnard (II). Father-in-law of Claude Hays (I), to whom he sold two houses in Fenchurch Street [Wagner Pedigrees *sub* Hays, supplementary material]. In partnership with Etienne Noguier when importing 2463 gallons of overproof brandy, 1685 [*CTB, 1685–9*, 338]; also a trading partner with Charles Marescoe [Roseveare, 74].

NAME: **David CONGNARD** (II)
BORN: London, 1662 [HSQS XIII, 165]
IN OFFICE: D 1688–9; discharged because he no longer had a house in town [FCL, MS 7, p. 465].
FAMILY OR TRADE CONNECTIONS WITH OTHER CHURCH OFFICERS: Son of David Congnard (I). Brother-in-law of Claude Hays (I).

NAME: **Jean de CONING** (Coninck, Coninq, Koning, Kuning)
BORN: Rouen [FCL, MS 7, p. 397]
ENDENIZED/NATURALIZED: De Coning arrived in England from Rotterdam with his wife in 1687 [HSQS XXI, 69], and was endenized that same year [HSQS XVIII, 196].
IN OFFICE: D 1688–90, drowned in Amsterdam while in office [FCL, MS 7, p. 505].
TRADE, WEALTH, SOCIAL STATUS: Presumed merchant, the de Conings being a well-established Dutch merchant family [see *BSHPF* LXXII (1923), 97 ff, which also shows Jean had been born 1662].

NAME: **Antoine COQUART** (Cocart, Cockart, Cocquard, Quoqar)
BORN: Beauvaisis?
ENDENIZED/NATURALIZED: End 1662
IN OFFICE: D 1651–3; A 1669–74, 1677–80

NAME: **David COQUEAU** (Cocqueau, Coquiau, Quoqueau)
BORN: Canterbury
IN OFFICE: D 1650–3; A 1659–62, 1667–70; declined a further term in 1675.
TRADE, WEALTH, SOCIAL STATUS: Weaver [HSQS XXXIII, 19, 22].
FAMILY OR TRADE CONNECTIONS WITH OTHER CHURCH OFFICERS: Brother-in-law of Charles Marescoe and Pierre Marescoe [HSQS XIII, 37; Wagner Pedigrees *sub* Marescoe].

NAME: **Abraham COSSART** (Cossard)
BORN: Rouen
ENDENIZED/NATURALIZED: End 1687, Nat 1696
IN OFFICE: D 1694–8; A 1701–5
TRADE, WEALTH, SOCIAL STATUS: Member of a wealthy Rouen merchant family. Merchant, in 1695–6 importing hemp from the Baltic and exporting small quantities of new draperies to Cadiz and near Europe [D.W. Jones (1971), 417].
FAMILY OR TRADE CONNECTIONS WITH OTHER CHURCH OFFICERS: Connected with the Le Plastriers [Du Pont (1923), I, 226, and II, chaps. 19–23]. A lawsuit brought by his brother Jean Cossart, who alleged he had cheated him of £1000, brought him into opposition to Pierre Reneu, who acted on Jean's behalf [FCL, MS 8, f. 207v, 210, 213–5, 226r].

NAME: **Bon COULON** (Colon, Coullon)
BORN: Tournai [HSQS XIII, 27]
ENDENIZED/NATURALIZED: End 1662
IN OFFICE: D 1658–60 [FCL, MS 135A]. Later he donated £30 to the church at the time of the Plague [FCL, MS 218, 24 Sept. and 18 Oct. 1665].
FAMILY OR TRADE CONNECTIONS WITH OTHER CHURCH OFFICERS: Father of Moise Coulon; father-in-law of Jacques Le Quien (II) [HSQS XIII, 100, 114, 188].

NAME: **Moise COULON**
BORN: London, 1645 [HSQS XIII, 100]
IN OFFICE: D 1676–9; A 1684–8 [unusually elected in Aug. 1684 following Philippe Le Keux's death, FCL, MS 7, p. 199].

TRADE, WEALTH, SOCIAL STATUS, ENGLISH POLITICAL AFFILIATION: Merchant. Joined the Eastland Company, 1683 [Roseveare, 41]. An 'Adventurer' in the stock raised to establish French refugee linen manufacture at Ipswich, 1681–2 [Papillon, 119].
FAMILY OR TRADE CONNECTIONS WITH OTHER CHURCH OFFICERS: Son of Bon Coulon. Brother-in-law of Jacques Le Quien (II). Clerk to Charles Marescoe by 1667. Put up £1000 in partnership with Jacob David and others, 1670 [Roseveare, 4, 25, 121].

NAME: **Pierre COUSSIRAT** (Cosserat, Causirat)
BORN: Oleron, Béarn
ENDENIZED/NATURALIZED: Nat 1704; his petition states he had served King William in the wars [HSQS XXVII, 37].
IN OFFICE: D 1705–8; A 1711–?, later elected again 1723–7 [Eg. 2734].

NAME: **Jacob COUTRIS** (Couteris, Coutry)
BORN: Bordeaux
ENDENIZED/NATURALIZED: End 1687, Nat 1698
IN OFFICE: D 1692–4
TRADE, WEALTH, SOCIAL STATUS: Substantial London inhabitant, liable to surtax in 1695 Assessment as having a personal estate valued over £600 [Glass, 74]. 'Merchant alias broker' acting for two women from Eltham, Kent, in dealing with Bank stock, 1699 [BEA, AC28/1513, 11 Feb. 1699]. Member of the Broderers Company, and Whig [*A List of the Poll for John Ward ... for Members of Parliament For the City of London* (1713), p. 6].

D

NAME: **Ruben DAMPURÉ** (d'Ampure, Dempuré, Denpurer)
BORN: Pons
IN OFFICE: D 1669–71; A 1676–9
FAMILY OR TRADE CONNECTIONS WITH OTHER CHURCH OFFICERS: Father-in-law of Pierre Guerin [HSQS XIII, 49].

NAME: **Abraham DANBRINE** or **DAMBRIN** (Dambrane, d'Ambrin, d'Anbrune, Denbrine, Dombrain)
BORN: London
IN OFFICE: D 1690–3
TRADE, WEALTH, SOCIAL STATUS: The will of Daniel Danbrine, dated and proved 1718, left £2000 to his nephew Abraham Danbrine,

weaver, of Spitalfields [HSQS LX, 82]. The will of 'Abraham Danbrine of London, gentleman', dated 1728, was proved in 1735; it included a £10 bequest to the Threadneedle Street church [HL, Wagner Wills, A, p. 17].

NAME: **Bon** (Good) **DANBRINE** or **DAMBRIN**
BORN: Lille
ENDENIZED/NATURALIZED: Nat 1657, again 1664
IN OFFICE: D 1650–3. In 1657 he was a supporter of Elie Delmé [*Consistoire* [1657]].
TRADE, WEALTH, SOCIAL STATUS: Foreign master weaver [HSQS XXXIII, 15].
FAMILY OR TRADE CONNECTIONS WITH OTHER CHURCH OFFICERS: Married Elizabeth, daughter of Abraham Desquien [HSQS XIII, 31d].

NAME: **Jacques DANBRINE** or **DAMBRIN**
BORN: Lille
ENDENIZED/NATURALIZED: Nat 1657
IN OFFICE: D 1639–43; A 1644–51. He was used on deputations sent to Norwich and Canterbury in 1646–7 to try to resolve problems, in both cases with another supporter of De la Marche, Barthélemi Caulier (I) [HSQS LIV, letters 41, 43, 51–3, 57; CCL, U47-H-1, no. 71]. The consistory sent the same two officers to defend De la Marche against allegations made at the 1647 Synod [FCL, MS 5, p. 333]. In 1657, Danbrine was a strong supporter of Elie Delmé [*Consistoire* [1657]]. Estranged from the consistory in 1658 [Hessels, 2401], he was evidently reconciled with it in 1661 [FCL, MS 5, p. 404] but did not again serve as elder before his death in 1665.
TRADE, WEALTH, SOCIAL STATUS, ENGLISH POLITICAL AFFILIATION: Weaver and gentleman [HSQS XXXIII, 12]. Parliamentarian and strong supporter of de La Marche against Hérault in 1643 as well as later [FCL, MS 5, f. 142a; Hessels, 1970].
FAMILY OR TRADE CONNECTIONS WITH OTHER CHURCH OFFICERS: Father of Joseph Danbrine [Rothstein (1989), 47].

NAME: **Joseph DANBRINE** or **DAMBRIN**
BORN: London
IN OFFICE: D 1670–3; A 1685–8, when he served as treasurer of donations for l'Eglise de l'Hôpital and helped oversee the building of the new church [FCL, MS 7, pp. 358, 368, 387, 393].
TRADE, WEALTH, SOCIAL STATUS: Joseph was on the books of the Weavers Company from 1662 [HSQS XXXIII, 12], but in fact was a

merchant factor, with an important role in marketing the goods produced by Canterbury weavers. He was admitted a member of the Artillery Company in 1666 [*HSP* XV, 306]. By his death in 1705, when he left £400 to each of his four surviving sons and £1000 to each of his two daughters, he had retired to Enfield, and had extensive house property in Spitalfields and elsewhere including his 'old dwelling house in Pettycoat Lane' [Rothstein (1989), 39–42, 47]. He subscribed £1000 to the Million Bank in 1695 [TNA, C/114/16].
FAMILY OR TRADE CONNECTIONS WITH OTHER CHURCH OFFICERS: Eldest son of Jacques Danbrine.

NAME: **Jacques DANTIER** (d'Antier, Dentiere)
IN OFFICE: A 1657–60 [for date of election, see Northampton R.O., P(L) 241, p. 3]

NAME: **Etienne DAUBUZ**
BORN: Nérac
ENDENIZED/NATURALIZED: Nat 1707
IN OFFICE: D 1708–?
TRADE, WEALTH, SOCIAL STATUS: Merchant; his daughter was to marry into the formidable Van Neck family [Jacob M. Price, *France and the Chesapeake* (University of Michigan Press, 1973), 543].

NAME: **Jacob DAVID**
BORN: Rouen
ENDENIZED/NATURALIZED: End 1675, Nat 1677
IN OFFICE: D 1676–8; A 1684–6 (he was absent from October 1685, having fled to Amsterdam to avoid legal pursuit and his debtors [Roseveare, 8], but was not discharged from office until June 1686. He died in May 1689.)
TRADE, WEALTH, SOCIAL STATUS: Merchant, with widespread business interests in the Baltic, France, the Netherlands and the Mediterranean, and a near monopoly of the London copper-wire market in the 1670s. In the same decade he was the London agent for Dutch-financed distribution of pitch and tar. He joined the Eastland Company, 1682 [for the rise and collapse of his business fortunes, see Roseveare, *passim*]. One of the 'principaux de l'Eglise' consulted about the refugees, 1681; his many gifts to the church included £100 in 1680–1 [FCL, MS 7, p. 80, and MS 218]. He was fined £2000 and committed to Newgate by the Court of Aldermen in 1681 for marrying his daughter-in-law, who had £12,000 in the Chamber of London, to a poor Frenchman [TNA, Adm./77/1, no. 114, f. 194v].

FAMILY OR TRADE CONNECTIONS WITH OTHER CHURCH OFFICERS: Married Leonora, daughter of Jean Lethieullier, after the death of her previous husband, Charles Marescoe, for whom he had acted as chief clerk. Lethieullier and Moise Coulon were trading venture partners [Roseveare, 4–5].

NAME: **François Touvois** (Thouvois, Touvoye, Tuvois) **dit DECHAMP** (de Champ, Dechamps, Deschamps). When entering his charge as elder in 1701 the officer signed his name as Touvois, but twice as many references encountered in the records style him by some variant of Dechamp. His marriage entry in 1678 shows that his father was also 'Louis Touvoi dit de Champ' [HSQS XIII, 56].
BORN: Tours
IN OFFICE: D 1694–7; A 1701–5
TRADE, WEALTH, SOCIAL STATUS: (Master) weaver, in 1700 in Black Eagle Street, Spitalfields [HSQS XVI, 202k]. His stock was assessed as having a taxable value of £200, and the extensive inventory made in 1707 following his death listed goods and more particularly investments and bonds totalling over £4000 [G. Parker (2014), 162–5]. He was an original subscriber to the 1697 issue to enlarge the Bank's capital stock, with £960 [BEA, M1/6, A, no.221].
FAMILY OR TRADE CONNECTIONS WITH OTHER CHURCH OFFICERS: Brother-in-law of Jacques Caron, and of Nicolas Dufay?

NAME: **Jean DELEDICQUE** or **DELDICK** (d'Eldit, del Dik)
ENDENIZED/NATURALIZED: Named in a naturalization bill that did not become an Act, 1670–1.
IN OFFICE: D 1673–6. He had been in London since 1659, and died by the end of 1681 [HSQS XXI, 77, and 138 *sub* 'Heldick'].
TRADE, WEALTH, SOCIAL STATUS: Foreign master weaver; his namesake son took up the same trade [HSQS XXXIII, 40, 44].

NAME: **Jean DELFOSS** (Delfos, De Le Fose, Delfosse)
BORN: Valenciennes
ENDENIZED/NATURALIZED: Nat 1696
IN OFFICE: D 1691–4; A 1699–1702, appears to have left or died in the first half of 1702.
TRADE, WEALTH, SOCIAL STATUS: Weaver [HSQS XXXIII, 54]
FAMILY OR TRADE CONNECTIONS WITH OTHER CHURCH OFFICERS: Brother-in-law of Adrian Denis (married the same day) [HSQS XIII, 61].

DE LILLERS, see LILLERS

NAME: **Jean DELMÉ** (Dalme, Delmet, Del Mee, de le Mer)
BORN: Canterbury, 1633
IN OFFICE: D 1668–70; A 1677–9, 1686–8. The son of the Canterbury minister Philippe Delmé (1588–1653) [Gwynn (2015), 261–2], whose papers were eventually printed in 1701 as *The Method of Good Preaching, being the Advice of a French Reform'd Minister to his Son*, Jean Delmé had decided opinions and took an active interest in the government of the Threadneedle Street church whether in or out of office. In 1688 he successfully sought the establishment of 'petites écoles' in which the children of the poor could be taught reading, writing and the catechism [FCL, MS 7, p. 394]. He also unavailingly protested at the manner of Piozet's nomination in 1683; urged in 1688 that unemployed refugee ministers be allowed to preach at l'Eglise de l'Hôpital; called for the convocation of a Colloquy in 1698, in which year he also complained about beggars at the church doors and asked that Threadneedle Street contribute to the establishment of a new French church; and opposed the discharge given to the minister Jacques Saurin in 1706 [FCL, MS 7, pp. 144, 395, 400, 403, 447, and MS 8, ff. 60–2, 245v]. Apart from his Threadneedle Street connections, Delmé presented a substantial number of books to the church of La Patente, Spitalfields [Burn (1846), 169n].
TRADE, WEALTH, SOCIAL STATUS: Merchant factor, with an important role in marketing the goods produced by Canterbury weavers [Rothstein (1989), 39–42]. Jean Delmé showed early interest in the Bank of England, attending its second General Court [BEA, G7/1 1694–1701, 10 Aug. 1694]. He was an original subscriber to the Bank in 1694, with £500 [BEA, M1/1, p. 6], and also to the 1697 issue to enlarge its capital stock, with £4020, when he was described as being of St Pancras, Soper Lane [BEA, M1/6, Book A, 2 June, and Book B, 19 June]. He held £3020 bank stock in 1709 [P.G.M. Dickson, pers. com.]. Before the advent of the Bank, Delmé was a regular provider of £300 loans in the early years of William III's government [*CTB*, *1689–92*, 1972, 1977, 1982, 1994, 2001]. He was buried at the Dutch Church of Austin Friars in 1712 [Moens (1884), 150, 169].
FAMILY OR TRADE CONNECTIONS WITH OTHER CHURCH OFFICERS: Brother of Pierre Delmé. Nephew of Pierre Du Quesne.

NAME: **Pierre DELMÉ**
BORN: Canterbury, 1630
IN OFFICE: D 1662–5; A 1672–5, 1682–5. Pierre Delmé was a member of deputations to Secretary Coventry in 1674 to express the consistory's reluctance to accept Bonhomme as minister, and later to settle differences

between the church and Mayor Sharp, 1682–3 [FCL, MS 5, p. 617, and MS 7, p. 116]. He took over some of Guillaume Carbonnel's accounting work for the new refugees in 1684, when he began the document now FCL, MS 55 [FCL, MS 7, p. 182].

TRADE, WEALTH, SOCIAL STATUS, ENGLISH POLITICAL AFFILIATION: Wealthy merchant and Dyer of London [Agnew (1886), I, 61–2 where his will is given in full, 186]. Common Councilman of London [Woodhead (1965), 59]. One of the 'principaux de l'Eglise' consulted about the refugees, 1681 [FCL, MS 7, p. 80]. An 'Adventurer' in the stock raised to establish French refugee linen manufacture at Ipswich, 1681–2 [Papillon, 119]. His will, proved in the first week of 1687, shows he held city property in the Poultry, Old Jury, Conyhoope Lane and elsewhere. Whig: 'French Presbyterian, ye best in ye pack', 1681 [Woodhead (1965), 59, citing TNA, SP/29/417/144].

His eldest son, Pierre, served as a member of the English Committee supervising public charity administration, 1705 [*Estat* for that year]. Pierre junior was knighted, became Governor of the Bank of England (1715–17) and Lord Mayor of London (1723), and was worth over £300,000 on his death in 1728 [*HSP* XV, 243; D.W. Jones, 'London Merchants and the Crisis of the 1690s', in Clark and Slack (1972), 329].

FAMILY OR TRADE CONNECTIONS WITH OTHER CHURCH OFFICERS: Brother of Jean Delmé. Nephew of Pierre Du Quesne.

NAME: **Isaac DELPECH** (Delpeche)
BORN: Bergerac
ENDENIZED/NATURALIZED: End 1701 ('Delpeth'); Nat 1707
IN OFFICE: D 1704–7; A 1709–?, later elected again 1721–3 [Eg. 2734].

NAME: **Jacques** (James) **DENEU** (de Neu, Denew, Denieu, de Noeu, Denue)
BORN: London
IN OFFICE: D 1654–6, 1664–7; A 1670–3, 1678–81. In June 1656, he abandoned his charge because he objected to the deacons being excluded from consistorial debates concerning Elie Delmé, whom he supported [FCL, MS 135A; Hessels, 2401–2; *Consistoire* [1657]].

TRADE, WEALTH, SOCIAL STATUS, ENGLISH POLITICAL AFFILIATION: Born 1627, died 1705 [*HSP* XV, 241]. Trustee of, and an 'Adventurer' in, the stock raised to establish refugees in the linen manufacture at Ipswich, 1681–2 [FCL, MS 7, p. 66; Papillon, 119]. Member of the English Committee supervising public charity administration, c.1699–1705 [LP, MS 941, no. 87; *Estat* for 1705].

Jacques Deneu was a citizen and Dyer of London, Prime Warden of the

Dyers' Company in 1678–9. He was a merchant of Mark Lane and a Common Councilman [Woodhead (1965), 59]. He had warehouses near the Tower but was described as of Barking in his will [HSQS LX, 133]. As a wine merchant, his trading area included Portugal, 1685 [TNA, SP/31/5, f. 11r]. He acted as agent for at least one Dutch investor in the English Million loan of 1693 [Dickson (1967), plate facing p. 298]. He himself lent £950 on the 4/- Aid, Poll Tax and Tontine in 1693–4 [D.W. Jones (1971), p. 484]. He became one of the original directors of the Bank of England, to which he subscribed £2000 in 1694, followed by £2810 towards the enlargement of the Bank stock in 1697 [BEA, M1/1, p. 4, and M1/6, Book B nos. 6, 109, and Book C, no. 55]. He was part owner of two ships engaged in privateering in the 1690s [D.W. Jones (1971), pp. 498, 509].

A Whig City leader, he aroused the wrath of the Court by defending Thomas Papillon before the Mayor of London in 1683 [Papillon, chap. XI; FCL, MS 7, pp. 132–3]. He was identified as a 'disaffected and suspicious person' to be arrested and detained at the time of Monmouth's rebellion, 1685 [LMA, CLA/050/02/002, pp. 37, 43, 61].

FAMILY OR TRADE CONNECTIONS WITH OTHER CHURCH OFFICERS: In partnership with his brother Nathaniel Deneu. Father of Jean Deneu. Son-in-law of Jean de Lillers. Brother-in-law of Guillaume Carbonnel. Uncle of Delillers Carbonnel.

NAME: **Jean DENEU**
BORN: London
IN OFFICE: D 1691–3; A 1696–9, 1701–4. Notably active as elder, during 1699 he was involved in various deputations to the Lord Chancellor or Secretary Vernon, the Bishop of London, and the Solicitor-General; and to the General Assembly considering the possible establishment of a refugee colony in Yorkshire [FCL, MS 8, ff. 82v, 84v, 90–1]. In 1702–3 he worked with Joseph Ducasse seeking to ensure the French and Dutch churches' exemption from any legislation on Occasional Conformity [ibid., ff. 189–90; Hessels, 2737, 2746].

TRADE, WEALTH, SOCIAL STATUS: Citizen and Dyer of London. Gentleman [Glass, p. 87] and merchant [HSQS LX, 133]. Member of the English Committee supervising public charity administration, c.1699–1709 [LP, MS 941, no. 87; *Estats* for 1706–9]; in this capacity he examined many of the relevant accounts now in the London Metropolitan Archives. He subscribed £260 towards the enlargement of the Bank's capital stock in 1697 [BEA, M1/6, Book D no. 10].

FAMILY OR TRADE CONNECTIONS WITH OTHER CHURCH OFFICERS: Son of Jacques Deneu. Son-in-law of Claude Hays (I) [Evelyn G.M. Carmichael (ed.), 'Family Note Book of Stephen Peter Godin',

The Genealogist, N.S. XXVIII:3, Jan. 1912, 129–41] (as was David Bosanquet).

NAME: **Nathaniel DENEU**
BORN: London
IN OFFICE: D 1668–71; A 1674–7. As deacon he was used on deputations to the Court of Aldermen, Lord Arlington, and the Weavers Company, and helped draw up a petition to the Council of Trade in 1669 [FCL, MS 5, pp. 539, 553–4, 546].
TRADE, WEALTH, SOCIAL STATUS: Common Councilman of London. Merchant and Dyer of Mark Lane [Woodhead (1965), 59]. On his death in 1690, his personal estate was valued at £8595, his trade connections being 'confined wholly to Lisbon, Port Saint Mary, Alicante, Venice and Genoa' [D.W. Jones (1988), 264].
FAMILY OR TRADE CONNECTIONS WITH OTHER CHURCH OFFICERS: In partnership with his brother Jacques Deneu. Son-in-law of Isaac de Lillers (I). Brother-in-law of Jacob de Lillers.

NAME: **Adrien DENIS** (Denise, Dennis)
BORN: Valenciennes
ENDENIZED/NATURALIZED: Nat 1698
IN OFFICE: D 1692–5; A 1700–2, 1707–?
TRADE, WEALTH, SOCIAL STATUS: Silk weaver [HSQS XVI, 177]
FAMILY OR TRADE CONNECTIONS WITH OTHER CHURCH OFFICERS: Brother-in-law of Jean Delfoss (married the same day).

NAME: **Jean DENIS**
BORN: Valenciennes
IN OFFICE: D?–1639; A 1641–3

NAME: **Samuel DE SANTHUNS** (I) (Santhune, Santun)
BORN: Canterbury
IN OFFICE: A 1667–70
TRADE, WEALTH, SOCIAL STATUS: Weaver, as was his son, another Samuel [references in HSQS XXXIII *sub* Desantine]. He remarried a cousin of Samuel Pepys, and the diarist was struck when De Santhuns specially sought him out in his house to return eighteen pence that he had been overpaid in error months previously [HSQS XIII, 44f; Latham and Matthews (1970), V, 342].

NAME: **Samuel DE SANTHUNS** (II)
IN OFFICE: A 1710–? [Eg. 2734].

NAME: **Samuel DESBOUVERIES** (Desbouverye)
BORN: London
IN OFFICE: D 1646–8

NAME: **Pierre DESCHAMPS** (De Champ, Des Champs)
BORN: (Poitou)
ENDENIZED/NATURALIZED: Yes, see below.
IN OFFICE: D 1697–1700; later elected A 1724–7 [Eg. 2734].
TRADE, WEALTH, SOCIAL STATUS: Merchant of Mark Lane, All Hallows, Barking [HSQS LX, 138]. Agent for three original subscribers to the Bank of England in 1694, Isaac Beranger, Francis Le Coq and Samuel de Ravenel, but not himself a subscriber [BEA, M1/1, pp. 10, 27, and M1/3, 22 June 1694].
FAMILY OR TRADE CONNECTIONS WITH OTHER CHURCH OFFICERS: His son Pierre married Catherine, daughter of Jean Ghiselin [Wagner pedigrees]. Precise identification is difficult. 'Peter Deschamps, born at Crollow in the Province of Poitou in France, son of Gabriel Deschamps by Jane, his wife' was naturalized in 1699 [HSQS XVIII, 271]. 'Peter Deschamps' was endenized in 1700 [ibid., 314]. 'Peter Deschampz, son of Peter Deschampz, by Mary his wife, born at Poitiers in Poitou' was naturalized in 1702 [HSQS XXVII, 22]. Two Pierre Deschamps became Directors of the French Hospital, one in 1736, the other in 1757 [Murdoch and Vigne (2009), 96].
FAMILY OR TRADE CONNECTIONS WITH OTHER CHURCH OFFICERS: Brother-in-law of Jean Motteux.

NAME: **Jacques DESMAISTRES**
BORN: 'Collein in Germany' [HSQS XVIII, 10]
ENDENIZED/NATURALIZED: Nat 1607
IN OFFICE: A continuously 1622–48 [HSQS LIV, 2 n. 8].
TRADE, WEALTH, SOCIAL STATUS: Described when naturalized as 'James Desmaistres, of East Smithfeild in the parish of St. Buttolphes without Algate in ... Middlesex, brewer'. The Threadneedle Street church received a legacy of £100 in 1650 following his death [FCL, MS 62, f. 8r].

NAME: **Daniel DESMARETS** (Demaré, Desmare, Desmarez)
BORN: Norwich
IN OFFICE: D 1643–7; A 1647–51, 1665–6, died in office [FCL, MS 5, p. 500]. In 1657 he was a strong supporter of Elie Delmé [*Consistoire* [1657]]. Estranged from the consistory in 1658 [Hessels, 2401], he was evidently reconciled with it in 1661 [FCL, MS 5, p. 404].

TRADE, WEALTH, SOCIAL STATUS: Weaver ['Desmaris', HSQS XXXIII, 12]. He volunteered a short-term loan of £100 when the church poor fund was exhausted in 1648 [FCL, MS 5, p. 341].

NAME: **Samuel DESPAIGN** (Despagne, Despaigne, d'Espagne)
BORN: Canterbury
IN OFFICE: D 1671–5; A 1680–2, dead by September 1682 [FCL, MS 90].
A man of this name had been a deacon of the French church of Canterbury in 1659 [CCL, U47-H-2, no. 86].
TRADE, WEALTH, SOCIAL STATUS: Admitted a foreign weaver in London, 1671, having served his apprenticeship at Canterbury [HSQS XXXIII, 36].
FAMILY OR TRADE CONNECTIONS WITH OTHER CHURCH OFFICERS: Married Marie, daughter of Jacques Baudry (I). Brother-in-law of Jacques Baudry (II) and Pierre Baudry, and of Nicolas (de la Fontaine, dit) Wicart.

NAME: **Abraham DESQUIEN** (Deskeen, Deskiens, Desqueene, Desquin)
BORN: London
IN OFFICE: D?-1638, 1644–6
TRADE, WEALTH, SOCIAL STATUS: Weaver [HSQS XXXIII, 15, 17].
FAMILY OR TRADE CONNECTIONS WITH OTHER CHURCH OFFICERS: His daughters Elizabeth and Suzanne married respectively Bon Danbrine and Daniel Du Prie (II) [HSQS XIII, 31d, 32k].

NAME: **Daniel DESVILLE** (Dellvill, Delvil, Desvilles) dit CITY
BORN: London
IN OFFICE: D 1645–7

NAME: **Benjamin DIDIER**
BORN: Canterbury, 1671 [HSQS V, 264].
IN OFFICE: D 1695–8, having been elected soon after arriving from Canterbury [HSQS XXI, 87]; A 1703–6.
TRADE, WEALTH, SOCIAL STATUS, ENGLISH POLITICAL AFFILIATION: Weaver [HSQS XXXIII, 74].
FAMILY OR TRADE CONNECTIONS WITH OTHER CHURCH OFFICERS: Brother-in-law of Samuel Hannott and of Charles Lason; cousin of Peter Le Keux [HSQS LX, 144. His will was proved 7 July 1721].

NAME: **Jacques DOBY** (Dobi, Dobie, Dobye)
IN OFFICE: D 1682; his insistence on resigning from office after only a year's service was accepted with reluctance [FCL, MS 7, p. 117].

NAME: **Paul DOBY**
BORN: London
IN OFFICE: D?-1638, 1641–4; A 1652–8, 1673–6
TRADE, WEALTH, SOCIAL STATUS, ENGLISH POLITICAL
AFFILIATION: Common Councilman of London; at his death in 1680,
his will shows him to be a merchant owning city property [Woodhead
(1965), 60]. Upper Bailiff of the Weavers' Company, 1668 [Plummer
(1972) 452]. Member of the Artillery Company, 1635–43; Captain of the
Red Trained Band Regiment, 1661 [*HSP* XV, 307]. Probably a moderate
politically; he testified against seditious preaching by De la Marche, 1646,
and brought charges against him at the 1647 Synod [Hessels, 1971; FCL,
MS 5, p. 335], but was at odds with the strongly royalist Hérault [FCL,
MS 5, f. 134b, and MS 6, pp. 607, 645].
FAMILY OR TRADE CONNECTIONS WITH OTHER CHURCH
OFFICERS: Son-in-law of Jean Edlin [HSQS IX, 30, 108].

NAME: **Paul DOCMINIQUE** (Docmyne, Docqmesnil, Docque Mesineque,
Dogminigue, Donckmenique)
BORN: Lille
ENDENIZED/NATURALIZED: Nat 1657, End 1662
IN OFFICE: D 1652–4; A 1660–3, 1667–9, 1676–9. In 1669 he was
involved in petitioning the Council of Trade on behalf of foreign weavers
in England [FCL, MS 5, pp. 546–7, 556].
TRADE, WEALTH, SOCIAL STATUS: Weaver [HSQS XXXIII, 17,
21–2 ('Duckmanis', 'Duikmanee')] and merchant of Stepney. Later he was
based at Hackney. He acquired the 5½-acre Holcroft's estate in Fulham,
a property he surrendered to his only son (also Paul) in 1675 [C.J. Feret,
Fulham Old and New (1900), ii, 161]. Gifts to the French Church of
London included £100 towards rebuilding after the Fire, and (jointly with
his wife) the land on which l'Eglise de l'Hôpital was later built [FCL, MS
62, f. 20v, and MS 43, p. 25]. He died in December 1680 [FCL, MS 7,
p. 36].
His son, Paul (II), native of London, declined office as deacon in 1677.
He became a merchant of note, Governor of the White Paper Makers
Company in 1696 and with a holding of £4000 in the Million Bank by
1701 [*HSP* XIX, 220; TNA, C/114/16], an M.P. and a Lord of Trade and
Plantations [Wagner Pedigrees]. In the early years after the Revolution he
agreed to loan the Exchequer over £9000 in 1690 and £10,000 in 1692,
and became an army clothing contractor [*CTB, 1689–92*, 621, 1742–3
and elsewhere].
FAMILY OR TRADE CONNECTIONS WITH OTHER CHURCH
OFFICERS: Brother-in-law of Pierre Tordereau [HSQS XIII, 21k, 24i].

Father-in-law of Benjamin Le Nud and of Etienne Lauze [Wagner Pedigrees].

NAME: **Jean DRIGUÉ** (Driguier, Driguer, Driquée, Driguy)
BORN: London
IN OFFICE: D 1654–7, 1661–4; he signed FCL, MS 135A as 'Jean Drigue le jeune'). A 1669–72, 1678–81, 1684–7. He contributed £40 towards rebuilding the church after the Fire, and made frequent donations to the library [FCL, MS 62 (f. 26v), and MS 5, pp. 607, 648, 673, 683, 694, 699, 719].
TRADE, WEALTH, SOCIAL STATUS: One of the 'principaux de l'Eglise' consulted about the refugees, 1681 [FCL, MS 7, p. 80]. An 'Adventurer' in the stock raised to establish French refugee linen manufacture at Ipswich, 1681–2 [Papillon, 118]. Upper Bailiff of the Weavers Company, 1689; he donated to it a large folio bible and £50 for the annual relief of two poor weavers in Bishopsgate [Plummer (1972), 259, 428, 452]. 'Esquire' in Bank of England records when he acquired £1400 of stock on 12 April 1695 [BEA, AC 28/32233].
FAMILY OR TRADE CONNECTIONS WITH OTHER CHURCH OFFICERS: His daughter and sole heir, Judith, married Herman Olmius [HSQS XIII, 51g].

NAME: **Ferri DUBOIS** (du Bois, Duboys)
BORN: Haubourdin, Flanders
IN OFFICE: D 1671–3
TRADE, WEALTH, SOCIAL STATUS, ENGLISH POLITICAL AFFILIATION: Admitted foreign master weaver, 1666 [HSQS XXXIII, 17].

NAME: **Jean DUBOIS**
BORN: Canterbury, 1622
IN OFFICE: D 1657–60; A 1670–2. With Thomas Papillon, although both were only deacons, he represented the consistory against the Delmé faction before the Council of State, 1657 [Papillon, 48–53].
TRADE, WEALTH, SOCIAL STATUS, ENGLISH POLITICAL AFFILIATION: Although declining a second term in office in 1677, as a man of importance in English society Jean Dubois was frequently approached when the French church became involved with the civil authorities. In 1676 he assisted a deputation to the Privy Council from the Canterbury church [FCL, MS 5, p. 673]. When in 1680 the Threadneedle Street consistory wanted advice about a possible Act of Parliament in favour of Protestant foreigners coming to work in England, it turned to

Dubois and Thomas Papillon because they were MPs [FCL, MS 7, p. 36]. These two men were also the first to be asked to become trustees of the fund for establishing the silk manufacture in Ipswich in 1681 [ibid., p. 66]. Dubois was again consulted about the refugees by the consistory the following year [ibid., p. 86], and was involved in supervising refugee relief on a national scale from 1681 [*The Currant Intelligence*, no. 42, 13–17 Sept. 1681]. In 1676–7 he received money from the Archbishop of Canterbury for the education at Oxford of two men designed for the ministry in the Piedmont [BT, MS xl, f. 4r].

Dubois was a Common Councilman of London [Woodhead (1965), 62], Upper Bailiff of the Weavers Company in 1682 [Plummer (1972), 452], and a leading Whig merchant trading with France [Priestley (1956)]. For his wealth, see *Past and Present* 46 (1970), 92: he 'divided his £16,189 between East India stock, ships and leases'. His will, proved in 1684, shows he had land in Carmarthen, Kent and Surrey, and after his death his personal estate was valued at £35,205 [Woodhead]. He claimed to be instrumental in promoting a £100,000 loan to the government in London on the credit of the Poll Act in the 1670s [*CTB, 1676–9*, 1375]. He was however a strong supporter of Exclusion, a member of the Grand Jury that dismissed the charges against the Earl of Shaftesbury in 1681, and one of the Whig candidates in the controversial 1682 election for sheriff of London and Middlesex (the other being Thomas Papillon) [Gwynn (2018), 254].

NAME: **Philippe DUBOIS**
BORN: Canterbury
IN OFFICE: D 1672–5
TRADE, WEALTH, SOCIAL STATUS: Merchant [*CTB, 1660–7*, 732]

DUCANE, see Du Quesne

NAME: **Joseph DUCASSE de la Couture** (Du Case, Du Casse)
BORN: Nérac
ENDENIZED/NATURALIZED: End 1687; took the oaths for a naturalization Bill that was never concluded, 1690; Nat 1698.
IN OFFICE: D 1689–92, after joining the church in 1686 [HSQS XXI, 91]; A 1694–8, 1701–5, 1708–?. With Jean Deneu, Ducasse had oversight during 1696–8 of tallies worth £4000 for refugee relief in England [FCL, MS 8, ff. 43, 64–5]. He showed particular concern for the plight of the galley slaves in France, helping transmit money for them to Lisbon [ibid., ff. 107v, 166r, 187r]. In 1703 he was again working alongside Deneu, seeking to ensure the French and Dutch churches' exemption from any

legislation on Occasional Conformity [ibid., ff. 189–90; Hessels, 2737, 2746].

TRADE, WEALTH, SOCIAL STATUS, ENGLISH POLITICAL AFFILIATION: Joseph was the eldest son of Jérémie Ducasse, *avocat au Parlement*. He left France in the livery of the future Republican martyr Algernon Sidney, joining his household in London in 1680–81 [Scott (1991), 85]. He became Sidney's valet and trusted secretary [*CSPD, July–Sept. 1683*, 142, 170] and later 'the custodian of his memory, as well as the guardian of his papers' [Carswell (1989), 159]. When Sidney was executed for high treason on Tower Hill at the end of 1683 following the discovery of the Rye House Plot, Ducasse was his sole servant at the scaffold. Later Ducasse safeguarded Sidney's *Apology*, reappearing with it in 1689–90, and spoke for him before the House of Lords enquiry [*LJ*, XIV, 390–1; Scott (1991), 294]. It is 'just possible' that Ducasse's wife Marie was Sidney's illegitimate daughter [Scott (1991), 86]. Ducasse was a merchant [HSQS XXI, 91], and an original subscriber to the Bank of England in 1694 with £500 [BEA, M1/1, p. 41].

NAME: **Louis DUCLOUX** (du Clou, du Cloux)
BORN: Sedan
ENDENIZED/NATURALIZED: End 1682?
IN OFFICE: D 1663–6; A 1674–6
TRADE, WEALTH, SOCIAL STATUS: Foreign weaver [HSQS XXXIII, 27 and other references as 'Decleux' and 'de Clew'].

NAME: **Jacques DUFAY** (Du Faye, Dufaij)
BORN: Boulogne
ENDENIZED/NATURALIZED: Nat 1685 [HSQS XVIII, 170].
IN OFFICE: A 1690–3, 1697–9, having arrived from Boulogne in 1681 [HSQS XXI, 92]. In 1690 he assisted the French Committee in making a collection for the refugees [HL, Bounty MS 6, 23 May and 2 June 1690]. At the December 1698 *Censures* it was ordered that he was not to be named in the list of discharged elders although his place was vacant [FCL, MS 8, f. 80r], and his accounts were rendered by Samuel Monck, the deacon of his *quartier*, throughout 1699 [FCL, MS 90].
TRADE, WEALTH, SOCIAL STATUS: Substantial merchant, with connections in France; he passed on £250 from Adrien Gorray of Paris to the Threadneedle Street Consistory in 1687 [FCL, MS 7, pp. 375, 378], and the Earl of Nottingham, Secretary of State, received anonymous information c.1690 that he had sent 4000 louis d'or to France in a single consignment [HMC 71: *Finch* II: p. 497]. Dufay invested £5000 in government securities 1692–3 [D.W. Jones (1971), 484], and was an

original subscriber to the Bank of England in 1694 with £2800 [BEA, M1/1, pp. 20, 28, 31]; his wife sometimes acted as his attorney [BEA, AC28/1513, 2 Aug. 1699]. Before the advent of the Bank, Dufay provided loans in the early years of William III's government, £2600 in 1689 and the same sum in 1690 [*CTB, 1689–92*, 1982–3, 2001, 2006: in the last of these references he is described as gentleman rather than merchant]. In 1695/6 he imported £2188 of currants from Zante and sent out £906 of new drapery exports to Lisbon and Near Europe [D.W. Jones (1971), 452]. According to Agnew, much of the Amonnet-Crommelin 'wealth was dissipated partly through the speculative mania of ... James Dufay' [Agnew (1886), II, 248].
FAMILY OR TRADE CONNECTIONS WITH OTHER CHURCH OFFICERS: In December 1684 Jacques Dufay married Jeanne Crommelin, widow of François Amonnet [HSQS XXVI, 122]. In 1697 he was close to a lawsuit with David Garric [FCL, MS 8, f. 48r].

NAME: **Nicolas DUFAY**
BORN: Boulogne
ENDENIZED/NATURALIZED: End 1682, Nat 1696 [HSQS XVIII, 142, 241]
IN OFFICE: D 1688–91, having arrived in 1678 with a *témoignage* from Canterbury [HSQS XXI, 92]; he found it difficult to fulfil all the obligations of his charge [FCL, MS 138, loose sheet by f. 322, and MS 51, p. 83].
FAMILY OR TRADE CONNECTIONS WITH OTHER CHURCH OFFICERS: Brother-in-law of Jacques Caron, and of François Touvoye dit de Champs.

NAME: **Jacques DUFOUR** (du Four)
BORN: Tours
ENDENIZED/NATURALIZED: Nat 1706
IN OFFICE: D 1702–5; A 1708–?
TRADE, WEALTH, SOCIAL STATUS: In 1703 he loaned £10 to the establishment of the French church of St Martin Orgars [LMA, MS 00994/I, p. 46]. He served on the French Committee, 1706–8 [*Estats* for 1706, 1708].

NAME: **Abraham DUGARD** (I) (Du Gar, Dugart, Duguar, d'Ugar)
BORN: Rouen
ENDENIZED/NATURALIZED: End 1687
IN OFFICE: A 1696–9, 1702–5
TRADE, WEALTH, SOCIAL STATUS: Merchant and goldsmith. Arrested

with his wife Elisabeth Saunier near Dieppe while trying to leave France; dragoons were maintained at the expense of his estate in his absence [Lesens, 28; Bianquis, 73]. Substantial London inhabitant, liable to surtax in 1695 Assessment as having a personal estate valued over £600 [Glass, 93]. In the early years of William III's government he loaned the Exchequer £300 in 1689 and £400 in 1690 [*CTB*, *1689–92*, 1985, 1992]. Member of the French Committee administering public charity, 1692–4 [HL, Bounty MS 6, 14 July 1692–4 April 1694]; he later complained that the Committee was denying to the poor the assistance ordered for them by the English Committee [*Malversations* (1708), 26]. See also:

NAME: **Abraham DUGARD** (II)
BORN: Rouen
IN OFFICE: D 1700–3
TRADE, WEALTH, SOCIAL STATUS: Merchant. Many references cannot be allocated with certainty between Abraham (I) and (II). Abraham and his wife Elizabeth were endenized in 1687 [HSQS XVIII, 197]. One Abraham produced his *témoignage* from Rouen in 1684 [HSQS XXI, 93]. Louis and an Abraham Dugard jointly contributed £10 to the loan at the establishment of the St Martin Orgars church, 1703 [LMA, MS 00994/I, p. 46]; they were merchants in partnership with another refugee from Rouen, Isaac Caillouel [HL, Caillouel MSS]. One of the Abrahams, of Basinghall Street, contributed £500 to the 1695 subscription for the Million Bank [TNA, C/114/16], and one was nominated by the Threadneedle Street Consistory to join the French Committee in 1701 [FCL, MS 8, f. 149r].

NAME: **Antoine DUGUA** (Du Gas, Du Guast, Dugast)
BORN: Nîmes
ENDENIZED/NATURALIZED: Nat 1675
IN OFFICE: D 1684–7

NAME: **Jean DU MAISTRE** (Dumaitre)
BORN: Bordeaux
ENDENIZED/NATURALIZED: End 1683, Nat 1685
IN OFFICE: D 1685–7
TRADE, WEALTH, SOCIAL STATUS, ENGLISH POLITICAL AFFILIATION: Merchant. An original subscriber to the Bank of England in 1694, with £500 [BEA, M1/1, p. 7]. Substantial London inhabitant, liable to surtax in 1695 Assessment as having a personal estate valued over £600 [Glass, p. 87 *sub* 'Demastre']. In 1695/6 he had a turnover of £506 old drapery exports and over £5570 imports, principally Italian silk

[D.W. Jones (1971), 454 (arithmetic reworked)]. Ordered by Parliament to be tried in the Westminster Courts for trading with the enemy during wartime, 1698 [*HSP* XV, 419, 424; *CJ* XII, 300].

NAME: **Jean DUMESNIL**
BORN: Calais
ENDENIZED/NATURALIZED: Nat 1677
IN OFFICE: D 1679–81. His activities on behalf of the new refugees included accompanying those going to settle in Ipswich, 1681 [FCL, MS 7, pp. 80–2, 84].
TRADE, WEALTH, SOCIAL STATUS: Merchant.
FAMILY OR TRADE CONNECTIONS WITH OTHER CHURCH OFFICERS: Sometimes worked with Jacob David [Roseveare, 182, 551].

NAME: **Huber DUMONS** (Dumont)
BORN: Valenciennes
IN OFFICE: D 1702–4

NAME: **Jacques DU MOUTIER** (Motie, Moultier, Moustier)
BORN: Blois
ENDENIZED/NATURALIZED: Yes
IN OFFICE: D 1681–4; A 1688–91, 1700–4. He was absent in Holland in July 1691, when he sought discharge, and still there when he was discharged six months later [FCL, MS 7, pp. 449, 523, 534–5].
TRADE, WEALTH, SOCIAL STATUS: Merchant [Roseveare, 515, 517]

NAME: **Simon DUPORT** (du Port)
BORN: Ile de Ré
ENDENIZED/NATURALIZED: End 1686, Nat 1696
IN OFFICE: D 1689–91; A 1694–7, 1703–6. He also petitioned in favour of a new French church in London, c.1686 [BT, xcii, f. 185v], and contributed £10 to the loan at the establishment of the French church of St Martin Orgars, 1703 [LMA, MS 00994/I, p. 46]. His wife and four children were detained near Deal in 1693 when trying to rejoin him in London [*CSPD, 1693*, 177].
TRADE, WEALTH, SOCIAL STATUS: Substantial London inhabitant, liable to surtax in the 1695 Assessment as having a personal estate valued over £600 [Glass, p. 95]. Merchant, with imports 1695/6 of £550 of currants from Zante and £1203 of port and wine [D.W. Jones (1971), 441, 450]. He was bankrupted in 1708 and died in King's Lynn in early 1724 [HSQS LX, 156].

FAMILY OR TRADE CONNECTIONS WITH OTHER CHURCH OFFICERS: Married Suzanne, daughter of Jean Strang, 1690 [HSQS, XVI, 17i].

NAME: **Daniel DU PRIE** (I) (Peré, Perrier, Pree, Prié, Prier, Prye)
BORN: Valenciennes
ENDENIZED/NATURALIZED: End 1632
IN OFFICE: D 1639–41; A 1644–?, 1649–53. He had died by mid-1654 [HSQS XIII, 35].
TRADE, WEALTH, SOCIAL STATUS: Weaver [HSQS XVIII, 46].
FAMILY OR TRADE CONNECTIONS WITH OTHER CHURCH OFFICERS: His daughter Susanne married the son of Deric Petit [HSQS XIII, 35].

NAME: **Daniel DU PRIE** (II)
BORN: London, 1625
IN OFFICE: D 1664–7; A 1672–5, 1679–82. Before the Restoration, he had been a supporter of Elie Delmé [*Consistoire* [1657]]. While deacon, he preserved the church library at his house following the Fire of London [FCL, MS 5, p. 503]. As elder he was named on deputations to Secretary Williamson (1675), and to thank the Bishop and Mayor of London and the King for their help to the new refugees (1681) [FCL, MS 5, p. 634, and MS 7, pp. 57, 70]. He was an 'Adventurer' in the stock raised to establish refugees in the linen manufacture at Ipswich, 1681–2 [Papillon, 119]. He became landlord of the Spitalfields *Maison de Charité* [HL, *Maison de Charité, Journal* 1693ff, f. 7a].
TRADE, WEALTH, SOCIAL STATUS: Merchant, of St Botolph's Without, Bishopsgate. By his will dated 23 August 1688 and proved 9 May 1694, he left £550 to each of seven children, specified house property, and referred to his goods adventured at sea at Cadiz, in the West Indies and elsewhere [PCC, 98, Box].
FAMILY OR TRADE CONNECTIONS WITH OTHER CHURCH OFFICERS: Married to Suzanne Desquien, 1650 [HSQS XIII, 32k]. André Willau and Herman Olmius were named as trustees in his will. His daughter Judith was the second wife of the minister David Primerose.

NAME: **Elie DUPUY** (Depuy, du Puis)
BORN: Bordeaux
ENDENIZED/NATURALIZED: End 1687, Nat 1698 [HSQS XVIII, 181, 184, 217, 252]
IN OFFICE: A 1690–3, 1698–1701. During his second term as elder, he organized a safe route for money being sent to the *galériens*, evidently

through a member of his family at Lisbon [FCL, MS 8, ff. 98r, 109r, 187r, and MS 91, f. 194].
TRADE, WEALTH, SOCIAL STATUS: Former *bourgeois* and merchant of Bordeaux [Meller (1902), 12]. Substantial London inhabitant, liable to surtax in the 1695 Assessment as having a personal estate valued over £600 [Glass, p. 95]. In 1695/6 he had a turnover of £2463 in port and Spanish wine imports, and he contributed £3000 to the East India Loan in 1698 [D.W. Jones (1971), 441, 478].

NAME: **Benjamin DU QUESNE** or **DUCANE** (Ducayne, Dukaine) (1613–90)
BORN: London. Baptized as Benjamin Du Quesne in 1613 [HSQS IX, 89], as a church officer he signed the *Discipline* as Ducane [FCL, MS 135A; Eg. 2734].
IN OFFICE: D 1647–9; A 1671–4. In 1657 he was a supporter of Elie Delmé [*Consistoire* [1657]].
TRADE, WEALTH, SOCIAL STATUS, ENGLISH POLITICAL AFFILIATION: Merchant and Common Councilman of London. Admitted a member of the Artillery Company, 1642; captain of horse regiment, 1660; Lieutenant-Colonel of the Green Auxiliary Regiment, 1660–6 [Woodhead (1965), 62; HSP XV, 307]. He served as Upper Bailiff of the Weavers' Company in the difficult years of 1666 and 1667 to the 'great satisfaction' of 'the whole Yeomanry and divers of the commonalty'; he contributed £20 to the rebuilding of the Company hall after the Fire, and was presumably partly responsible for encouraging the French and Dutch congregations to provide £49 10s for the same purpose in 1667–8 despite the financial problems involved in rebuilding the French church itself [Plummer (1972), 203, 207]. Treasurer of Bridewell and Bethlem Hospital [Du Cane (1876), 17]. Whig [De Krey (1978), 636]. He died in 1690 [Woodhead (1965), 62].
FAMILY OR TRADE CONNECTIONS WITH OTHER CHURCH OFFICERS: Younger brother of Jean (II) and Pierre Du Quesne. Brother-in-law of Isaac Le Quesne [Du Cane (1876), 16–17] and of Jacques Houblon.

NAME: **Jean DU QUESNE** (I) (c.1576–1646)
BORN: Valenciennes
ENDENIZED/NATURALIZED: End 1636
IN OFFICE: A 1637–43 [FCL, MS 5, ff. 123b, 141a]
TRADE, WEALTH, SOCIAL STATUS: Weaver [HSQS XVIII, 54]. Probably the Jean Du Quesne who was born about 1576, married in Valenciennes in 1601 and for the second time in London 1637 [Leslie Du

Cane, pers. com.; HSQS, XIII, 16l]. He died in Canterbury in 1646, when he was described as a gentleman [HSQS V, 595].
FAMILY OR TRADE CONNECTIONS WITH OTHER CHURCH OFFICERS: Jean (I) was only remotely related to the other church officers named Du Quesne. Father-in-law of Isaac de Lillers.

NAME: **Jean DU QUESNE** (II) (1601–84)
BORN: London
IN OFFICE: D 1638–41, A 1645–8 [FCL, MS 5, ff. 124b, 131a, 148 and p. 341].
TRADE, WEALTH, SOCIAL STATUS, ENGLISH POLITICAL AFFILIATION: BA, Trinity College, Cambridge, then incorporated MA at Oxford (Foster (1891): *Alumni Oxoniensis 1500–1714* sub Ducane). Merchant (T.C. Dale, *The Inhabitants of London in 1638* (Society of Genealogists, 1931), 295a: Register of Marriages, St John, Croydon, Surrey, 23 August 1638). Parliamentarian; supporter of de La Marche, 1646, and Elie Delmé, 1657 [Hessels, 1970; *Consistoire* [1657]].
FAMILY OR TRADE CONNECTIONS WITH OTHER CHURCH OFFICERS: Elder brother of both Benjamin and Pierre Du Quesne.

NAME: **Pierre DU QUESNE** (1609–1672)
BORN: London
ENDENIZED/NATURALIZED: [The 'Peter Du Quesne, born in Valentienne, son of John Du Quesne', who was naturalized in 1660 [HSQS XVIII, 78], was a different man, the son of Jean Du Quesne (I).]
IN OFFICE: D 1641–4; A 1647–9. In the 1650s he was a strong supporter of Elie Delmé [*Consistoire* [1657]], and for a time, like Jacques Houblon, was estranged from the consistory after refusing to accept the compromise agreement that otherwise settled the disputes of that decade [Hessels, 2401].
TRADE, WEALTH, SOCIAL STATUS, ENGLISH POLITICAL AFFILIATION: Merchant and Alderman of London, with city property; Renter Warden (1659) and Prime Warden (1660) of the Dyers Company; died in 1672 [Woodhead (1965), 62]. From 1650, Pierre occupied extensive premises at St Pancras Soper Lane, described in detail in D.J. Keene and Vanessa Harding, 'St. Pancras Soper Lane 145/14–15', in *Historical Gazetteer of London Before the Great Fire Cheapside; Parishes of All Hallows Honey Lane, St Martin Pomary, St Mary Le Bow, St Mary Colechurch and St Pancras Soper Lane* (London, 1987), pp. 713–723. [*British History Online*, http://www.british-history.ac.uk/no-series/london-gazetteer-pre-fire/pp713-723 [accessed 9 July 2019]]. Holding strong Nonconformist beliefs, he was described 1667 as a 'wicked, dangerous, seditious sectary,

who joined in an illegal conventicle' (Margaret Butler, *Local Life in the Reign of Charles II* (Barnes and Mortlake History Society, 2012), p. 8). FAMILY OR TRADE CONNECTIONS WITH OTHER CHURCH OFFICERS: Brother of Benjamin Du Quesne and Jean (II) Du Quesne. Brother-in-law of Jacques Houblon. Uncle of Jean Delmé and Pierre Delmé. His daughter Jeanne married into the Lethieullier family [Agnew (I, p. 180)]. His son Pierre Du Quesne (1646–1714) (for whom Pierre Houblon and Anne de Lillers were sponsors at his baptism) was a London merchant [Roger L'Estrange, *Collection of the Names of the Merchants...*, 1677] and initial subscriber to the Bank of England in 1694 with £4000, who also subscribed £8500 for others including several Lethieulliers and a James Ducane [BEA, M1/1, p. 19].

NAME: **Daniel DUTHAIS** (Du Tais, Tay, Tee, Tez, Thaix, Thays)
BORN: Plymouth
IN OFFICE: D 1662–4; A 1674–7, 1680–3. In 1675 he was empowered to act on behalf of the Piedmont churches [FCL, Misc. Papers 31, deed dated 11 June]. A generous supporter of the church, he contributed £86 between 1673 and 1677 [FCL, MS 218]. In his final term of office he repeatedly represented the church on deputations to important people, including the King, the Bishop and Mayor of London, and Secretary Jenkins [HSQS LVIII, 63, 66, 102, 107]. He went to Ipswich to assess its suitability for a refugee colony and signed the proposal for a settlement there in 1681, and in London helped consult the 'principaux de l'Eglise' about the new refugees and assisted with charity distribution [FCL, MS 7, pp. 61, 80, 89].
TRADE, WEALTH, SOCIAL STATUS: Duthais was a merchant [*Little London Directory* of 1677] and large-scale vinegar maker in Southwark. In 1695, following a fire that destroyed two warehouses and 25 tons of vinegar, he claimed to have paid many thousands of pounds in excise over the years. The authorities were sufficiently sympathetic to refund £118 duty paid on the lost 25 tons, and the following year a royal brief was issued on his behalf and that of four Englishmen, to compensate them for the loss of £4469 through the fire [*CSPD, 1693–6*, 1219, 1326; FCL, MS 8, ff. 38–9].
FAMILY OR TRADE CONNECTIONS WITH OTHER CHURCH OFFICERS: Together with Claude Hays (I) and François Amonnet, he patented an invention of the manufacture of 'draped milled stockings', 29 July 1682 [*Subject-Matter Index (made from Titles only) of Patents of Inventions ...1617...to 1852* (2 vols, 1854), patent no. 221, where 'Duthais' has been misread as 'Guthard'].

DU TILLIEUX, see GIRARDOT

E

NAME: **Jean EDLIN** (Edelyn, Edling, Hedelin)
BORN: Frankfurt
ENDENIZED/NATURALIZED: End 1632
IN OFFICE: Edlin had served as deacon, perhaps more than once, in the 1620s [HSQS IX, 130, 143]. In our period he served as an elder 1639–47, 1650–3, 1658–61. He frequently acted as the consistory's spokesman in dealing with Hérault in 1643, when he seems to have tried to hold a moderate position, and he opposed De la Marche in 1646 [FCL, MS 5, ff. 134b, 136a, 142; Hessels, 1972–3]. In his second term as elder he oversaw the collection for the church repair in 1650, and was involved in a bid to come to terms with Jean d'Espagne's congregation [FCL, MS 62, f. 9v, and MS 5, pp. 355–6].
TRADE, WEALTH, SOCIAL STATUS: Weaver [HSQS XVIII, 46]. He owned property in London [P.E. Jones (1966), I, decree B.606, p. 160].
FAMILY OR TRADE CONNECTIONS WITH OTHER CHURCH OFFICERS: Father-in-law of Paul Doby [HSQS IX, 30, 108].

NAME: **Jean ESSELBRONN** (Asselbronne, Elsbron, Esselbroun, Heselbron)
BORN: Alzey, Palatinate
ENDENIZED/NATURALIZED: Nat 1685, after the failure of several previous attempts [HSQS XVIII, 168; TNA, SP/31/3, f. 1].
IN OFFICE: D 1688–91, having been received a member in 1676 [FCL, MS 20, f. 114v]; A 1695–8.
TRADE, WEALTH, SOCIAL STATUS, ENGLISH POLITICAL AFFILIATION: Substantial merchant, liable to surtax in the 1695 Assessment as having a personal estate valued over £600 [Glass, 101 *sub* Eselborne]. He sent about £6900 in cloth exports to Near Europe in 1695–6 [D.W. Jones (1971), 189a, 396]. He was buried at the Dutch Church of Austin Friars in 1719 [Moens (1884), 151, 190].

NAME: **Jonathan EVERARD** (Evrard)
BORN: Calais
IN OFFICE: D 1683–5

F

NAME: **Pierre FABROT**
BORN: Nîmes

ENDENIZED/NATURALIZED: Nat 1702
IN OFFICE: D 1703–6; A 1708–?, later elected again 1718 [Eg. 2734].
His company had earlier loaned the St Martin Orgars church £20 at its
opening [LMA, MS 00994/I, p. 46]. In 1705 he was a director of the
Spitalfields Maison de Charité [HL, *Maison de Charité, Deliberations
1695–1718*, f. 76a].
TRADE, WEALTH, SOCIAL STATUS: In 1709 Fabrot held £5885 Bank
stock, and £8266 East India stock [Dickson (1967), 264], apart from a
further £660 in trust [P.G.M. Dickson, pers. com.]. He had strong Swiss
connections [*CSPD, 1702–3*, 552–3; Dickson (1967), 318].

NAME: **Pierre FACQUIER** (Faquier)
BORN: Amiens
IN OFFICE: D 1701; he died during the year [FCL, MS 8, f. 158r].

NAME: **Michel FALLET** (Fallett)
BORN: Caen
ENDENIZED/NATURALIZED: Nat 1685
IN OFFICE: D 1686–9. He had arrived from Caen in 1675 [HSQS XXI,
101].
TRADE, WEALTH, SOCIAL STATUS: Fallet was employed in the Bank
of England accountancy office from February 1694, bound with London
merchants John Lambert and Stephen Creagh [BEA, M5/674]; he was still
in office in 1703 [BEA, M5, p. 136]. Around the start of that employment,
a privateer that he had outfitted was successful in taking prizes [BEA,
G4/1, p. 159]. See above, p. 130.

NAME: **Paul FANJOUX** (Fanioux, Fanjou)
BORN: Tours
ENDENIZED/NATURALIZED: End 1697, Nat 1702
IN OFFICE: D 1701–3
TRADE, WEALTH, SOCIAL STATUS: Apothecary [FCL, MS 7, p. 517].
His brother Mathieu was appointed an Anglican rector in 1697 [Gwynn
(2015), 286].

NAME: **Jean FARBU** (Ferbu)
BORN: Valenciennes
IN OFFICE: D 1651–2, died in office [FCL, MS 5, p. 362].

NAME: **Daniel FARVACQUES** (many variants including Fairfax, Faiwak,
Farfax, Farvacks, de Farvaques, Fervacques, de Fervaques)
BORN: Norwich

IN OFFICE: A 1648–52, 1661–5, 1667–9, died October 1669 [Plummer (1972), 31]. In 1657 he was a supporter of Elie Delmé [*Consistoire* [1657]]. During his second term in office he was deputed to see the Bishop of London, 1661, and to help pacify the Canterbury church, 1662 [FCL, MS 5, 412, 432]. In his third term he was extensively involved in the church rebuilding after the Fire [ibid., 519, 546, 552]. During the 1665 Plague, while not in office, he volunteered to distribute *méreaux* in the Blackfriars *quartier* following David Bouquet's death [Gwynn (2015), 65].
TRADE, WEALTH, SOCIAL STATUS: Member of the Artillery Company, 1635–43 [*HSP* XV, 308]. Common Councilman of London [Woodhead (1965), 67]. Upper Bailiff of the Weavers' Company, 1664 [Plummer (1972), 452].
FAMILY OR TRADE CONNECTIONS WITH OTHER CHURCH OFFICERS: Possible Le Poutre connection; he had married Elizabeth le Poultre near Norwich, 1629 [HSQS IX, 28].

NAME: **Jean FARVACQUES**
BORN: London
IN OFFICE: D 1671–3

NAME: **Nicolas FARVACQUES**
BORN: Tournai
IN OFFICE: A 1651–4
TRADE, WEALTH, SOCIAL STATUS: Weaver; admitted a foreign brother of the London Weavers' Company, upon a certificate from its Canterbury equivalent, in 1654 [HSQS XXXIII, 10, 21]. Other records show a Nicolas de Farvacques, perhaps the same man, to have been a deacon at Canterbury at least 1645–8 and elder 1659–61 [Gwynn (2018), 294]; he contributed £100 towards the rebuilding of the London church after the Fire [FCL, MS 62 (f. 21r)].

NAME: **Aaron FASCON** (Facon, Falcon, Faucon, Faulcon)
BORN: London
IN OFFICE: D 1670–3; A 1679–82
TRADE, WEALTH, SOCIAL STATUS: Weaver [HSQS XXXIII, 17].

NAME: **Pierre FAUCONNIER** (Fauconier, Faulconniere)
BORN: Angoulême
ENDENIZED/NATURALIZED: End 1685, later sought naturalization [HSQS XVIII, 174, 218, 287].
IN OFFICE: D 1686–9, after arriving from Angoulême in 1685 [HSQS

XXI, 102]. He had signed a petition in favour of a new French church in London c.1685–6 [BT, xcii, f. 185v], and apparently ceased to support the Threadneedle Street church after 1692 [FCL, MS 8, f. 3r].

TRADE, WEALTH, SOCIAL STATUS, ENGLISH POLITICAL AFFILIATION: Admitted to the Freedom of the City by redemption in the Company of Haberdashers, June 1686 [LMA, Court of Aldermen, Rep. 91, f. 94]. Fauconnier was viewed as hostile by James II's government, which issued an order, 6 November 1686, for his house near Artillery Ground to be searched and any arms found seized, and for his arrest [TNA, SP/44/337, p. 125]. He was an army clothing contractor in the 1690s; he and Etienne Faget contracted to clothe the Dutch Foot Guards in 1694, and the following year petitioned they had received only a third of the £15,250 due to them [*CTB, 1693–6*, 1062].

NAME: **Abraham FAULCON** (Faucon)
BORN: Rouen
IN OFFICE: D 1699–1701; A 1705–?

FAY, see Dufay

NAME: **Philippe FERMENT** (Fermant, Fermen)
BORN: Dieppe
ENDENIZED/NATURALIZED: End 1687; Nat on oath roll, 1709 [HSQS XXVII, 81].
IN OFFICE: D 1699–1702, A 1713–? [Eg. 2734].
TRADE, WEALTH, SOCIAL STATUS: Described as an engraver, of Blackfriars, when an original subscriber to the 1697 issue to enlarge the Bank's capital stock, with £255 [BEA, MS M1/6, B, no. 82]. He also subscribed £300 to the enlargement of the Million Bank stock in 1700 [TNA, C/114/16].

NAME: **Pierre FONTAINE** (Fountaine, Fontayne)
BORN: Caen
ENDENIZED/NATURALIZED: End 1637, named in unsuccessful naturalization bills 1641.
IN OFFICE: A 1637–41, 1648–9, died in office [FCL, MS 5, p. 349].
TRADE, WEALTH, SOCIAL STATUS: Merchant [HSQS XVIII, 61–2].

FOUR, see DUFOUR

NAME: **Paul FRANJOUX**
IN OFFICE: A 1708–? [Eg. 2734].

G

GARD, see DUGARD

NAME: **Michel GARNIER**
BORN: Caen
ENDENIZED/NATURALIZED: End 1687
IN OFFICE: Michel Garnier was elected D in 1689, but having accepted the charge he then declined it and persisted in his refusal to take up office; the Company of Deacons remained one man short for the next six months [FCL, MS 7, pp. 467–8].
TRADE, WEALTH, SOCIAL STATUS: Gentleman [Wagner Pedigrees *sub* Carbonnel] and also described as a merchant when he acted as attorney for a transfer of Bank stock [BEA, AC28/1513, 9 March 1696].
FAMILY OR TRADE CONNECTIONS WITH OTHER CHURCH OFFICERS: Supported Guillaume Carbonnel's claims to register his pedigree and coat of arms.

NAME: **David GARRIC** (Garicq, Garrick, Garrie, Garrigues, Guaric)
BORN: Montpellier.[1]
ENDENIZED/NATURALIZED: End 1686, Nat 1696; in 1690 he had been in a naturalization Bill that did not proceed [HSQS XVIII, 177, 217, 240].
IN OFFICE: D 1686–9; A 1692–5, 1703–5. He signed the petition for a new French church in London in 1686, and while deacon at Threadneedle Street was also a member of the congregation that later formed the church of St Martin Orgars [BT, xcii, f. 185v; LMA, CLC/197/MS 00998, list of pew holders].
TRADE, WEALTH, SOCIAL STATUS: The church officer, grandfather of the actor David Garrick, was a former *bourgeois* of Bordeaux [Meller (1902), 17]. He was a merchant, but not considered liable to surtax in the 1695 Assessment as having a personal estate valued over £600 [Glass, 117]. His trading relations seem principally to have been with Spain; in 1695–96 he imported £720 of iron from Bilbao and exported about £1000 in hosiery. He was also part owner of the privateer *The Protestant Cause* [D.W. Jones (1971), pp. 189, 398, 437, 501]. He had arrived in London on

---

1 The man elected as deacon was described as native of Bordeaux [FCL, MS 7, p. 260]; the man elected elder was twice described as native of Montpellier [FCL, MS 7, p. 546, and MS 8, f. 184v]. I have assumed that Bordeaux as birthplace was an error and that all references are to the same person.

5 October 1685 via Saintonge, Poitou, Brittany and Guernsey [C. Oman, *David Garrick* (1958), 3].
FAMILY OR TRADE CONNECTIONS WITH OTHER CHURCH OFFICERS: In 1697 he was close to a lawsuit with Jacques Dufay [FCL, MS 8, f. 48r].

NAME: **Pierre GARRON** (Garon)
BORN: Champdeniers, Poitou
ENDENIZED/NATURALIZED: End 1694, Nat 1698
IN OFFICE: D 1698–1701

GAS, GUAST, see DUGAST

NAME: **Charles GAUDELIER** (Godelier)
BORN: Lens, Artois
IN OFFICE: D 1641 (died in office that year) [FCL, MS 5, f. 131b].

NAME: **Henri GAULTIER** (Gautier, Gualtier)
BORN: Angoulême
ENDENIZED/NATURALIZED: Nat 1698
IN OFFICE: D 1705–?; A 1713–?. He served on the French Committee in 1707–8 [*Estats* for those years].
FAMILY OR TRADE CONNECTIONS WITH OTHER CHURCH OFFICERS: Brother of Jacques Gaultier.

NAME: **Jacques** (James) **GAULTIER**
BORN: Angoulême
ENDENIZED/NATURALIZED: Nat 1700
IN OFFICE: D 1702–5; he was in Holland when discharged [FCL, MS 8, f. 229v]. A 1709–?, later elected again 1717 [Eg. 2734].
TRADE, WEALTH, SOCIAL STATUS: A Director of the Bank of England, 1728–48.
FAMILY OR TRADE CONNECTIONS WITH OTHER CHURCH OFFICERS: Brother of Henri Gaultier [HSQS XVIII, 252, 296].

NAME: **Pierre GAUSSEN**
BORN: Lunel
ENDENIZED/NATURALIZED: End 1700; Nat 1704, following an unsuccessful Bill in 1703.
IN OFFICE: A 1713–?, later elected again 1723–8, 1734–8 [Eg. 2734]. He had served on the French Committee in 1709 [*Estat* for that year]. Later

he was a director, treasurer and deputy governor of the French Hospital [Murdoch and Vigne (2009), 30–1].

TRADE, WEALTH, SOCIAL STATUS: Admitted to the freedom of London by redemption in the Company of Glaziers, 1712 [LMA, Court of Aldermen, Rep. 116, ff. 442–3]. Merchant [*HSP* XV, 246; Frank Atkinson (ed.), *Some Aspects of the Eighteenth-Century Woollen and Worsted Trade in Halifax* (1956), 10–11]. The many charitable legacies in his will, proved 1759, included £500 to the Threadneedle Street church, £300 to the French Hospital and £100 to 'La Soupe' [HSQS LX, 182].

NAME: **Perrin GERARD** or **GIRARD** (Gerrard, Girrard)
BORN: Baccarat
IN OFFICE: D 1664–7

NAME: **Louis GERVAIZE** (I) (Cherves, Gervaise, Gervaisse, Gewayes, Jervaise)
BORN: Chauny, Picardy, c.1619
ENDENIZED/NATURALIZED: End 1682
IN OFFICE: A 1689–92. Probably because of his advanced age, special arrangements were made to see he was not overburdened in his *quartier* [HSQS LVIII, 293–4, 307].

TRADE, WEALTH, SOCIAL STATUS: Formerly merchant of Paris ('marchand linger') and an elder at Charenton. His house in Saint-Germain was valued at 50,000 livres. He was exiled to Gannat in 1685, then transferred elsewhere and later imprisoned in the château d'Angoulême until he was expelled from the kingdom in 1688 [Haag (1846), V, 256–7]. The two Louis Gervaizes are hard to disentangle. One arranged the financing for the Royal Lustring Company, 1692 [*CJ* XII, 221]. Both were original subscribers to the Bank of England in 1694 with £800 between them [BEA, M1/1, pp. 2, 17; see above pp. 127, 130]. One subscribed £3000 to the Million Bank in 1695, and a further £1500 in 1700 [TNA, C/114/16]. One developed a proposal to melt down and renew all the country's silver money, which was referred to the Warden of the Mint [*CTB, 1693–6*, 900]. Earlier, one described as 'gentleman' or 'merchant' had subscribed £2900 to government loans in the early years of William III's reign, 1689–90 [*CTB, 1689–92*, 1981–2, 1995].

FAMILY OR TRADE CONNECTIONS WITH OTHER CHURCH OFFICERS: Father of Louis Gervaize (II), with whom he lodged in London at Clock Lane, College Hill [*BSHPF* XVIII (1869), 551n; Douen (1894), II, 57–60; TNA, C/114/16].

NAME: Louis **GERVAIZE** (II)
BORN: Paris, 1653
ENDENIZED/NATURALIZED: End 1682
IN OFFICE: D 1684–7; A 1695–8. As deacon he was involved in discussions about transport for refugees heading for America, and as elder he proposed a Parliamentary Act to settle naturalized refugees in Yorkshire and other counties [FCL, MS 7, pp. 217–9, and MS 8, ff. 76v, 90–1, 93–4].
TRADE, WEALTH, SOCIAL STATUS: Formerly merchant of Paris ('marchand linger'). See the last entry; since he was much the younger man, it may well be that most of the references for the 1690s relate to Louis Gervaize (II). Although he settled in England in 1682, the French police noted that he regularly revisited Paris to confer with his father and other elders of Charenton on Huguenot matters, and when he was absent from the July 1684 *Censures* the Threadneedle Street minutes recorded he was away 'en voiage' ('absent en France' crossed out) [FCL, MS 7, p. 193]. Wagner suggests that '1686...found him interned in the *Oratoire*; and in 1687, after imprisonment in the Abbaye de Lagny, he was finally expelled from France', but Douen and the *BSHPF* apply these references to his father [*Miscellanea Genealogica et Heraldica*, 3rd series, II (1898), 59; *BSHPF* XVIII (1869), 551n; Douen (1894), II, 57–9].
FAMILY OR TRADE CONNECTIONS WITH OTHER CHURCH OFFICERS: Son of Louis Gervaize (I). Louis (II)'s wife Jacqueline was François Mariette's niece [Wagner Pedigrees *sub* Mariette].

NAME: **Guillaume GHISELIN** (Cheselyn, Gezelin, Ghilin, Gisseling, Guiselin)
BORN: Rouen
ENDENIZED/NATURALIZED: End 1682
IN OFFICE: D 1685–8
TRADE, WEALTH, SOCIAL STATUS: Diamond cutter [Edgar Samuel, 'Gems from the Orient: The activities of Sir John Chardin (1643–1713) as a diamond importer and East India merchant', *HSP* XXVII (1997–2002), 357].
FAMILY OR TRADE CONNECTIONS WITH OTHER CHURCH OFFICERS: Brother of Jean Ghiselin [Wagner Pedigrees]. Their aunt Sara Gontier née Ghiselin and her eldest daughter were imprisoned, and her second daughter shut up in a convent, when captured trying to escape from Rouen [Lesens, 38].

NAME: **Jean GHISELIN**
BORN: Rouen, 1653
ENDENIZED/NATURALIZED: End 1682, Nat 1698

IN OFFICE: D 1681–4; A 1692–5
TRADE, WEALTH, SOCIAL STATUS: Described as of Stoke Newington, gentleman, in his will proved 23 March 1711 [HSQS LX, 183].
FAMILY OR TRADE CONNECTIONS WITH OTHER CHURCH OFFICERS: Brother of Guillaume Ghiselin. His daughter Catherine married Pierre Deschamps, probably the son of the church officer [Wagner Pedigrees *sub* Deschamps].

NAME: **Jean GIRARDOT DE** (Du) **TILLIEUX** (Tilleul)
BORN: Château-Chinon
ENDENIZED/NATURALIZED: Possibly endenized 1686, as 'John Girardot'. Naturalized 1699, as 'John Girardott alias Girardott De Tillieux' [HSQS XVIII, 178, 270].
IN OFFICE: D 1694–7
TRADE, WEALTH, SOCIAL STATUS: Jean was a member of the rich timber and banking family of Girardot. His father Paul 'came to England in his coach, with painted-over gold fittings which he converted back into money on arrival' [*HSP* XXVI, 684]. Alice C. Carter has reflected on the variety of Jean's financial enterprises, noting that while in June 1697 he held £1850 of Bank stock, this 'hardly reflects the scale of his activities. His turnover before 1700 was well over £10,000 and about half of his clients had French names' [Carter (1954), 27, 33–4]. He also subscribed £2300 towards the enlargement of the Million Bank capital in 1700 [TNA, C/114/16]. Agnew notes that he became a Director of the South Sea Company in 1721, 'but seems to have got out of it in time, as his property was not confiscated by Parliament' [Agnew (1886), II, 402]. By 1739, when he made his will, Jean had moved to Putney. He left property there, £28,000 in trust for his nephew, and various small bequests including £200 to the Threadneedle Street church. He died on 27 September 1741 [HSQS LX, 187].

NAME: **Jean GOBAU** or **GOBEAU** (Goboe)
BORN: Valenciennes
IN OFFICE: D 1666–9
TRADE, WEALTH, SOCIAL STATUS: Weaver [HSQS XXXIII, 23].

NAME: **George GOSSELIN** (Gausselin, Goisselin, Goslin, Goslien, Gostlin)
BORN: Caen [HSQS XVIII, 111].
ENDENIZED/NATURALIZED: End 1655, 1662 and Nat 1675
IN OFFICE: D 1659–61

TRADE, WEALTH, SOCIAL STATUS, ENGLISH POLITICAL AFFILIATION: Surgeon for high-class society, specializing in dentistry. Gentleman. Inherited land in Jamaica, 1675 [*CTB*, *1672–5*, 705]. Considered well affected towards Cromwell's government, 1655 [HSQS XVIII, 68–9]. His legacy of £5 reached the church in 1698 [FCL, MS 218, p. 120].
FAMILY OR TRADE CONNECTIONS WITH OTHER CHURCH OFFICERS: He and Pierre de La Roche, another immigrant from Caen, 'both of which, and no others are sworn operators to the Kings teeth', shared a surgery 'about Fleet Bridge' after the Restoration [A.W. Lufkin, *A History of Dentistry* (2nd edn, 1948), 136]. Brother of:

NAME: Jacob GOSSELIN
BORN: Amsterdam
ENDENIZED/NATURALIZED: Nat 1657, 1660
IN OFFICE: D 1656–9; A 1666–70. Although not then in office, he accompanied two church officers to Dieppe in 1660 to secure the release of the minister Jacques Felles to serve Threadneedle Street [FCL, MS 5, pp. 395–6]. As elder, he acted repeatedly to help resolve trade disputes affecting church members [FCL, MS 5, pp. 533, 538–9, 542, 547].
TRADE, WEALTH, SOCIAL STATUS: Merchant. In 1650, he and Samuel Swaysoone gave £1000 recognizance that a ship they had sold would not be used against the Commonwealth [*CSPD*, *1650*, 34, 40, 53]. In 1661 he was seeking to export Turkey silk to France with Pierre Caulier [*CTB*, *1660–67*, 195]. Jacob died in Jamaica in March 1675, when the royal interest in any part of his estate that accrued to the Crown because he was an alien born was granted to his brother 'George Gosselyn, gent.' [*CTB*, *1672–5*, 705].
FAMILY OR TRADE CONNECTIONS WITH OTHER CHURCH OFFICERS: See previous paragraph. Jacob's son Jean was apprenticed to Jacob David, 1677–80 [Roseveare, 171, 204, 527–8, 565. Jean had been born in 1658]. His daughter Marie was engaged to Charles Trinquand (banns called), but died before marriage [HSQS XIII, 55].

NAME: Elie GOURBEIL (Gorbeil, Gourbiel, Gourbal, Gourbeille)
ENDENIZED/NATURALIZED: End 1686
IN OFFICE: D 1691–3
TRADE, WEALTH, SOCIAL STATUS: Substantial London inhabitant, liable to surtax in 1695 Assessment as having a personal estate valued over £600 [Glass, 125]. That same year he subscribed £300 to the Million Bank [TNA, C/114/16].

NAME: **Jean GRANDEL**
BORN: Lille
IN OFFICE: D 1650, died December 1650 [FCL, MS 135A].

NAME: **Jean de GRAVE** (I) (d'Egrave, de Graves)
BORN: London
IN OFFICE: D 1661–3, 1667–70; A 1674–7, 1682–5
TRADE, WEALTH, SOCIAL STATUS, ENGLISH POLITICAL
AFFILIATION: Leather merchant and Skinner [*CTB, 1676–9*, 312, 366].
One of the 'principaux de l'Eglise' consulted about the refugees, 1681
[FCL, MS 7, p. 80].

NAME: **Jean de GRAVE** (II)
BORN: London
IN OFFICE: D 1688–91. In 1703 he loaned £20 at the establishment of
the French church of St Martin Orgars [LMA, MS 00994/I, p. 46].
TRADE, WEALTH, SOCIAL STATUS, ENGLISH POLITICAL
AFFILIATION: Merchant. It is probably Jean de Grave (II) who suffered
directly from the *dragonnades* while residing at Rouen in 1685. As a
natural-born subject of the King of England, he petitioned the English
Council for assistance, claiming that so many soldiers had been quartered
on him that the charge amounted to twenty crowns a day. Sir William
Trumbull, Envoy Extraordinary at Paris, was instructed to help him but
could not do so because De Grave had taken out papers of naturalization
in France – when instructing that dragoons were to enter the houses of
the best Protestant citizens at Rouen 'with the intention of being master',
Marillac specified that De Grave was to be targeted [Bianquis, 73]. In
January 1686 Trumbull reported he believed 'that by this time all his goods
are seizd upon and sold and he is clappt up (if they have found him) in
prison'. In fact, however, De Grave and his wife managed to remain in
hiding at Rouen and eventually effected their escape [HMC 75: *Downshire
I pt. I*: pp. 61–2; see also references in Clark (1938)]. He was importing
wine and brandy in 1696, also Spanish wool and grocery from the
Mediterranean, and during the 1690s was a member of a highly successful
syndicate outfitting privateers on a grand scale that had 60 captures to
its credit [*CTB, 1696–7*, 281–2, 380; D.W. Jones (1971), pp. 253, 441].

NAME: **Christophe GREENWOOD**
BORN: Hamburg
ENDENIZED/NATURALIZED: End 1698, Nat 1700
IN OFFICE: D 1707–?

NAME: **David GRIEL** (Griell, Le Griel)
BORN: Dieppe
ENDENIZED/NATURALIZED: End 1655, Nat 1657 and 1660 [HSQS XVIII, 68–9, 78]. He signed his name in FCL, MS 135A, as Le Griel but was both endenized and naturalized simply as 'David Griell'.
IN OFFICE: D 1659–62
TRADE, WEALTH, SOCIAL STATUS, ENGLISH POLITICAL AFFILIATION: 'Drugster' [HSQS XVIII, 68]; and merchant, importing camphor and oil of nutmegs 1662, and brandy 1668 [*CTB, 1660–67*, 180, 433, and *1679–80*, 853 ('Lepriell')]. Considered well affected towards the Cromwellian government, 1655 [HSQS XVIII, 68–9].
FAMILY OR TRADE CONNECTIONS WITH OTHER CHURCH OFFICERS: Nephew of Daniel Sochon. See also *sub* Pierre Caulier [Wagner Pedigrees *sub* Chauvel]. Connected by marriage to Charles and Pierre Marescoe [HSQS XIII, 41a].

NAME: **François GRUEBER** (Gruber, Grubert)
BORN: Lion
ENDENIZED/NATURALIZED: End 1682, Nat 1685
IN OFFICE: D 1691–3; A 1705–8, 1713–? [Eg. 2734]
TRADE, WEALTH, SOCIAL STATUS: Merchant of Sweething Lane, convicted of silk smuggling in the 1690s; it seems however that his involvement in this activity ceased c.1695 [*CJ* XII, 211, 214, 235; *HSP* XV, 412n, 424–5]. Gentleman. The proprietor of gunpowder mills at Faversham, which supplied gunpowder to the Ordnance Office in 1701, he died in 1730 and was buried in Faversham church [Gwynn (2018), 68; pers. com. from K.R. Fairclough and Arthur Percival].
FAMILY OR TRADE CONNECTIONS WITH OTHER CHURCH OFFICERS: Son-in-law of François Amonnet [Wagner Pedigrees *sub* Grubert]. The mother of his wife Suzanne remarried to Jacques Dufay. Brother-in-law of Robert Caillé.

NAME: **Pierre GUEPIN** (Gepin, Gipin, Guespin, Guipin)
BORN: Dieppe
ENDENIZED/NATURALIZED: End 1687
IN OFFICE: A 1694–7, when he served as the church's representative on the French Committee in early 1696 and obtained for the Committee a listing of all the poor assisted by the church [FCL, MS 8, f. 34v, and MS 52, p. 211].
TRADE, WEALTH, SOCIAL STATUS: Merchant, importing £652 of wine in 1695–6 [D.W. Jones (1971), 189].

NAME: Pierre GUERIN
BORN: Pons
IN OFFICE: Elected deacon 1680, having arrived from Saintonge in 1669 [HSQS XXI, 130], after declining office in 1677. He seems to have died or moved during the year of his election, since his *quartier* was reallocated at the start of 1681 [FCL, MS 51, pp. 46–7].
FAMILY OR TRADE CONNECTIONS WITH OTHER CHURCH OFFICERS: Son-in-law of Ruben Dampuré.

NAME: Daniel GUIS (Gui, Guise, Guy)
BORN: Montélimar
ENDENIZED/NATURALIZED: End 1685
IN OFFICE: D 1687–90; A 1697–1700. Daniel's family seems to have been on the move from the late 1670s; a Jacques Guy from Montélimar had been received as a *bourgeois* of Geneva in 1677 [Samuel Mours, *l'Eglise Réformée de Montélimar* (Montélimar, 1957), 101], and Daniel presented a *témoignage* from Charenton in 1683 [HSQS XXI, 132]. As deacon, he disagreed so strongly with a consistorial decision about the election of a particular surgeon for the treatment of the poor cared for by the church that he temporarily refused to carry out his duties in 1689 [FCL, MS 51, p. 70, and MS 7, pp. 471, 473]. As elder he was deputed to General Assemblies considering the establishment of a French colony in Yorkshire (1699) and a new translation of the Psalms (1700) [FCL, MS 8, ff. 90–1, 93r, 117v].
TRADE, WEALTH, SOCIAL STATUS: Surgeon, licensed in 1686 [LMA, MS 10,116/12]

GUISELIN, see GHISELIN

NAME: Jacques (James) GUYOTT (Guyot)
BORN: London
IN OFFICE: D 1648–50
FAMILY OR TRADE CONNECTIONS WITH OTHER CHURCH OFFICERS: Jacques Guyot entered a marriage contract in 1646 with Dame Anne Bulteel, widow of the late Jacques Maurois, and so was connected by marriage with Pierre Bulteel [HSQS V, 721].

H

NAME: Jean HANET (Anet, Hannet)
BORN: Corbigny

ENDENIZED/NATURALIZED: End 1686, Nat 1698 [HSQS XVIII, 178, 253]
IN OFFICE: D 1695–8; A 1703–6
TRADE, WEALTH, SOCIAL STATUS: Loaned £10 at the establishment of the French church of St Martin Orgars, 1703 [LMA, MS 00994/I, p. 46].

NAME: **Samuel HANNOTT** (Anau, Hanaut, Henau, Hannot, Hanot)
BORN: London
IN OFFICE: D 1688–91; A 1700–3
TRADE, WEALTH, SOCIAL STATUS: Weaver [HSQS XXXIII, 67] and silk dyer, so described when acting as attorney for a Yarmouth relative in acquiring £600 Bank stock [BEA, AC28/1513, 7 Nov. 1699]. The will of Samuel Hannott of Walthamstow, Esq., made in 1730 and proved in August 1732, disposed of land in Hertfordshire, Kent and elsewhere [HSQS LX, 206].
FAMILY OR TRADE CONNECTIONS WITH OTHER CHURCH OFFICERS: Brother-in-law of Benjamin Didier and of Charles Lason. Probable connection with the Le Keux family; both he and a Jean Le Keux signed a testimonial for the Rev. Luke Milbourn who had been ministering to a congregation in Spitalfields, 1694 [*A Vindication of the Case of Spittle-Fields, against an Uncharitable Paper...*, p. 8], and a Peter Le Keux, made free of the Weavers Company in 1713, had been Hannott's apprentice [HSQS XXXIII, 67]. Probable Whig [*A List of the Poll for John Ward ... for Members of Parliament For the City of London* (1713), p. 13].

NAME: **Christophe HARFORD** (Hartford)
BORN: Newton, Somerset
IN OFFICE: D 1689–92; A 1701–4. He had been admitted to communion in 1682 [FCL, MS 49, p. 65].

NAME: **Pierre HARLEY** (Harlai, Harle)
BORN: near St Quentin
ENDENIZED/NATURALIZED: Nat 1706 [HSQS XXVII, 50]
IN OFFICE: D 1694–7; A 1701–5, 1710–? [Eg. 2734]
TRADE, WEALTH, SOCIAL STATUS: Weaver [HSQS XXXIII, 73]

NAME: **Jean de HAUSSY** (Daussi, d'Hausi)
BORN: Mons
ENDENIZED/NATURALIZED: End 1682?
IN OFFICE: D 1665–8; A 1673–5, 1681–4

NAME: **Claude HAYS** (I) (Hais, Hayes)
BORN: Calais, 1643
ENDENIZED/NATURALIZED: Nat 1667 [HSQS XVIII, 99]
IN OFFICE: D 1672–5; A 1681–4, 1692–5. His first period of eldership came at a critical time, and Hays did much work on behalf of the new refugees from 1681, when he conferred with Secretary Jenkins about their denization, with the 'principaux de l'Eglise' about their needs, and with the Savoy church about their use of the Clerkenwell Hospital [FCL, MS 7, pp. 64–5, 80, 84]. One of the original trustees of the settlement fund for the Ipswich colony, he became 'treasurer for sealing the woollen manufacture' there [ibid., pp. 66, 80, and LMA, COL/CHD/PR/06/001/A, no. 252]. He was further engaged in refugee relief work on a national scale [Gwynn (2018), 268–9], and took over Guillaume Carbonnel's accounting for money paid to the church from the Chamber of London [FCL, MS 63, preface, p. 4]. Hays was often also employed by the consistory on deputations it sent to influential people such as the Secretary of State and Bishop and Mayor of London at times of delicate political situations [FCL, MS 5, p. 617, and MS 7, pp. 74–6, 134–5].
TRADE, WEALTH, SOCIAL STATUS, ENGLISH POLITICAL AFFILIATION: Substantial merchant and insurance underwriter [Roseveare, 583], son of an 'honorable homme' of Calais [HSQS III, 144]. His trading commodities ranged from copper plates to brandy to drapery [*CTB, 1672–5*, 578, and *1679–80*, 853; D.W. Jones (1971), 401]. He made significant loans on government securities in the early part of William's reign, £400 in 1689, £1000 in 1690, £5600 in 1692–3 [*CTB 1689–92*, 1982, 1993, 1997; D.W. Jones (1971), 483–4]. Hays' legacy of £40 reached the church in October 1696 [FCL, MS 218, p. 113].
Whig. With William and John Carbonnel, Hays was a witness in 1681 to the will of Robert de Lunars, of whom the Hertford Quarter Sessions were informed the following year that he 'entertains Castair [the Scottish Presbyterian William Carstairs, imprisoned and tortured in Scotland 1683 on suspicion of involvement in the Rye House plot] in his house' [Anthony Kirby, pers. com.].
FAMILY OR TRADE CONNECTIONS WITH OTHER CHURCH OFFICERS: Son-in-law of David Congnard (I). Father of Claude Hays (II). Half-brother of Daniel Hays. Brother-in-law of David Congnard (II). Father-in-law of David Bosanquet and of Jean Deneu [Wagner Pedigrees]. Together with Daniel Duthais and François Amonnet, Hays patented an invention of the manufacture of 'draped milled stockings', 29 July 1682 [*Subject-Matter Index (made from Titles only) of Patents of Inventions ... 1617...to 1852* (2 vols, 1854), patent no. 221].

NAME: **Claude HAYS** (II)
BORN: London, 1678
IN OFFICE: D 1697–1700
TRADE, WEALTH, SOCIAL STATUS: Turkey merchant. Common Councilman of London, Coleman Street, 1709 [LMA, COL/CC/13/03/002, p. 65]. Held £4018 in East India Company stock, 1709 [P.G.M. Dickson, pers. com.]. Member of the Dyers Company, and Whig [*A List of the Poll for John Ward ... for Members of Parliament For the City of London* (1713), p. 13].
FAMILY OR TRADE CONNECTIONS WITH OTHER CHURCH OFFICERS: Son of Claude Hays (I). Nephew of Daniel Hays. Brother-in-law of David Bosanquet and of Jean Deneu.

NAME: **Daniel HAYS**
BORN: Calais
ENDENIZED/NATURALIZED: took the oaths in connection with a naturalization bill that did not become an Act, 1690. Nat 1696 [HSQS XVIII, 218, 240].
IN OFFICE: A 1694–7, 1707–?. His initial election led to protests from the deacons' consistory because he had never served as a deacon [FCL, MS 8, ff. 16r, 19r].
TRADE, WEALTH, SOCIAL STATUS, ENGLISH POLITICAL AFFILIATION: 'Eminent merchant' [*Gentleman's Magazine*, 1732, II, 930]; his connections included France – he transmitted a collection of £350 to Marseilles for the *galériens*, 1709 [FCL, MS 91, f. 196]. Assistant of the Royal Africa Company, 1706, 1708, 1710–12 [Davies (1957)]. 'Daniel Hays is believed to have left Calais in 1670, going first to Ireland, and not coming to England till 1688. He was a man of wealth, leaving £20,000 to his son, and £10,000 apiece to his five daughters, after having, by deed in 1724, put £20,000 at his wife's disposition.' A family tradition, recorded in writing in 1842, had it that he came to England in the same ship as William of Orange [Wagner Pedigrees]. He was an original subscriber to the Bank of England in 1694, with £1000 [BEA, M1/1, p. 14]. In 1709 he held £4000 bank stock, £20,180 of East India Company stock and £7700 in the loan to the Emperor of Germany [P.G.M. Dickson, pers. com.].
FAMILY OR TRADE CONNECTIONS WITH OTHER CHURCH OFFICERS: Half-brother of Claude Hays (I), uncle of Claude Hays (II).

NAME: **Mathieu HEBERT** (I)
BORN: Dieppe
ENDENIZED/NATURALIZED: Nat 1670 [HSQS XVIII, 102, 104].

IN OFFICE: D 1673–5; A 1680–3. In December 1681 he helped see Huguenot fishermen settled in at Rye, and assessed the state of Clerkenwell Hospital for the use of the refugees [FCL, MS 7, pp. 82, 84].

TRADE, WEALTH, SOCIAL STATUS: Dyer, of Wandsworth, where he died in 1703, aged 63; he was buried there at Mt Nod [*HSP* I, 266, 296].

FAMILY OR TRADE CONNECTIONS WITH OTHER CHURCH OFFICERS: Mathieu (I) married Lovington Pamplin's daughter Mary and was brother-in-law of Michel Savary. Mathieu is a common name in the family, and the nature of the connection between the two Mathieu Heberts has not been established; they were perhaps uncle and nephew.

NAME: **Mathieu HEBERT** (II)
BORN: Dieppe
ENDENIZED/NATURALIZED: End 1690; Nat 1706 [HSQS XXVII, 53]
IN OFFICE: D 1696–9
TRADE, WEALTH, SOCIAL STATUS: Citizen and Skinner of London, probably the merchant given in his will as of Spital Square but with a house at Walthamstow [HSQS LX, 209 *sub* Matthew Hebert (1739)].
FAMILY OR TRADE CONNECTIONS WITH OTHER CHURCH OFFICERS: Possibly nephew of Mathieu Hebert (I), see above.

NAME: **Denis HELOT** (Hellot)
BORN: Paris
ENDENIZED/NATURALIZED: End 1685; Nat on Oath Roll 1709 [HSQS XVIII, 173, and XXVII, 82]
IN OFFICE: D 1688–91

NAME: **Pierre HEMARD** (Aimart, Aymar, Eimar, Emar, Hamar, Haymard, Heimard)
BORN: Vitry-le-François
ENDENIZED/NATURALIZED: End 1697; Nat on Oath Roll 1709 [HSQS XVIII, 247, and XXVII, 80]
IN OFFICE: D 1694–7; A 1700–2
TRADE, WEALTH, SOCIAL STATUS: Admitted a foreign master weaver, 1684 [HSQS XXXIII, 51–2].

NAME: **Samuel HERVIEU** (Harvie, Hervie, Hervieux)
BORN: Rouen
IN OFFICE: D 1639–43; A 1650?-52. He was elected again in 1659, but immediately replaced because he was not in town.
TRADE, WEALTH, SOCIAL STATUS, ENGLISH POLITICAL AFFILIATION: A probable royalist, he evidently spoke on Louis Hérault's

behalf in 1643 and opposed Jean de La Marche in 1645 [FCL, MS 5, f. 142 and p. 304].

NAME: **Abraham de HEULLE** (Deheulle, de Heule, de Heullee)
BORN: Bolbec, Normandy
ENDENIZED/NATURALIZED: End 1682; Nat 1706 [HSQS XVIII, 141, and XXVII, 53]
IN OFFICE: D 1706–?; A 1711–? [Eg. 2734]
TRADE, WEALTH, SOCIAL STATUS, ENGLISH POLITICAL AFFILIATION: Weaver, admitted foreign master 1715 having previously worked only with the status of foreign weaver [HSQS XXXIII, 65, 71]. His son, another Abraham, who had been his apprentice, was to follow him both as church elder 1736–40 [Eg. 2734] and as a highly successful silk weaver of consequence, who was able to offer 47 men to serve the crown against the Young Pretender in 1745 [Murdoch (1985), 98] and served in 1756 as Upper Bailiff of the Weavers Company.

NAME: **Pierre HOCHART** (Hauchart, Hauthart, Hochar, Hoshart, Hushar)
BORN: Norwich
IN OFFICE: D 1647–50, 1653–6; A 1680–2. He abandoned his charge in June 1656 because he objected to the deacons being excluded from consistorial debates concerning Elie Delmé, whom he supported [FCL, MS 135A; Hessels, 2401–2; *Consistoire* [1657]].
FAMILY OR TRADE CONNECTIONS WITH OTHER CHURCH OFFICERS: Son-in-law of Barthélemi Caulier (I) [HSQS XIII, 7g, 26p]. Brother-in-law of Barthélemi (II) Caulier, Pierre Caulier and Jean Beauvarlet.

NAME: **Isaac HOGUEL** (de Hoguel, Hauguel, Oguel)
BORN: Dieppe
ENDENIZED/NATURALIZED: End 1687; Nat 1706 [HSQS XVIII, 195, and XXVII, 53]
IN OFFICE: D 1697–1700; A 1703–6. When he died in office in 1706 he was said to have served the church with much faithfulness and care [FCL, MS 8, f. 247v].
TRADE, WEALTH, SOCIAL STATUS: In 1709, £250 of Bank stock remained held in his name [P.G.M. Dickson, pers. com.].

NAME: **Jacques HOUBLON** (Hobelon, Houbelon, Hublond) (1592–1682)
BORN: London
IN OFFICE: A 1637–40; 1643–6, serving as the lay representative of the

church at the 1646 Colloquy [HSQS II, 88]. He did not hold office again as elder, declining in 1662 and 1664. Until his death, a few days short of the age of 90 in 1682, he continued to be an active communicant member and weekday and Sunday attender of the Threadneedle Street church when in the city [Gilbert Burnet, *A Sermon Preached at the Funeral of Mr James Houblon* (London, 1682), 27, 31]. His donations to the church included £50 towards rebuilding after the Fire, and a legacy of £100 [FCL, MS 62, f. 21v, and MS 218, p. 63]; he urged his children to 'be especially charitable to the French Church: I know not any charity better bestowed or more faithfully managed' [*Pious Memoirs of Mr. James Houblon* (London, 1886), 12].

TRADE, WEALTH, SOCIAL STATUS, ENGLISH POLITICAL AFFILIATION: The son and grandson of refugees from Lille, Jacques Houblon came to be recognized by John Strype as 'a very eminent merchant of London, and as eminent for his plainness and piety' [Strype (1720), I, ii, 162]. His epitaph, written by Samuel Pepys, described him as 'Londinensis Bursae Pater', 'the Father of the London Exchange' [Houblon (1907), I, 95–6]. His sons were to be instrumental in the foundation of the Bank of England. A member of the Artillery Company, Houblon was seriously injured in 1635 by an explosion in the Artillery Garden, otherwise he would surely have served with the Parliamentarian forces. Instead he outfitted a soldier to serve on his behalf, and engaged in committee and financial work for the Parliamentarian cause [Houblon (1907), I, 99–100, 106 ff], while within the church he opposed the reception of Louis Hérault and was a strong supporter of Jean de La Marche and later Elie Delmé [FCL, MS 5, f. 138b; Hessels, 1970, 2388; *Consistoire* [1657]]. He had married Marie Du Quesne in 1620 [HSQS IX, 19], and the connections of these two families were at the heart of the La Marche faction's influence in the 1640s and that of Elie Delmé in the 1650s. Houblon's refusal to accept a compromise agreement that otherwise settled the disputes of the 1650s led to a short-lived estrangement from the consistory in 1658 which was resolved by a reconciliation shortly after the Restoration [Hessels, 2401; FCL, MS 5, pp. 404, 477, and MS 6, pp. 101–2].

FAMILY OR TRADE CONNECTIONS WITH OTHER CHURCH OFFICERS: Uncle of Pierre Houblon. Connections with the Jorion and Lordell families through the marriages of his daughters Anne and Sara to Jacob Jorion and Jacques Lordell respectively. Amongst Jacques's sons in order of age, Peter, James, John, Isaac and Abraham were all notable merchants (Jacob was not, but became an Anglican minister). Jacques Lordell was frequently associated with Houblon transactions and like James and John was prominent in trade with the Iberian Peninsula.

NAME: Pierre **HOUBLON** (1627–91)
BORN: London
IN OFFICE: D 1645–7, 1651–4
According to the family chronicler, the Pierre who was a deacon at the Threadneedle Street church was not Jacques Houblon's eldest son (1623–92), who also had that Christian name, but rather the eldest son of Jacques's brother Pierre (born 1615) [Houblon (1907), I, 94]. Evidence shows this man was, and remained, connected with the church; his legacy of £5 reached it in 1692 [FCL, MS 218, p. 101]. The identification has therefore been accepted here, but confusion abounds and it is quite likely that there were two different men of the same name who each served one term as a deacon. If so, they were both first cousins and brothers-in-law!
TRADE, WEALTH, SOCIAL STATUS, ENGLISH POLITICAL AFFILIATION: Whichever Pierre was the officer was a merchant of standing in London society – one of the two was Prime Warden of the Dyers' Company in 1670–1 and shared Jacques Houblon's views in support of the Delmé faction in the church [*Le Consistoire de l'Eglise Françoise de Londres* (1657)]. The entire Houblon clan was Whig later in the century. Pierre Houblon aroused the wrath of the Court by defending Thomas Papillon before the Mayor of London in 1683, and was one of the 'disaffected and suspicious persons' arrested and detained at the time of Monmouth's rebellion, 1685 [Papillon, chap. XI; FCL, MS 7, pp. 132–3; LMA, CLA/050/02/002, pp. 39, 42].
FAMILY OR TRADE CONNECTIONS WITH OTHER CHURCH OFFICERS: See previous entry.

IJK

NAME: Claude **JAMINEAU** (Jamino)
BORN: Loudun, 1658 [Jean-Luc Tulot, 'Les Huguenots de Loudun ...', undated typescript in HL, part i, pp. 5n, 10].
ENDENIZED/NATURALIZED: End 1687, Nat 1700
IN OFFICE: D 1702–4; A 1707–?, elected again 1715 [Eg. 2734]
TRADE, WEALTH, SOCIAL STATUS: Merchant of St Martin Lane, near Cannon Street [HSQS XVI, 238]. He contributed £500 to the Loan for the Emperor of Germany in 1706 [BEA, M1/20, no. 112], and in 1709 held £1607 East India stock [P.G.M. Dickson, pers. com.].
FAMILY OR TRADE CONNECTIONS WITH OTHER CHURCH OFFICERS: Brother of Daniel Jamineau [HSQS XVIII, 240, 296].

NAME: **Daniel JAMINEAU**
BORN: Loudun, 1653 [Jean-Luc Tulot, 'Les Huguenots de Loudun…', undated typescript in HL, part i, p. 5n]
ENDENIZED/NATURALIZED: End 1687, Nat 1696
IN OFFICE: D 1692–5; A 1698–1700. As elder he was responsible for sending donations totalling over £300 to the Huguenot galley slaves in France, 1699–1700 [FCL, MS 8, f. 133v].
TRADE, WEALTH, SOCIAL STATUS: Substantial merchant, of St Swithins: in 1706 of Oxford Court, Walbrook [Wagner Pedigrees], with interests covering a very broad range. Shortly after the Revolution he can be found providing clothing for the army, and lending money for that purpose [*CTB, 1689–92*, 830, 2000]. Over nine years he sent merchandise to Africa with an aggregate sworn value of £6637 [K.G. Davies (1957), 372]. In 1695/6 he imported £2691 of currants from Zante and £200 of sugar and ginger from Barbados, and exported over £1050 of drapery and leather gloves to Hamburg and Venice, while in 1698 he invested £500 in the New East India Loan [D.W. Jones (1971), pp. 189c, 452, 480].
FAMILY OR TRADE CONNECTIONS WITH OTHER CHURCH OFFICERS: Brother of Claude Jamineau.

NAME: **Jean JAQUIN** (Jacquin)
BORN: Bédarieux, Languedoc
ENDENIZED/NATURALIZED: Nat 1696
IN OFFICE: D 1701–3
TRADE, WEALTH, SOCIAL STATUS: Merchant, as was his father Peter who subscribed £500 to the Bank of England in 1695 [HSQS XVIII, 240, and XVI, 208g; BEA, AC 28/32233, 26 Feb. 1695].

NAME: **Benjamin de JENNES** (Desjenne, Genes, Genne, Ienne, Jean, Jeane, Jesne, Jane, Yenne)
BORN: London
IN OFFICE: D 1667–70, 1673–6; A 1681–3, 1688–91. During his first period of office as elder he was sent to Ipswich to assess its suitability for refugees and became an 'Adventurer' in the stock raised to establish a linen manufacture there, and loaned houses for lodging refugees in London and discussed their needs with the 'principaux de l'Eglise' [FCL, MS 7, pp. 61, 78, 80; Papillon, 119].
TRADE, WEALTH, SOCIAL STATUS: Gentleman [*CTB, 1689–92*, 1979], and haberdasher living in Hackney according to his will by which he left the church half the residue of his estate after debts and legacies had been paid; in October 1707 this was expected to produce £221 9s 11d [FCL, MS 8, ff. 265v, 267, 272–4]. He had been admitted a foreign brother

weaver in 1662 [HSQS XXXIII, 13]. In the early years after the Revolution he loaned the Exchequer £200 in 1689 [*CTB, 1689–92*, 1676, 1979], and in 1697 he held £845 bank stock [BEA, M1/6, Book B, nos. 137, 241–2].

NAME: **Jacques de JENNES**
BORN: Ligny
IN OFFICE: D 1654–7; A 1662–6, 1670–3. In 1663 he was molested by some Englishmen, and was granted leave by the consistory because he was retiring to the country for reasons of health, but he does not appear to have gone; presumably the church was successful in its plea to the mayor to put an end 'au trouble qu'on fait a Mr de Jennes quy demeure dans la juridiction de la tour' [FCL, MS 5, pp. 447–8].
TRADE, WEALTH, SOCIAL STATUS: 'James Dejane, stranger, having been here about 20 years' was admitted foreign master weaver in 1662. He had taken apprentices since at least 1651, and in 1657 was living in Stepney [HSQS XXXIII, 14, 15, 18]. He donated £50 towards rebuilding the church after the Fire [FCL, MS 62, f. (25v)].

NAME: **Pierre de JENNES**
BORN: Ligny
IN OFFICE: D July–December 1657, when he was discharged to become A 1658–61.

NAME: **Jacob JORION** (Gaurion, Gorion, Jurian, Jurin, Jurion)
BORN: London
IN OFFICE: D 1644–6
TRADE, WEALTH, SOCIAL STATUS: Admitted member of the Artillery Company, 1643 [*HSP* XV, 310]. Dead by July 1653 [HSQS XIII, 131].
FAMILY OR TRADE CONNECTIONS WITH OTHER CHURCH OFFICERS: Son-in-law of Jacques Houblon.

NAME: **Jean JORION**
BORN: London [FCL, MS 5, p. 337].
IN OFFICE: A 1640–4, 1648–50, 1665–9, 1674–7
TRADE, WEALTH, SOCIAL STATUS, ENGLISH POLITICAL AFFILIATION: Four generations of Jean Jorions or Jurins must be distinguished across the seventeenth century, of whom the elder is the second. The first Jean, born overseas, was endenized in 1635 [HSQS XVIII, 54]; the third, probably the son of the *ancien*, was elected deacon in 1662 but refused to come to the consistory [FCL, MS 5, p. 418]; the fourth, son of the third, was admitted to membership of the Threadneedle Street church at the age of sixteen in 1673 [HSQS XXI, 147].

The Jean Jorion who was the *ancien* contributed £15 to the repair of the church in 1650 and £100 to its rebuilding after the Fire [FCL, MS 62, ff. 8v (20v)]. An outspoken man, he was frequently at the centre of disturbances within the congregation. Initially a close partisan of Jean de La Marche, he later turned against him [FCL, MS 6, pp. 609, 613–6]. In the 1650s he was a firm adherent of the Delmé faction, refusing to be judged by Coetus because it was an 'assemblie, merelie, and onelie for consulting and ordering of Civill affairs, and hath no power or influence at all upon matters of Church government since the establishing of our Colloquies'. When the Colloquy he desired met, it censured him for publishing his *True, and exact Relation* ... (1657), from which the quotation is taken, but it succeeded in reconciling him with his consistory in 1658 [Hessels, 2402]. The next major dispute within the church, in the 1670s, again saw Jorion involved, Louis Hérault complaining bitterly that he had called him a traitor unworthy of the company of people of honour [FCL, MS 6, pp. 607, 613–6]. His relationships with the church pastors prove that Jean Jorion was Parliamentarian in the Civil War.

He was a merchant (at St Dunstans Hill in 1677), Prime Warden of the Dyers' Company in 1656–7, and a Common Councilman and Alderman of London. He held £500 of the original stock of the Royal African Company (1671), and had an estate in Barbados where his namesake son died [Woodhead (1965), 100, and Beaven (1908), I, 126, both *sub* John Jurin]. His will, proved 12 October 1680, explains that his estate has been much impoverished in recent years [TNA, PROB 11/364/122].

NAME: **Pierre JORION**
BORN: London
IN OFFICE: D 1653–6, 1664–7. In June 1656 he abandoned his charge because he objected to the deacons being excluded from consistorial debates concerning Elie Delmé, whom he supported [FCL, MS 135A; Hessels, 2386–7, 2389–90, 2401–2].

NAME: **Louis JOURDAIN** (Jordan)
BORN: La Rochelle
ENDENIZED/NATURALIZED: End 1687; Nat 1698
IN OFFICE: D 1704–6; A 1711–? [Eg. 2734]. Jourdain had first arrived in London in 1685, when the consistory accepted there were personal and family reasons why he should make *reconnaissance* before it rather than more publicly [FCL, MS 7, p. 237]. He signed a petition in favour of a new French church in London c.1685–6 [BT, xcii, f. 185v].

NAME: **Roger JUGLEBERT**
BORN: Tournai
IN OFFICE: D 1653, died 19 April 1653 [FCL, MS 135A].

L

NAME: **Pierre** (de) **LA BALE** (Ball, Balle)
BORN: Rouen
IN OFFICE: A 1688–9; died in office, leaving a legacy of £8 15s to the church [FCL, MS 218, p. 98].
TRADE, WEALTH, SOCIAL STATUS: Surgeon [HSQS LX, 98. His will, dated 17 November 1689, was witnessed by Claude Hays (I) and Daniel Le Conte]. He had been threatened with arrest in Rouen in 1672, as pressure on Protestants increased [Lesens, 25], and reached London in 1685 via Rotterdam [HSQS XXI, 71].

NAME: **Jean de LA CLEF**
BORN: (Poitou)
ENDENIZED/NATURALIZED: Nat 1657
IN OFFICE: D 1654–6

NAME: **Paul Minvielle** (Menviel) (de) **LA COZE** (Cause, Cose, Cosse)
BORN: Bordeaux
ENDENIZED/NATURALIZED: End 1682, Nat 1685
IN OFFICE: D 1686–9, having presented his *témoignage* from Bordeaux in 1683 [FCL, MS 20, f. 60r]; A 1695–8. He distributed poor relief for the French Committee to those of the meaner sort in Spitalfields, 1698–99 [HL, Bounty MS 17, pt. 2, and pt. 4 p. 51].
TRADE, WEALTH, SOCIAL STATUS: He was a merchant, based in 1700 at Mincing Lane when he contributed £1500 towards the enlargement of Million Bank stock plus a further £3300 on behalf of eight others. His will was dated and proved in 1723 [TNA, C/114/16; HL, Wagner Wills, F, p. 22].

LA FONTAINE, see WICART

NAME: **Jacques** (Jacob) **de LA FORTERIE** (Forteri, Fortree, Fortrey)
BORN: London
IN OFFICE: D 1639–41, A 1643–7
TRADE, WEALTH, SOCIAL STATUS, ENGLISH POLITICAL AFFILIATION: Merchant [*HSP* XIX (ii), 77]. He was strongly opposed to

Jean de La Marche 'medling with state matters', 1646, when he protested by temporarily withdrawing from the consistory [Hessels, 1970; FCL, MS 5, p. 322].

NAME: **Jean Pierre LAMBLOIS** (Lamblour, Lambloy) or **PETERS**
BORN: London
IN OFFICE: D 1691–4; A 1706–?, later elected again 1731–5 by which time he signed his name as 'Jean Peters Lamblois' [Eg. 2734].
TRADE, WEALTH, SOCIAL STATUS: Weaver [HSQS XXXIII, 71, records Francis Peter being apprenticed in 1715 to 'John Peters alias Lamblois, foreign weaver'].

NAME: **Louis LANSAC** (Lanzac)
ENDENIZED/NATURALIZED: End 1687 ('Lewis de Lansac').
IN OFFICE: D 1699–1701

NAME: **Jacques LAOUST** (Lahou, Laourt)
IN OFFICE: D 1687–8
TRADE, WEALTH, SOCIAL STATUS: Weaver [HSQS XXXIII, 47, 'James Slaoust'].
FAMILY OR TRADE CONNECTIONS WITH OTHER CHURCH OFFICERS: No reason for his early discharge is given. A Londoner, Jacques l'Aoust, marred Marie Six, daughter of Abraham Six and Elizabeth Le Keux, at Canterbury in October 1685 [HSQS V, 529]; if this is the same man, perhaps he returned permanently to Canterbury?

NAME: **Jacques de LA PORTE**
BORN: Caen
ENDENIZED/NATURALIZED: Nat 1657 and 1660
IN OFFICE: D 1647–50, 1654–6

NAME: **Pierre** (Blanchers, dit) **de LA ROCHE**
BORN: Caen
IN OFFICE: A 1652–6
TRADE, WEALTH, SOCIAL STATUS, ENGLISH POLITICAL AFFILIATION: Dentist for high-class society. He testified against seditious preaching by De la Marche, 1646 [Hessels, 1971], and laid charges against him before the 1647 Synod [FCL, MS 5, p. 333].
FAMILY OR TRADE CONNECTIONS WITH OTHER CHURCH OFFICERS: He and George Gosselin, another immigrant from Caen, 'both of which, and no others are sworn operators to the Kings teeth', shared a surgery 'about Fleet Bridge' after the Restoration [A.W. Lufkin,

A History of Dentistry (2nd edn, 1948), 136]. Samuel Pepys's wife was another who benefited from La Roche's ministrations: 'she hath got her teeth new done ... and are endeed now pretty handsome' [Latham and Matthews (1970), II, 53].

NAME: **Charles LASON** (Lanson, Lansoon, Lasson, Lawson)
BORN: Valenciennes
ENDENIZED/NATURALIZED: End 1682, Nat 1698
IN OFFICE: D 1679–82; A 1687–90, 1695–8
TRADE, WEALTH, SOCIAL STATUS: Weaver, the subject of a complaint in 1683 that he employed more French journeymen than English [HSQS XXXIII, 49]. Burn [(1846), 256], followed by Weiss [(1854), 252], attributed to 'Lauson, Mariscot, and Monceaux' the chief production of the flowered silks manufactured in late seventeenth-century London; Burn seems to have had inside information but does not indicate his sources.
FAMILY OR TRADE CONNECTIONS WITH OTHER CHURCH OFFICERS: Father of Jean Lason. Brother-in-law of Samuel Hannott [HSQS LX, 206], Abraham Didier and Pierre Lernoult.

NAME: **Jean LASON**
BORN: London
IN OFFICE: D 1708–?
TRADE, WEALTH, SOCIAL STATUS: Weaver. He entered apprenticeship with his father in 1693; 'Mr John Lason' was admitted foreign master in 1713 [HSQS XXXIII, 57, 67].
FAMILY OR TRADE CONNECTIONS WITH OTHER CHURCH OFFICERS: Son of Charles Lason [HSQS XIII, 232e].

NAME: **Noel de LAUNAY** (Delony, Laune, Launé, Lonnay)
BORN: near Senlis
ENDENIZED/NATURALIZED: 'Noah de Launay, a native of France' was endenized 1673 [HSQS XVIII, 109].
IN OFFICE: D 1674–6; A 1683–6
TRADE, WEALTH, SOCIAL STATUS: Button maker and seller, harassed by English competitors while a deacon [TNA, SP/29/382, nos. 192–3].

NAME: **Paul de LAUNE**
BORN: London, c.1585 [Littleton (1996), p. 146].
IN OFFICE: A 1651–4
TRADE, WEALTH, SOCIAL STATUS: Eminent physician, M.D. Padua 1614, Senior Censor of the Royal College of Physicians of London 1643, Professor of Physic in Gresham College 1643–52, appointed

Physician-General to the fleet 1654 [Gwynn (1976B), wrongly discounted this identification. There is no other possible Paul de Laune in the family tree].

NAME: **Jean LAURENS** (Laurans, Laurentz, Lawrence, Lorrans)
ENDENIZED/NATURALIZED: End 1682; Nat on Oath Roll 1709 [HSQS XXVII, 78].
IN OFFICE: D 1682–5. A Jean Laurens took refuge from Rouen with his wife Marguerite Jansse, abandoning '*rentes*' there; but since the officer was elected in January 1682, he cannot be the Jean Laurence with a témoignage from Rouen in May 1682. The church records do not give the officer's birthplace, but his wife was Anne Chalon [HSQS XIII, 265d].

NAME: **Marc LAURENS**
BORN: Rouen
ENDENIZED/NATURALIZED: Nat 1657 and 1660
IN OFFICE: D 1655–8; A 1664–9
TRADE, WEALTH, SOCIAL STATUS: Artist or illustrator; in 1671 he presented a copy of the Ten Commandments to the church, in 1678 he gave 'tableaux' to the consistory, and in March 1707, following his death, the deacons were considering the sale of pictures he had left for the poor [FCL, MS 5, pp. 567, 695, and MS 56, p. 120].
FAMILY OR TRADE CONNECTIONS WITH OTHER CHURCH OFFICERS: Brother of Pierre Laurens [HSQS XVIII, 78, 94].

NAME: **Pierre LAURENS**
BORN: Rouen
ENDENIZED/NATURALIZED: Nat 1657 and 1664
IN OFFICE: D 1659–61, 1668–71
FAMILY OR TRADE CONNECTIONS WITH OTHER CHURCH OFFICERS: Brother of Marc Laurens.

NAME: **Esaie LAURIER** (Lorié, Loryé)
BORN: Canterbury
IN OFFICE: D 1680–3
TRADE, WEALTH, SOCIAL STATUS: Admitted a foreign master weaver 1673, having come from Canterbury (where he had served the first five years of his apprenticeship) in 1667 [HSQS XXXIII, 18, 38].

NAME: **Etienne LAUZE** (Lause, Louse)
BORN: Nîmes

ENDENIZED/NATURALIZED: Nat 1675 [HSQS XVIII, 111].
IN OFFICE: D 1679–82. He became a member of the Jewin Street congregation on its foundation [BT, MS xcii, f. 189r].
TRADE, WEALTH, SOCIAL STATUS: Merchant?; he petitioned for the restoration of three pieces of alamode seized at Bristol, 1696 [*CTB, 1693–6*, 1294].
FAMILY OR TRADE CONNECTIONS WITH OTHER CHURCH OFFICERS: Son-in-law of Paul Docminique [FCL, MS 7, p. 36].

NAME: **Jacques LE CLERCQ** (Clarcq, Clerc)
BORN: (Artois)
IN OFFICE: D 1649–50, died in office February 1650 [FCL, MS 135A].

NAME: **Philippe LE COCQ** (Cock)
BORN: Lille
ENDENIZED/NATURALIZED: End 1640
IN OFFICE: D 1654–7

NAME: **Daniel LE CONTE** (Compte, Comte, Count)
BORN: Rouen
ENDENIZED/NATURALIZED: Nat 1675
IN OFFICE: D 1683–6; A 1689–92
TRADE, WEALTH, SOCIAL STATUS: Not considered liable to surtax in 1695 Assessment as having a personal estate valued over £600 [Glass, 182. HSQS XIII, 255 confirms that Daniel le Conte's wife was Ursula]. Watch and clock maker; there are watches by him at the Ashmolean Museum, and a long case clock at the Victoria and Albert Museum.

NAME: **Josias LE CONTE**
BORN: Rouen
ENDENIZED/NATURALIZED: Nat 1706
IN OFFICE: D 1705–8; A 1711–16, later elected again 1721–5 and in 1733; died in office Dec. 1733 [Eg. 2734].

NAME: **Louis LE CONTE**
BORN: Luynes, Touraine
ENDENIZED/NATURALIZED: End 1682
IN OFFICE: D 1689–92; A 1693–6, 1705–7, died in office.
TRADE, WEALTH, SOCIAL STATUS: Was he the Lewis Lecompt admitted to the Weavers' Company in 1684 [HSQS XXXIII, 51]?

NAME: **David LE COURT**
BORN: Rouen
ENDENIZED/NATURALIZED: End 1700
IN OFFICE: D 1706–?, A 1714–? [Eg. 2734].

NAME: **Isaac LE FORT**
BORN: Vitré, Brittany
ENDENIZED/NATURALIZED: End 1685; took oaths in connection
with a naturalization bill that did not become an Act, 1690 [HSQS XVIII,
173, 218].
IN OFFICE: D 1693–4, died in office [FCL, MS 8, f. 19r].

NAME: **Jean LE FRANC** (Lefranc)
BORN: La Ferté-sous-Jouarre
IN OFFICE: D 1708–?; A 1712–?, later elected again 1729–32 [Eg. 2734].

NAME: **Jacques LE KEUX** (Kueux, Queuche, Queux)
IN OFFICE: D 1669–72
TRADE, WEALTH, SOCIAL STATUS: Wholesale merchant factor
dealing with Canterbury weavers [Rothstein (1989), 40].
FAMILY OR TRADE CONNECTIONS WITH OTHER CHURCH
OFFICERS: The connection of Jacques with the other officers of this
name has not been established [he is not mentioned in Henry Wagner,
'The Huguenot Refugee Family of Le Keux', *Miscellanea Genealogica et
Heraldica*, III, N.S. (1880), 349–52, from which information on the other
members of the family has been taken].

NAME: **Jean LE KEUX** (I)
BORN: Canterbury, 1648 [HSQS V, 212].
IN OFFICE: D 1678–81; A 1688–91, 1697–9
TRADE, WEALTH, SOCIAL STATUS: Foreign master weaver [HSQS
XXXIII, 43]. Captain of the Tower Hamlets Trained Band, 1695–1714
[*HSP* XV, 310].
FAMILY OR TRADE CONNECTIONS WITH OTHER CHURCH
OFFICERS: Brother of Philippe Le Keux and Pierre Le Keux (II). Father
of Jean Le Keux (II). His daughter Jeanne married the eldest son and
namesake of François Mariette.

NAME: **Jean LE KEUX** (II)
BORN: London
IN OFFICE: D 1698–1701

TRADE, WEALTH, SOCIAL STATUS: The will of a John LeKeux, gentleman, of Artillery Ground, was proved 2 March 1726 [P.C.C. 52, Plymouth]. However, the Le Keux family was large and disentangling it is difficult; it is no more than a possibility that this is the same man.
FAMILY OR TRADE CONNECTIONS WITH OTHER CHURCH OFFICERS: Son of Jean Le Keux (I). Nephew of Philippe Le Keux and of Pierre Le Keux (II).

NAME: **Philippe LE KEUX**
BORN: Canterbury, 1646 [HSQS V, 207].
IN OFFICE: D 1675-8; A 1684, dying in office in August that year [FCL, MS 7, p. 199].
TRADE, WEALTH, SOCIAL STATUS: Dyer, and foreign master weaver [HSQS XXXIII, 43-4].
FAMILY OR TRADE CONNECTIONS WITH OTHER CHURCH OFFICERS: Brother of Jean (I) and Pierre (II) Le Keux. Uncle of Jean Le Keux (II).

NAME: **Pierre LE KEUX** (I)
BORN: Canterbury
IN OFFICE: D 1641-4

NAME: **Pierre LE KEUX** (II)
BORN: Canterbury, 1649 [HSQS V, 214].
IN OFFICE: D 1683-6; A 1691-4, 1699-1702, 1704-7. As elder he was employed on deputations to important men such as the Bishop of London, the Secretary of State, the Solicitor-General and the Mayor of London [FCL, MS 8, ff. 119v, 219v, 262v, 263v].
TRADE, WEALTH, SOCIAL STATUS: Foreign master weaver [HSQS XXXIII, 43]. Coetus took the unusual step of co-opting him to advise on the best method of preserving its privileges in the face of the threatened Act against Occasional Conformity in 1702 because he had 'a very great acquaintance with many Lords and Commons and ... was capable and no doubt willing to do his best to preserve the liberties and priviledges of the Dutch and French churches' [Hessels, 2740]. His 'wealth became assured by his marriage to a rich wife, Marie, daughter of Pierre Marescaux' in 1681 [Agnew (1886), I, 202]. He was a founder member (1692) and deputy governor (1698) of the Royal Lustring Company. Before his death in 1723 he had become a Justice of the Peace, Lieutenant-Colonel of the Tower Hamlets Trained Band, a Commissioner of Sewers and a Commissioner for Land Tax in the county of Middlesex [*HSP* XV, 310, 417, and XX, 78-9]. In his will he left seven houses in John Street, Spitalfields, to one

son; an estate in Fleet Lane to a second; and seven more houses, in Gravel Lane, to a third [HSQS LX, 241–2].
FAMILY OR TRADE CONNECTIONS WITH OTHER CHURCH OFFICERS: Brother of Jean (I) and Philippe Le Keux. Uncle of Jean Le Keux (II). Son-in-law of Pierre Marescoe. Cousin of Abraham Didier. 'Good friend' of Jean Blondel (I), who left him significant property [Agnew (1886), II, 259].

NAME: **Andrieu LE MAIRE**
BORN: (Flanders)
ENDENIZED/NATURALIZED: Nat 1657
IN OFFICE: D 1648–51. In 1657 he was a supporter of Elie Delmé [*Consistoire* [1657]].

NAME: **Pierre LEMAN** (Laiman, Laymant, Lemon)
BORN: Canterbury
IN OFFICE: D 1687–90; A 1694–6, 1702–5
TRADE, WEALTH, SOCIAL STATUS: Silk weaver. Pierre presented his *témoignage* from Amsterdam at the Threadneedle Street church in 1673 [HSQS XXI, 168], and in the following year was admitted to the Weavers' Company of London on proof of his service to his father in Amsterdam [HSQS XXXIII, 41]. By 1702 Pierre was living at Stewart Street, Artillery Ground, Spitalfields; it was under him that his son James Leman, many of whose early designs are now in the Victoria and Albert Museum, served his apprenticeship. Pierre died in 1712 [*HSP* XX, 69–70].

LE MOTEUX, see MOTTEUX

NAME: **David LE NOBLE**
BORN: Canterbury
IN OFFICE: D 1660–3; A 1664–5, died in office.
TRADE, WEALTH, SOCIAL STATUS: Merchant, of St Botolph without Aldgate. His will allocated £1400 between his four children, and referred to his tenement in St Peter's, Canterbury [HSQS LX, 244 *sub* David Le Noble (will dated 6 Oct. and proved 4 Nov. 1665)].
FAMILY OR TRADE CONNECTIONS WITH OTHER CHURCH OFFICERS: Brother of Pierre Le Noble. Pierre Delmé and Nicolas Wicart were unrelated but appointed his executors as his friends.

NAME: **Pierre LE NOBLE**
BORN: Canterbury
IN OFFICE: D 1663, died in office [FCL, MS 135A].

TRADE, WEALTH, SOCIAL STATUS: Merchant and Freeman of London [HSQS LX, 244 *sub* Peter Le Noble (will dated 21 Aug. and proved 7 Oct. 1663)].
FAMILY OR TRADE CONNECTIONS WITH OTHER CHURCH OFFICERS: Brother of David Le Noble.

NAME: **Benjamin LE NUD**
BORN: Rouen
ENDENIZED/NATURALIZED: Nat 1675
IN OFFICE: D 1674–6
TRADE, WEALTH, SOCIAL STATUS: Merchant of St Stephen's, Walbrook [Wagner Pedigrees *sub* Docminique].
FAMILY OR TRADE CONNECTIONS WITH OTHER CHURCH OFFICERS: Son-in-law of Paul Docminique.

NAME: **François LE PIPRE** (Pippre)
BORN: Armentieres
ENDENIZED/NATURALIZED: End 1632 ('Le Peper').
IN OFFICE: D 1637–40
TRADE, WEALTH, SOCIAL STATUS: Perhaps identifiable as the merchant Francis Lepipre who obtained the head lease of a messuage in Fenchurch Street in 1666 for £200 but died shortly afterwards [P.E. Jones (1970), II, decree D.168, p. 274].

NAME: **Jean LE PLASTRIER** (Le Platterier, Le Platrier)
BORN: Rouen, 1614
ENDENIZED/NATURALIZED: End 1686; his son, also Jean, was endenized the following year [HSQS XVIII, 178, 199].
IN OFFICE: A 1688–94; he was allocated a less strenuous *quartier* on account of his great age [FCL, MS 7, p. 421].
TRADE, WEALTH, SOCIAL STATUS: Substantial London inhabitant, liable to surtax in the 1695 Assessment as having a personal estate valued over £600 [Glass, 234 *sub* Platree]. He had been a merchant, goldsmith and *bourgeois* of Rouen, where he was an *ancien* and secretary of the Consistory. There he was specifically targeted by the French authorities when he sought shelter from persecution with a relative. Forced to abjure, he then took refuge with his second wife and their daughter, abandoning two houses. He died in London in 1703, where his namesake son, born in 1646, died before him, in 1695 [Bianquis, 38, 82–83; Lesens, 56; Du Pont (1923), II, 501ff]. One of the Jean Le Plastriers was a member of the French Committee administering public charity, 1689–92, being present at 90 out of the 107 meetings of the Committee for which attendance records

exist; this was probably the Threadneedle Street elder, since following his departure he was replaced by other members of the Consistory [HL, Bounty MS 6]. The Threadneedle Street elder was described as J. Le Plastrier senior, gentleman, when he became an original subscriber to the Bank of England in 1694, with £500 [BEA, M1/1, p. 28]. He also subscribed £500 to the Million Bank the following year, when he was resident at Throgmorton Street [TNA, C/114/16], and contributed to the loan to the Emperor of Germany [*HSP* XIX (iii), 37].
FAMILY OR TRADE CONNECTIONS WITH OTHER CHURCH OFFICERS: Father of Robert Le Plastrier.

NAME: **Robert LE PLASTRIER**
BORN: Rouen, 1651
ENDENIZED/NATURALIZED: End 1687; took oaths in connection with a naturalization bill that did not become an Act, 1690; Nat 1702 [HSQS XVIII, 199, 218, and XXVII, 12].
IN OFFICE: D 1693–6; A 1699–1702
TRADE, WEALTH, SOCIAL STATUS: Substantial London inhabitant, liable to surtax in the 1695 Assessment as having a personal estate valued over £600 [Glass, p. 234 *sub* Platree]. Merchant, dealing in a range of goods; before the Revolution he was importing alamode silk, lustrings and paper from France [*CTB, 1689–92*, 180, 254], in 1695 he was shipping a parcel of 'shellock' [*CTB, 1693–6*, 1204], and in 1695/6 his turnover of £1413 was primarily in grocery imports such as nutmeg and cloves [D.W. Jones (1971), 452]. He was an early subscriber to the Bank of England, with £200 [BEA, M1/1, p. 12], and to the Million Bank, with £300, when he lived near Fenchurch Street [TNA, C/114/16]. He has been instanced as 'an example of a merchant turned [stock] dealer. Before 1690, le Plastrier was, besides being concerned to some extent in loans to the City, a biggish buyer of skins from the Hudson's Bay Company. After that date he seems to turn more and more to finance, appearing in Bank and East India stock, and in the Million Bank' [Carter (1954), 37]. He returned to Rouen c.1709, apparently without his religion being questioned, and died there in 1715 [Du Pont (1923), II, 508].
FAMILY OR TRADE CONNECTIONS WITH OTHER CHURCH OFFICERS: Son of Jean Le Plastrier.

NAME: **Abraham LE POUTRE**
BORN: Canterbury
IN OFFICE: D 1639–43
TRADE, WEALTH, SOCIAL STATUS, ENGLISH POLITICAL AFFILIATION: Parliamentarian, joining with Beauvarlet and Jacques

Danbrine in 1643 in deposing that the royalist Louis Hérault had defamed Jean de La Marche [FCL, MS 5, f. 142a].

NAME: **Isaac LE QUESNE** (Cane)
BORN: Rouen
IN OFFICE: A 1637–43, 1652, died in office [FCL, MS 5, p. 359].
TRADE, WEALTH, SOCIAL STATUS: Merchant [CCL, U47-H-1, 66/3 and later references].
FAMILY OR TRADE CONNECTIONS WITH OTHER CHURCH OFFICERS: Brother-in-law of Benjamin Du Quesne [E.F. Du Cane (1876), 16–17].

NAME: **Jacques LE QUIEN** (I) (Kien, Kiene, Quen, Quin)
BORN: near Valenciennes
IN OFFICE: D 1647–51; A 1653–7

NAME: **Jacques LE QUIEN** (II)
IN OFFICE: D 1677–9
TRADE, WEALTH, SOCIAL STATUS: Admitted a member of the Artillery Company, 1672 [*HSP* XV, 311].
FAMILY OR TRADE CONNECTIONS WITH OTHER CHURCH OFFICERS: Son-in-law of Bon Coulon. Brother-in-law of Moise Coulon.

NAME: **Adrien LERNOULT** (I) (Larneau, Larnou, Lernou)
BORN: Amiens
ENDENIZED/NATURALIZED: Endenized either 1687 or 1688; in a naturalization bill that did not become an Act, 1690 [HSQS XVIII, 199, 206, 217].
IN OFFICE: A 1690–4, 1699–1701. He had served as *diacre reçeveur* at the Huguenot church at Calais, where he was subjected to the *dragonnades* in 1685 [*HSP* II, 435, 444–5, and VI, 140, 167].
TRADE, WEALTH, SOCIAL STATUS: Merchant. Substantial London inhabitant, liable to surtax in the 1695 Assessment as having a personal estate valued over £600 [Glass, 184 *sub* Lernault].
FAMILY OR TRADE CONNECTIONS WITH OTHER CHURCH OFFICERS: Brother of Pierre Lernoult. Father of Adrien Lernoult (II) [Wagner Pedigree, to which it has been added that Pierre and Adrien (I) were brothers]. See also:

NAME: **Adrien LERNOULT** (II)
BORN: Calais

ENDENIZED/NATURALIZED: End either 1687 or 1688; naturalized 1698, when described as the son of Adrian [HSQS XVIII, 199, 206, 252].
IN OFFICE: D 1695–8
TRADE, WEALTH, SOCIAL STATUS: Merchant, of Tottenham High Cross. Substantial London inhabitant, liable to surtax in the 1695 Assessment as having a personal estate valued over £600 [Glass, 184 *sub* Lernault]. Probably the Adrien imprisoned 'chez les Pères de l'Oratoire' 1686, while his sisters were put with the 'Hospitalières' of Calais [Douen, III, 195]. In the early years of William III's government one of the two Adriens loaned the Exchequer £500 in 1689 and again £500 in 1690 [*CTB*, *1689–92*, 1982, 1992]. One of the two was an original subscriber to the 1697 issue to enlarge the Bank's capital stock, with £650 for the use of Phillipp Lernoult of Canterbury, merchant [BEA, M1/6, Book B, no. 54]. The two Adriens jointly subscribed £300 to the Million Bank in 1695 and a further £400 in 1700 [TNA, C/114/16].
FAMILY OR TRADE CONNECTIONS WITH OTHER CHURCH OFFICERS: Son of Adrien Lernoult (I). Nephew of Pierre Lernoult. Son-in-law of Herman Olmius; one of Adrien's sons bore the name John Drigue Lernoult, a reminder of the Drigué connection, Jean Drigué's daughter and sole heiress having married Herman Olmius.

NAME: **Pierre LERNOULT**
BORN: Amiens
ENDENIZED/NATURALIZED: End 1682; in a naturalization bill that did not become an Act, 1690 [HSQS XVIII, 159, 218, 223].
IN OFFICE: A 1689–90, having recently come from Canterbury [HSQS XXI, 172]; died in office.
TRADE, WEALTH, SOCIAL STATUS: Merchant, of St Mary, Whitechapel. 'Very rich' [Douen, III, 195]. In the early years of William III's government, he loaned the Exchequer £500 in 1689 and the same sum in 1690 [*CTB*, *1689–92*, 1982, 1992].
FAMILY OR TRADE CONNECTIONS WITH OTHER CHURCH OFFICERS: Brother of Adrien Lernoult (I). Uncle of Adrien Lernoult (II). Brother-in-law of Charles Lason.

NAME: **Jean LE ROY**
BORN: Saumur
ENDENIZED/NATURALIZED: End 1655, Nat 1663
IN OFFICE: D 1656–8; A 1659–61. He was discharged as deacon and immediately elected an elder. However he did not have an easy time in the latter capacity, supporting Pierre Rousseau's objections to Felles as minister

[FCL, MS 5, pp. 394–5], and he may have moved to the Savoy church and later become an elder there [Gwynn (2018), 298].

TRADE, WEALTH, SOCIAL STATUS, ENGLISH POLITICAL AFFILIATION: Described when endenized in 1655 as John Le Roy of Westminster, jeweller, and as well affected towards Cromwell's government [HSQS XVIII, 68–9]. Le Roy, Rousseau and Trippier all had strong Westminster connections, all opposed the reception of Felles as minister, and they were naturalized together in 1663; they represented a discernible Westminster view more politically centrist than that of the City consistory as a whole.

NAME: **Jean LE SADE** (Sad)
IN OFFICE: D 1669–72
TRADE, WEALTH, SOCIAL STATUS: His widow was allocated a place in the Hospital church in 1688 although too poor to pay for it, in consideration of his faithful service as a church officer [HSQS MS 7, p. 416].

NAME: **Jacques LE SAGE**
BORN: Canterbury
IN OFFICE: D 1638–41
TRADE, WEALTH, SOCIAL STATUS, ENGLISH POLITICAL AFFILIATION: testified that De la Marche had preached sedition in 1646 [Hessels, 1971].

NAME: **Aaron LESTOURGEON** (l'Eturgeon, l'Etourgeon)
BORN: Dieppe
IN OFFICE: D 1694–7
TRADE, WEALTH, SOCIAL STATUS: If the church officer was the Aaron Lesturgeon whose will was dated 14 October 1700 and proved 9 January 1701, he left £140 between four daughters and a furred cloak to the fifth. The family is complicated (see Wagner Pedigrees), but this seems the most likely identification.

NAME: **JEAN LETHIEULLIER** or **LE THUILLIER** (Thyullier, Tullier, Twielier, Twillier)
BORN: Cologne, 1591
ENDENIZED/NATURALIZED: End 1632
IN OFFICE: A 1651. No reason for his early discharge is given, but he is known to have spent much of the 1640s at Amsterdam and may have returned there before later settling at Lewisham, Kent, where he died in 1679, aged 88 [Agnew (1886), I, 178].
TRADE, WEALTH, SOCIAL STATUS, ENGLISH POLITICAL

AFFILIATION: Grandson of a Protestant martyred at Valenciennes in 1568, the church elder (1591–1679) was the man who established his family in England. He was already a senior member of the London church before the start of our period, having represented it at the 1634 Synod [HSQS II, 68]. Clearly he was a prominent and successful London merchant, but his activities are less well recorded than those of his sons, two of whom were knighted – Sir John Lethieullier (1633–1719) and Sir Christopher (1639–90) – while a third, Samuel (1643–1710), was an extremely wealthy bachelor who was a foundation director of the Bank of England.
FAMILY OR TRADE CONNECTIONS WITH OTHER CHURCH OFFICERS: His daughter Leonora married Charles Marescoe, then after his death Jacob David [Roseveare, 1–4].

NAME: Jacob LIEGE
BORN: Lusignan
ENDENIZED/NATURALIZED: End 1682, although his *témoignage* from Lusignan was not presented at the French church until 1683; in a naturalization bill that did not proceed, 1690; Nat 1702 [HSQS XVIII, 148–9, 218; XXI, 178; and XXVII, 20].
IN OFFICE: D 1704–6; A 1710–?, later elected again 1722–6 [Eg. 2734].
TRADE, WEALTH, SOCIAL STATUS: Subscribed £500 to the Million Bank, 1695, when he was living in New Paternoster Row, Spitalfields [TNA, C/114/16].

NAME: Isaac de LILLERS (I) (Delier, Lilairs, Lilers, Lillars, Lilliers, Lisler) (1608–78)
BORN: Canterbury
IN OFFICE: D 1638–41; A 1645–8, 1653–6, 1662–5
TRADE, WEALTH, SOCIAL STATUS, ENGLISH POLITICAL AFFILIATION: Merchant [Agnew (1886), I, 266]. Parliamentarian and supporter of de La Marche, 1646 [Hessels, 1970]. Donated £50 towards rebuilding the church after the Fire [FCL, MS 62, f. (21r)].
FAMILY OR TRADE CONNECTIONS WITH OTHER CHURCH OFFICERS: Brother of Jean de Lillers. Father of Isaac (II) and Jacob de Lillers. Father-in-law of Nathaniel Deneu. Son-in-law of Jean Du Quesne (I). See also:

NAME: Isaac de LILLERS (II)
BORN: London
IN OFFICE: D 1678–80; A 1686–9. As elder, he helped solicit letters patent for the new building of l'Eglise de l'Hôpital [FCL, MS 7, pp. 349, 378].

TRADE, WEALTH, SOCIAL STATUS, ENGLISH POLITICAL AFFILIATION: Merchant, trading with Portugal [TNA, SP/31/5, f. 11r] and in 1690 importing sherry and oil from Cadiz in conjunction with his brother Jacob [*CTB, 1689–92*, 468]. Broker (1699) [HL, Beeman MS VII, 6(d)]. An 'Adventurer' in the stock raised to establish French refugee linen manufacture at Ipswich, 1681–2 [Papillon, 119]. Probably the 'De Lilla' whose premises near Aldgate were amongst the first to be searched for arms in connection with Monmouth's rebellion, 1685, being considered someone to be disarmed as disaffected to the government [LMA, CLA/050/02/002, p. 24].
FAMILY OR TRADE CONNECTIONS WITH OTHER CHURCH OFFICERS: Son of Isaac de Lillers (I). Brother of Jacob de Lillers. Nephew of Jean de Lillers. Brother-in-law of Nathaniel Deneu.

NAME: **Jacob de LILLERS**
BORN: London
IN OFFICE: D 1681–3; A 1689–92, 1698–1700
TRADE, WEALTH, SOCIAL STATUS, ENGLISH POLITICAL AFFILIATION: Citizen and Dyer [HSQS LX, 106 *sub* Ellen de Lillers (1709)]. An 'Adventurer' in the stock raised to establish French refugee linen manufacture at Ipswich, 1681–2 [Papillon, 119]. Substantial London inhabitant, liable to surtax in 1695 Assessment as having a personal estate valued over £600 [Glass, p. 86 *sub* 'Delaleer']. Merchant, trading with Portugal [TNA, SP/31/5, f. 11r] and Spain [see above under Isaac de Lillers II]; in 1695/6 he had a turnover of £1464 drapery exports to Near Europe and Iberia [D.W. Jones (1971), 394]. Given as of Leadenhall Street when he contributed £142 to the 1697 subscription to increase the Bank's capital stock [BEA, M1/6, Book A, no. 329]. Whig [De Krey (1978), III, 482].
FAMILY OR TRADE CONNECTIONS WITH OTHER CHURCH OFFICERS: Son of Isaac de Lillers (I). Brother of Isaac de Lillers (II). Nephew of Jean de Lillers. Brother-in-law of Nathaniel Deneu.

NAME: **Jean de LILLERS**
BORN: Cambrai
ENDENIZED/NATURALIZED: End 1635
IN OFFICE: A 1641–7, 1651–4, 1659–62, 1666–9, died in office. A strong supporter of Elie Delmé, he declined to submit to Colloquy in 1658 [Hessels, 2344–5, 2401], but must have been reconciled with the consistory shortly afterwards since he was re-elected elder in 1659. A generous contributor to the church, he gave £20 towards its repair in 1650, £60 towards its rebuilding after the Fire and £56 for other purposes 1665–69, and left it a legacy of £50 [FCL, MS 62, ff. 6r (20v); MS 218;

and MS 101]. He also left £30 to the poor elderly of the Canterbury church [HSQS V, 747].

TRADE, WEALTH, SOCIAL STATUS, ENGLISH POLITICAL AFFILIATION: Merchant [Woodhead (1965), 59]. Parliamentarian and supporter of De la Marche, 1646 [Hessels, 1970].

FAMILY OR TRADE CONNECTIONS WITH OTHER CHURCH OFFICERS: Brother of Isaac de Lillers (I). Uncle of Isaac (II) and Jacob de Lillers. Father-in-law of Jacques Deneu (through Marie, daughter of his first wife Marie de l'Epine), and of Guillaume Carbonnel (through Elizabeth, daughter of his second wife Anne Maurois).

NAME: **Jacques LIZÉ** (Lisée, Lizy)
BORN: possibly Canterbury, where a Jaques Lesie was baptized in May 1649 [HSQS V, 213].
IN OFFICE: D 1682–4. He was elected an elder in 1691, but immediately replaced because he could not be located [FCL, MS 7, p. 506].
TRADE, WEALTH, SOCIAL STATUS: Weaver [HSQS XXXIII, 53]. A James Lizy held £4300 bank stock in trust in 1709 [P.G.M. Dickson, pers. com.].

NAME: **Pierre LOMBARD** (Lombar)
BORN: Nîmes, 1642
ENDENIZED/NATURALIZED: End 1677, Nat 1685
IN OFFICE: D 1681–3; A 1690–3, 1705–?
TRADE, WEALTH, SOCIAL STATUS: Tailor. 'Gentleman' in Bank records when he acquired £500 of stock, 15 Nov. 1694 [BEA, AC28/32233]. In the early years of William III's government he loaned the Exchequer £500 in 1690 [*CTB, 1689–92*, 2005]. When he became an original subscriber with £2682 to the 1697 issue to enlarge the Bank's capital stock, he is given as of York Buildings in the Strand [BEA, M1/6, Book A, no. 197, and Book C, no. 80]. He developed excellent connections; one daughter married Isaac Le Heup, British Envoy to Sweden (1727) and M.P., the other married the younger brother of Prime Minister Robert Walpole [Henry Wagner, 'Peter Lombard of Nismes and his Immediate Descendants', *The Genealogist*, N.S., XXXV (July 1918)]. His will, made in 1720 and proved 1725, bequeathed household property in Norfolk, and talks of his servants, coach and horses, and plate [Wagner Pedigrees].

NAME: **Benjamin LONGUET** (Longet, Lonquett)
BORN: London, 1678 [HSQS XIII, 229h; compare XIII, 207z and 233y, and see HSQS LX, 261 *sub* Mary Longuet, for evidence he was the son of Jean (not Benjamin) Longuet and Marie Loffroy].

IN OFFICE: D 1705–8; later elected A 1716–? [Eg. 2734].
TRADE, WEALTH, SOCIAL STATUS: Merchant. He became a director (from 1734 until his death in 1761), deputy governor (1745–7) and governor (1747–9) of the Bank of England.
FAMILY OR TRADE CONNECTIONS WITH OTHER CHURCH OFFICERS: Son of Jean Longuet.

NAME: **Jean LONGUET**
BORN: Bayeux
ENDENIZED/NATURALIZED: Nat 1664
IN OFFICE: D 1669–72, 1676–8; A 1687–90
TRADE, WEALTH, SOCIAL STATUS: Gentleman [Glass, p. 188]. In the early years of William III's government he loaned the Exchequer £1000 on the 4/- Aid, 1692–3 [D.W. Jones (1971), 485]. Merchant, with a turnover in 1695/6 of £510 in wool and iron imports from Bilbao [D.W. Jones (1971), 437]. His legacy of £20 reached the church in December 1697 [FCL, MS 218, p. 116].
FAMILY OR TRADE CONNECTIONS WITH OTHER CHURCH OFFICERS: Father of the Benjamin Longuet who became Governor of the Bank of England.

NAME: **Henri LOO** (Lo, Loe, Looe)
BORN: London
IN OFFICE: D 1650–3; A 1663–6, 1670–3, 1677–80
TRADE, WEALTH, SOCIAL STATUS: Gentleman, 'Monsieur' or 'Sieur' in church records [HSQS XIII, 164e, 178k]. Jeweller [TNA, C 11/29/17]. Buried 22 August 1688 at All Hallows, London Wall.
FAMILY OR TRADE CONNECTIONS WITH OTHER CHURCH OFFICERS: connections with Du Quesne family (he married Sara Du Quesne 1645, HSQS XIII 28c) and with Marc Laurens (see HSQS XIII 142u, 178k).

NAME: **Jacques** (James) **LORDELL** (Laudel, Lordel, Lourdelle)
BORN: London
IN OFFICE: D 1644–7; A 1670–3. In 1657 he was a supporter of Elie Delmé [*Consistoire* [1657]].
TRADE, WEALTH, SOCIAL STATUS: Merchant.
FAMILY OR TRADE CONNECTIONS WITH OTHER CHURCH OFFICERS: Married to Sara, daughter of Jacques Houblon [HSQS XIII, 27k]. Brother and partner of Jean Lordell in New Fish Street [*HSP* XV, 240]. Father of the Jean Lordell who was a foundation director of the Bank of England, see the next entry:

NAME: **Jean LORDELL**
BORN: London
IN OFFICE: D 1640–4, 1647–9
TRADE, WEALTH, SOCIAL STATUS: Merchant; his trading connections included Portugal [TNA, SP/31/5, f. 11r]. Acres (1934) and Crouzet (1996) identify this Jean Lordell, the brother of Jacques, as a foundation director of the Bank of England, remaining a director 'until his death in 1726 at a very advanced age' [*HSP* XV, 240; Crouzet (1996), 228]. However the strong likelihood is that the brothers were born in 1612 (Jean) and 1617 (Jacques) [HSQS IX, 86, 107], which would have the bank director dying at the highly improbable age of 114. I suggest the bank director is a different Jean Lordell, the son of Jacques Lordell (above) and Sara Houblon, born in 1651 [HSQS XIII, 125a]. That same Jean is also likely to have been the member of the English Committee supervising public refugee charity administration in the late 1690s and until 1705 [LP, MS 941, no. 87; *Estat* for 1705].
FAMILY OR TRADE CONNECTIONS WITH OTHER CHURCH OFFICERS: Brother and partner of Jacques Lordell, see above.

NAME: **Pierre de LORIÉ** (Laurier)
BORN: near Calais
ENDENIZED/NATURALIZED: Probably endenized 1636 [HSQS XVIII, 54].
IN OFFICE: D 1642–4, 1651–3, died in office in April 1653 [FCL, MS 135A].
TRADE, WEALTH, SOCIAL STATUS, ENGLISH POLITICAL AFFILIATION: If he was the Peter Lorier endenized in 1636 he may well have been a merchant, since his denization was tagged with a clause to pay customs and subsidy with strangers [HSQS XVIII, 54]. A moderate or royalist in the Civil War, he testified against seditious preaching by De la Marche, 1646 [Hessels, 1971].

NAME: **Jean Louis LOUBIER** (Loubar)
BORN: Nîmes
ENDENIZED/NATURALIZED: Unless there were two Jean Louis Loubiers involved, he was both endenized (in March) and naturalized (the following month) in 1700 [HSQS XVIII, 296, 315].
IN OFFICE: D 1701–4; A 1730–4 [Eg. 2734].
TRADE, WEALTH, SOCIAL STATUS: The Loubiers were an important mercantile family in eighteenth-century London, prominent in the re-export market [Ormrod (1993), 204]. Two successive men of this name were directors of the London Assurance, 1732–5 and 1735–65 [*HSP* XVIII, 90].

NAME: **Mathieu LYS**
BORN: Bois, Saintonge
ENDENIZED/NATURALIZED: End 1700, Oath Roll naturalization 1709.
IN OFFICE: D 1705–?, A 1716–?. He or another Mathieu Lys had previously served as an elder at the second church of the Artillery, 1695–7 [Gwynn (2018), 306].
TRADE, WEALTH, SOCIAL STATUS: Foreign weaver [HSQS XXXIII, 57].

M

NAME: **Charles MARESCOE** (Marscot, Marecau, Marescau, Morisco)
BORN: Lille
ENDENIZED/NATURALIZED: Nat 1657 and 1660
IN OFFICE: D 1663–5
TRADE, WEALTH, SOCIAL STATUS: Merchant. He 'combined East Indian shipping interests with exchange dealings and building speculation' [*Past and Present*, 46 (1970), 92–3], carrying on business in the Baltic, Iberia and the Mediterranean [Roseveare, 1] and monopolizing the importation of Swedish tar as agent for the Dutch-dominated Swedish tar company [Latham and Matthews (1970), VI, 166]. He was worth £13,000 in mid-1664, rising to nearly £40,000 by the end of 1667 following the onset of the Second Anglo-Dutch War [Roseveare, 2]. His legacy of £150 reached the Threadneedle Street church in October 1670 [FCL, MS 137]. His eldest daughter was said to have a dowry exceeding £10,000 when she married Thomas Frederick in 1675 [Verney (1899), 224].
FAMILY OR TRADE CONNECTIONS WITH OTHER CHURCH OFFICERS: Brother of Pierre Marescoe. Brother-in-law of David Coqueau. Brother-in-law of David Griel. Charles Marescoe married Leonora, daughter of Jean le Thuillier. Jacob David was Charles's chief clerk, Moise Coulon another clerk.

NAME: **Pierre MARESCOE**
BORN: Lille
ENDENIZED/NATURALIZED: Nat 1657, End 1662
IN OFFICE: D 1659–62, 1666–9; A 1677–9, 1683–6, 1689–93
TRADE, WEALTH, SOCIAL STATUS: Foreign master weaver (admitted 1666) and gentleman [HSQS XXXIII, 17, 22]. Burn [(1846), 256], followed by Weiss [(1854), 252], attributed to 'Lauson, Mariscot, and

Monceaux' the chief production of the flowered silks manufactured in late seventeenth-century London; Burn seems to have had inside information but does not indicate his sources. 'Rich old Mr Marisco' [*Political State of Great Britain*, commenting on the death of Pierre Le Keux (II) (2 April 1723) who had married Pierre Marescoe's daughter Mary, cited in Henry Wagner, 'The Huguenot Refugee Family of Le Keux', *Miscellanea Genealogica et Heraldica*, III, N.S. (1880), 349]. Pierre Marescoe was an original subscriber to the 1697 issue to enlarge the Bank's capital stock, with £1125 [BEA, M1/6, Book C, no. 131]. He died in 1710, and a full inventory of his goods and chattels made in June 1711 is held in TNA, PROB 32/54/43.
FAMILY OR TRADE CONNECTIONS WITH OTHER CHURCH OFFICERS: Brother of Charles Marescoe. Brother-in-law of David Coqueau. Brother-in-law of David Griel. Father-in-law of Pierre Le Keux (II).

NAME: **Jansien** (Gentien) **MARIA**
BORN: Mer
ENDENIZED/NATURALIZED: End 1682
IN OFFICE: D 1695-7
TRADE, WEALTH, SOCIAL STATUS: A man of this name had been admitted foreign journeyman weaver upon certificate from Paris in 1670-1, and master in 1676 [HSQS XXXIII, 32, 36, 46].

NAME: **François MARIETTE** (Marriett)
BORN: Orléans
ENDENIZED/NATURALIZED: End 1686
IN OFFICE: A 1688-97, an unusually lengthy continuous period. He helped the French Committee in visiting important men to seek contributions for the refugees [HL, Bounty MS 6, 23 May 1690].
TRADE, WEALTH, SOCIAL STATUS: Formerly a wealthy wine merchant of Place Maubert, Paris, François was the son of Guillaume Mariette, Sieur de la Courtoisie. Having made preparations for evacuation before the Revocation, he escaped successfully with his family in 1685 and was endenized with his wife and five children early the following year [HSQS XVIII, 177-8]. He left behind several properties and vineyards in France worth over 90,000 livres, but it had been claimed he was worth 600,000 livres in all [Douen, III, 367-8, and II, 455, 497]. In the early days of William III's government he loaned the Exchequer £600 on the 2/- Aid, 1690 [*CTB, 1689-92*, 1992]. He also subscribed £300 to the Tontine in 1693 [P.G.M. Dickson, pers. com.], and was an original subscriber to the Bank of England in 1694, with £500 [BEA, M1/1, pp. 8, 35], on each of

these occasions being described as a 'Gentleman' of Soho rather than as a 'merchant'.
FAMILY OR TRADE CONNECTIONS WITH OTHER CHURCH OFFICERS: Connected by marriage with Louis Gervaize (II) [HSQS XVI, 50k]. His eldest son François married Jeanne Le Keux, daughter of Jean Le Keux (I).

NAME: **Jean MARIETTE**
BORN: Paris
ENDENIZED/NATURALIZED: End 1698, Nat 1702
IN OFFICE: D 1705–?

NAME: **Jacob MARION** (Marrion)
BORN: Havre-de-Grace
IN OFFICE: D 1677–9, having come from Amsterdam in late 1675 [HSQS XXI, 190].

NAME: **Balthazar de** (le) **MARQUE** (Marcq)
BORN: Valenciennes
ENDENIZED/NATURALIZED: End 1635
IN OFFICE: D 1643–?
TRADE, WEALTH, SOCIAL STATUS: Possibly a merchant, since his denization was tagged with a clause to pay customs and subsidy with strangers [HSQS XVIII, 54].

NAME: **Guillaume MARTEL** (Martell)
BORN: (Picardy)
IN OFFICE: A?-1637, 1643–7, 1650–2
TRADE, WEALTH, SOCIAL STATUS, ENGLISH POLITICAL AFFILIATION: Tailor and gentleman; enregistered as 'Mr' when buried 1654 [W. Bruce Bannerman (ed), *The Registers of St Olave, Hart Street, London, 1563–1700* (Harleian Society, 1916), 186]. Left a legacy to the Threadneedle Street church of rents from two houses he owned in Fenchurch Street [TNA, PCC PROB 11/234]. An opponent of Jean de La Marche [Hessels, 1972–3], so probably moderate in the Civil War.
FAMILY OR TRADE CONNECTIONS WITH OTHER CHURCH OFFICERS: Father of Laurens Martel.

NAME: **Laurens MARTEL**
BORN: London
IN OFFICE: D 1648–51; A 1658–60, 1669–72

TRADE, WEALTH, SOCIAL STATUS: Merchant, of Fenchurch Street. Left bequests totalling over £16,000 [HSQS LX, 270 (will dated 29 Sept. 1676, proved 5 March 1677)].
FAMILY OR TRADE CONNECTIONS WITH OTHER CHURCH OFFICERS: Son of Guillaume Martel. Father of Pierre Martel.

NAME: **Pierre MARTEL**
BORN: London?
IN OFFICE: D 1686–8
TRADE, WEALTH, SOCIAL STATUS, ENGLISH POLITICAL AFFILIATION: Merchant, of Fenchurch Street [De Krey (1978), III, 576]. Liable to surtax in the 1695 Assessment as having a personal estate valued over £600 [Glass, 196]. He lent £100 on the 4/- Aid, 1692–3 [D.W. Jones (1971), 483].
FAMILY OR TRADE CONNECTIONS WITH OTHER CHURCH OFFICERS: Son of Laurens Martel [HSQS XXI, 191].

NAME: **Isaac MAUBERT** (Mauberte)
BORN: Rouen
ENDENIZED/NATURALIZED: Possibly the 'Isaac Mobert' naturalized in 1657, but this entry could equally refer to the Isaack Maubert endenized after the Restoration in 1662 [HSQS XVIII, 72, 88]. The church officer died between those dates, on 11 October 1660 [FCL, MS 135A].
IN OFFICE: D 1639–40, 1659–60.
TRADE, WEALTH, SOCIAL STATUS, ENGLISH POLITICAL AFFILIATION: Testified against seditious preaching by De la Marche, 1646 [Hessels, 1971].
FAMILY OR TRADE CONNECTIONS WITH OTHER CHURCH OFFICERS: Son-in-law of David Bouquet [HSQS XIII, 35].

NAME: **Marc MAUBERT**
BORN: Rouen
ENDENIZED/NATURALIZED: Nat 1675
IN OFFICE: D 1677–9; A 1683–6
TRADE, WEALTH, SOCIAL STATUS: Merchant; wine importer? [*CTB*, 1676–9, 346, 'Mark Manbret']. He purchased diamonds in association with Nicolas Maubert in the early 1680s [Edgar Samuel, pers. com.]. One of the 'principaux de l'Eglise' consulted about the new refugees, 1681 [FCL, MS 7, p. 80].
FAMILY OR TRADE CONNECTIONS WITH OTHER CHURCH OFFICERS: Connections with Etienne Beaumont (*q.v.*).

NAME: **Nicolas MAUBERT**
BORN: Rouen
ENDENIZED/NATURALIZED: End 1662
IN OFFICE: D 1663–6, 1671–4; A 1684–7
TRADE, WEALTH, SOCIAL STATUS: Important jeweller and diamond merchant [Mitchell (2017), 62]. Large-scale purchaser of diamonds in East India Company sales, 1684, almost certainly for the Parisian jewellery trade [East India Co. ledger L/A/G/1/1, ff. 295, 405; I am endebted to Edgar Samuel for this reference and comment]. One of the 'principaux de l'Eglise' consulted about the new refugees, 1681 [FCL, MS 7, p. 80].
FAMILY OR TRADE CONNECTIONS WITH OTHER CHURCH OFFICERS: Connections with Etienne Beaumont and with Louis Berchere (*q.v.*). Son-in-law of David Bouquet [HSQS XIII, 42].

NAME: **Jean MAURICE** (Mauris, Maurisse)
BORN: Rouen
ENDENIZED/NATURALIZED: End 1682, Nat 1685 [HSQS XVIII, 150, 171].
IN OFFICE: D 1685–8. Absent, on voyage, from the June 1687 *Censures*, he was apparently discharged without seeking leave the following year [FCL, MS 7, pp. 339, 414]. The church receipts for January 1691 include £32 from Jean Maurice for 'the obligation he owes' [FCL, MS 139].

NAME: **Salomon MAURICE**
BORN: Frankfurt
IN OFFICE: A 1651–4

NAME: **Etienne MAZIEQ** (Masick, Mazicq, Mazyke)
BORN: Ile de Ré
ENDENIZED/NATURALIZED: End 1687. In a naturalization bill that did not become an Act, 1690 [HSQS XVIII, 188, 217].
IN OFFICE: D 1691–4
TRADE, WEALTH, SOCIAL STATUS: Merchant [Mazieq came from a Dutch family that had settled in the Ile de Ré for commercial purposes (Dez, 1936), 47)]. He moved to Dublin, where he became a freeman in 1697, and in 1721 was a potential subscriber to the proposed National Bank of Ireland scheme [*HSP* XXIX, 77].

NAME: **Jean MERCIER** (Mercye, Meisier)
BORN: Canterbury? – see below.
IN OFFICE: D 1673–6; A 1679–82. He had presented his *témoignage* from Canterbury in 1670 [HSQS XXI, 196].

TRADE, WEALTH, SOCIAL STATUS: Admitted a foreign master weaver by the Weavers' Company of London on certificate from Canterbury, 1670 [HSQS XXXIII, 34 ('Merchié') and later references to Mercier]. The Merciers were a well-established family in Canterbury, and Jean may have been both born, and later returned there; a Jean Mercier was serving as an elder of the Canterbury church in 1694, and evidently had London connections [CCL, U47-A-7, 24 May and 23 Aug. 1694].

NAME: **Bennet METCALFE** (Metcalf)
BORN: Oxford
IN OFFICE: D 1691–4; A 1706–?, 1715–? [Eg. 2734].
TRADE, WEALTH, SOCIAL STATUS: Wholesale merchant factor, dealing with Canterbury weavers [Rothstein (1989), 40]; given in 1724 as of Queen Street, London [Crisp (1888), 19]. He acquired £1200 Bank stock between July 1695 and January 1696 [BEA, AC28/32233, 26 July and 17 Sept. 1695, 10 and 23 Jan. 1696].

NAME: **Samuel MONCK** (Monk)
BORN: London
IN OFFICE: D 1698–1701; A 1709–12, later elected again 1717–22 [Eg. 2734].
TRADE, WEALTH, SOCIAL STATUS: Merchant of Lothbury, according to the entry when he subscribed £510 to the enlargement of the Bank's capital stock in 1697 [BEA, M1/6, Book A, no. 218].

[Pierre MONET of Niort was elected as a deacon in 1705 but immediately resigned following a report about some irregularity in his conduct unbefitting the office] [FCL, MS 8, f. 224].

NAME: **Abraham MONFORT** (Montford)
BORN: Chinon
ENDENIZED/NATURALIZED: End 1697, Nat 1698
IN OFFICE: D 1692–4; A 1698–1700, 1706–?. While deacon he acted in 1692 as governor of the Spitalfields *Maison de Charité* [FCL, MS 51, p. 85].
TRADE, WEALTH, SOCIAL STATUS: Weaver of Spitalfields, according to the entry when he subscribed £125 to the enlargement of the Bank's capital stock in 1697 [BEA, M1/6, Book C, no. 1].

NAME: **Salomon MONNEREAU**
BORN: La Rochelle
ENDENIZED/NATURALIZED: End 1687
IN OFFICE: D 1706–?

NAME: **Etienne MONTEAGE** (Montyage)
BORN: Chartres
ENDENIZED/NATURALIZED: End 1613
IN OFFICE: A 1637–40, 1644. Monteage had been in office previously, for instance as elder in 1633 [HSQS IX, 183]. He served as the lay representative of the church at the 1644 Colloquy and Synod, and was also named as part of a deputation to the Walloon Synod of the Low Countries seeking Elie Delmé as minister [HSQS II, 78, 85, and LIV, 34]. However at the end of the year he successfully demanded to be released from his service as elder, maintaining that Jean de La Marche had preached contrary to pure doctrine [FCL, MS 5, f. 147]. He brought a further complaint against La Marche before Synod in 1647 [HSQS II, 113].
TRADE, WEALTH, SOCIAL STATUS, ENGLISH POLITICAL AFFILIATION: Since he had also opposed the election of Louis Hérault in 1643 [FCL, MS 5, f. 138], Monteage might be viewed as a moderate at the time of the Civil War.

NAME: **Daniel MOTET** (Mottet, Moutelt)
BORN: Loudun
ENDENIZED/NATURALIZED: End 1688 [HSQS XVIII, 207]. He had reached London via Jersey the previous year [HSQS XXI, 204].
IN OFFICE: A 1692–6
TRADE, WEALTH, SOCIAL STATUS: Merchant of Leadenhall Street, partner of his son-in-law Samuel Dufresnay, mercer [Wagner Pedigrees]. His customers included the church, to which he sold black cloth for clerical garb [FCL, Misc. Papers 56, 31 Jan. and 26 May 1695]. His will, dated at Greenwich 17 Sept. 1702, was proved the following January.
FAMILY OR TRADE CONNECTIONS WITH OTHER CHURCH OFFICERS: Father-in-law of Samuel Stringer [Wagner Pedigrees].

NAME: **Jean** (Jean Antoine) **MOTTEUX** (Lemoteux, Moteux)
BORN: Rouen
ENDENIZED/NATURALIZED: Yes, 1693, 1704; see below.
IN OFFICE: D 1698–1701; A 1704–7, later elected again 1723–31, 1735–8 [Eg. 2734]. His work in office included actions against the French 'prophets' [FCL, MS 8, f. 261r, and BR, MS C 984], and joining the French Committee administering public charity, 1705–7 [FCL, MS 8, ff. 233r, 242v, 266v; *Estat* for 1706].
TRADE, WEALTH, SOCIAL STATUS: Jean Motteux's father, another Jean Motteux from Rouen, abandoned five properties in and near that city when taking refuge in England [Lesens, 55]. Jean senior sought naturalization in 1690, but the Bill did not proceed. He was then endenized in

1693 with his children John, Antony, Timothy, Peter, Judith, Catherine and Martha Mary, before being naturalized in 1696 [HSQS XVIII, 217, 231, 240; the endenization entry mistakenly records John and Antony as separate sons]. His eldest child was also naturalized in 1704, after an earlier unsuccessful attempt the previous year, but on these occasions he is described as John Anthony Motteux [HSQS XXVII, 25, 30]. When in 1747 his sister Catherine made her will, she confirmed the identification, describing him both as her 'late brother John' and as her 'late brother John Anthony' [HSQS LX, 138]. The church officer became 'an eminent Hamburgh merchant' [*Gentleman's Magazine*, 26 Dec. 1741] and a Director of the French Hospital.
FAMILY OR TRADE CONNECTIONS WITH OTHER CHURCH OFFICERS: Brother-in-law of Pierre Deschamps.

NAME: **Robert MYRÉ** (Meree, Miré)
BORN: Rouen
ENDENIZED/NATURALIZED: End 1687, Nat 1701 [HSQS XVIII, 200, and XXVII, 3–4].
IN OFFICE: D 1692–5; A 1701–4. As elder he represented the church at two General Assemblies, became a member of the French Committee 1702–6, and helped Coetus in its opposition to the proposed Act against Occasional Conformity [FCL, MS 8, ff. 154–5, 166v, 231v, 199r; *Estat* for 1705; Hessels, 2738].
TRADE, WEALTH, SOCIAL STATUS: Substantial London inhabitant, liable to surtax in the 1695 Assessment as having a personal estate valued over £600 [Glass, 211]. Myré was born in 1662 and died in 1732. When naturalized, he was listed as an officer of Col. Foxe's regiment of foot, lately disbanded in the West Indies. Family tradition says he fought at the Battle of the Boyne, 1690, and his portrait, by Sir Peter Lely, depicts him as a soldier in armour [*Fragments of Family History ... the Family of Wilkinson* (London: Hodder Brothers, 1896), 45, 46e]. He became a member of the Shipwrights' Company and a Freeman of London. He was at Oxford Court, Cannon Street when he subscribed £500 to the Million Bank, 1695 [TNA, C/114/16]. Retiring from business in London, he removed to Dublin c.1726 [*HSP* XI, 430]. He left an estate of about £11,800 after £5500 had been paid to three children on marriage [Wagner Pedigrees].
FAMILY OR TRADE CONNECTIONS WITH OTHER CHURCH OFFICERS: Son-in-law of Thomas Verbecq [*HSP* XI, 430].

NOPQ

NAME: **Pierre NEPUEU** (Neveu)
BORN: Dover
IN OFFICE: D 1678–81. Elected A. January 1692, but immediately replaced because he was absent from London [FCL, MS 7, p. 537].
TRADE, WEALTH, SOCIAL STATUS, ENGLISH POLITICAL AFFILIATION: Substantial London merchant, liable to surtax in the 1695 Assessment as having a personal estate valued over £600 [Glass, p. 212 *sub* Peter Nepven]. His trading areas included Portugal and Near Europe [D.W. Jones (1971), 183, 471]. He was an original subscriber to the Bank of England in 1694, with £300 [BEA, M1/1, p. 27], and held £750 Bank stock in 1709 [P.G.M. Dickson, pers. com.].

De NEU or De NEW, see DENEU

NAME: **Etienne NOGUIER** (Naugier, Nogee, Nogier)
BORN: Nîmes
ENDENIZED/NATURALIZED: Stephen Noguier, son of Stephen, was naturalized in 1677 [HSQS XVIII, 118].
IN OFFICE: D 1685–8
TRADE, WEALTH, SOCIAL STATUS: Merchant; in 1693 he was importing thrown silks from Genoa and Italy [*CTB, 1693–6*, 151], while in 1695/6 he sent £4917 in drapery exports to various parts of Europe from the Baltic to the Mediterranean [D.W. Jones (1971), 406]. He subscribed £500 to the Million Bank in 1695, when he was living at Old Jewry [TNA, C/114/16], £375 to the enlargement of the Bank of England's capital stock in 1697 [BEA, M1/6, Book A, no. 471], and £1500 to the East India Loan of 1698 [D.W. Jones (1971), 481].
FAMILY OR TRADE CONNECTIONS WITH OTHER CHURCH OFFICERS: In partnership with David Congnard when importing 2463 gallons of overproof brandy, 1685 [*CTB, 1685–9*, 338].

NAME: **Pierre NOUAL** (Noel, Noele)
BORN: Nîmes
ENDENIZED/NATURALIZED: End 1688 [HSQS XVIII, 207, 'Novel'].
IN OFFICE: D 1695–8

NAME: **Daniel OLIVIER**
BORN: Champdeniers
ENDENIZED/NATURALIZED: Nat 1694 [HSQS XVIII, 232–3].
IN OFFICE: D 1700–2

TRADE, WEALTH, SOCIAL STATUS: Substantial London inhabitant and merchant, liable to surtax in 1695 Assessment as having a personal estate valued over £600 [Glass, p. 219 *sub* Oliver; HSQS XVI, 186m]. From his base in Pancras Lane, Olivier was particularly active in promoting the increasing of the Million Bank's capital in 1700, contributing £3400 himself (including £1400 'to complete the subscription') and also lodging 24 contributions from others totalling £14,300 [TNA, C/114/16].

NAME: **Herman OLMIUS**
BORN: Lochem, Gelderland
ENDENIZED/NATURALIZED: Nat 1677
IN OFFICE: D 1674–7; A 1684–7, 1691–4. During his first term as elder, he helped present the petition to build the new Eglise de l'Hôpital to the state authorities [FCL, MS 7, p. 349].
TRADE, WEALTH, SOCIAL STATUS: Olmius was one of the 'principaux de l'Eglise' consulted about the refugees, and an 'Adventurer' in the stock raised to establish refugees in the linen manufacture at Ipswich, in 1681–2 [FCL, MS 7, p. 80; Papillon, 119]. Gulston's Biographical Dictionary of Foreigners describes him as a prosperous merchant who 'got great riches by trading' and purchased the manor of Waltham Bury, Essex from the Earl of Manchester in 1701 [BL, MS 34,283, f. 141]. His connections included Germany, where in 1703 he delivered £850 from the proceeds of the 1699 Brief for French and Vaudois refugees to a Frankfurt merchant for onwards distribution [LMA, COL/CHD/PR/06/004, ex-GH MS 352/4], and the Netherlands.
In the early years of William III's government Olmius loaned the Exchequer £700 in 1689 and £500 in 1690 [*CTB, 1689–92*, 1982, 1992]. He subscribed £1511 to the 1697 issue to enlarge the Bank's capital stock [BEA, M1/6, Book C, no. 120], and became 'a prominent Bank stock proprietor, and one of the commissioners for the Bank subscription of 1709; his son John was later a Bank director' [Dickson (1967), 427].
FAMILY OR TRADE CONNECTIONS WITH OTHER CHURCH OFFICERS: He married the daughter and sole heir of Jean Drigué. Father-in-law of Adrien Lernoult (II). A trustee for Daniel Du Prie (II). One known trading venture with Jacob David [Roseveare, 183, 393].

NAME: **Paul ORARD** (Aurard, Herard, Horard, Orar)
BORN: Autun [FCL, MS 8, f. 69r].
ENDENIZED/NATURALIZED: A Paul Horard was naturalized in 1696 but was described as born at Mizoen, Dauphiné [HSQS XVIII, 241].
IN OFFICE: D 1698–1701. He distributed poor relief for the French

Committee to those of the meaner sort in Spitalfields, 1700 [HL, Bounty MS 17, pt. 4, p. 51].
TRADE, WEALTH, SOCIAL STATUS: Merchant [HSQS XVI, 198f].

NAME: **André PALLARDY** (Palardy)
BORN: (Poitou)
ENDENIZED/NATURALIZED: Nat 1706
IN OFFICE: D 1702–4; A 1710–? [Eg. 2734].
TRADE, WEALTH, SOCIAL STATUS: Foreign weaver [HSQS XXXIII, 62, 75].

NAME: **Lovington PAMPLIN** (Pamphlin)
BORN: Cambridge, 1618
IN OFFICE: D 1648–51
FAMILY OR TRADE CONNECTIONS WITH OTHER CHURCH OFFICERS: The son of a minister, Pamplin married into the Deneu family in 1647. He became the father-in-law of Mathieu Hebert (I) and of Michel Savary [HSQS XIII, 29w, 50p ('Ramplain'), 222b].

NAME: **Esaie PANTIN** (Pantaine, Panthin, Pontin)
BORN: Rouen
ENDENIZED/NATURALIZED: End 1682? [HSQS XVIII, 153].
IN OFFICE: D 1662–4; A 1677–9
TRADE, WEALTH, SOCIAL STATUS: Almost certainly a goldsmith, as were his father, his son and his brother. He was the first of this family of gold and silversmiths to come to England [see David McKinley, 'The Foundation of Huguenot Silversmithing in London', *HSJ* XXX:5 (2017), 648–9, 652–5].
FAMILY OR TRADE CONNECTIONS WITH OTHER CHURCH OFFICERS: Connected with the Maubert and Bouquet families. He married Elizabeth, daughter of David Maubert, in 1658, and following her death remarried, 1666, to Marie Bouquet, the widow of Isaac Maubert [HSQS XIII, 40t, 48c].

NAME: **David PAPILLON** (Papillion)
BORN: Paris, 1581
IN OFFICE: A 1648–9, following previous service in office for the church dating back to at least 1614, when he was a deacon [HSQS IX, 94]. He requested discharge at the end of 1649 because his business in the country prevented him staying in London and expenses in the city were too great [Northampton R.O., MS P(L) 5].
TRADE, WEALTH, SOCIAL STATUS, ENGLISH POLITICAL

AFFILIATION: Born 1581, died 1659. David Papillon was an architect and military engineer, and between 1642 and 1646 treasurer for Leicestershire, where he acquired an estate. He published *A Practicall Abstract of the Arts of Fortification and Assailing* in 1645, and fortified Gloucester for Parliament in 1646. He approved the English form of government 'though some of its sovereigns, in imitation of the French kings, would have reduced it to an absolute monarchy but for the courage and resolution of Parliament' [*DNB*; *HSP* XVIII, 51–2]. He took the oath of fidelity to 'the Commonwealth of England, as it is now established without a King or house of Lords' in November 1650 [Northampton R.O., MS P(L) 6].
FAMILY OR TRADE CONNECTIONS WITH OTHER CHURCH OFFICERS: Father of Thomas Papillon.

NAME: **Thomas PAPILLON**
BORN: Roehampton, Surrey, 1623.
IN OFFICE: D 1656–9. His working book as deacon has survived and is now in the Northampton Record Office, MS P(L) 241; it includes a monthly breakdown of all church members in the *quartier* for which he was responsible and their financial contributions (if any). With Jean Dubois, although both were only deacons, he represented the Consistory against the Delmé faction before the Council of State, 1657 [Papillon, 48–53].
Although he never again held office in the Threadneedle Street church, Papillon continued to influence its government and development. In 1660 he helped prepare an argument for presentation to Coetus in favour of receiving Felles as minister [FCL, MS 5, p. 398]. In 1669 he urged the Consistory to petition the Council of Trade on behalf of weavers and other artisans [FCL, MS 5, p. 546]. His unpopularity at Court following his election as sheriff of London caused the Consistory concern; the Bishop of London represented that the King resented church members having supported his election and his defence before the Mayor, and the affair may have been the direct cause of the royal order in June 1683 that Piozet be elected a minister of the church [FCL, MS 7, pp. 132–5, 141–5; TNA, SP/44/53, p. 84].
TRADE, WEALTH, SOCIAL STATUS, ENGLISH POLITICAL AFFILIATION: Merchant, Common Councilman of London. Active member of the Council of Trade. Bought the manor of Acrise, Kent, 1666. Twice Master of the Mercer's Company. Director of the East India Company (Deputy Governor 1680–2). M.P. for Dover 1678–81. He was a supervisor of national refugee relief work at its inception in 1681 [Gwynn (2018), 268–9], and again a member of the English Committee in 1689 [BR, MS A 306, p. 39].

Papillon was a Whig City leader, a strong supporter of Exclusion, and one of the Whig candidates in the controversial 1682 election for sheriff of London and Middlesex (the other was Jean Dubois) [Gwynn (2018), 254–5]. As a result he found himself in exile in Holland from the end of 1684 to the Revolution, although he did his best to keep away from political activism while there. He assured his family at the beginning of 1685 that he ever had been and would remain a true, faithful and loyal subject to the King, and reiterated to his wife in March that 'whatever the Gazetteer might say, or any other imagine, I am resolved not to intermeddle with any affaires of State, or to converse with any that are obnoxious to the Government' [HL, Emily C. Papillon, 'The Papillons in France and England' (unpublished typescript, ed. T.L. Papillon, 1923), pp. 695, 713]. Perhaps this determination lessened after James II's accession, since the historian Richard Greaves offers some evidence for classifying him as a radical [Greaves (1992), 301, 314, 341].

After Papillon's return from exile, he resumed as M.P. for Dover 1689–95, then became M.P. for London 1695–1700. He was First Commissioner to the Victualling Office under William III. His will shows he had a personal estate of at least £20,000 in 1701 [Woodhead (1965), 125]. He acquired £1000 of Bank stock in 1694 and held it thereafter [BEA, AC 28/32233, 22 Sept. 1694; Crouzet (1996), 260 n.4].

Papillon continued a lifelong member of the Threadneedle Street church, his family sitting in the place reserved for its most distinguished members [FCL, MS 7, p. 528]. In 1699 the consistory agreed he should be given communion in his seat, his gout preventing him coming up to the table [FCL, MS 8, f. 103v]. When he died in May 1702, he left £100 to the poor of the church, and £25 to each of its ministers [Papillon, 382]. For Papillon's career and convictions, see Papillon (1887) and Scouloudi, (1947).

FAMILY OR TRADE CONNECTIONS WITH OTHER CHURCH OFFICERS: Son of David Papillon.

NAME: **Pierre PATTE**
BORN: Canterbury
IN OFFICE: A 1639–43

NAME: **Pierre PERCHARD** (Peshart, Pitchard)
BORN: Guernsey
IN OFFICE: D 1691–4; A 1698–1700
TRADE, WEALTH, SOCIAL STATUS: The Perchards were one of several families of Guernsey origin who became merchant bankers in London in

the eighteenth century [G.S. Cox (1999), 26]. With reference to a later Peter Perchard who was Lord Mayor of London in 1805 and died the following year aged 76, Wagner writes that it is known only that he came to London 'under the patronage of a wealthy uncle' and that he belonged to a Guernsey family now extinct [Wagner Pedigrees]. Some distant connection with the church officer is likely but has not been identified.

NAME: **Daniel PERREAU** (Parreau, Perau)
BORN: La Rochelle
ENDENIZED/NATURALIZED: End 1687
IN OFFICE: D 1693–6
TRADE, WEALTH, SOCIAL STATUS: Not considered liable to surtax in 1695 Assessment as having a personal estate valued over £600 [Glass, p. 230 *sub* Perro].

PETERS, see LAMBLOIS

NAME: **Deric** (Theodoric) **PETIT** (Pettit, Pety)
BORN: Bar-le-Duc
IN OFFICE: D 1644–7; A 1654–8
TRADE, WEALTH, SOCIAL STATUS: Foreign weaver [HSQS XXXIII, 25].
FAMILY OR TRADE CONNECTIONS WITH OTHER CHURCH OFFICERS: His son married Susanne, daughter of Daniel Du Prie (I) [HSQS XIII, 35]. His daughter Suzanne married Jacques Baudry (II).

PLASTRIER, see LE PLASTRIER

PORT(E), see DUPORT and LA PORTE

NAME: **Daniel PORTEN** (Portin, Porton)
BORN: Dover
IN OFFICE: D 1667–70; A 1677–80
TRADE, WEALTH, SOCIAL STATUS: Merchant, with connections with Italy and the Netherlands [CTB, 1676–9, 535]. One of the 'principaux de l'Eglise' consulted about the refugees, 1681 [FCL, MS 7, p. 80].

NAME: **Germain PORTERET** (Portrait)
BORN: Rouen
IN OFFICE: D 1703–6; A 1707–? He served on the French Committee in 1709 and 1710 [*Estats* for those years].

NAME: **François POUSSET** (Poucet)
ENDENIZED/NATURALIZED: End 1682; Nat on Oath Roll 1710
[HSQS XVIII, 152, and XXVII, 95].
IN OFFICE: D 1690–3
TRADE, WEALTH, SOCIAL STATUS: Weaver. He joined with Pierre
Sené and others to petition the House of Commons on behalf of Protestant
stranger weavers who were members of the Weavers' Company but
threatened by private prosecutions, 1690 [*TNA*, SP/32/13, ff. 140–2; *CJ*
X, 416]. He patented inventions for 'preparing crapes, woollen stuffs and
silks, in flowers and other figures, before being dyed, which appear, after
the goods are dyed, in different colours and on the same piece', 1694; and
for making black and white silk crape, 1698 [*Subject-Matter Index (made
from Titles only) of Patents of Inventions ... 1617 ... to 1852* (2 vols,
1854), patent nos. 332, 357].

NAME: **David PRIMEROSE** (Primrose)
BORN: London
IN OFFICE: D 1705–?; A 1712–? [Eg. 2734].
TRADE, WEALTH, SOCIAL STATUS: The son of the church minister
David Primerose and his second wife Judith Du Prie, born in 1679, this
officer was educated at Merchant Taylors' School. Henry Wagner suggests
he was the David Primerose made free of the Apothecaries' Company in
1703, and the Apothecary of London who made his will in 1716; the will
was proved in 1721 [*Miscellanea Genealogica et Heraldica*, 3rd series, II
(1898), 77–9].

R

NAME: **Jean RAMET** (Ramé, Ramett)
BORN: Valenciennes
ENDENIZED/NATURALIZED: Oath roll naturalization 1709 [HSQS
XXXV, 14].
IN OFFICE: D 1695–8; A 1702–5
TRADE, WEALTH, SOCIAL STATUS: Weaver [HSQS XXXIII, 60, 62].

NAME: **Abraham RATTE** (Le Rat, Ratté)
ENDENIZED/NATURALIZED: End 1655, Nat 1657
IN OFFICE: D 1658–60
TRADE, WEALTH, SOCIAL STATUS, ENGLISH POLITICAL
AFFILIATION: In 1653, the Goldsmiths' Company ordered proceedings
against him as a stranger jeweller [Mitchell (2017), 57]. When endenized

he was described as an enameller, and as well affected towards Cromwell's government [HSQS XVIII, 68–9, 71].

NAME: **Pierre RENEU** or **RENU** (Renew) (I)
BORN: Bordeaux
ENDENIZED/NATURALIZED: Nat 1677 [HSQS XVIII, 118].
IN OFFICE: D 1677–80; A 1685–8, 1693–6, 1701–4. He had presented his *témoignage* from Bordeaux in December 1676 [HSQS XXI, 231], was naturalized in April 1677 and was elected deacon in July 1677, so he clearly came determined to stay in England. He married Elizabeth, daughter of John Cox, merchant, in 1679 [Gauci (2001), 75].
TRADE, WEALTH, SOCIAL STATUS: He and his brother Hilaire were wealthy men with significant connections, and Pierre was one of the most important newcomers to join the Threadneedle Street church. He was one of the 'principaux de l'Eglise' consulted about the refugees in 1681 [FCL, MS 7, p. 80], and an 'Adventurer' in the stock raised to organize the linen manufacture at Ipswich, 1681–2 [Papillon, 119]. His main work on the refugees' behalf lay in his distribution of public charity. During and after his first term as elder, he acted as a distributor for the French Committee [FCL, MS 7, p. 446]. He was reputed to be a leading member of that Committee in 1696 [TNA, SP/32/6 (part II), no. 125, p. 16], and seems to have been largely responsible for the arrangement whereby tallies nominally worth £4000, which if sold in 1696 would have been heavily discounted, were instead lodged with the City church and a loan raised on their security [FCL, MS 8, ff. 42, 64–5, and see the French Committee's accounts in HL and LMA]. By 1699 he had become a member of the English Committee, to which he still belonged a decade later [LP, MS 941, no. 87, p. 3; *Estats* for 1705–9]. He was a foundation Director of the French Protestant Hospital *La Providence* [Murdoch and Vigne (2009), 12].
Reneu was a substantial merchant and, later, stock dealer. At least initially, he had very good connections in France [De Beer (1976), II, 165, 178]. Shortly after arriving in England his imports included wine, brandy and honey [*CTB, 1676–9,* 1004–5, 1009]; in 1695/6 he and his partner imported £1590 of Spanish wine and port [D.W. Jones (1971), 446]. He contributed a loan of just over £900 on the Additional 12d Aid in 1690 [*CTB, 1689–82,* 2008]. He was an original subscriber to the Bank of England in 1694, with £2000 for himself and a further £2000 on behalf of his brother Hilaire [BEA, M1/1, pp. 28, 40], and also an original subscriber to the enlargement of the Bank's capital stock in 1697, with £3920 [BEA, M1/6, Book B, no. 97]. In addition, he subscribed £600 to the Tontine in 1693 and £4000 to the East India loan in 1698, and by 1701 had a significant

holding (£3425) in the Million Bank [D.W. Jones (1971), 240, 478, 485].
He died in Putney in 1729 [for his will, see HSQS LX, 321].

Reneu was an active spy for the Williamite cause. In March 1692 the
secretary-at-war, the Earl of Nottingham, procured a royal pardon for him
and another London merchant, William Lewen, for having 'severall times
since We declared Warr with France traded to that Kingdom ... with a
designe to gaine as much intelligence as possible in matters relating to the
French Fleet, and other things of importance to Our Service, whereof they
gave us constantly advice' [BL, Add MS 28939, f. 207]. Reneu continued to
provide such intelligence for the Secretary of State – and for Pierre Jurieu
in the Netherlands – after Nottingham's fall [BL, Add MS 40771, f. 73,
and see also HMC, *Finch V*, p. xliii].
FAMILY OR TRADE CONNECTIONS WITH OTHER CHURCH
OFFICERS: uncle of Pierre Reneu (II).

NAME: **Pierre RENEU** (II)
BORN: Bordeaux
ENDENIZED/NATURALIZED: Nat 1698 [HSQS XVIII, 255]
IN OFFICE: D 1702–4
TRADE, WEALTH, SOCIAL STATUS: Pierre Reneu junior of London
was the son of Pierre (I)'s brother, Hilaire. He is described as 'gentleman' in
Bank records when acting as attorney for Hilaire and transferring £1625 in
1699, unlike Pierre senior and Hilaire who are both described as merchants
[BEA, AC28/1513, 19 Jan. 1699]. Perhaps it was Pierre (II) who deposited
£7925 for a group of people (including £1800 for himself) when the stock
of the Million Bank was increased in 1700 [TNA, C/114/16].
FAMILY OR TRADE CONNECTIONS WITH OTHER CHURCH
OFFICERS: See above. Baptismal entries suggest friendship between the
Reneu and Hays families [HSQS XIII, 239t, and XVI, 292u].

NAME: **Jean RENIER**
IN OFFICE: A?-1641

NAME: **Nicolas ROMAIN** (Roman)
BORN: Paris
IN OFFICE: D 1695–8
TRADE, WEALTH, SOCIAL STATUS: Admitted foreign weaver by the
Weavers' Company between 1676 and 1684 [HSQS XXXIII, 43, 45, 53].

NAME: **Isaac ROMIEU** (Romier, Roumieu)
ENDENIZED/NATURALIZED: End 1634
IN OFFICE: D 1638–41

TRADE, WEALTH, SOCIAL STATUS: Described as a jeweller when endenized [HSQS XVIII, 49].
FAMILY OR TRADE CONNECTIONS WITH OTHER CHURCH OFFICERS: An Isaac Romieu of London, son of the late Isaac and of Jeanne Hardret, married Marthe Bouquet, daughter of David Bouquet and Marie de Bourg, in January 1663 [HSQS XIII, 44].

NAME: **Pierre ROUSSEAU** (Rosseau, Rousau)
BORN: Saintes
ENDENIZED/NATURALIZED: End 1655, Nat 1663
IN OFFICE: D?-1638; A 1654–8. In 1660 he led opposition to the reception of Jacques Felles as minister of the church, appealing to Coetus when overruled by the consistory. Coetus upheld his arguments, but the consistory convoked a Colloquy, which refused to hear Rousseau when he declined to submit beforehand to its judgement. Rousseau then printed an account of the matter, and when cited before the consistory in 1661 for this 'libelle' refused to accept its jurisdiction, saying he was no longer a member of the church [FCL, MS 5, pp. 394–401, 405, 407, and Misc. Papers 53, 1660 Colloquy; LMA, CLC/180/MSO7412/001, pp. 77–80]. However, he contributed £20 to its poor in 1665 [FCL, MS 218, p. 27].
TRADE, WEALTH, SOCIAL STATUS, ENGLISH POLITICAL AFFILIATION: Silkweaver of Westminster [HSQS XVIII, 68]. Possibly the Peter Rousseau of Wandsworth, gentleman, whose will, dated 27 March 1683 and proved 15 April 1684, mentions his 'greate age' [P.C.C. (47, Hare)]. He appears to have been a political moderate during the Interregnum – he testified against seditious preaching by Jean de La Marche and laid charges against him at the 1647 Synod [Hessels, 1971; FCL, MS 5, p. 333], but was considered well affected towards Cromwell's government in 1655 [HSQS XVIII, 68–9]. Rousseau, Le Roy and Trippier all had strong Westminster connections, all opposed the reception of Felles as minister, and they were naturalized together in 1663; they represented a discernible Westminster view more politically centrist than that of the City consistory as a whole.

NAME: **Jacques ROUSSY** (Roucy, Roussey)
BORN: Vigan, Cévennes
ENDENIZED/NATURALIZED: Nat 1704 [HSQS XXVII, 27].
IN OFFICE: A 1707–?, later elected again 1717–22, 1726–32 [Eg. 2734].
TRADE, WEALTH, SOCIAL STATUS: 'James Roussey' held £504 East India stock in 1709 [P.G.M. Dickson, pers. com.]. Merchant. Director of the French Hospital, to which he left £100 by his will, dated December

1732 and proved the following year [Murdoch and Vigne (2009), 101; HSQS LX, 331].

NAME: **Jean ROY**
BORN: Saugeon, Saintonge
ENDENIZED/NATURALIZED: Various men named John Roy were endenized, the most likely candidate in 1700 [HSQS XVIII, 314].
IN OFFICE: D 1705–7; A 1712–? [Eg. 2734].

NAME: **Nicolas RUFFIN** (Rufin, Rufine)
BORN: Verchin, near Valenciennes
IN OFFICE: D 1657–9; A 1666–9
TRADE, WEALTH, SOCIAL STATUS: Weaver, having been in England for 30 years when admitted a member of the Weavers' Company in 1662 [HSQS XXXIII, 11].

NAME: **Henri de RUSMES** (Rucham)
BORN: Sedan
IN OFFICE: D 1638–41

S

SANTHUNE or SANTHUNS, see DE SANTHUNS

NAME: **David SARRAZIN** (Sarasin, Sarrazen, Sarrusin)
BORN: (Auvergne)
ENDENIZED/NATURALIZED: End 1682, Nat 1685
IN OFFICE: D 1680–3; A 1686–90, 1694–7
TRADE, WEALTH, SOCIAL STATUS: The church registers, in recording the baptisms of the fifteen children born to him by his second wife Marie Minuel, describe him variously as merchant, skinner, and 'mofe maker'; his property adjoined the Threadneedle Street church [HSQS XVI, 179, 196, 219, 240, 256]. He sent £862 in drapery exports to Near Europe in 1695/6 [D.W. Jones (1971), 409]. Despite being born in Auvergne, he took refuge from Rouen [Lesens, 77; HSQS XIII, 59 confirms he was married to Anne Ablin].
FAMILY OR TRADE CONNECTIONS WITH OTHER CHURCH OFFICERS: Probably brother of Jacques Sarrazin.

NAME: **Jacques SARRAZIN**
BORN: Ségur, Auvergne

ENDENIZED/NATURALIZED: End 1682
IN OFFICE: D 1698–1700; A 1705–8
TRADE, WEALTH, SOCIAL STATUS: Goldsmith [HSQS XVI, pp. 181, 200, 224]. Not considered liable to surtax in the 1695 Assessment as having a personal estate valued over £600 [Glass, p. 258 *sub* Sarazine].
FAMILY OR TRADE CONNECTIONS WITH OTHER CHURCH OFFICERS: Probably brother of David Sarrazin.

NAME: **Daniel SAUVAGE** (Savage, Sovage)
BORN: Dieppe
IN OFFICE: D 1666–9
TRADE, WEALTH, SOCIAL STATUS: Foreign weaver, as was his son, another Daniel [HSQS XXXIII, 11, 35]. He could only make his mark 'DS' when signing the *Discipline* [FCL, MS 135A].

NAME: **Michel SAVARY** (Savarie, Savery)
BORN: Dieppe
ENDENIZED/NATURALIZED: Nat 1677
IN OFFICE: D 1680–3; A 1692–5
TRADE, WEALTH, SOCIAL STATUS, ENGLISH POLITICAL AFFILIATION: Not considered liable to surtax in 1695 Assessment as having a personal estate valued over £600 [Glass, p. 259 *sub* Saveree]. Member of the Lorriners Company, and Whig [*A List of the Poll for John Ward ... for Members of Parliament For the City of London* (1713), p. 22].
FAMILY OR TRADE CONNECTIONS WITH OTHER CHURCH OFFICERS: Married Lovington Pamplin's daughter Elizabeth; brother-in-law of Mathieu Hebert (I) [HSQS XIII, 50p, 222b].

NAME: **Jean SEALE**
BORN: Jersey
IN OFFICE: D 1707–? Possibly the man elected A in January 1739 who died on 23 December that year [Eg. 2734].

NAME: **Etienne SEIGNORET** (Seingnoret, Siegnieuret)
BORN: 'Lion' [FCL, MS 8, p. 34].
ENDENIZED/NATURALIZED: End 1686, Nat 1698
IN OFFICE: A 1694–7; he was a director of the Spitalfields *Maison de Charité* in 1695 [HL, *Maison de Charité, Deliberations* 1695–1718, f. 1b], and organized a route to get money to the *galériens* [FCL, MS 8, ff. 28r, 30v, 43v]. Previously he had been a founder member of the Jewin Street congregation [BT, xcii, ff. 179r, 185v, 189r], and helped the French Committee in visiting important men to seek contributions for the refugees

[HL, Bounty MS 6, 23 May 1690]. Later he contributed £40 to the loan at the establishment of the French church of St Martin Orgars, 1703 [LMA, MS 00994/I, p. 46], was a founding director of the French Hospital *La Providence* in 1718, and on his death in 1719 bequeathed £70 per annum for apprenticing children of refugees to useful trades [*HSP* VI, 49, 63, 71]. TRADE, WEALTH, SOCIAL STATUS, ENGLISH POLITICAL AFFILIATION: Formerly a silk merchant of Lyons, Seignoret established himself in Lombard Street. He was extremely wealthy. His wife Elizabeth Got was said to be worth £40,000 [*HSP* VII, 208]. D.W. Jones summarizes his activities: 'in the mid 1690's we find him as a big import/export merchant exporting £9377 worth of cloth to Hamburg, Rotterdam, Lisbon and Cadiz, and importing wrought silk from Italy and the Low Countries, and cochineal from Spain. He invested £2950 in the Bank subscription of 1694, and handled some of the remittance business for the government in the later stages of the Nine Years war' [D.W. Jones (1971), 190]. However, Seignoret's attempts to continue trading with France in the wartime conditions of the 1690s – one of his relatives organized the connections of the silk smugglers between London and Lyons – resulted in two convictions, for the smuggling of taffetas in 1694 and for trading in silks in 1698. On the latter occasion he was fined £10,000, being officially estimated to be worth between £80,000 and £100,000, and by Hilaire Reneu to be worth £50,000 [*HSP* XV, 420]. Earlier he had also subscribed £1100 to the Tontine in 1693, and by 1701 he held the largest individual holding in the Million Bank (£6581) [D.W. Jones (1971), 240, 483]. In addition to his initial Bank subscription in 1694, he subscribed a further £5365 in 1697, plus also £4438 'for my selfe and René Baudouin my partner' [BEA, M1/6, Book A, no. 395, and Book B, nos. 156, 239, 279]. Again in 1708 he subscribed £6800 to the doubling of the Bank of England's capital, and in that year he also held £14,187 of East India stock [Dickson (1967), 264]. He played a significant role in 1704 in bringing the important French financier Huguetan over to the allied side [D.W. Jones (1988), 260]. Member of the Merchant Taylors Company, and Whig [*A List of the Poll for John Ward ... for Members of Parliament For the City of London* (1713), p. 25]. Seignoret's will was dated October 1721 and proved a year later [Henry Wagner, 'Huguenot Refugee Family of Seignoret', *Miscellanea Genealogica et Heraldica*, IV, N.S. (1884), 321–2]. FAMILY OR TRADE CONNECTIONS WITH OTHER CHURCH OFFICERS: In partnership with René Baudouin in 1697, see above.

NAME: **Pierre SENÉ** or **SNEE**
BORN: Amiens
ENDENIZED/NATURALIZED: Nat 1698

IN OFFICE: D 1694–7; A 1700–3. He had come from Amiens as a young man in 1675 [HSQS XXI, 244]. Another man of this name was an elder of the Hungerford Market church, 1690–4 [Gwynn (2018), 302].
TRADE, WEALTH, SOCIAL STATUS: Weaver [HSQS XXXIII, 46]. He joined with François Pousset and others to petition the House of Commons on behalf of Protestant stranger weavers who were members of the Weavers' Company but threatened by private prosecutions, 1690 [*TNA*, SP/32/13, ff. 140–2; *CJ* X, 416].

NAME: **Pierre** (Le) **SERRURIER** (Serurier)
BORN: St Quentin
ENDENIZED/NATURALIZED: End 1683
IN OFFICE: D 1684–5, having arrived from St Quentin in 1682 [HSQS XXI, 173]. His discharge was abrupt [FCL, MS 7, p. 238].

NAME: **Melchior SIEGE** or **SIEGIE**
BORN: Comines
IN OFFICE: D 1664–5, died in September 1665 [FCL, MS 135A].

NAME: **Daniel SOCHON** (Chocon, Choson, Sachon, Shocon)
BORN: Dieppe
ENDENIZED/NATURALIZED: Nat 1657 ('Gochon'), again 1660 [HSQS XVIII, 71, 78].
IN OFFICE: D 1652–4; A 1658–61, 1665 (died in office that summer) [FCL, MS 5, p.489].
TRADE, WEALTH, SOCIAL STATUS: Merchant, licensed to import hemp and other commodities for ships from France, 1653. He petitioned for fishing rights off Newfoundland as owner of the *Prophet of Dieppe*, 1655, noting that 'that kind of fishing' was 'used only by the French' [*CSPD, 1651–2*, 337; *1652–3*, 466; and *1655*, 187]. He was also an insurance underwriter [Roseveare, 582].
FAMILY OR TRADE CONNECTIONS WITH OTHER CHURCH OFFICERS: Uncle of David Griel [Wagner Pedigrees *sub* Chauvel].

NAME: **David STRANG** (Strange, Streing, Strong)
BORN: Pittenweem, Fife, Scotland
IN OFFICE: D 1683–6; A 1690–4, 1698–1700, 1705–?
FAMILY OR TRADE CONNECTIONS WITH OTHER CHURCH OFFICERS: Brother of Jean Strang. Nephew of Abraham Carris.

NAME: **Jean STRANG**
BORN: Pittenweem, Fife, Scotland

IN OFFICE: A 1693–7, 1702–3, died in office January 1703 [FCL, MS 8, f. 185r].

TRADE, WEALTH, SOCIAL STATUS: Scottish born, Jean Strang had been a merchant factor in Bordeaux for over twenty years, and had acquired *bourgeois* status [Meller (1902), 25], when he was imprisoned for his religion in 1685. Being a naturalized French subject, his appeals to Sir William Trumbull (Envoy Extraordinary at Paris) and the English Council were ineffective, and in December 1685 Trumbull reported that Louis XIV was resolved 'that all persons naturalizd should have no passeports; so that Mr. John Strang and others of his Majesties subjects, either such as are in prison, as such as have the Dragoons quarterd upon them till they change their religion, have no more hopes of obtaining releif, or leave to go away' [HMC 75: *Downshire I pt. I*: pp. 46, 57, 65, 71; and Clark (1938), 51]. Strang probably escaped during 1687 and headed first for his native country, since he presented his *témoignage* from the French church of Edinburgh at Threadneedle Street on 29 January 1689 [FCL, MS 20, f. 83r]. It is not certain whether he was the 'John Strange' of Bread Street who subscribed £1000 to the Million Bank in 1695 [TNA, C/114/16] and acquired £662 10s of Bank stock at the time of its enlargement in 1697 [BEA, M1/6, Book B, no.241].

FAMILY OR TRADE CONNECTIONS WITH OTHER CHURCH OFFICERS: Brother of David Strang. Nephew of Abraham Carris. His daughter Suzanne married Simon Du Port, 1690 [HSQS XVI, 17i].

NAME: **Samuel STRINGER** (Stringar)
BORN: London, c.1669
IN OFFICE: D 1697–1700. Prior to becoming a deacon, he had been serving as a director of the Spitalfields *Maison de Charité* in 1695 [HL, *Maison de Charité, Deliberations* 1695–1718, f. 1b].

TRADE, WEALTH, SOCIAL STATUS: Apothecary in Bishopsgate Street [HSQS XVI, 213k], later Doctor of Physic in Surrey; his will was proved in 1738 [Wagner Pedigrees *sub* Motet].

FAMILY OR TRADE CONNECTIONS WITH OTHER CHURCH OFFICERS: Son-in-law of Daniel Motet.

NAME: **Abraham SY** (Cy)
BORN: Canterbury
IN OFFICE: D 1653–6, 1664–5, died in office September 1665 [FCL, MS 135A]. In 1657 he was a supporter of Elie Delmé [*Consistoire* [1657]].

TRADE, WEALTH, SOCIAL STATUS: Another 'Abraham See' was active in the Weavers' Company 1668–77 [HSQS XXXIII, 22, 25, 47].

T

NAME: **Jacques TAINE** (I) (Tain, Tainne, Tayne, Tein, Thaine)
BORN: Cambrai
ENDENIZED/NATURALIZED: End 1680
IN OFFICE: D 1676–9; A 1683–6
TRADE, WEALTH, SOCIAL STATUS: Merchant [HSQS XVIII, 123].
Another man of this name, apparently also from Cambrai, was admitted
a foreign weaver in 1667 [HSQS XXXIII, 18, 32]; was this his father?
FAMILY OR TRADE CONNECTIONS WITH OTHER CHURCH
OFFICERS: Father of Jacques Taine (II) [FCL, MS 49, 1 Jan. 1684].

NAME: **Jacques TAINE** (II)
BORN: London
IN OFFICE: D 1690–3; A 1706–?
FAMILY OR TRADE CONNECTIONS WITH OTHER CHURCH
OFFICERS: Son of Jacques Taine (I).

NAME: **Florentin TAINTURIER** (Teinturier, Tinturie)
BORN: Lorquin, Lorraine
ENDENIZED/NATURALIZED: End 1628, Nat 1656
IN OFFICE: A 1639–43, 1647–50, 1655–7. A senior member of the
consistory, he was deputed to protest to the duc de Soubise about Jean
d'Espagne's services being held in his house, 1642 [FCL, MS 5, f. 132a],
and appointed church representative at the Colloquy and Synod of 1647
[HSQS II, 103, 109].
TRADE, WEALTH, SOCIAL STATUS: Tailor [HSQS XVIII, 42]. He had
moved in 1626 from Lorquin to London, where he developed a high-class
clientele which included Sir Thomas Fairfax and Sir Oliver Cromwell, the
uncle of the Lord Protector. He possessed extensive holdings in London in
addition to his house in Blackfriars – he had properties on Ludgate Hill,
near Fleet Bridge, in St Martin's Lane, Long Acre and Covent Garden,
in Axe Yard, Westminster and at Stepney – and in 1647 he acquired the
manors of North Willingham and Ludford in Lincolnshire [Jean Imray,
'The Boucherett Family Archives', *The Lincolnshire Historian*, vol. 2 no. 3
(1955–6), 12–13]. His legacy of £40 reached the church in 1664 [FCL,
MS 101].
FAMILY OR TRADE CONNECTIONS WITH OTHER CHURCH
OFFICERS: Father-in-law of Mathieu Boucheret.

NAME: **Jean TAVERNIER**
BORN: Amsterdam
ENDENIZED/NATURALIZED: Probably the 'John Taverner' endenized in 1676; the 'John Tavernier' endenized in 1682 is more likely to be the man who presented a *témoignage* from Charenton in 1681 [HSQS XVIII, 116, 155, and XXI, 250].
IN OFFICE: D 1660–3, 1666–9; A 1676–9, 1686–9. In 1657 he was a supporter of Elie Delmé [*Consistoire* [1657]]. During his final period in office, he served as adjoint to Joseph Danbrine in supervising the building of the Hospital church, 1688 [FCL, MS 7, p. 387].
TRADE, WEALTH, SOCIAL STATUS: Weaver [HSQS XXXIII, 22 and other references]. Tavernier was an 'Adventurer' in the stock raised to establish the French refugee linen manufacture at Ipswich, 1681–2 [Papillon, 119]. His legacy of £20 reached the church in 1692 [FCL, MS 218, p. 102].

NAME: **Pierre TORDEREAU** (Tordreau)
BORN: Valenciennes
ENDENIZED/NATURALIZED: Nat 1657
IN OFFICE: D 1661–3
TRADE, WEALTH, SOCIAL STATUS: Weaver and gentleman [HSQS XXXIII, 16 ('Taurdiraw')].
FAMILY OR TRADE CONNECTIONS WITH OTHER CHURCH OFFICERS: Brother-in-law of Paul Docminique [HSQS XIII, 21k, 24i].

NAME: **Charles TRINQUAND** (Trainkand, Tringuand)
BORN: Mirebeau
ENDENIZED/NATURALIZED: Nat 1675
IN OFFICE: D 1677–9; A 1685. He had arrived at the church in 1674 [HSQS XXI, 256]. No reason is given for his early release from his eldership.
TRADE, WEALTH, SOCIAL STATUS, ENGLISH POLITICAL AFFILIATION: Merchant and gentleman [W. Bruce Bannerman (ed), *The Registers of St Olave, Hart Street, London, 1563–1700* (Harleian Society, 1916), 219, 223, 235, 281]. In 1695–6 he had a turnover of £5182 paper imports [D.W. Jones (1971), 457]. Member of the Skinners Company, and Whig [*A List of the Poll for John Ward ... for Members of Parliament For the City of London* (1713), p. 29].
FAMILY OR TRADE CONNECTIONS WITH OTHER CHURCH OFFICERS: Guardian of Etienne Allemand, who inherited £1400 from Etienne Beaumont which was held for him by the Threadneedle Street

consistory 1681–8 [FCL, MS 7, p. 211, and Misc. Papers 18]. Trinquand was engaged to Jacob Gosselin's daughter Marie (banns called), but she died before marriage.

NAME: **Daniel TRIPPIER** (Trepier, Treippeer, Tripier, Trippiere)
BORN: Le Mans
ENDENIZED/NATURALIZED: End 1636, Nat 1657 and 1663
IN OFFICE: D 1651–3; A 1656–60, 1665–9. He tried to reconcile the divisions in the London church after De la Marche's death in 1651, and later opposed Felles's reception as minister in 1660 [FCL, MS 5, pp. 356, 394–6].
TRADE, WEALTH, SOCIAL STATUS, ENGLISH POLITICAL AFFILIATION: Trippier, Le Roy and Rousseau all had strong Westminster connections, all opposed the reception of Felles as minister, and they were naturalized at the same time in 1663; they represented a discernible Westminster view more politically centrist than that of the City consistory as a whole.

NAME: **Machelar TROUDE** (Theroude)
BORN: Dieppe
ENDENIZED/NATURALIZED: Nat 1696
IN OFFICE: D 1695–8

UV

NAME: **Jacques VAISSIER** (Vaisier, Vaissiere, Vessier)
BORN: Montpellier
ENDENIZED/NATURALIZED: End 1624
IN OFFICE: A 1642–4

NAME: **Jacques VANCOURT** (Vancour, Wancourt)
BORN: Canterbury
IN OFFICE: D 1642–5; A 1653–6, when he was outspoken in his support of Cisner and Stouppe against the Delmé faction [Jurin (1657), dedicatory epistle].
TRADE, WEALTH, SOCIAL STATUS, ENGLISH POLITICAL AFFILIATION: Member of the Artillery Company, 1636–9; Lieutenant of the Green Trained Band, 1642 [*HSP* XV, 315].

NAME: **Allard VAN DER WOUDE** (Vanderwood)
BORN: Lille
IN OFFICE: D 1638–40

NAME: **Isaac VANNÉ** (Vane, Vannay, Vannet, Wanné)
BORN: Bohain, Picardy
IN OFFICE: D 1642–4; A 1653–8, 1662–6 [Northampton R.O., P(L) 241, p. 9, for his discharge at the end of 1658].
TRADE, WEALTH, SOCIAL STATUS, ENGLISH POLITICAL AFFILIATION: Foreign weaver and gentleman [HSQS XXXIII, 13, 20]. Vanné testified that Jean de La Marche had preached sedition in 1646 [Hessels, 1971] and supported the more moderate element in consistory against the Delmé faction a decade later [*Consistoire* (1657), 6, 14].
FAMILY OR TRADE CONNECTIONS WITH OTHER CHURCH OFFICERS: Father-in-law of Martin Warlop [HSQS XIII, 29a].

NAME: **François VAURIGAUD** (Vaurigau)
BORN: Pons (?)
ENDENIZED/NATURALIZED: End 1687 or 1694; Nat 1698 (?) [HSQS XVIII, 203, 235, 252].
IN OFFICE: D 1703–5. In 1703 he loaned £10 at the establishment of the French church of St Martin Orgars [LMA, MS 00994/I, p. 46].
TRADE, WEALTH, SOCIAL STATUS: Merchant, importing £660 of port in 1695/6 [D.W. Jones (1971), 449].

NAME: **Thomas VERBECQ** (Verbeck, Werbecq)
BORN: Paris
ENDENIZED/NATURALIZED: Nat 1663
IN OFFICE: D 1666–9. He contributed the largest sum given by a deacon, £50, towards rebuilding the Threadneedle Street church after the Fire [FCL, MS 62, f. 20v].
TRADE, WEALTH, SOCIAL STATUS: Gentleman and merchant, dealing with important people and significant sums including a warrant for £27,000 from the Queen Mother [*CTB, 1660–67*, 637; *1667–68*, 14–15, 362; *1669–72*, 554], but bankrupted in the commercial stagnation of the late 1660s [Roseveare, 89, 313]. 'Possibly the son of *La veuve Verbeck* (widow of Thomas Verbeck the elder who supplied much notable silver to Louis XIV, including great chased pots for orange trees)' [Mitchell (2017), 59].
FAMILY OR TRADE CONNECTIONS WITH OTHER CHURCH OFFICERS: Father-in-law of Robert Myré [*HSP* XI, 430].

NAME: **Jean VERDON** (Verdun, Vodon)
BORN: London
IN OFFICE: D 1688–91; A 1695–8. While deacon he acted in 1691 as governor of the Spitalfields *Maison de Charité* [FCL, MS 51, pp. 82, 84].
TRADE, WEALTH, SOCIAL STATUS: Subscribed £500 to the loan to the Emperor of Germany, 1706 [BEA, M1/20, no. 277].
FAMILY OR TRADE CONNECTIONS WITH OTHER CHURCH OFFICERS: son-in-law of Martin Warlop [HSQS XIII, 54n, 114g].

NAME: **Pierre VIGNIER** (Vigné, Vinier)
BORN: Antwerp
IN OFFICE: A 1637–40, 1657–60
TRADE, WEALTH, SOCIAL STATUS, ENGLISH POLITICAL AFFILIATION: Vignier testified that Jean de La Marche had preached sedition, 1646 [Hessels, 1971], and supported the more moderate element in consistory against the Delmé faction a decade later [*Consistoire* (1657), 14].

NAME: **Samuel VINCENT** (Vancaint, Vinsant)
BORN: London
IN OFFICE: A 1644–7, 1654–7
TRADE, WEALTH, SOCIAL STATUS, ENGLISH POLITICAL AFFILIATION: Not a supporter of Jean de La Marche [Hessels, 1972–3]. Note: A Samuel Vincent was baptized at Threadneedle Street in 1618, but age 26 would be too young for election as elder. Another Samuel Vincent, native of Rouen, was elected A. and had a quartier allocated in 1650 [FCL, MS 5, pp. 349–50] but does not seem to have taken up office and does not appear in FCL, MS 90.

NAME: **Claude VOISIN**
BORN: St Martin, Ile de Ré
ENDENIZED/NATURALIZED: Nat 1657
IN OFFICE: D 1660–2. It is possible that he later became a member and elder of the Savoy church [BR, MS C 984, f. 221].
TRADE, WEALTH, SOCIAL STATUS: Goldsmith? David Mitchell identifies him as having been endenized in 1629 and as having at some stage become free of the Leathersellers' Company, but the difference in time between endenization and holding office as deacon suggests two different men may be involved here [Mitchell (2017), 62].

WXYZ

NAME: **Valentin WANLEY** (Vandelay, Vanlé, Vanneley, Wanlye)
BORN: Basle
ENDENIZED/NATURALIZED: End 1634, Nat 1656 after an earlier attempt in 1642 had passed the House of Commons only [HSQS XVIII, 52, 62, 73].
IN OFFICE: D 1641–5; A 1647–51, 1657–60. In his first period as elder he worked in Coetus to protect foreign weavers in London in 1648 [Hessels, 2123–4], and gave £20 towards the repair of the church, 1650 [FCL, MS 62, f. 8v].
TRADE, WEALTH, SOCIAL STATUS: Tailor [HSQS XVIII, 52] and gentleman. Wanley was the diarist Samuel Pepys's landlord in 1660 [Latham and Matthews (1970), I, 6, 245]. In 1661(?) it was stated that his estate in St Margaret's, Westminster, value £1000 p.a., had fallen to the crown because it had been purchased before his letters of denization were issued [*CSPD, 1661–2,* 209]. However, he eventually left lands in Westminster, Gloucestershire and Lambeth [*CSPD, 1665–6,* 494–5]. His will, proved in 1666, gave the church deacons £6 p.a. for 500 years from the rent of property in King Street, Westminster, and an immediate gift of £80 [FCL, MS 209, p. 47; MS 51, p. 93; and MS 222, f. 1].
FAMILY OR TRADE CONNECTIONS WITH OTHER CHURCH OFFICERS: Connections with David Collivaulx and (through his wife Marie Wanley née Buizard) with the Buizard family.

NAME: **Martin WARLOP** (Warlo, Werlope)
BORN: Calais
IN OFFICE: D 1655–8; he was elected elder in 1681, but declined on grounds of infirmity [FCL, MS 7, p. 38].
FAMILY OR TRADE CONNECTIONS WITH OTHER CHURCH OFFICERS: Son-in-law of Isaac Vanné; father-in-law of Jean Verdon [HSQS XIII, 29a, 54n, 114g].

NAME: **Nicolas** (de la Fontaine, dit) **WICART** (Wicar, Wickart)
BORN: Valenciennes
ENDENIZED/NATURALIZED: Nat 1657, End 1662
IN OFFICE: D 1650–3, 1656–9; A 1660–4, 1666–9, 1674–6. He was the church lay representative at the 1660 Colloquy [FCL, Misc. Papers 53]. During his final term as elder he was closely involved with Hérault's retirement, which took him on deputations to Secretary Coventry, Secretary Williamson and the Bishop of London [FCL, MS 5, pp. 617, 634, 667].

TRADE, WEALTH, SOCIAL STATUS: Weaver and gentleman [HSQS XXXIII, 22].
FAMILY OR TRADE CONNECTIONS WITH OTHER CHURCH OFFICERS: He married, firstly, Lea, daughter of Pierre Bourla, in 1644; and secondly, Esther, daughter of Jacques Baudry (I), in 1653. Brother-in-law of Jacques Baudry (II) and Pierre Baudry, and of Samuel Despaign.

NAME: Noé de la Fontaine (dit) WICART
BORN: Valenciennes
ENDENIZED/NATURALIZED: Nat 1704 [HSQS XXVII, 27].
IN OFFICE: D 1706–?; A 1712–? [Eg. 2734].

NAME: André WILLAU (Villiau, Wailleau, Willow, Willaw)
BORN: London
IN OFFICE: D 1676–8; A 1683–6, 1691–3
TRADE, WEALTH, SOCIAL STATUS: Citizen and grocer of London [HSQS LX, 157]. Left a legacy of £200 to the Threadneedle Street church, 1701 [FCL, MS 140].
FAMILY OR TRADE CONNECTIONS WITH OTHER CHURCH OFFICERS: Son of Jean Willau. A trustee for Daniel Du Prie (II).

NAME: Jean WILLAU
BORN: London
IN OFFICE: D 1643–7; A 1647–51, 1664–6, 1670–3, 1679–82. In 1657 he was a supporter of Elie Delmé [*Consistoire* [1657]]. In his final term of office, he was one of those deputed to thank the King for his kindness towards the new refugees [FCL, MS 7, p. 70].
TRADE, WEALTH, SOCIAL STATUS: Weaver and gentleman [HSQS XXXIII, 21–2]. In 1648 he worked in Coetus to protect foreign weavers in London [Hessels, 2123–4], and in 1684 helped promote new refugee skills in working with silk [Plummer (1972), 138]. He was an 'Adventurer' in the stock raised to establish French refugee linen manufacture at Ipswich, 1681–2 [Papillon, 119]. Common Councilman of London, Bishopsgate Without, 1673? [LMA, COL/CC/13/03/002, p. 22].
FAMILY OR TRADE CONNECTIONS WITH OTHER CHURCH OFFICERS: Father of André Willau, who gave the church £80 in his memory in 1686 [FCL, MS 218, p. 80].

NAME: François WILLETT (Willet)
BORN: London
IN OFFICE: D 1698–1701

TRADE, WEALTH, SOCIAL STATUS, ENGLISH POLITICAL AFFILIATION: Merchant, with £2629 linen imports from Bremen in 1695/6 [D.W. Jones (1971), 436]. He acted as attorney for Claude Rondeau and Philip Lernoult of Canterbury in dealing with Bank stock [BEA, MS AC28/1513, July–Aug. 1698]. Gary de Krey classifies both François and Humfroy Willett as Whigs, Presbyterians, members of the Clothworkers' Company, and merchants with a special focus on Near Europe [De Krey (1978), 508, 603].
FAMILY OR TRADE CONNECTIONS WITH OTHER CHURCH OFFICERS: Son of Humfroy Willett.

NAME: **Humfroy WILLETT**
BORN: Rouen
IN OFFICE: D 1672–5; A 1687–9
TRADE, WEALTH, SOCIAL STATUS, ENGLISH POLITICAL AFFILIATION: See previous entry. Before the Revolution of 1688, Humfroy Willett had good connections in France and Italy, and his activities included organizing ships being laden in the Netherlands for direct consignment to French ports [*CTB, 1676–9*, 758, 870]. In 1695/6 his imports of £4194 were mostly of linen from Bremen with some iron from Bilbao, while he exported small quantities of draperies to Near Europe and alum to Bruges [D.W. Jones (1971), 436]. When in 1702 he petitioned the Earl of Nottingham, principal Secretary of State, for authorization to bring prisoners back to England 'now the cartell is setled', he offered any security demanded, claiming 'I have been a generall tradeing merchant in the City of London, these 38 years, a member of the Turky Company, past all offices in the said City both civill and military, except Sherriff; and Mayor ... there is neither Our Lord Mayor, Alderman or any considerable merchant in London but know me'. At that time his London house was in Copt Hall Court, Throgmorton Street, near the Exchange [BL, Add. MS 29,588, f. 377]. He was an original subscriber to the Bank of England in 1694, with £1200 [BEA, M1/1, pp. 10, 27], and to the Million Bank the following year, with £500 [TNA, C/114/16].
His premises were amongst the first to be searched for arms in connection with Monmouth's rebellion, 1685, when he was considered someone who should be disarmed as disaffected to James II's government; he was arrested and briefly detained [LMA, CLA/050/02/002, pp. 24, 58]. An Edouard Willet with an English father, forced to flee Rouen as a refugee and abandoning three houses in the process, was almost certainly a relation but presumably not Humfroy's son Edouard, who was born in 1676 and so aged only 9 at the time of the Revocation [Lesens, 87; HSQS XIII, 220a].

FAMILY OR TRADE CONNECTIONS WITH OTHER CHURCH OFFICERS: Father of François Willett.

NAME: **Abraham YONE**
BORN: Pays de Caux
IN OFFICE: D 1702–?
TRADE, WEALTH, SOCIAL STATUS: Presumably the Abraham Yon or Yong, weaver or cloth seller, of Wheeler Street, Spitalfields, who died in 1705 [HSQS XVI, 194r, 219g, 266e].

Errata and Corrigenda for Volumes 1 and 2

I am indebted to researchers who have offered helpful corrections and additions to material in the first two volumes of *The Huguenots in Later Stuart Britain*: Kathleen Chater, Barbara Julien, Lonnie Lee, Robert Nash, Sugiko Nishikawa, Elizabeth Randall, Marcia Watson, Philippa Woodcock. Where I have seen the evidence, the sources are provided. In other cases I have simply provided the information I have been given.

ARANDE, Elie Paul d' [vol. I, p. 206]. See further the entry by Andrew Spicer in the Oxford *DNB*.

BAIGNOUX. Timothée Baignoux, given in vol. I, p. 211, as 'born about 1633', was born at Blois in 1635.

BARBAT, Samuel. Much more information than is provided in vol. I, p. 213, about Samuel Barbat, clerk, from Réalville, will be found in Julien (2015), HSQS vol. LXII, 119, n.151. Evidently, he did not pursue a career as a minister but instead became a successful merchant grocer.

BASCLE, Théodore. Add 'Barcle' to the alternative spellings in vol. I, p. 217. He was elected *lecteur* of Le Tabernacle, Soho on 5 April 1696 [HL, MS J8, p. 10].

BAUDET. Delete entry in vol. I, p. 218, see instead Jean Boudet on p. 230.

BERTRAND, Jean and Paul [vol. I, p. 223] were brothers. In 1681 Jean may have been acting as domestic chaplain to the large French Protestant household in Castle Street 'near the Black Bull's Head' headed by Louis Casimir de La Rochefoucaud Esq., sieur de Fontrouet [LMA,

MR/R/R/032/08]. The unpublished manuscript by Lonnie H. Lee, 'The Rappahannock Refuge of John Bertrand and Charlotte Jolly' (2018), discusses Jean's career after he and his wife went to Virginia in 1687. He died there in 1701, and she twenty years later.

BINEAUD, Guillaume. Theology student in 1689 [HSQS XI, 3], omitted from the biographical dictionary in vol. I.

BOSNAUD, Nicolas. This proselyte had arrived in England with references from the Genevan Academy [LMA, MS 10,116/14].

BOUDET, Jean [vol. I, p. 230]. Add after '4 April 1706', 'apparently to serve as temporary *ministre lecteur* at Le Carré,' and add after 'MS 941, no.64', 'HL, MS J10, p. 57'. See vol. II, chap. 2, Le Carré, note.

Jean CAIRON was licensed as a schoolmaster in 1697 [LMA, MS 10,116/14].

CALVET, Jean [vol. I, p. 237]. Calvet was still active at Plymouth in the mid-1690s [LMA, ACC/2079/A1/14].

CAVALLIER, Pierre. Lay *lecteur* at St Jean, Spitalfields, omitted from the Biographical Dictionary in vol. I. See vol. II, p. 123.

CISNER, Christophe [vol. I, p. 247]. On his marriage (16 Sept. 1647), Cisner was described as the son of the late Jean, minister [Crisp (1888), 15].

COUGOT, Antoine [vol. I, p. 252]. Cougot married Antoinette de Gineste, widow of Abbel de Terson, sieur de la Surette, on 3 Jan. 1685/6. Both Antoine and Antoinette came from Puy Laurens, Languedoc. Antoine is given as the son of the late Antoine Cougot and of Dlle. Judith de Tard-dieu [Crisp (1888), 15–16].

DÈZE, François [vol. I, p. 266]. Dèze owed his two English benefices to the patronage of the Whig MP Isaac Rebow. Dèze died in November 1717, and his widow in January 1734; both were buried at the church of St Nicholas, Colchester [*HSP* XXIV, 509].

DUBOURDIEU, Isaac and Jean [vol. I, pp. 268–9]. More information on the French background of these ministers, father and son, and about the financial loss they suffered in taking refuge, can be found in Henri

Teisserenc, 'The Family of Pastor Isaac Dubourdieu: Montpellier 1650–83 and London 1683–94', *HSJ* 31 (2018), 102–16.

DUPONT, Philippe [vol. I, p. 277]. Philippa Woodcock has established that rather than being the father of François Loumeau Dupont, Philippe Dupont [vol. 1, p. 277] was his younger brother. She cites the registers for the reformed church of Saint-Claud, AN TT 269 Saint-Claud, some of the records being printed in Bujeaud, *Supplément au Tableau des Eglises de la Saintonge et de l'Angoumois* pp. 15–18.

François DURETTE [vol. I, p. 280], was a minister at l'Ancienne Patente, 1700 [LMA, MS 10,326/30 *sub* Saurin].

DUROUSOIR. With Papin de Prefontaine, Durousoir was serving the non-conformist 'church near the Greek Church' in the West London suburbs and that at Quaker Street, Spitalfields, at the time of Bishop Compton's enquiry in late 1700 [LMA, DL/A/F/040/MS 09657/003, list of churches]. Nothing else is known of him, and he was omitted from the biographical dictionary of ministers in vol. I.

FORNES, Antoine. Vol I p. 293, 4 lines from the bottom of the entry, for 'St James's Square', read 'Swallow Street'.

FOUACE, Etienne [vol. I, p. 293]. Lonnie Lee advises that Fouace arrived in Virginia in 1688 and served parishes in York County there until 1702, when he left for England after a dispute with the governor, Francis Nicholson. Fouace was a charter trustee of the College of William and Mary at its foundation in 1693. She cites Park Rouse junior, *James Blair of Virginia* (University of North Carolina Press, Chapel Hill, NC, 1971), 160–3.

GARIOT, Thomas. Omitted in error in vol. I; see vol. II, p.26.

GUILLEMIN, François. Guillemin [vol. 1, p. 307] later officiated at a marriage at Le Carré in May 1728, when he signed his name as 'F. Guillemain, prof[esseur] ecclés[iastique]' [HSQS XXV, 35].

JARLAN, Théodore, and LARDEAU, Jean. Barbara Julien has discovered among the Colchester wills those for the ministers Jarlan, 11 Nov. 1729 [PROB 11/633/176] and Lardeau, 11 July 1733 [PROB 11/660/135]. The former gives Jarlan's Christian name as Theosodine.

Anthony Marie de **LA CROZE** was not included in the biographical dictionary of ministers in vol. I. Late in Queen Anne's reign, this Huguenot refugee was vicar of Old Windsor, and actively promoted the idea of building an Anglican church at Geneva. See Sugiko Nishikawa, '"When in Rome ...": Religious practice by Anglicans on the continent in the seventeenth and early eighteenth centuries', in Katsumi Fukasawa and others (eds), *Religious Interactions in Europe and the Mediterranean World* (Routledge, 2017), 98–99.

LA MOTHE, Charles [vol. I, p. 323]. Ordained deacon in 1704, Charles La Mothe is identifiable as the Reverend Charles Lamotte (c.1679–1742) who served as a steward for the second Duke of Montagu and held the living of Weekley, bordering Boughton House park; see the note on him by P.H. McKay in *HSJ* XXX (2015), 437.

LA MOTTE, Joseph de [vol. I, p. 325]. Between 1691 and 1694 he served the four united London conformist churches, mostly only as an assistant, see vol. II, p. 114.

LARDEAU. See above *sub* Jarlan

LA SALLE, Jean de and Jean François de [vol. 1, p. 334]. Kathleen Chater advises that her recent research demonstrates that Jean and Jean François are one and the same minister [*HSJ* XXX (2017), 664 n.25].

LA SERRE, Louis. Mr 'Lasserer' or 'La Ferte', a chaplain paid £20 around the beginning of 1695 because he was going to the Plantations [*CTB, 1693–1696*, pp. 865, 875, 883] seems identifiable with Louis La Serre [vol. I, p. 335].

LA VALLETTE, François [vol. I, p.337]. Following the public scandal he had caused, La Vallette was given £15 from relief funds at the express order of Bishop Compton, on condition he left for Scotland [LMA, MS COL/CHD/PR/05/02/073, acquittance no.27]. In LP [YY 10. 10.17] is a work published in London [for R. Bassett, 1701], *Two Letters, one from the Bishop of Blois to Monsieur de la Vallette, with Promises and Threatnings to prevent his turning Protestant. The other from Monsieur de la Vallette, to his brethren the Clergy of Blois, laying before them the gross errors of their Church, and the necessity to follow his example for their salvation.*

LE MASSON. Add to the list of lay *lecteurs* at Threadneedle Street in vol. II, p. 107, Mr Maçon or Le Masson in 1640–47 [FCL, MS 5, f. 128a and p. 333].

MASSON, Jean (I) and (II) [vol. I, p. 356]. The distinctions made in the biographical dictionary between these two identically named ministers, father and son, depended on published information that Jean (II) was a child aged about five at the time of the Revocation. It has now been suggested that Jean (II) was born much earlier, rendering both entries invalid without more research.

MAZEL, David. Vol I p. 357 last line, for 'La Patente, Soho' read 'l'Ancienne Patente, Soho'.

MILITARY CHAPLAINCIES. Further information regarding military chaplaincies held by the following men who were listed in the 'Biographical Dictionary of Huguenot Ministers' in vol. I, pp. 203–423, can be found in the Jones cards forming the basis for Appendix 1 in the present volume on Huguenot officers serving in the armies of William and Anne:

BRISSAC or BRISAC, Jean Pierre
DUBOURDIEU or DU BORDIEU, Pierre
DESCAIRAC or d'ESCAIRAC, Alexandre
GALLY de GAUJAC, Pierre
LAUSSAC, Antoine Dastor de
LE SUEUR, Pierre
L'HERONDELLE or L'HIRONDELLE, François Alexandre
MAJOU, Jean
MATURIN or MATHURIN, Pierre
PAPIN de PREFONTAINE, François (for the period 1720–21)
RICHON, Bernard
TREPSAC or TRAPSACK, Jean.

NABES, Antoine. Nabes [vol. 1, p. 367] has now been shown to have also been minister at Rye, 1701–4 [vol. II, p. 72].

NOÉ, Charles and Jacques [vol. I, p. 368]. Robert Nash's work on the Channel Islands has established it was Jacques who became a minister in Jersey and then forfeited relief assistance by leaving his post [parish register of St Ouen (Channel Island Family History Society Transcript L/D/21/B9/3/1), 23 Nov. 1689].

NUMBERS OF HUGUENOTS IN BRITAIN. One of the 'imponderables' on which vol. II could reach no conclusion concerned the number of refugees in the Channel Islands (see vol. II, pp. 195–6). See the preface to the present volume.

Laurent PAYAN [vol. I, p. 371]. Add after 'did not have a degree', 'but drew strong support as a teacher' [LMA, MS 10,116/14].

PESSEU and **LA PILLONIERE** [vol. I, pp. 326–7, 374]. Evidence from 1714–15 demonstrates that these were entirely different proselyte ministers [HL, Bounty MSS 34 and 43/1].

PROSELYTES. The work *Two Letters*, noted above sub La Vallette, includes a list of 40 named proselytes. Some of these have not been included in the 'Biographical Dictionary of Huguenot Ministers' in vol. I, while others provide more information than is given there about their French backgrounds.

ROSSIER or ROUSSIER [vol. I, p. 394]. 'Roussié le filz' was received into the ministry by the Walloon Synod of the Low Countries in early 1707, after being called by the church of Dartmouth [Bost (2008), 424].

SCOFFIER, Claude [vol. I, p. 404]. Scoffier was a member of the French Committee by 1714 [HL, Bounty MS 34].

SEVERIN, Jacques and Jean [vol. I, p. 405; vol. II, p. 84]. There is evidence that these men, who were brothers, were both together at Greenwich in 1692 [Huguenot Society, new series volume 4, p. 266]. If they were living and working together, it confuses the picture of which of them may have been doing what, and when, in Greenwich and in Ireland in the 1690s.

SICQUEVILLE, Jacob Gédéon (de) [vol. I, pp. 406–7]. The minister's subscription to the Bank of England is not easy to square with the need portrayed by the minister and his wife Elisabet when petitioning Charles, sixth Earl of Dorset, for assistance [Kent History and Library Centre, U269 Miscellanea Sackville MSS, C121].

TORDEREAU, Charles François. Lay *lecteur* at l'Eglise de l'Hôpital 1688–9. Omitted from Biographical Dictionary in vol. I. See vol II, p. 107 and note.

WANDSWORTH SETTLEMENT. Kathleen Chater's article 'The Huguenots in Wandsworth: new research' (*HSJ* XXX (2017), 657–669), appeared in 2017. Volume II of *The Huguenots in Later Stuart Britain* (2018) also presented substantial new information on the Wandsworth settlement. The two authors have emphasized differing sources of evidence and reached different conclusions. Readers should consider and weigh the merits of both approaches.

Select Consolidated Bibliography (Volumes I–III)

The bibliography is divided into four sections:

(1) manuscript sources;
(2) works printed before 1800;
(3) primary sources in editions published since 1800; and
(4) secondary works printed since 1800.

Printed works were published in London unless otherwise stated.

It is not practicable to list every source consulted across half a century of research, and selections for the bibliography are weighted towards material with a specific Huguenot component on the grounds that such material tends to be less well known to most historians.

1. MANUSCRIPT SOURCES
ARCHIVES OF THE FRENCH PROTESTANT CHURCH OF LONDON, SOHO SQUARE. [Fuller descriptions of these manuscripts will be found in the handlist compiled by Raymond Smith, HSQS L (1972).]

MSS

5, 6, 7, 8	Consistory *Actes* 1615–1708
298, 45, 135	Letter books 1643–1754
292 (Misc. Papers 75)	Royal approbations of ministers
296	Orders of the Consistory
Misc. Papers 28	Papers regarding Louis Hérault
49	Examinations for communion 1656–91
20	*Témoignages* 1669–1719
62	Special collections 1650–1747
90, 91	*Bourse des Nécessités* 1650–1747

94, 222	Elders' *Livres de La Ville* 1669–1731
Misc. Papers 18, 31	Trust funds
Misc. Papers 56	Accounts and receipts 1680–98
209	Church properties
135A, 205	Discipline and signatures of deacons 1649–94
51	Deacons' *Actes* 1661–1719
98, 114	Deacons' rough books 1669–85
101, 137, 221, 138–40	*Grands livres des diacres* 1663–79, 1686–1701
252, 129, 35	Deacons' capital accounts 1648–1738
218	Register of donations 1649–1700
191	Rent of St. Anthony's chapel 1626–63
52, 56	Deacons' *livres des deliberations* 1688–1711
63, 64, 102	Refugee relief
Misc. Papers 47	Refugee relief
73, 74	*Livres des hardes* 1666–99
128	Inventories 1613–74
Misc. Papers 53	Colloquies 1654 and 1660
43	Transcriptions (1761–2) of important documents
294, Misc. Papers 60	Church of La Patente, Spitalfields
187, Misc. Papers 37	Church of the Artillery (II), Spitalfields

LIBRARY OF THE HUGUENOT SOCIETY OF GREAT BRITAIN AND IRELAND, UNIVERSITY COLLEGE, LONDON. [Fuller descriptions of many of these manuscripts will be found in the handlist compiled by Raymond Smith, HSQS LI (1974).]

(a) Burn Donation

MS J2	Hungerford Market / Castle Street church, *Actes* 1688–1758
MS J8	Glasshouse Street / Leicester Fields church, *Actes* 1693–1729
MS J10	Church of Le Carré, *Actes* 1691–1744
MS J25	St James's Square / Swallow Street church, *Actes* 1689–96, also minutes of the meetings of the four united conformist churches
MS J26	West Street church, *Actes* 1693–1741
MS J28	Church of Thorpe-le-Soken, *Actes* 1684–1726

(b) Savoy Church Archive

| MS K2 | *Actes*, 1736–1810 |
| MS K6 | Royal grant, 1675 |

(c) Bounty MSS

MSS for the reigns of James II, William and Mary, and Anne, as calendared in schedules A–E of the Smith handlist. Particular use was made of the *Journal* of the French Committee 1689–94, MS 6.

[New digitized microfiches of part of the Royal Bounty archive recently became available in the Members' Area of the Huguenot Society's website.]

(d) Records of the Spitalfields Maison de Charité ('La Soupe')

Journal 1693–7
Deliberations 1695–1718

(e) Records of the Dover church (nos. ii and iii as described in *HSP* IV (1891–3), 94)

(f) Allix family papers (especially the first three volumes as described in HSQS LXI, 21–2; see also *HSP* XXVIII, 438–9)

(g) Henry Wagner, Huguenot genealogical material, pedigrees and abstracts of Huguenot wills.

(h) George Hilton Jones, cards on Huguenot army officers. T/28.

BODLEIAN LIBRARY, OXFORD

(a) Tanner MSS

28–36, 40, 42, 44–5, 92, 124–5, 138, 147. Papers of William Sancroft, Archbishop of Canterbury. MS 92, from f. 70 onwards, is of especial importance.

(b) Rawlinson MSS

A 17–20	Thurloe's papers; Stouppe as agent
A 306	Secret service payments
A 477–8	William Bridgeman MSS
C 109	John Barbot, Timothy Baignoux
C 392	Bishop Robinson
C 982–5	Henry Compton, Bishop of London. MSS 982 and 984 are of especial importance.

D 436	Jean Forent
D 480	Timothy Baignoux
D 641	French Protestants, including Forent papers

CHRIST CHURCH LIBRARY, OXFORD
| Wake MSS | Especially MSS xxvii–xxviii (much on proselytes) |

PUBLIC RECORD OFFICE, THE NATIONAL ARCHIVES, KEW
(a) London French church *actes* or registers

RG/4/4545	Le Carré
RG/4/4547	Milk Alley (II)
RG/4/4563	Pearl Street (I) and Crispin Street
RG/4/4590	St Jean, Spitalfields
RG/4/4612	Artillery (II)
RG/4/4614	La Patente, Spitalfields

(b) State Papers

Series 8	King William's Chest
Series 18, 25	Domestic, Interregnum
Series 29, 30	Domestic, Charles II
Series 31	Domestic, James II
Series 32	Domestic, William and Mary
Series 34	Domestic, Anne
Series 44	Entry books
Series 63	Ireland
Series 77	Flanders
Series 78	France

(c) Transcripts

| Series 3 | Baschet's transcripts of Paris archives |

(d) Other Material

| Adm./77 | Admiralty, Greenwich Hospital, Newsletters |
| C/114/16 | Million Bank |

LAMBETH PALACE LIBRARY
(a) MSS

929–30, 932–4, 941–2	Gibson MSS; much concerning Archbishop Tenison
952–4, 1028–9, 1834	Miscellaneous
1122	Foreign Protestants

(b) Former Fulham Palace Papers (London)
Box 'Chapels Royal', MS 124

Box labelled 'French Protestants', now dispersed and filed under individual bishops

BRITISH LIBRARY, MANUSCRIPT DEPARTMENT
(a) Additional MSS

5853	Letters to Rev. John Strype
28,887	Ellis papers
29,561, 29,584, 29,586–8	Hatton–Finch papers
32,093	Miscellaneous papers including material on the Savoy church in the Interregnum
34,280–5	Gulston's biographical dictionary of foreigners in England
34,502	Mackintosh collections: letters from D.P. Ronquillo
52,279	Sir William Trumbull, Diary 1685–91
70,083	Harley papers

(b) Others

Egerton MS 1717	Refugee correspondence
Egerton MSS 2568, 2734	*Discipline*, with signatures, of French churches of Norwich (1589–1712) and London (1666–1745)
Stowe MSS 119, 163	Miscellaneous
Lansdowne MSS 256, 486	Includes material on naturalization
Lansdowne MS 1215	Funding the war effort, 1694
MS Loan 29/48	Harley papers

DR WILLIAMS'S LIBRARY, LONDON

| MS 34.4 | John Evans list of Dissenting congregations |

John Quick MSS and transcripts

MSS of Roger Morrice, P and Q; now published, see Goldie and others (2007).

LONDON METROPOLITAN ARCHIVES
(A). Formerly in Corporation of London Record Office.
Court of Aldermen, Repertories 64–128 (1656–1724)
Court of Common Council, Journals 41–55 (1654–1712)
Remembrancia, IX (1660–4), nos. 71–2
MS list of Common Councilmen
Papers concerning Refugee Relief, 1681–1710:

> Account books, formerly Guildhall Library MSS 279–80
>
> Chamber vouchers and warrants for payments, formerly Guildhall Library MSS 344–7, 352
>
> Other accounts etc. listed by A.H. Thomas in *HSP* XII (1917–23), 263–87

(B). Formerly in Guildhall Library.
MSS

994 (3 vols), 996, 998	French church of St. Martin Orgars, 1691–1728
7412 (2 vols)	Coetus minute books
9531/17	Bishop Compton's Registers 1675–1715, part 1
9657, bundles 2 and 3	Papers relating to diocese of London
9899	Society of Parisians
9535/3	Ordinations by Bishop of London 1676–1718
10,326/1 – 10,326/46	Material supporting ordination applications, 1676–1716

(C). Formerly in St. Paul's Cathedral Library, London.
Brief returns, Cambridgeshire, 1688

(D). Others.

CLA/050/02/002	Searches and detentions at the time of Monmouth's Rebellion, 1685
COL/CHD/PR/05/01/011	The master account for auditing payments made to disbanded soldiers in 1699, summarized in this volume as Appendix 2

WESTMINSTER CITY LIBRARIES

Rate Books A3 – A17	For St Anne's Soho, King's Square division, 1691–5
MS A.2202a	Survey of Inhabitants, St Anne's, Soho, 1711

KENSINGTON AND CHELSEA PUBLIC LIBRARIES, Chelsea Branch
Dr John King's manuscript account of Chelsea

BANK OF ENGLAND ARCHIVES

M1/1	Original subscriptions to Bank capital, 1694
M1/3	Bank stock, 1694–1704
M1/6	Bank stock, original subscribers to 1697 issue
M1/20	Loan for Emperor of Germany, 1706–10
M6/87	Powers of Attorney
AC28/32233	Stock transfers between stockholders 1694–5
AC28/1513	Stock transfers between stockholders 1695–9
G4/1	Minutes of the Court of Directors
G7/1	Minutes, General Court of Proprietors, 1694–1701

CAMBRIDGE UNIVERSITY LIBRARY

MS Add. 7519	Abraham de La Pryme manuscripts
MSS Add. 2, 5–7	Strype correspondence

CANTERBURY CATHEDRAL LIBRARY

U47-A- 5, 6, 7 and 8	Walloon Church of Canterbury, *Actes*, fragments between 1651 and 1709
U47-C- 2 and 3	Walloon Church of Canterbury, deacons' accounts 1641–60, 1686–1707
U47-H- 1, 2, 3, 4 and 5	Walloon Church of Canterbury, mostly letters regarding schism of Interregnum period

CORNWALL RECORD OFFICE

DDX 230	Daubuz family papers

CUMBRIA RECORD OFFICE
D/Lons/W 2/1/20 and D/Lons/W 2/1/21 and Lowther Correspondence
Huguenots at Whitehaven

DEVON RECORD OFFICE
MS QS/17/3   Oath roll naturalizations of foreign Protestants 1709–11

Principal Registry of the Bishop of Exeter, ordination papers Refugee community at Bideford 1687

MS Dioc./Basket/D/17/22 & CC/181/136
         French congregation at Dartmouth, 1711

MS Dioc./Chanter 51   Ordinations 1668–1701

MS DD59584   Needy French Protestants at Swanfields

DUBLIN, MARSH'S LIBRARY
MS Z.2.2.3   Diary of Narcissus Marsh

Diary of Elie Bouhéreau

DUBLIN, NATIONAL LIBRARY OF IRELAND
MSS 476–7   'A Light to the Blind; whereby they may see the Dethronement of James the Second King of England'. 2 volumes.

MS 4166   'An Account of the more Remarkable Transactions w[hich] Brigad[ie]r Stearne has been Engaged in with the Royal Regiment of Foot in Ireland'

DUBLIN, ROYAL IRISH ACADEMY
MS H.I.3   'A Journal. From London To the Relief of London-Derry'. 1689.

GENEVA, BIBLIOTHÈQUE DE GENÈVE
Arch. Tronchin 54   Correspondence from Daniel Chamier to Louis Tronchin

GUERNSEY, PRIAULX LIBRARY
Diary of Jean de La Marche

NORFOLK RECORD OFFICE, NORWICH
FC/29/17   Walloon church of Norwich, *Actes*

FC/29/11 and 12   Bishop of Norwich to Dr. de Laune 1637/8

Norwich City Records 16.b.25   Mayor's Court Book 1677–95

Cozens-Hardy deposit 12/2/75, T188D
         Needy refugees at Plymouth, 1693

NORTHAMPTON RECORD OFFICE
P(L) 4–7, 13–14, 224, 241 Papillon papers. MS 241 includes Thomas
                         Papillon's notes as deacon of the Threadneedle
                         Street church.

PARIS, LIBRARY OF THE SOCIÉTÉ DE L'HISTOIRE DU
PROTESTANTISME FRANÇAIS
MSS 335, 765   Ferry papers
MSS 785 (2), (3)   Schickler papers
MS 713 (especially (3)) Letters (especially Tessereau/Bouhereau)

SOUTHAMPTON CITY RECORD OFFICE
D/FC 1   French church of Southampton *Actes*
                       1702–1939
D/FC 3   Letters regarding the French church of
                       Southampton's intent to conform, 1712

SUFFOLK RECORD OFFICE, Ipswich Branch
C/2/2/2/3, C/4/3/1/7   Huguenot settlement at Ipswich

2. WORKS PUBLISHED BEFORE 1800

NOTE. For many works other than newspapers published between 1641
and 1700, the reference number is supplied by D. Wing (comp.), *Short-Title
Catalogue of Books … 1641–1700* (2nd edn, 3 vols, New York, 1972–88).
In some cases, where works might be difficult to trace, the location of the
copy consulted is given.

[Abbadie, Jacques]. *Defense de la Nation Britannique: Ou les droits de
    Dieu, de la Nature, et de la Societé clairement établis au sujet de
    la revolution d'Angleterre, contre l'auteur de L'avis important aux
    Refugiés.* La vefue Mallet, 1692.
Abbé Le Blanc. *Letters on the English and French Nations.* 2 vols.
    J. Brindley and others, 1747.
*An Abstract of the Proceedings of the Commissioners for the Relief of
    Poor Proselytes, from the 30ᵗʰ of April, 1718, to the 30th of April,
    1719.* 1719. [Huguenot Library, University College, London]
*An Account of the Barbarous Attempt of the Jesuites upon Mr. De
    Luzancy, upon his Conversion to the Protestant Religion* [1675].
    Wing A239.
*An Account of the Late Persecution of the Protestants in the Vallys of
    Piemont, by the Duke of Savoy and the French King, in the year
    1686.* For John Crosley, Oxford, 1689. Wing A315.

An Account of the Life and Writings of Mr. John Le Clerc, ... to this present year MDCCXI. 1712.

[Allix, Pierre]. *An Examination of the Scruples of Those who refuse to take the Oath of Allegiance. By a Divine of the Church of England.* 1689.

The Ambitious Practices of France: Or, a relation of the ways and methods used by them to attain to that supream grandeur.... [1689].

Animadversions upon the French King's Declaration against the Protestants. Given at Versailles the 17th of June 1681. 1681. Wing A3206.

An Apology for the Protestants of France, in reference to the Persecutions they are under at this day; In six letters.... 1683. Wing A3555.

Barrow, Isaac. *A Brief State of the Socinian Controversy, concerning a Trinity in Unity.* 1698. Wing B930.

Baxter, Richard. *Reliquiae Baxterianae: Or, Mr Richard Baxter's narrative of the most memorable passages of his life and times.* T. Parkhurst and others, 1696.

[Benoît, Elie]. *Histoire de l'Edit de Nantes, contenant les choses les plus remarquables qui se sont passées en France avant et après sa publication ... jusques à l'Edit de Revocation, en Octobre 1685....* 3 vols in 5, Adrien Beman, Delft, 1693–5.

Bion, John. *An Account of the Torments the French Protestants endure aboard the Galleys.* 1708.

Birch, Thomas. *A Collection of the State Papers of John Thurloe Esq....* 7 vols, 1742.

Birch, Thomas. *The Life of the Most Reverend Dr. John Tillotson, Lord Archbishop of Canterbury. Compiled chiefly from his original papers and letters.* 1752.

Bolde, Sa[muel]. *A Sermon against Persecution, preached March 26, 1682. Being ... the time when the Brief for the persecuted Protestants in France was read....* 1682. Wing B3488–91 [Four 1682 editions].

[Bossuet, Jacques Bénigne]. *A Pastoral Letter from the Lord Bishop of Meaux, to the New Catholics of his Diocess, exhorting them to keep their Easter ... with Reflections upon the Pretended Persecution.* 1686. Wing B3787–8 [Two 1686 editions].

Bourdillon, Jacob. *Sermon de Jubilé, prononcé dans l'Eglise Françoise de l'Artillerie en Spital-Fields, le 13e Janvier 1782.* 1782. [Huguenot Library, University College, London]

A Brief Narrative of the State of the Protestants in Hungary; and the Sufferings and Persecutions of the Ministers of Christ for Religion in that Kingdom. T. Parkhurst, 1677.

Brief Observations concerning Trade and Interest of Money. (1668).

A Brief Relation of the Persecution and Sufferings of the Reformed Churches of France. 1668. Wing B4628.

[Brousson, Claude]. *The Support of the Faithful in Times of Persecution, or, a Sermon preach'd in the Wilderness ... by ... M. Brousson ... who was broke upon the Wheel at Montpelier, Nov. 6 N.S. 1698.* By Tho. Snowden for Tho. Parkhurst, 1699. Wing B5003.

B[ulteel], J[ohn]. *A Relation of the Troubles of the Three Forraign Churches in Kent. Caused by the Injunctions of William Laud Archbishop of Canterbury....* Sam. Enderbie, 1645. Wing B5452.

Bulteel, John. *A Sermon preached in the French Church, in London on the 29. day of August 1652, at the Imposition of Hands on Mr Stouppe.* By T.M. for Edward Archer, 1654. Wing B5453g.

[Burnet, Gilbert]. *News from France: In a letter giving a relation of the present state of the difference between the French King and the Court of Rome....* 1682. Wing B5839.

[Burnet, Gilbert]. *An Apology for the Church of England, with relation to the Spirit of Persecution: for which She is accused.* [Amsterdam, 1688]. Wing B5762.

Burnet, Gilbert. *A Relation of the Barbarous and Bloody Massacre of about an Hundred Thousand Protestants, begun at Paris, and carried on over all France by the Papists, in the Year 1572.* For Richard Chiswel, 1678.

Burnet, Gilbert. *A Sermon Preached at the Funeral of Mr. James Houblon, Who was buried at St. Mary Wolnoth Church in Lombard-Street, June 28, 1682.* For Richard Chiswell, 1682.

Burnet, Gilbert. *Some Letters, containing, an Account of what seemed most remarkable in Switzerland, Italy, etc.* Rotterdam, 1686. Wing B5915.

The Case concerning the Wallons of the City of Canterbury, that are not of Mr. Jannon's Congregation; and those Wallons there, who are of Mr. Jannon's Congregation. [Canterbury?, 1662]. [Broadside in Canterbury Cathedral Library, U47-H-2, no.89]

The Case of the Persecuted and Oppressed Protestants in Some Parts of Germany and Hungary: Laid open in a memorial. Thomas Newcomb, 1675.

The Case of the Poor French Refugees. [1695, not 1697 as in Wing, see *Journals of the House of Commons,* XI, p. 297, 9 April 1695]. Wing C1141.

The Cevenois Relieved, or else, Europe enslav'd.... John Nutt, 1703.

Chabbert, John. *The Most Humble Remonstrances presented to ... the House of Commons, ... 1. Concerning the Proofs, whereby the French Gentlemen Commissioners ... may be convinced, that in their Hands, there are still remaining great Summs of Money....* 1696 [TNA, SP/32/6 (part II), no.125].

Child, Sir Josiah. *A New Discourse of Trade* ... (4th edn, no date).

[Claude, Jean]. *An Account of the Persecutions and Oppressions of the Protestants in France.* 1686. Wing C4588–9 [two 1686 editions].

[Claude, Jean]. *A Short Account of the Complaints, and Cruel Persecutions of the Protestants in the Kingdom of France.* W. Redmayne, 1707.

Complainte de l'Eglise Francoise de Londres sur l'Assechement des Eaux de Siloè. 1645. Wing C5624.

A Complete Collection of State-Trials, and Proceedings upon High-Treason and other Crimes. 2nd edn, 1730.

Considerations upon the Mischiefs that may arise from granting too much Indulgence to Foreigners. Occasioned by the late election of Broad-street Ward. T. Boreman, 1735.

Le Consistoire de l'Eglise Françoise de Londres [et] ... Sieur Delmé et ... ses Adherans.... [1657]. Not in Wing. This is the preamble to a tract in the Huguenot Library, University College, London, now lacking a title page but perhaps originally entitled *Réponse aux Allégations du Sr. Delmé,* see Schickler (1892) II, p. 194 n.1.

[Convenent, Jean]. *A Short History of the Revolutions that have befallen the Principality of Orange, in the Reign of Lewis XIV....* For A. & J. Churchill, 1703.

Copie de la Récusation que les Pauvres Réfugiez opprimez par le Committé François, ont fait de plusieurs Commissaires que ledit Committé prétendoit faussement avoir été nommez par Sa Majesté pour examiner les Plaintes desdits Pauvres opprimez.... [1705?]. [LP, H.9455.4 (10)]

Corpus Disciplinae: *Or the Discipline, together with the Form of all Ecclesiasticall Administrations used in the Dutch-Churches within this Kingdom* ... 1645. Wing C6344.

The Currant Intelligence, nos 1–70, 26 April–24 December 1681 [Bodleian Library, Ash. 1675].

Dalrymple, John. *Memoirs of Great Britain and Ireland. From the Dissolution of the last Parliament of Charles II, until the Sea-battle off La Hogue. Volume II.* 2nd edn, London and Edinburgh, 1773.

[Davenant, Charles]. *An Essay upon the Probable Methods of making a People Gainers in the Ballance of Trade.* James Knapton, 1699.

The Declaration and Manifesto of the Protestants of the Vallies of Piedmont, called the Vaudois, to all Christian Princes and States, of the Reasons of their taking up Arms just now against the Duke of Savoy. 1690. Wing D531A.

[Defoe, Daniel]. *The True-Born Englishman. A Satyr.* No place, 1700 [1701]. Wing D849.

[Delmé, Philippe]. *The Method of Good Preaching, Being the Advice of a French Reform'd Minister to his Son.* 1701.

The Deplorable State and Condition of the Poor French Protestants commiserated ... with reasons for a Protestant League. Richard Janeway, 1681. Wing D1076.

Denis, John Baptist. *A Plot Discovered: Carried on boldly, these many years by false brethren against the new converts from Popery to the Protestant religion, ... wherein is set forth, the insolence and ingratitude, of the greatest part of the French refugees, towards the English, their benefactors....* Privately printed [1722]. [BL, 700.f. 9(4)]

La Dicipline [sic] *de la Societé de Dauphiné.* 1710 [FCL, X.c.25].

Domestick Intelligence, or News both from City and Country, later *The Protestant (Domestick) Intelligence, or, News both from City and Country.* 1679–81.

[Drelincourt, Charles]. *Recueil des Diverses Pieces concernant la Religion en Angleterre. Et le Rétablissement du serenissime Roy de la Grand Bretagne.* Geneva, 1661.

Dubourdieu, John-Armand. *An Appeal to the English Nation: Or, the body of the French Protestants, and the honest proselytes, vindicated from the calumnies cast on them by one Malard and his associates....* J. Roberts, 1718. [A second edition was published the same year, with additions concerning the Bangorian controversy; citations given are from the first edition.]

Du Bourdieu, Isaac. *A Discourse of Obedience unto Kings and Magistrates ... 29 May 1684.* Samuel Lowndes, 1684.

Du Bourdieu, Isaac. *Sermon Prononcé en L'Eglise de la Savoye ... Le 29 de May, jour de la Naissance et du Rétablissement du Roy* [1684].

Du Maresq, Richard. *Sermon prêché dans l'Eglise Francoise de la Savoye, le 28ᵐᵉ de Novemb. 1675. Jour de l'abjuration de deus persones de l'Eglise Romaine.* By J.M. for Moyse Pitt. 1675.

[Du Moulin, Louis]. *A True Report of a Discourse between Monsieur de L'Angle, Canon of Canterbury, and Minister of the French Church in the Savoy, and Lewis du Moulin; the 10ᵗʰ of February, 1678/9.* 1679 [Guildhall Library].

Du Moulin, Pierre. *A Replie to a Person of Honour, his pretended Answer to the Vindication of the Protestant Religion in the Point of Obedience to Soveraigns, and to the Book of Papal Tyranny.* Henry Brome, 1675.

Durel, John. *The Liturgy of the Church of England asserted in a Sermon. Preached at the Chappel of the Savoy, before the French Congregation ... upon the first day that Divine Service was there celebrated according to the Liturgy of the Church of England.* 1662. Wing D2692. [A second edn was printed 1688, Wing D2693.]

Durel, J. *A View of the Government and Publick Worship of God in the Reformed Churches beyond the Seas. Wherein is shewed their Conformity and Agreement with the Church of England, as it is established by the Act of Uniformity.* R. Royston, 1662. Wing D2695.

Durette, Rev. *A Treatise concerning the Abuse of Confessions of Faith: Or, an answer to Mr Graverol's book, entitl'd, A Defence of the Reform'd Religion, of its Synods, and Pastors....* Translated by Francis de la Pillonniere. 1718. [Huguenot Library, University College, London]

An Edict of the French King, prohibiting all Publick Exercise of the Pretended Reformed Religion in his Kingdom.... 1686. Wing L3120.

d[']Espagne, Jean. *Essay des Merveilles de Dieu en l'Harmonie des Temps ..., première partie.* 1657 [BL, 1016.d.15(1)]. Translated as *An Essay of the Wonders of God*, with introduction by Henry Browne, 1662. [Bodleian Library, Vet. A 3 f. 979]

d[']Espagne, Jean. *Les Oeuvres de Jean Despagne, Ministre du Saint Evangile en l'Eglise Françoise de Londres, au Quartier de Westmunster [sic].* 2 vols. La Haye, chez Arnout Leers, 1674. [BL, 12239.a.10]

Establissement de la Societé des Enfans de Nismes. 1683. Wing E3364A.

Estat de la Distribution de la Somme de Douze Mille Livres Sterling, accordée par la Reine aux Pauvres Protestants François Refugiez en Angleterre, pour l'An 1705 ... Paul Vaillant, 1707. [LP, H.9455.5.14]

Estats de la Distribution de la Somme de Douze Mille Livres Sterling, accordée par la Reine aux Pauvres Protestants François Refugiez dans La Grande Bretagne. Pour l'Année, 1707.... Paul Vaillant, 1708. [LP, H.9455.5.17]

Estats de la Distribution de la Somme de Douze Mille Livres Sterling, accordée par la Reine aux Pauvres Protestants François Refugiez en Angleterre, receüe par le Committé François le 18 de décembre 1706.... Paul Vaillant, 1708. [LP, H.9455.5.16]

Estats de la Distribution du Reliqua de la Beneficence de 1707, et de la Beneficence de 1708, accordée par la Reine aux Pauvres Protestants François Refugiez en Angleterre, et administrée par le Committé François, jusqu'au 25 de Mars, 1709.... Paul Vaillant, 1709. [LP, H.9455.5.18]

Estats de la Distribution du Reliqua de la Beneficence de 1708, et de la Beneficence de 1709, accordée par la Reine aux Pauvres Protestants François Refugiez en Angleterre, et administrée par le Committé François jusqu'au 25 de Mars, 1710.... Paul Vaillant, 1710. [LP, H.9455.5.19]

E[verard], E[dmund]. *The Great Pressures and Grievances of the Protestants in France....* 1681. Wing E3529.

An Exact Copy of the Petition of the Protestants in France to their Sovereign Lewis XIV, for Redress of their Present Oppressions. 1680.

A Faithful Account of the Cruelties done to the Protestants, on Board the French King's Gallies, on the Account of the Reformed Religion. J. Nutt, 1700. Wing F261.

Festeau, Paul. *A New and Easie French Grammar.* Thornycroft, 1667.

Forms of Prayer used in the Reformed Churches in France before their Persecution and Destruction.... 1699. [LP, H9427]

Gailhard, Jean. *Apologie des Puritains d'Angleterre à Messieurs les Pasteurs et Anciens des Eglises Reformées en France.* Jean Colin, Geneva, 1663.

[Gaujac, Peter Gally de]. *The Bloudy Babylon: Or, a collection of some particulars concerning the Persecution raging in France against the Protestants, from the Peace of Reswick, to the Martyrdom of the Reverend Monsieur Brousson, inclusively. In a letter to a Lord.* 1698. Wing G373E.

Gaujac, Peter Gally de. *A True Relation of what hath been transacted in behalf of those of the Reformed Religion, during the Treaty of Peace at Reswick. With an account of the present persecution in France.* 1698.

Graverol, Jean. *Projet de Reunion entre les Protestans de la Grande Bretagne.* 'Chez B.G. pour la Veuve René Pean', 1689.

Grey, Anchitell. *Debates of the House of Commons, from the Year 1667 to the Year 1694.* 10 vols. For T. Becket and P.A. de Hondt, 1769.

[Gualtier, François de, de St Blancard]. *A Letter of Several French Ministers fled into Germany upon the account of the Persecution in France, to such of their Brethren in England as approved the Kings Declaration touching Liberty of Conscience.* [1688]. Wing L1575.

[Guybert, René]. *Les Soupirs et les Larmes de l'Afligé: Ou le recours du malade aux remédes de ses maux.* Jean Mayos, 1704. [LP, H.5133.780(6)]

Herault, Louis. *Le Pacifique Royal en Deuil. Compris en deux sermons faits sur la mort de Charles I, roy de la Grande Bretagne et d'Irlande, etc.* Saumur: Jean Lesnier. 1650.

Herault, Louis. *Remerciment faict au Roy au nom des Eglises Estrangeres de ce Royaume, pour sa Royale Protection dont il â pleu a Sa Majeste les asseurer tout de nouveam [sic] par sa derniere Declaration. Prononcé a Whithall, le Vendredy Quinziesme Mars, 1665/6.* Octavian Pulleyn, 1666. Wing H1491.

Herault, Louys. *Le Pacifique Royal en Joye. Compris en Vingt Sermons sur divers texts de l'Escriture.* Amsterdam, Pierre le Grand, 1665. [BL, C128. e. 1]

[Herbert, Guillaume]. *Reponse aux Questions de Mr Despagne, adressées à l'Eglise Françoise de Londres.* 1657. Wing H1545.

Hickes, George. *The True Notion of Persecution stated. In a Sermon preached at the Time of the Late Contribution for the French Protestants.* For Walter Kettilby, 1681. Wing H1876.

An Historical Account of the Sufferings and Death of the Faithful Confessor and Martyr, M. Isaac le Fevre, an Advocate of Parliament. Who after 18 years imprisonment, died a slave in the French King's gallies. Together with a particular relation of the condition of the other miserable prisoners there. 1704.

The History of the Persecutions of the Reformed Churches in France, Orange, and Piedmont. From the year 1655, to this time.... Tho. Newborough & John Nicholson, 1699. Wing H2174.

The History of the Wars in Ireland, between Their Majesties Army, and the Forces of the late King James. For Benj. Johnson, 1690.

The Horrible Persecution of the French Protestants in the Province of Poitou truly set forth by a Gentleman of Great Quality, an eye witness. For Randolph Taylor, 1681.

d'Huisseau, I[saac]. *La Discipline des Eglises Refformées de France. Ou l'ordre par lequel elles sont conduites et gouvernées.* Orléans, 1675.

The Humble Petition of the Protestants of France, lately presented to His Most Christian Majesty, by the Mareschal Schomberg, and the Marquis of Ruvigny. No date [1685].

The Intolerable Grievances of the Poor French.... [Two similar Broadsides with this opening, both in Chetham's Library, Manchester, HP 2579 and 2580.]

[Jurieu, Pierre]. *L'Esprit de Monsieur Arnaud: Tiré de sa conduit, et des Ecrits de luy et de ses Disciples, particulierement de l'Apologie pour les Catholiques*, 2 vols. Deventer, les Heritiers de Jean Colombius. 1684.

Jurieu, Pierre. *Lettres Pastorales addressées aux Fideles de France, qui gemissent sous la Captivité de Babylon....* Seconde Année, Rotterdam, 1688.

[Jurieu, Pierre]. *The Policy of the Clergy of France, to destroy the Protestants of that Kingdom. Wherein is set down the Ways and Means that have been made use of for these twenty Years last past, to root out the Protestant Religion. In a Dialogue between two Papists....* 1681. Wing J1210.

Jurieu, Pierre. *Seasonable Advice to All Protestants in Europe Of what Persuasion soever. For Uniting and Defending themselves against Popish Tyranny.* For R. Baldwin, 1689.

Jurin, John. *A True, and Exact Relation of the Difference between Mr. Christopher Cisner, one of the Pastors of the French Church in London, and others of the Consistory thereof, and John Jurin senior, Merchant, a Member of the same Church....* 1657. Wing J1213A.

A Justification of the Proceedings of the French-Church in London, about the Suspension of Mr. Elijah Delmey. 1656. Wing J1262A.

Kane, Richard (1747). *Campaigns of King William and the Duke of Marlborough: With remarks, on the stratagems by which every battle was won or lost, from 1689, to 1712.* J. Millan.

Kazner, J.F.A. (1789). *Leben Friederichs von Schomberg, oder Schoenburg.* Mannheim, 2 vols.

Keach, Benjamin. *Sion in Distress: Or, the groans of the Protestant Chruch* [sic]. 1681.

[Kennett, White] (1706). *A Complete History of England ... to the Death of his Late Majesty King William III.* 3 vols.

Kennett, White (1744). *An Historical Register and Chronicle of English Affairs: before and after the Restoration of King Charles II.* Charles Marsh.

La Mothe, Claude Groteste de. *Correspondance Fraternelle de l'Eglise Anglicane, avec les autres Eglises Réformées et étrangéres; Prouvée par une dissertation historique, et par plusieurs sermons prononcez à l'occasion des Réfugiez d'Orange.* La Haye, 1705 [LP, H.31.1].

La Mothe, Claude Groteste de. *Entretiens sur la Correspondance Fraternelle de l'Eglise Anglicane, avec les autres Eglises Reformées.* Amsterdam, 1707 [LP, H.31.1].

La Mothe, Claude Groteste de. *Two Discourses concerning the Divinity of our Saviour. Whereunto are added some Articles subscribed by all the French Divines in or about London, in Opposition to the Socinians.* 1693. Wing L299.

La Motte, Franc[ois] de. *The Abominations of the Church of Rome: Discovered in a Recantation-Sermon, lately preached in the French Church of the Savoy....* 1675. Wing L303.

A Letter to the French Refugees concerning their Behavior to the Government. 1710.

Lettre d'un Protestant à un de ses Amis de la Contrée. [London, 1706?] [LP, H.9455.4 (12)]

[Levassor, Michel]. *The Sighs of France in Slavery, breathing after Liberty. By way of memorial.* 1689. Wing L1796.

Lex Talionis: Or, an enquiry into the most proper ways to prevent the persecution of the Protestants in France. 1698.

The Life and Death of Monsieur Claude the famous Minister of Charenton in France. 1688.

Lions, Jean. *Apologie de Jean Lions Ministre, avec des Réflexions sur les Ecrits des Sieurs Pégorier, Lamote et Rival.* 1708 [Huguenot Library, University College, London].

Lions, Jean. *Examen de la Prétenduë Refutation de l'Apologie de Jean Lions Ministre.* 1708.

Lions, Jean. *Relation de ce qui s'est passé entre Jean Lions Ministre, et ses Consistoires.* 1707.

Liste des Protestans François Refugiez en Angleterre, qui étant dans le besoin, ont part a l'Assistance Charitable de Quinze Mille Livres Sterlings ... accordées tous les Ans dans ce ... Royaume. [Chez Robert Roger, 1703]. [LP, H.9455.5.12]

Livre Synodal contenant les Articles résolus dans les Synodes des Eglises Walonnes des Provinces Unies du Pais-Bas. [This is the title as published in 1688, no place. The Walloon Synod continued to print a very small run of its minutes, primarily for its member churches. No copies have been located in Britain. For the minutes up to 1690, see *sub* Commission de l'Histoire des Eglises Wallonnes in the next section. The minutes for the 1690s and early eighteenth century were consulted at the Stadsarchief Amsterdam, reference 201/405–409.]

La Liturgie. C'est a dire, le Formulaire des Prieres Publiques, de l'Administration des Sacramens ... selon l'Usage de l'Eglise Anglicane.... 1667. Wing D2688. [For the many seventeenth century editions of Durel's version of the liturgy, first produced in 1661, see *HSP* XXII (1972), 108–9.]

London Gazette. Especially for the 1680s.

Luzancy, [Hippolite du Chastelet] de. *Sermon du Sieur De Luzancy, Licentié en Théologie. Prononcé dans l'Eglise de la Savoy, le Unzieme de Juillet* ... 1675. Translated as *A Sermon preached in the Savoy, July 11, 1675* ... *on the Day of his Abjuration.* 1675.

Lysons, Daniel. *The Environs of London.* A. Strahan, 1792.

Maitland, William (1739). *History of London, from its Foundation* ... *to the Present Time.* Samuel Richardson, 2 vols.

Malard, Michael (1717). *The case, and the humble petition of Michael Malard* ... *to the* ... *Committee* ... *for the Relief of Proselytes.*

Malard, Michael (1718). *The French Plot found out against the English Church: Or, a manifesto upon the unequalness of the distribution* ... *of the money of the Royal Beneficence, given every year to the French Protestants.* 'Printed for the Ecclesiastick Proselytes'.

Malard, Michael (1720). *Proselytish Hercules against the mystery of iniquity, or, a true light into the plot of the French Committee and its league against the Church of England.*

Les Malversations du Committé Francois, prouvées manifestement par de justes et solides remarques sur le conte rendu par ce Committé l'An 1707, pour la Distribution de l'Année 1705.... 1708. [LP, H.9455.3.(5)]

[Marvell, Andrew]. *An Account of the Growth of Popery, and Arbitrary Government in England.* Amsterdam, 1677. Wing M860.

*Memoires envoiés de Londres a M. *. par M. *. Au sujet de l'Etablissement d'un Conseil pour veiller sur la Conduite des Protestans François Refugiés en Angleterre.* 'Cologne' [probably Holland], 1699. [LP, H.9455.1.(3)]

Mesnard, Philippe. *Essai sur le Socinianisme. Ou réflexions sur quelques articles de la doctrine de M. le Clerc touchant les Sociniens. Et examen de quelques passages de son Nouveau Testament François.* La Haye: la veuve d'Abraham Troyel, 1709.

Misson, [Maximilien]. *Memoirs and Observations in his Travels over England....* 1719.

Misson, Maximilien. *Le Théâtre Sacré des Cevennes: Ou, récit de diverses merveilles nouvellement operées dans cette partie de la province de Languedoc. Première partie.* Robert Roger, 1707. Translated into English as *A Cry from the Desart: Or, testimonials of the miraculous things lately come to pass in the Cevennes* (B. Bragg, 1707).

[Mossom, Charles]. *An Account of the Disposal of the Money, collected upon the late Brief for the French Protestants, together with the Present State of those* ... *to be relieved....* [1688]. Wing M2858.

Neau, Elias. *An Account of the Sufferings of the French Protestants, slaves on board the French Kings Galleys.* Richard Parker, 1699. Wing N363.

Newcourt, Ric. *Repertorium Ecclesiasticum Parochiale Londinense: an ecclesiastical parochial history of the diocese of London....* 2 vols. Benj. Motte, 1708–10.

[Nye, Stephen]. *The Life of Mr. Thomas Firmin, late Citizen of London ... with a sermon on Luke X. 36, 37. Preach'd on the occasion of his death. Together with an account of his religion, and of the present state of the Unitarian Controversy.* A.Baldwin, 1698. Wing N1508.

A Particular and full Account of the Routing the whole Irish Army at Aghrim. Upon Sunday the 12ᵗʰ of July, 1691. With a list of the Principall Persons that were Killed and taken Prisoners. 'Published by Authority.' Dublin, by Andrew Crook for Peter Thornton, 1691. [National Library of Ireland; call number Dublin L.B. 1691]

The Pastoral Letters of the Incomparable Jurieu, directed to the Protestants in France groaning under the Babylonish Tyranny, translated ... Unto which is added, a brief account of the Hungarian persecution. For T. Fabian, 1689.

[Pineton, Jacques, de Chambrun, the younger]. *The History of the Persecutions of the Protestants by the French King, in the Principality of Orange, from ... 1660, to ... 1687... 1689.* Wing P2265.

Popish Treachery: Or, a short and new account of the horrid cruelties exercised on the Protestants in France. Being a true prospect of what is to be expected from the most solemn promises of Roman Catholick princes. London, Richard Baldwin: also Edinburgh: 1689. Wing P2958–9.

Portrait au Naturel du Committé François, ou l'on voit le Dessein que les Commissaires dudit Committé eurent en priant les Eglises Françoises de nommer et de se choisir des Personnes d'entre leur Anciens, pour être Distributeurs aux Bureaux établis pour faire aux Commun Peuple la Distribution de la Beneficence Royale.... 1706.

The Present State of the Protestants in France. In three letters. 1681. Wing P3274.

Preuves tres-claires, tres-fortes, et en trés-grand nombre des Malversations et des Injustices du Committé François dans l'Administration des Charitez Publiques et Particuliéres qui lui sont confiées.... No place or date. [LP, H.9455.3 (2)]

Primerose, David. *Sermon sur ces Paroles [Numbers 23 v.10] ... prononcé le 21 jour de May. A l'enterrement de feu Monsieur Michely Pasteur de l'Eglise Françoise de Londres.* 1674. Wing P3474A.

Prynne, William. *Canterburies Doome. Or, the first part of a compleat history of the commitment, charge, tryall, condemnation, execution of William Laud late Arch-Bishop of Canterbury.* John Macock for Michael Spark senior. 1646. Wing P3917.

Quick, John. *Synodicon in Gallia Reformata: Or, the acts, decisions, decrees, and canons of those famous National Councils of the Reformed Churches in France.* 2 vols. T.Parkhurst and J.Robinson, 1692.

R[ichard] H[aines]. *The Prevention of Poverty: Or, a discourse of the causes of the decay of trade, fall of lands, and want of money throughout the nation....* 1674.

Raport du Committe de la Chambre des Communes, nommé au sujèt de la Requete de la Compagnie Royale des Lustrez en Angleterre.... Sam. Gellibrand, 1698. [LP, H.9455.5.8]

Reasons humbly offered by several of the Principal Inhabitants of the Parish of St. Martin Orgars London, against the passing an Ingrossed Bill (from the Lords) for erecting a Church for the French in the Church-Yard of that Parish. [1699]. Wing R530A.

Relation dans laquelle on fait voir l'Etablissement des Bureaux, et des Distributeurs, commis pour distribuer l'Argent de la Bénéficence Royale aux Pauvres François Réfugiez ... [1706] [LP, H.9455.3 (3)].

A Relation of what most Remarkably happened during the Last Campaign in Ireland, betwixt His Majesties Army Royal, and the Forces of the Prince of Orange, sent to Joyn the Rebels, under the Command of the Count de Schomberg. Dublin, for Alderman James Malone, 1689. [National Library of Ireland]

Renoult, [Jean-Baptiste]. *Motifs qui ont engagé Mr. Renoult, cy devant Prestre et Predicateur dans la Grande Province des Cordeliers de France, a se separer de l'Eglise Romaine. Pour se ranger dans la Reformée.* La veufue Marret & Henry Ribotteau, 1696.

Rey, Claudius. *An Account of the Cruel Persecutions, rais'd by the French Clergy, since their taking Sanctuary here, against several worthy Ministers, Gentlemen, Gentlewomen, and Tradesmen, dissenting from their Calvinistical Scheme....* 1718. [Huguenot Library, University College, London]

The Rights and Liberties of Englishmen Asserted. A. Baldwin, 1701.

Rival, Pierre. *Apologie de Pierre Rival, Ministre de la Chapelle Françoise au Palais de St. James.* 1716.

Rocque, John. *Exact Survey of the Cities of London and Westminster ... with the Country near Ten Miles Round.* 1746.

Rocquigny, Adrian de. *La Muse Chrestienne: Reveuë, embellie et augmentee d'une seconde partie par l'Autheur.* 1634.

A Satyr against the French. 1691. Wing S714.

A Seasonable Warning for Old England; Being remarks upon the Government of France; Together with an Essay discovering the True Reasons of the Persecution of the French Protestants. 1704.

A Seasonble [sic] Warning to Protestants; from the cruelty and treachery of the Parisian Massacre, August the 24ᵗʰ. 1572: wherein, the snares laid for the innocent are detected, and posterity cautioned not to believe.... 1680. Wing S2247.

Seconde Lettre d'un Protestant à un de ses Amis de la Contrée. [1706?] [LP, H.9455.4 (13)]

Several Letters written by some French Protestants now refug'd in Germany, from the Tyrannical Persecution of France, concerning the Unity of the Church.... 1690.

A Short Memorial of the Most Grievous Sufferings of the Ministers of the Protestant Churches in Hungary. William Nott, 1676.

Smith's Protestant Intelligence: Domestick and Foreign. February–April 1681.

Smythies, William. *An Earnest Exhortation to Charity for the Relief of the French-Protestants. And Objections against it Answered.* [For T. Milbourn, 1688.] [Huguenot Library, University College, London, Beeman Pamphlets box 4.]

[Souverain, Jacques.] *Le Platonisme dévoilé. Ou Essai touchant le Verbe Platonicien, divisé en deux parties.* 'Cologne, P. Marteau', 1700.

The State of Savoy. In which a full and distinct account is given of the persecution of the Protestants, by means of the French Councils.... 1691. Wing S5304A.

Stillingfleet, Edward. *The Unreasonableness of Separation, or, an impartial account of the history, nature, and pleas of the present separation from the communion of the Church of England: To which several late letters are annexed of eminent Protestant divines abroad concerning the nature of our differences and the way to compose them.* For Henry Mortlock, 1681.

Story, George. *An Impartial History of the Wars of Ireland, With a Continuation thereof. In Two Parts. From the Time that Duke Schonberg landed with an Army in that Kingdom, to the 23d of March, 1691/2, when their Majesties Proclamation was published, declaring the War to be ended.* For Ric. Chiswell, 1693.

Stouppe, Jean Baptiste. *A Collection or Narative [sic] sent to his Highness the Lord Protector ... concerning the Bloody and Barbarous Massacres ... in the Valleys of Piedmont....* H. Robinson, 1655. Wing S5746B.

Strype, John (ed.). *A Survey of the Cities of London and Westminster: ... written at first in the year MDXCVIII, by John Stow, ... corrected, improved, and very much enlarged: and ... brought down ... to the present time....* 6 books in 2 vols, 1720.

Tillotson, John. *The Works of the Most Reverend Dr. John Tillotson ... published from the originals by Ralph Barker, D.D., Chaplain to his Grace.* 2 vols, 1712.

The Trade of England Revived. 1681. Wing T2004.

The True News: or, Mercurius Anglicus. Being the Weekly Occurrences faithfully transmitted. 1679–80.

The True and Perfect Relation of the New Invented Way of persecuting the Protestants in France. Richard Janaway, 1682.

The True Protestant Mercury: Or, occurrences forei[g]n and domestick. Nos. 1–188, 28 Dec. 1680–25 Oct. 1682 [Bodleian Library, Ash. 1675].

Two Letters, one from the Bishop of Blois to Monsieur de la Vallette, with Promises and Threatnings to prevent his turning Protestant. The other from Monsieur de la Vallette, to his brethren the Clergy of Blois, laying before them the gross errors of their Church, and the necessity to follow his example for their salvation ... Translated by Mr Hale. For R. Bassett, 1701 [LP, YY 10. 10.17].

Wake, William. *The case of the Exiled Vaudois, and French Protestants, stated: And their relief recommended to all good Christians....* 1699.

Walker, George (1689). *A True Account of the Siege of London-Derry.* 3rd edn, corrected, for Robert Clavel and Ralph Simpson.

A Wonderful Instance of God's Appearance for, and Presence with His People in a Day of Suffering: Or, a narrative of the most holy life, and triumphant death of Mr. Fulcran Rey: who was put to death in France, for being a publick preacher. 1688.

3. PRIMARY SOURCES IN EDITIONS PUBLISHED SINCE 1800

Adams, Leonard (1988). *William Wake's Gallican Correspondence and Related Documents, 1716–1731*, vols I–II [1716–21]. Peter Lang, New York, etc.

Ailesbury, Thomas, Earl of [d.1741] (1890). *Memoirs of Thomas, Earl of Ailesbury, written by himself.* 2 vols. Roxburghe Club, Westminster.

Arber, Edward (1908). *The Torments of Protestant Slaves in the French King's Galleys, and in the Dungeons of Marseilles. 1686–1707 A.D.* Elliot Stock.

Armet, Helen (1962). *Extracts from the Records of the Burgh of Edinburgh 1689 to 1701.* Oliver & Boyd, Edinburgh and London, for the Corporation of the City of Edinburgh.

Armet, Helen (1967). *Extracts from the Records of the Burgh of Edinburgh 1701 to 1718.* Oliver & Boyd, Edinburgh and London, for the Corporation of the City of Edinburgh.

Axtell, James L. (1968). *The Educational Writings of John Locke: A critical edition.* Cambridge University Press.

D'Avaux, Jean-Antoine de Mesmes, Count (1934). *Négociations de M. le Comte d'Avaux en Irelande 1689–90.* Irish Manuscripts Commission, Dublin.

Barrell, Rex A. (1980). *French Correspondence of Philip Dormer Stanhope, Fourth Earl of Chesterfield.* 2 vols. Borealis Press, Ottawa.

Barrell, Rex A. (1992). *The Correspondence of Abel Boyer Huguenot Refugee 1667–1729.* Edwin Mellen Press, Lewiston, NY.

Bellingham, Thomas (1908). Diary of Thomas Bellingham, an Officer under William III. Complete transcript and notes by Anthony Hewitson. Geo. Toulmin & Sons, Preston.

Bond, Shelagh (1966). *The Chapter Acts of the Dean and Canons of Windsor 1430, 1523–1672.* Historical monographs relating to St. George's Chapel, Windsor Castle, vol. 13. Windsor.

Bost, Charles (1931). *Memoires Inédits d'Abraham Mazel et d'Elie Marion sur la Guerre des Cevennes 1701–1708.* HSQS XXXIV.

Bost, Hubert (2008). *Le Consistoire de l'Eglise Wallonne de Rotterdam, 1681–1706.* Honoré Champion, Paris.

Bramston, Sir John [1611–1700] (1845). *The Autobiography of Sir John Bramston, K.B., ...* Camden Society, First Series, vol. XXXII.

Browning, Andrew (1936). *Memoirs of Sir John Reresby: The complete text and a selection from his letters.* Jackson, Glasgow; 2nd edn, Royal Historical Society, 1991.

Browning, Andrew (1966). *English Historical Documents 1660–1714.* Eyre & Spottiswoode.

Bryant, Sir Arthur (1968). *The Letters, Speeches and Declarations of King Charles II.* Cassell.

Burnet, [Gilbert, 1643–1715] (1833). *Bishop Burnet's History of his Own Time: With notes by the Earls of Dartmouth and Hardwicke, Speaker Onslow, and Dean Swift....* 2nd enlarged edn, 6 vols. Oxford University Press.

Cartwright, Thomas [1634–89] (1843). *The Diary of Dr. Thomas Cartwright, Bishop of Chester*...[Aug. 1686–Oct. 1687]. Camden Society, First Series, vol. XXII.

Chamier, Adrian Charles (1890). *Les Actes des Colloques des Eglises Françaises et des Synodes des Eglises Etrangères refugiées en Angleterre 1581–1654.* HSQS II.

Cobbett, [William] (1808). *Parliamentary History of England.* Vols III (1642–1660), IV (1660–1688) and V (1688–1702).

Cole, G.H.D., and Browning, D.C. (1962). *Daniel Defoe, A Tour through the Whole Island of Great Britain.* 2 vols. J.M. Dent, Everyman's Library.

Colyer-Fergusson, T[homas] C. (1906). *The Registers of the French Church, Threadneedle Street, London. Volume III.* HSQS XVI.

Colyer-Fergusson, T[homas] C. (1916). *The Registers of the French Church, Threadneedle Street, London. Volume IV.* HSQS XXIII.

Commission de l'Histoire des Eglises Wallonnes (1896). *Livre Synodal contenant les Articles résolus dans les Synodes des Eglises Wallonnes des Pays-Bas. I, 1563–1685.* Martinus Nijhoff, La Haye.

Commission de l'Histoire des Eglises Wallonnes (1904). *Livre Synodal contenant les Articles résolus dans les Synodes des Eglises Wallonnes des Pays-Bas. II, 1686–1688* [but extends beyond that date]. Martinus Nijhoff, La Haye [see also *Livre Synodal* in the previous section].

Cooper, William Durrant (1858). *Savile Correspondence. Letters to and from Henry Savile Esq., Envoy at Paris....* Camden Society, First Series, vol. LXXI.

Cooper, William Durrant (1861). 'Protestant Refugees in Sussex'. *Sussex Archaeological Collections* XIII, 180–208.

Cox, Janice V. (2011). *The Travels of Francis Tallents in France and Switzerland 1671–1673.* Huguenot Society, new series no.5.

Coxe, William (1821). *Private and Original Correspondence of Charles Talbot, Duke of Shrewsbury, with King William.* Longman, Hurst and others.

Crespin, Théodore (1859). 'Lettre Inédite de Crespin, de Canterbury, à Vincent, Ministre de La Rochelle, 1650(?)'. *BSHPF* VIII, 138–45.

Crisp, F.A. (1888). *Registers of the French Church at Dover, Kent.* Privately printed, no place.

Dalton, Charles (1892). *English Army Lists and Commission Registers, 1661–1714.* 6 vols, 1892–1904. Eyre & Spottiswoode.

Danaher, K. and Simms, J.G. (1962), *The Danish Force in Ireland 1690–1691.* Irish Manuscripts Commission. Stationery Office, Dublin.

Dangeau, Marquis de (1689–91). *Journal du Marquis de Dangeau* 3, Firmin Didot Frères, Paris, 1854.

De Beer, E.S. (1955). *The Diary of John Evelyn.* 6 vols. Clarendon Press, Oxford.

De Beer, E.S. (1976). *The Correspondence of John Locke.* 8 vols. Clarendon Press, Oxford. 1976–89.

[Dicconson, William] (1816). *The Life of James the Second, King of England, etc, collected out of memoirs writ of his own hand ... published from the original Stuart Manuscripts in Carlton-House, by the Rev. J.S. Clarke.* 2 vols. Longman and others, London.

Drenth, Wienand (2012). *A Regimental List of the Half-Pay Officers for the Year 1714 on the English and Irish Establishments.* Drenth Publishing, Eindhoven.

Drenth, Wienand (2013). *A Regimental List of the Reduced Officers for the Year 1699 on the English, Scots, and Irish Establishments.* Drenth Publishing, Eindhoven.

Ellis, George Agar (1829). *The Ellis Correspondence. Letters written during...1686, 1687, 1688 and addressed to John Ellis Esq....* 2 vols.

Elton, G.R. (1965). *The Tudor Constitution: documents and commentary.* Cambridge University Press.

England. *Calendars of State Papers. Domestic Series.*

England. *Calendars of Treasury Books.*

England, Parliament. *Journals of the House of Commons.* Vols 2–16, 1640–1711.

England, Parliament. *Journals of the House of Lords.* Vols 4–19, 1628–1714.

England, Privy Council. *Acts of the Privy Council, Colonial Series.* Vol. 2, 1680–1720.

Fenwick, Kenneth (1957). *Galley Slave: the autobiography of Jean Marteilhe.* Folio Society.

Foster, Joseph (1891). *Alumni Oxonienses: The members of the University of Oxford, 1500–1714.* 4 vols. Parker, Oxford. 1891–2.

Fountainhall, Lord [Sir John Lauder of Fountainhall, 1646–1722] (1822). *Chronological Notes of Scottish Affairs, from 1680 till 1701; Being chiefly taken from the diary of Lord Fountainhall.* Archibald Constable, Edinburgh.

French Church of London [1915]. *Discipline Ecclésiastique de l'Église Protestante Française de Londres établie par le Roi Édouard VI. Observée es Églises de la Langue Française recueillies en ce Roiaume d'Angleterre selon qu'elle a esté revue par le Synode des dittes Églises l'An MDCXLI.* Frederick Savage & Co. [In both French and English. Subsequently reprinted in HSQS LIV.]

Garrisson, Robert (1936). *Mémoires de Samuel de Pechels 1685–1692 et Documents sur la Révocation à Montauban.* Musée du Désert, Cévennes.

Gilbert, John T (1892). *A Jacobite Narrative of the War in Ireland, 1688–1691.* Joseph Dollard, Dublin.

Godfray, Humphrey Marett (1890). *Registre des Baptesmes, Mariages et Mortz, et Jeusnes, de l'Église Wallonne et des Isles de Jersey, Guernesey, Serq, Origny, etc., établie à Southampton par Patente du Roy Edouard Six^e et de la Reine Elizabeth.* HSQS IV.

Godfrey, Walter H. (1951). *Le Guide de Londres (1693) by F. Colsoni.* Cambridge University Press for the London Topographical Society.

Goldie, Mark and others (2007). *The Entring Book of Roger Morrice 1677–1691.* 7 vols, 2007–9. Boydell Press in association with the Parliamentary History Yearbook Trust, Woodbridge, Suffolk.

Granville, Denis [1637–1703] (1860). *The Remains: Comprising his farewell sermons, letters to the Earl of Bath, etc., and miscellaneous correspondence.* In Surtees Society *Miscellanea*, Surtees Society Publications, vol. XXXVII (1861 for 1860).

Granville, Denis (1865). *The Remains: Being a further selection from his correspondence, diaries, and other papers.* Surtees Society Publications, vol. XLVII.

Gwynn, Robin D. (1979). *A Calendar of the Letter Books of the French Church of London from the Civil War to the Restoration, 1643–1659.* HSQS LIV.

Gwynn, Robin D. (1994). *Minutes of the Consistory of the French Church of London, Threadneedle Street, 1679–1692: Calendared with an historical introduction and commentary.* HSQS LVIII.

Hands, A.P., and Scouloudi, Irene (1971). *French Protestant Refugees relieved through the Threadneedle Street Church, London, 1681–1687.* HSQS XLIX.

Hessels, Joannes H. (1897). *Ecclesiae Londino-Batavae Archivum. Tomi Tertii, Pars Secunda. Epistulae et Tractatus cum Reformationis tum Ecclesiae Londino-Batavae Historiam Illustrantes.* Cambridge.

Historical Manuscripts Commission. *Reports*, especially

HMC 29: Portland III (Harley MSS, 1582–1700)

HMC 29: Portland IV (Harley MSS, 1700–11)

HMC 9th Report, part II: House of Lords (House of Lords MSS, 1671–8)

HMC 37: 14th Report, VIII: Corporation of Lincoln

HMC 56: Stuart I (Stuart MSS, 1685–1716)

HMC 71: Finch II (Finch MSS, 1670–90)

HMC 75: Downshire I part I (Trumbull MSS, 1645–95).

- Finch V (papers of Earl of Nottingham, 1691–4, edited by Sonia P. Anderson).

Horwitz, Henry (1972). *The Parliamentary Diary of Narcissus Luttrell 1691–1693*. Clarendon Press, Oxford.

[Houblon, James] (1886). *Pious Memoirs of Mr. James Houblon, Senior, … who died … 1682*. Pickering.

Hovenden, Robert (1891). *The Registers of the Wallon or Strangers' Church in Canterbury*. 3 parts, 1891–8. HSQS V.

Howarth, R.G. (1932). *Letters and the Second Diary of Samuel Pepys*. J.M. Dent, London and Toronto, and E.P. Dutton, New York.

Hyde, Henry, Earl of Clarendon (1828). *The Correspondence of … and of his brother, Laurence Hyde, Earl of Rochester*. 2 vols. Henry Colburn.

Jessopp, Augustus (1890). *The Lives of the Right Hon. Francis North, Baron Guilford; the Hon. Sir Dudley North; and the Hon. and Rev. Dr. John North. By the Hon. Roger North, together with the Autobiography of the Author*. 3 vols. G. Bell & Sons.

Jones, P.E. (1966–70). *The Fire Court: Calendar to the judgments and decrees of the Court of Judicature appointed … after the Great Fire*. 2 vols, 1966–70.

Julien, Barbara (2015). *The Consistory Minutes and Poor Relief Accounts of the French Church at Thorpe-le-Soken, 1683–1763*. HSQS LXII.

Kenyon, John P. (1966). *The Stuart Constitution 1603–1688: Documents and commentary*. Cambridge University Press.

Kenyon, John P. (1969). *Halifax: Complete Works*. Penguin Books, Harmondsworth, Middlesex.

Kerr, Russell J., and Duncan, Ida Coffin (1928). *The Portledge Papers: Being extracts from the letters of Richard Lapthorne, Gent., of Hatton Garden London, to Richard Coffin Esq. of Portledge, Bideford, Devon from December 10th 1687–August 7th 1697*. Jonathan Cape.

Lart, Charles Edmund (1912). *Registers of the French Churches of Bristol, Stonehouse, and Plymouth*. HSQS XX.

Latham, Robert, and Matthews, William (1970). *The Diary of Samuel Pepys: A new and complete transcription*. 11 vols. G. Bell/Bell & Hyman, 1970–83.

La Touche, J.J. Digges (1893). *Registers of the French Conformed Churches of St. Patrick and St. Mary, Dublin*. HSQS VII.

Le Fanu, Thomas Philip (1901). *Registers of the French Non-Conformist Churches of Lucy Lane and Peter Street, Dublin*. HSQS XIV.

Le Fanu, Thomas Philip (1908). *Registers of the French Church of Portarlington, Ireland.* HSQS XIX.

Le Fanu, Thomas Philip and Manchee, W.H. (1946). *Dublin and Portarlington Veterans: King William III's Huguenot army.* HSQS XLI.

Lenihan, Pádraig and Sidwell, Keith (2018). *Poema de Hibernia: A Jacobite Latin epic on the Williamite wars.* Irish Manuscripts Commission, Dublin.

Lesens, Emile (1874). *Histoire de la Persécution faite à l'Église de Rouen sur la Fin du XVIIe Siècle, par Philippe Legendre.* Léon Deshays, Rouen, and Sandoz et Fischbacher, Paris.

Lord, George de F. (1975). *Anthology of Poems on Affairs of State: Augustan satirical verse 1660–1714.* Yale University Press, New Haven.

Luttrell, Narcissus [1657–1732] (1857). *A Brief Historical Relation of State Affairs from September 1678 to April 1714.* 6 vols. Oxford.

Mackay, Major General Hugh (1833). *Memoirs of the War carried on in Scotland and Ireland. MDCLXXXIX–MDCXCI.* Maitland Club, Edinburgh.

Migault, Jean [d.1707] (1825). *Journal de Jean Migault, ou Malheurs d'une Famille Protestante du Poitou, à l'Époque de la Révocation de l'Édit de Nantes.* Henry Servier, Paris.

Migault, Jean (1995). *Journal de Jean Migault ou Malheurs d'une Famille Protestante du Poitou...*, edited by Yves Krumenacker, Max Chaleil, Paris.

Minet, Susan (1938). *Register of the Church of Saint Jean, Spitalfields 1687–1827.* HSQS XXXIX.

Minet, Susan (1948). *Register of the Church of the Artillery, Spitalfields 1691–1786.* HSQS XLII.

Minet, Susan (1956). *Registers of the Churches of La Patente de Soho, Wheeler Street, Swanfields and Hoxton, also the Répertoire Général.* HSQS XLV.

Minet, William (1888). 'Isaac Minet's Narrative'. *HSP* II (1887–8), 428–45.

Minet, William and Susan (1909). *Livre des Tesmoignages de l'Eglise de Threadneedle Street 1669–1789.* HSQS XXI.

Minet, William and Susan (1914). *Livre des Conversions et des Reconnoissances faites à l'Eglise Françoise de la Savoye 1684–1702.* HSQS XXII.

Minet, William and Susan (1921). *Registers of the Church of Le Carré and Berwick Street 1690–1788.* HSQS XXV.

Minet, William and Susan (1922). *Registres des Eglises de la Savoye, de Spring Gardens et des Grecs 1684–1900.* HSQS XXVI.

Minet, William and Susan (1924). *Registres des Eglises de la Chapelle Royale de Saint James 1700–1756 et de Swallow Street 1690–1709.* HSQS XXVIII.

Minet, William and Susan (1926). *Registers of the Churches of the Tabernacle, Glasshouse Street and Leicester Fields 1688–1783.* HSQS XXIX.

Minet, William and Susan (1927). *Register of the Church of Rider Court 1700–1738.* HSQS XXX.

Minet, William and Susan (1928). *Register of the Church of Hungerford Market, later Castle Street ... with a sketch of its history as of that of the Carré founded on the Actes of the two churches.* HSQS XXXI.

Minet, William and Susan (1929). *Registres des Quatre Eglises du Petit Charenton, de West Street, de Pearl Street et de Crispin Street.* HSQS XXXII.

Minet, William and Susan (1932). *A Supplement to Dr. W.A. Shaw's Letters of Denization and Acts of Naturalization which formed volumes XVIII and XXVII of the Publications of the Huguenot Society of London.* HSQS XXXV.

Minet, William and Susan (1935). *Register of the Church of Saint Martin Orgars with its History and that of Swallow Street.* HSQS XXXVII.

Minet, William and Waller, William Chapman (1891). *Transcript of the Registers of the Protestant Church at Guisnes, from 1668 to 1685.* HSQS III.

Minet, William and Waller, William Chapman (1898). *Registers of the Church known as La Patente in Spittlefields from 1689 to 1785.* HSQS XI.

Mitchell, Alex. F., and Struthers, John (1874). *Minutes of the Sessions of the Westminster Assembly of Divines.* W. Blackwood & Sons, Edinburgh and London.

Moens, William John Charles (1884). *The Marriage, Baptismal, and Burial Registers ... of the Dutch Reformed Church, Austin Friars, London.* Lymington.

Moens, William John Charles (1887). *The Walloons and their Church at Norwich: Their history and registers, 1565–1832. In two parts.* HSQS I, 1887–8.

Moens, William John Charles (1896). *The Registers of the French Church, Threadneedle Street, London. Volume I.* HSQS IX.

Moens, William John Charles (1899). *The Registers of the French Church, Threadneedle Street, London. Volume II.* HSQS XIII.

Morris, Christopher (1947). *The Journeys of Celia Fiennes.* Cresset Press, 1947.

Nash, Robert (2020). *A Directory of Huguenot Refugees on the Channel Islands, 1548–1825.* HSQS LXIII.

Papillon, A.F.W. (1887). *Memoirs of Thomas Papillon, of London, Merchant (1623–1702).* Joseph J. Beecroft, Reading.

Peet, Henry (1903). *Register of Baptisms of the French Protestant Refugees settled at Thorney, Cambridgeshire, 1654–1727.* HSQS XVII.

Pryme, Abraham de la [1672–1704] (1870). *The Diary of Abraham de la Pryme, the Yorkshire Antiquary.* Surtees Society, LIV, 1870 for 1869.

Ressinger, Dianne W. (1992). *Memoirs of the Reverend Jaques Fontaine 1658–1728.* Huguenot Society, new series no.2.

Ressinger, Dianne W. (2005). *Memoirs of Isaac Dumont de Bostaquet, a Gentleman of Normandy: before and after the Revocation of the Edict of Nantes.* Huguenot Society, new series no.4.

Roseveare, Henry (ed.) (1987). *Markets and Merchants of the Late Seventeenth Century: The Marescoe – David letters, 1668–1680.* Oxford University Press for the British Academy: Records of social and economic history, new series vol. XII.

Rouffignac, Jacob de [1640–1720] and others (1891). *'Lettres du Pasteur de Rouffignac et de Quelques Réfugiés de Mauvezin'.* BSHPF XL (1891), 39–50, 76–89, 207–13.

Rules to be observed by the Friendly Benefit Society ... instituted in the year 1687 as the Society of Parisians. 1882. A copy will be found in LMA, CLC/144/MS 09899.

Russell, Lady Rachel [1636–1723] (1809). *Letters of Lady Rachel Russell....* 7th edn. J. McCreery, London.

Schickler, Baron Fernand de (1892). *Les Églises du Refuge en Angleterre*, vol. 3. Librairie Fischbacher, Paris.

Shaw, William A. (1911). *Letters of Denization and Acts of Naturalization for Aliens in England and Ireland, 1603–1700.* HSQS XVIII.

Shaw, William A. (1923). *Letters of Denization and Acts of Naturalization for Aliens in England and Ireland, 1701–1800.* HSQS XXVII.

Surman, Charles E. (1953). *The Register-Booke of the Fourth Classis in the Province of London, 1646–59.* Harleian Society Publications LXXXII–LXXXIII for 1952–3.

Swedenberg, H.T., and others (1956). *The Works of John Dryden.* 4 vols. University of California Press, Berkeley and Los Angeles, 1956–74.

Tanner, J.R. (1926). *Private Correspondence and Miscellaneous Papers of Samuel Pepys 1679–1703 in the possession of J. Pepys Cockerell.* 2 vols. G. Bell & Sons.

Thirsk, Joan and Cooper, J.P. (1972). *Seventeenth-Century Economic Documents.* Clarendon Press, Oxford.

Thompson, Edward Maunde (1875). *Letters of Humphrey Prideaux sometime Dean of Norwich to John Ellis, sometime Under-Secretary of State, 1674–1722.* Camden Society Publications, N.S. 15.

Turner, Winifred (1940). *The Aufrère Papers: Calendar and selections.* HSQS XL.

Venn, John and J.A. (1922). *Alumni Cantabrigienses. A biographical list of all known students, graduates and holders of office at the University of Cambridge ... Part I, from the earliest times to 1751.* 4 vols. Cambridge University Press, 1922–27.

Verney, Margaret M. (1899). *Memoirs of the Verney Family, vol. IV: From the Restoration to the Revolution, 1660 to 1696.* Longmans, Green.

Waller, William Chapman (1912). *The Register of the French Church at Thorpe-le-Soken in Essex 1684–1726.* HSQS XX (part 2).

Waller, William Chapman (1931). *Extracts from the Court Books of the Weavers Company of London 1610–1730.* HSQS XXXIII.

Welch, Edwin (1979). *The Minute Book of the French Church at Southampton 1702–1939.* (Southampton Records Series vol. XXIII.) Southampton University Press.

Williams, E. Neville (1960). *The Eighteenth Century Constitution 1688–1815: Documents and commentary.* Cambridge University Press.

Wood, Anthony à (1813). *Athenae Oxonienses. An exact history of all the writers and bishops who have had their education in the University of Oxford. To which are added the Fasti, or the annals of the said university.* New edn, with additions, and a continuation by Philip Bliss. 4 vols. F.C. and J. Rivington and others, London. 1813–20.

Wood, Marguerite. *Extracts from the Records of the Burgh of Edinburgh 1663–1680.*

Wood, Marguerite and Armet, Helen (1954). *Extracts from the Records of the Burgh of Edinburgh 1681 to 1689.* Oliver & Boyd, Edinburgh and London, for the Corporation of the City of Edinburgh.

4. SECONDARY WORKS PUBLISHED SINCE 1800

Acres, W. Marston (1934). 'Huguenot Directors of the Bank of England'. *HSP* XV (1933–7), 238–48.

Agnew, David C.A. (1886). *Protestant Exiles from France, chiefly in the Reign of Louis XIV. Or, the Huguenot Refugees and their Descendants in Great Britain and Ireland.* 3rd edn, privately printed, no place, 2 vols.

Ainslie, James L. (1940). *The Doctrines of Ministerial Order in the Reformed Churches of the Sixteenth and Seventeenth Centuries.* T. & T. Clark, Edinburgh.

Almagor, Joseph (1989). *Pierre Des Maiseaux (1673–1745), Journalist and English Correspondent for Franco-Dutch Periodicals, 1700–1720, with the Inventory of his Correspondence and Papers at the British Library (Add. MSS. 4281–4289), London.* APA-Holland University Press, Amsterdam and Maarssen.

Analytical Index to the … Remembrancia … of the City of London … 1579–1664. 1878.

Anderson, Sonia P. (2005). 'The Adventures of Peter Fontaines, Naval Surgeon and Intelligence Agent'. *HSP* XXVIII:3 (2005), 336–49.

Archdeacon, T.J. (1976). *New York City, 1664–1710.* Cornell University Press.

Archer, Ian W. (1991). *The Pursuit of Stability: Social relations in Elizabethan London.* Cambridge University Press.

Armstrong, Brian G. (1969). *Calvinism and the Amyraut Heresy: Protestant Scholasticism and Humanism in seventeenth-century France.* University of Wisconsin Press.

Ascoli, Georges (1930). *La Grande-Bretagne devant l'Opinion Française au XVIIe Siècle.* 2 vols. Librairie Universitaire J. Gamber, Paris.

Ashley, Maurice (1977). *James II.* J.M. Dent, London, Toronto and Melbourne.

Baird, Henry M. (1895). *The Huguenots and the Revocation of the Edict of Nantes.* 2 vols. New York.

Balleine, G.R. (1950). *A History of the Island of Jersey.* Staples Press, London and New York.

Baxter, Stephen B. (1966). *William III.* Longmans.

Beaven, A.B. (1908). *The Aldermen of the City of London.* 2 vols, 1908–13.

Beeman, George B. (1902). 'Notes on the City of London Records dealing with the French Protestant Refugees, especially with reference to the Collections made under Various Briefs'. *HSP* VII (1901–4), 108–92.

Beeman, George B. (1905). 'Notes on the Sites and History of the French Churches in London'. *HSP* VIII (1905–8), 13–59.

Beier, A.L., and Finlay, Roger (eds) (1986). *London 1500–1700: The making of the metropolis.* Longman.

Bell, H.E., and Ollard, R.L. (eds) (1963). *Historical Essays 1600–1750 presented to David Ogg.* Adam & Charles Black.

Bell, W.G. (1923). *The Great Fire of London in 1666* (3rd edn). John Lane (Bodley Head).

Benedict, Philip (1991). *The Huguenot Population of France, 1600–1685: The demographic fate and customs of a religious minority.* Transactions of the American Philosophical Society, vol. 81, part 5. Philadelphia.

Benedict, Philip (2001). *The Faith and Fortunes of France's Huguenots, 1600–1685.* Ashgate, Aldershot.

Bennett, G.V. (1975). *The Tory Crisis in Church and State 1688–1730.* Oxford.

Bert, Paul (1908). *Histoire de la Révocation de l'Edit de Nantes à Bordeaux et dans le Bordelais (Diocèse de Bordeaux) (1653–1715).* Bordeaux.

[Jean Bianquis and] Emile Lesens (1885). *La Révocation de l'Edit de Nantes à Rouen.* Rouen.

Birnstiel, Eckart (ed.) (2001). *La Diaspora des Huguenots: Les réfugiés protestants de France et leur dispersion dans le monde (XVIe– XVIIIe siècles).* Honoré Champion, Paris.

Boles, Laurence Huey (1997). *The Huguenots, the Protestant Interest, and the War of the Spanish Succession, 1702–1714.* Peter Lang, New York.

Bosher, J.F. (1995). 'Huguenot Merchants and the Protestant International in the Seventeenth Century', *William and Mary Quarterly*, 3rd series, 52:1, 77–100.

Bosher, Robert S. (1951). *The Making of the Restoration Settlement.* Dacre Press.

Bost, Charles (1898A). 'Le Guide Paul Berger Ragatz'. *BSHPF* XLVII (1898), 507–17.

Bost, Charles (1898B). 'Les Routes de l'Exil: Itinéraires suivis par les fugitifs du Languedoc à la Révocation'. *BSHPF* XLVII (1898), 561–93, 634–51.

Bots, Hans (1999). 'La Migration Huguenote dans les Provinces-Unies, 1680–1715: Un nouveau bilan'. In Henry, Philippe and de Tribolet, Maurice (eds). *In Dubiis Libertas. Mélanges d'Histoire offerts au Professeur Rémy Scheurer* (Gilles Attinger, Hauterive), pp. 271–81.

Bots, J.A.H., and Posthumus Meyjes, G.H.M. (eds) (1986). *La Révocation de l'Édit de Nantes et les Provinces-Unies 1685*. APA-Holland University Press, Amsterdam and Maarssen.

Boulton, Jeremy (1987). *Neighbourhood and Society: A London suburb in the seventeenth century*. Cambridge University Press.

Brett-James, Norman G. (1935). *The Growth of Stuart London*. London & Middlesex Archaeological Society and George Allen & Unwin.

Brewer, John (1989). *The Sinews of Power: War, money and the English state, 1688–1783*. Unwin Hyman.

Brockett, Allan (1962). *Nonconformity in Exeter 1650–1875*. Manchester University Press.

Bultmann, Phyllis and William A. (1959). 'Claude Groteste de la Mothe and the Church of England, 1685 to 1713'. *HSP* XX (1958–64), 89–101.

Buranelli, Vincent (1962). *The King and the Quaker*. University of Pennsylvania Press, Philadelphia.

Burke, Peter (1992). *The Fabrication of Louis XIV*. Yale University Press.

Burn, John Southerden (1846). *The History of the French, Walloon, Dutch, and other Foreign Protestant Refugees settled in England....* Longman, Brown, Green & Longmans.

Butler, Jon (1983). *The Huguenots in America: A refugee people in New World society*. Harvard University Press, Cambridge, MA.

Caldicott, C.E.J., Gough, H. and Pittion, J.-P. (eds) (1987). *The Huguenots and Ireland: Anatomy of an emigration*. Glendale Press, Dublin.

Campbell, John (1970). 'The Walloon Community in Canterbury, 1625–1649'. PhD thesis, University of Wisconsin.

Capp, B.S. (1972). *The Fifth Monarchy Men: A study in seventeenth-century English millenarianism*. Faber & Faber.

Carlo, Paula Wheeler (2005). *Huguenot Refugees in Colonial New York: Becoming American in the Hudson Valley*. Sussex Academic Press, Brighton and Portland.

Carpenter, Edward (1948). *Thomas Tenison, Archbishop of Canterbury: His life and times*. SPCK.

Carpenter, Edward (1956). *The Protestant Bishop: Being the life of Henry Compton, 1632–1713, Bishop of London*. Longmans, Green.

Carré, Albert (1937). *L'Influence des Huguenots Français en Irlande au XVIIe et XVIIIe Siècles*. Presses Universitaires de France, Paris.

Carruthers, Bruce G. (1996). *City of Capital: Politics and markets in the English Financial Revolution*. Princeton University Press.

Carswell, John (1989). *The Porcupine: The Life of Algernon Sidney.* John Murray.

Carter, Alice Clare (1954). 'The Huguenot Contribution to the Early Years of the Funded Debt, 1694–1714'. *HSP* XIX (1952–8), iii, 21–41.

Carter, Alice Clare (1964). *The English Reformed Church in Amsterdam in the Seventeenth Century.* Scheltema & Holkema, Amsterdam.

Carter, Alice Clare (1975). *Getting, Spending and Investing in Early Modern Times: Essays on Dutch, English and Huguenot economic history.* Van Gorcum, Assen.

Chalklin, C.W. (1965). *Seventeenth-Century Kent: A social and economic history.* Longmans.

Chamayou, Fabienne (2001). 'Le Refuge dans les Îles Britanniques'. In Birnstiel (2001), pp. 43–62.

Chambrier, Mme Alexandre de (1910). *Henri de Mirmand et les Réfugiés de la Révocation de l'Édit de Nantes, 1650–1721.* Attinger Frères, Neuchâtel.

Champion, J.A.I. (1992). *The Pillars of Priestcraft Shaken: The Church of England and its enemies, 1660–1730.* Cambridge University Press.

Champion, Justin, and John Coffey, Tim Harris and John Marshall (eds) (2019). *Politics, Religion and Ideas in Seventeenth-Century Britain: Essays in honour of Mark Goldie.* Boydell Press, Woodbridge.

Chappell, Carolyn Lougee (1999). '"The Pains I took to save My/His Family": Escape accounts by a Huguenot mother and daughter after the Revocation of the Edict of Nantes'. *French Historical Studies*, 22:1 (1999), 1–64.

Childs, John (1980). *The Army, James II and the Glorious Revolution.* Manchester University Press.

Childs, John (1987). *The British Army of William III, 1689–1702.* Manchester University Press.

Childs, John (1988). 'A Patriot for Whom? "For God and for Honour": Marshal Schomberg'. *History Today*, 38 (July 1988), 46–52.

Childs, John (1991). *The Nine Years' War and the British Army 1688–97.* Manchester University Press.

Childs, John (2007). *The Williamite Wars in Ireland 1688–1691.* Hambledon Continuum.

Clapham, Sir John (1944). *The Bank of England: A History. Volume I, 1694–1797.* Cambridge University Press.

Clark, Peter, and Slack, Paul (eds) (1972). *Crisis and Order in English Towns 1500–1700. Routledge and Kegan Paul.*

Clark, Ruth (1932). *Strangers and Sojourners at Port Royal: Being an account of the connections between the British Isles and the Jansenists of France and Holland.* Cambridge University Press [reprint, Octagon Books, 1972].

Clark, Ruth (1938). *Sir William Trumbull in Paris 1685–1686.* Cambridge University Press.

Claydon, Tony (1996). *William III and the Godly Revolution.* Cambridge University Press.

Claydon, Tony (2009). 'The recent English Historiography of the Glorious Revolution' and 'British Networks and the Glorious Revolution' in *Odysseus* 1, 27–42, 70–86.

Coleman, D.C. (1956). 'The Early British Paper Industry and the Huguenots'. *HSP* XIX (1952–8), 210–25.

Coleman, D.C. (1958). *The British Paper industry 1495–1860: A study in industrial growth.* Clarendon Press, Oxford.

Collinson, Patrick (1967). *The Elizabethan Puritan Movement.* Jonathan Cape.

Collinson, Patrick (1979). *Archbishop Grindal 1519–1583: The struggle for a Reformed church.* Jonathan Cape.

Collinson, Patrick (1982). *The Religion of Protestants: The church in English society 1559–1625.* Oxford University Press.

Conlon, Pierre M. (1966). *Jean-François Bion et sa Relation des Tourments soufferts par les Forçats Protestants.* Librairie Droz, Geneva.

Conner, Philip (2002). *Huguenot Heartland: Montauban and Southern French Calvinism during the Wars of Religion.* Ashgate, Aldershot.

Cooper, William Durrant (1861). 'Protestant Refugees in Sussex'. *Sussex Archaeological Collections* XIII, 180–208.

Cosmos, Georgia (2006). *Huguenot Prophecy and Clandestine Worship in the Eighteenth Century: 'The Sacred Theatre of the Cévennes'.* Ashgate, Aldershot.

Cottret, Bernard (1985). *Terre d'Exil: l'Angleterre et ses réfugiés Français et Wallons, de la Réforme à la Révocation de l'Édit de Nantes, 1550–1700.* Aubier, Paris.

Cottret, Bernard (1991). *The Huguenots in England: Immigration and settlement c.1550–1700.* Cambridge University Press/Editions de la Maison des Sciences de l'Homme, Cambridge and Paris.

Coward, Barry (1980). *The Stuart Age: England, 1603–1714.* Longman. Second edn, 1994.

Cox, Gregory Stevens (1999). *St Peter Port 1680–1830: The history of an international entrepôt.* Boydell Press, Woodbridge.

Cross, Claire (1976). *Church and People 1450–1660: The triumph of the laity in the English Church*. Fontana/Collins, Glasgow.

Cross, Francis (1898). *History of the Walloon and Huguenot Church at Canterbury*. HSQS XV.

Crouzet, François M. (1990). 'Walloons, Huguenots and the Bank of England', *HSP* XXV (1989–93), 167–78.

Crouzet, François M. (1996). *Britain, France and International Commerce: From Louis XIV to Victoria*. Variorum.

Crouzet, François M. (1998). 'Some Remarks on the *Metiers d'Art*'. In Fox, R. and Turner, A., *Luxury Trades and Consumerism in Ancien Régime Paris: Studies in the history of the skilled workforce* (Ashgate), pp. 263–86.

Cruickshanks, Eveline (ed.) (1989). *By Force or Default? The Revolution of 1688–1689*. John Donald, Edinburgh.

Cullen, L.M. (2009). 'The Eighteenth-Century Jacobite Network' and 'The International Huguenot Network' in *Odysseus* 1, 115–41.

Cunningham, W. (1897). *Alien Immigrants to England*. Swan Sonnenschein.

Daireaux, Luc (2010). '*Réduire les Huguenots*': *Protestants et pouvoirs en Normandie au XVIIe siècle*. Honoré Champion, Paris.

Daullé, Alfred (1905). *La Réforme à Saint-Quentin et aux Environs du XVIe à la Fin du XVIIIe Siècle*. Revised edn, St Quentin.

Davies, C. Stella (1961). *A History of Macclesfield*. Manchester University Press.

Davies, K.G. (1957). *The Royal African Company*. Longmans, Green.

Davis, Ralph (1962). *The Rise of the English Shipping Industry in the Seventeenth and Eighteenth Centuries*. David & Charles, Newton Abbot.

Daynes, John Norman (1965). *A Short History of the Ancient Mistery of the Dyers of the City of London*.

De Beer, E.S. (1950). 'The Revocation of the Edict of Nantes and English Public Opinion'. *HSP* XVIII (1947–52), 292–310.

De Beer, E.S. (1966). 'The Huguenots and the Enlightenment'. *HSP* XXI (1965–70), 179–95.

De Krey, Gary Stuart (1978). 'Trade, Religion, and Politics in London in the Reign of William III'. PhD Dissertation, Princeton University, 3 vols.

De Krey, Gary Stuart (1985). *A Fractured Society: The politics of London in the first age of party 1688–1715*. Clarendon Press, Oxford.

Deyon, Solange (1976). *Du Loyalisme au Refus: Les Protestants Français et leur Deputé Général entre la Fronde et la Révocation.* Université de Lille III.

Dez, Pierre (1936). *Histoire des Protestants et des Églises Réformées du Poitou.* New edn, volume 1. Imprimerie de l'Ouest, La Rochelle.

Dickinson, H.T. (1967). 'The Poor Palatines and the Parties'. *English Historical Review* LXXXII, 464–85.

Dickson, P.G.M. (1967). *The Financial Revolution in England: A study in the development of public credit, 1688–1756.* Macmillan.

Dillon, Patrick (2006). *The Last Revolution: 1688 and the Creation of the Modern World.* Jonathan Cape.

Dodge, Guy H. (1947). *The Political Theory of the Huguenots of the Dispersion: With special reference to the thought and influence of Pierre Jurieu.* Columbia University Press, New York.

Doherty, Richard (2008). *The Siege of Derry 1689: The military history.* Spellmount edn, Stroud, 2010.

Douen, O. (1894). *La Révocation de l'Édit de Nantes à Paris d'après des Documents Inédites.* 3 vols. Librairie Fischbacher, Paris.

DuBourdieu, William J. (1967). *Baby on her Back: A history of the Huguenot family DuBourdieu.* Privately printed, Illinois.

Du Cane, E.F. (1876). *Some Account of the Family of Du Quesne.* Harrison & Sons.

Duffy, Michael (1986). *The Englishman and the Foreigner.* Chadwyck-Healey, Cambridge.

Dunan-Page, Anne (ed.) (2006). *The Religious Culture of the Huguenots, 1660–1750.* Ashgate, Aldershot.

Dunan-Page, Anne, and Munoz-Teulié, Marie-Christine (2008). *Les Huguenots dans les Iles Britanniques de la Renaissance aux Lumières: 'Ecrits religieux et representations'.* Honoré Champion, Paris.

Dunn, Richard M. (1973). 'The London Weavers' Riot of 1675'. *Guildhall Studies in London History*, 1:1 (1973), 13–23.

Du Pont, H.A. (1923). *The Early Generations of the Du Pont and Allied Families.* 2 vols. New York.

Durand, René (1908). 'Louis XIV et Jacques II à la Vieille de la Révolution de 1688. Les Trois Missions de Bonrepaus en Angleterre, 1686, 1687, 1688.' *Revue d'Histoire Moderne et Contemporaine* X (1908), 28–44, 111–25, 192–204.

Earle, Peter (1989). *The Making of the English Middle Class: Business, society and family life in London, 1660–1730.* Methuen.

Evans, Joan (1933). 'Huguenot Goldsmiths in England and Ireland'. *HSP* XIV (1929–33), 496–554, with supplement in *HSP* XV (1933–7), 516–20.

Evans, John T. (1979). *Seventeenth-Century Norwich*. Clarendon Press, Oxford.

Fatio, Olivier (1999). 'Rester à Neuchâtel? Les hesitations d'un jeune ministre réfugié, Daniel Chamier (1685–1691)'. In Henry, Philippe and de Tribolet, Maurice (eds), *In Dubiis Libertas. Mélanges d'Histoire offerts au Professeur Rémy Scheurer* (Gilles Attinger, Hauterive), pp. 247–70.

Faulkner, Thomas (1813). *An Historical and Topographical Account of Fulham: Including the hamlet of Hammersmith*. J. Tilling.

Faulkner, Thomas (1829). *An Historical and Topographical Description of Chelsea, and its Environs*. Chelsea, 2 vols.

Félice, Paul de (1898). *Les Protestants d'Autrefois. Vie Intérieure des Églises: Moeurs et usages. Les Pasteurs – vie officielle – vie privée*. Librairie Fischbacher, Paris.

Ferguson, Kenneth (1990). 'The Organisation of King William's Army in Ireland, 1689–92'. *The Irish Sword* XVIII (1970), pp. 62–79.

Finlay, Roger (1981). *Population and Metropolis: The demography of London 1580–1650*. Cambridge University Press.

Fisher, F.J. (1990). *London and the English Economy, 1500–1700*, eds Corfield, P.J. and Harte, N.B. Hambledon Press.

Fitch, J.A. (1967). 'Balthazar Gardemau: A Huguenot squarson and his library'. *HSP* XXI (1965–70), 241–72.

Fletcher, C.R.L. (1925). 'Some Troubles of Archbishop Sancroft'. *HSP* XIII (1923–9), 209–61.

Flick, Andreas, and Schulz, Walter (2008). *From Sweden to South Africa: Proceedings of the international Huguenot conference in Emden 2006*. Deutschen Hugenotten-Gesellschaft, Bad Karlshafen.

Foxcroft, H.C. (1946). *A Character of the Trimmer ... the First Marquis of Halifax*. Cambridge University Press.

Free, Richard W. (1888). *Lux Benigna, being the History of Orange Street Chapel, otherwise called Leicester Fields Chapel....*

Frijhoff, Willem. 'Uncertain Brotherhood: The Huguenots in the Dutch Republic'. In Van Ruymbeke and Sparks (2003).

Galland, A. (1928). 'Les Pasteurs Français Amyraut, Bochart, etc., et la Royauté de Droit Divin, de l'Edit d'Alais à la Révocation (1629–1685)'. *BSHPF* LXXVII (1928), 14–20, 105–34, 225–41, 413–23.

Garrisson, Janine (1985). *L'Edit de Nantes et sa Révocation: Histoire d'une intolerance*. Editions du Seuil, Paris.

Gauci, Perry (2001). *The Politics of Trade: The Overseas Merchant in State and Society, 1660–1720*. Oxford University Press.

Gautier, Etienne, and Henry, Louis (1958). *La Population de Crulai Paroisse Normande*. Institut National d'Etudes Démographiques, travaux et documents cahier no.33, Paris.

Gibbs, G.C. (1971). 'The Role of the Dutch Republic as the Intellectual Entrepôt of Europe in the Seventeenth and Eighteenth Centuries'. *Bijdragen en Mededelingen betreffende de geschiedenis der Nederlanden*, 86 (1971), 323–49.

Gibbs, G.C. (1975). 'Some Intellectual and Political Influences of the Huguenot Emigrés in the United Provinces, c.1680–1730'. *Bijdragen en Mededelingen betreffende de geschiedenis der Nederlanden* 90, 255–87.

Giuseppi, John (1966). *The Bank of England: A history from its foundation in 1694*. Evans Brothers.

Glass, D.V. (1966). *London Inhabitants within the Walls 1695*. London Record Society.

Glass, D.V., and Eversley, D.E.C. (eds) (1965). *Population in History: Essays in historical demography*. Edward Arnold.

Glass, D.V., and Revelle, Roger (eds) (1972). *Population and Social Change*. Edward Arnold.

Glozier, Matthew (2002). *The Huguenot Soldiers of William of Orange and the 'Glorious Revolution' of 1688: The Lions of Judah*. Sussex Academic Press, Brighton and Portland.

Glozier, Matthew (2005). *Marshal Schomberg 1615–1690: International soldiering and the formation of state armies in seventeenth-century Europe*. Sussex Academic Press, Brighton and Portland.

Goldie, Mark (1987). 'The Huguenot Experience and the Problem of Toleration in Restoration England'. In Caldicott and others (1987), pp. 175–203.

Goldie, Mark (1992). 'John Locke's Circle and James II'. *Historical Journal* 35:3 (1992), 557–86.

Goldie, Mark (1993). 'James II and the Dissenters' Revenge: The Commission of Enquiry of 1688'. *Bulletin of the Institute of Historical Research* 66 (1993), 53–88.

Goldie, Mark (2009). 'The *Entring Book* of Roger Morrice'. *HSP* XXIX:2, 157–67.

Goldie, Mark (2016). *Roger Morrice and the Puritan Whigs: The Entring Book, 1677–1691*. Boydell Press, Woodbridge.

Goose, Nigel, and Luu, Lien (eds) (2005). *Immigrants in Tudor and Early Stuart England*. Sussex Academic Press, Brighton and Portland.

Goubert, Pierre (1960). *Beauvais et le Beauvaisis de 1600 à 1730*. Paris.

Grant, A.J. (1934). *The Huguenots*. Thornton Butterworth.

Grant, Alison, and Gwynn, Robin D. (1985). 'The Huguenots of Devon'. *Report and Transactions of the Devonshire Association for the Advancement of Science, Literature and the Arts* 117 (1985), 161–94.

Grave, J.W. de (1895). 'A Refugee Pasteur at the Revocation: Jacob de Rouffignac and his descendants'. *HSP* V (1894–6), 251–88.

Greaves, Richard L. (1990). *Enemies under his Feet: Radicals and nonconformists in Britain, 1664–1677*. Stanford University Press.

Greaves, Richard L. (1992). *Secrets of the Kingdom: British radicals from the Popish Plot to the Revolution of 1688–1689*. Stanford University Press.

Greaves, Richard L. (1994). 'The Rye House Plotting, Nonconformist Clergy, and Calvin's Resistance Theory'. In W. Fred Graham (ed.), *Later Calvinism: International Perspectives*, Sixteenth Century Essays and Studies XXII, 505–24.

Green, I.M. (1978). *The Re-establishment of the Church of England 1660–1663*. Oxford University Press.

Grell, Ole Peter (1989). *Dutch Calvinists in Early Stuart London: The Dutch Church in Austin Friars 1603–1642*. E.J. Brill, Leiden.

Grell, Ole Peter, Israel, J.I. and Tyacke, N. (eds) (1991). *From Persecution to Toleration: The Glorious Revolution and religion in England*. Clarendon Press, Oxford.

Griffiths, D.N. (1972). 'The French Translations of the English Book of Common Prayer'. *HSP* XXII (1970–6), 90–114.

Guyot, H.D. (1906). *Le Marquis de Venours, Protecteur des Victimes de l'Intolérance de Louis XIV*. Groningue.

Gwynn, Robin D. (1968A). 'The Arrival of Huguenot Refugees in England 1680–1705'. *HSP* XXI (1965–70), 366–73.

Gwynn, Robin D. (1968B). 'The Distribution of Huguenot Refugees in England'. *HSP* XXI (1965–70), 404–36.

Gwynn, Robin D. (1971). 'Louis Hérault and his "*Advis*"'. *HSP* XXII (1970–6), 41–50.

Gwynn, Robin D. (1976A). 'The Distribution of Huguenot Refugees in England, II: London and its environs'. *HSP* XXII (1970–6), 509–68.

Gwynn, Robin D. (1976B). 'The Ecclesiastical Organization of French Protestants in England in the Later Seventeenth Century, with Special Reference to London'. PhD thesis, University of London.

Gwynn, Robin D. (1977). 'James II in the Light of his Treatment of Huguenot Refugees in England, 1685–1686'. *English Historical Review* XCII, 820–33.

Gwynn, Robin D. (1983). 'The Number of Huguenot Immigrants in England in the Late Seventeenth Century'. *Journal of Historical Geography* 9:4, 384–95.

Gwynn, Robin D. (1987). 'Patterns in the Study of Huguenot Refugees in Britain: Past, present and future' in Scouloudi (1987), pp. 217–35.

Gwynn, Robin D. (1991). 'Disorder and Innovation: The reshaping of the French churches of London after the Glorious Revolution'. In Grell, Israel and Tyacke (eds), (1991), pp. 251–73.

Gwynn, Robin D. (1995). 'Marital Problems and the Position of Women in the French Church of London in the Later 17th Century'. *HSP* XXVI, 214–29.

Gwynn, Robin D. (1998). *The Huguenots of London*. Alpha Press, Brighton and Portland.

Gwynn, Robin D. (2001). *Huguenot Heritage: The history and contribution of the Huguenots in Britain*. 2nd revised edn, Sussex Academic Press, Brighton and Portland.

Gwynn, Robin D. (2006A). 'Conformity, Non-conformity and Huguenot Settlement in England in the Later Seventeenth Century'. In Dunan-Page (2006), pp. 23–41.

Gwynn, Robin D. (2006B). 'Roger Morrice and the Huguenot Refugees'. In McElligott (2006), pp. 32–48.

Gwynn, Robin D. (2008). 'Huguenots in English Sea Port Towns in the Late Seventeenth Century'. *Journal of Port Cities Studies* 3 (2008) [Port Cities Research Center, Kobe, Japan], 15–29.

Gwynn, Robin D. (2009). 'International Huguenot Networks in the 1680s and 1690s'. *Odysseus* 1, 3–25.

Gwynn, Robin D. (2011). 'Strains of Worship: The Huguenots and non-conformity'. In Trim (2011), pp. 121–51.

Gwynn, Robin D. (2015). *The Huguenots in Later Stuart Britain. Volume I – Crisis, Renewal, and the Ministers' Dilemma*. Sussex Academic Press, Brighton, Portland and Toronto.

Gwynn, Robin D. (2018). *The Huguenots in Later Stuart Britain. Volume II – Settlement, Churches, and the Role of London*. Sussex Academic Press, Brighton, Portland and Toronto.

Gwynn, Robin D. (2019). 'Britain's Significance in the Huguenot Diaspora of the Late Seventeenth Century'. *HSJ* 32, 1–14.

Haag, Eugène and Émile (1846). *La France Protestante (ou Vies des Protestants Français ...)*. 10 vols. E. Thunot, Paris, 1846–59.

Haag, Eugène and Émile (1877). *La France Protestante (ou Vies des Protestants Français ...)*. 2nd edn, 6 vols, A to G only. Paris, 1877–88.

Haley, K.H.D. (1953). *William of Orange and the English Opposition 1672–4.* Clarendon Press, Oxford.

Haley, K.H.D. (1968). *The First Earl of Shaftesbury.* Clarendon Press, Oxford.

Hardy, W.J. (1888). 'Foreign Refugees at Rye', *HSP* II (1887–8), 406–27, 567–87.

Harris, Tim (1987). *London Crowds in the Reign of Charles II: Propaganda and politics from the Restoration until the Exclusion Crisis.* Cambridge University Press.

Harris, Tim (1993). *Politics under the Later Stuarts: Party conflict in a divided society 1660–1715.* Longman.

Harris, Tim (1997). 'What's New about the Restoration?', *Albion* 29:2.

Harris, Tim (2005). *Restoration: Charles II and his kingdoms, 1660–1685.* Allen Lane.

Harris, Tim (2006). *Revolution: The great crisis of the British monarchy, 1685–1720.* Allen Lane.

Harris, Tim (2019). 'Constitutional Royalism Reconsidered: Myth or Reality?', in Champion and others (2019), 19–37.

Hart, A. Tindal (1949). *The Life and Times of John Sharp Archbishop of York.* SPCK for the Church Historical Society.

Hart, A. Tindal (1952). *William Lloyd 1627–1717.* SPCK for the Church Historical Society.

Hatton, Ragnhild (1972). *Louis XIV and his World.* Thames & Hudson.

Hatton, Ragnhild (1976). *Louis XIV and Europe.* Macmillan.

Hay, Malcolm V. (1938). *The Enigma of James II.* Sands & Co.

Hayes-McCoy, G.A. (1969). *Irish Battles.* Longman.

Hayward, J.F. (1959). *Huguenot Silver in England 1688–1727.* Faber & Faber.

Hayward, J.F. (1964). 'The Huguenot Gunmakers of London'. *HSP* XX (1958–64), 649–63.

Hazard, Paul (1964). *The European Mind 1680–1715.* Penguin.

Henning, Basil Duke (ed.) (1983). *The House of Commons 1660–1690.* 3 vols. Secker & Warburg for the History of Parliament Trust.

Herbert, W. (1834). *History of the Twelve Great Livery Companies of London.* 2 vols, 1834–7.

Holmes, Geoffrey (1982). *Augustan England: Professions, state and society, 1680–1730.* George Allen & Unwin.

Holmes, Geoffrey (1993). *The Making of a Great Power: Late Stuart and early Georgian Britain 1660–1722.* Longman.

Home Office (1913). *Report with Evidence and Appendices of the Committee appointed by the Secretary of State for the Home Department to inquire as to the History and Constitution of the French Protestant Church of London.*

Hoppit, Julian (2000). *A Land of Liberty? England 1689–1727.* New Oxford History of England, Oxford University Press.

Horwitz, Henry (1977). *Parliament, Policy and Politics in the Reign of William III.* Manchester University Press.

Houblon, Lady Alice Archer (1907). *The Houblon Family: Its story and times.* 2 vols. Archibald Constable & Co.

Houston, R.A. (1992). *The Population History of Britain and Ireland 1500–1700.* Macmillan Education, Basingstoke.

Hugo. E-letter of the Huguenot Society of Australia Inc.

Huguenot Society of Great Britain and Ireland (formerly of London). *Proceedings.* 1885–2012, vols I–XXIX.

Huguenot Society of Great Britain and Ireland (formerly of London). *Huguenot Society Journal.* Continues the above from vol. XXX, 2013 (in progress).

Hunt, Margaret R. (1996). *The Middling Sort: Commerce, gender, and the family in England, 1680–1780.* University of California Press, Berkeley.

Hylton, Raymond (1982). 'The Huguenot Settlement at Portarlington, 1692–1771'. MA thesis, National University of Ireland, University College, Dublin.

Hylton, Raymond (2005). *Ireland's Huguenots and their Refuge, 1662–1745: An unlikely haven.* Sussex Academic Press, Brighton and Portland.

Israel, Jonathan I. (ed.) (1991). *The Anglo-Dutch Moment: Essays on the Glorious Revolution and Its World Impact.* Cambridge University Press.

Israel, Jonathan I. (1995). *The Dutch Republic: Its Rise, Greatness, and Fall, 1477–1806.* Clarendon Press, Oxford.

Jalland, Beatrice M. (1944). 'John Cosin and the French Reformed Church'. *Church Quarterly Review* 138, 192–203.

James, Margaret (1930, 1966). *Social Problems and Policy during the Puritan Revolution, 1640–1660.* Routledge & Kegan Paul.

Jaulmes, Yves (1993). *The French Protestant Church of London and the Huguenots.* Église Protestante Française de Londres.

Jones, D.W. (1971). 'London Overseas-Merchant Groups at the End of the Seventeenth Century and the Moves against the East India Company'. DPhil thesis, University of Oxford.

Jones, D.W. (1988). *War and Economy in the Age of William III and Marlborough.* Basil Blackwell, Oxford.

Jones, George Hilton (1969). 'The Problem of French Protestantism in the Foreign Policy of England, 1680–8', *Bulletin of the Institute of Historical Research* XLII (1969), 145–57.

Jones, George Hilton (1990). *Convergent Forces: Immediate causes of the Revolution of 1688 in England.* Iowa State University Press.

Jones, J.R. (1966). *Britain and Europe in the Seventeenth Century.* Edward Arnold.

Jones, J.R. (1970). *The First Whigs: The politics of the Exclusion Crisis, 1678–1683.* Oxford University Press.

Jones, J.R. (1972). *The Revolution of 1688 in England.* Weidenfeld & Nicolson.

Jones, J.R. (1978). *Country and Court: England 1658–1714.* Edward Arnold.

Joutard, Philippe (1985). 'The Revocation of the Edict of Nantes: End or renewal of French Calvinism?'. In Prestwich (ed.) (1985), pp. 339–68.

Joutard, Philippe (2018). *La Révocation de l'Édit de Nantes.* Éditions Gallimard, Paris.

Kenyon, John P. (1958). *Robert Spencer, Earl of Sunderland 1641–1702.* Longmans, Green.

Kenyon, John P. (1972). *The Popish Plot.* Heinemann.

Knights, Mark (1994). *Politics and Opinion in Crisis, 1678–81.* Cambridge University Press.

Knights, Mark (1997). 'A City Revolution: The remodelling of the London Livery Companies in the 1680s'. *English Historical Review* 112, 1141–78.

Knights, Mark (2006). 'Judging Partisan News and the Language of Interest', in McElligott, *Fear, Exclusion, and Revolution*, 204–20.

Laborie, Lionel (2015). *Enlightening Enthusiasm: Prophecy and religious experience in early eighteenth-century England.* Manchester University Press.

Labrousse, Elisabeth (1985). *'Une foi, une loi, un roi?'. Essai sur la Révocation de l'Edit de Nantes.* Labor et Fides, Geneva.

Lacey, Douglas R. (1969). *Dissent and Parliamentary Politics in England, 1661–1689: A study in the perpetuation and tempering of Parliamentarianism.* Rutgers University Press, New Brunswick, New Jersey.

Lachenicht, Susanne (2006). 'Differing Perceptions of the Refuge?'. In Dunan-Page (2006), pp. 43–53.

Lachenicht, Susanne (2007). 'Huguenot Immigrants and the Formation of National Identities, 1548–1787'. *Historical Journal* 50:2, 1–23.

Lambert, David E. (2010). *The Protestant International and the Huguenot Migration to Virginia*. Peter Lang, New York, etc. (Studies in Church History, vol. 12.)

Landers, John (1993). *Death and the Metropolis: Studies in the demographic history of London 1670–1830*. Cambridge University Press.

Lane, Jane (1949). *Titus Oates*. Andrew Dakers.

Larminie, Vivienne (2018). *Huguenot Networks, 1560–1780: The interactions and impact of a Protestant minority in Europe*. Routledge.

Lart, Charles E. (1904). 'The Huguenot Settlements and Churches in the West of England'. *HSP* VII (1901–4), 286–98.

Lart, Charles E. (1911). 'The Huguenot Regiments', *HSP* IX (1909–11), 476–529.

Lart, Charles E. (1928A). *Huguenot Pedigrees*. 2 vols. C. Guimaraens & Co.

Lart, Charles E. (1928B). 'The French Colony and Church at Sunbury-on-Thames'. *HSP* XIII (1923–9), 474–82.

Laslett, Peter (1971) *The World We Have Lost*. 2nd edn, Methuen.

Lee, Grace Lawless (1936). *The Huguenot Settlements in Ireland*. Longmans, Green.

Lee, Grace Lawless (1966). *The Story of the Bosanquets*. Phillimore, Canterbury.

Le Fanu, Thomas Philip (1905). 'The Huguenot Churches of Dublin and their Ministers'. *HSP* VIII (1905–8), 87–139.

Le Fanu, Thomas Philip (1932). 'The Life and Sufferings of Benjamin de Daillon'. *HSP* XIV (1929–33), 458–78.

Le Moine, H.G.B., Moens, W.J.C. and Overend, G.H. (1887). 'Huguenots in the Isle of Axholme'. *HSP* II (1887–8), 265–331.

Lenihan, Pádraig (2001) (ed.). *Conquest and Resistance: War in Seventeenth-Century Ireland*. Brill, Leiden.

Lenihan, Pádraig (2005). *1690 Battle of the Boyne*. Tempus Publishing, Stroud.

Lenihan, Pádraig (2009). 'Schomberg at Dundalk, 1689'. *Journal of the County Louth Archaeological and Historical Society* 27:1, 39–52.

Lenihan, Pádraig and Sheridan, Geraldine (2005), 'A Swiss Soldier in Ireland, 1689–90'. *Irish Studies Review* 13:4 (Nov.), pp. 479–97.

Léonard, Émile G. (1961). *Histoire Générale du Protestantisme*. 3 vols. Presses Universitaires de France, Paris, 1961–4.

Léonard, Émile G. (1967). *A History of Protestantism: 2, the Establishment*. Nelson. [Translation of volume II of this work.]

Léoutre, Marie M. (2018). *Serving France, Ireland and England: Ruvigny, Earl of Galway, 1648–1720.* Routledge, London and New York.

Le Roy Ladurie, Emmanuel (1991). 'Glorious Revolution, Shameful Revocation'. Afterword to Cottret (1991), 285–305.

Lesens, Emile (1885). See *sub* Bianquis, Jean (1885).

Levillain, Charles-Edouard (2006). 'London Besieged? The City's Vulnerability During the Glorious Revolution', chap. 5 in McElligott (2006).

Levin, Jennifer (1969). *The Charter Controversy in the City of London, 1660–1688, and its Consequences.* Athlone Press.

Li, Ming-Hsun (1963). *The Great Recoinage of 1696 to 1969.* Weidenfeld & Nicolson.

Ligou, Daniel (1968). *Le Protestantisme en France de 1598 à 1715.* Société d'édition d'enseignement, Paris.

Lindeboom, J. (1950). *Austin Friars: History of the Dutch Reformed Church in London 1550–1950.* Martinus Nijhoff, The Hague.

Linden, David van der (2015). *Experiencing Exile: Huguenot refugees in the Dutch Republic, 1680–1700.* Ashgate, Farnham and Burlington.

Lipson, E. (1934). *The Economic History of England: III, The Age of Mercantilism.* 2nd edn.

Littleton, Charles Galton (1996). 'Geneva on Threadneedle Street: The French Church of London and its Congregation, 1560–1625'. Ph.D thesis, University of Michigan.

London County Council. *Survey of London.*, particularly vols 27 (Spitalfields and Mile End New Town, 1957) and 33–34 (St Anne Soho, 1966).

Lough, John (1985). *France observed in the Seventeenth Century by British Travellers.* Oriel Press, Stocksfield.

Lüthy, Herbert (1959). *La Banque Protestante en France de la Révocation de l'Édit de Nantes à la Révolution.* 2 vols. SEVPEN, Paris, 1959–61.

Macaulay, Lord (1913–15). *The History of England from the Accession of James the Second.* Illustrated edn, ed. C.H. Firth, 6 vols.

Macrory, Patrick (1980). *The Siege of Derry.* Oxford University Press, 1988 paperback edn.

Magdelaine, Michelle. 'Conditions et Préparation de l'Intégration: Le voyage de Charles de Sailly en Irlande (1693) et le projet d'Edit d'accueil', in Vigne and Littleton (2001), 435–41.

Magdelaine, M., and Von Thadden, R. (1985). *Le Refuge Huguenot.* Armand Colin, Paris.

Maillard, T. (1900). 'Les Routes de l'Exil: Du Poitou vers les îles Normandes et l'Angleterre. Le guide Pierre Michaut'. *BSHPF* XLIX (1900), 281–91.

Manchée, William Henry (1915). 'Marylebone, and its Huguenot Associations'. *HSP* XI (1915–17), 58–128, 249–54.

Manchée, William Henry (1916). 'Huguenot Clergy List. 1548–1916'. *HSP* XI (1915–17), 263–92, 387–99.

Manchée, William Henry (1921). 'Huguenot London: Charing Cross and St. Martin's Lane'. *HSP* XII (1917–23), 346–81.

Manchée, William Henry (1924). 'Huguenot London: Covent Garden, Savoy and the Strand'. *HSP* XIII (1923–9), 54–76.

Manchée, William Henry (1930). 'Huguenot London: The City of Westminster: Soho'. *HSP* XIV (1929–33), 144–90 and 399–400.

Manchée, William Henry (1935). 'Some Huguenot Smugglers. The Impeachment of London Silk Merchants, 1698'. *HSP* XV (1933–7), 406–27.

Manchée, William Henry (1938). 'The First and Last Chapter of the Church of "Les Grecs", Charing Cross Road'. *HSP* XVI (1937–41), 140–58.

Manchée, William Henry (1946). 'Huguenot London: Greater Soho'. *HSP* XVII (1942–6), 423–45.

Marmoy, C.F.A. (1970). 'The Huguenots and their Descendants in East London'. *East London Papers* XIII:2 (1970–1), 72–88.

Marshall, John (2001). 'Huguenot Thought after the Revocation of the Edict of Nantes: Toleration, 'Socinianism', integration and Locke'. In Vigne and Littleton (2001), pp. 383–96.

Marshall, John (2010). *John Locke, Toleration and Early Enlightenment Culture.* Cambridge University Press.

Martin, Odile (1986). *La Conversion Protestante à Lyon (1659–1687).* Geneva.

Mason, John (1945). 'The Weavers of Picardy', *Book of the Old Edinburgh Club* XXV (1945), 1–33.

Mayo, Ronald (1966). 'Les Huguenots à Bristol (1681–1791)'. PhD thesis, Faculté des Lettres et Sciences Humaines de Lille.

Mayo, Ronald (1985). *The Huguenots in Bristol.* Bristol Branch of the Historical Association.

Mayor, J.E.B. (ed.) (1911). *Cambridge under Queen Anne.* Cambridge Antiquarian Society.

McElligott, Jason (2004). 'Roger Morrice, Sir Henry Hobart, and a New Eyewitness Account of the Battle of the Boyne'. *The Irish Sword* XXIV (2004–5), 31–43.

McElligott, Jason (ed.) (2006). *Fear, Exclusion, and Revolution: Roger Morrice and Britain in the 1680s*. Ashgate, Aldershot and Burlington.

McKee, Jane (2002). 'The Importance of Reputation, Contacts and Patronage in making a Successful Life Abroad: The case of the Drelincourt family', Huguenot Society of South Africa, *Bulletin* 39 (Proceedings of the Third International Huguenot Conference), 138–48.

McKee, Jane (2012). 'Anglicanism and the Huguenots: The experience of two generations of the Drelincourt family'. *HSP* XXIX (2008–12), 623–39.

McKee, Jane and Vigne, Randolph (eds) (2013). *The Huguenots: France, exile and diaspora*. Sussex Academic Press, Brighton, Portland and Toronto.

McLachlan, H. John (1951). *Socinianism in Seventeenth-Century England*. Oxford University Press.

McNally, Michael (2008). *The Battle of Aughrim 1691*. History Press, Stroud.

McNeill, John T. (1954). *The History and Character of Calvinism*. Oxford University Press.

McShane, Angela (2007). 'A Resounding Silence? Huguenots and the Broadside Ballad in the Seventeenth Century'. *HSP* XXVIII:5, 604–25.

Meller, Pierre (1902). *Les Familles Protestantes de Bordeaux*. Bordeaux.

Mentzer, Raymond A., and Spicer, Andrew (eds) (2002). *Society and Culture in the Huguenot World, 1559–1685*. Cambridge University Press.

Mettam, Roger (ed.) (1977). *Government and Society in Louis XIV's France*. Macmillan.

Michelet, J. (1860). *Louis XIV et la Révocation de l'Edit de Nantes*. Chamerot, Libraire-Editeur, Paris.

Miller, John (1973). *Popery and Politics in England 1660–1688*. Cambridge University Press.

Miller, John (1978). *James II: A Study in Kingship*. Wayland Publishers, Hove.

Miller, John (1991). *Charles II*. Weidenfeld & Nicolson.

Miller, John (2003). 'The Fortunes of the Strangers in Norwich and Canterbury, 1565–1700'. In Van Ruymbeke and Sparks (2003), pp. 110–27.

Minet, William (1893). 'The Fourth Foreign Church at Dover, 1685–1731'. *HSP* IV (1891–3), 93–217.

Minet, William. 'Notes on the Threadneedle Street Registers', undated typescript in the Huguenot Library, University College London.

Mitchell, D.M. (2017). *Silversmiths in Elizabethan and Stuart London: Their lives and their marks.* Boydell Press, Woodbridge.

Mours, Samuel (1958). *Les Eglises Réformées en France: Tableaux et cartes.* Librairie Protestante, Paris, and Lib. Oberlin, Strasbourg.

Mours, Samuel (1966). *Essai Sommaire de Geógraphie du Protestantisme Réformé Français au XVIIe Siècle.* Librairie Protestante, Paris.

Mours, Samuel (1967). *Le Protestantisme en France au XVIIe Siècle (1598–1685).* Librairie Protestante, Paris.

Mours, Samuel (1968). 'Les Pasteurs à la Révocation de l'Édit de Nantes'. *BSHPF* 114 (1968), 67–105, 292–316, 521–4.

Murdoch, Tessa (comp.) (1985). *The Quiet Conquest: The Huguenots 1685 to 1985.* Museum of London.

Murdoch, Tessa (ed.) (1992). *Boughton House: The English Versailles.* Faber/Christie's.

Murdoch, Tessa (1997). 'Jean, René and Thomas Pelletier, a Huguenot Family of Carvers and Gilders in England 1682–1726'. *Burlington Magazine*, 2 parts, 139 (1997), 732–42 and 140 (1998), 363–74.

Murdoch, Tessa and Randolph Vigne (2009). *The French Hospital in England: Its Huguenot history and collections.* John Adamson, Cambridge.

Murtagh, Harman (1987). 'Huguenot Involvement in the Irish Jacobite War, 1689–91'. In Caldicott and others (1987), 223–38.

Murtagh, Harman (1995). 'The Irish Jacobite Army, 1689–91'. In Bernadette Whelan (1995), 69–82.

Murtagh, Harman (2006). *The Battle of the Boyne 1690: A guide to the battlefield.* Boyne Valley Honey Company, Drogheda.

Murtagh, Diarmuid and Harman (1990). 'The Irish Jacobite Army, 1689–1691'. *The Irish Sword* XVIII, pp. 32–47.

Nishikawa, Sugiko (1998). 'English Attitudes toward Continental Protestants with Particular Reference to Church Briefs c.1680–1740'. PhD thesis, University of London.

Nishikawa, Sugiko (2001). 'Henry Compton, Bishop of London (1676–1713) and Foreign Protestants'. In Vigne and Littleton (2001), pp. 359–65.

Nishikawa, Sugiko (2005). 'The SPCK in Defence of Protestant Minorities in Early Eighteenth-Century Europe'. *Journal of Ecclesiastical History* 56:4, 730–48.

Nishikawa, Sugiko (2021). 'Henri Arnaud in London, 1699' in Rivista della Società di Studi Valdesi, *Riforma e Movimenti Religiosi*, 171–90.

Nusteling, Hubert P.H. (1986). 'The Netherlands and the Huguenot émigrés'. In Bots and Posthumus Meyjes (eds) (1986), pp. 17–34.

Odysseus 1. 2009. [ISSN 1345-0557. A Japanese journal with English text, the whole number is devoted to the international context of the 'Glorious Revolution'.]

Ogg, David (1955). *England in the Reigns of James II and William III*. Clarendon Press, Oxford.

Ogier, D.M. (1996). *Reformation and Society in Guernsey*. Boydell Press, Woodbridge.

Onnekink, David (2009). '"The Embarrassment of Power … 1688" and "A Common Philosophy"'. *Odysseus* 1, 43–65, 87–104.

Orcibal, Jean (1951). *Louis XIV et les Protestants*. Librairie Philosophique J. Vrin, Paris.

Ormrod, David (1993). 'The Atlantic Economy and the "Protestant Capitalist International", 1651–1775', *Historical Research* 66, 197–208.

Overend, G.H. (1889). 'Strangers at Dover'. *HSP* III (1888–91), 91–171, 286–330.

Papillon, Emily C. (1923). 'The Papillons in France and England: the story of a Huguenot house'. 4 vols. Unpublished typescript, ed. T.L. Papillon, in the Huguenot Library, University College, London.

Parker, Greig (2014). *Probate Inventories of French Immigrants in Early Modern London*. Ashgate, Aldershot.

Parker, William Riley (1968). *Milton: A biography*. 2 vols. Clarendon Press, Oxford.

Parry, Clive (1957). *Nationality and Citizenship Laws of the Commonwealth and of the Republic of Ireland*. Stevens.

Pascal, C. (1900). 'Les Ordres du Consistoire de l'Église Réformée Française de Londres'. *BSHPF* XLIX (1900), 260–9.

Pettegree, Andrew (1986). *Foreign Protestant Communities in Sixteenth-Century London*. Clarendon Press, Oxford.

Pettegree, Andrew (1991). 'The French and Walloon Communities in London, 1550–1688'. In Grell and others, *From Persecution to Toleration*, pp. 77–96.

Picard, Liza (1997). *Restoration London*. Weidenfeld & Nicolson (paperback edn, Phoenix, 1998).

Pickard, Col. R. (1937). 'The Huguenots in Exeter'. *Report and Transactions of the Devonshire Association for the Advancement of Science, Literature and Art* LXVIII (1937), 261–97, and LXXVI (1945), 129–31.

Pincus, Steven C.A. (1995). 'From Butterboxes to Wooden Shoes: The shift in English popular sentiment from anti-Dutch to anti-French in the 1670s'. *Historical Journal* 38:2, 333–61.

Pincus, Steven C.A. (1996). *Protestantism and Patriotism: Ideologies and the making of English foreign policy, 1650–1668.* Cambridge University Press.

Pincus, Steven C.A. (2009). *1688: The first modern revolution.* Yale University Press, New Haven and London.

Pinkham, Lucile (1969). *William III and the Respectable Revolution: The part played by William of Orange in the Revolution of 1688.* Archon Books.

Pitassi, Maria Cristina (1987). *Entre croire et savoir: Le problème de la méthode critique chez Jean Le Clerc.* Brill, Leiden.

Plummer, Alfred (1972). *The London Weavers' Company 1600–1970.* Routledge & Kegan Paul, London and New York.

Poole, Reginald Lane (1880). *A History of the Huguenots of the Dispersion at the Recall of the Edict of Nantes.* Macmillan.

Préclin, E. and Jarry, E. (1955). *Les Luttes Politiques et Doctrinales aux XVIIe et XVIIIe Siècles.* Histoire de l'Eglise depuis les origines jusqu'à nos jours, vol. 19. Paris.

Prestwich, Menna (ed.) (1985). *International Calvinism 1541–1715.* Clarendon Press, Oxford.

Priestley, Margaret (1951). 'Anglo-French Trade and the "Unfavourable Balance" Controversy, 1660–1685'. *Economic History Review,* 2nd series, IV (1951–2), 37–52.

Priestley, Margaret (1956). 'London Merchants and Opposition Politics in Charles II's Reign'. *Bulletin of the Institute of Historical Research* XXIX, 205–19.

Rappaport, Steve (1989). *Worlds within Worlds: Structures of life in sixteenth-century London.* Cambridge.

Redstone, Vincent B. (1920). 'The Dutch and Huguenot Settlements of Ipswich'. *HSP* XII (1917–23), 183–204.

Reese, Charles (2015). 'Huguenot Members of the Honourable Artillery Company in the 17th and Early 18th Century'. *HSJ* XXX:3, 358–68.

Robb, Nesca A. (1966). *William of Orange: A personal portrait. Volume Two: 1674–1702.* Heinemann.

Roberts, Richard, and Kynaston, David (eds) (1995). *The Bank of England: Money, power and influence 1694–1994*. Clarendon Press, Oxford.

Robbins, Caroline (1962). 'A Note on General Naturalization under the Later Stuarts and a Speech in the House of Commons on the Subject in 1664'. *Journal of Modern History* XXXIV, 168–77.

Rossier, L. (1861). *Histoire des Protestants de Picardie*. Paris.

Rothstein, Natalie (1987). 'Huguenots in the English Silk Industry in the Eighteenth Century'. In Scouloudi (1987), 125–40.

Rothstein, Natalie (1989). 'Canterbury and London: the silk industry in the late seventeenth century'. *Textile History* 20:1, 33–47.

Rousset, C. (1865). *Histoire de Louvois et de son administration politique depuis la Paix de Nimègue*. 2 vols. Didier, Paris.

Rumbold, Margaret E. (1991). *Traducteur Huguenot: Pierre Coste*. Peter Lang, New York.

Sanxay, Theodore F. (1907). *The Sanxay Family, and Descendants of Rev. Jacques Sanxay....* Privately printed, New York.

Schickler, Baron Fernand de (1885). 'Les Églises Françaises de Londres après la Révocation'. *HSP* I (1885–6), 95–115.

Schickler, Baron Fernand de (1890). '"Reconnoissances" et Abjurations dans les Églises de la Savoie et de Hungerford à Londres (1684–1733)'. *BSHPF* XXXIX (1890), 86–97.

Schickler, Baron Fernand de (1892). *Les Églises du Refuge en Angleterre*. 3 vols. Librairie Fischbacher, Paris.

Schickler, Baron Fernand de (1900). 'Un Chapitre de l'Histoire des Églises du Refuge de Langue Française en Angleterre après la Révocation de l'Édit de Nantes: Les Deux Patentes'. *HSP* VI (1898–1901), 268–94.

Schwartz, Hillel (1980). *The French Prophets: The history of a millenarian group in eighteenth-century England*. University of California Press.

Schwarz, L.D. (1992). *London in the Age of Industrialisation: Entrepreneurs, labour force and living conditions, 1700–1850*. Cambridge University Press.

Schwoerer, Lois G. (1988). *Lady Rachel Russell: 'One of the Best of Women'*. Johns Hopkins University Press, Baltimore and London.

Schwoerer, Lois G. (2001). *The Ingenious Mr Henry Care, Restoration Publicist*. Johns Hopkins University Press, Baltimore and London.

Scott, Jonathan (1990). 'England's Troubles: Exhuming the Popish Plot', in Tim Harris and others (eds), *The Politics of Religion in Restoration England*. Basil Blackwell, Oxford.

Scott, Jonathan (1991). *Algernon Sidney and the Restoration Crisis, 1677–1683*. Cambridge University Press.

Scott, William Robert (1912). *The Constitution and Finance of English, Scottish and Irish Joint-Stock Companies to 1720*. 3 vols. Cambridge University Press.

Scouloudi, Irene (1937). 'Alien Immigration and Alien Communities in London 1558–1640'. MSc (Econ) thesis, University of London.

Scouloudi, Irene (1947). 'Thomas Papillon, Merchant and Whig, 1623–1702'. *HSP* XVIII (1947–52), 49–72.

Scouloudi, Irene (ed.) (1987). *Huguenots in Britain and their French Background, 1550–1800*. Macmillan.

Scoville, Warren C. (1952). 'The Huguenots and the Diffusion of Technology'. *Journal of Political Economy* LX, 294–311, 392–411.

Scoville, Warren C. (1960). *The Persecution of Huguenots and French Economic Development 1680–1720*. University of California Press, Berkeley and Los Angeles.

Selwood, Jacob (2010). *Diversity and Difference in Early Modern London*. Ashgate, Farnham and Burlington.

Shaw, R.A., Gwynn, R.D. and Thomas, P. (1985). *Huguenots in Wandsworth*. Wandsworth Borough Council.

Shaw, William A. (1895). 'The English Government and the Relief of Protestant Refugees'. *HSP* V (1894–6), 343–423 [an enlarged version of the article of the same title in the *English Historical Review* IX (1894), 662–83].

Shaw, William A. (1900). *A History of the English Church during the Civil Wars and under the Commonwealth 1640–1660*. 2 vols. Longmans, Green.

Shepherd, Robert (1990). *Ireland's Fate: The Boyne and After*. Aurum Press.

Sheppard, Francis H.W. (1968). 'The Huguenots in Spitalfields and Soho'. *HSP* XXI (1965–70), 355–65.

Simms, J.G. (1969). *Jacobite Ireland 1685–91*. London: Routledge & Kegan Paul, and Toronto University Press.

Simms, J.G. (1971). 'Schomberg at Dundalk, 1689'. *The Irish Sword* X (1971–2), 14–25.

Simon, Walter G. (1965). *The Restoration Episcopate*. Bookman Associates, New York.

Smiles, Samuel (1867). *The Huguenots: Their settlements, churches, and industries in England and Ireland*. John Murray.

Smith, J.W. Ashley (1956). 'French Influence on English Higher Education in the Later Seventeenth and Early Eighteenth Century 1660–1730'. PhD thesis, University of Leeds.

Smith, M.G. (1964). 'The Administration of the Diocese of Exeter during the Episcopate of Sir Jonathan Trelawny, 1689–1707'. BD thesis, University of Oxford.

Smith, Raymond (1972). *The Archives of the French Protestant Church of London: A handlist.* HSQS vol. L.

Smith, Raymond (1973). 'Financial Aid to French Protestant Refugees 1681–1727: Briefs and the Royal Bounty'. *HSP* XXII (1971–6), 248–56.

Smith, Raymond (1974). *Records of the Royal Bounty and Connected Funds, the Burn Donation, and the Savoy Church in the Huguenot Library, University College, London: A handlist.* HSQS LI.

Speck, W.A. (1987). 'The Orangist Conspiracy against James II', *Historical Journal* 30, 453–62.

Speck, W.A. (1988). *Reluctant Revolutionaries: Englishmen and the Revolution of 1688.* Oxford University Press.

Speck, W.A. (2002). *James II.* Longman.

Spence, Craig (2000). *London in the 1690s: A social atlas.* Centre for Metropolitan History, Institute of Historical Research, University of London.

Spicer, Andrew (1997). *The French-speaking Reformed Community and their Church in Southampton, 1567–c.1620.* Huguenot Society, new series no.3.

Spicer, Andrew (2007). 'The Consistory Records of Reformed Congregations and the Exile Churches'. *HSP* XXVIII:5, 640–63.

Spicer, Andrew (2017). 'Aliens, Native Englishmen and Migration: William Herbert's *Considerations in the behalf of Foreiners*', in Spicer, Andrew, and Stevens Crawshaw, Jane L. (eds), *The Place of the Social Margins, 1350–1750.* Routledge, New York.

Spurr, John (1991). *The Restoration Church of England, 1646–1689.* Yale University Press, New Haven and London.

Spurr, John (ed.) (2011). *Anthony Ashley Cooper, first Earl of Shaftesbury 1621–1683.* Ashgate, Farnham and Burlington.

Squire, John Traviss (1886). 'The Huguenots at Wandsworth in the County of Surrey...'. *HSP* I (1885–6), 229–42, 261–312.

Stankiewicz, W.J. (1960). *Politics and Religion in Seventeenth-Century France.* University of Toronto Press.

Statt, Daniel (1995). *Foreigners and Englishmen: The controversy over immigration and population, 1660–1760.* Associated University Presses, Cranbury, New Jersey.

Stephenson, H.W. (1950). 'Thomas Firmin, 1632–1697'. DPhil thesis, University of Oxford.

Strayer, Brian E. (2002). *Huguenots and Camisards as Aliens in France, 1598–1789*. Edwin Mellen Press, Lewiston, NY.

Sundstrom, Roy A. (1972). 'Aid and Assimilation: A study of the economic support given French Protestants in England, 1680–1727'. PhD thesis, Kent State University.

Sundstrom, Roy A. (c.1975). 'The Huguenots in England 1680–1876: A study in alien assimilation'. Typescript in the Huguenot Library, University College, London.

Sundstrom, Roy A. (1976). 'French Huguenots and the Civil List, 1696–1727: A study of alien assimilation in England'. *Albion* 8, 219–35.

Swindlehurst, Catherine. '"An Unruly and Presumptuous Rabble": The reaction of the Spitalfields weaving community to the settlement of the Huguenots, 1660–90'. In Vigne and Littleton (2001), 366–74.

Sykes, Norman (1948). *The Church of England and Non-Episcopal Churches in the Sixteenth and Seventeenth Centuries: An essay towards an historical interpretation of the Anglican tradition from Whitgift to Wake*. SPCK, 'Theology' Occasional Papers, new series, no.11.

Sykes, Norman (1956). *Old Priest and New Presbyter*. Cambridge University Press.

Terry, Ken (2007). 'The Huguenots in East Anglia. A study of seventeenth century Huguenot immigration. Why they came, how they were received and where they went'. BA History Dissertation, University of Essex.

Thirsk, Joan (1978). *Economic Policy and Projects: The development of a consumer society in early modern England*. Clarendon Press, Oxford.

Thomas, A.H. (1920). 'The Documents relating to the Relief of French Protestant Refugees, 1693 to 1718, preserved in the Records Office at the Guildhall, London'. *HSP* XII (1917–23), 263–87.

Thomson, Gladys Scott (1950). *Life in a Noble Household 1641–1700*. Jonathan Cape.

Thornton, Peter, and Rothstein, Natalie (1959). 'The Importance of the Huguenots in the London Silk Industry'. *HSP* XX (1958–64), 60–88.

Thorp, Malcolm R. (1976). 'The Anti-Huguenot Undercurrent in Late-Seventeenth-Century England'. *HSP* XXII (1970–6), 569–80.

Tolmie, Murray (1977). *The Triumph of the Saints: The separate churches of London 1616–1649*. Cambridge University Press.

Tournier, Gaston (1943). *Les Galères de France et les Galériens Protestants des XVIIe et XVIIIe Siècles*. 3 vols. Cevennes, 1943–9.

Treasure, Geoffrey (2013). *The Huguenots*. Yale University Press, New Haven and London.

Trevelyan, G.M. (1932). *England under Queen Anne*. 3 vols, 1932–4. Longmans.

Trim, David J.B. (ed.) (2011). *The Huguenots: History and memory in transnational context. Essays in honour and memory of Walter C. Utt*. Brill, Leiden and Boston.

Tulot, Jean Luc. 'Les Huguenots de Loudun …'. Undated typescript in HL.

Turner, F.C. (1948). *James II*. Eyre & Spottiswoode.

Tyacke, N. (1987). *Anti-Calvinists: The rise of English Arminianism, c.1590–1640*. Oxford University Press.

Utt, Walter C., and Strayer, Brian E. (2003). *The Bellicose Dove: Claude Brousson and Protestant resistance to Louis XIV, 1647–1698*. Sussex Academic Press, Brighton and Portland.

Van Ruymbeke, Bertrand and Sparks, Randy J. (eds) (2003). *Memory and Identity: The Huguenots in France and the Atlantic diaspora*. University of South Carolina Press.

Vareilles, Robert (2009). *L'Itinéraire Pastoral de Jean d'Espagne*. Rumeur des Ages, La Rochelle. An earlier draft, 'L'Itinéraire Pastoral ou les Controverses de Jean D'Espagne…', includes more reproductions of original documents [HL, XH.7.DES].

Varley, E.H. (1939). 'The Occupations of Protestant Refugees in the Seventeenth Century'. *Geography* XXIV, 131–4.

Vigne, Randolph, and Littleton, Charles (eds) (2001). *From Strangers to Citizens: The integration of immigrant communities in Britain, Ireland and Colonial America, 1550–1750*. Huguenot Society of Great Britain and Ireland and Sussex Academic Press, Brighton and Portland.

Viola, Giorgio (2001). 'The Revd J.B. Stouppe's Travels in France in 1654 as Cromwell's Secret Agent'. *HSP* XXVII, 509–26.

Walker, G. Goold (1935). 'Huguenots in the Trained Bands of London and the Honourable Artillery Company'. *HSP* XV (1933–7), 300–16.

Waller, William Chapman (1899). 'Early Huguenot Friendly Societies'. *HSP* VI (1898–1901), 201–35, and VIII (1905–8), 280–90.

Waller, William Chapman (1913). 'The French Church of Thorpe-le-Soken'. *HSP* X (1912–14), 265–97.

Walton, Clifford (1894). *History of the British Standing Army A.D. 1660 to 1700*. Harrison & Sons, London.

Watts, Diane (2007). 'Pierre Allix, the Huguenot Diaspora and the Problem of Conformity in late seventeenth-century England'. MA thesis, University of Reading.

Watts, Michael R. (1978). *The Dissenters*. Clarendon Press, Oxford.

Wauchope, Piers (1992). *Patrick Sarsfield and the Williamite War*. Irish Academic Press, Dublin.

Weil, Rachel (2013). *A Plague of Informers: Conspiracy and political trust in William III's England*. Yale University Press, New Haven and London.

Weiss, Charles (1852). 'Mémoire sur les Protestants de France au 17e Siècle', Séances et Travaux de l'Académie des Sciences Morales et Politiques, XXI.

Weiss, Charles (1853). *Histoire des Réfugiés Protestants de France depuis la Révocation de l'Edit de Nantes jusqu'à nos Jours*. 2 vols. Paris.

Weiss, Charles (1854). *History of the French Protestant Refugees from the Revocation of the Edict of Nantes to the Present Time*. William Blackwood & Sons, Edinburgh.

Western, J.R. (1972). *Monarchy and Revolution: The English State in the 1680s*. Blandford Press.

Whelan, Bernadette (ed.) (1995). *The Last of the Great Wars: Essays on the War of the Three Kings in Ireland 1688–91*. University of Limerick Press.

Whelan, Ruth (1996). 'Points of View: Benjamin de Daillon, William Moreton and the Portarlington affair'. *HSP* XXVI (1994–7), 463–89.

Whelan, Ruth (1997). 'The Huguenots, the Crown and the Clergy: Ireland, 1704'. *HSP* XXVI (1994–7), 601–10.

Whelan, Ruth, and Baxter, Carol (eds) (2003). *Toleration and Religious Identity: The Edict of Nantes and its implications in France, Britain and Ireland*. Four Courts Press, Dublin and Portland.

Whiteman, Anne (1962). 'The Restoration of the Church of England'. In Nuttall, Geoffrey F., and Chadwick, Owen (eds), *From Uniformity to Unity 1662–1962*, pp. 19–88. SPCK.

Whiting, C.E. (1931). *Studies in English Puritanism from the Restoration to the Revolution, 1660–1688*. SPCK.

Williamson, Fiona (2014). *Social Relations and Urban Space: Norwich, 1600–1700*. Boydell Press, Woodbridge.

Wolf, John B. (1968). *Louis XIV*. Panther History edn, 1970.

Woodhead, J.R. (1965). *The Rulers of London 1660–1689: A biographical record of the Aldermen and Common Councilmen of the City of London*. London and Middlesex Archaeological Society, Bristol.

Wormald, B.H.G. (1964). *Clarendon: Politics, history and religion 1640–1660*. Cambridge University Press.

Wrigley, E.A. (ed.) (1966). *An Introduction to English Historical Demography from the Sixteenth to the Nineteenth Century.* Weidenfeld & Nicolson.

Wrigley, E.A. and Schofield, R.S. *The Population History of England, 1541–1871: A reconstruction.* Cambridge University Press, 1989, 1981.

Yardeni, Myriam (1985). *Le Refuge Protestant.* Presses Universitaires de France, Paris.

Yardeni, Myriam (1993). 'Naissance et Essor d'un Mythe: La Révocation de l'Édit de Nantes et le déclin économique de la France', *BSHPF* 139, 79–96.

Yardeni, Myriam (1995). 'La Querelle de la Nouvelle Version des Psaumes dans le Refuge Huguenot', in Brigitte Maillard (ed.), *Foi, Fidelité, Amitié en Europe à la Période Moderne. Mélanges offerts à Robert Sauzet.* Université de Tours.

Yardeni, Myriam (2008). *Huguenots et Juifs.* Honoré Champion, Paris.

Yungblut, Laura Hunt (1996). *Strangers settled here amongst us: Policies, perceptions and the presence of aliens in Elizabethan England.* Routledge.

Zuber, Roger, and Theis, Laurent (eds) (1986). *La Révocation de l'Édit de Nantes et le Protestantisme Français en 1685.* Société de l'Histoire du Protestantisme Français, Paris.

Index